**"THE BEST HISTORY OF WESTERN THOUGHT
I HAVE READ. . . . MASTERFUL."**
Robert A. McDermott
Chairman, Philosophy Department
Baruch College, City University of New York

"An extraordinary piece of scholarship. It not only places the history of Western thought in perspective, but derives new insights concerning the evolution of our thinking and the future of the whole human enterprise. . . . A truly important publishing event."
John E. Mack
Professor of Psychiatry, Harvard Medical School
Pulitzer Prize–winning author of *A Prince of Our Disorder* and *The Alchemy of Survival*

"This is the most creative and comprehensive treatment of the history of Western thought I know. . . . The book is a real masterpiece."
Stanislav Grof
author of *Realms of the Human Unconscious* and *Beyond the Brain*

"I revelled in the intellectual pleasure and stimulation it gave me from beginning to end. And when I got to the end, I wanted to read it all over again. . . . I have added it to a small set of books—about ten, and including my dictionary, the Bible, etc.—which sit in my 'permanent collection' on my desk. . . . A perfect book, without flaw. No accolade would be excessive."
Kenneth Ring
Professor of Psychology, University of Connecticut
Author of *The Omega Project*

"AN INTELLECTUAL ADVENTURE,
this challenging synthesis throws a sharp light on ideas central to
the modern outlook."
Publishers Weekly

"Brilliantly conveys the drama of conflicting questions about mind
and matter, faith and reason, cosmology and science, freedom and
determinism. . . . An essential guidebook to the permanent wisdom of past philosophers."
Joseph F. Keppler
The Seattle Times/Post-Intelligencer

"No other such overview provides, in equal compass, as clear and
cogent a survey. Its scholarship is impeccable."
Huston Smith, Professor of Religious Studies
University of California, Berkeley, author of
The World's Religions and Beyond the Postmodern Mind

"Richard Tarnas speaks to our condition as humans alive at the
end of the 20th century. . . . Tarnas has accumulated a staggering
amount of data, yet he spares us the confusion this knowledge
could create in our minds. How does he manage this? He tells us
not primarily about the things his mind has grasped, but rather
about the things that have grasped his mind. Thus, his account
grasps the reader's mind, too."
David Steindl-Rast
coauthor of Belonging to the Universe

The
PASSION
of the
WESTERN
MIND

Understanding the Ideas
That Have Shaped Our World View

Richard Tarnas

Ballantine Books • New York

To Heather

This edition published by arrangement with Harmony Books, a division of Crown Publishers, Inc., New York.

Library of Congress Catalog Card Number: 92-90050
ISBN: 0-345-36809-6

Cover design by James R. Harris
Cover painting: Thomas Cole. *The Architect's Dream* (1840), oil on canvas, 53 × 84¹/₁₆ inches. The Toledo Museum of Art, Toledo, Ohio. Purchased with funds from the Florence Scott Libbey Bequest in Memory of Her Father, Maurice A. Scott.

Manufactured in the United States of America

First Ballantine Books Edition: April 1993

10 9 8 7 6 5 4 3 2 1

Contents

Preface

This book presents a concise narrative history of the Western world view from the ancient Greek to the postmodern. My aim has been to provide, within the limits of a single volume, a coherent account of the evolution of the Western mind and its changing conception of reality. Recent advances on several fronts—in philosophy, depth psychology, religious studies, and history of science—have shed new light on this remarkable evolution. The historical account presented here has been greatly influenced and enriched by these advances, and at the end of the narrative I have drawn on them to set forth a new perspective for understanding our culture's intellectual and spiritual history.

We hear much now about the breakdown of the Western tradition, the decline of liberal education, the dangerous lack of a cultural foundation for grappling with contemporary problems. Partly such concerns reflect insecurity and nostalgia in the face of a radically changing world. Yet they also reflect a genuine need, and it is to that growing number of thoughtful men and women who recognize such a need that this book is addressed. How did the modern world come to its present condition? How did the modern mind arrive at those fundamental ideas and working principles that so profoundly influence the world today? These are pressing questions for our time, and to approach them we must recover our roots—not out of uncritical reverence for the views and values of ages past, but rather to discover and integrate the historical origins of our own era. I believe that only by recalling the deeper sources of our present world and world view can we hope to gain the self-understanding necessary for dealing with our current dilemmas. The West's cultural and intellectual history can thus serve as a preparatory education for the challenges that face us all. Through this book I have hoped to make an essential part of that history more readily accessible to the general reader.

Yet I also simply wanted to tell a story I thought worth telling. The history of Western culture has long seemed to possess the dynamics, scope, and beauty of a great epic drama: ancient and classical Greece, the Hellenistic era and imperial Rome, Judaism and the rise of Christianity, the Catholic Church and the Middle Ages, the Renaissance, Reformation, and Scientific Revolution, the Enlightenment and Romanticism and onward to our own compelling time. Sweep and grandeur, dramatic conflicts and astonishing resolutions have marked the Western mind's sustained attempt to comprehend the nature of reality—from Thales and Pythagoras to Plato and Aristotle, from Clement and Boethius to Aquinas and Ockham, from Eudoxus and Ptolemy to Copernicus and Newton, from Bacon and Descartes to Kant and Hegel, and from all these to Darwin, Einstein, Freud, and beyond. That long battle of ideas called "the Western tradition" has been a stirring adventure whose sum and consequence we all bear within ourselves. An epic heroism has shone forth in the personal struggles of Socrates, of Paul and Augustine, of Luther and Galileo, and in that larger cultural struggle, borne by these and by many less visible protagonists, which has moved the West on its extraordinary course. There is high tragedy here. And there is something beyond tragedy.

The following account traces the development of the major world views of the West's mainstream high culture, focusing on the crucial sphere of interaction between philosophy, religion, and science. Perhaps what Virginia Woolf said of great works of literature could be said as well of great world views: "The success of the masterpieces seems to lie not so much in their freedom from faults—indeed we tolerate the grossest errors in them all—but in the immense persuasiveness of a mind which has completely mastered its perspective." My goal in these pages has been to give voice to each perspective mastered by the Western mind in the course of its evolution, and to take each on its own terms. I have assumed no special priority for any particular conception of reality, including our present one (which is itself multiple and in profound flux). Instead, I have approached each world view in the same spirit that I would approach an exceptional work of art—seeking to understand and appreciate, to experience its human consequences, to let its meaning unfold.

Today the Western mind appears to be undergoing an epochal transformation, of a magnitude perhaps comparable to any in our civilization's history. I believe we can participate intelligently in that transformation only to the extent to which we are historically informed. Every age must remember its history anew. Each generation must examine and think through again, from its own distinctive vantage point, the ideas that have shaped its understanding of the world. Our task is to do so from the richly complex perspective of the late twentieth century. I hope this book will contribute to that effort.

R. T.

The
Passion
of the
Western
Mind

The world is deep:
deeper than day can comprehend.

Friedrich Nietzsche
Thus Spoke Zarathustra

Introduction

A book that explores the evolution of the Western mind places special demands on both reader and writer, for it asks us to enter into frames of reference that are sometimes radically different from our own. Such a book invites a certain intellectual flexibility—a sympathetic metaphysical imagination, a capacity for viewing the world through the eyes of men and women from other times. One must in a sense wipe the slate clean, attempt to see things without the benefit or burden of a preconceived outlook. Of course such a pristine, malleable state of mind can only be striven for, never achieved. Yet to aspire to that ideal is perhaps the single most important prerequisite for an enterprise such as this. Unless we are able to perceive and articulate, on their own terms and without condescension, certain powerful beliefs and assumptions that we no longer consider valid or defensible—for example, the once universal conviction that the Earth is the stationary center of the cosmos, or the even more enduring tendency among Western thinkers to conceive of and personify the human species in predominantly masculine terms— then we will fail to understand the intellectual and cultural foundations of our own thought. Our constant challenge is to remain faithful to the historical material, allowing our present perspective to enrich, but not distort, the various ideas and world views we examine. While that challenge should not be underestimated, I believe that today, for reasons that will become clear in the later chapters of the book, we are in a better position to engage this task with the necessary intellectual and imaginative flexibility than at perhaps any time in the past.

The following narrative is organized chronologically according to the three world views associated with the three major eras that have traditionally been distinguished in Western cultural history—the classical, the medieval, and the modern. Needless to say, any division of history into "eras" and "world views" cannot in itself do justice to the actual complexity and diversity of Western thought during these centuries. Yet to discuss such an immense mass of material fruitfully, one must first introduce some provisional principles of organization. Within these overarching generalities, we may then better address the complications and ambiguities, the internal conflicts and unanticipated changes that have never ceased to mark the history of the Western mind.

We begin with the Greeks. It was some twenty-five centuries ago that the Hellenic world brought forth that extraordinary flowering of culture that marked the dawn of Western civilization. Endowed with seemingly primeval clarity and creativity, the ancient Greeks provided the Western mind with what has proved to be a perennial source of insight, inspiration, and renewal. Modern science, medieval theology, classical humanism—all stand deeply in their debt. Greek thought was as fundamental for Copernicus and Kepler, and Augustine and Aquinas, as for Cicero and Petrarch. Our way of thinking is still profoundly Greek in its underlying logic, so much so that before we can begin to grasp the character of our own thought, we must first look closely at that of the Greeks. They remain fundamental for us in other ways as well: Curious, innovative, critical, intensely engaged with life and with death, searching for order and meaning yet skeptical of conventional verities, the Greeks were originators of intellectual values as relevant today as they were in the fifth century B.C. Let us recall, then, these first protagonists of the Western intellectual tradition.

Note: A detailed chronology for the events discussed in this book appears at the end of the text (page 446), while dates of birth and death for each historical figure cited can be found next to the individual's name in the Index. A discussion of gender and language in the text appears at the beginning of the Notes (page 468).

I

The
Greek World View

To approach what was distinctive in a vision as complex and protean as that of the Greeks, let us begin by examining one of its most striking characteristics—a sustained, highly diversified tendency to interpret the world in terms of archetypal principles. This tendency was in evidence throughout Greek culture from the Homeric epics onward, though it first emerged in philosophically elaborate form in the intellectual crucible of Athens between the latter part of the fifth century B.C. and the middle of the fourth. Associated with the figure of Socrates, it there received its foundational and in some respects definitive formulation in the dialogues of Plato. At its basis was a view of the cosmos as an ordered expression of certain primordial essences or transcendent first principles, variously conceived as Forms, Ideas, universals, changeless absolutes, immortal deities, divine *archai*, and archetypes. Although this perspective took on a number of distinct inflections, and although there were important countercurrents to this view, it would appear that not only Socrates, Plato, and Aristotle, and Pythagoras before them and Plotinus after, but indeed Homer and Hesiod, Aeschylus and Sophocles all expressed something like a common vision, reflecting a typically Greek propensity to see clarifying universals in the chaos of life.

Speaking in these broad terms, and mindful of the inexactness of such generalities, we may say that the Greek universe was ordered by a plurality of timeless essences which underlay concrete reality, giving it form and meaning. These archetypal principles included the mathematical forms of geometry and arithmetic; cosmic opposites such as light and dark, male and female, love and hate, unity and multiplicity; the forms of man (*anthrōpos*) and other living creatures; and the Ideas of the Good, the Beautiful, the Just, and other absolute moral and aesthetic values. In the pre-philosophical Greek mind, these archetypal principles took the form of mythic personifications such as Eros, Chaos, Heaven and Earth (Ouranos and Gaia), as well as more fully personified figures such as Zeus, Prometheus, and Aphrodite. In this perspective, every aspect of existence was patterned and permeated by such fundamentals. Despite the continuous flux of phenomena in both the outer world and inner experience, there could yet be distinguished specific immutable structures or essences, so definite and enduring they were believed to possess an independent reality of their own. It was upon this apparent immutability and independence that Plato based both his metaphysics and his theory of knowledge.

Because the archetypal perspective outlined here provides a useful point of departure for entering into the Greek world view, and because Plato was that perspective's preeminent theoretician and apologist, whose thought would become the single most important foundation for the evolution of the Western mind, we shall begin by discussing the Platonic doctrine of Forms. In subsequent chapters, we shall pursue the historical development of the Greek vision as a whole, and thereby attend to the complex dialectic that led to Plato's thought, and to the equally complex consequences that followed from it.

Yet to approach Plato, we must bear in mind his unsystematic, often tentative, and even ironic style of presenting his philosophy. We should bear in mind too the inevitable and no doubt often deliberate ambiguities inherent in his chosen literary mode, the dramatic dialogue. Finally, we must recall the range, variability, and growth of his thought over a period of some fifty years. With these qualifications, then, we may make a provisional attempt to set forth certain prominent ideas and principles suggested by his writings. Our tacit guide in this interpretive effort will be the Platonic tradition itself, which preserved and developed a specific philosophical perspective it regarded as originating with Plato.

Having established that pivotal position within the Greek mind, we can then move backward and forward—retrospectively to the early mythological and Presocratic traditions, and then onward to Aristotle.

The Archetypal Forms

What has been commonly understood as Platonism revolves around its cardinal doctrine, the asserted existence of the archetypal Ideas or Forms. That assertion demands a partial shift, though a profound one, from what has come to be our usual approach to reality. To understand this shift, we must first ask, "What is the precise relation between the Platonic Forms or Ideas and the empirical world of everyday reality?" Upon this question turns the entire conception. (Plato used the Greek words *idea* and *eidos* interchangeably. *Idea* was taken over into Latin and English, while *eidos* was translated into Latin as *forma* and into English as "form.")

It is crucial to the Platonic understanding that these Forms are primary, while the visible objects of conventional reality are their direct derivatives. Platonic Forms are not conceptual abstractions that the human mind creates by generalizing from a class of particulars. Rather, they possess a quality of being, a degree of reality, that is superior to that of the concrete world. Platonic archetypes form the world and also stand beyond it. They manifest themselves within time and yet are timeless. They constitute the veiled essence of things.

Plato taught that what is perceived as a particular object in the world can best be understood as a concrete expression of a more fundamental Idea, an archetype which gives that object its special structure and condition. A particular thing is what it is by virtue of the Idea informing it. Something is "beautiful" to the exact extent that the archetype of Beauty is present in it. When one falls in love, it is Beauty (or Aphrodite) that one recognizes and surrenders to, the beloved object being Beauty's instrument or vessel. The essential factor in the event is the archetype, and it is this level that carries the deepest meaning.

It could be objected that this is not the way one experiences an event of this sort. What actually attracts one is not an archetype but a specific person, or a concrete work of art, or some other beautiful object. Beauty is only an attribute of the particular, not its essence. The Platonist argues, however, that this objection rests on a limited perception of the event. It is true, he answers, that the ordinary person is not directly aware of an archetypal level, despite its reality. But Plato described how a philosopher who has observed many objects of beauty, and who has long reflected on the matter, may suddenly glimpse absolute beauty—Beauty itself, supreme, pure, eternal, and not relative to any specific person or thing. The philosopher thereby recognizes the Form or Idea that underlies all beautiful phenomena. He unveils the authentic reality behind the appearance. If something is beautiful, it is so because it "participates" in the absolute Form of Beauty.

Plato's mentor, Socrates, had sought to know what was common to all virtuous acts, so that he could evaluate how one should govern one's conduct in life. He reasoned that if one wishes to choose actions that are good, one must know what "good" is, apart from any specific circumstances. To evaluate one thing as "better" than another assumes the existence of an absolute good with which the two relative goods can be compared. Otherwise the word "good" would be only a word whose meaning had no stable basis in reality, and human morality would lack a secure foundation. Similarly, unless there was some absolute basis for evaluating acts as just or unjust, then every act called "just" would be a relative matter of uncertain virtue. When those who engaged in dialogue with Socrates espoused popular notions of justice and injustice, or of good and evil, he subjected these to careful analysis and showed them to be arbitrary, full of internal contradictions and without any substantial basis. Because Socrates and Plato believed that knowledge of virtue was necessary for a person to live a life of virtue, objective universal concepts of justice and goodness seemed imperative for a genuine ethics. Without such changeless constants that transcended the vagaries of human conventions and political institutions, human beings would possess no firm foundation for ascertaining true values, and would thus be subject to the dangers of an amoral relativism.

Beginning with the Socratic discussion of ethical terms and the search for absolute definitions, Plato ended with a comprehensive theory of reality. Just as man as moral agent requires the Ideas of justice and goodness to conduct his life well, so man as scientist requires other absolute Ideas to understand the world, other universals by which the chaos, flux, and variety of sensible things can be unified and made intelligible. The philosopher's task encompasses both the moral and the scientific dimensions, and the Ideas provide a foundation for both.

It seemed evident to Plato that when many objects share a common property—as all human beings share "humanness" or as all white stones share "whiteness"—that property is not limited to a specific material instance in space and time. It is immaterial, beyond spatiotemporal limitation, and transcendent to its many instances. A particular thing may cease to be, but not the universal property that the particular thing embodied. The universal is a separate entity from the particular and, because it is beyond change and never passes away, is superior in its reality.

One of Plato's critics once stated, "I see particular horses, but not horseness." Plato answered, "That is because you have eyes but no intelligence." The archetypal Horse, which gives form to all horses, is to Plato a more fundamental reality than the particular horses, which are merely specific instances of the Horse, embodiments of that Form. As such, the archetype is apparent not so much to the limited physical senses, though these can suggest and lead the way, as to the more penetrating eye of the soul, the illuminated intellect. Archetypes reveal themselves more to the inner perception than to the outer.

The Platonic perspective thus asks the philosopher to go through the particular to the universal, and beyond the appearance to the essence. It assumes not only that such insight is possible, but that it is mandatory for the attainment of true knowledge. Plato directs the philosopher's attention away from the external and concrete, from taking things at face value, and points "deeper" and "inward," so that one may "awaken" to a more profound level of reality. He asserts that the objects one perceives with one's senses are actually crystallizations of more primary essences, which can be apprehended only by the active, intuitive mind.

Plato maintained a strong distrust of knowledge gained by sense perceptions, since such knowledge is constantly changing, relative, and private to each individual. A wind is pleasantly cool for one person but uncomfortably cold for another. A wine is sweet to a person who is well but sour to the same person when ill. Knowledge based on the senses is therefore a subjective judgment, an ever-varying opinion without any absolute foundation. True knowledge, by contrast, is possible only from a direct apprehension of the transcendent Forms, which are eternal and beyond the shifting confusion and imperfection of the physical plane. Knowledge derived from the senses is merely opinion and is fallible by any nonrelative standard. Only knowledge derived directly from the Ideas is infallible and can be justifiably called real knowledge.

For example, the senses never experience true or absolute equality, since no two things in this world are ever exactly equal to each other in every respect. Rather, they are always only more or less equal. Yet because of the transcendent Idea of equality, the human intellect can comprehend absolute equality (which it has never known concretely) independently of the senses, and can therefore employ the term "equality" and recognize approximations of equality in the empirical world. Similarly, there are no perfect circles in nature, but all approximate circles in nature derive their "circleness" from the perfect archetypal Circle, and it is on this latter reality that the human intelligence depends to recognize any empirical circles. So too with perfect goodness or perfect beauty. For when one speaks of something as "more beautiful" or "more good" than something else, this comparison can be made only against an invisible standard of absolute beauty or goodness—Beauty itself and the Good itself. Everything in the sensible world is imperfect, relative, and constantly shifting, but human knowledge needs and seeks absolutes, which exist only on the transcendent level of pure Ideas.

Implicit in Plato's conception of the Ideas is his distinction between being and becoming. All phenomena are in a never-ending process of transformation from one thing into another, becoming this or that and then perishing, changing in relation to one person and another, or to the same person at different times. Nothing in this world *is*, because everything is always in a state of becoming something else. But one thing does enjoy real being, as distinguished from merely becoming, and this is the Idea—the only stable reality, that which underlies, motivates, and orders the flux of phenomena. Any particular thing in the world is actually a complexly determined appearance. The perceived object is a meeting place of many Forms which at different times express themselves in varying combinations and with varying degrees of intensity. Plato's world, therefore, is dynamic only in that all phenomenal reality is in a state of constant becoming and perishing, a movement governed by the shifting participation of Ideas. But the ultimate reality, the world of Ideas wherein resides true being, not just becoming, is in itself changeless and eternal, and is therefore static. The relation of being to becoming for Plato was directly parallel to the relation of truth to opinion—what is apprehensible by the illuminated reason in contrast to what is apprehensible by the physical senses.

Since the Forms endure, while their concrete expressions come and go, the Forms can be said to be immortal, and therefore similar to gods. Though a particular incarnation of the moment may die, the Form that was temporarily embodied within that particular continues to manifest itself in other concrete things. A person's beauty passes, but Aphrodite lives on—archetypal Beauty is eternal, neither vulnerable to the passing of time nor touched by the transience of its particular manifestations. The individual trees of the natural world eventually fall and rot away, but the archetypal Tree continues to express itself in and through other trees. A good person may fall and perform evil acts, but the Idea of the Good stands forever. The archetypal Idea comes into and out of being in a multiplicity of concrete forms, yet simultaneously remains transcendent as a unitary essence.

Plato's use of the word "idea" (which in Greek denoted the form, pattern, essential quality, or nature of something) clearly differs from our contemporary usage. In the usual modern understanding, ideas are subjective mental constructs private to the individual mind. By contrast, Plato meant something that exists not only in human consciousness but outside of it as well. Platonic Ideas are objective. They do not depend on human thought, but exist entirely in their own right. They are perfect patterns embedded in the very nature of things. The Platonic Idea is, as it were, not merely a human idea but the universe's idea, an ideal entity that can express itself externally in concrete tangible form or internally as a concept in the human mind. It is a primordial image or formal essence that can manifest in various ways and on various levels, and is the foundation of reality itself.

The Ideas are thus the fundamental elements of both an ontology (a theory of being) and an epistemology (a theory of knowledge): they constitute the basic essence and deepest reality of things, and also the means by which certain human knowledge is possible. A bird is a bird by virtue of its participation in the archetypal Idea of the Bird. And the human mind can know a bird by virtue of the mind's own participation in that same Idea of the Bird. The red color of an object is red because it participates in archetypal redness, and human perception registers red by virtue of the mind's participation in the same Idea. The human mind and the universe are ordered according to the same archetypal structures or essences, because of which, and only because of which, true understanding of things is possible for the human intelligence.

The paradigmatic example of Ideas for Plato was mathematics. Following the Pythagoreans, with whose philosophy he seems to have been especially intimate, Plato understood the physical universe to be organized in accordance with the mathematical Ideas of number and geometry. These Ideas are invisible, apprehensible by intelligence only, and yet can be discovered to be the formative causes and regulators of all empirically visible objects and processes. But again, the Platonic and Pythagorean conception of mathematical ordering principles in nature was essentially different from the conventional modern view. In Plato's understanding, circles, triangles, and numbers are not merely formal or quantitative structures imposed by the human mind on natural phenomena, nor are they only mechanically present in phenomena as a brute fact of their concrete being. Rather, they are numinous and transcendent entities, existing independently of both the phenomena they order and the human mind that perceives them. While the concrete phenomena are transient and imperfect, the mathematical Ideas ordering those phenomena are perfect, eternal, and changeless. Hence the basic Platonic belief—that there exists a deeper, timeless order of absolutes behind the surface confusion and randomness of the temporal world— found in mathematics, it was thought, a particularly graphic demonstration. The training of the mind in mathematics was therefore deemed by Plato essential to the philosophical enterprise, and according to tradition, above the door to his Academy were placed the words "Let no one unacquainted with geometry enter here."

The position described thus far represents a fair approximation of Plato's most characteristic views concerning the Ideas, including those set forth in his most celebrated dialogues—the *Republic,* the *Symposium,* the *Phaedo,* the *Phaedrus,* and the *Timaeus*—as well as in the *Seventh Letter,* his one probably genuine extant letter. Yet a number of ambiguities and discrepancies remained unresolved in the corpus of Plato's work. At times Plato seems to exalt the ideal over the empirical to such an extent that all concrete particulars are understood to be, as it were, only a series of footnotes to the transcendent Idea. At other times he seems to stress the intrinsic nobility of created things, precisely because they are embodied expressions of the divine and eternal. The exact degree to which the Ideas are transcendent rather than immanent—whether they are entirely separate from sensible things, with the latter only imperfect imitations, or whether they are in some manner present in sensible things, with the latter essentially sharing in the Ideas' nature—cannot be determined from the many references in the different dialogues. Generally speaking, it seems that as Plato's thought matured, he moved toward a more transcendent interpretation. Yet in the *Parmenides,* probably written after most of the dialogues cited above, Plato presented several formidable arguments against his own theory, pointing out questions concerning the nature of the Ideas—how many kinds are there, what are their relations to each other and to the sensible world, what is the precise meaning of "participation," how is knowledge of them possible—the responses to which raised seemingly unsolvable problems and inconsistencies. Some of these questions, which Plato posed perhaps as much out of dialectical vigor as from self-criticism, became the basis for later philosophers' objections to the theory of Ideas.

Similarly, in the *Theaetetus*, Plato analyzed the nature of knowledge with extraordinary acuity and with no firm conclusions, never adducing the theory of Ideas as a way out of the epistemological impasse he depicted. In the *Sophist*, Plato ascribed reality not just to the Ideas but also to change, life, soul, and understanding. Elsewhere he pointed to the existence of an intermediate class of mathematical objects between Ideas and sensible particulars. On several occasions he posited a hierarchy of Ideas, yet different dialogues suggested different hierarchies, with the Good, the One, Existence, Truth, or Beauty variously occupying supreme positions, sometimes simultaneously and overlapping. Clearly Plato never constructed a complete, fully coherent system of Ideas. Yet it is also evident that, despite his own unresolved questions concerning his central doctrine, Plato considered the theory true, and that without it human knowledge and moral activity could have no foundation. And it was this conviction that formed the basis for the Platonic tradition.

To sum up: From the Platonic perspective, the fundamentals of existence are the archetypal Ideas, which constitute the intangible substrate of all that is tangible. The true structure of the world is revealed not by the senses, but by the intellect, which in its highest state has direct access to the Ideas governing reality. All knowledge presupposes the existence of the Ideas. The archetypal realm, far from being an unreal abstraction or imaginary metaphor for the concrete world, is here considered to be the very basis of reality, that which determines its order and renders it knowable. To this end, Plato declared direct experience of the transcendent Ideas to be the philosopher's primary goal and ultimate destination.

Ideas and Gods

All things are indeed "full of gods," Plato asserted in his final work, the *Laws*. And here we must address a peculiar ambiguity in the nature of archetypes—an ambiguity central to the Greek vision as a whole—that suggested the existence of an underlying connection between ruling principles and mythic beings. Although at times Plato favored a more abstract formulation of archetypes, as with the mathematical Ideas, at other times he spoke in terms of divine figures, mythical personages of exalted stature. On many occasions, Socrates's way of speaking in the Platonic dialogues has a distinctly Homeric tone, treating various philosophical and historical matters in the form of mythological figures and narratives.

A taut irony, a playful seriousness, colors Plato's use of myth, so that one cannot pin down precisely the level on which he wishes to be understood. He often prefaced his mythical excursions with the ambiguous ploy, at once affirming and self-distancing, of declaring that it was "a likely account" or that "either this or something very like it is true." Depending on a specific dialogue's context, Zeus, Apollo, Hera, Ares, Aphrodite, and the rest could signify actual deities, allegorical figures, character types, psychological attitudes, modes of experience, philosophic principles, transcendent essences, sources of poetic inspiration or divine communications, objects of conventional piety, unknowable entities, imperishable artifacts of the supreme creator, heavenly bodies, foundations of the universal order, or rulers and teachers of mankind. More than only literalistic metaphors, Plato's gods defy strict definition, in one dialogue serving as fanciful characters in a didactic fable, in another commanding an undoubted ontological reality. Not infrequently, these personified archetypes are used in his most philosophically earnest moments, as if the depersonalized language of metaphysical abstraction were no longer suitable when directly confronting the numinous essence of things.

We see this memorably illustrated in the *Symposium*, where Eros is discussed as the preeminent force in human motivations. In a fine succession of elegantly dialectical speeches, the several participants in Plato's philosophical drinking party describe Eros as a complex and multidimensional archetype which at the physical level expresses itself in the sexual instinct, but at higher levels impels the philosopher's passion for intellectual beauty and wisdom, and culminates in the mystical vision of the eternal, the ultimate source of all beauty. Yet throughout the dialogue that principle is represented in personified and mythical terms, with Eros considered a deity, the god of love, with the principle of Beauty referred to as Aphrodite, and with numerous allusions to other mythic figures such as Dionysus, Kronos, Orpheus, and Apollo. Similarly, in the *Timaeus*, when Plato sets forth his views on the creation and structure of the universe, he does so in almost entirely mythological terms; so too in his many discussions of the nature and destiny of the soul (*Phaedo, Gorgias, Phaedrus, Republic, Laws*). Specific qualities of character are regularly attributed to specific deities, as in the *Phaedrus*, where the philosopher who seeks after wisdom is called a follower of Zeus, while the warrior who would shed blood for his cause is said to be attendant upon Ares. Often there is little doubt that Plato is employing myth as pure allegory, as when in the *Protagoras* he has the Sophist teacher use the ancient myth of Prometheus simply to make an anthropological point. In his theft of fire from the heavens, giving it to mankind with the other arts of civilization, Prometheus symbolized rational man's emergence from a more primitive state. At other times, however, Plato himself seems swept up into the mythic dimension, as when, in the *Philebus*, he has Socrates describe his dialectical method of analyzing the world of Ideas as "a gift of heaven, which, as I conceive, the gods tossed among men by the hands of a new Prometheus, and therewith a blaze of light."

By philosophizing in such a manner, Plato gave expression to a unique confluence of the emerging rationalism of Hellenic philosophy with the prolific mythological imagination of the ancient Greek psyche—that primordial religious vision, with both Indo-European and Levantine roots extending back through the second millennium B.C. to Neolithic times, which provided the Olympian polytheistic foundation for the cult, art, poetry, and drama of classical Greek culture. Among ancient mythologies, that of Greece was singularly complex, richly elaborated, and systematic. As such, it provided a fertile basis for the evolution of Greek philosophy itself, which bore distinct traces of its mythic ancestry not only in its initial emergence but in its Platonic apogee. Yet it was not just the language of myth in Plato's dialogues, but rather the underlying functional equivalence of deities and Ideas implicit in much of his thought, that made Plato so pivotal in the development of the Greek mind. As the classicist John Finley has noted, "Just as the Greek gods, variable though they may have been in cult, corporately comprise an analysis of the world—Athena as mind, Apollo as random and unpredictable illumination, Aphrodite as sexuality, Dionysus as change and excitement, Artemis as untouchedness, Hera as settlement and marriage, Zeus as order dominant over all—so the Platonic forms exist in their own right, lucent and eternal above any transitory human participation in them. . . . [Like the forms, the gods] were essences of life, by contemplation of which any individual life took on meaning and substance."[1]

Plato often criticized poets for anthropomorphizing the gods, yet he did not cease from teaching his own philosophical system in striking mythological formulations and with implicitly religious intent. Despite the high value he placed on intellectual rigor, and despite his dogmatic strictures concerning poetry and art in his political doctrines, the distinct implication in many passages of the dialogues is that the imaginative faculty, both poetic and religious, was as useful in the quest for attaining knowledge of the world's essential nature as any purely logical, let alone empirical, approach. But of especial importance for our present inquiry was the effect of Plato's vision on the unstable and problematic condition of the Greek world view. For by speaking of Ideas on one page and gods on another in such analogous terms, Plato resolved, tenuously yet with weighty and enduring consequences, the central tension in the classical Greek mind between myth and reason.

The Evolution of the Greek Mind
from Homer to Plato

The Mythic Vision

The religious and mythological background of Greek thought was profoundly pluralistic in character. When successive waves of Greek-speaking Indo-European nomadic warriors began sweeping into the lands of the Aegean around the turn of the second millennium B.C., they brought with them their heroic patriarchal mythology, presided over by the great sky-god Zeus. Although the ancient matriarchal mythologies of the indigenous pre-Hellenic societies, including the highly developed Minoan goddess-worshiping civilization on Crete, were eventually subordinated to the religion of the conquerors, they were not entirely suppressed. For the northern male deities mated with and married the ancient southern goddesses, as Zeus did Hera, and this complex amalgamation which came to constitute the Olympian pantheon did much to ensure the dynamism and vitality of classical Greek myth. Moreover, this pluralism in the Hellenic inheritance was further expressed in the continuing dichotomy between, on the one hand, Greek public religion, with its polis festivals and civic rituals focused on the major Olympian deities, and, on the other, the widely popular mystery religions—Orphic, Dionysian, Eleusinian—whose esoteric rites drew on pre-Greek and Oriental religious traditions: death-rebirth initiations, agricultural fertility cults, and worship of the Great Mother Goddess.

Given the oath-bound secrecy of the mystery religions, it is difficult from the present vantage point to judge the relative significance of the various forms of Hellenic religious belief for individual Greeks. What is evident, however, is the pervasive archetypal resonance of the archaic Greek vision, expressed above all in the foundational epic poems of Greek culture that have come down to us, the Homeric *Iliad* and *Odyssey*. Here, at the luminous dawn of the Western literary tradition, was captured the primordial mythological sensibility in which the events of human existence were perceived as intimately related to and informed by the eternal realm of gods and goddesses. The archaic Greek vision reflected an intrinsic unity of immediate sense perception and timeless meaning, of particular circumstance and universal drama, of human activity and divine motivation. Historical persons lived out a mythic heroism in war and wandering, while Olympian deities watched and intervened over the plain of Troy. The play of the senses on an outflung world bright with color and drama was never separated from a comprehension of the world's meaning that was both ordered and mythic. Keen apprehension of the physical world—of seas and mountains and dawns, of banquets and battles, of bows, helmets, and chariots—was permeated with the felt presence of the gods in nature and human destiny. The immediacy and freshness of the Homeric vision was paradoxically tied to a virtually conceptual understanding of the world governed by an ancient and venerable mythology.

Even the towering figure of Homer himself suggested a peculiarly indivisible synthesis of the individual and the universal. The monumental epic poems were brought forth from a greater collective psyche, creations of the Hellenic racial imagination passed on, developed, and refined generation after generation, bard after bard. Yet within the established formulaic patterns of oral tradition that governed the epics' composition there also lived an unmistakably personal particularity, a flexible individualism and spontaneity of style and vision. Thus "Homer" was ambiguously both an individual human poet and a collective personification of the entire ancient Greek memory.

The values expressed in the Homeric epics, composed around the eighth century B.C., continued to inspire successive generations of Greeks throughout antiquity, and the many figures of the Olympian pantheon, systematically delineated somewhat later in Hesiod's *Theogony*, informed and pervaded the Greek cultural vision. In the various divinities and their powers lay a sense of the universe as an ordered whole, a cosmos rather than a chaos. The natural world and the human world were not distinguishable domains in the archaic Greek universe, for a single fundamental order structured both nature and society, and embodied the divine justice that empowered Zeus, the ruler of the gods. Although the universal order was especially represented in Zeus, even he was ultimately bound by an impersonal fate (*moira*) that governed all and that maintained a certain equilibrium of forces. The gods were indeed often capricious in their actions, with human destinies in the balance. Yet the whole cohered, and the forces of order prevailed over those of chaos—just as the Olympians led by Zeus had defeated the Giants in the primeval struggle for rulership of the world, and just as Odysseus after his long and perilous wanderings at last triumphantly achieved home.[2]

By the fifth century B.C., the great Greek tragedians Aeschylus, Sophocles, and Euripides were employing the ancient myths to explore the deeper themes of the human condition. Courage, cunning and strength, nobility and the striving for immortal glory were the characteristic virtues of the epic heroes. Yet however great the individual, man's lot was circumscribed by fate and the fact of his mortality. It was above all the superior man whose actions could draw the destructive wrath of the gods upon him, often because of his hubris, sometimes seemingly unjustly. Against the backdrop of that opposition between human endeavor and divine stricture, between free will and fate, sin and retribution, the moral struggle of the protagonist unfolded. In the hands of the tragedians, the conflicts and sufferings that had been straightforwardly and unreflectively portrayed in Homer and Hesiod were now subjected to the psychological and existential probings of a later, more critical temperament. What had been long-accepted absolutes were now searched, questioned, suffered through with a new consciousness of the human predicament. On the stage of the Dionysian religious festivals in Athens, the pronounced Greek sense of the heroic, balanced against and in integral relation to an equally acute awareness of pain, death, and fate, discharged itself in the context of mythic drama. And just as Homer was called the educator of Greece, so too were the tragedians expressive of the culture's deepening spirit and shapers of its moral character, with the theatrical performances as much communal religious sacrament as artistic event.

For both archaic poet and classical tragedian, the world of myth endowed human experience with an ennobling clarity of vision, a higher order that redeemed the wayward pathos of life. The universal gave comprehensibility to the concrete. If, in the tragic vision, character determined fate, yet both were mythically perceived. Compared with the Homeric epics, Athenian tragedy reflected a more conscious sense of the gods' metaphorical significance and a more poignant appreciation of human self-awareness and suffering. Yet through profound suffering came profound learning, and the history and drama of human existence, for all its harsh conflict and wrenching contradiction, still held overarching purpose and meaning. The myths were the living body of that meaning, constituting a language that both reflected and illuminated the essential processes of life.

The Birth of Philosophy

With its Olympian order, the mythic world of Homer and Sophocles possessed a complex intelligibility, but this persistent desire for system and clarity in the Greek vision, as well as the growing humanism visible in the tragedies, was beginning to take new forms. The great shift had already commenced in the early sixth century B.C. in the large and prosperous Ionian city of Miletus, situated in the eastern part of the Greek world on the coast of Asia Minor. Here Thales and his successors Anaximander and Anaximenes, endowed with both leisure and curiosity, initiated an approach to understanding the world that was radically novel and extraordinarily consequential. Perhaps they were impelled by their Ionian location, where they were confronted with neighboring civilizations that possessed mythologies differing both from each other and from the Greek. Perhaps, too, they were influenced by the social organization of the Greek polis, which was governed by impersonal, uniform laws rather than the arbitrary acts of a despot. Yet whatever their immediate inspiration, these prototypical scientists made the remarkable assumption that an underlying rational unity and order existed within the flux and variety of the world, and established for themselves the task of discovering a simple fundamental principle, or *archē*, that both governed nature and composed its basic substance. In so doing, they began to complement their traditional mythological understanding with more impersonal and conceptual explanations based on their observations of natural phenomena.

At this pivotal stage, there was a distinct overlap of the mythic and scientific modes, visible in the principal statement attributed to Thales in which he affirmed both a single unifying primary substance and a divine omnipresence: "All is water, and the world is full of gods." Thales and his successors proposed that nature arose from a self-animated substance that continued to move and change itself into various forms.[3] Because it was author of its own ordered motions and transmutations, and because it was everlasting, this primary substance was considered to be not only material but also alive and divine. Much like Homer, these earliest philosophers perceived nature and divinity as yet intertwined. They also maintained something of the old Homeric sense of a moral order governing the cosmos, an impersonal fate that preserved the world's equilibrium amidst all its changes.

But the decisive step had been taken. The Greek mind now strove to discover a natural explanation for the cosmos by means of observation and reasoning, and these explanations soon began to shed their residual mythological components. Ultimate, universal questions were being asked, and answers were being sought from a new quarter—the human mind's critical analysis of material phenomena. Nature was to be explained in terms of nature itself, not of something fundamentally beyond nature, and in impersonal terms rather than by means of personal gods and goddesses. The primitive universe ruled by anthropomorphic deities began to give way to a world whose source and substance was a primary natural element such as water, air, or fire. In time, these primary substances would cease to be endowed with divinity or intelligence, and would instead be understood as purely material entities mechanically moved by chance or blind necessity. But already a rudimentary naturalistic empiricism was being born. And as man's independent intelligence grew stronger, the sovereign power of the old gods grew weak.

The next step in this philosophical revolution, a step no less consequential than that of Thales a century earlier, was taken in the western part of the Greek world in southern Italy (Magna Graecia) when Parmenides of Elea approached the problem of what was genuinely real by means of a purely abstract rational logic. Again, as with the early Ionians, Parmenides's thought possessed a peculiar combination of traditional religious and novel secular elements. From what he described as a divine revelation emerged his achievement of an unprecedentedly rigorous deductive logic. In their search for simplicity in explaining nature, the Ionian philosophers had stated that the world was one thing, but had become many. But in Parmenides's early struggle with language and logic, "to be" something made it impossible for it to change into something it is not, for what "is not" cannot be said to exist at all. Similarly, he argued that "what is" can never have come into being or pass away, since something cannot come from nothing or turn into nothing if nothing cannot exist at all. Things cannot be as they appear to the senses: the familiar world of change, motion, and multiplicity must be mere opinion, for the true reality by logical necessity is changeless and unitary.

These rudimentary but foundational developments in logic necessitated thinking through for the first time such matters as the difference between the real and the apparent, between rational truth and sensory perception, and between being and becoming. Of equal importance, Parmenides's logic eventually forced into the open the distinction between a static material substance and a dynamic ordering life-force (which had been presumed identical by the Ionians), and thereby highlighted the basic problem of what caused motion in the universe. But most significant was Parmenides's declaration of the autonomy and superiority of the human reason as judge of reality. For what was real was intelligible—an object of intellectual apprehension, not of sense perception.

These two advancing trends of naturalism and rationalism impelled the development of a series of increasingly sophisticated theories to explain the natural world. Obliged to reconcile the conflicting demands of sensory observation with the new logical rigor, Empedocles, Anaxagoras, and finally the atomists attempted to explain the world's apparent change and multiplicity by reinterpreting and modifying Parmenides's absolute monism—reality as one, motionless, and changeless—in terms of more pluralistic systems. Each of these systems adhered to Parmenides's view that what was real could not ultimately come into being or pass away, but they interpreted the apparent birth and destruction of natural objects as being the consequence of a multiplicity of fundamental unchanging elements which alone were truly real, and which moved into and out of various combinations to form the objects of the world. The elements themselves did not come into being or pass away. Only their constantly shifting combinations were subject to such change. Empedocles posited four ultimate root elements—earth, water, air, and fire—which were eternal, and which were moved together and apart by the primary forces of Love and Strife. Anaxagoras proposed that the universe was constituted by an infinite number of minute, qualitatively different seeds. But instead of explaining matter's movement in terms of blind semimythic forces (such as Love and Strife), he postulated a transcendent primordial Mind (*Nous*), which set the material universe into motion and gave it form and order.

But the most comprehensive system in this development was that of atomism. In an attempt to fulfill the Ionians' search for an elementary substance constituting the material world, while also overcoming the Parmenidean argument against change and multiplicity, Leucippus and his successor Democritus constructed a complex explanation of all phenomena in purely materialistic terms: The world was composed exclusively of uncaused and immutable material atoms—a unitary changeless substance, as Parmenides required, though of infinite number. These invisibly minute and indivisible particles perpetually moved about in a boundless void and by their random collisions and varying combinations

produced the phenomena of the visible world. The atoms were qualitatively identical, different only in shape and size—i.e., in quantitative
and hence measurable terms. Democritus further answered Parmenides's
objection by stating that what "is not" could indeed exist, in the sense of
a void—an empty but real space which made room for the atoms to move
and combine. The atoms were moved mechanically, not by any cosmic
intelligence such as the *Nous,* but by the blind chance of natural
necessity (*anankē*). All human knowledge was derived simply from the
impact of the material atoms on the senses. Much of human experience,
however, such as that of hot and cold or bitter and sweet, derived not
from the atoms' inherent qualities but from human "convention." Qualities were subjective human perceptions, for the atoms possessed only
quantitative differences. What was real was matter in space, atoms
moving randomly in the void. When a man died, his soul perished;
matter, however, was conserved and did not perish. Only the specific
combinations of atoms changed, with the same atoms constantly col-
liding and forming different bodies in various stages of increase and
decrease, conglomerating and breaking apart, thereby creating and dissolving over time an infinite number of worlds throughout the void.

In atomism, the mythological residue of the earliest philosophers'
self-animated substance was now fully removed: the void alone caused
the random motions of the atoms, which were entirely material and
possessed neither divine order nor purpose. For some, this explanation
succeeded as the most lucid rational effort to escape the distortions of
human subjectivity and desire, and to grasp the unadorned mechanisms
of the universe. For others, however, much was left unresolved—the
issue of forms and their duration, the question of purpose in the world,
the need for a more satisfying answer to the problem of a first cause of
motion. Significant advances in understanding the world seemed to be
developing, yet much that had been certain for the primitive, pre-
philosophical mind was now problematic. By implication of these early
philosophical forays, not only the gods but the immediate evidence of
one's own senses might be an illusion, and the human mind alone must
be relied upon to discover rationally what is real.

There was one major exception to this intellectual progress among the
Greeks away from the mythic and toward the naturalistic, and this was
Pythagoras. The dichotomy of religion and reason seems to have not so
much pressed Pythagoras antithetically away from one in favor of the
other, but rather provided for him an impetus toward synthesis. Indeed,

his reputation among the ancients was that of a man whose genius was as much religious as scientific. Yet little can be said about Pythagoras with any definiteness. A rule of strict secrecy was maintained by his school, and an aura of legend surrounded it from its beginnings. Originally from the Ionian island of Samos, Pythagoras probably traveled and studied in Egypt and Mesopotamia before migrating westward to the Greek colony of Croton in southern Italy. There he established a philosophical school and religious brotherhood centered on the cult of Apollo and the Muses, and dedicated to the pursuit of moral purification, spiritual salvation, and the intellectual penetration of nature—all of which were understood as intimately interconnected.

Where the Ionian physicists were interested in the material substance of phenomena, the Pythagoreans focused on the forms, particularly mathematical, that governed and ordered those phenomena. And while the main current of Greek thought was breaking away from the mythological and religious ground of archaic Greek culture, Pythagoras and his followers conducted philosophy and science in a framework permeated by the beliefs of the mystery religions, especially Orphism. To comprehend scientifically the order of the natural universe was the Pythagorean *via regia* to spiritual illumination. The forms of mathematics, the harmonies of music, the motions of the planets, and the gods of the mysteries were all essentially related for Pythagoreans, and the meaning of that relation was revealed in an education that culminated in the human soul's assimilation to the world soul, and thence to the divine creative mind of the universe. Because of the Pythagorean commitment to cultic secrecy, the specifics of that meaning and of the process by which that meaning was disclosed remain largely unknown. What is certain is that the Pythagorean school charted its independent philosophical course according to a belief system that decisively maintained the ancient structures of myth and the mystery religions while advancing scientific discoveries of immense consequence for later Western thought.

But the general tenor of Greek intellectual evolution was otherwise, as from Thales and Anaximander to Leucippus and Democritus a naturalistic science matured in step with an increasingly skeptical rationalism. Although none of these philosophers commanded universal cultural influence, and although for most Greeks the Olympian gods were never seriously in doubt, the gradual rise of these different strands of early philosophy—Ionian physics, Eleatic rationalism, Democritean atomism—represented the seminal vanguard of Greek thought in its development out of the era of traditional belief into the era of reason. With the exception of the relatively autonomous Pythagoreans, the Hellenic mind before Socrates followed a definite, if at times ambiguous, direction away from the supernatural and toward the natural: from the divine to the mundane, from the mythical to the conceptual, from poetry and story to prose and analysis. To the more critical intellects of this later age, the gods of the ancient poets' stories seemed all too human, made in man's own image, and increasingly dubious as real divine entities. Already near the start of the fifth century B.C. the poet-philosopher Xenophanes had disparaged the popular acceptance of Homeric mythology, with its anthropomorphic gods engaged in immoral activities: if oxen, lions, or horses had hands with which to make images, they would undoubtedly form gods with bodies and shapes like their own. A generation later, Anaxagoras declared that the Sun was not the god Helios but was rather an incandescent stone larger than the Peloponnese, and that the Moon was composed of an earthy substance which received its light from the Sun. Democritus considered that human belief in gods was no more than an attempt to explain extraordinary events like thunderstorms or earthquakes by means of imagined supernatural forces. An equivocal skepticism toward the ancient myths could be seen even in Euripides, the last of the great tragedians, while the comic dramatist Aristophanes openly parodied them. In the face of such diverging speculations, the time-honored cosmology was no longer self-evident.

Yet the more the Greek developed a sense of individual critical judgment and emerged from the collective primordial vision of earlier generations, the more conjectural became his understanding, the more narrow the compass of infallible knowledge. "As for certain truth," Xenophanes asserted, "no man has known it, nor will he know it." Philosophical contributions such as the irresolvable logical paradoxes of Zeno of Elea, or Heraclitus's doctrine of the world as constant flux, often seemed only to exacerbate the new uncertainties. With the advent of reason, everything seemed open to doubt, and each succeeding philosopher offered solutions differing from his predecessor's. If the world was governed exclusively by mechanical natural forces, then there remained no evident basis upon which firm moral judgments could be founded. And if the true reality was entirely divorced from common experience, then the very foundations of human knowledge were called into question. It seemed that the more man became freely and consciously self-determining, the less sure was his footing. Still, that price appeared well worth paying if human beings could be emancipated from the superstitious fears and beliefs of conventional piety and allowed insight, however provisional, into the genuine order of things. Despite the continual emergence of new problems and new attempted solutions, a heartening sense of intellectual progress seemed to override the various confusions accompanying it. Thus Xenophanes could affirm: "The gods did not reveal, from the beginning, all things to us; but in the course of time, through seeking, men find that which is the better. . . ."[4]

The Greek Enlightenment

This intellectual development reached its climax in Athens as the various streams of Greek thought and art converged there during the fifth century B.C. The age of Pericles and the building of the Parthenon saw Athens at the peak of its cultural creativity and political influence in Greece, and Athenian man asserted himself within his world with a new sense of his own power and intelligence. After its triumph over the Persian invaders and its establishment as leader of the Greek states, Athens rapidly emerged as an expansive commercial and maritime city with imperial ambitions. Its burgeoning activities provided Athenian citizens with increased contact with other cultures and outlooks and a new urban sophistication. Athens had become the first Greek metropolis. The development of democratic self-government and technical advances in agriculture and navigation both expressed and encouraged the new humanistic spirit. Earlier philosophers had been relatively isolated in their speculations, with one or perhaps a few disciples to carry on their work. Now in Athens such speculation became more representative of the city's intellectual life as a whole, which continued to move toward conceptual thought, critical analysis, reflection, and dialectic.

In the course of the fifth century, Hellenic culture attained a delicate and fertile balance between the ancient mythological tradition and the modern secular rationalism. Temples to the gods were erected with an unprecedented zeal to capture a timeless Olympian grandeur. Yet in the monumental buildings, sculptures, and paintings of the Parthenon, in the artistic creations of Phideas and Polyclitus, this grandeur was accomplished not least through meticulous analysis and theory, through a vigorous effort to combine human rationality with the mythic order in concrete form. The temples to Zeus, Athena, and Apollo seemed to celebrate man's triumph of rational clarity and mathematical elegance as much as they offered homage to the divine. Similarly, the Greek artists' renderings of gods and goddesses were renderings of Greek men and women—ideal, spiritualized, yet manifestly human and individual. Still, the characteristic object of artistic aspiration continued to be the gods, and there remained a sense of man's proper limits in the universal scheme. The new creative treatment of myth by Aeschylus and Sophocles, or the odes of the great choral poet Pindar, who saw intimations of the gods in the athletic feats of the Olympic games, suggested that man's own developing abilities could enhance and give exalted expression to the divine powers. Yet both tragedies and choral hymns upheld the boundaries of human ambition, beyond which lay danger and impossibility.

As the fifth century advanced, the balance continued to shift in favor of man. Hippocrates's seminal work in medicine, Herodotus's observant histories and travel descriptions, Meton's new calendrical system, Thucydides's penetrating historical analyses, the bold scientific speculations of Anaxagoras and Democritus—all extended the scope of the Hellenic mind and forwarded its grasp of things in terms of rationally comprehensible natural causes. Pericles himself was intimate with the rationalist philosopher and physicist Anaxagoras, and a new intellectual rigor, skeptical of the old supernatural explanations, was widespread. Contemporary man now perceived himself as more a civilized product of progress from savagery than a degeneration from a mythical golden age.[5] The commercial and political rise of an active middle class further moved against the aristocratic hierarchy of the old gods and heroes. The long-stable society celebrated by Pindar for his aristocratic patrons was giving way to a new order that was more fluidly egalitarian and aggressively competitive. With that change was also left behind Pindar's conservative maintenance of the old religious values and sanctions against uninhibited human endeavor. Belief in the traditional deities of the Athenian polis was being undermined, and a more critical and secular spirit was strongly on the ascent.

The most acute stage in this evolution was reached in the latter half of the fifth century with the emergence of the Sophists. The leading protagonists of the new intellectual milieu, the Sophists were itinerant professional teachers, secular humanists of a liberal spirit who offered both intellectual instruction and guidance for success in practical affairs. With the expanded possibilities for political participation in the democratic polis, the services of the Sophists were in high demand. The general tenor of their thought was marked by the same rationalism and naturalism that had characterized the development of philosophy before them, and that increasingly reflected the spirit of the age. But with the Sophists, a new element of skeptical pragmatism entered Greek thought, turning philosophy away from its earlier, more speculative and cosmological concerns. According to Sophists such as Protagoras, man was the measure of all things, and his own individual judgments concerning everyday human life should form the basis of his personal beliefs and conduct—not naive conformity to traditional religion nor indulgence in far-flung abstract speculation. Truth was relative, not absolute, and differed from culture to culture, from person to person, and from situation to situation. Claims to the contrary, whether religious or philosophical, could not stand up to critical argument. The ultimate value of any belief or opinion could be judged only by its practical utility in serving an individual's needs in life.

This decisive shift in the character of Greek thought, encouraged by the contemporary social and political situation, owed as much to the problematic condition of natural philosophy at that time as to the decline in traditional religious belief. Not only were the old mythologies losing their hold on the Greek mind, but the current state of scientific explanation was reaching a point of crisis. The extremes of Parmenidean logic with its obscure paradoxes, and of atomistic physics with its hypothetical atoms, both of which controverted the tangible reality of common human experience, were beginning to make the entire practice of theoretical philosophy seem irrelevant. In the Sophists' view, the speculative cosmologies neither spoke to practical human needs nor appeared plausible to common sense. From Thales on, each philosopher had proposed his particular theory as to what was the true nature of the world, with each theory contradicting the others, and with a growing tendency to reject the reality of more and more of the phenomenal world revealed by the senses. The result was a chaos of conflicting ideas, with no basis upon which to certify one above the rest. Moreover, the natural philosophers seemed to have been constructing their theories about the external world without adequately taking into account the human observer, the subjective element. By contrast, the Sophists recognized that each person had his own experience, and therefore his own reality. In the end, they argued, all understanding is subjective opinion. Genuine objectivity is impossible. All a person can legitimately claim to know is probabilities, not absolute truth.

Yet, according to the Sophists, it did not matter if man had no certain insight into the world outside him. He could know only the contents of his own mind—appearances rather than essences—but these constituted the only reality that could be of valid concern to him. Other than appearances, a deeper stable reality could not be known, not only on account of man's limited faculties, but more fundamentally because such a reality could not be said to exist outside of human conjecture. Yet the true aim of human thought was to serve human needs, and only individual experience could provide a basis for achieving that aim. Each person should rely on his own wits to make his way through the world. Acknowledgment of the individual's intellectual limitations would therefore be a liberation, for only in that way could a man seek to make his thought stand on its own, sovereign, serving himself rather than illusory absolutes arbitrarily defined by unreliable sources external to his own judgment.

The Sophists proposed that the critical rationalism that had previously been directed toward the physical world could now more fruitfully be applied to human affairs, to ethics and politics. The evidence of travelers' reports, for example, suggested that social practices and religious beliefs were not absolutes but merely local human conventions, received pieties varying according to each nation's customs with no fundamental relation either to nature or to divine commandment. The recent physical theories were drawn on to suggest the same conclusion: If the experience of hot and cold had no objective existence in nature but was merely an individual person's subjective impression created by a temporary arrangement of interacting atoms, then so too might the standards of right and wrong be equally insubstantial, conventional, and subjectively determined.

The existence of the gods could similarly be recognized as an undemonstrable assumption. As Protagoras said, "Concerning the gods, I have no means of knowing whether they exist or not, nor of what form they are; for there are many obstacles to such knowledge, including the obscurity of the subject and the shortness of human life." Another Sophist, Critias, suggested that the gods were invented to instill fear in those who would otherwise have acted in an evil manner. Much like the physicists with their mechanistic naturalism, the Sophists considered nature an impersonal phenomenon whose laws of chance and necessity bore little concern for human affairs. The evidence of unbiased common sense suggested that the world was constituted by visible matter, not invisible deities. The world was therefore best viewed apart from religious prejudices.

Hence the Sophists concluded in favor of a flexible atheism or agnosticism in metaphysics and a situational morality in ethics. Since religious beliefs, political structures, and rules of moral conduct were now seen to be humanly created conventions, these were all open to fundamental questioning and change. After centuries of blind obedience to restrictive traditional attitudes, man could now free himself to pursue a program of enlightened self-interest. To discover by rational means what was most useful for man seemed a more intelligent strategy than to base one's actions on belief in mythological deities or the absolutist assumptions of unprovable metaphysics. Since it was futile to seek absolute truth, the Sophists recommended that young men learn from them the practical arts of rhetorical persuasion and logical dexterity, as well as a broad spectrum of other subjects ranging from social history and ethics to mathematics and music. The citizen could thereby be best prepared to play an effective role in the polis democracy and, more generally, assure for himself a successful life in the world. Because the skills for achieving excellence in life could be taught and learned, a man was free to expand his opportunities through education. He was not limited by traditional assumptions such as the conventional belief that one's abilities were forever fixed as a result of chance endowment or the status of one's birth. Through such a program as that offered by the Sophists, both the individual and the society could better themselves.

Thus the Sophists mediated the transition from an age of myth to an age of practical reason. Man and society were to be studied, methodically and empirically, without theological preconceptions. Myths were to be understood as allegorical fables, not revelations of a divine reality. Rational acuity, grammatical precision, and oratorical prowess were the prime virtues in the new ideal man. The proper molding of a man's character for successful participation in polis life required a sound education in the various arts and sciences, and thus was established the paideia—the classical Greek system of education and training, which came to include gymnastics, grammar, rhetoric, poetry, music, mathematics, geography, natural history, astronomy and the physical sciences, history of society and ethics, and philosophy—the complete pedagogical course of study necessary to produce a well-rounded, fully educated citizen.

The Sophists' systematic doubting of human beliefs—whether the traditional belief in the gods or the more recent but, in their view, equally naive faith in human reason's capacity genuinely to know the nature of something as immense and indeterminate as the cosmos—was freeing thought to take new and unexplored paths. As a result, man's status was greater than ever before. He was increasingly free and self-determining, aware of a larger world containing cultures and beliefs besides his own, aware of the relativity and plasticity of human values and customs, aware of his own role in creating his reality. Yet he was no longer so significant in the cosmic scheme, which, if it existed at all, had its own logic heedless of man and Greek cultural values.

Other problems were presented by the Sophists' views. Despite the positive effects of their intellectual training and establishment of a liberal education as a basis for effective character formation, a radical skepticism toward all values led some to advocate an explicitly amoral opportunism. Students were instructed how to devise ostensibly plausible arguments supporting virtually any claim. More concretely disturbing was the con-current deterioration of the political and ethical situation in Athens to the point of crisis—the democracy turning fickle and corrupt, the conse-quent takeover by a ruthless oligarchy, the Athenian leadership of Greece becoming tyrannical, wars begun in arrogance ending in disaster. Daily life in Athens saw minimally humane ethical standards un-scrupulously violated—visible not least in the exclusively male Athenian citizenry's routine and often cruel exploitation of women, slaves, and foreigners. All these developments had their own origins and motives, and could hardly be laid at the feet of the Sophists. Yet in such critical circumstances, the philosophical denial of absolute values and sophistical commendation of stark opportunism seemed both to reflect and to exacerbate the problematic spirit of the times.

The Sophists' relativistic humanism, for all its progressive and liberal character, was not proving wholly benign. The larger world opened by Athens's earlier triumphs had destabilized its ancient certainties and now seemed to require a larger order—universal, yet conceptual—within which events could be comprehended. The Sophists' teachings provided no such order, but rather a method for success. How success itself was to be defined remained moot. Their bold assertion of human intellectual sovereignty—that through its own power man's thought could provide him with sufficient wisdom to live his life well, that the human mind could independently produce the strength of equilibrium—now seemed to require reevaluation. To more conservative sensibilities, the foundations of the traditional Hellenic belief system and its previously timeless values were being dangerously eroded, while reason and verbal skill were coming to have a less than impeccable reputation. Indeed, the whole development of reason now seemed to have undercut its own basis, with the human mind denying itself the capacity for genuine knowledge of the world.

Socrates

It was in this highly charged cultural climate that Socrates began his philosophical search, as skeptical and individualistic as any Sophist. A younger contemporary of Pericles, Euripides, Herodotus, and Protagoras, and growing up in an era when he could see the Parthenon built on the Acropolis from start to finish, Socrates entered the philosophical arena at the height of tension between the ancient Olympian tradition and the vigorous new intellectualism. By virtue of his extraordinary life and death, he would leave the Greek mind radically transformed, establishing not only a new method and new ideal for the pursuit of truth, but also, in his own person, an enduring model and inspiration for all subsequent philosophy.

Despite the magnitude of Socrates's influence, little is known with certainty about his life. Socrates himself wrote nothing. The richest and most coherent portrait of the man is that contained in Plato's *Dialogues*, but precisely to what extent the words and ideas attributed there to Socrates reflect the subsequent evolution of Plato's own thought remains unclear (a problem we shall address at the end of the chapter). The extant reports of other contemporaries and followers—Xenophon, Aeschines, Aristophanes, Aristotle, later Platonists—though helpful, are generally secondhand or fragmentary, often ambiguous, and sometimes contradictory. Nevertheless, a reasonably reliable picture can be pieced together by drawing on the early Platonic dialogues in combination with the other sources.

It is evident from these that Socrates was a man of singular character and intelligence, who was imbued with a passion for intellectual honesty and moral integrity rare for his or any other age. He insistently sought answers to questions that had not before been asked, attempted to undermine conventional assumptions and beliefs to provoke more careful thinking about ethical matters, and tirelessly compelled both himself and those with whom he conversed to seek a deeper understanding of what constituted a good life. His words and deeds embodied an abiding conviction that the act of rational self-criticism could free the human mind from the bondage of false opinion. Because of his dedication to the task of discovering wisdom and drawing it forth from others, Socrates neglected his private affairs, spending all his time instead in earnest discussion with his fellow citizens. Unlike the Sophists, he did not charge for his instruction. Although intimate with the elite of Athens, he was altogether indifferent to material wealth and conventional standards of success. Socrates gave the impression of being a man unusually at one with himself, though his personal character was full of paradoxical contrasts. Disarmingly humble yet presumptuously confident, puckishly witty yet morally urgent, engaging and gregarious yet solitary and contemplative, Socrates was above all a man consumed by a passion for truth.

As a young man Socrates appears to have studied the natural science of his time with some enthusiasm, examining the various contemporary philosophies concerned with speculative analysis of the physical world. Eventually, however, he found these unsatisfying. The welter of conflicting theories brought more confusion than clarity, and their explanations of the universe solely in terms of material causation, ignoring the evidence of purposive intelligence in the world, seemed to him inadequate. Such theories, he judged, were neither conceptually coherent nor morally useful. He therefore turned from physics and cosmology to ethics and logic. How one should live, and how to think clearly about how one should live, became his overriding concern. As Cicero would declare three centuries later, Socrates "called down philosophy from the skies and implanted it in the cities and homes of men."

Such a shift was indeed already reflected in the ideas of the Sophists, who also resembled Socrates in their concern with education, language, rhetoric, and argument. But the character of Socrates's moral and intellectual aspirations was sharply different. The Sophists offered to teach others how to live a successful life, in a world in which all moral standards were conventions and all human knowledge was relative. Socrates believed such an educational philosophy was both intellectually misconceived and morally detrimental. In opposition to the Sophist view, Socrates saw his own task as that of finding a way to a knowledge that transcended mere opinion, to inform a morality that transcended mere convention.

At an early date in the young philosopher's life, the oracle of Apollo at Delphi had declared that no man was wiser than Socrates. Seeking, as he later put it with characteristic irony, to disprove the oracle, Socrates assiduously examined the beliefs and thinking of all who considered themselves wise—concluding that he was indeed wiser than all others, for he alone recognized his own ignorance. But while the Sophists had held genuine knowledge to be unattainable, Socrates held rather that genuine knowledge had not yet been achieved. His repeated demonstrations of human ignorance, both his own and that of others, were intended to elicit not intellectual despair but rather intellectual humility. The discovery of ignorance was for Socrates the beginning rather than the end of the philosophical task, for only through that discovery could one begin to overcome those received assumptions that obscured the true nature of what it was to be a human being. Socrates conceived it his personal mission to convince others of their ignorance so that they might better search for a knowledge of how life should best be lived.

In Socrates's view, any attempt to foster true success and excellence in human life had to take account of the innermost reality of a human being, his soul or psyche. Perhaps on the basis of his own highly developed sense of individual selfhood and self-control, Socrates brought to the Greek mind a new awareness of the central significance of the soul, establishing it for the first time as the seat of the individual waking consciousness and of the moral and intellectual character. He affirmed the Delphic motto "Know thyself," for he believed that it was only through self-knowledge, through an understanding of one's own psyche and its proper condition, that one could find genuine happiness. All human beings seek happiness by their very nature, and happiness, Socrates taught, is achieved through living the kind of life that best serves the nature of the soul. Happiness is the consequence not of physical or external circumstances, of wealth or power or reputation, but of living a life that is good for the soul.

Yet to live a genuinely good life, one must know what is the nature and essence of the good. Otherwise one will be acting blindly, on the basis of mere convention or expediency, calling something good or virtuous whenever it conforms to popular opinion or serves the pleasure of the moment. By contrast, Socrates argued, if a man does know what is truly good—what is beneficial for him in the deepest sense—then he will naturally and inevitably act in a good manner. Knowing what is good will necessarily cause one to act on that basis, for no man deliberately chooses that which he knows would harm himself. It is only when he mistakes an illusory good for a genuine good that he falls into erroneous conduct. No one ever does wrong knowingly, for it is the very nature of the good that when it is known, it is desired. In this sense, Socrates held, virtue is knowledge. A truly happy life is a life of right action directed according to reason. The key to human happiness, therefore, is the development of a rational moral character.

But for a person to discover what is genuine virtue, hard questions must be asked. To know virtue, one has to discover the common element in all virtuous acts: i.e., the essence of virtue. One has to take apart, analyze, test the worth of every statement about the nature of virtue in order to find its true character. It is not enough to cite examples of various kinds of virtuous actions and say that this is virtue itself, for such an answer does not reveal the single essential quality within all the examples that makes them genuine instances of virtue. So also with goodness, justice, courage, piety, beauty. Socrates criticized the Sophist belief that such terms were ultimately only words, mere names for currently established human conventions. Words could indeed distort and deceive, giving the impression of truth when actually they lacked solid foundation. But words could also point, as to a precious invisible mystery, to something genuine and enduring. To find one's way to that genuine reality was the task confronting the philosopher.

It was in the course of pursuing this task that Socrates developed his famous dialectical form of argument that would become fundamental to the character and evolution of the Western mind: reasoning through rigorous dialogue as a method of intellectual investigation intended to expose false beliefs and elicit truth. Socrates's characteristic strategy was to take up a sequence of questions with whomever he was in discussion, relentlessly analyzing one by one the implications of the answers in such a way as to bring out the flaws and inconsistencies inherent in a given belief or statement. Attempts to define the essence of something were rejected one after another as being either too wide or too narrow, or as missing the mark altogether. Often it happened that such an analysis ended in complete perplexity, with Socrates's fellow discussants feeling as if they had been numbed by a stingray. Yet at such times it was clear that philosophy for Socrates was concerned less with knowing the right answers than with the strenuous attempt to discover those answers. Philosophy was a process, a discipline, a lifelong quest. To practice philosophy in the Socratic manner was continually to subject one's thoughts to the criticism of reason in earnest dialogue with others. Genuine knowledge was not something that could simply be received from another secondhand like a purchased commodity, as with the Sophists, but was rather a personal achievement, won only at the cost of constant intellectual struggle and self-critical reflection. "The life not tested by criticism," Socrates declared, "is not worth living."

Because of his incessant questioning of others, however, Socrates was not universally popular, and his active encouraging of a critical skepticism among his pupils was regarded by some as a dangerously unsettling influence which undermined the proper authority of tradition and the state. In his painstaking effort to find certain knowledge, Socrates had spent much of his life outdoing the Sophists at their own game, but ironically it was with the Sophists that Socrates was classed when, in the politically unstable period in Athens following the disastrous Peloponnesian War, two citizens accused him of impiety and of corrupting the young. Caught in a backlash against a number of political figures, some of whom had once been in his circle, Socrates was sentenced to death. In such a situation it would have been customary to propose an alternative punishment of exile, and this was probably what his accusers desired. But Socrates refused at every stage of the trial to compromise his principles, and rejected all efforts to escape or modify the consequences of the verdict. He affirmed the rightness of the life he had led, even if his mission to awaken others now brought him death—which he did not fear, but rather welcomed as a portal to eternity. Cheerfully drinking the poison hemlock, Socrates became an unreluctant martyr to the ideal of philosophy that he had so long championed.

The Platonic Hero

The friends and disciples who gathered around Socrates in his last days were drawn to a man who, to a singular degree, had embodied his own ideal. With its unique synthesis of *eros* and *logos*—of passion and mind, friendship and argument, desire and truth—Socrates's philosophy appears to have been a direct expression of his personality. Each Socratic idea and its articulation bore the mark of, and seemed to have been born of, the very core of his personal character. Indeed, as he was portrayed in the full course of Plato's dialogues, it was this very fact—that Socrates spoke and thought with an intellectual and moral confidence based on profound self-knowledge, rooted as it were in the depths of his psyche— that gave him the capacity to express a truth that was in some sense universal, grounded in divine truth itself.

Yet it was not only this charismatic profundity of mind and soul that Plato emphasized in his portrait of the master. The Socrates commemorated by Plato also developed and set forth a specific epistemological position that in effect brought the dialectical Socratic strategy to its metaphysical fulfillment. And here we shall extend our discussion of this pivotal figure by drawing on the more elaborated—and more decisively "Platonic"—interpretation of Socrates contained in the great middle dialogues of Plato. Beginning with the *Phaedo,* and in fully developed form in such dialogues as the *Symposium* and the *Republic,* the character of Socrates increasingly voices positions that move beyond those attributed to him in the earlier dialogues and by other sources such as Xenophon and Aristotle. Although the evidence may be interpreted in several ways, it would appear that Plato, in reflecting upon the legacy of his teacher in the course of his own intellectual evolution, gradually made explicit in these more developed positions what he understood to be implicit in both Socrates's life and his arguments.

As the dialogues progress (and their exact order is not entirely clear), the earlier account of Socrates—pressing hard his demands for logical coherence and meaningful definitions, criticizing all the presumed certainties of human belief—begins to move forward to a new level of philosophical argument. After having investigated every current system of thought, from the scientific philosophies of nature to the subtle arguments of the Sophists, Socrates had concluded that all of them lacked sound critical method. To clarify his own approach, he decided to concern himself not with facts but with statements about facts. These propositions he would analyze by treating each as a hypothesis, deducing its consequences, and thereby judging its value. A hypothesis whose consequences were found to be true and consistent would be provisionally affirmed, though not proved, since it in turn could be certified only by appeal to a more ultimate accepted hypothesis.

Finally, according to Plato's middle dialogues, after exhaustive argument and meditation on these matters, Socrates put forth his own fundamental postulate to serve as that ultimate foundation for knowledge and moral standards: When something is good or beautiful, it is so because that thing partakes of an archetypal essence of goodness or beauty that is absolute and perfect, that exists on a timeless level that transcends its passing particular manifestation, and that is ultimately accessible only to the intellect, not to the senses. Such universals have a real nature beyond mere human convention or opinion, and an independent existence beyond the phenomena they inform. The human mind can discover and know these timeless universals, through the supreme discipline of philosophy.

As described by Plato, this hypothesis of the "Forms" or "Ideas," though never proved, seems to have represented something more than a plausible result of logical discussion, standing rather as an apodictic—absolutely certain and necessary—reality beyond all the conjectures, obscurities, and illusions of human experience. Its philosophical justification was finally epiphanic, self-evident to the lover of truth who had attained the distant goal of illumination. Plato's implication seemed to be that in Socrates's resolute attention to his mind and soul, to moral virtue as well as intellectual truth, the world order itself had been contacted and revealed. In Plato's Socrates, human thought no longer stood precariously on its own, but had found a confidence and certainty grounded in something more fundamental. Thus, as dramatically set forth by Plato, the paradoxical denouement of Socrates's skeptical pursuit of truth was his final arrival at the conception, or vision, of the eternal Ideas—absolute Good, Truth, Beauty, and the rest—in contemplation of which he ended his long philosophical search and fulfilled it.

The age of mythic heroes and gods seemed long past for the modern urban Athenians, but in Plato's Socrates the Homeric hero was reborn, now as hero of the intellectual and spiritual quest for absolutes in a realm endangered by the Scylla of sophistry and the Charybdis of traditionalism. It was a new form of immortal glory that Socrates revealed as he faced his death, and it was in this act of philosophical heroism that the Homeric ideal took on fresh significance for Plato and his followers. For through Socrates's intellectual labor had been born a spiritual reality apparently so fundamental and all-comprehensive that even death did not dim its existence, but on the contrary served as its gateway. The transcendent world unveiled in Plato's dialogues—themselves great works of literature like the epic poems and dramas already gracing

Hellenic culture—bespoke a new Olympian realm, a realm that reflected the new sense of rational order while also recalling the exalted grandeur of the ancient mythic deities. The Socrates of Plato's report had remained true to the Greek development of reason and individualistic humanism. But in the course of his intellectual odyssey, critically employing and synthesizing his predecessors' insights, he had forged a new connection to a timeless reality, one now endowed with philosophical significance as well as mythic numinosity. In Socrates, thought was confidently embraced as a vital force of life and an indispensable instrument of the spirit. Intellect was not just a profitable tool of Sophists and politicians, nor just the remote preserve of physical speculation and obscure paradox. It was, rather, the divine faculty by which the human soul could discover both its own essence and the world's meaning. That faculty required only awakening. However arduous the path of awakening, such divine intellectual power lay potentially resident in humble and great alike.

Thus stood the figure of Socrates for Plato—the resolution and climax of the Greek quest for truth, the restorer of the world's divine foundation, the awakener of the human intellect. What for Homer and the archaic mind had been an inseparable connection between the empirical and the archetypal, a connection that was increasingly challenged in the naturalism of the Ionian physicists and the rationalism of the Eleatics, and eliminated altogether in the materialism of the atomists and the skepticism of the Sophists, was now reformulated and restored on a new level by Socrates and Plato. In contrast to the undifferentiated archaic vision, the perceived relation between the archetypal and the empirical had now become more problematic, dichotomized, and dualistic. This step was a crucial one. But the underlying, rediscovered commonality with the primordial mythic vision was equally crucial. In the Platonic understanding, the world was again illuminated by universal themes and figures. Its governing principles were again knowable by the human mind. Divine absolutes once more ruled the cosmos and provided a foundation for human conduct. Existence was again endowed with transcendent purpose. Intellectual rigor and Olympian inspiration no longer stood opposed. Human values were again rooted in nature's order, both of which were informed by divine intelligence.

With Socrates and Plato, the Greek search for clarity, order, and meaning in the manifold of human experience had come full circle, bringing an intellectual restoration of the numinous reality known in Hellenic culture's distant Homeric childhood. Thus Plato joined his conception with, and gave new life and significance to, the archaic archetypal vision of the ancient Greek sensibility.

>+X+<

Socrates is the paradigmatic figure of Greek philosophy—indeed, of all Western philosophy—yet we possess nothing written by him that could represent his ideas directly. It was largely through the powerful prism of Plato's understanding that his life and thought were passed on to posterity. Socrates's impact on the young Plato was potent enough that the Platonic dialogues seem to bear the Socratic imprint on almost every page, carrying in their very form the dialectical spirit of Socratic philosophy, and making any final distinctions between the two philosophers' thought virtually impossible. The character of Socrates plays the major role and expresses the central themes in most of the important dialogues, and does so with a large degree of what appears to be faithfully portrayed personal idiosyncrasy. Where the historical Socrates ends and the Platonic Socrates begins is notoriously ambiguous. His self-effacing claim of ignorance seemingly contrasts with the Platonic knowledge of absolutes; yet the latter appears to have grown directly from the former, as if an unconditional intellectual humility were the eye of the needle giving passage to universal wisdom. Certainly Socrates's lifelong pursuit of truth and order would seem to have implicitly depended on a faith in the ultimate existence of that truth and order.[6] Moreover, the character and direction of his arguments, as represented not only in the early Platonic dialogues but also in the reports of others, strongly suggest that Socrates was at least logically committed to what would later be seen to be a theory of universals.

The trial and execution of Socrates by the Athenian democracy left a profound impression on Plato, persuading him of the untrustworthiness of both a rudderless democracy and a standardless philosophy: hence the necessity of an absolute foundation for values if any political or philosophical system was to be successful and wise. On the basis of the available historical and literary evidence, it would appear that Socrates's personal search for absolute definitions and moral certainty, and very possibly his suggestion of some early form of the doctrine of Ideas, was developed and extended through Plato's more encompassing sensibility into a comprehensive system. Additional insights were incorporated by Plato from the various Presocratics, particularly Parmenides (the changeless and unitary nature of intelligible reality), Heraclitus (the constant flux of the sensible world), and above all the Pythagoreans (the intelligibility of reality via mathematical forms). Socrates's more focused concerns and strategies thereby became the basis for Plato's broader enunciation of the major outlines and problems for subsequent Western philosophy in all its diverse areas—logic, ethics, politics, epistemology, ontology, aesthetics, psychology, cosmology.

Plato expressed that deepening and expansion by using the figure of Socrates to articulate the philosophy that he believed Socrates's life had nobly exampled. For in Plato's vision, Socrates appeared as a living embodiment of goodness and wisdom, the very qualities Plato considered to be the foundational principles of the world and the highest goals of human aspiration. Socrates thus became not only the inspiration for but also the personification of the Platonic philosophy. From Plato's art emerged the archetypal Socrates, the avatar of Platonism.

In this view, Plato did not provide a verbatim documentary of Socrates's thought; nor, in the opposite extreme, did he use Socrates merely as a mouthpiece for his own completely independent ideas. Rather, Plato's relationship to Socrates appears to have been more complicated, more mysterious, more interpretive and creative, as he elaborated and transformed his master's ideas to bring them to what he understood to be their inherent, systematically argued, metaphysically articulate conclusions. Socrates often referred to himself as an intellectual midwife, through his dialectical skill bringing to birth the latent truth in another's mind. Perhaps Platonic philosophy itself was the final and fullest fruit of that labor.

The Philosopher's Quest
and the Universal Mind

For all its devotion to dialectical precision and intellectual rigor, Plato's philosophy was permeated with a kind of religious romanticism that affected both its ontological categories and its epistemological strategy. As in his discussion of Eros in the *Symposium*, Plato described the Ideas not so much as neutral objects of dispassionate rational apprehension but as transcendent essences that, when directly experienced by the pure philosopher, evoke intense emotional response and even mystical rapture. The philosopher is literally a "lover of wisdom" and approaches his intellectual task as a romantic quest of universal significance. For Plato, the ultimate reality is not only ethical and rational in nature, but also aesthetic. The Good, the True, and the Beautiful are effectively united in the supreme creative principle, at once commanding moral affirmation, intellectual allegiance, and aesthetic surrender. As the most accessible of the Forms, visible in part even to the physical eye, Beauty opens up human awareness to the existence of the other Forms, drawing the philosopher toward the beatific vision and knowledge of the True and the Good. Hence Plato suggested that the highest philosophical vision is possible only to one with the temperament of a lover. The philosopher must permit himself to be inwardly grasped by the most sublime form of Eros—that universal passion to restore a former unity, to overcome the separation from the divine and become one with it.

Plato described knowledge of the divine as being implicit in every soul, but forgotten. The soul, immortal, experiences direct and intimate contact with the eternal realities prior to birth, but the postnatal human condition of bodily imprisonment causes the soul to forget the true state of affairs. The goal of philosophy is to free the soul from this deluded condition in which it is deceived by the finite imitation and veiling of the eternal. The philosopher's task is to "recollect" the transcendent Ideas, to recover a direct knowledge of the true causes and sources of all things.

In the *Republic*, Plato illustrated the difference between authentic knowledge of reality and the illusion of appearances with a striking image: Human beings are like prisoners chained to the wall of a dark subterranean cave, where they can never turn around to see the light of a fire that is higher up and at a distance behind them. When objects outside the cave pass in front of the light, the prisoners mistake as real what are merely shadows created on the wall. Only one who is freed from his chains and leaves the cave to enter into the world beyond can glimpse true reality, though when first exposed to the light he may be so overwhelmed by its dazzling luminosity as to be unable to recognize its actual character. Yet once he habituates himself to the light and comes to recognize the true causes of things, he would hold precious the clarity of his new understanding. Recalling his former fate among the other prisoners, where all incessantly devote their minds to the understanding of mere illusions, he would, like Homer, prefer to endure anything in the real world rather than be forced to live in the underworld of shadows. Indeed, were he required to return to the cave and, unaccustomed to its darkness, contend with the others in their usual activity of "understanding" the shadows, he would likely only provoke their ridicule, and be unable to persuade them that what they were perceiving was only a dim reflection of reality.

For Plato, then, the great task facing the philosopher was to emerge from the cave of ephemeral shadows and bring his darkened mind back into the archetypal light, the true source of being. When speaking of this higher reality, Plato repeatedly linked light, truth, and goodness. In the *Republic*, he described the Idea of the Good as being to the intelligible realm what the Sun is to the visible realm: in the same way that the Sun allows objects of the visible world to grow and to be visible, so does the Good grant to all objects of reason their existence and their intelligibility. The philosopher's attainment of virtue consists in his discovering that luminous knowledge which brings harmony between the human soul and the cosmic order of archetypes, an order governed and illuminated by the supreme Idea of the Good.

Yet to achieve liberation from the unenlightened state requires extraordinarily sustained intellectual and moral effort, so that the intellect—considered by Plato the highest part of the soul—can rise above the merely sensible and physical to reattain the lost knowledge of the Ideas. In some dialogues (such as the *Republic*), Plato emphasized the power of dialectic, or rigorously self-critical logic, to accomplish this aim, while elsewhere (such as in the *Symposium* and the *Seventh Letter*), he spoke more of a spontaneous recognition by the intuitive intellect—a visitation or moment of grace, as it were, after long discipline. In either case, the recollection of the Ideas is both the means and the goal of true knowledge.

And so Plato's primary directive for philosophy focused on the strenuous development of the intellect and will, motivated by a ceaseless desire to reattain the lost union with the eternal. Through the labor of philosophical recollection, the human mind can bring to birth the divine wisdom that was its former possession. Education, therefore, is in the service of the soul and the divine, and not, as for the Sophists, of the secular and human alone. Moreover, education is a process through which truth is not introduced into the mind from without, but is "led out" from within. The mind then finds revealed within itself a knowledge both of its own nature and of the universe, a knowledge otherwise clouded by the obscurities of mundane existence. Under Plato's guidance, the classical *paideia* assumed the deeper metaphysical and spiritual dimensions of the Academy, an institution as much monastery as university, holding forth the ideal of inner perfection realized through disciplined education.

Philosophical illumination, then, is a reawakening to and remembrance of forgotten knowledge, a reestablishment of the soul's happy intimacy with the transcendent Ideas that inhere in all things. Here Plato asserted the redemptive aspect of philosophy, for it is the soul's direct encounter with eternal Ideas that reveals to the soul its own eternity. In Plato's account of Socrates's last hours, it would appear that Socrates so highly valued this state of archetypal awareness transcending physical existence that he expressed equanimity, even eagerness, in anticipation of his death by hemlock. His entire life, he declared, had been directed toward this moment of embracing death, when the soul could at last return to the glory of its immortal state. Such passionately affirmed confidence in the reality of the eternal, accompanied by the dialogues' frequent references to myth and the sacred mysteries, suggests that Socrates and Plato themselves may have been intimately involved with the Greek mystery religions. In the Platonic vision, not only did the divine exist, as in traditional Greek public religion, but through the philosophical path the human soul could attain knowledge of its own divine immortality. Such a belief set Plato apart from the Homeric tradition, which had kept relatively strict limits between mortal humans and eternal gods, and placed him rather in the company of the mystery religions, in which initiation brought a revelation of immortality, and in the company of the Pythagoreans, for whom philosophy itself provided the highest path to mystical illumination and assimilation to the divine. Plato's affinity with such groups was also reflected in his belief that the highest truths should not be communicated to all, lest they be abused. Hence he preferred not the straightforward treatise, but the more ambiguous dialogue, which could conceal—and, for the properly prepared, reveal—the deepest truths of his philosophy.

It could be said that the dualism of the characteristic Platonic values— the philosopher over the common man, the mind and soul over matter, the pre-existing ideal Forms over the phenomenal world, the absolute over the relative, the posthumous spiritual life over the present physical life—reflected Plato's reaction to the political, moral, and intellectual crises of Athens during his lifetime. Whereas the fifth century at its height during the Periclean age had embraced the notion of mankind's autonomous achievement of progress from primitive ignorance to civilized sophistication, Plato often tended toward the earlier Greek view, set forth by Hesiod, that mankind's state had gradually degenerated from an earlier golden age. Plato saw not only contemporary man's technical progress but also his moral decline from the simpler innocence of the men of old, "who were better than ourselves and dwelt nearer the gods." Human achievement per se was relative and precarious. Only a society founded on divine principles and governed by divinely informed philosophers could save mankind from its destructive irrationality; and the best life was one directed away from mundane life and toward the world of the eternal Ideas. The changeless spiritual realm preceded and would forever be superior to whatever human beings tried to accomplish in the temporal world. The spiritual alone held genuine truth and value.

Yet for all his seeming antiworldly pessimism, Plato's outlook was marked by a certain cosmic optimism, for behind the obscure flux of events he posited the providential design of divine wisdom. And despite, or rather underlying, his flights of rhapsodic mysticism, Plato's philosophy was fundamentally rationalist in character—though his rationalism rested on what he regarded as a universal and divine foundation rather than a merely human logicality. For at the heart of Plato's conception of the world was the notion of a transcendent intelligence that rules and orders all things: divine Reason is "the king of heaven and earth." The universe is ultimately ruled not by chance, materialistic mechanics, or blind necessity, but rather by "a wondrous regulating intelligence."

Plato also recognized in the world's composition an irreducible element of stubborn errancy and irrationality, which he referred to as *anankē*, or Necessity. In the Platonic understanding, the irrational was associated with matter, with the sensible world, and with instinctual desire, while the rational was associated with mind, with the transcendent, and with spiritual desire.[7] *Anankē*, the refractory purposelessness and random irrationality in the universe, resists full conformity to the creative Reason. It shadows the archetypal perfection, obscuring its pure expression in the concrete world. Reason overrules Necessity in the greatest part of the world so that it conforms to good purpose, but on some points Reason cannot overcome the errant cause—hence the existence of evil and disorder in the world. As a finite creation, the world is necessarily imperfect. Yet precisely because of its problematic nature, *anankē* serves as an impulsion for the philosopher's ascent from the visible to the transcendent. Although wayward chance and irrational necessity are real and have their place, they exist within a greater structure informed and governed by the universal intelligence, Reason, which moves all things in accordance with an ultimate wisdom, the Idea of the Good.

Here Plato made fully articulate the principle that had been broached in earlier Greek philosophy, and that would play a central role in its subsequent development. Anaxagoras in Periclean Athens had proposed that *Nous*, or Mind, was the transcendent source of the cosmic order. Both Socrates and Plato were attracted by Anaxagoras's first principle, with its suggestion of a rational teleology as the basis of the universe's existence. They were disappointed, however, as was Aristotle later, that Anaxagoras had not developed the principle further in his own philosophy (which was predominantly materialistic, like that of the atomists), and particularly that he had not made explicit the intentional goodness of the universal mind. But about a half-century before Anaxagoras, the poet-philosopher Xenophanes, having criticized the anthropomorphic deities of naive popular tradition, had posited instead a single supreme God, a universal divinity who influenced the world through pure intellection, and who was in essence identified with the world itself. Shortly afterward, another Presocratic philosopher, the solitary and enigmatic Heraclitus, introduced a similarly immanent conception of divine intelligence with his use of the term *logos* (originally meaning word, speech, or thought) to signify the rational principle governing the cosmos. All things are in constant flux, and yet are fundamentally related and ordered through the universal Logos, which is also manifest in the human being's power of reason. Heraclitus associated the Logos with the element of fire, which, like the Heraclitean world as a whole, is born of strife, ever-consuming, and in constant movement. It is the law of the universal Logos that everything is defined by, tends toward, and is ultimately balanced by its opposite, so that all opposites ultimately constitute a unity. The finest harmony is composed of elements that are in tension with each other. Heraclitus asserted that most human beings, by not understanding the Logos, live as if asleep in a false dream of the world, and consequently in a state of constant disharmony. Human beings should seek to comprehend the Logos of life, and thereby awaken to a life of intelligent cooperation with the universe's deeper order.

But it was the Pythagoreans, perhaps above all other philosophical schools, who stressed the world's intelligibility, and especially taught the spiritual value of scientifically penetrating its mysteries to achieve ecstatic union between the human soul and the divine cosmos. For Pythagoreans, as later for Platonists, the mathematical patterns discoverable in the natural world secreted, as it were, a deeper meaning that led the philosopher beyond the material level of reality. To uncover the regulative mathematical forms in nature was to reveal the divine intelligence itself, governing its creation with transcendent perfection and order. The Pythagorean discovery that the harmonics of music were mathematical, that harmonious tones were produced by strings whose measurements were determined by simple numerical ratios, was regarded as a religious revelation. Those mathematical harmonies maintained a timeless existence as spiritual exemplars, from which all audible musical tones derived. The Pythagoreans believed that the universe in its entirety, especially the heavens, was ordered according to esoteric principles of harmony, mathematical configurations that expressed a celestial music. To understand mathematics was to have found the key to the divine creative wisdom.

Pythagoreans also taught that these forms are brought to light first in the human mind, and then in the cosmos. The mathematical laws of numbers and figures are recognized in the external world only after they have been established by the human intelligence. By this means the human soul discovers its own essence and intelligence to be the same as that hidden within nature. Only then does the meaning of the cosmos dawn within the soul. Through intellectual and moral discipline, the human mind can arrive at the existence and properties of the mathematical Forms, and then begin to unravel the mysteries of nature and the human soul. The word *kosmos,* which signified a peculiarly Greek combination of order, structural perfection, and beauty, was traditionally supposed to have been first applied to the world by Pythagoras, after whose time it was frequently understood in that Pythagorean sense. As restated by Plato, to discover *kosmos* in the world was to reveal *kosmos* in one's own soul. In the thought life of man, the world spirit revealed itself. Here the Socratic dictum "Know thyself" was seen not as the creed of an introspective subjectivist, but as a directive to universal understanding.

The belief that the universe possesses and is governed according to a comprehensive regulating intelligence, and that this same intelligence is reflected in the human mind, rendering it capable of knowing the cosmic order, was one of the most characteristic and recurring principles in the central tradition of Hellenic thought. After Plato, the terms *logos* and *nous* were both regularly associated with philosophical conceptions of human knowledge and the universal order, and through Aristotle, the Stoics, and later Platonists, their meanings were increasingly elaborated. As ancient philosophy progressed, *logos* and *nous* were variously employed to signify mind, reason, intellect, organizing principle, thought, word, speech, wisdom, and meaning, in each case relative to both human reason and a universal intelligence. The two terms eventually came to denote the transcendent source of all archetypes, as well as the providential principle of cosmic order that, through the archetypes, continuously permeates the created world. As the means by which human intelligence could attain universal understanding, the Logos was a divine revelatory principle, simultaneously operative within the human mind and the natural world. The highest quest of the philosopher was to achieve inner realization of this archetypal world Reason, to grasp and be grasped by this supreme rational-spiritual principle that both ordered and revealed.

The Problem of the Planets

Among many other significant themes and concepts discussed in the Platonic dialogues, one in particular requires our present attention. For this aspect of Plato's thought was to prove uniquely consequential for the evolution of the Western world view, not only forming a basis for the cosmology of the later classical world, but emerging again as a crucial force in the birth of modern science. It may well have been the single most important factor giving both dynamism and continuity to the Western mind's attempt to comprehend the physical cosmos.

Plato repeatedly recommended one area of study, astronomy, as especially important for the attainment of philosophical wisdom, and in this study he specified one outstanding problem that especially required solution. Moreover, this problem—how to explain mathematically the erratic movements of the planets—was so significant for Plato that he described the need for its resolution as if it were a matter of religious urgency. The nature of the problem—indeed, its very existence—clearly illuminates the character of Plato's world view, underscoring not only its own inner tensions, but also its pivotal position between the ancient mythological cosmos and the universe of modern science. For the riddle of the planets as formulated by Plato, and the long and arduous intellectual struggle to solve it, would culminate two thousand years later in the work of Copernicus and Kepler and their initiation of the Scientific Revolution.

But to pursue this remarkable line of thinking from Plato to Kepler, we must first briefly attempt to reconstruct the ancient view of the heavens prior to Plato, specifically that associated with the earliest astronomer-astrologers from the ancient Mesopotamian kingdom of Babylonia. For it was from these distant origins nearly two millennia before Christ that the cosmology of the West would first emerge.

It would appear that from very early times ancient observers noticed a fundamental distinction between the celestial and terrestrial realms. While earthly life was everywhere marked by change, unpredictability, generation and decay, the heavens seemed to possess an eternal regular-

ity and luminous beauty that established them as a realm of an entirely
different and superior order. While observations of the heavens continued to disclose this unchanging regularity and incorruptibility night after
night, century after century, observations of mundane existence by
contrast revealed incessant change—with plants and animals, the seas
and the weather undergoing ceaseless alteration, with human beings
dying and being born, with entire civilizations rising and passing away.
The heavens appeared to possess an order of time that transcended
human time, an order of time suggestive of eternity itself. It was also
evident that the movements of the heavenly bodies influenced earthly
existence in various ways—bringing dawn after every night, for example,
or spring after every winter, with unfailing constancy. Certain major
seasonal fluctuations in climatic conditions, droughts, floods, and tides
seemed to coincide with specific phenomena in the heavens. And while
the heavens appeared as a vast distant space beyond human reach,
populated by insubstantial, jewel-like points of bright light, the earthly
environment was immediate, tangible, and composed of patently grosser
materials like rock and dirt. The celestial realm seemed to express—
indeed it seemed to be—the very image of transcendence. Perhaps
because the heavens were distinguished by these extraordinary qualities—luminous appearance, timeless order, transcendent location, terrestrial effects, and an all-encompassing majesty—the ancients viewed
the celestial realm as the residence of the gods. The starry sky reigned
above as an eternal revolving illustration of the mythic deities, their
visible incarnation. From this perspective, the heavens were not so much
a metaphor for the divine, but rather the divine's very embodiment.

The divine character of the heavens compelled human attention to
the patterns and movements of the stars, with significant events in the
celestial realm considered indicative of parallel events in terrestrial life.
In the imperial cities of ancient Babylonia, centuries of continuous and
increasingly precise observations, for omens as well as for calendrical
calculations, gave rise to a large body of systematic astronomical records.
But when these observations, as well as their mythological correspondences, reached the cultural environment of the early Greek philosophers, and there met the Hellenic demand for coherent rational and
natural explanation, a fundamentally new dimension in cosmological
speculation was created. While for other contemporary cultures the
heavens remained, like the overall world view, principally a mythological phenomenon, for the Greeks the heavens became linked as well to

geometrical constructions and physical explanations, which in turn became basic components of their evolving cosmology. The Greeks thereby bestowed to the West a tradition which demanded that a cosmology not only must satisfy the human need to exist in a meaningful universe—a need already served by the archaic mythological systems—but must also delineate a coherent physical and mathematical structure of the universe accounting for detailed systematic observations of the heavens.[8]

In accord with their newly naturalistic outlook, early Greek philosophers such as the Ionians and the atomists began regarding the heavens as composed of various material substances whose movements were mechanically determined. But the evidence that the celestial motions maintained a consistent order in perfect conformity to mathematical patterns was for many Greeks a fact pregnant with significance. For Plato in particular, that mathematical order revealed the heavens as the visible expression of the divine Reason and the embodiment of the *anima mundi*, the living soul of the universe. In his cosmological dialogue, the *Timaeus*, Plato described the stars and planets as visible images of immortal deities whose perfectly regulated movements were paradigms of the transcendent order. God, the primordial artist and craftsman (Demiurge) who had formed the world from a chaos of primordial matter, had created the heavens as a moving image of eternity, revolving precisely according to perfect mathematical Ideas, which in turn created and established the patterns of time. Plato believed it was man's encounter with the celestial movements that had first given rise to human reasoning about the nature of things, to the divisions of the day and the year, to numbers and mathematics, and even to philosophy itself, that most liberating of the gods' gifts to mankind. The universe was the living manifestation of divine Reason, and nowhere was that Reason more fully manifest than in the heavens. If earlier philosophers had thought the latter comprised nothing more than material objects in space, for Plato their evident mathematical order proved otherwise. Far from being merely a soulless domain of moving stones and dirt, the heavens contained the very sources of the world order.

Plato therefore stressed the value of studying the movements of the heavens, for the harmonious symmetry of the celestial revolutions constituted a spiritual perfection directly accessible to human understanding. By devoting himself to things divine, the philosopher could awaken divinity within himself and bring his own life into intelligent harmony with the celestial order. In the spirit of his Pythagorean forebears, Plato elevated astronomy to high status among those studies demanded in his ideal education for the philosopher-ruler, for astronomy revealed the eternal Forms and divinities governing the cosmos. Only the person who had fully applied himself to such studies, and through his long labor of education comprehended the divine ordering of things both in the heavens and on Earth, could be capable of being the just guardian of a political state. An unthinking traditional belief in the existence of the gods was acceptable for the masses, but a prospective ruler should be expected to have mastered all possible proofs of the universe's divinity. He must be able to regard the many and perceive the one, the divine intelligent unity of design behind all apparent diversity. The paradigmatic field for this philosophical imperative was astronomy, for above all the passing phenomena of the world stood the timeless perfection of the heavens, whose manifest intelligence could inform the philosopher's life and awaken wisdom in his soul.

Beginning with Thales (renowned for having predicted an eclipse) and Pythagoras (credited with being the first to conclude that the Earth was a sphere, rather than a flat circular disc as in Homer and Hesiod), each of the major Greek philosophers had brought new insights concerning the apparent structure and character of the cosmos. By Plato's time, the continuing observations of the heavens had revealed a cosmos that seemed to most thoughtful observers to be structured in two concentric spheres, with the vast outer sphere of stars revolving diurnally westward around the much smaller sphere of the Earth, and with the Earth stationary in the exact center of the universe. The Sun, Moon, and planets revolved in approximate synchrony with the outer starry sphere, moving in a space somewhere between the Earth and the stars. The conceptual clarity of this two-sphere scheme, which readily explained the overall diurnal motion of the heavens, gradually allowed Greek astronomers to discern what Babylonians had earlier observed but what was to the Greeks, with their passion for lucid geometrical understanding, a disturbing phenomenon. Indeed, the phenomenon now fully revealed was so problematic as to challenge the entire science of astronomy and to place the divine scheme of the heavens in jeopardy. For it had become evident that several celestial bodies did not move with the same eternal regularity as did the rest, but instead they "wandered" (the Greek root for the word "planet," *planētēs*, meant "wanderer," and signified the Sun and Moon as well as the other five visible planets—Mercury, Venus, Mars, Jupiter, and Saturn). Not only did the Sun (in the course of a year) and the Moon (in a month) move gradually eastward across the starry sphere in an opposite direction from the westward diurnal movement of the entire heavens. More puzzling, the other five planets had glaringly inconsistent cycles in which they completed those eastward orbits, periodically appearing to speed up or slow down relative to the fixed stars, and sometimes to stop altogether and reverse direction while emitting varying degrees of brightness. The planets were inexplicably defying the perfect symmetry and circular uniformity of the heavenly motions.

Because of his equation of divinity with order, of intelligence and soul with perfect mathematical regularity, the paradox of the planetary movements seems to have been felt most acutely by Plato, who first articulated the problem and gave directions for its solution. To Plato, the proof of divinity in the universe was of the utmost importance, for only with such certainty could human ethical and political activity have a firm foundation. In the *Laws*, he cited two reasons for belief in divinity—his theory of the soul (that all being and motion is caused by soul, which is immortal and superior to the physical things it animates), and his conception of the heavens as divine bodies governed by a supreme intelligence and world soul. The planetary irregularities and multiple wanderings seemingly contradicted that perfect divine order, thereby endangering human faith in the divinity of the universe. Therein lay the significance of the problem. Part of the religious bulwark of Platonic philosophy was at stake. Indeed, Plato considered it blasphemous to call any celestial bodies "wanderers."

But Plato not only isolated the problem and defined its significance. He also advanced, with remarkable confidence, a specific—and in the long run extremely fruitful—hypothesis: namely, that the planets, in apparent contradiction to the empirical evidence, actually move in single uniform orbits of perfect regularity. Although there would seem to have been little but Plato's faith in mathematics and the heavens' divinity that could have supported such a belief, he enjoined future philosophers to grapple with the planetary data and find "what are the uniform and ordered movements by the assumption of which the apparent movements of the planets can be accounted for"—i.e., to discover the ideal mathematical forms that would resolve the empirical discrepancies and reveal the true motions.[9] Astronomy and mathematics were to be mastered in order to penetrate the riddle of the heavens and comprehend their divine intelligence. Naive empiricism, which took the appearance of erratic and multiple planetary movements at face value, was to be overcome by critical mathematical reasoning, thereby revealing the simple, uniform, and transcendent essence of the celestial motions. The philosopher's task was to "save the phenomena"—to redeem the apparent disorder of the empirical heavens through theoretical insight and the power of mathematics.

Of course, "saving the phenomena" was in some sense the main goal of all Platonic philosophy: to discover the eternal behind the temporal, to know the truth hidden within the apparent, to glimpse the absolute Ideas that reign supreme behind and within the flux of the empirical world. But here Plato's philosophy was put on the line, so to speak, in open confrontation with a specific empirical problem under the full gaze of future generations. The problem itself was significant only because of the Greeks', and particularly Plato's, assumptions about geometry and divinity—that the two were intrinsically associated with each other and with the heavens. But the long-term consequences of those assumptions—consequences that would develop directly from the centuries-long struggle with the planetary movements—were to be singularly antithetical to their Platonic foundation.

Here, then, we find many of the most characteristic elements of Platonic philosophy: the search for and belief in the absolute and unitary over the relative and diverse, the divinization of order and the rejection of disorder, the tension between empirical observation and ideal Forms, the consequently ambivalent attitude toward empiricism as something to be employed only to be overcome, the juxtaposition of the primordial mythic deities with the mathematical and rational Forms, the further juxtaposition of the many gods (the celestial deities) with the single God (the Creator and supreme Intelligence), the religious significance of scientific research, and finally the complex and even antithetical consequences which Plato's thought would hold for later developments in Western culture.

>·X·<

Before moving onward past Plato, let us briefly review the various methods for acquiring knowledge suggested in the course of the Platonic dialogues. Knowledge of the transcendent Ideas that were the governing principles of the divine intelligence was the foundation of Platonic philosophy, and access to this archetypal knowledge was said to be mediated by several different (and usually overlapping) cognitive modes, involving different degrees of experiential directness. The Ideas could be known most directly through an intuitive leap of immediate apprehension, which was also considered to be a recollection of the immortal soul's prior knowledge. The logical necessity of the Ideas could also be discovered by meticulous intellectual analysis of the world of empirical experience, both through dialectic and through mathematics. In addition, the transcendent reality could be encountered through the astronomical contemplation and understanding of the heavens, which displayed the moving geometry of the visible gods. The transcendent could also be approached through myth and the poetic imagination, as well as by attending to a kind of aesthetic resonance within the psyche touched off by the presence of the archetypal in veiled form within the phenomenal world. Thus intuition, memory, aesthetics, imagination, logic, mathematics, and empirical observation each played a specific role in Plato's epistemology, as did spiritual desire and moral virtue. But of all these, the empirical was typically depreciated and, at least in its uncritical employment, considered more hindrance than help in the philosophical enterprise. This was the legacy that Plato passed on to his most brilliant pupil, Aristotle, who studied for twenty years in Plato's Academy before setting forth his own distinctive philosophy.

Aristotle and the Greek Balance

With Aristotle, Plato was, as it were, brought down to earth. And if, from a Platonic view, the luminosity of Plato's universe based on the transcendent Ideas was diminished in the process, others would point to a decisive gain in the articulate intelligibility of the world as described by Aristotle, and would indeed consider his outlook to be a necessary modification of Plato's idealism. To understand the basic tenor of Aristotle's philosophy and cosmology is prerequisite for comprehending the further movement of Western thought and its succession of world views. For Aristotle provided a language and logic, a foundation and structure, and, not least, a formidably authoritative opponent—first against Platonism and later against the early modern mind—without which the philosophy, theology, and science of the West could not have developed as they did.

The problem of discovering the exact character and development of Aristotle's thought presents a different set of difficulties from that facing the interpreter of Plato. Virtually none of Aristotle's extant works were apparently intended for publication. Works that were published by Aristotle are now lost, these being highly Platonic in doctrine and written in popular literary form, while those that survive are concentrated treatises composed for school use in the form of lecture-course notes and texts for students. These surviving manuscripts were compiled, edited, and titled by Aristotelians several centuries after the philosopher's death. The modern attempt to trace Aristotle's development from this much-transformed body of material has not brought forth unequivocal results, and his judgments on certain issues remain obscure. Yet the overall character of his philosophy is clear, and a general theory of its evolution can be surmised.

It would seem to be that after an initial period when his thought still reflected a more unreservedly Platonic influence, Aristotle began to construct a philosophical position sharply distinguished from his master's. The crux of their difference involved the precise nature of the Forms and their relation to the empirical world. Aristotle's intellectual temperament was one that took the empirical world on its own terms as fully real. He could not accept Plato's conclusion that the basis of reality

existed in an entirely transcendent and immaterial realm of ideal entities. True reality, he believed, was the perceptible world of concrete
objects, not an imperceptible world of eternal Ideas. The theory of Ideas
seemed to him both empirically unverifiable and fraught with logical
difficulties.

To counter that theory, Aristotle put forth his doctrine of categories.
Things can be said "to be" in many ways. A tall white horse is in one
sense "tall," in another sense "white," and in another sense a "horse." Yet
these different ways of being are not equivalent in ontological status, for
the tallness and whiteness of the horse depend for their existence entirely
on the primary reality of the particular horse. The horse is substantial in
its reality in a way that the adjectives describing it are not. To distinguish
between these different ways of being, Aristotle introduced the notion of
categories: the particular horse is a substance, which constitutes one
category; its whiteness is a quality, which constitutes another category
altogether. The substance is the primary reality, upon which the quality
depends for its existence. Among the ten categories established by
Aristotle, only substance ("this horse") signifies concrete independent
existence, while the others—quality ("white"), quantity ("tall"), relation
("faster"), and the rest—are derivative ways of being in that they exist
solely relative to an individual substance. A substance is ontologically
primary, while the various other types of being that may be predicated of
it are derivative. Substances underlie and are the subjects of everything
else. If substances did not exist, nothing would exist.

For Aristotle, the real world is one of individual substances which are
distinct and separate from each other, yet which are characterized by
qualities or other types of being held in common with other individual
substances. This commonality, however, does not signify the existence
of a transcendent Idea from which the common quality is derived. The
common quality is a universal recognizable by the intellect in sensible
things, but it is not a self-subsistent entity. The universal is conceptually
distinguishable from the concrete individual, but is not ontologically
independent. It is not itself a substance. Plato had taught that things like
"whiteness" and "tallness" possessed an existence independent of any
concrete things in which they might appear, but for Aristotle that
doctrine was untenable. The error, he held, lay in Plato's confusion of
categories, whereby he treated a quality, for example, as a substance.
Many things can be beautiful, but that does not mean there is a transcendent Idea of the Beautiful. Beauty exists only if at some point a concrete

substance is beautiful. The individual man Socrates is primary, while his "humanness" or "goodness" exists only to the extent that it is found in the concrete particular Socrates. In contrast to the primary reality of a substance, a quality is only an abstraction—though it is not merely a mental abstraction, for it is based on a real aspect of the substance in which it resides.

By replacing Plato's Ideas with universals, common qualities that the mind could grasp in the empirical world but that did not exist independently of that world, Aristotle turned Plato's ontology upside down. For Plato, the particular was less real, a derivative of the universal; for Aristotle, the universal was less real, a derivative of the particular. Universals were necessary for knowledge, but they did not exist as self-subsistent entities in a transcendent realm. Plato's Ideas were for Aristotle an unnecessary idealist duplication of the real world of everyday experience, and a logical error.

But further analysis of the world, specifically of change and motion, suggested to Aristotle the need to introduce a more complex account of things—an account that paradoxically made his philosophy closer in spirit to Plato's yet also more distinctly his own. A substance, Aristotle concluded, is not simply a unit of matter, but is an intelligible structure or form (*eidos*) embodied in matter. Although the form is entirely immanent, and does not exist independently of its material embodiment, it is the form that gives to the substance its distinctive essence. Thus a substance is not only "this man" or "this horse" in simple contrast to its qualities and other categories, for what makes these substances what they are is their specific composition of matter and form—i.e., the fact that their material substrate has been structured by the form of a man or a horse. Yet form for Aristotle was not static, and it was especially here that Aristotle both sustained certain elements of Plato's philosophy and added a fundamentally new dimension.

For in Aristotle's view, form gives to a substance not only its essential structure but also its developmental dynamic. Organic biology, rather than abstract mathematics, was Aristotle's characteristic science, and in lieu of Plato's static ideal reality Aristotle brought a more pronounced recognition of nature's processes of growth and development, with each organism striving to move from imperfection to perfection: from a state of potentiality to a state of actuality, or realization of its form. While Plato emphasized the imperfection of all natural things compared with the Forms they imitated, Aristotle taught that an organism moves from an imperfect or immature condition in a teleological development toward achievement of a full maturity in which its inherent form is actualized: the seed is transformed into a plant, the embryo becomes the child, the child becomes the adult, and so on. The form is an intrinsic principle of operation that is implicit in the organism from the latter's inception, as the form of the oak is implicit in the acorn. The organism is drawn forward by the form from potentiality to actuality. After this formal realization is achieved, decay sets in as the form gradually "loses its hold." The Aristotelian form bestows an indwelling impulse in each organism which orders and motivates its development.

The essence of something is the form into which it has grown. The nature of something is to actualize its inherent form. Yet for Aristotle, "form" and "matter" are relative terms, for the actualization of a form can in turn lead to its being the matter out of which a higher form can grow. Thus the adult is the form of which the child was matter, the child the form of which the embryo was matter, the embryo the form of which the ovum was matter. Every substance is composed of that which is changed (the matter) and that into which it is changed (the form). "Matter" here does not simply mean a physical body, which in fact always possesses some degree of form. Matter is, rather, an indeterminate openness in things to structural and dynamic formation. Matter is the unqualified substrate of being, the possibility of form, that which form molds, impels, brings from potentiality to actuality. Matter becomes realized only because of its composition with form. Form is matter's actuality, its purposefully completed figuration. All of nature is in the process—is itself the process—of this conquest of matter by form.

Though a form is not itself a substance, as in Plato's view, every substance *has* a form, an intelligible structure, that which makes the substance what it is. Moreover, every substance not only possesses a form; one could say it is also possessed by a form, for it naturally strives to realize its inherent form. It strives to become a perfect specimen of its kind. Every substance seeks to actualize what it already is potentially.

In Aristotle's conception, the being-becoming distinction that had been developed by Plato from the differing views of reality given by Parmenides and Heraclitus has now been placed entirely in the context of the natural world, where it is seen as actuality and potentiality. Plato's distinction, with "being" the object of true knowledge and "becoming" the object of sense-perceived opinion, had reflected his elevation of real Forms above relatively unreal concrete particulars. Aristotle, by contrast, gave to the process of becoming its own reality, asserting that the governing form itself is realized in that process. Change and movement are not signs of a shadowy unreality but are expressive of a teleological striving for fulfillment.

This understanding was achieved through the Aristotelian idea of "potentiality," an idea uniquely capable of providing a conceptual basis for both change and continuity. Parmenides had not allowed the rational possibility of real change, because something that "is" cannot change into something that it is not, for what "is not" cannot exist, by definition. Plato, mindful too of Heraclitus's teaching that the natural world is in constant flux, had therefore located reality in the changeless Forms transcending the empirical world. He also, however, pointed out a verbal distinction that shed light on Parmenides's problem. Parmenides was not distinguishing between two significantly different meanings of the term "is," for on the one hand one could say that something "is" in the sense that it exists, while on the other hand one could say that something "is hot" or "is a man" in the sense of a predicable. Building upon this important distinction, Aristotle asserted that something can change into something else if there is a continuing substance that undergoes change from a potential to an actual state as determined by the substance's inherent form. Thus Aristotle moved toward reconciling the Platonic Forms with the empirical facts of dynamic natural processes, and more deeply stressed the human intellect's capacity to recognize these formal patterns in the sensible world.

While Plato distrusted knowledge gained by sense perception, Aristotle took such information seriously, contending that knowledge of the natural world derives first from the perception of concrete particulars in which regular patterns can be recognized and general principles formulated. All living things require powers of nutrition to survive and grow (plants, animals, man), while some also require powers of sensation to be aware of objects and distinguish between them (animals, man). In the case of man, who is further endowed with reason, these powers enable him to store up his experience, to make comparisons and contrasts, to calculate and reflect and draw conclusions, all of which make possible knowledge of the world. Human understanding of the world thus begins with sense perception. Before any sensory experience, the human mind is like a clean tablet on which nothing is written. It is in a state of potentiality with regard to intelligible things. And man requires sensory experience to bring his mind, with the help of mental images, from potential knowledge to actual knowledge. Empiricism, if perhaps humbler than Plato's direct intuition of absolute Ideas, is dependably tangible.

Yet it is man's reason that allows sense experience to be the basis for useful knowledge, and Aristotle was above all that philosopher who articulated the structure of rational discourse so the human mind might apprehend the world with the greatest degree of conceptual precision and effectiveness. Establishing systematic rules for the proper employment of logic and language, Aristotle built on principles already worked out by Socrates and Plato, but brought new clarity, coherence, and innovations of his own. Deduction and induction, the syllogism, the analysis of causation into material, efficient, formal, and final causes, basic distinctions such as subject-predicate, essential-accidental, matter-form, potential-actual, universal-particular, genus-species-individual, the ten categories of substance, quantity, quality, relation, place, time, position, state, action, and affection: all were defined by Aristotle and established thereafter as indispensable instruments of analysis for the Western mind. Where Plato had placed direct intuition of the transcendent Ideas as the foundation of knowledge, Aristotle now placed empiricism and logic.

Yet Aristotle believed that the mind's greatest power of cognition derived from something beyond empiricism and the rational elaboration of sensory experience. Although it is difficult to discern his precise meaning from the brief and somewhat obscure statements he made concerning the issue, it would seem that Aristotle regarded the mind not only as that which is activated by sensory experience, but also as something that is eternally active, and indeed divine and immortal. This aspect of mind, the active intellect (*nous*), alone gave man the intuitive capacity to grasp final and universal truths. Empiricism renders particular data from which generalizations and theories can be derived, but these are fallible. Man can attain necessary and universal knowledge only through the presence of another cognitive faculty, the active intellect. Just as light makes potential colors into actual colors, so does the active intellect actualize the mind's potential knowledge of forms and provide man with the fundamental principles that make possible certain rational knowledge. It illuminates the processes of human cognition while it yet remains beyond them, eternal and complete. Only because man shares in the divine *nous* can he apprehend infallible truth, and the *nous* constitutes the only part of man that "comes in from outside." In Aristotle's view, the individual human soul might cease to exist with death, since the soul is vitally joined to the physical body it animates. The soul is the form of the body, just as the body is the matter of the soul. But the divine intellect, of which each man has a potential share and which distinguishes man from other animals, is immortal and transcendent. Indeed, man's highest happiness consists in the philosophical contemplation of eternal truth.

As Aristotle agreed finally with Plato's evaluation of the human intellect as divine despite his new regard for sense perception, so also, despite his diminishing the ontological status of the Forms, Aristotle still maintained their objective existence and their crucial role in the economy of nature and the processes of human knowledge. Like Plato, he believed that a philosophy such as Democritus's atomism, based solely on material particles and lacking a decisive concept of form, was unable to account for the fact that nature, despite constant change, contains a visible order with distinct and lasting formal qualities. Also like Plato, Aristotle believed the deepest cause for things must be sought not in the beginning of things but in their end—their *telos*, their purpose and final actuality, that to which they aspire. Although the Aristotelian forms (with one exception) are wholly immanent in nature and not transcendent, they are essentially changeless and are thus recognizable by the human intellect amidst the flux of organic development and decay. Cognition takes place when the mind receives the form of a substance into itself, even though in the world that form never exists apart from its particular material embodiment. The mind conceptually separates, or abstracts, what is not separated in reality. Yet because reality possesses inherent structure, cognition is possible. An empirical approach to nature is meaningful because of nature's intrinsic openness to rational description, by which it can be cognitively organized according to forms, categories, causes, genera, species, and the like. Thus Aristotle continued and brought new definition to the Platonic conception of an ordered and humanly knowable cosmos.

In essence, Aristotle realigned Plato's archetypal perspective from a transcendent focus to an immanent one, so it was fully directed to the physical world with its empirically observable patterns and processes. By emphasizing the Forms' transcendence, Plato had found it difficult to explain how particulars participated in Forms, a difficulty rooted in his ontological dualism, which in its more extreme formulations entailed a virtual severance of Forms from matter. Aristotle, by contrast, pointed to a vital composite entity produced by the uniting of form with matter in a substance. Unless a form is incorporated in a substance—as the form of a man is found in the individual person Socrates—that form cannot be said to exist. Forms are not beings, for they possess no independent existence. Rather, beings exist *through* forms. Aristotle's form thereby took on several roles—as intrinsic pattern, as intelligible structure, as governing dynamic, and as end or purpose. He eliminated the numinosity and independence of Plato's Forms, yet gave them new functions to make possible a rational analysis of the world and enhance the power of scientific explanation.

The early foundations of science had already been established by, on the one side, the Ionian and atomistic philosophies of matter, and, on the other, the Pythagorean and Platonic philosophies of form and mathematics. But by directing his Platonically educated attention to the empirical world, Aristotle placed a new and fruitful stress on the value of observation and classification within a Platonic framework of form and purpose. More emphatically than Plato, Aristotle considered both the Ionians' focus on material causes and the Pythagoreans' focus on formal causes necessary for a full understanding of nature. It was this unique comprehensiveness that distinguished much of Aristotle's achievement. The Greek sense of confidence in the power of human thought to comprehend the world rationally, a confidence begun with Thales, now found in Aristotle its fullest expression and climax.

Aristotle's universe possessed a remarkable logical consistency throughout its complex and multifaceted structure. All motion and process in the world was explicable by his formal teleology: Every being is moved from potentiality to actuality according to an inner dynamic dictated by a specific form. No potentiality is brought into actuality unless there exists an already actual being, a being that has already realized its form: a seed must have been produced by a mature plant, as a child must have a parent. Hence the dynamism and structured develop-ment of any entity requires an external cause—a being that serves simultaneously as efficient cause (initiating the motion), formal cause (giving the entity form), and final cause (serving as goal of the entity's development). To account for the entire universe's order and movement, therefore, especially for the great movement of the heavens (and here he faulted Democritus and the atomists for not dealing adequately with the first cause of motion), Aristotle posited a supreme Form—an already existing actuality, absolute in its perfection, the only form existing entirely separate from matter. Since the greatest universal motion is that of the heavens, and since that circular motion is eternal, this prime mover must also be eternal.

Aristotle's logic could be represented in the following way: (a) All motion is the result of the dynamism impelling potentiality to formal realization. (b) Since the universe as a whole is involved in motion, and since nothing moves without an impulse toward form, the universe must be moved by a supreme, universal form. (c) Since the highest form must already be perfectly realized—i.e., not in a potential state—and since matter is by definition the state of potentiality, the highest form is both entirely immaterial and without motion: hence the Unmoved Mover, the supreme perfect Being that is pure form, God.

This absolute Being, here posited by logical necessity rather than religious conviction, is the first cause of the universe. Yet this Being is wholly self-absorbed, since for it to take any heed of physical nature would diminish its perfect undisturbed character and immerse it in the flux of potentialities. As perfect actuality, the Unmoved Mover is characterized by a state of eternal unhindered activity—not the struggling process (*kinesis*) of moving from potential to actual, but the forever enjoyable activity (*energeia*) made possible only in a state of complete formal realization. For the supreme Form, that activity is thought: eternal contemplation of its own being, unqualified by the change and imperfection of the physical world it ultimately motivates. Aristotle's God is thus pure Mind, with no material component. Its activity and pleasure is simply that of eternal consciousness of itself.

In its absolute perfection, the primary Form moves the physical universe by drawing nature toward itself. God is the goal of the universe's aspirations and movement—a more conscious goal for man, a less conscious instinctual dynamism for other forms of nature. Every individual being in the universe is striving to imitate, each in its specific limited way, the perfection of the supreme Being. Each seeks to fulfill its purpose, to grow and mature, to achieve its realized form. God "moves as the object of desire." But of all living things, man alone shares in God's nature, by virtue of his possessing intelligence, the *nous*. Because the supreme Form is so removed from the world, there is considerable distance between man and God. Yet because man's highest faculty, his intellect, is divine, he can by cultivating that intellect—that is, by imitating the supreme Form in the way most appropriate to man—bring himself into a kind of communion with God. The Prime Mover is not the creator of the world (which Aristotle considered eternal and coeval with God). Rather nature, in its movement toward imitating this supreme immaterial Form, is involved in an eternal process of creating itself. Although there is no beginning or end to this striving, Aristotle suggested the existence of regular cycles that depended on the movements of the heavens, which, like Plato, he considered divine.

In Aristotle, Greek cosmology achieved its most comprehensive and systematic development. His view of the cosmos was a synthesis of his many predecessors' insights, from the Ionians' and Empedocles's ideas concerning natural elements to Plato's astronomy and the problem of the planets. The Earth was the stationary center of the universe, around which the heavenly bodies rotated. The whole cosmos was finite and circumscribed by a perfect sphere, within which were set the fixed stars. Aristotle based the Earth's uniqueness, centrality, and immobility not only on self-evidence and common sense, but also on his theory of the elements. The heavier elements, earth and water, moved according to their intrinsic nature toward the universe's center (the Earth), while the lighter elements, air and fire, intrinsically moved upward away from the center. The lightest element was aether—transparent, purer than fire, and divine—the substance of which the heavens were composed, and its natural motion, unlike that of the terrestrial elements, was circular.

One of Plato's pupils and Aristotle's contemporaries, the mathematician Eudoxus, had taken up the problem of the planetary movements and provided its first answer. To preserve the ideal of perfect circularity while also saving the appearances of the erratic motions, Eudoxus devised a complex geometrical scheme whereby each planet was set in the inner sphere of a group of interconnected rotating spheres, with the fixed stars at the universe's periphery constituting the outermost sphere. Although every sphere was centered on the Earth, each one had a different rate and axis of rotation, by which means Eudoxus was able to construct—using three spheres each for the Sun and Moon, and four each for the more complex movements of the other planets—an ingenious mathematical solution accounting for the planetary movements, including their retrograde periods. Eudoxus thus achieved the first scientific explanation of the irregular motions of the planets, providing an influential initial model for the subsequent history of astronomy.

It was this solution, somewhat elaborated by Eudoxus's successor Callippus, that Aristotle integrated into his cosmology. Each of the aetheric spheres, beginning with the outermost one, communicated its motion to the next one by means of a frictional drive, so that the motions of the inner spheres were the combined product of the peripheral sphere along with the relevant adjoining ones. (Aristotle also added intermediate counteracting spheres to separate properly the planetary motions from each other, while maintaining the overall motion of the heavens.) In turn, the celestial spheres affected the other, sublunary elements—fire, air, water, and earth—which because of those movements did not remain purely separated in what would be their natural state in successive spheres around the Earth, but instead were pushed into varying admixtures, thereby creating the great multiplicity of natural substances on the Earth. The ordered movement of the heavens was caused ultimately by the primary Unmoved Mover, and the other movements of the planetary spheres from Saturn down through the Moon were caused in turn by other timeless, immaterial, and self-thinking intellects. These heavenly bodies Aristotle considered to be gods, a fact he considered to have been accurately conveyed by the ancient myths (although in other matters he believed the myths were an unreliable source of knowledge). All terrestrial processes and change were therefore caused by the celestial movements, which were ultimately caused by the highest formal and final cause, God.

It was especially in regard to his theories concerning astronomy and the supreme Form that Aristotle approached a Platonic sort of idealism, and in some respects went even further than Plato. By so strongly emphasizing the transcendent quality of mathematical Forms, Plato had occasionally portrayed even the heavens as only an approximate reflection of the perfect divine geometry—a judgment also reflecting Plato's notion of *ananke*, the imperfect irrationality shadowing the physical creation. But for Aristotle, Mind was in a sense more fully omnipotent and immanent in nature, and in his earlier years he concluded that the ordered mathematical perfection of the heavens and the existence of the astral deities affirmed the heavens themselves as a visible embodiment of the divine. In so doing, he joined together more explicitly the Platonic focus on the eternal and mathematical with the tangible world of physical reality within which man found himself. He upheld the natural world as a worthy expression of the divine, and not, as Plato often strongly implied, something merely to be seen through or left behind altogether as an encumbrance to absolute knowledge. Despite the generally secular cast of his thought, Aristotle defined the role of philosophy in his influential work *De Philosophia* (extant now only in fragments), which was to mold the ancient conception of the philosopher's profession: to move from the material causes of things, as in natural philosophy, to the formal and final causes, as in divine philosophy, and thus to discover the intelligible essence of the universe and the purpose behind all change.

>+X+<

Yet as distinguished from Plato's idealism and stress on the need for immediate intuitions of a spiritual reality, the overall thrust of Aristotle's philosophy was decidedly naturalistic and empiricist. The world of nature was of primary interest to Aristotle, who was the son of a physician and early exposed to biological science and medical practice. In this sense his thought could be said to reflect the Homeric and Ionian sense of life characteristic of the heroic age, in which the present life was the preferred, more real realm of existence (in contrast to shadowy Hades, where the disembodied soul lacked virtually all vitality), and the physical body's active involvement in love, war, and feasting was recognized as the essence of a good life. Concerning such matters as the body's worth, the soul's immortality, and man's relation to God, Plato's sensibility was less Homeric and Ionian, and more reflective of the mystery religions and the Pythagoreans. Aristotle's attention to and high valuation of the body more directly reflected the widespread classical Greek appreciation for the human body as expressed in athletic prowess, personal beauty, or artistic creation. Plato's attitude in this regard, while often genuinely admiring, was distinctly ambivalent. In the end, Plato's loyalty lay with the transcendent archetype.

Aristotle's renunciation of self-subsistent Ideas also had major implications for his ethical theory. For Plato, a person could properly direct his actions only if he knew the transcendent basis of any virtue, and only the philosopher who had attained knowledge of that absolute reality would be capable of judging the virtue of any action. Without the existence of an absolute Good, morality would have no certain basis, and so for Plato ethics was derived from metaphysics. For Aristotle, however, the two fields were of fundamentally different character. What actually existed was not an Idea of the Good relevant to all situations, but only good persons or good actions in many varying contexts. One could not attain absolute knowledge in ethical matters as one could in scientific philosophy. Morality lay in the realm of the contingent. The best one could do would be to derive rules empirically for ethical conduct that held probable value in meeting the complexities of human existence.

The proper aim in ethics was not to determine the nature of absolute virtue, but to be a virtuous person. That task was necessarily complex and ambiguous, evading final definition, and required practical solutions to specific problems rather than absolute principles that were universally true. For Aristotle, the goal of human life was happiness, the necessary precondition for which was virtue. But virtue itself had to be defined in terms of rational choice in a concrete situation, where virtue lay in the mean between two extremes. Good is always a balance between two opposite evils, the midpoint between excess and defect: temperance is a mean between austerity and indulgence, courage a mean between cowardice and foolhardiness, proper pride a mean between arrogance and abasement, and so forth. Such a mean can be found only in practice, in individual cases relative to their specific conditions.

In each of Aristotle's concepts in contrast to Plato's—yet always within the Platonic framework of form and purpose—there was a new stress on this world and this life, on the visible, the tangible, and the particular. Although both Aristotle's ethics and his politics were founded on definitions and goals, they remained linked to the empirical, the contingent and individual. Although his universe was teleological and not randomly mechanical, his was generally an unconscious natural teleology, based on the empirical perception that nature draws forward each individual thing to its formal realization, "doing nothing in vain." Form was still the determining principle in Aristotle's universe, but it was primarily a natural principle. Similarly, Aristotle's God was essentially the logical consequence of his cosmology, a necessary existent on physical grounds, rather than the mystically apprehended supreme Good of Platonic thought. Aristotle assumed the power of reason strenuously forged by Socrates and Plato, and applied it systematically to the many kinds of phenomena that existed in the world; but while Plato employed reason to overcome the empirical world and discover a transcendent order, Aristotle employed reason to discover an immanent order within the empirical world itself.

The Aristotelian legacy was thus predominantly one of logic, empiricism, and natural science. The Lyceum, the school which Aristotle founded in Athens and where he conducted his peripatetic discussions, reflected this legacy, being more a center for scientific research and data collection than a semireligious philosophical school like Plato's Academy. Although in ancient times Plato was generally judged the greater master, that evaluation would be dramatically counterbalanced in the high Middle Ages, and in many respects it would be Aristotle's philosophical temperament that would come to define the dominant orientation of the Western mind. So considerable was his encyclopedic system of thought that most scientific activity in the West until the seventeenth century was carried out on the basis of his fourth-century B.C. writings, and even when moving beyond him modern science would continue his orientation and use his conceptual tools. Yet in the last analysis, it was in the spirit of his master Plato, though in a decisively new direction, that Aristotle proclaimed the power of the developed human intellect to comprehend the world's order.

In Aristotle and Plato together, then, we find a certain elegant balance and tension between empirical analysis and spiritual intuition, a dynamic beautifully rendered in Raphael's Renaissance masterpiece *The School of Athens*. There, in the center of the many Greek philosophers and scientists gathered in lively discussion, stand the elder Plato and the younger Aristotle, with Plato pointing upward to the heavens, to the invisible and transcendent, while Aristotle motions his hand outward and down to the earth, to the visible and immanent.

The Dual Legacy

This, then, was the achievement of classical Greek thought: Reflecting the archaic mythological consciousness from which it emerged, informed by the artistic masterworks that preceded and accompanied it, influenced by the mystery religions with which it was contemporaneous; forged through a dialectic with skepticism, naturalism, and secular humanism; and in its commitment to reason, empiricism, and mathematics conducive to the development of science in succeeding centuries—the thought of the great Greek philosophers was an intellectual consummation of all the major cultural expressions of the Hellenic era. It was a global metaphysical perspective, intent on encompassing both the whole of reality and the multiple sides of the human sensibility.

Above all, it was an attempt to know. The Greeks were perhaps the first to see the world as a question to be answered. They were peculiarly gripped by the passion to understand, to penetrate the uncertain flux of phenomena and grasp a deeper truth. And they established a dynamic tradition of critical thought to pursue that quest. With the birth of that tradition and that quest came the birth of the Western mind.

Let us now attempt to distinguish some of the principal elements in the classical Greek conception of reality, especially as these influenced Western thought from antiquity through the Renaissance and Scientific Revolution. For our present purposes, we may describe two very general sets of assumptions or principles inherited by the West from the Greeks. The first set of tenets formulated below represents that unique synthesis of Greek rationalism and Greek religion which played such a significant role in Hellenic thought from Pythagoras through Aristotle, and which was most fully embodied in the thought of Plato:

(1) The world is an ordered cosmos, whose order is akin to an order within the human mind. A rational analysis of the empirical world is therefore possible.

(2) The cosmos as a whole is expressive of a pervasive intelligence that gives to nature its purpose and design, and this intelligence is

directly accessible to human awareness if the latter is developed and focused to a high degree.

(3)   Intellectual analysis at its most penetrating reveals a timeless order that transcends its temporal, concrete manifestation. The visible world contains within it a deeper meaning, in some sense both rational and mythic in character, which is reflected in the empirical order but which emanates from an eternal dimension that is both source and goal of all existence.

(4)   Knowledge of the world's underlying structure and meaning entails the exercise of a plurality of human cognitive faculties— rational, empirical, intuitive, aesthetic, imaginative, mnemonic, and moral.

(5)   The direct apprehension of the world's deeper reality satisfies not only the mind but the soul: it is, in essence, a redemptive vision, a sustaining insight into the true nature of things that is at once in-tellectually decisive and spiritually liberating.

The immense influence on the subsequent evolution of Western thought exerted by these remarkable convictions, at once idealist and rationalist in character, can scarcely be exaggerated. But the Hellenic legacy was a dual one, for the Greek mind also fathered a very different, equally influential set of intellectual assumptions and tendencies, which to some degree overlapped the first set but to a crucial extent acted in tense counterpoint to it. This second set of principles can be summarized roughly as follows:

(1)   Genuine human knowledge can be acquired only through the rigorous employment of human reason and empirical observation.

(2)   The ground of truth must be sought in the present world of human experience, not in an undemonstrable otherworldly reality. The only truth that is humanly accessible and useful is immanent rather than transcendent.

(3)   The causes of natural phenomena are impersonal and physical, and should be sought within the realm of observable nature. All mythological and supernatural elements should be excluded from caus-al explanations as anthropomorphic projections.

(4) Any claims to comprehensive theoretical understanding must be measured against the empirical reality of concrete particulars in all their diversity, mutability, and individuality.

(5) No system of thought is final, and the search for truth must be both critical and self-critical. Human knowledge is relative and fallible and must be constantly revised in the light of further evidence and analysis.

Very generally speaking, both the evolution and the legacy of the Greek mind can be said to have resulted from the complex interaction of these two sets of assumptions and impulses. While the first set was especially visible in the Platonic synthesis, the second set gradually evolved out of the bold, many-sided intellectual development that dialectically impelled that synthesis—namely, the Presocratic philosophical tradition of naturalistic empiricism from Thales, of rationalism from Parmenides, of mechanistic materialism from Democritus, and of skepticism, individualism, and secular humanism from the Sophists. Both of these sets of tendencies in Hellenic thought had deep nonphilosophical roots in the Greek religious and literary traditions, from Homer and the mysteries to Sophocles and Euripides, with each set drawing on different aspects of those traditions. Moreover, these two impulses shared a common ground in their uniquely Greek affirmation, often only implicit, that the final measure of truth was found not in hallowed tradition, nor in contemporary convention, but rather in the autonomous individual human mind. Most consequentially, both impulses found their paradigmatic embodiment in the richly ambiguous figure of Socrates, both found vivid contrapuntal expression in the Platonic dialogues, and both found a brilliant and seminal compromise in the philosophy of Aristotle.

The constant interplay of these two partly complementary and partly antithetical sets of principles established a profound inner tension within the Greek inheritance, which provided the Western mind with the intellectual basis, at once unstable and highly creative, for what was to become an extremely dynamic evolution lasting over two and a half millennia. The secular skepticism of the one stream and the metaphysical idealism of the other provided a crucial counterbalance to each other, each undermining the other's tendency to crystallize into dogmatism, yet the two in combination eliciting new and fertile intellectual possibilities. The Greek search for and recognition of universal archetypes in the chaos of particulars was fundamentally countered by an equally robust impulse to value the concrete particular in and for itself—a combination that resulted in the profoundly Greek tendency to perceive the empirical individual in all its concrete exceptionality as something that could itself reveal new forms of reality and new principles of truth. An often problematic yet immensely productive polarization thereby emerged in the Western mind's understanding of reality, a division of allegiance between two radically different kinds of world view: on the one hand, to a sovereignly ordered cosmos; on the other, to an unpredictably open universe. It was with this unresolved bifurcation at its very basis, with the accompanying creative tension and complexity, that the Greek mind flourished and endured.

The West has never ceased to admire the extraordinary vitality and profundity of the Greek mind, even when subsequent intellectual developments have placed in question one aspect or another of Hellenic thought. The Greeks were supremely articulate in the service of their evolving vision, and in cases beyond counting, what may have long been considered a peculiar error or confusion in Greek thought has later, in the light of new evidence, been discovered to be an astonishingly accurate intuition. Perhaps the Greeks, coming at the dawn of our civilization, perceived the world with a certain innate clarity that authentically reflected the universal order they were seeking. Certainly the West continues to turn again and again to its ancient progenitors, as to a fount of immortal insight. As Finley remarked, "Whether the Greeks saw things most freshly because they came first or it is pure good luck that, having come first, they answered life with unmatched alertness, they in either case keep ageless sparkle, as of the world lit by a kind of six-o'clock-in-the-morning light and the dew imperishably on the grass. The Greek mind remains in ours, because this untarnished freshness leaves it, like youth itself, our first exemplar."[10]

It is as if, for the Greeks, heaven and earth had not yet been fully rent asunder. But instead of our now attempting to sort out what is permanently valuable and what problematic in the Hellenic vision, let us observe history engage that task as the Western culture that Greece initiated moved forward—building upon the Greek legacy, transforming it, criticizing it, amplifying it, disregarding it, reintegrating it, negating it . . . yet never, in the end, truly leaving it.

II

The
Transformation
of the Classical Era

J ust when the Greek intellectual achievement had reached its climax during the fourth century B.C., Alexander the Great swept down from Macedonia through Greece and onward to Persia, conquering lands and peoples from Egypt to India and creating an empire that was to encompass most of the known world. The very qualities that had served Greece's brilliant evolution—restless individualism, proud humanism, critical rationalism—now helped precipitate its downfall, for the divisiveness, arrogance, and opportunism that shadowed the Greeks' nobler qualities left them myopic and fatally unprepared for the Macedonian challenge. Yet the Hellenic achievement was not fated for extinction. Tutored by Aristotle as a youth in his father's court and inspired by the Homeric epics and Athenian ideals, Alexander carried with him and disseminated the Greek culture and language throughout the vast world he conquered. Thus Greece fell just as it culminated, yet spread triumphantly just as it submitted.

As planned by Alexander, the large cosmopolitan cities of the empire—above all Alexandria, which he founded in Egypt—became vital centers of cultural learning, in whose libraries and academies the classical Greek inheritance survived and flourished. Alexander seems also to have been inspired by a vision of mankind's universal kinship beyond all political divisions, and he attempted to bring about such a unity, a massive cultural fusion, by means of his immense military ambition. After his early death, however, Alexander's empire did not hold together. Following a long period of dynastic struggles and shifting sovereignties, Rome emerged as the center of a new empire, with both its focal point and its outlying regions now further west.

Despite the Roman conquest, Greek high culture still presided over the educated classes of the greater Mediterranean world and was rapidly absorbed by the Romans. The most significant scientists and philosophers continued to work within the Greek intellectual framework. The Romans modeled their Latin works on the Greek masterpieces and carried on the development and expansion of a sophisticated civilization, but their more pragmatic genius lay in the realm of law, political administration, and military strategy. In philosophy, literature, science, art, and education, Greece remained the most compelling cultural force in the ancient world. As the Roman poet Horace noted, the Greeks, captive, took the victors captive.

Crosscurrents of the Hellenistic Matrix

The Decline and Preservation of the Greek Mind

Despite Greece's continuing cultural power after Alexander's conquest and throughout the period of Roman hegemony, the original cast of the classical Greek mind did not hold under the impact of so many new forces. With the Hellenistic world extending all the way from the western Mediterranean to central Asia, the reflective individual of the later classical era was exposed to an enormous multiplicity of viewpoints. The initial expansion of Greek culture eastward was in time complemented by a strong influx of Oriental (from east of the Mediterranean) religious and political currents to the West. In important respects Greek culture was as enriched by this new influx as were the non-Greek cultures by the Hellenic expansion. Yet in other respects the polis-centered Greek mind lost something of its earlier confident lucidity and bold originality. Just as the critical individualism of classical Greece had produced its great art and thought yet also contributed to the disintegration of its social order, rendering it vulnerable to Macedonian subjugation, so too did the centrifugal vitality of Greek culture lead not only to its successful propagation but also to its eventual dilution and fragmenting as the classical polis was opened to the contrasting influences of a much larger, heterogeneous cultural environment. The unprecedented cosmopolitanism of the new civilization, the breakup of the old order of small city-states, and the succeeding centuries of constant political and social upheaval were profoundly disorienting. Both individual freedom in and responsibility to the polis community were undermined by the massiveness and confusion of the new political world. Personal destinies appeared to be determined more by large impersonal forces than by individual volition. The old clarity no longer seemed available, and many felt they had lost their bearings.

Philosophy reflected and attempted to address these changes. While Plato and Aristotle continued to be studied and followed, the two dominant philosophical schools originating in the Hellenistic era, the Stoic and Epicurean, were of a different character. Though owing much to the earlier Greeks, these new schools were primarily ethical and exhortatory, noble philosophical defenses with which to endure troubled and uncertain times. This shift in the nature and function of philosophy was partly a consequence of a new intellectual specialization in the wake of Aristotle's expansion and classification of the sciences, a specialization that gradually separated science from philosophy, narrowing the latter to moral positions backed by relevant metaphysical or physical doctrines. Yet beyond this insulation of philosophy from broader intellectual concerns, the characteristic philosophical impulse of the Hellenistic schools arose less from the passion to comprehend the world in its mystery and magnitude, and more from the need to give human beings some stable belief system and inner peace in the face of a hostile and chaotic environment. The result of this new impulse was the emergence of philosophies more limited in scope and more prone to fatalism than their classical predecessors. Disengagement from the world or from one's own passions was the principal choice, and in either case philosophy took on a more dogmatic tone.

Yet Stoicism, the most broadly representative of the Hellenistic philosophies, possessed a loftiness of vision and moral temper that would long leave its mark on the Western spirit. Founded in Athens in the early third century B.C. by Zeno of Citium, who had studied at the Platonic Academy, and later systematized by Chrysippus, Stoicism would be especially influential in the Roman world of Cicero and Seneca, Epictetus and Marcus Aurelius. In the Stoic view, all reality was pervaded by an intelligent divine force, the Logos or universal reason which ordered all things. Man could achieve genuine happiness only by attuning his life and character to this all-powerful providential wisdom. To be free was to live in conformity with God's will, and what mattered finally in life was the virtuous state of the soul, not the circumstances of the outer life. The Stoic sage, marked by inner serenity, sternness in self-discipline, and conscientious performance of duty, was indifferent to the vagaries of external events. The existence of the world-governing reason had another important consequence for the Stoic. Because all human beings shared in the divine Logos, all were members of a universal human community, a brotherhood of mankind that constituted the World City, or Cosmopolis, and each individual was called upon to participate actively in the affairs of the world and thereby fulfill his duty to this great community.

At heart, Stoicism was a development of central elements of Socratic and Heraclitean philosophy, transposed to the less circumscribed and more ecumenical Hellenistic period. By contrast, its contemporary rival Epicureanism distinguished itself from the Stoic devotion to moral virtue and the world-governing Logos, as well as from traditional religious notions, by asserting the primary value of human pleasure—defined as freedom from pain and fear. Mankind must overcome its superstitious belief in the fickle, anthropomorphic gods of popular tradition, Epicurus taught, for it is above all this belief, and the anxiety about divine retribution after death, that caused human misery. One need not fear the gods, for they do not concern themselves with the human world. Nor need one fear death, for it is merely the extinction of consciousness and not a prelude to a painful punishment. Happiness in this life can best be achieved through withdrawal from the world of affairs to cultivate a quiet existence of simple pleasure in the company of friends. The physical cosmology from which the Epicurean system drew was Democritus's atomism, with material particles forming the substance of the world, including the mortal human soul. Such a cosmology and contemporary human experience were not unrelated, for citizens of the Hellenistic era, deprived of the defined, centered, organically ordered world of the polis—the general character of which was not unlike the Aristotelian cosmos—may well have sensed a certain parallel between their own fate and that of Democritean atoms, moving randomly at the behest of impersonal forces in the centerless void of a disorientingly expanded universe.

A more radical reflection of the era's intellectual shift was the systematic Skepticism represented by thinkers such as Pyrrho of Elis and Sextus Empiricus, who held that no truths could be known to be certain and that the only appropriate philosophical stance was the complete suspension of judgment. Developing powerful arguments to refute all dogmatic claims to philosophical knowledge, Skeptics pointed out that any conflict between two apparent truths could be settled only by appeal to some criterion; yet that criterion could itself be justified only by appeal to some further criterion, which would thereby require an infinite regress of such criteria, none foundational. "Nothing is certain, not even that," said Arcesilaus, a member of the Platonic Academy (which, significantly, also embraced Skepticism at this time, renewing a central aspect of its Socratic origins). It is true that in Hellenistic philosophy, logic was often skillfully employed to demonstrate the futility of much of the human enterprise, particularly the pursuit of metaphysical truth. Yet Skeptics such as Sextus argued that people who believed they could know reality were subject to constant frustration and unhappiness in life. If they would genuinely suspend judgment, recognizing that their beliefs about reality were not necessarily valid, they would achieve peace of mind. Neither affirming nor denying the possibility of knowledge, they should remain in a state of open-minded equanimity, waiting to see what might emerge.

While important and attractive in their different ways, these several philosophies did not entirely satisfy the Hellenistic spirit. Divine reality was seen as either insensitive and irrelevant to human affairs (Epicureanism), implacably deterministic if providential (Stoicism), or altogether beyond human cognition (Skepticism). Science too became more thoroughly rationalistic, shedding the virtually religious impetus and goal of divine comprehension formerly visible in Pythagoras, Plato, and even Aristotle. Hence the culture's emotional and religious demands were met most directly by the various mystery religions—Greek, Egyptian, Oriental—which offered salvation from the imprisonment of the world, and which flourished throughout the empire with ever-increasing popularity. But these religions, with their festivals and secret rites devoted to their different deities, failed to compel the allegiance of many in the educated classes. For them, the old myths were dying, good at best as allegorical instruments for reasonable discourse. And yet the austere rationalism of the dominant philosophies left a certain spiritual hunger. That uniquely creative unity of intellect and feeling of earlier times had now bifurcated. In the midst of an extraordinarily sophisticated cultural milieu—busy, urbanized, refined, cosmopolitan—the reflective individual was often without compelling motivation. The classical synthesis of pre-Alexandrian Greece had come apart, its potency spent in the process of diffusion.

Yet the Hellenistic era was an exceptionally rich age with several remarkable and, from the perspective of the modern West, indispensable cultural accomplishments to its credit. Not least was its recognition of the earlier Greek achievement and its consequent preservation of the classics from Homer to Aristotle. The texts were now collected, systematically examined, and painstakingly edited to prepare a definitive canon of masterworks. Humanistic scholarship was founded. New disciplines of textual and literary criticism were developed, interpretive analyses and commentaries produced, and the great works set forth as revered cultural ideals for the enrichment of future generations. In Alexandria, the Greek translation of the Hebrew Bible, the Septuagint, was similarly compiled, edited, and canonized with the same meticulous scholarship as that accorded to the Homeric epics and Platonic dialogues.

Education itself became systematized and widespread. Large and elaborately organized academic institutions were established for the pursuit of scholarly research in the major cities—Alexandria with its Museum, Pergamum with its Library, and Athens with its still-thriving philosophical academies. The royal rulers of the major Hellenistic empire-states subsidized the public institutions of learning, employing scientists and scholars as salaried officials of the state. Public educational systems existed in almost every Hellenistic city, gymnasia and theaters were plentiful, and advanced instruction in Greek philosophy, literature, and rhetoric became widely available. The Greek *paideia* flourished. Thus the earlier Hellenic achievement was scholastically consolidated, geographically extended, and vitally sustained for the remainder of the classical era.

Astronomy

As for original contributions, it was in the field of natural science that the Hellenistic period especially excelled. The geometer Euclid, the geometer-astronomer Apollonius, the mathematical physicist Archimedes, the astronomer Hipparchus, the geographer Strabo, the physician Galen, and the geographer-astronomer Ptolemy all produced scientific advances and codifications that would remain paradigmatic for many centuries. The development of mathematical astronomy was particularly consequential. The problem of the planets had found its first solution in Eudoxus's interconnected homocentric spheres, which both explained retrograde motion and gave approximately accurate predictions. It did not, however, explain the variations of brightness when the planets were retrograde, since the rotating spheres necessarily kept the planets at constant distance from the Earth. It was this theoretical failing that provoked subsequent mathematicians and astronomers to explore alternative geometrical systems.

A few, such as the Pythagoreans, made the radical suggestion that the Earth moved. Heraclides, a member of Plato's Academy, proposed that the diurnal movement of the heavens was actually caused by the Earth's rotating on its axis, and that Mercury and Venus, which always appeared close to the Sun, did so because they revolved about the Sun rather than the Earth. A century later, Aristarchus went so far as to hypothesize that the Earth and all the planets revolved around the Sun, and that the Sun, like the outer sphere of stars, remained stationary.[1]

These various models were generally rejected, however, for sound mathematical and physical reasons. No annual stellar parallax was ever observed, and such a shift should have occurred if the Earth revolved around the Sun and thus traveled such vast distances relative to the stars (unless, as Aristarchus suggested, the outer sphere of stars was inconceivably large). Moreover, a moving Earth would entirely disrupt the comprehensive coherence of Aristotelian cosmology. Aristotle had definitively treated the physics of falling bodies, demonstrating that heavy objects move toward the Earth because it is the universe's fixed center. If the Earth moved, then this well-reasoned and virtually self-evident account of falling bodies would be undermined with no theory of comparable power to replace it. Perhaps even more fundamentally, a planetary Earth would contravene the ancient and also self-evident terrestrial-celestial dichotomy based on the transcendent majesty of the heavens. Finally, theoretical and religious issues aside, common sense dictated that a moving Earth would force objects and persons on it to be knocked about, clouds and birds would be left behind, and so forth. The unambiguous evidence of the senses argued for a stable Earth.

On the basis of such considerations, the majority of Hellenistic astronomers decided in favor of an Earth-centered universe, and continued working with various geometrical models for explaining the planetary positions. The cumulative result of these efforts was codified in the second century A.D. by Ptolemy, whose synthesis established the working paradigm for astronomers from that time through the Renaissance. The essential challenge presented to Ptolemy remained as before: how to account for the numerous discrepancies between, on the one hand, the basic structure of the Aristotelian cosmology, which demanded that the planets move uniformly in perfect circles around a central immobile Earth, and, on the other hand, astronomers' actual observations of the planets, which appeared to move with varying speeds, directions, and degrees of brightness. Building on the recent advances of Greek geometry, on the Babylonians' continued observations and linear computational techniques, and on the work of the Greek astronomers Apollonius and Hipparchus, Ptolemy outlined the following scheme: The outermost revolving sphere of the fixed stars daily carried the entire heavens westward about the Earth. Within that sphere, however, each planet, including the Sun and Moon, revolved eastward at varying slower rates, each in its own large circle called a deferent. For the more complex movements of the planets other than the Sun and Moon, another smaller circle, called an epicycle, was introduced, which rotated uniformly around a point that continued to rotate on the deferent. The epicycle solved what Eudoxus's spheres could not, since the rotating epicycle automatically brought the planet closer to the Earth whenever it was retrograde, and thus made the planet appear brighter. By adjusting the different rates of revolution for each deferent and epicycle, astronomers could approximate the variable movements of each planet. The simplicity of the deferent-epicycle scheme, plus its explanation of variable brightness, made it the acknowledged victor in the quest for a viable astronomical model.

Yet when applied, this scheme revealed further minor irregularities, to explain which Ptolemy employed further geometrical devices: eccentrics (circles whose centers were displaced from the center of the Earth), minor epicycles (additional smaller circles that rotated about a major epicycle or deferent), and equants (which further explained variable speeds by positing another point away from the circle's center about which motion was uniform). Ptolemy's elaborate model of compound circles was able to give the first systematic quantitative account of all the celestial motions. Moreover, its versatility, whereby new conflicting observations could be met by adding new geometrical modifications (e.g., adding another epicycle to an epicycle, or an eccentric to an eccentric), gave the model a flexible power that sustained its reign throughout the classical and medieval periods. The Aristotelian cosmology, with its fixed central Earth, its circling aetheric spheres, and its elemental physics, had provided the basic framework for Hellenistic astronomers to forge this scheme, and the synthesized Ptolemaic-Aristotelian universe in turn became the fundamental world conception informing the West's philosophical, religious, and scientific vision for most of the subsequent fifteen centuries.

Astrology

In the classical world, however, mathematical astronomy was not an entirely secular discipline. For the ancient understanding of the heavens as the locus of the gods was inextricably wedded to the rapidly developing astronomy to form what was considered the science of astrology, of which

Ptolemy was the classical era's culminating systematizer. Indeed, a large part of the impetus for the development of astronomy derived directly from its ties to astrology, which employed those technical advances to improve its own predictive power. In turn, the widespread demand for astrological insight—whether in the imperial courts, the public marketplace, or the philosopher's study—encouraged astronomy's further evolution and continued social significance, the two disciplines forming essentially one profession from the classical era through the Renaissance.

With the greatly increased precision of astronomical computations, the ancient Mesopotamian conception of celestial events indicating terrestrial events—the doctrine of universal sympathy, "as above, so below"—was now placed into a more sophisticated and systematic Greek framework of mathematical and qualitative principles. This system was then applied by Hellenistic astrologers to render predictions not only for large collectivities such as nations and empires, but also for individual persons. By calculating the exact positions of the planets at the moment of a person's birth, and by drawing out archetypal principles from the perceived correspondence of specific mythic deities to specific planets, astrologers derived conclusions concerning the individual's character and destiny. Further insights emerged by employing various Pythagorean and Babylonian principles pertaining to the structure of the cosmos and its intrinsic relation to the microcosm, man. Platonists elaborated on the means by which specific planetary alignments could bring about an assimilation of the planet's character with the individual, an archetypal unity between agent and receiver. In turn, Aristotelian physics, with its impersonal terminology and its mechanical explanation of celestial influence on terrestrial phenomena via the elemental spheres, provided an appropriate scientific framework for the developing discipline. The accumulated elements of classical astrological theory were brought by Ptolemy into a unified synthesis, in which he catalogued the meanings of the planets, their positions and geometrical aspects, and their various effects on human affairs.

With the emergence of the astrological perspective, it was widely believed that human life was ruled not by capricious chance, but by an ordered and humanly knowable destiny defined by the celestial deities according to the movements of the planets. Through such knowledge it was thought that man could understand his fate and act with a new sense of cosmic security. The astrological conception of the world closely reflected the essential Greek concept of *kosmos* itself, the intelligibly ordered patterning and interconnected coherence of the universe, with man an integral part of the whole. In the course of the Hellenistic era, astrology became the one belief system that cut across the boundaries of science, philosophy, and religion, forming a peculiarly unifying element in the otherwise fragmented outlook of the age. Radiating outward from the cultural center of Alexandria, belief in astrology pervaded the Hellenistic world and was embraced alike by Stoic, Platonic, and Aristotelian philosophers, by mathematical astronomers and medical physicians, by Hermetic esotericists and members of the various mystery religions.

Yet the central basis of the astrological understanding was interpreted in different ways by the different groups, each according to its own world view. For Ptolemy and his colleagues, astrology seems to have been regarded primarily as a useful science—a straightforward study of how specific planetary positions and combinations coincided with specific events and personal qualities. Ptolemy noted that astrology could not claim to be an exact science like astronomy, since astronomy dealt exclusively with the abstract mathematics of the perfect celestial movements, while astrology applied that knowledge to the necessarily less predictable imperfect arena of terrestrial and human activity. But while its inherent inexactness and susceptibility to error left astrology open to criticism, Ptolemy and his era believed it worked. It shared with astronomy the same focus on the orderly motions of the heavens, and because of the powers of causation exercised by the celestial spheres, astrology possessed a rational foundation and firm principles of operation, which Ptolemy undertook to define.

In a more philosophical spirit, the astrological correspondences were interpreted by the Greek and Roman Stoics as signifying the fundamental determinism of human life by the celestial bodies. Hence astrology was regarded as the best method for interpreting the cosmic will and aligning one's life with the divine reason. With their conviction that a cosmic fate ruled all things, and with their belief in a universal sympathy or law unifying all parts of the cosmos, the Stoics found astrology highly congenial to their world view. The mystery religions expressed a similar understanding of the planets' dominion over human life, but perceived in addition a promise of liberation: beyond the last planet, Saturn (the deity of fate, limitation, and death), presided the all-encompassing sphere of a greater Deity whose divine omnipotence could lift the human soul out of the bound determinism of mortal existence into eternal freedom. This highest God ruled all the planetary deities, and could thus suspend the laws of fate and liberate the devout individual from the web of determinism.[2] Platonists similarly held the planets to be under the ultimate government of the supreme Good, but tended to view the celestial configurations as indicative rather than causal, and not absolutely determining for the evolved individual. A less fatalistic view was also implicit in Ptolemy's approach, in which he stressed the strategic value of such studies and suggested that man could play an active role in the cosmic scheme. But whatever the particular interpretation, the belief that the planetary movements possessed an intelligible significance for human life exercised an immense influence on the cultural ethos of the classical era.

Neoplatonism

One other field of thought sought to bridge the Hellenistic schism between the rational philosophies and the mystery religions. During the several centuries following Plato's death in the mid-fourth century B.C., a continuing stream of philosophers had developed his thought by focusing on and amplifying its metaphysical and religious aspects. In the course of this development, the highest transcendent principle began to be called "the One"; new emphasis was placed on "the flight from the body" as necessary for the soul's philosophical ascent to the divine reality; the Forms began to be located within the divine mind; and increased concern was shown for the problem of evil and its relation to matter. This stream found its culmination in the third century A.D. in the work of Plotinus, who, by integrating a more explicitly mystical element into the Platonic scheme while incorporating certain aspects of Aristotelian thought, formulated a "Neoplatonic" philosophy of considerable intellectual power and universal scope. In Plotinus, Greek rational philosophy reached its end point and passed over into another, more thoroughly religious spirit, a suprarational mysticism. The character of a new era, with a psychological and religious sensibility fundamentally different from that of classical Hellenism, was becoming apparent.

For in Plotinus's thought, the rationality of the world and of the philosopher's quest is but the prelude to a more transcendent existent beyond reason. The Neoplatonic cosmos is the result of a divine emanation from the supreme One, which is infinite in being and beyond all description or categories. The One, also called the Good, in an overflow of sheer perfection produces the "other"—the created cosmos in all its variety—in a hierarchical series of gradations moving away from this ontological center to the extreme limits of the possible. The first creative act is the issuing forth from the One of the divine Intellect or *Nous*, the pervasive wisdom of the universe, within which are contained the archetypal Forms or Ideas that cause and order the world. From the *Nous* comes the World Soul, which contains and animates the world, is the source for the souls of all living beings, and constitutes the intermediate reality between the spiritual Intellect and the world of matter. The emanation of divinity from the One is an ontological process which Plotinus compared to the light that moves gradually outward from a candle until it at last disappears into darkness. The several gradations, however, are not separate realms in a temporal or spatial sense, but are distinct levels of being timelessly present in all things. The three "hypostases"—One, Intellect, and Soul—are not literal entities but rather spiritual dispositions, just as the Ideas are not distinct objects but rather different states of being of the divine Mind.

The material world, existing in time and space and perceptible to the senses, is the level of reality furthest from unitary divinity. As the final limit of creation, it is characterized in negative terms as the realm of multiplicity, restriction, and darkness, as lowest in ontological stature—holding the least degree of real being—and as constituting the principle of evil. Yet it is also, despite its deep imperfection, characterized in positive terms as a creation of beauty, an organic whole produced and held together by the World Soul in a universal harmony. It imperfectly reflects on the spatiotemporal level the glorious unity in diversity that exists on a higher level in the spiritual Intellect's world of Forms: The sensible is a noble image of the intelligible. Although evil exists within this harmony, that negative reality plays a necessary role in a larger design, and ultimately affects neither the perfection of the One nor the well-being of the philosopher's highest self.

Man, whose nature is soul-in-body, has potential access to the highest intellectual and spiritual realms, though this is dependent on his liberation from materiality. Man can rise to the consciousness of the World Soul—thereby becoming in actuality what he already is potentially—and thence to the universal Intellect; or he can remain bound to the lower realms. Because all things emanate from the One through the Intellect and the World Soul, and because the human imagination at its highest participates in that primal divinity, man's rational soul can imaginatively reflect the transcendent Forms and thus, through this insight into the ultimate order of things, move toward its spiritual emancipation. The entire universe exists in a continual outflow from the One into created multiplicity, which is then drawn back to the One—a process of emanation and return always moved by the One's superfluity of perfection. The philosopher's task is to overcome the human bondage to the physical realm by moral and intellectual self-discipline and purification, and to turn inward to a gradual ascent back to the Absolute. The final moment of illumination transcends knowledge in any usual sense, and cannot be defined or described, for it is based on an overcoming of the subject-object dichotomy between the seeker and the goal: it is a consummation of contemplative desire that unites the philosopher with the One.

Thus Plotinus articulated an elaborately coherent rationalist and idealist metaphysics which found its fulfillment in a unitary mystical apprehension of the supreme Godhead. With confident and meticulous precision, and in often startlingly beautiful prose, Plotinus described the complex nature of the universe and its participation in the divine. Basing his philosophy on the Platonic doctrine of transcendent Ideas, he then added or drew out several new, defining features—teleological dynamism, hierarchy, emanation, and a suprarational mysticism. In this form, Neoplatonism became the final expression of classical pagan philosophy, and it assumed the role of Platonism's historical carrier in subsequent centuries.

Both Neoplatonism and astrology transcended the intellectual bifurcation of the Hellenistic era, and, like much else in classical culture, both were the result of Greek thought-forms' penetrating and intermingling with non-Hellenic cultural impulses. Each in its own way would have an enduring, if sometimes hidden, influence on later Western thought. Yet despite astrology's near-universal popularity in the Hellenistic world, and despite Neoplatonism's well-received renovation of pagan philosophy in the last years of the academies, by the late classical era new, powerful forces had begun to impinge on the Greco-Roman consciousness. In the end, the restless spirit of the Hellenistic era was to seek its redemption in a new quarter altogether.

With the several important exceptions already cited, the later efforts of Hellenic culture in the classical period appeared to lack the daring intellectual optimism and curiosity that had been characteristic of the earlier Greeks. At least on the surface, Hellenistic civilization seemed remarkable more for its variety than its force, more for its worldly intelligence than its inspired genius, more for its sustaining and elaboration of past cultural achievements than its origination of new ones. Many significant currents were at work, but the whole did not cohere. The cultural outlook was unsettled, alternately skeptical and dogmatic, syncretistic and fragmented. The highly organized centers of learning seemed to have a discouraging effect on individual genius. Already by the time of Rome's conquest of Greece in the second century B.C., the Hellenic impulse was fading, displaced by the more Oriental view of human subordination to the overwhelming powers of the supernatural.

Rome

In Rome, however, classical civilization experienced an expansive autumnal flowering, spurred first by the Republic's militaristic and libertarian ethos, and then nourished by the *Pax Romana* established during the long imperial reign of Caesar Augustus. With political shrewdness and steadfast patriotism, and fortified by belief in their guiding deities, the Romans succeeded not only in conquering the entire Mediterranean basin and a large part of Europe, but also in fulfilling their perceived mission of extending their civilization throughout the known world. Without that conquest, made possible by the ruthless military tactics and ambitious political genius of leaders like Julius Caesar, it is unlikely the positive legacy of classical culture would have survived, in the West or the East, the pressures of later barbarian and Oriental assaults.

Roman culture itself contributed significantly to the classical achievement. Cicero, Virgil, Horace, and Livy brought the Latin language, under the influence of the Greek masters, to an eloquent maturity. The Greek *paideia* found new life in the Roman aristocracy's *humanitas* (Cicero's Latin translation of *paideia*), the liberal education founded on the classics. Greek mythology was conflated with and preserved in Roman mythology, and through the works of Ovid and Virgil passed on to Western posterity. Roman legal thought, containing a new sense of objective rationality and natural law derived from the Greek concept of the universal Logos, introduced systematic clarity into commercial and legal interactions throughout the empire, cutting through the welter of divergent local customs and evolving principles of contract law and property ownership crucial for the West's later development.

The sheer energy and massiveness of the Roman enterprise commanded the awe of the ancient world. But Rome's cultural splendor was an *imitatio*, albeit inspired, of Greece's glory, and its magnitude alone could not indefinitely sustain the Hellenic spirit. Although nobility of character often evidenced itself in the turmoil of political life, the Roman ethos gradually lost its vitality. The very success of the empire's inordinate military and commercial activity, divorced from deeper motivations, was weakening the fiber of the Roman citizenry. Most scientific activity, let alone genius, radically diminished in the empire soon after Galen and Ptolemy in the second century, and the excellence of Latin literature began to wane in the same period. Faith in human progress, so broadly visible in the cultural florescence of fifth-century B.C. Greece, and sporadically expressed, usually by scientists and technologists, in the Hellenistic age, virtually disappeared in the final centuries of the Roman Empire. Classical civilization's finest hours were by then all in the past, and the various factors that brought on Rome's fall—oppressive and rapacious government, overambitious generals, constant barbarian incursions, an aristocracy grown decadent and effete, religious crosscurrents undermining the imperial authority and military ethos, drastic sustained inflation, pestilential diseases, a dwindling population without resilience or focus—all contributed further to the apparent death of the Greek-inspired world.

Yet beneath the glittering decay of classical culture, and from within the wellspring of the Hellenistic religious matrix, a new world had been slowly and inexorably taking form.

The Emergence of Christianity

Considered as a single entity, classical Greco-Roman civilization arose, flourished, and declined in the course of a thousand years. At about the midpoint of this millennium, in the remote districts of Galilee and Judaea on the periphery of the Roman Empire, the young Jewish religious leader Jesus of Nazareth lived, taught, and died. His radical religious message was embraced by a small but fervently inspired group of Jewish disciples, who believed that after his death by crucifixion, Jesus had risen again and revealed himself as the Christ ("the anointed one"), the world's Lord and Savior. A new stage in the religion was reached with the advent of Paul of Tarsus, who was Jewish by birth, Roman by citizenship, and Greek by culture. While on his way to Damascus to restrain further spread of what he viewed as a heretical sect dangerous to Judaic orthodoxy, Paul was overwhelmed by a vision of the risen Christ. He then ardently espoused the very religion of which he had been the most forceful opponent, and indeed became its preeminent missionary and foundational theologian. Under Paul's leadership, the small religious movement rapidly spread to the other parts of the empire—Asia Minor, Egypt, Greece, to Rome itself—and began to constitute itself as a world church.

In the course of the unsettled Hellenistic era, something like a spiritual crisis appears to have arisen in the culture, its members impelled by newly conscious needs for personal significance in the cosmos and personal knowledge of life's meaning. To these needs the various mystery religions, public cults, esoteric systems, and philosophical schools all spoke, but it was Christianity that, after intermittent periods of severe persecution by the Roman state, gradually emerged as the victor. The turning point of this process came in the early fourth century with the epochal conversion of the Roman emperor Constantine, who thereafter committed himself and his imperial power to Christianity's propagation.[3]

The classical world was drastically transformed in its final centuries by the influx of the Christian religion from the east and the massive invasions of the Germanic barbarians from the north. By the end of the fourth century, Christianity had become the official state religion of the Roman Empire, and by the end of the fifth, the last Roman emperor in the West had been deposed by a barbarian king. On the face of it, classical civilization had been snuffed out in the West, its great works and ideas left to the Byzantines and later the Moslems to be preserved as in a museum. As Edward Gibbon would pointedly epitomize his *History of the Decline and Fall of the Roman Empire,* "I have described the triumph of barbarism and religion." But from a long view of the West's complex evolution, these new forces did not entirely eliminate or supplant the Greco-Roman culture as much as they engrafted their own distinctive elements onto the highly developed and deeply rooted classical foundation.[4]

Despite the decline of Europe into cultural isolation and inactivity during the following centuries (especially as compared with the flourishing Byzantine and Islamic empires), the restless enterprising vigor of the Germanic peoples combined with the civilizing influence of the Roman Catholic Church to forge a culture that was, in another thousand years, to give birth to the modern West. These "Middle" Ages between the classical era and the Renaissance were thus a gestation period of considerable consequence. The Church served as the one institution uniting the West and sustaining a connection with classical civilization. The barbarians for their part did two remarkable things: they converted to Christianity, while they simultaneously set about the enormous task of learning and integrating the rich intellectual heritage of the classical culture they had just conquered. This great scholastic labor, slowly carried out over the thousand-year period first in the monasteries and later in the universities, encompassed not only Greek philosophy and letters as well as Roman political thought, but also the now impressive body of theological writings by the ancient Christian fathers culminating in the work of Augustine—who wrote in the early fifth century just as the Roman Empire was collapsing around him under the impact of the barbarian invasions. It was from this complex fusion of racial, political, religious, and philosophical elements that there gradually arose a comprehensive world view common to Western Christendom. Succeeding that of the classical Greeks as the governing vision of the culture, the Christian outlook would inform and inspire the lives and thinking of millions until the modern era—and, for many, continues to do so.

III

The
Christian World View

O ur next task is to attempt an understanding of the Christian belief system. Any recapitulation of our cultural and intellectual history must address this task with care, for Christianity has presided over Western culture for most of the latter's existence, not only bearing its central spiritual impulse for two millennia but also influencing its philosophical and scientific evolution well on through the Renaissance and Enlightenment. Even now, in less obvious but no less significant ways, the Christian world view still affects—indeed, permeates—the Western cultural psyche, even when the latter is most apparently secular in disposition.

Precisely what the historical Jesus of Nazareth said, did, or believed himself to be cannot now be ascertained. Like Socrates, Jesus wrote nothing for posterity. It is relatively well established by historical studies and scriptural exegesis that he preached, within the Judaic religious tradition, a call for repentance in anticipation of the imminent coming of God's Kingdom, that he saw this dawning Kingdom as already present in his own words and deeds, and that for these claims he was put to death under the Roman procurator Pontius Pilate in about 30 A.D. Whether he knew himself to be the Son of God is not unequivocally established, and many of the other major elements of Jesus's life held sacred by the Christian faith—the dramatic nativity narrative, the various miracle stories, Jesus's knowledge of the Trinity, his intention to found a new religion—cannot be conclusively verified from the historical and textual evidence.

It was not until the later part of the first century that the four Gospels of the New Testament were composed and the foundations of Christian belief laid out by the descendants of Jesus's immediate followers, and by then an elaborate and at times inconsistent belief structure had developed. This structure involved not only the remembered facts of Jesus's life, but also various oral traditions, legends, parables and sayings, subsequent visions and prophecies, hymns and prayers, apocalyptic beliefs, the young Church's didactic requirements, interpolated parallels with the Hebrew Scriptures, other Jewish, Greek, and Gnostic influences, and a complex redemptive theology and view of history—all unified by the biblical authors' commitment of faith to the new religion. How much this final compound reflected the actual events and teachings of Jesus's life remains problematic. The earliest extant Christian documents are the letters of Paul, who never met Jesus. Hence the Jesus that history came to know is the Jesus portrayed—recalled, reconstructed, interpreted, embellished, vividly imagined—in the New Testament by writers living one or two generations after the period covered by their narratives, the authorship of which they ascribed to Jesus's original disciples.

Even these writings were gradually selected as God's authentic revelation by the early Church hierarchy out of a larger group of such materials, some of which (generally composed later) offered radically different perspectives on the events in question. The orthodox Church that made these judgments, so decisive for the subsequent formation of the Christian belief system, understood itself to be an authority founded with the first apostles and divinely sanctioned by Holy Scripture. The Church was God's representative on earth, a sacred institution whose continuing tradition would serve as the exclusive interpreter of God's revelation to humanity. With the Church's gradual emergence as the dominant structure and influence in the early Christian religion, the writings that now constitute the New Testament, added to the Hebrew Bible, were established as the canonical basis for the Christian tradition, and these effectively determined the parameters of the evolving Christian world view.

These writings will therefore serve as the basis for our present study of the Christian phenomenon. Because our topic is the nature of and dynamic relationship between the dominant world views of Western civilization, our main concern here is with the tradition of Christianity that held cultural sway over the West from the fall of Rome to the modern era. What the Christian West believed to be true about the world and the human being's place in it is our specific interest, and that world view was grounded in the canonical revelation, and gradually modified, developed, and extended by various subsequent factors largely under the authoritative guidance of Church tradition. That it was the Church that established the divine authority of the scriptural canon, and the scriptural canon that established the divine authority of the Church, may appear circuitous, but that symbiotic mutual endorsement, affirmed in faith by the continuing Church community, effectively ruled the formation of the Christian outlook. This tradition, then, both in its foundational biblical form and in its later developments, is the subject of our inquiry.

To begin, let us turn our attention to that from which Christianity emerged—the intensely focused, morally rigorous, richly religious tradition of the Israelites, the descendants of Abraham and Moses.

Judaic Monotheism
and the Divinization of History

Theology and history were inextricably conjoined in the Hebrew vision. Acts of God and the events of human experience constituted one reality, and the biblical narrative of the Hebrew past was intended rather to reveal its divine logic than to reconstruct an exact historical record. As with Christianity, legend and fact in the early history of Judaism cannot now be clearly distinguished. Nevertheless, although later biblical interpolations obscure the precise emergence in the ancient Near East of a specific people with a monotheistic religion out of an earlier background (extending to the patriarchs Abraham, Isaac, and Jacob in the early second millennium B.C.) of seminomadic tribes with elements of polytheism in their worship, there would appear to be a definite historical core to the traditional Judaic self-understanding.

Certainly the history and mission of the Hebrew people and its religion were unlike any other in the ancient world. In the midst of many nations, often more powerful and advanced than their own, the Hebrews came to experience themselves as the Chosen People, singled out as a nation whose history would have weighty spiritual consequences for the entire world. In the midst of a land where a multiplicity of nature deities were worshiped by surrounding tribes and nations, the Hebrews came to believe that they existed in a unique and direct relationship to the one absolute God who stood above and beyond all other beings as both creator of the world and director of its history. Indeed, the Hebrews perceived their own history as continuous with and reflective of the very beginnings of Creation, when God had made the world and, in his own image, man. With Adam and Eve's primal disobedience and expulsion from the Garden of Eden, the drama of man's exile from divinity had begun, to be renewed again and again—Cain and Abel, Noah and the Flood, the Tower of Babel—until Abraham was called forth in faith to follow God's plan for his people.

It was in the course of the Exodus, when Moses led the Hebrews out of bondage from Egypt, that the sacred covenant was established by which Israel identified itself and recognized its God, Yahweh, as the saving Lord of history.[1] On this historical foundation rested the Israelites' continuing faith in God's promise for their future fulfillment. By accepting the divine commandments revealed on Mount Sinai, the Hebrews betrothed themselves in obedience to their God and his insuperable and inscrutable will. For the God of the Hebrews was a God of miracle and purpose, who saved nations or crushed them at will, who brought forth water from rocks, food from heaven, children from the barren womb, to accomplish his plan for Israel. Their God was not only creator but liberator, and had assured his people a glorious destiny if they would remain faithful and obedient to his law.

The imperative of trust in the Lord, and fear of the Lord, dominated Jewish life as the prerequisite for enjoying his saving power in the world. Here was the overriding sense of moral urgency, of ultimate fate's being decided by present human actions, of the individual's direct accountability to the all-seeing and all-just God. Here too was the denunciation of an unjust society, the contempt for hollow secular success, the prophetic call for moral regeneration. A divine summons had been given to the Jews to recognize God's sovereignty over the world, and to aid in the realization of his purpose—to bring peace, justice, and fulfillment to all mankind. This final design became explicit in the later centuries of ancient Israel's fluctuating history, during the Babylonian captivity (sixth century B.C.) and afterward, when there developed an increasing sense of the coming "Day of the Lord." Then the Kingdom of God would be established, the righteous would be elevated and the wicked punished, and Israel would be honored as the spiritual light of mankind. Then the present sufferings of the Chosen People would bring forth a new era of universal justice, true piety, and the revelation of God's full glory to the world. After the centuries of anguish and defeat, a messianic figure would appear, through whose divine power history itself would find its triumphant end. Israel's "Promised Land," flowing with milk and honey, had now expanded to become Israel's bringing the Kingdom of God to all humanity. It was this faith, this hope in the future, this unique historical impulse carried forward by the prophets and compellingly recorded in the poetry and prose of the Bible, that had sustained the Jewish people for two millennia.

When Jesus of Nazareth began his ministry, he did so in a Jewish cultural ambiance in which expectations of a messiah and an apocalyptic denouement of history had reached extreme proportions. Such a context gave singularly dramatic weight to Jesus's announcement to his fellow Galileans that in his person the time had at last arrived for the fulfillment of the biblical prophecies: "The Kingdom of God is at hand." But it was not just Jesus's teachings about the dawning Kingdom that inspired the new faith, nor the eschatological expectations aroused by wandering preachers like John the Baptist. Most decisive was the reaction by Jesus's disciples to his death by crucifixion and their fervent belief in his resurrection. For in that resurrection, the Christian faithful perceived the triumph of God over mortality and evil, and recognized the type and promise of their own resurrection. Whatever the basis for that belief—the intense conviction of which can scarcely be overestimated—it would seem that not long after Jesus's death his followers had achieved a remarkably rapid and comprehensive recasting of their religious faith that exploded old assumptions and initiated a new understanding of God and humanity.

This new vision emerged soon after the crucifixion from a series of revelatory experiences, through which a number of Jesus's followers became convinced their master was again alive. These "appearances," later bolstered by Paul's visionary experience of the risen Christ, led the disciples to believe that Jesus in some sense had been wholly restored by God's power, and reunited in glory with God to share his eternal life in heaven. Jesus, then, was not just a man, nor even a great prophet, but was the Messiah himself, the Son of God, the long awaited divine savior whose passion and death had inaugurated the world's redemption and the birth of a new aeon. The Judaic biblical prophecies could now be properly understood: The Messiah was not a mundane king but a spiritual one, and God's Kingdom not a political victory for Israel but a divine redemption for humanity, bringing a new life suffused with God's Spirit. Thus the bitterly disappointing event of their leader's crucifixion was mysteriously transformed in the minds of his disciples into the basis for a seemingly unlimited faith in the ultimate salvation of mankind, and an extraordinarily dynamic impulse to propagate that faith.

Jesus had challenged his fellow Jews to accept God's saving activity in history, an activity visible in his own person and ministry. This challenge was paralleled—developed, reformulated, magnified—by the early Church in its call to recognize Jesus as the Son of God and Messiah.[2] Thus did Christianity claim to be the fulfillment of the Judaic hopes: The longed for future of God had now entered history in Christ. In a paradoxical combination of the linear and the timeless, Christianity declared that Christ's presence in the world was the presence of God's promised future, just as God's future lay in the full realization of the presence of Christ. The Kingdom of God was now already present, and yet was just dawning, to be fulfilled at the end of history with Christ's triumphant return. For in Christ, the world had been reconciled, but it had not yet been fully redeemed. Christianity thereby both culminated the Judaic hope and yet also continued a hope for a cosmic spiritual triumph in the imminent future, when there would come a new creation and a new humanity enjoying the unhindered presence of God.

Just as the Exodus provided the historical root of the Judaic hope in the future Day of the Lord, so too did Christ's resurrection and reunion with God provide the foundation for the Christian hope in mankind's future resurrection and reunion with God. And just as the Jewish Bible, with its revelation of God's law and promises in counterpoint with the history of his people, had sustained the Jews through the centuries and permeated their lives with its principles and its hopes, so now the sustaining basis for the new religion and its traditions became the Christian Bible, with a "New Testament" joined to the "Old" (the Jewish Bible). The Church was the new Israel. Christ was the new covenant. Thus it was that the character of the new age ushered in with Christianity was stamped with the altogether un-Hellenic character of the small nation of Israel.

Of all the characteristics of the new religion, Christianity's claims to universality and historical fulfillment were pivotal, and those claims derived from Judaism. The Judaeo-Christian God was not one tribal or polis deity among many, but was the one true supreme God—the Maker of the universe, the Lord of history, the omnipotent and omniscient King of Kings whose unequaled reality and power justly commanded the allegiance of all nations and all mankind. In the history of the people of Israel, that God had entered decisively into the world, spoken his Word through the prophets, and called forth humanity to its divine destiny: what would be born of Israel would have world-historic significance. To the quickly growing numbers of Christians who now proclaimed their message far and wide in the Roman Empire, what was born of Israel was Christianity.

Classical Elements
and the Platonic Inheritance

Considering the singular nature of its essential doctrine and message, Christianity spread at an astonishing rate from its tiny Galilean nucleus eventually to encompass the Western world. Within a generation after Jesus's death, his followers had forged a religious and intellectual synthesis within the framework of their new faith that not only inspired many to undertake the often dangerous mission of extending that faith into the surrounding pagan environment, but also was capable of addressing, and eventually fulfilling, the religious and philosophical aspirations of a sophisticated urbanized world empire. Yet Christianity's self-conception as a world religion was profoundly facilitated by its relation to the larger Hellenistic world. While Christianity's claim to religious universality originated in Judaism, both its effective universality—its success in propagation—and its philosophical universality owed much to the Greco-Roman milieu of its birth. Ancient Christians did not consider it accidental that the Incarnation occurred at the historical moment of conjunction between the Jewish religion, Greek philosophy, and the Roman Empire.

Significantly, it was not the Galilean Jews who had been closest to Jesus, but Paul, the Roman citizen of Greek cultural background, who effectively turned Christianity toward its universal mission. Although virtually all of the earliest Christians were Jewish, only a relatively small fraction of Jews eventually became Christian. In the long run, the new religion appealed much more broadly and successfully to the larger Hellenistic world.[3] The Jews had long awaited a messiah, but had expected either a political monarch, like their ancient king David, who would assert Israel's sovereignty in the world, or a manifestly spiritual prince—the "Son of man"—who would arrive from the heavens in angelic glory at the dramatic end of time. They did not expect the apolitical, unmilitant, manifestly human, suffering and dying Jesus. Moreover, although the Jews understood their special relation to God would have important consequences for all mankind, the Judaic religion was by character intensely nationalistic and separatist, almost wholly centered on the people of Israel—a spirit that continued in those early Christian Jews in Jerusalem who opposed the full inclusion of non-Jews into the community of faith until all of Israel was awakened. While the Jerusalem Christians, under the leadership of James and Peter, continued for some time to require the observance of traditional Jewish rules against common eating, thus circumscribing the new religion into the Judaic framework, Paul asserted, amidst much opposition, that the new Christian freedom and hope for salvation was already universally present, for Gentiles without the Judaic Law as well as Jews within it. All of mankind needed, and could embrace, the divine Savior. In that first fundamental doctrinal controversy within the early Church, it was Paul's universalism that prevailed over Judaic exclusivism, with large repercussions for the classical world.

For the reluctance on the part of most Jews to embrace the Christian revelation, and the success of Paul's reaction—bringing Christianity to the Gentiles—combined with political events to shift the new religion's center of gravity from Palestine to the larger Hellenistic world. After Jesus's death, the messianic political revolutionary movements led by the Zealot party continued among the Jews against the Romans, reaching a critical peak a generation later in a widespread Palestinian revolt. In the ensuing war, Roman troops crushed the rebellion, captured Jerusalem, and destroyed the Jewish Temple (70 A.D.). The Christian community in Jerusalem and Palestine was thereby dispersed, and the closest link of the Christian religion to Judaism—maintained and symbolized by the Jerusalem Christians—was severed. Christianity thereafter was more a Hellenistic than a Palestinian phenomenon.

It must also be noted that, compared with Judaism, Greco-Roman culture was in many respects more consistently nonsectarian and universal in both its practice and its vision. The Roman Empire and its laws transcended all nationalities and previous political boundaries, granting citizenship and rights to conquered peoples as well as to Romans. The cosmopolitan Hellenistic age, with its great urban centers and trade and travel, joined together the civilized world as never before. The Stoic ideal of the brotherhood of mankind and the Cosmopolis, or World City, affirmed that all human beings are free and equal children of God. The universal Logos of Greek philosophy transcended all apparent oppositions and imperfections—the divine Reason ruling all humanity and the cosmos yet immanent in human reason and potentially available to every individual of whatever nation or people. But above all, a universal Christian religion of world proportions was made feasible by the prior existence of the Alexandrian and Roman empires, without which the lands and peoples surrounding the Mediterranean would still have been divided into an enormous multiplicity of separate ethnic cultures with widely diverging linguistic, political, and cosmological predispositions. Despite the understandable antagonism felt by many early Christians toward their Roman rulers, it was precisely the *Pax Romana* that afforded the freedom of movement and communication that was indispensable to the propagation of the Christian faith. From Paul, at the start of Christianity, to Augustine, its most influential protagonist at the end of the classical era, the character and aspirations of the new religion were decisively molded by its Greco-Roman context.

These considerations apply not only to the practical side of Christianity's dissemination but also to the elaborated Christian world view as it came to rule the Western mind. Although the Christian outlook may be imagined as an entirely independent and monolithic structure of belief, we may more accurately distinguish not only opposing tendencies within the whole, but also a historical continuity with the metaphysical and religious conceptions of the classical world. It is true that, with the rise of Christianity, the pluralism and syncretism of Hellenistic culture, with its various intermingling philosophical schools and polytheistic religions, were replaced by an exclusive monotheism derived from the Judaic tradition. It is also true that Christian theology established the biblical revelation as absolute truth and demanded strict conformity to Church doctrine from any philosophical speculations. Within these limits, however, the Christian world view was fundamentally informed by its classical predecessors. Not only did there exist crucial parallels between the tenets and rituals of Christianity and those of the pagan mystery religions, but in addition, as time passed, even the most erudite elements of Hellenic philosophy were absorbed by, and had their influence on, the Christian faith. Certainly Christianity began and triumphed in the Roman Empire not as a philosophy but as a religion—eastern and Judaic in character, emphatically communal, salvational, emotional, mystical, depending on revelatory statements of faith and belief, and almost fully independent of Hellenic rationalism. Yet Christianity soon found Greek philosophy to be not just an alien pagan intellectual system with which it was forced to contend, but, in the view of many early Christian theologians, a divinely prearranged matrix for the rational explication of the Christian faith.

The essence of Paul's theology lay in his belief that Jesus was not an ordinary human being but was the Christ, the eternal Son of God, who incarnated as the man Jesus to save mankind and bring history to its glorious denouement. In Paul's vision, God's wisdom ruled all of history in a hidden manner, but had at last become manifest in Christ, who reconciled the world with the divine. All things had been made in Christ, who was the very principle of divine wisdom. Christ was the archetype of all creation, which was patterned after him, converged in him, and found its triumphant meaning in his incarnation and resurrection. Christianity thus came to understand the entire movement of human history, including all of its various religious and philosophical strivings, as an unfolding of the divine plan that was fulfilled in the coming of Christ.

The correspondences between this conception of Christ and that of the Greek Logos did not go unnoticed by Hellenistic Christians. The remarkable Hellenistic Jewish philosopher Philo of Alexandria, an older contemporary of Jesus and Paul, had already broached a Judaic-Greek synthesis pivoted on the term "Logos."[4] But it was with the opening words of the Gospel according to John, "In the beginning was the Logos," that Christianity's relationship to Hellenic philosophy was potently initiated. Soon afterward, an extraordinary convergence of Greek thought and Christian theology was in progress that would leave both transformed.

Faced with the fact that there already existed in the greater Mediterranean culture a sophisticated philosophical tradition from the Greeks, the educated class of early Christians rapidly saw the need for integrating that tradition with their religious faith. Such an integration was pursued both for their own satisfaction and to assist the Greco-Roman culture in understanding the Christian mystery. Yet this was considered no marriage of convenience, for the spiritually resonant Platonic philosophy not only harmonized with, it also elaborated and intellectually enhanced, the Christian conceptions derived from the revelations of the New Testament. Fundamental Platonic principles now found corroboration and new meaning in the Christian context: the existence of a transcendent reality of eternal perfection, the sovereignty of divine wisdom in the cosmos, the primacy of the spiritual over the material, the Socratic focus on the "tending of the soul," the soul's immortality and high moral imperatives, its experience of divine justice after death, the importance of scrupulous self-examination, the admonition to control the passions and appetites in the service of the good and true, the ethical principle that it is better to suffer an injustice than to commit one, the belief in death as a transition to more abundant life, the existence of a prior condition of divine knowledge now obscured in man's limited natural state, the notion of participation in the divine archetype, the progressive assimilation to God as the goal of human aspiration. Despite its having entirely distinct origins from the Judaeo-Christian religion, for many ancient Christian intellectuals the Platonic tradition was itself an authentic expression of divine wisdom, capable of bringing articulate metaphysical insight to some of the deepest of Christian mysteries. Thus as Christian culture matured during its first several centuries, its religious thought developed into a systematic theology, and although that theology was Judaeo-Christian in substance, its metaphysical structure was largely Platonic. Such a fusion was advanced by the major theologians of the early Church—first by Justin Martyr, then more fully by Clement of Alexandria and Origen, and finally, most consequentially, by Augustine.

In turn, Christianity was regarded as the true consummation of philosophy, with the gospel as the great meeting ground of Hellenism and Judaism. The Christian proclamation that the Logos, the world Reason itself, had actually taken human form in the historical person of Jesus Christ compelled widespread interest in the Hellenistic cultural world. In their understanding of Christ as the incarnate Logos, early Christian theologians synthesized the Greek philosophical doctrine of the intelligible divine rationality of the world with the Judaic religious doctrine of the creative Word of God, which manifested a personal God's providential will and gave to human history its salvational meaning. In Christ, the Logos became man: the historical and the timeless, the absolute and the personal, the human and the divine became one. Through his redemptive act, Christ mediated the soul's access to the transcendent reality and thus satisfied the philosopher's ultimate quest. In terms strongly reminiscent of Platonism with its transcendent Ideas, Christian theologians taught that to discover Christ was to discover the truth of the cosmos and the truth of one's own being in one unitary illumination.

The Neoplatonic philosophical structure, developing simultaneously alongside early Christian theology in Alexandria, seemed to offer an especially fitting metaphysical language within which could be better comprehended the Judaeo-Christian vision. In Neoplatonism, the ineffable transcendent Godhead, the One, had brought forth its manifest image—the divine Nous or universal Reason—and the World Soul. In Christianity, the transcendent Father had brought forth his manifest image—the Son or Logos—and the Holy Spirit. But Christianity now brought dynamic historicity into the Hellenic conception by asserting that the Logos, the eternal truth which had been present from the creation of the world, had now been sent forth into world history in human form to bring that creation, by means of the Spirit, back to its divine essence. In Christ, heaven and earth were reunited, the One and the many reconciled. What had been the philosopher's private spiritual ascent was now, through the Incarnation of the Logos, the historical destiny of the entire creation. The Word would awaken all mankind. Through the indwelling of the Holy Spirit would occur the world's return to the One. That supreme Light, the true source of reality shining forth outside Plato's cave of shadows, was now recognized as the light of Christ. As Clement of Alexandria announced, "By the Logos, the whole world is now become Athens and Greece."

It is indicative of this intimacy between Platonism and Christianity that Plotinus and Origen, the central thinkers, respectively, of the last school of pagan philosophy and the first school of Christian philosophy, shared the same teacher in Alexandria, Ammonius Saccas (a mysterious figure about whom virtually nothing is known). Plotinus's philosophy, in turn, was pivotal in Augustine's gradual conversion to Christianity. Augustine saw Plotinus as one in whom "Plato lived again," and regarded Plato's thought itself as "the most pure and bright in all philosophy," so profound as to be in almost perfect concordance with the Christian faith. Thus Augustine held that the Platonic Forms existed within the creative mind of God and that the ground of reality lay beyond the world of the senses, available only through a radical inward-turning of the soul. No less Platonic, although thoroughly Christian, was Augustine's paradigmatic statement that "the true philosopher is the lover of God." And it was Augustine's formulation of Christian Platonism that was to permeate virtually all of medieval Christian thought in the West. So enthusiastic was the Christian integration of the Greek spirit that Socrates and Plato were frequently regarded as divinely inspired pre-Christian saints, early communicators of the divine Logos already present in pagan times— "Christians before Christ," as Justin Martyr claimed. In ancient Christian icons, Socrates and Plato were portrayed among the redeemed whom Christ led forth from the underworld after his storming of Hades. In itself classical culture may have been finite and perishable, but from this view it was being reborn through Christianity, endowed with new life and new meaning. Thus Clement declared that philosophy had prepared the Greeks for Christ, just as the Law had prepared the Jews.

Yet however profound this metaphysical affinity with Platonic thought, the essential thrust of Christianity derived from its Judaic foundation. In contrast to the Greeks' atemporal balancing of many archetypal beings with different qualities and areas of dominance, Judaic monotheism bestowed to Christianity a particularly forceful sense of the divine as a single supreme personal being with a specific historical plan of salvation for mankind. God acted in and through history with definite intent and direction. In comparison with the Greeks, Judaism condensed and intensified the sense of the holy or sacred, regarding it as emanating from a single omnipotent Deity who was both Creator and Redeemer. Although monotheism certainly existed in various Platonic conceptions of God—the universal Mind, the Demiurge, the highest Form of the Good, and especially the Neoplatonic supreme One—the God of Moses was by his own declaration unequivocally unique in his divinity, and was more personal in his relationship to humanity and more freely active in human history than was the transcendent Platonic absolute. Although the Judaic tradition of exile and return bore a striking resemblance to the Neoplatonic doctrine of the cosmos's outgoing and return to the One, the former possessed a communally witnessed historical concreteness and ritually consecrated emotional passion that were not characteristic of the latter's more interior, intellectual, and individualized approach.

While the Hellenic sense of history was generally cyclical, the Judaic was decisively linear and progressive, the gradual fulfillment in time of God's plan for man.[5] While Hellenic religious thought tended toward the abstract and analytic, Judaism's mode was more concrete, dynamic, and apodictic. And where the Greek conception of God leaned toward the idea of a supreme ruling intelligence, the Judaic conception emphasized that of a supreme ruling will. For the essence of the Judaic faith rested on a burning expectation that God would actively renew his sovereignty over the world in a dramatic transfiguration of human history, and by Jesus's time this expectation centered on the appearance of a personal messiah. Christianity integrated the two traditions by proclaiming, in effect, that the true and highest divine reality—God the Father and Creator, the Platonic eternal transcendent—had fully penetrated the imperfect and finite world of nature and human history through the flesh-and-blood incarnation of his Son Jesus Christ, the Logos, whose life and death had commenced a liberating reunion of the two previously separate realms—transcendent and mundane, divine and human—and thus a rebirth of the cosmos through man. The world Creator and Logos had broken anew into history with fresh creative power, inaugurating a universal reconciliation. In the transition from Greek philosophy to Christian theology, the transcendent was made immanent, the eternal was made historical, and human history itself was now spiritually significant: "And the Logos became flesh and dwelt among us."

The Conversion of the Pagan Mind

In the course of the Hellenistic period, even Jewish culture had been penetrated by Hellenic influences. The broad geographical dispersion of Jewish communities throughout the Mediterranean empire had accelerated this influence, reflected in later Jewish religious literature such as the Wisdom books, in the Septuagint and the biblical scholarship of Alexandria, and in the Platonic religious philosophy of Philo. But with Christianity, and particularly with Paul's mission to expand its gospel beyond the confines of Judaism, the Judaic impulse in turn began a countervailing movement that radically transformed the Hellenic contribution to the Christian world view emerging in the later centuries of the classical era. The powerful currents of Greek metaphysics, epistemology, and science, the characteristic Greek attitudes toward myth, religion, philosophy, and personal fulfillment—all were transfigured in the light of the Judaeo-Christian revelation.

The status of the transcendent Ideas, so central to the Platonic tradition and widely recognized by the pagan intelligentsia, was now significantly altered. Augustine agreed with Plato that the Ideas constituted the stable and unchangeable forms of all things and provided a solid epistemological basis for human knowledge. But he pointed out that Plato lacked an adequate doctrine of creation to explain the participation of particulars in the Ideas. (Plato's Creator, the Demiurge of the *Timaeus,* was not an omnipotent supreme being, since the chaotic world of becoming upon which he imposed the Ideas already existed, as did the Ideas themselves; nor was he omnipotent vis-à-vis *anankē,* the errant cause.) Augustine therefore argued that Plato's metaphysical conception could be fulfilled by the Judaeo-Christian revelation of the supreme Creator, who freely wills the creation into existence *ex nihilo*, yet who does so in accordance with the seminal ordering patterns established by the primordial Ideas residing in the divine mind. Augustine identified the Ideas as the collective expression of God's Word, the Logos, and viewed all archetypes as contained within and expressive of the being of Christ. Here the emphasis was placed more on God and his creation, rather than on the Ideas and their concrete imitation, with the former framework employing and subsuming the latter much as Christianity in general employed and subsumed Platonism.

To this metaphysical correction of Plato, Augustine added an episte-mological modification. Plato had based all human knowledge on two pos-sible sources, the first derived from sense experience, which is unreliable, and the second derived from direct perception of the eternal Ideas, knowl-edge of which is innate but forgotten and requires recollection, and which provide the only source of certain knowledge. Augustine agreed with this formulation, asserting that man can have no intellectual ideas arise in his mind that are not illuminated there by God, as by an inner spiritual Sun. Thus the soul's only genuine teacher is an inner one, and is God. But Augustine added one more source for human knowledge—Christian reve-lation—a source necessitated by man's fall from grace and bestowed on man with the coming of Christ. This truth, revealed in the biblical testa-ments and taught by Church tradition, fulfilled Platonic philosophy just as it fulfilled the Judaic Law, both preparations for the new order.

Although in theory Augustine's Platonism was definite, in practice Christianity's emphatic monotheism reduced the metaphysical signifi-cance of the Platonic Ideas. A direct relationship to God based on love and faith was more important than an intellectual encounter with the Ideas. Any reality possessed by the Ideas was contingent on God and thus less significant in the Christian scheme of things. The Christian Logos, the active Word—creating, ordering, revealing, redeeming—ruled all. The fact of the archetypes' plurality argued further against their playing a major role in Christianity's generally monistic spiritual reality. More-over, the Neoplatonic doctrine of a hierarchy of being, with reality stratified into successively diminishing levels of divinity, was countered by certain aspects of the primitive Christian revelation (from the first century A.D.), which stressed a fundamental unification and divinization of all creation, a democratic explosion of all former categories and hierarchies. Conversely, other elements of the Judaeo-Christian tradi-tion emphasized the absolute dichotomy between God and his creation, a dichotomy that Neoplatonism attenuated in favor of the One's emana-tion of divinity through intermediate levels—such as the Ideas—to the entire cosmos. But perhaps most important, the biblical revelation pro-vided a more accessible and readily grasped truth for the body of the Christian faithful than did any subtle philosophical arguments regarding the Platonic Ideas.

Yet Christian theologians employed archetypal thinking in many of the most important doctrines of the Christian religion: the participation of all mankind in the sin of Adam, who was thus the primal archetype of unredeemed man; Christ's passion as encompassing the totality of human suffering, with his redemptive act, as the second Adam, effecting redemption for all; Christ as the archetype of perfect humanity, with every human soul potentially participating in the universal being of Christ; the invisible universal Church as fully existing in all the individual churches; the single supreme God as fully existing in each of the three persons of the Trinity; Christ as the universal Logos, constituting the entirety and essence of the creation. And biblical archetypes such as the Exodus, the Chosen People, and the Promised Land never ceased to play a significant role in the cultural imagination. Although the Platonic Ideas per se were not central to the Christian belief system, the ancient and medieval mind was generally predisposed toward thinking in terms of types, symbols, and universals, and Platonism offered the most philosophically sophisticated framework for comprehending that mode of thought. Indeed the existence of the Ideas and the issue of their independent reality would become matters of intense debate in later Scholastic philosophy—a debate whose outcome would have lasting repercussions beyond philosophy proper.

The pagan deities were more explicitly antithetical to biblical monotheism, and thus more forcefully dispensed with. First viewed as real forces, though as lesser demon-like beings, they were eventually rejected altogether and regarded as false gods, multiple idols of pagan fantasy, the active belief in which was not only foolishly superstitious but dangerously heretical. The old rituals and mysteries constituted a widespread impediment to the propagation of the Christian faith and were therefore combated by Christian apologists in terms not unlike those of the skeptical philosophers of classical Athens, but in a new context and with different intent. As Clement reasoned with the pagan intellectuals of Alexandria, the world was not a mythological phenomenon full of gods and daimones, but was rather a natural world providentially governed by the one supreme self-subsistent God. In truth, the pagan statues of deities were no more than stone idols, the myths merely primitive anthropomorphic fictions. Only the one invisible God and the one biblical revelation were authentic. The Presocratic philosophies, like those of Thales or Empedocles with their deification of the material elements, were no better than the primitive myths. Matter should not be worshiped, but rather the Maker of matter. The heavenly bodies were not divine, but rather the Creator of those bodies. Now man could be liberated from the old superstitions and illuminated by the true divine light of Christ. The myriad sacred objects of the primitive imagination could now be recognized as nothing more than natural things naively endowed with nonexistent supernatural powers. Men—not animals or birds, trees or planets—were the true messengers of divine communication, chosen as God's prophets. The supremely just Judaeo-Christian God, not the fickle Hellenic Zeus, was the true universal ruler. The historical Christ, not the mythological Dionysus or Orpheus or Demeter, was the true saving deity. The darkness of paganism was now dispelled by the Christian dawn. Clement described the late pagan Greco-Roman world as being like the seer Tiresias—old, wise, but blind and dying—and exhorted him to shed his decaying life and ways, cast off the old revels and divinations of paganism, and be initiated into the new mystery of Christ. If he would now discipline himself for God, he could see again, see heaven itself, and become the ever-new child of Christianity.

And so the old gods died and the one true Christian God was revealed and glorified. Yet a more subtle and differentiated process of assimilation occurred in the conversion of paganism, for in the process of the Hellenistic world's adoption of Christianity, many essential features of the pagan mystery religions now found successful expression in the Christian religion: the belief in a savior deity whose death and rebirth brought immortality to man, the themes of illumination and regeneration, the ritual initiation with a community of worshipers into the salvational knowledge of cosmic truths, the preparatory period before initiation, demands for cultic purity, fasting, vigils, early morning ceremonies, sacred banquets, ritual processions, pilgrimages, the giving of new names to initiates. But while some of the mystery religions emphasized the evil imprisonment of matter, which only initiates could transcend, early Christianity heralded Christ as inaugurating the redemption of even the material world. Christianity further introduced an essential public and historical element into the mythological framework: Jesus Christ was not a mythical figure but an actual historical person who fulfilled the Judaic messianic prophecies and brought the new revelation to a universal audience, with potentially all of mankind as the new initiates rather than a select few. What was to the pagan mysteries an esoteric mythological process—the death-rebirth mystery—had in Christ become concrete historical reality, enacted for all humanity to witness and openly participate in, with a consequent transformation of the entire movement of history. From this viewpoint, the pagan mysteries were not so much an impediment to the growth of Christianity as they were the soil from which it could more readily spring.

But unlike the mystery religions, Christianity was proclaimed and recognized as the exclusively authentic source of salvation, superseding all previous mysteries and religions, alone bestowing the true knowledge of the universe and a true basis for ethics. Such a claim was decisive in the triumph of Christianity in the late classical world. Only thus were the anxieties of the Hellenistic era, with its conflicting religious and philosophical pluralism, and with its large amorphous cities filled with the rootless and dispossessed, resolved in the new certitudes. Christianity offered mankind a universal home, an enduring community, and a clearly defined way of life, all of which possessed a scriptural and institutional guarantee of cosmic validity.

The Christian assimilation of the mysteries extended to the various pagan deities as well, for as the Greco-Roman world gradually embraced Christianity, the classical gods were consciously or unconsciously absorbed into the Christian hierarchy (as later would occur with the Germanic deities and those of other cultures penetrated by the Christian West). Their characters and properties were retained but were now understood and subsumed in the Christian context, as in the figures of Christ (Apollo and Prometheus, for example, as well as Perseus, Orpheus, Dionysus, Hercules, Atlas, Adonis, Eros, Sol, Mithra, Attis, Osiris), God the Father (Zeus, Kronos, Ouranos, Sarapis), the Virgin Mary (Magna Mater, Aphrodite, Artemis, Hera, Rhea, Persephone, Demeter, Gaia, Semele, Isis), the Holy Spirit (Apollo, Dionysus, Orpheus, as well as aspects of the procreative feminine deities), Satan (Pan, Hades, Prometheus, Dionysus), and a host of angels and saints (the conflation of Mars with Michael the archangel, Atlas with Saint Christopher). As the Christian religious understanding emerged out of the classical polytheistic imagination, the different aspects of a single complex pagan deity were applied to corresponding aspects of the Trinity, or, in the case of a pagan deity's shadow aspect, to Satan. Apollo as the divine Sun god, the luminous prince of the heavens, was now seen as a pagan precursor of Christ, while Apollo as the bringer of sudden illumination and the giver of prophecy and oracles was now recognized as the presence of the Holy Spirit. Prometheus as the suffering liberator of mankind was now subsumed by the figure of Christ, while Prometheus as the hubristic rebel against God was subsumed by the figure of Lucifer. The spirit of ecstatic possession once ascribed to Dionysus was now ascribed to the Holy Spirit, Dionysus as the self-sacrificing redemptive deity of death and rebirth was now transfigured into Christ, and Dionysus as the unleashed erotic and aggressive instincts, the demonic deity of unregenerate elemental energy and mass frenzy, was now recognized as Satan.

Thus the ancient mythic deities were transformed into the doctrinally established figures that constituted the Christian pantheon. A new conception of spiritual truth arose as well. The narratives and descriptions of divine reality and divine beings, that which had been myth in the pagan era—malleable, undogmatic, open to imaginative novelty and creative transformation, subject to conflicting versions and multiple interpretations—were now characteristically understood as absolute, historical, and literal truths, and every effort was made to clarify and systematize those truths into unchanging doctrinal formulae. In contrast to the pagan deities, whose characters tended to be intrinsically ambiguous—both good and evil, Janus-faced, variable according to context—the new Christian figures, in official doctrine at least, possessed no such ambiguity and maintained solid characters definitely aligned with good or evil. For the core drama of Christianity, like that of Judaism (and its seminal Persian relative, the prototypically dualistic religion of Zoroastrianism), centered on the historical confrontation between the primeval opposing principles of good and evil. And ultimately Christianity's dualism of good and evil, God and Satan, was a derivation of its final monism, since Satan's existence was finally contingent upon God, supreme Creator and Lord of all.

Compared with the pagan outlook, the Christian world view was still structured by a transcendent principle, but it was now a decisively monolithic structure, absolutely governed by one God. Among the Greeks, Plato had been one of the most monotheistic, yet even for him "God" and "the gods" were often interchangeable. For Christians, there was no such ambiguity. The transcendent was still primary, as with Plato, but no longer pluralistic. The Ideas were derivative, and the gods anathema.

>✳<

Despite the influence of Platonism and Augustine's intellectuality, the Christian approach to truth was substantially different from that of the classical philosophers. Certainly reason played a role in Christian spirituality, for, as Clement emphasized, it was by virtue of man's reason that he was capable of receiving the revealed Logos. Human reason was itself the gift of God's original creation, in which the Logos was agent of the creative principle. And it was Christianity's superior welding of intellect and cult, compared with paganism's more ambivalent dichotomy, that played such a crucial role in Christianity's ascendance in the late classical era. Yet in contrast to the Greeks' philosophical program of independent intellectual self-development in relation to the empirical world and to the transcendent sphere of absolute knowledge which ordered that world, the Christian approach centered on the revelation of one person, Jesus Christ, and thus the devout Christian sought enlightenment by reading Holy Scripture. Intellectuality alone was not sufficient to grasp cosmic truth, as it had been for many Greek philosophers such as Aristotle, not even if supplemented by the moral purity stressed by Plato or Plotinus. In the Christian understanding, the pivotal role was played by faith—the soul's active, freely willed embrace of Christ's revealed truth, with man's commitment of belief and trust working in mysterious interaction with God's freely bestowed grace. For Christianity proclaimed a personal relation to the transcendent. The Logos was not just an impersonal Mind, but a divinely personal Word, an act of love by God, revealing to all the numinous essence of man and cosmos. The Logos was God's saving Word; to believe was to be saved.

Hence faith was the primary means, and reason a distant second, for comprehending the deeper meaning of things. Augustine experienced his final conversion as an overcoming of his sophisticated intellectual pretensions and a humble embrace of Christian faith. Except for Platonism, the effects of a purely philosophical development of his rational intellect had only increased Augustine's skepticism concerning the possibility of discovering truth. For Augustine, even Neoplatonic philosophy, the most religiously profound of pagan thought systems, had its fundamental imperfections and unfulfilling aspects, for nowhere in it could he find that personal intimacy with God he so desired, nor that miraculous revelation that the transcendent Logos had become flesh.[6] It was, by contrast, reading the letters of Paul that awakened in Augustine the knowledge he experienced as spiritually liberating. From that point, he held a new strategy for acquiring truth: "I have faith in order to understand." Here Augustine's theory of knowledge displayed its Judaic foundation, for right knowledge utterly depended on man's right relation to God. Without the initial commitment to God, the entire track of intellectual inquiry and comprehension could not avoid being thrown off into disastrously erroneous directions.

In the Christian view, human reason might once have been sufficient when, in the paradisiacal state, it still possessed its original resonance with divine intelligence. But after man's rebellion and fall from grace, his reason was increasingly obscured and the need for revelation became absolute. Relying on and developing an exclusively human reason was bound to result in dangerous ignorance and error. Indeed, man's fall itself was caused by his stealing the fruit from the Tree of Knowledge of Good and Evil, his first and fatal step toward intellectual independence and proud self-reliance, and a moral transgression of God's exclusive sovereignty. By grasping such knowledge out of the divine order, man had instead been intellectually blinded, and could now be illuminated only by God's grace. Thus was the secular rationality so esteemed by the Greeks considered of doubtful value for salvation, with empirical observation largely irrelevant except as an aid to moral improvement. In the context of the new order, the simple faith of a child was superior to the abstruse reasonings of a worldly intellectual. Christian theologians continued to philosophize, to study the ancients, and to debate doctrinal subtleties—but all within the defined boundaries of Christian dogma. All learning was subservient to theology, now the most important of all studies, and theology found its unshakable basis in faith.

In a sense, the Christian focus was more narrow and sharp than the Greek, and entailed less need for educational breadth. The highest metaphysical truth was the fact of the Incarnation: the miraculous divine intervention into human history, the effect of which was to liberate humanity and reunite the material world with the spiritual, the mortal with the immortal, creature with Creator. The mere grasp of that stupendous fact was enough to satisfy the philosophical quest, and that fact was fully described in the Church scriptures. Christ was the exclusive source of truth in the cosmos, the all-comprehending principle of Truth itself. The Sun of the divine Logos illuminated everything. Moreover, in the new self-awareness of the late classical and early Christian era, most acutely epitomized in Augustine, the individual soul's concern for its spiritual destiny was far more significant than the rational intellect's concern with conceptual thinking or empirical study. Faith alone in the miracle of Christ's redemption was enough to bring the deepest saving truth to man. Despite his erudition and appreciation for the intellectual and scientific achievements of the Greeks, Augustine proclaimed:

> When, then, the question is asked what we are to believe in regard to religion, it is not necessary to probe into the nature of things, as was done by those whom the Greeks call *physici*; nor need we be in alarm lest the Christian should be ignorant of the force and number of the elements; the motion, and order, and eclipses of the heavenly bodies; the form of the heavens; the species and the natures of animals, plants, stones, fountains, rivers, mountains; about chronology and distances; the signs of coming storms; and a thousand other things which those philosophers either have found out, or think they have found out. . . . It is enough for the Christian to believe that the only cause of all created things, whether heavenly or earthly, whether visible or invisible, is the goodness of the Creator, the one true God; and that nothing exists but Himself that does not derive its existence from Him.[7]

With the rise of Christianity, the already decadent state of science in the late Roman era received little encouragement for new developments. Early Christians experienced no intellectual urgency to "save the phenomena" of this world, since the phenomenal world held no significance compared with the transcendent spiritual reality. More precisely, the all-redeeming Christ had already saved the phenomena, so there was little need for mathematics or astronomy to perform that task. The study of astronomy in particular, being tied to astrology and the cosmic religion of the Hellenistic era, was discouraged. The monotheistic Hebrews had already had occasion to condemn foreign astrologers, and this attitude persisted in the Christian context. With its planetary deities and aura of polytheistic paganism, and with its proneness to a determinism antithetical to both divine grace and human responsibility, astrology was officially condemned by Church councils (with Augustine especially seeing the need for confuting the astrological "mathematicians"), as a result of which it gradually declined despite its occasional theological defenders. In the Christian world view, the heavens were devoutly perceived as the expression of God's glory and, more popularly, as the abode of God and his angels and saints, and the realm from which Christ would return at the Second Coming. The world as a whole was understood simply and preeminently as God's creation, and thus efforts at

scientifically penetrating nature's inherent logic no longer seemed necessary or appropriate. Its true logic was known to God, and what man could
know of that logic was revealed in the Bible.

God's will ruled every aspect of the universe. Because miraculous
intervention was always possible, the processes of nature were at all times
subservient to divine providence rather than to merely natural laws. The
scriptural testaments were thus the final and unchanging repository of
universal truth, and no subsequent human efforts were going to enhance
or modify, let alone revolutionize, that absolute statement. The relationship of the good Christian to God was that of child to father—typically a
very young and naive child to the infinitely greater, omniscient and
omnipotent Father. Because of the great distance between Creator and
creature, the human capacity to comprehend the creation's inner workings was radically circumscribed. Truth was therefore approached primarily not through self-determined intellectual inquiry, but through
Scripture and prayer, and faith in the teachings of the Church.

Both Paul and Augustine testified to the overwhelming power and
supremacy of God's will, in the potential spiritual devastation of God's
damning judgment of an impure soul, but also most benignly in Christ's
redemptive act for mankind by his death on the cross. Both men had
experienced their own religious conversions—Paul on the road to
Damascus, Augustine in the garden at Milan—as dramatic biographical
turning points, forcefully impelled by the intervention of divine grace.
Only by such intervention were they saved from continuing a life the
self-defined direction of which could now be seen as futile and destructive. In light of these experiences, all merely human activity,
whether independent willfulness or intellectual curiosity, now appeared
secondary—superfluous, misleading, even sinful—except as it might lead
to fully God-directed activity. God was the exclusive source of all good
and of man's salvation. All heroism, so central to the Greek character,
was now concentrated in the figure of Christ. The human surrender to
the divine was the only existential priority. All else was vanity. Martyrdom, the ultimate surrender of the self to God, represented the highest
Christian ideal. As Christ was self-giving in the highest degree, so should
all Christians strive to be like their Redeemer. Humility, not pride, was
the distinguishing Christian virtue, requisite for salvation. Selflessness in

action and thought, devotion to God and service to others: only through such an emptying of self would the power of God's grace fully enter and transform the soul.

Yet humanity was not considered diminished by such an asymmetrical relationship, for God's grace and love alone were all-sufficient for humanity's true needs and deepest desires. In comparison with these divine gifts, all worldly satisfactions were pale imitations, of no ultimate value. Indeed, here was the astounding proclamation made by Christians to the world: God loved mankind. God was not only the source of the world order, not only the goal of philosophical aspiration, not only the first cause of all that exists. Nor was he just the inscrutable ruler of the universe and stern judge of human history. For in the person of Jesus Christ, God had reached out from his transcendence and displayed for all time and all humanity his infinite love for his creatures. Here was the basis for a new way of life, grounded in the experience of God's love, the universality of which created a new community in mankind.

Thus Christianity bequeathed to its members a pervasive sense of a personal God's direct interest in human affairs and vital concern for every human soul, no matter what level of intelligence or culture was brought to the spiritual enterprise, and without regard to physical strength or beauty or social status. In contrast to the Hellenic focus on great heroes and rare philosophers, Christianity universalized salvation, asserting its availability to slaves as well as kings, to simple souls as well as profound thinkers, to the ugly as well as the beautiful, to the sick and suffering as well as the strong and fortunate, even tending to reverse the former hierarchies. In Christ, all divisions of humanity were overcome—barbarian and Greek, Jew and Gentile, master and slave, male and female—all were now as one. The ultimate wisdom and heroism of Christ made redemption possible for all, not just the few: Christ was the Sun, who shone alike on all mankind. Christianity therefore placed high value on each individual soul as one of God's children, but in this new context the Greek ideal of the self-determining individual and the heroic genius was diminished in favor of a collective Christian identity. This elevation of the communal self, the human reflection of the Kingdom of Heaven, founded on the shared love of God and faith in Christ's redemption, encouraged an altruistic sublimation, and at times subjugation, of the individual self in favor of a greater allegiance to the good of others and the will of God. Yet on the other hand, by granting immortality and value to the individual soul, Christianity encouraged the growth of the individual conscience, self-responsibility, and personal autonomy relative to temporal powers—all decisive traits for the formation of the Western character.

In its moral teachings, Christianity brought to the pagan world a new sense of the sanctity of all human life, the spiritual value of the family, the spiritual superiority of self-denial over egoistic fulfillment, of unworldly holiness over worldly ambition, of gentleness and forgiveness over violence and retribution; a condemnation of murder, suicide, the killing of infants, the massacre of prisoners, the degradation of slaves, sexual licentiousness and prostitution, bloody circus spectacles—all in the new awareness of God's love for humanity, and the moral purity that love required in the human soul. Christian love, whether divine or human, was not so much the realm of Aphrodite, nor even primarily the Eros of the philosophers, but was the love, epitomized in Christ, that expressed itself through sacrifice, suffering, and universal compassion. This Christian ethical ideal of goodness and charity was strongly promulgated and at times widely observed, an ideal certainly not lacking in the moral imperatives of Greek philosophy—particularly in Stoicism, which in several ways anticipated Christian ethics—but now having a more pervasive influence on the mass culture in the Christian era than had Greek philosophical ethics in the classical world.

The more formidable intellectualized quality of the Greek notion of the Godhead and the philosopher's individual ascent (however passionate that process was for Plato or Plotinus) was replaced in Christianity by the emotional and communally shared intimacy of a personal, familial relationship with the Creator, and by the pious embrace of revealed Christian truth. In contrast to the previous centuries of metaphysical perplexity, Christianity offered a fully worked out solution to the human dilemma. The potentially distressing ambiguities and confusions of a private philosophical search without religious guideposts were now replaced by an absolutely certain cosmology and an institutionally ritualized system of salvation accessible to all.

But again, with the truth so firmly established, philosophical inquiry was seen by the early Church as less vital to spiritual development, and intellectual freedom, basically irrelevant, was carefully circumscribed.[8] True freedom was found not in unlimited intellectual speculation but in Christ's saving grace. The Christian religion was not to be considered on a par with Hellenic philosophy, let alone with the pagan religions, for its unique revelation held the utmost significance for man and the world.

The Christian mystery was not the arguable result of ingenious metaphysical reasoning, nor another viable alternative to the various pagan mysteries and mythologies. Rather, Christianity was the authentic proclamation of the supreme God's absolute truth, belief in which would change not only the individual's personal fate but the destiny of the world. A sacred doctrine had been entrusted to Christians, and fidelity to that trust, as well as the integrity of that doctrine, needed to be maintained at all costs. Eternal salvation was at stake for all humanity.

Safeguarding the faith was thus the first priority in any question of philosophical or religious dialogue; hence that dialogue was often curtailed altogether lest the devil of doubt or unorthodoxy gain a foothold in the vulnerable minds of the faithful. The more intellectually esoteric and doctrinally unconstrained forms of early Christianity, such as the widespread Gnostic movements, were condemned and eventually suppressed with as much intense antagonism as was shown to paganism. It was especially the antihierarchical Gnostics who pressed the orthodox Church to a firm definition of Christian doctrine in the second and third centuries. For to protect what was perceived by the postapostolic Church as the unique and, in a sense, fragile essence of the Christian revelation—the simultaneous humanity and divinity of Christ, the simultaneous unity and trinity of God, the original goodness of the Creation yet its need for redemption, the New Testament as the dialectical fulfillment of the Old—against a growing number of conflicting sects and doctrines, leading early Christians concluded that the beliefs of the faithful must be established, disseminated, and sustained by an authoritative Church structure. Thus the institutional Church, as the living embodiment of the Christian dispensation, became the official guardian of the final truth and the highest court of appeal in any matters of ambiguity—indeed, not only the court, but also the prosecuting and punitive arm of the religious law.

The shadow side of the Christian religion's claim to universality was its intolerance. The Church's view of Christian conversion as a private religious experience fully contingent on individual freedom and spontaneous faith stood in stark counterpoint to a not infrequent policy of forcibly imposed religious conformity. With the final ascendance of Christianity at the end of the classical era, the pagan temples were systematically demolished and the philosophical academies officially closed.[9] Just as the strict ethical puritanism that Christianity had inherited from Judaism opposed the unrestrained sensuality and immorality it perceived in pagan culture, so too with equal stringency did Christianity develop a theological puritanism that posited itself against the teachings of pagan philosophy and any unorthodox conceptions of Christian truth. There were not many true paths, nor many gods and goddesses, differing from one place to the next and from one person to the next. There was but one God and one Providence, one true religion, one plan of salvation for the entire world. All mankind deserved to know and have this one saving faith. And so it was that the pluralism of classical culture, with its multiplicity of philosophies, its diversity of polytheistic mythologies, and its plethora of mystery religions, gave way to an emphatically monolithic system—one God, one Church, one Truth.

Contraries Within the Christian Vision

Here we may begin to recognize the outlines of two significantly different aspects of the Christian world view. Indeed, on first impression one might discern two entirely distinct world views that coexisted and overlapped within Christianity, and that were in continual tension with each other: whereas the one outlook was rapturously optimistic and all-embracing, its complement was sternly judgmental, restrictive, and prone to a dualistic pessimism. But in fact the two outlooks were inextricably united, two sides of the same coin, light and shadow. For the Church contained both perspectives, and at its essence was their effective point of intersection. Both views were enunciated in the Bible, in both New and Old Testaments, and both found simultaneous expression, in varying ratios, in all the major theologians, councils, and doctrinal syntheses of the Church. Yet it will be useful for us to distinguish the two perspectives and define them separately, thereby clarifying some of the complexities and paradoxes of the Christian vision. Let us attempt first to describe this internal dichotomy, and then to understand how the Church endeavored to resolve it.

The emphasis of the first view considered here was on Christianity as an already existent spiritual revolution that was now progressively transforming and liberating both the individual soul and the world in the dawning light of God's revealed love. In this understanding, Christ's self-sacrifice had initiated the fundamental reunion of humanity and the created world with God, a reunion prefigured and commenced by Christ and reaching fulfillment in a coming age with Christ's return. The stress here was on the inclusiveness of redemption, the breadth and power of the Logos and the Spirit, God's present immanence in man and the world, and the resulting joy and freedom of the Christian faithful who constituted the Church, the living body of Christ.

The other side of the Christian vision focused more emphatically on the present alienation of man and the world from God. It therefore stressed the futurity and otherworldliness of redemption, the ontological finality of God's "otherness," the need for strict inhibition of worldly activities, a doctrinal orthodoxy defined by the institutional Church, and a salvation narrowly limited to the small portion of mankind constituting the Church faithful. Underlying and consequent to these tenets was a pervasive negative judgment regarding the present status of the human soul and the created world, especially relative to the omnipotence and transcendent perfection of God.

Again, neither side of this inner polarity within the Christian framework was ever separated from the other. Both Paul and Augustine, the first and last of the ancient theologians who defined the Christian religion passed on to the West, were strongly expressive of both views in an indissoluble though somewhat uneasy compound. Yet because the differences in emphasis between the two sides were so marked, and because the two perspectives often seemed to derive from entirely different psychological sources and religious experiences, it will be valuable to treat them with separate and highly dichotomized descriptions, as if they were in fact fully distinguished from each other.

The first side examined here found its primary articulation in the letters of Paul to the early Christian communities and in the Gospel according to John. The other three Gospels and the Acts of the Apostles often supported this view as well, however, and no one source encompassed this perspective in its entirety. The dominant insight expressed in this understanding was that in Christ the divine had entered the world, and that the redemption of humanity and nature was now already dawning. If the Judaic religion was a great yearning, Christianity was its glorious fulfillment. The Kingdom of Heaven had broken into the field of history and was now actively transforming it, progressively impelling humanity toward a new and previously inconceivable perfection. The life, death, and resurrection of Christ had attained the miracle of the ages, and the resulting emotion was therefore one of ecstatic joy and gratitude. The greatest battle had already been won. The cross was the sign of victory. Christ had liberated a mankind held captive by its own ignorance and error. Because the principle of divinity was already present in the world and working its wonders, the pivot of the spiritual quest was to acknowledge in faith the reality of that sublime fact and, in the light of this new faith, to participate directly in the divine unfolding. The coming Kingdom's redemptive potency shone forth in the person of Christ, whose charismatic power brought all human beings together into a new community. Christ had introduced a new life into the world: He was himself that new life, the breath of the eternal. By means of Christ's passion, a new creation had been given birth, now taking place within and through man. Its climax would be the establishment of a new heaven and a new earth, and the merging of finite time with eternity.

The peculiar sense of cosmic joy and immense thanksgiving expressed in early Christianity seemed to derive from the belief that God, in a gratuitous overflow of love for his creation, had miraculously broken through the imprisonment of this world and poured forth his redeeming power into humanity. The divine essence had fully reentered into materiality and history, initiating their radical transformation. Because God himself, in the person of Jesus Christ, had become fully human— experiencing within himself all the suffering to which mortal flesh is heir, taking on the universal burden of human guilt, and overcoming within himself the moral errancy to which the free human will is subject—God had thereby ransomed mankind from its state of alienation from the divine. The meaning of Jesus's life was not just that he had brought new teachings and spiritual insight to the world. Rather, by sacrificing his divine transcendence to a full immersion in the agonies of human life and death, within the definite historical conditions of a specific time and place—"suffered under Pontius Pilate"—Christ had forged a fundamentally new reality. Within this new historical aeon, a new human destiny could unfold in communion with divine wisdom and love. Christ's death had seeded the world with God's Spirit, whose continuing presence in mankind would bring about its divine transfiguration.

In this view, the "repentance" Jesus called for was not so much a prerequisite as it was a consequence of the experience of the dawning Kingdom of Heaven. It was less a backward-moving and paralyzing regret for past sinfulness than a progressive embrace of the new order, which made one's old life appear inauthentic and misdirected by comparison. It was a returning to the divine source from which flowed all innocence and new beginnings. The Christian experience of redemption was an inner transformation based on an awakening to what was already being born— within the individual and within the world. In the eyes of many early Christians, the time for rejoicing was already present.

Nevertheless, as the second pole of the Christian vision made clear, this same revelation led to other, very different consequences, in which Christ's redemptive action in an alienated world was perceived as part of a dramatic battle between good and evil whose outcome was by no means already accomplished, nor assured for all. As a counterbalance to the more positive, exultant, and unitive element in Christianity, much of the New Testament put emphasis not so much on an already realized redemptive transformation as on the demand for a taut watchfulness and heightened moral rectitude in expectation of Christ's return, especially in consideration of the perils of the present corrupt world and the risks of eternal damnation. Such a view was expressed not only in the three Synoptic Gospels—the Gospels of Matthew, Mark, and Luke—but in Paul's and John's writings as well. Here was stressed how completely humanity's final salvation awaited God's external activity in the future, through an apocalyptic end of history and the Second Coming. The battle between Christ and Satan was still continuing, and the tremendous dangers and sufferings of the present time were lightened by faith in the historical Jesus, the risen Lord, and in his saving return—rather than by the confident Johannine sense of Christ's already decisive victory over evil and death, God's new immanence in the world, and the believer's already present share in the eternal life of the glorified Christ. Hope in the Redeemer was paramount in both sides of the Christian polarity, but in this second understanding, the present suffered an imprisonment of spiritual darkness that made the redemptive hope more urgent, even desperate, and pressed the locus of redemption more exclusively into the future and into God's external activity.

This more fully anticipatory side of Christianity bore resemblance to certain dominant elements of Judaism, which thereby continued to structure the Christian vision. The experience of evil pervading man and nature, the deep alienation between human and divine, the sense of grimly waiting for a definitive sign of God's redeeming presence in the world, the need for fastidious adherence to the Law, the attempt to preserve a pure and faithful minority against incursions from a hostile and contaminating environment, the expectation of an apocalyptic punishment—all these elements of the Judaic sensibility emerged anew in the Christian understanding. That tone of religious vision was, in turn, reinforced and given a new context by the continued delay of Christ's Second Coming, and by the Church's historical and theological evolution accompanying that delay.

In its more extreme form, which was not uncharacteristic of the mainstream Christian tradition in the West after Augustine, this more dualistic understanding emphasized mankind's inherent unworthiness and consequent inability to experience the potency of Christ's redemption in this life, except in a proleptic manner through the Church.

Reflecting and magnifying the Judaic conception of Adam's fall and the resultant separation between God and man, the Christian Church inculcated a pronounced sense of sin and guilt, the danger or even likelihood of damnation, and consequently a need for strict observance of religious law and an institutionally defined justification of the soul before God. The exultant image of God as both an immanent and transcendent being mysteriously unifying man, nature, and spirit was here juxtaposed by the image of an entirely transcendent juridical authority separate from and even antagonistic toward man and nature. The stern and often ruthless God of the Old Testament, Yahweh, was now embodied in Christ the Judge, who damned the disobedient as readily as he redeemed the obedient. And the Church itself—here understood more as hierarchical institution than as mystical community of the faithful—took on that judicial role with considerable cultural authority. The unitive early Christian ideal of becoming one with the resurrected Christ and with the Christian community, and the Hellenic-inspired mystical philosophical union with the divine Logos, receded as explicit religious goals in favor of the more Judaic concept of strict obedience to the will of God—and, by extrapolation, obedience to the decisions of the Church hierarchy. Christ's suffering and death were here often portrayed as further cause for human guilt, rather than as effecting the removal of that guilt. The crucifixion in its horrific aspect became the dominant image, rather than the resurrection or the two together. The relationship of guilty child to stern father, as in much of the Old Testament, largely overshadowed the happy reconciliation with the divine essence proclaimed in the other side of early Christianity.

Yet the two poles of the Christian vision were not as unrelated as these distinctions might suggest, and the Church not only carried the meaning of both sides, it understood itself to be the resolution of that dichotomy. To comprehend how such apparently divergent messages could have been united in the same religion, we must attempt to grasp the process by which the Christian Church evolved, both in its self-conception and in history, and the pressure of those events, personalities, and movements which governed that evolution. Even that investigation, however, depends on first grasping, or at least glimpsing, the primitive Christian proclamation in something like its first-century form.

Exultant Christianity

In the New Testament, especially in certain passages of Paul's letters and John's Gospel, it was clear that the infinite schism between the human and divine had in some sense already been bridged. The guilt and pain of that separation (caused by Adam's sin) had been overcome by the victory of Christ (the "second Adam"), and the believing Christian directly participated in the new union. That option, so to speak, was now at last open to humanity. Christ had sacrificed himself so that mortal man could attain immortal life: God united himself with man so that man could now unite himself with God. With Christ's departure from the world, his Spirit had descended and was now immanent in humanity, effecting humanity's spiritual transformation—indeed, its deification.

The new Christian perception of God was different from the traditional Judaic image. Not only was Christ the Messiah foretold by the Hebrew prophets, fulfilling the Jewish religious mission in history. He was also the Son of God, one with God; and with his self-sacrifice, the righteous Yahweh of the Old Testament, who demanded justice and exacted vengeance, had become the loving Father of the New Testament, who bestowed grace and forgave all sins. Early Christians also affirmed the new immediacy and intimacy of God, who was further transfigured from the remote severity of Yahweh into the human Jesus Christ, and who now acted less as vengeful judge than as compassionate liberator.

The coming of Christ was therefore a break from, as well as a fulfillment of, the Judaic tradition. (Hence the conscious distinction made by early Christians between the "Old" Testament and the "New"—with the latter's declaration of the "new life," the "new man," the "new nature," the "new way," the "new heaven and the new earth.") Christ's confrontation with and triumph over death, suffering, and evil had made possible that triumph for all human beings, and allowed them to perceive their own tribulations in a greater context of rebirth. To die with Christ was to rise with him into the new life of the Kingdom. Christ was here understood as a point of perpetual newness, a boundless birth of divine light in the world and in the soul. His crucifixion represented the birth pangs of a new humanity and a new cosmos. A process of divine transfiguration had been initiated in both man and nature by Christ's redemption, here seen as a cosmic event affecting the whole universe. Instead of condemnation of a sinful humanity in a fallen world, there was here a greater emphasis on God's limitless grace, the Spirit's presence, the Logos's love of man and the world, sanctification, deification, and universal rebirth. On the evidence of their writings, it was as if many early Christians had experienced a sudden cosmic reprieve from certain death, a reversal of certain damnation, an unexpected gift of new life—indeed, not only new life, but eternal life. Under the impact of this miraculous revelation, they set out to spread the "good news" of humanity's salvation.

So fully was Christ's redemption here viewed as an absolute and positive fulfillment of human history and of all human suffering that Adam's original sin, the archetypal origin of human alienation and mortality, was paradoxically celebrated as "*O felix culpa!*" ("O blessed sin!") in the Easter liturgy. The Fall—man's primal error bringing the dark knowledge of good and evil, the moral perils of freedom, the experience of alienation and death—was here viewed not so much as an unmitigatedly heinous and tragic disaster, but as an early and, in retrospect, integral part of man's existential development caused by his infantile lack of discerning awareness, his naive susceptibility to deception. In the misuse of his God-given freedom, choosing to love and elevate himself over God, man had ruined the perfection of creation and divorced himself from the divine unity. Yet it was just through a painfully acute consciousness of this sin that man could now experience the infinite joy of God's forgiveness and embrace of his lost soul. Through Christ, the primal separation was being healed and the perfection of creation restored on a new and more comprehensive level. Human weakness thus became the occasion for God's strength. Only from man's sense of defeat and finitude could he open himself freely to God. And only by man's fall could God's inconceivable glory and love fully reveal itself by righting the unrightable. Even God's apparent wrath could now be understood as a necessary element in his infinite benevolence, and human suffering seen as the necessary prelude to unbounded happiness.[10]

For in Christ's overcoming of death, in man's recognition of his potential rebirth into the eternal, all temporal evil and suffering ceased to have ultimate significance except as a preparation for redemption. The negative element in the universe rather served to bring about, according to the logic of a divine mystery, the birth of a greater positive state of being which all Christian believers could enjoy. One could place absolute trust in the Almighty, abandoning all anxiety for the future to live with the simplicity of "the lilies of the field." Just as the hidden seed was brought forth from winter's cold shadow to flower into the warm light and life of spring, so even in the darkest hour was God's mysterious wisdom working its exalted design. The whole drama from the Creation to the Second Coming could now be recognized as the sublime product of the divine plan, the unfolding of the Logos. Christ was both the beginning and the end of the Creation, "the Alpha and the Omega," its original wisdom and its final consummation. What was hidden had become manifest. In Christ the meaning of the cosmos was fulfilled and revealed. All this was celebrated by early Christians in ecstatic metaphor: With Christ's incarnation, the Logos had reentered the world and created a celestial song, tuning the discords of the universe into perfect harmony, sounding the joy of the cosmic wedding between heaven and earth, God and humanity.

This primitive Christian proclamation of redemption was at once mystical, cosmic, and historical. On the one hand was the experience of fundamental interior transformation: To experience God's dawning Kingdom was to be inwardly grasped by divinity, suffused by an inner light and love. Through Christ's grace the old, separate and false self died to allow the birth of a new self, the true self at one with God. For Christ was the true self, the deepest core of the human personality. His birth in the human soul was not so much an external arrival as an emergence from within, an awakening to the real, an unanticipatedly radical irruption of divinity into the heart of human experience. Yet on the other hand, in association with this inner transfiguration, the entire world was being transformed and restored to its divine glory—not just as if by subjective illumination but in some essential ontological way that was historically and collectively significant.

Here an unprecedented cosmic optimism was asserted. In its physicality and historicity, Christ's resurrection held forth the promise that everything—all history both of individuals and of mankind, all striving, all mistakes and sins and imperfections, all materiality, the entire drama and reality of Earth—would somehow be swept up and perfected in a final victorious reunion with the infinite Godhead. All that was cruel and absurd would then be made meaningful in the full revelation of Christ, the hidden meaning of creation. Nothing would be left out. The world was not an evil imprisonment, not a dispensable illusion, but the bearer of God's glory. History was not an endless cycle of deteriorating

stages, but the matrix of humanity's deification. Through God's omnipotence, grim Fate itself was miraculously transmuted into benevolent
Providence. Human anguish and despair could now find not just respite,
but divine fulfillment. The Gates of Paradise, implacably closed at the
Fall, had been reopened by Christ. The infiniteness of God's compassion
and power would inevitably conquer, and thereby consummate, the
entire universe.

Many early Christians appear to have lived in a state of continuous
astonishment at the miraculous historical redemption they believed had
just taken place. The unification of the cosmos was now dawning, and
the finality of the old dualisms—man and God, nature and spirit, time
and eternity, life and death, self and other, Israel and the rest of
mankind—had been overcome. While they eagerly anticipated Christ's
Second Coming, the Parousia ("Presence"), when he would return from
the heavens in full glory before the entire world, their awareness was
centered on the liberating fact that Christ had already initiated the
redemptive process—a triumphant process in which they could directly
participate. On this basis was constituted the overriding Christian attitude of hope. Through the Christian faithful's continuing act of hope in
God's compassionate power and plan for humanity, the trials and terrors
of the present could be transcended. Humanity could now look forward,
in humble confidence, to a glorious future fulfillment which its own
attitude of hope was in some way helping to realize.

Of especial importance here was the belief that in Christ, God had
become man—that the all-encompassing infinite Creator had fully become an individual human person in history. For this merging in Christ
had brought humanness and divinity into a fundamentally new relationship, a redemptive unity in which the value of humanity itself was
exalted. The language about the coming Christ used by Paul, John, and
early Christian theologians such as Irenaeus seemed to suggest not only
that Christ's return was going to take place as an external event, a
descent from heaven at some unspecified time in the future, but that it
would also take the form of a progressive birth from within the natural
and historical development of all human beings, who were being perfected in and through Christ. Here Christ was seen both as the heavenly
bridegroom, who had impregnated humanity with the seed of divinity,
and as the goal of human evolution, the realization of that seed's
promise. In his continuing and progressive incarnation into humanity
and into the world, Christ would bring the creation to its fruition. The

seed might be hidden now in the ground, but it was already at work, active, slowly growing, moving toward perfection in a glorious unfolding of the divine mystery. As Paul wrote in his Letter to the Romans, "the whole creation groaneth in travail" for the birth of this divine being, just as all Christians were pregnant with the Christ within—pregnant with a new self that would be born to a new and more authentic life in the full consciousness of God. Human history was an immense education into divinity, a leading forth of man's being to God. Indeed, not only was man to be fulfilled in God, but God was to be fulfilled in man, achieving a self-revelation through his realization in human form. For God had chosen man as the vessel of his image, in which his divine essence could be most fully incarnate.

In this perspective, man was a noble participant in God's creative unfolding. In his alienation from God the least happy of creatures, man could yet play the central role in repairing the riven state of creation and restoring its divine image. The Logos had descended into man so that man, by participating in Christ's passion and now containing the Logos himself, could ascend to God. Because Christ had freely given himself to man and fully experienced the humiliation and weakness of the human condition, he had given to man the capacity to share in God's own power and glory. Hence there was no limit as to what man's future in God might become. In the doctrinal formulation of the fourth-century theologian Athanasius, the ideal of human deification found in Paul and John was made explicit: "God became man in order that we become God." In the light of the evolutionary deification heralded in the New Testament, all the historical traumas and devastations, the wars and famines and earthquakes, the immeasurable sufferings of humanity, were comprehensible as the necessary birth labor of the divine in man. In the new light of Christian revelation, mankind's labors were not in vain. Man was to bear affliction, Christ's cross, so that he could bear God. Jesus Christ was the new Adam who had initiated a new humanity, evolving new powers of spiritual awareness and freedom that would be fulfilled in the future—but the divine was already gloriously immanent and active in man and in the present world.

Dualistic Christianity

Paul warned, however, that the exultant element in Christianity, though valid in itself, could easily lead to negative spiritual consequences should its stress swing too far away from Christ and toward man, away from the future and toward the present, away from faith and toward knowledge. Such a distortion he perceived, and hastened to correct, in certain "enthusiasts" or proto-Gnostics among the early Church congregations he had helped found.

In Paul's eyes, their beliefs and moral behavior revealed the dangers of a too-exultant interpretation of the Christian message, which could thereby degenerate into a sinful overestimation of the self, an irresponsible indifference to the world and its still-present evil, and an inflated elevation of personal spiritual powers and esoteric knowledge over love, humility, and practical moral discipline. Christ had indeed commenced a new age and a new humanity, but these had not yet arrived, and man deceived himself if he thought anyone but God could effect that sublime transfiguration whose full reality still lay ahead. The world was pregnant with the divine and was in the throes of labor, but it had not yet given birth. Although Christ's activity was already present in man, Paul's own persecutions and personal sufferings (his "thorn in the flesh") were evidence that fulfillment lay in the future, and that the true way of glory was the way of the cross. One must suffer with Christ to be glorified with Christ.

Paul especially combated the enthusiasts' tendency to lose what he regarded as the proper balance between the religious aspirations of the individual and those of the larger Christian community. For to lose that balance was to lose the essence of the true Christian gospel. Their assertion of an already realized personal redemption in a world that clearly remained unredeemed could lead to spiritual elitism, to licentiousness in behavior, even to denial of a future collective resurrection because personal resurrection was already deemed present. Human hubris, rather than divine compassion, was the effect of such teachings. It was necessary for man to know his limits and his faults, and to put his faith in Christ. For the present, the true Christian's mandate was to labor with his fellow believers in building up a community of love and moral purity worthy of God's glorious future. Joy in what had already been experienced through Christ was in order, but so too was moral rigor, personal sacrifice, and humble faith in the future transformation.

Thus Paul taught a partial dualism in the present to affirm a greater cosmic unity in the future, lest a premature claim of redemption now preclude the greater salvation of the world later. These corrective teachings by Paul were supported as well by the religious vision contained in the three Synoptic Gospels of Mark, Matthew, and Luke. As a group, and in contrast to the Gospel according to John, these narratives tended to emphasize Jesus's humanity, his historical life and suffering, and the satanic dangers of the present time prior to the apocalyptic end time, with less of the Johannine sense of Christ's spiritual glory already suffusing the present age. The perspective expressed in the Synoptic Gospels therefore encouraged an intense anticipation of divine activity that would relieve the trials of the present time, and suggested a more critical opinion of man's present spiritual position. Such a view lent itself to a dualism between the present world and the coming Kingdom of Heaven, and between God's omnipotence and man's helplessness. That dualism, however, was mitigated by God's gift of the Spirit to mankind, and would soon be overcome altogether with Christ's Second Coming.

Yet, paradoxically, that dualism was enhanced and given a different significance by certain elements of John's Gospel, the last of the four Gospels to be written (near the end of the first century), and the most theologically developed. Since the Second Coming did not arrive as soon as the first-generation Christians had expected, the dualism that had an anticipatory form in the Synoptics took on a more mystical and ontological dimension under the influence of John's Gospel. The Johannine vision was permeated by the theme of light versus darkness, of good versus evil, a cosmic division that was readily applicable to a dualism between spirit and matter which concretized and reinforced the distinction between Christ's transcendent kingdom and the world under Satan. Although John's "realized eschatology"—his teaching that the salvational end of history was already being actualized in the wake of the resurrection—affirmed man's present participation in Christ's glorification, this was increasingly understood as a spiritual participation that transcended the material world and the physical body, which thereby became irrelevant to the redemptive process and even inhibitory. Such a mystical and ontological dualism was supported and amplified by the Gnostics, as well as by the Neoplatonist stream within Christian theology, and was further confirmed by the continued historical delay of the Parousia. But while for the Gnostics esoteric knowledge was thought to mediate that transcendence, and while for the Neoplatonists mystical illumination could do so, for the larger mainstream Christian tradition, which had anticipated the Second Coming as the necessary solution, that mediating role would be fulfilled by the ongoing sacramental Church.

Thus John's Gospel affirmed a present unity of Christ and believer, but at the expense of an implied ontological dualism. Moreover, despite the fundamental Johannine proclamation that "the Logos became flesh," the sheer magnitude of luminous divinity possessed by the Christ of John's Gospel—portrayed there in glory as the exalted Lord from the beginning of his ministry—seemed to far transcend the present potentialities of all other human beings, and consequently tended to highlight the spiritual inferiority and darkness of the natural man and the natural world. It would be the Church that would fill that gap, as the numinous representation of Christ's continuing presence in the world and the vehicle of humanity's sacramentalization. The Johannine Christ was opened to man's being in a mystical way: those who obeyed his commandment of love and who knew him as the Son could participate in his unitary relationship with the transcendent Father. But this special relationship was viewed in contrast with the rest of those who were "of the world," thereby establishing another division—as the Gnostic elite were distinct from the irredeemable majority of mankind, or the enlightened philosopher was distinct from the unenlightened, or, most broadly for the Christian tradition, those within the Church were distinct from everyone outside it. This division sustained and strengthened that tendency throughout the Old and New Testaments to view salvation in terms of an elect minority of believers who alone were dear to God, and who would be gratuitously saved from the masses of a mankind that was by nature opposed to God and destined for damnation.

It was this general trend—an unusually potent and durable compound of the anticipatory view of redemption found in the Synoptic Gospels, Paul's moral admonitions, and John's mystical dualism, with all these combined with the continuing impact of pre-Christian Judaic themes, the delay of the Second Coming, and the requirements of the developing institutional Church—that encouraged the other side of the Christian vision, the character of which in the long run would significantly redefine the primitive Christian message. With a moderate shift or intensification of emphasis, the same Gospels and Epistles that together proclaimed the exultant Christian message could lend themselves to another synthesis of strikingly different hue, especially as the historical context changed and cast a different light on the revelation. At its root, this understanding reflected a heightened sense of the divisions of existence—between God and man, heaven and earth, good and evil, the faithful and the damned. Here was stressed the corruption to which both man and this world had succumbed and, in consequence, the transcendent divine activity necessary to save human souls. On this scriptural foundation, and on the basis of their own experience of the present world's negative condition and their own spiritual longing, devout Christians focused their attention more exclusively on the future and the unworldly, in the form either of the promised Second Coming or of a Church-mediated redeemed afterlife. In either case there resulted a pronounced tendency to negate the intrinsic value of the present life, the natural world, and humanity's status in the divine hierarchy.

Only God's intervention could save the righteous remnant of mankind, an intervention that in the first generations after Christ was expected to take the form of an apocalyptic irruption that would end history. Such an expectation was possibly encouraged by Jesus's own words concerning the imminence of such an event, although he was also reported to have discouraged calculations concerning its precise timing or details. In any case an urgent anticipation of the end time was then widespread among Jews and other religious sects critical of the evil contemporary world. But after several generations had passed without such an apocalypse, and especially after Augustine, salvation was seen less in such dramatic historical and collective terms, and more as a Church-mediated process that could occur only through the institutional sacraments, and could be fulfilled only when the soul left behind the physical world and entered the celestial state. Such a salvation, like that of the apocalypse, was perceived as due entirely to God's will rather than to human effort, though it required that the believer during this lifetime strictly conform his actions and beliefs to those sanctioned by the Church. In both instances, man's positive role was diminished or negated in favor of God's, this world's value was diminished or negated in favor of the next, and only a scrupulous conformity to specific moral principles and ecclesiastical regulations could preserve the believing soul from condemnation. The struggle with overwhelming evil was of paramount concern, making the authoritative activity of God and Church mandatory.

On such a basis most Christians, and the ongoing Christian tradition in the West, while acknowledging in principle much of the exultant unitary conception, in practice subscribed to a form of Christianity that was more static, circumscribed, and dualistic. The cosmic dimension of primitive Christianity—humanity and nature as the progressive bearer of Christ, history as an emergent process of the birth of the divine in the world—was attenuated in favor of a more dichotomized conception. In the latter view, the ideal Christian was conceived as an obedient and relatively passive receptor of the divine, whose presence could be fully known by the human soul only in a radical break from this world— variously understood as taking place through an externally effected apocalyptic Second Coming, through ascetic monastic withdrawal from the world, through the sacramental mediation of an unworldly or anti-worldly Church, or through a fully transcendent, extramundane salvation in the afterlife.

In this sense it could be said that much of Christianity was still waiting for its redeemer—not unlike Judaism, though now with a more after-worldly emphasis. Here the spiritual significance of Christ's Second Coming, or Christ's coming to the soul after death, tended to outweigh that of his first coming, except as the latter initiated the Church, provided teachings and a moral example, and brought hope for a future salvation. As regards the first coming, the suffering and crucified Jesus, bearing humanity's guilt, tended to displace the triumphant resurrected Christ, bearing humanity's liberation. For the world itself appeared to have undergone little essential change or divinization. Indeed, it had crucified God when he had become man, thus further defining its sinful fate. Humanity's hope lay in the future, in God's transcendent power, in the afterworld, and, for the present, in the bulwark of the Church.

Thus all the "immanence" of God's Kingdom was now contained in the Church. Yet that Church was perceived as decisively against the world in which it existed, or rather with which it was forced to coexist. On a deeper level, the immanent dynamism of the "new man" and "new creation" that had characterized the primitive Christian awareness was here transformed into an eager longing for an afterworldly newness, a radiantly celestial future, an entirely transcendent illumination. The present world was an alien stage, the relatively static context into which man had been placed at creation and within which he was to work out his salvation via the Church. That salvation, in turn, would consist in man's being taken up by Christ into heaven, where his earthly imperfections would be left behind. As destitute and depraved as was the present world, so much the more exalted would be the happiness of the redeemed condition in paradise. Painfully aware of their own sinfulness and the world's grave defects, most faithful Christians conscientiously devoted their efforts to preparing for such an afterworldly salvation, spurred by the belief that only a few elect would be saved, while the vast majority of corrupt mankind would meet perdition.

In this perspective, the idea of human deification became either meaningless or blasphemous. The human contribution to the salvational enterprise was limited, and the nature of that salvation was defined less as assimilation to God and more as ecclesiastical justification and inclusion in God's heavenly court. The believing Christian was not so much made divine like God as he was made righteous in God's eyes, freed from his personal and hereditary guilt. Here the Christian concept of man's nobility and freedom as God's greatest creation, made in God's own image and exalted by Christ's uniting of divine and human, was largely overshadowed by the sense of man's unworthiness and absolute spiritual dependence on God and the Church. Man was an intrinsically sin-permeated being who had willfully set himself in opposition to God. Hence his will was impotent against the evil within and outside him, and his salvation lay solely in the possibility that God might mercifully overlook the believer's culpability, viewing his own Son's death as atonement, and save the believer from the damnation that, like the rest of mankind, he genuinely deserved.

Because God's action alone was spiritually potent, human pretensions to heroism of the ancient Greek type could be viewed only as reprehensible vainglory. It is true that for many primitive and later mystical Christians, one could participate in the heroic to the extent that one directly participated in Christ, the indwelling principle of universal divinity. Such a view often underlay the testaments of martyrs in the early Church. Yet to later mainstream Christianity, that ultimate heroism typically lay beyond human capabilities altogether. In this perspective, Christ was an entirely external figure, whose historical manifestation in Jesus was unique and whose divine heroism was absolute, in comparison with which human beings were at best indebted creatures, at worst wretched sinners. All good came from God and was spiritual in origin, while all evil derived from man's own sinful nature and was carnal in origin. Here the ancient dualism was virtually as absolute as before the birth of Christ, and the tragic image of the crucifixion served to reinforce the sense of schism in the universe between God and man, and between the present life in this world and a future life in the spiritual world. The Church alone could bridge that great hiatus.

>+*+<

The existence of these two radically different though intertwined modes of experiencing Christianity reflected a similar dichotomy within the Jewish faith, the continuing influence of which in this respect constituted an additional factor in the evolving Christian world view. The highly developed Judaic sense of the divine and its potency was complemented by an equally acute sense of the profane, the idolatrous, and the insignificance of the merely human. Similarly, Israel's special relationship to God, and special historical responsibility for carrying out its mandate to renew God's sovereignty in the world, gave it a consciousness not only of its unique spiritual importance, but also of its all-too-human failure and guilt. In the spirit of Zoroastrianism's cosmic dualism of good and evil, but with the historically consequential difference that it was *man*'s fall that caused the cosmic fall rather than vice versa, the biblical tradition placed on man's shoulders a moral responsibility of universal dimensions. God's Chosen People were both exalted and burdened by their special role, and God's image varied accordingly.

On the one hand, many passages of the Hebrew Bible—such as in the Psalms, Isaiah, or the Song of Songs—testified to the Judaic experience of God's mercy, goodness, and intimate love. Jewish religious literature was distinguished above all for its pronounced sense of God's personal relation to and concern for man and his history. Yet on the other hand, so much of the spirit and narrative of the Old Testament was dominated by the figure of a jealous God of stern justice and ruthless vengeance— arbitrarily punitive, obsessively self-referential, militantly nationalistic, patriarchal, moralistic, "an eye for an eye" and so forth—that God's cherished compassionate qualities were often difficult to discern. Trust in God was constantly balanced against fear of God. In certain crucial encounters with Yahweh, it was only man's plea for an equitable or merciful judgment that mitigated the full brunt of God's wrath against those he perceived as disobedient. On some occasions it was as if the Jew's own sense of moral justice surpassed that of Yahweh; yet the former evidently emerged from the encounter with the latter.[11] The sacred covenant between God and man paradoxically required both autonomy and compliance from the human partner, and on the basis of that tension the Judaic ethos evolved.

Tension was central to the Judaic religious experience, for despite significant exceptions, the Hebrew God generally disclosed himself as intransigently "Other." Duality pervaded the Judaic vision: God and man, good and evil, sacred and profane. But God's nearness, counter-balancing his otherness, was visible in history. And in the Judaic vision, the presence of the divine in the world was especially manifested through and measured by Israel's obedience to Yahweh, an obligation in which it alternately triumphed and faltered. Everything rested on that drama. The Judaic dialectic between God's fearsome omnipotence and man's ontological separateness from God was resolved through God's historical plan of salvation, and this plan required man's total submission. Thus the divine command for unswerving obedience tended to outweigh the divine outpouring of reconciliatory love.

Yet that love was experienced nonetheless, especially as a perceived numinous presence drawing forward the Jewish nation to fulfillment, to the Promised Land in its various and constantly evolving forms. The redemptive and unitary aspect of God's love for man seemed to be more of a fervently awaited condition that would be realized by a messiah in a future era, while the present age was distressingly colored by the darkness and desolation of man's sin and God's anger. The Jewish experience of divinity was inextricably bound up with an unyielding sense of judgment, just as man's love for God was fully entwined with scrupulous obedience to God's law. This combination was in turn inherited and reasserted by Christianity, for which Christ's redemption did not altogether eliminate God's vengeful nature.

The writings of Paul, John, and Augustine all expressed a peculiar mixture of the mystical and the juridical, and the Christian religion of which they were principal shapers reflected those divergent tendencies. God was an absolutely good supreme being, but that good God could act toward the disobedient man, as in the apocalyptic Last Judgment of John's Revelation, with the most relentless and unforgiving severity. (It was not theologically insignificant that the "*O felix culpa!*" passage of the Easter liturgy was expunged by certain medieval churches and monasteries.) As in Judaism, the Christian experience of God oscillated between that of a sublime love relationship, indeed a divine romance, and that of a horrifically punitive antagonism and juridical condemnation. Thus did Christian hope and faith coexist with Christian guilt and fear.

Further Contraries
and the Augustinian Legacy

Matter and Spirit

The inner conflict in Christianity between redemption and judgment, and between the unification of God with the world and a highly charged dualistic distinction, was especially prominent in its attitudes toward the physical world and the physical body—a fundamental ambivalence that Christianity never entirely resolved. More explicitly than other religious traditions, Judaism and Christianity asserted the full reality, grandeur, beauty, and rightness of God's original freely willed creation: not an illusion, a falsehood, a divine error; not an imperfect imitation or a necessary emanation. God created the world, and it was good. Moreover, man was created, body and soul, in the image of God. But with man's sin and fall, both man and nature lost their divine inheritance, and thus began the Judaeo-Christian drama of man's vicissitudes in relation to God, amidst a backdrop of a spiritually destitute and alienated world. As exalted as was the Judaeo-Christian vision of the original pristine creation, so much the more tragic was its view of the world's fall.

The Christian revelation, however, asserted that in Christ, God had become man, flesh and blood, and after his crucifixion had risen again in what the apostles believed was a full spiritual transfiguration and renewal of his physical body. In these central miracles of the Christian faith—the Incarnation and Resurrection—was founded the belief not only in the soul's immortality, but even in the redemption and resurrection of the body, and of nature itself. Because of Christ, not just the human soul but the human body and its activities were being changed, spiritualized, and made holy again. Even the conjugal union was here seen as a reflection of Christ's intimate bond with humanity, and therefore as possessing sacred significance. Christ's incarnation had effected the restoration of God's image in man. In Jesus, the archetypal Logos had merged with its derivative image, man, thereby restoring the latter's full divinity. The redemptive triumph was a new man in his entirety, not just a spiritual transcendence of his physicality. In its teaching that "the

Logos was made flesh," and in its faith in the rebirth of the whole man, lay an explicitly material dimension that distinguished Christianity from other, more exclusively transcendent mystical conceptions.

This redemptive Christian understanding reaffirmed and brought new meaning to the original Hebrew view of man as created body and soul in the image of God, a conception parallel to the later Neoplatonic idea of man as microcosm of the divine, but with Judaism's decisively greater stress on man—body and soul—as an integrated unit of vital power. The body was the vessel of the spirit, its temple and incarnate expression. In addition, Jesus's ministry had been centrally involved with the act of healing, body and soul considered together. In the early Church, there was repeated reference to "Christ the physician," and the apostles as well were often recognized as charismatic healers. The primitive Christian faith perceived the nature of spiritual salvation in explicitly psychosomatic terms. Paul's dominant image for mankind's resurrection was that of the one body of Christ, all humanity composing its members, matured into the fullness of Christ who was its head and consummation. Yet not just man was being restored to divinity, but also nature, which had been riven by man's fall and longed for its salvation. Paul wrote in his Letter to the Romans: "For the creation waits with eager longing for the revealing of the children of God." Early Church fathers believed that as Christ would restore the severed relation between man and God, so would he restore that between man and nature, which since the Fall and man's misuse of freedom had been subject to man's selfish arrogation.

Christ's incarnation into and redemption of the world were here seen not just as exclusively spiritual events, but rather as an unparalleled development within temporal materiality and world history, and as representing the spiritual completion of nature—not nature's antithesis, but its fulfillment. For the Logos, the divine wisdom, had been present in the creation from its beginning. Now Christ had made the implicit divinity of the world explicit. Creation was the ground of redemption, just as birth was the precondition of rebirth. In this view, nature was regarded as God's noble handiwork and the present locus of his self-revelation, and was thus worthy of reverence and understanding.

But equally characteristic of Christian thinking was an opposing view, especially dominant in later Western Christianity, in which nature was perceived as that which must be overcome to attain spiritual purity. Nature as a whole was corrupt and finite. Only man, the head of creation, was capable of salvation, and in man only his soul was essentially redeemable. In this understanding, man's soul was in direct conflict with the base instincts of his own biological nature and was endangered by the potential entrapment of carnal pleasures and the material world. Here the physical body was often deplored as the residence of the devil and the occasion of sin. The early Judaeo-Christian belief in redemption of the whole man and the natural world shifted in emphasis, especially under the influence of the Neoplatonist Christian theologians, to a belief in a purely spiritual redemption in which man's highest faculties alone—the spiritual intellect, the divine essence of the human soul—would be reunited with God. While the Platonic element in Christianity overcame the divine-human dualism by conceiving of man as directly participating in the divine archetype, it simultaneously encouraged a different dualism between body and spirit. The focus for the Platonic divine-human identity was the *nous*, the spiritual intellect; the physical body did not participate in this identity, but rather impeded it. In its more extreme forms, Platonism encouraged in Christianity a view of the body as the soul's prison.

As with the physical body, so with the physical world. Plato's doctrine of the supremacy of the transcendent reality over the contingent material world reinforced in Christianity a metaphysical dualism that in turn supported a moral asceticism. Like Plato's Socrates, the devout Christian perceived himself as a citizen of the spiritual world, and his relation to the transitory physical realm was that of a stranger and pilgrim. Man had once possessed a blissful divine knowledge but had fallen into dark ignorance, and only the hope of recovering that lost spiritual light motivated the Christian soul while detained in this body and this world. Only when man awakened from the present life would he attain true happiness. Death, as a spiritual liberation, was more highly valued than mundane existence. At best the concrete natural world was an imperfect reflection of and preparation for the higher spiritual kingdom to come. But more likely the mundane world, with its deceptive attractions, its spurious pleasures and debasing arousal of the passions, would pervert the soul and deprive it of its celestial reward. Hence all human intellectual and moral effort was properly directed toward the spiritual and the afterlife, away from the physical and this life. In all these ways, Platonism gave an emphatic philosophical justification to the potential spirit-matter dualism in Christianity.

Yet this later theological development had numerous antecedents: Stoicism, Neopythagoreanism, Manichaeism, and other religious sects such as the Essenes all possessed marked tendencies toward religious dualism and asceticism that affected the Christian view. And Judaism itself, with its characteristic imperative against worldly and fleshly defilement of the divine and holy, lent support to such tendencies from the outset of the new religion. But it was certain streams of dualistic Gnosticism, probably originating from the penetration of mystical Judaism by Zoroastrian dualism, that were the most extreme in this regard during Christianity's first centuries, holding an absolute division between an evil material world and a good spiritual realm. The resulting syncretistic Gnostic theology radically transformed the orthodox Christian conception by maintaining that the creator of the physical world, the Old Testament Yahweh, was an imperfect and tyrannical subordinate deity, who was overthrown by the spiritual Christ and the compassionate Father of the New Testament revelation (which the Gnostics augmented with other texts and edited to remove the remnants of the Hebrew faith which they considered false). Man's spirit was entrapped in an alien body in an alien material world, which could be transcended only by the esoterically knowledgeable, the Gnostic elect. Such a vision amplified related tendencies in John's Gospel stressing the divisions between light and darkness, between Christ's kingdom and the world under Satan, between the spiritual elect and the worldly unredeemed, as well as between Yahweh and Christ, Old Testament and New. Although the earliest authoritative orthodox Christian theologians, such as Irenaeus, argued forcefully for the continuity of the Old and New Testaments, for the divine plan's unity from Genesis to Christ, much of the tenor of Gnostic dualism left its traces in later Christian theology and piety.

For primitive Christianity itself, like its Judaic progenitor, tended ambiguously toward a matter-spirit dualism and a negative view of nature and this world. The New Testament referred to Satan as the prince of this world; thus Christian trust in a world ruled by Providence was juxtaposed with Christian fear of a world ruled by Satan. Moreover, to distance itself from the highly sexualized contemporary pagan culture, much of early Christianity stressed the need for a spiritual purity that held little room for nature's spontaneous instincts, particularly sexuality. Celibacy was the ideal state, and marriage a necessary allowance for human cupidity so that it be kept within defined boundaries. Communal and charitable forms of Christian love were instead emphasized—*agapē* rather than *eros*. Especially important here was the expectation of Christ's imminent return, which dominated the early Church sensibility and which made procreative and marital considerations seem irrelevant. The arrival of the Kingdom of Heaven, an event most early Christians expected would take place in their own lifetime, would eliminate all material and social forms of the old order. More generally, the desire to overcome the perceived materialistic excesses of pagan culture, as well as Christianity's repeated encounter with state-sanctioned persecutions, impelled early Christians to negate the values of the present world in favor of the next. Withdrawal from and transcendence of this world, whether in the manner of the desert hermits or, more absolutely, through martyrdom, held great attraction for the fervent Christian. Apocalyptic expectations often arose from and engendered intensely negative evaluations of the present world.

The need to keep holy and blameless in anticipation of Christ's imminent coming was the foremost imperative for the early Christian. And the nature of that holiness and moral purity was defined in Paul's radical opposition of "flesh" to "spirit," with the former evil and the latter good. It is true that Paul made a distinction between "flesh" (*sarx*) as unredeemed nature, and "body" (*soma*) as something connoting the whole man—less part of a Greek body-soul dichotomy and more the biblical unity, susceptible to sin yet open to redemption. He suggested a positive evaluation of "body" in such images as the body of Christ, the body of Church members, the resurrection of the body, the body as temple of the Holy Spirit. He often employed "flesh" to refer less to the physical per se than to man's mortal weakness, and specifically to a principle of narrow self-elevation that caused a moral inversion of the proper human personality, a subjection of the human soul and body to lower negative forces at the expense of a loving openness to the greater spiritual reality of God. Sin was not so much mere carnality—though the sinful life was carnal in its obsessions—as it was the perverse elevation over God of that which, good in itself in proper measure, was rightly subordinate to God.

Yet Paul's flesh-body distinction was often ambiguous, both in his doctrinal statements and in his practical ethics. And his choice of "flesh" as the constellating term for such authoritative moral and metaphysical disparagement was a consequential one. It was not without Paul's assumed support that many subsequent Christians characteristically viewed the physical, the biological, and the instinctual as inherently prone to the demonic and responsible for man's fall and continued corruption. In Paul's flesh-spirit polarity, compounded by similar tendencies in other parts of the New Testament, lay the seeds of an antiphysical dualism in Christianity that Platonic, Gnostic, and Manichaean influences would later amplify.

Augustine

What was implicit in Paul was made explicit by Augustine. And here we must focus more directly on that individual whose effect on Christianity in the West would be uniquely pervasive and enduring. For in Augustine all these factors—Judaism, Pauline theology, Johannine mysticism, early Christian asceticism, Gnostic dualism, Neoplatonism, and the critical state of late classical civilization—combined with the peculiarities of his own character and biography to define an attitude toward nature and this world, toward human history, and toward man's redemption that would largely mold the character of medieval Western Christianity.

Son of a pagan father and a devoutly Christian mother, Augustine was endowed with a character the intensity of which further charged his biographical polarities. Highly sensual by nature, living the life of a young bon vivant in the libidinous environment of pagan Carthage, fathering an illegitimate child by his mistress, pursuing the worldly career of a professor of rhetoric, he was nevertheless progressively drawn to the supersensible and spiritual by philosophical preference and religious aspiration, and, not least, by maternal concern. In a series of psychologically dramatic experiences, Augustine moved away from his earlier, secularly oriented existence through a sequence of stages holding considerable meaning for his later religious understanding: first espousing the higher life of philosophy after reading Cicero's *Hortensius*; then a long involvement with the highly dualistic semi-Gnostic sect of Manichaeism; followed by an increasing attraction to philosophical Neoplatonism; and finally, after encountering Ambrose, the Neoplatonist Christian bishop of Milan, ending his search in a full embrace of the Christian religion and the Catholic Church. Each element in this sequence left its mark on his mature vision, which in turn left its mark on subsequent Christian thinking in the West through the medium of his extraordinarily compelling writings.

Augustine's self-consciousness as a volitional, responsible moral agent was acute, as was his awareness of the burdens of human freedom—error and guilt, darkness and suffering, severance from God. In a sense, Augustine was the most modern of the ancients: he possessed an ex-

istentialist's self-awareness with his highly developed capacity for introspection and self-confrontation, his concern with memory and consciousness and time, his psychological perspicacity, his doubt and
remorse, his sense of the solitary alienation of the human self without
God, his intensity of inner conflict, his intellectual skepticism and
sophistication. It was Augustine who first wrote that he could doubt
everything, but not the fact of the soul's own experience of doubting, of
knowing, willing, and existing—thereby affirming the certain existence
of the human ego in the soul. Yet he also affirmed the absolute contingency of that ego on God, without whom it could not exist, let alone be
capable of attaining knowledge or fulfillment. For Augustine was also the
most medieval of the ancients. His Catholic religiosity, his monolithic
predispositions, his otherworldly focus, and his cosmic dualism all fore-
tokened the succeeding age—as did his keen sense of the invisible, of
God's will, of the Mother Church, of miracles, grace, and Providence, of
sin, evil, and the demonic. Augustine was a man of paradox and extremes, and his legacy would be of the same character.

It was certainly the quality and power of Augustine's conversion—the
experience of an overwhelming influx of grace from God turning him
away from the corrupt and egoistic blindness of his natural self—that was
the culminating factor in his theological vision, imprinting in him a
conviction of the supremacy of God's will and goodness and the im-
prisoned poverty of his own. The luminous potency of Christ's positive
intervention in his life left the human person in relative shadow. Yet
what may have especially influenced his religious understanding was the
pivotal role played by sexuality in Augustine's religious quest. Although
mindful of nature's inherently divine ordering (and often more unstint-
ing in his praise of the creation's beauty and bounty than a Platonist),
Augustine placed extreme emphasis in his own life on the ascetic denial
of his sexual instincts as the prerequisite for full spiritual illumination—a
point of view supported by his encounters with both Neoplatonism and
Manichaeism, yet reflective of deeper roots in his own personality and
experience.

Love of God was the quintessential theme and goal of Augustine's
religiosity, and love of God could thrive only if love of self and love of
the flesh were successfully conquered. In his view, succumbing to the
flesh was at the heart of man's fall; Adam's eating the fruit from the Tree
of Knowledge of Good and Evil, the original sin in which all mankind
participated, was tied directly to concupiscence (and indeed the biblical

"knowing" had always possessed sexual connotations). For Augustine, the evil character of fleshly lust was visible in the shame that attended its expression, uncontrolled by the rational will, and that attended the mere nakedness of the sexual organs. Procreation in Paradise before the Fall would not have entailed such bestial impulsiveness and shame. Marriage now at least could realize some good out of the inherited evil, since it brought offspring, enduring commitment, and a limitation of sexuality to procreative purposes. But the primal sin infected all born of carnal generation, so that all humanity was condemned to pain in childbirth, to suffering and guilt in life, and to the final evil of death. Only by Christ's grace and with the resurrection of the body would all traces of that sin be removed and man's soul be freed from the curse of his fallen nature.

It is true that Augustine held that the root of evil did not reside in matter, as the Neoplatonists suggested, for matter was God's creation and therefore good. Rather, evil was a consequence of man's misuse of his free will. Evil lay in the act of turning itself—of turning away from God—not in what was turned to. Yet in Augustine's linking of that sinful abuse of freedom to concupiscence and sexuality, and to the pervasive corruption of nature thereafter, the germ of the Neoplatonic and more extreme Manichaean dualism lived on.

On this pivot rested the tenor of Augustine's moral theology. Creation—man as well as nature—was indeed an infinitely marvelous product of God's benevolent fecundity, but with man's primal sin that creation was set so fundamentally awry that only the next, heavenly, life would restore its original integrity and glory. Man's fall was precipitated by his willful rebellion against the proper divine hierarchy, a rebellion founded in the assertion of the values of the flesh against those of the spirit. He was now enslaved to the passions of the lower order. Man was no longer free to determine his life simply by virtue of his rational will, not only because circumstances beyond his control presented themselves, but also because he was unconsciously constrained by ignorance and emotional conditioning. His initial sinful thoughts and actions had become ingrained habits and finally ineluctable chains imprisoning him in a state of wretched alienation from God. Only the intervention of divine grace could possibly break the vicious spiral of sin. Man was so bound by his vanity and pride, so desirous of imposing his will on others, as to be incapable of transforming himself by his own powers. In his present, fallen state, positive freedom for man could consist only in the acceptance of God's grace. Only God could free man, since no action by man on his own could be sufficient to move him toward salvation. And God already knew for all time who were the elect and who the damned based upon his omniscient foreknowledge of their different responses to his grace. Although official Christian doctrine would not always accept Augustine's more extreme formulations of predestination or his nearly complete denial of any active human role in the process of salvation, the subsequent Christian view of man's moral corruption and imprisonment was one largely congruent with Augustine's.

Thus it was that the man who so decisively declared God's love and liberating presence in his own life also recognized, with a potency that never ceased to permeate the Western Christian tradition, the innate bondage and powerlessness of the human soul as perverted by Original Sin. From this antithesis arose the necessity for Augustine of a divinely provided means of grace in this world: an authoritative Church structure, within which haven man could satisfy his overriding needs for spiritual guidance, moral discipline, and sacramental grace.

Augustine's critical view of human nature had its corollary in his evaluation of secular history. As an influential bishop in his own era, Augustine was dominated in his later life by two pressing concerns—the preservation of Church unity and doctrinal uniformity against the entropic impact of several major heretical movements, and the historical confrontation with the fall of the Roman Empire under the barbarian invasions. Faced with the crumbling empire and the apparent demise of civilization itself, Augustine saw little possibility for any genuine historical progress in this world. With its manifest evils and cruelties, wars and murders, with man's greed and arrogance, licentiousness and vice, with the ignorance and suffering all human beings were forced to experience, he instead saw evidence of the absolute and enduring power of Original Sin, which made of this life a torment, a hell on earth from which only Christ could save man. Augustine answered the great criticism aimed at the Christian religion by the surviving pagan Romans—that Christianity had undermined the integrity of Roman imperial power and thereby opened the way for barbarian triumph—with a different set of values and a different vision of history: All true progress was necessarily spiritual and transcended this world and its negative fate. What was important for man's welfare was not the secular empire but the Catholic Church. Because divine Providence and spiritual salvation were the ultimate factors in human existence, the significance of secular history, with its passing values and its fluctuating and generally negative progress, was accordingly diminished.

Yet history, like all else in creation, was a manifestation of God's will. It embodied God's moral purpose. Man could not fully grasp that purpose in the present time of darkness and chaos, for its meaning would be vindicated only at the end of history. But although world history was still under God's command and spiritual in design (indeed, Augustine compared it to a great melody by some ineffable composer, with the parts of that melody being the dispensations suitable to each epoch), its secular aspect was not positively progressive. Rather, because of Satan's continuing power in this world, history was destined to enact, as in the eternal Manichaean battle of good versus evil, a deteriorating and divisive evolution of the spiritual elect and the mass of the worldly damned. In the course of this drama, God's motives were often hidden but ultimately just. For whatever apparent successes or defeats happened to individuals in this life, they were as nothing compared with the eternal fates their souls had earned. The particulars and achievements of secular history were of no ultimate importance in themselves. Actions in this life were significant mainly for their afterworldly consequences, divine reward or punishment. The individual soul's search for God was primary, while history and this world merely served as the stage for that drama. Escape from this world to the next, from self to God, from flesh to spirit, constituted the deepest purpose and direction of human life. The one great saving grace in history was the Church founded by Christ.

Instead of the early Christian anticipation of an immanent, as well as imminent, world change, Augustine gave up the field of this world, whose fallen tendency was naturally negative. In Augustine's vision, Christ had indeed already defeated Satan, but in the transcendent spiritual realm, the only realm that genuinely mattered. The true religious reality was not subject to the vagaries of this world and its history, and that reality could be known only through the individual's interior experience of God as mediated by the Church and its sacraments.

Here the Neoplatonic influence—inward, subjective, the individual spiritual ascent—joined, and to an extent took precedence over, the Judaic principle of a collective, exterior, historical spirituality. The penetration of Christianity by Neoplatonism both augmented and explicated the mystical and interior element of the Christian revelation, especially that of John's Gospel. But in so doing, it simultaneously diminished the historical and collectively evolutionary element that primitive Christianity, especially Paul and very early theologians like Irenaeus, had inherited and radically developed from Judaism. Augustine's strong sense of God's government of history—as in his dramatic scenario of the two invisible societies of the elect and the damned, the city of God and the city of the world, battling throughout creation's history until the Last Judgment—still reflected the Judaic ethical vision of God's purposefulness in history. Indeed, the doctrine of the two cities would have much influence on subsequent Western history, affirming the autonomy of the spiritual Church vis-à-vis the secular state. But his fundamental depreciation of the secular, combined with his philosophical background, his psychological predispositions, and his historical context, transformed that vision in the direction of a personal and interior otherworldly religiosity.

In other essential aspects of Augustine's thought and the evolving Christian world view—as in the dualism of an omnipotent transcendent God versus the sin-enchained creaturely man, and the need for a doctrinally and morally authoritative religious structure governing the community of chosen believers—it was the Judaic sensibility that dominated. This was particularly visible in the evolution of Christianity's characteristic attitudes toward God's moral commandments.

Law and Grace

For the Jews, the Mosaic Law was a living guide, their pillar of existential solidity, that which morally ordered their lives and retained them in good relation to God. While the Judaic tradition, as represented in Jesus's time by the Pharisees, held forth the need for strict obedience to the Law, early Christianity asserted what it believed was a fundamentally contrasting view: The Law was made for man and was fulfilled in the love of God, which eliminated the need for repressive obedience and instead called up a liberating and wholehearted embrace of God's will as one's own. That union of wills was mediated only by divine grace, the unearned gift of salvation brought to mankind by Christ. In this view, the Law could establish, with its negative precepts written in stone, only an imperfect obedience by fear. By contrast, Paul declared, man could be genuinely justified only by faith in Christ, through whose saving act all believers could know the freedom of God's grace. The Law's strictures made man a sinner, divided against himself. Instead of being in "slavery" under the Law, the Christian believer was free, because by Christ's grace he participated in Christ's freedom.

Before his conversion, Paul himself had been a Pharisee and a fervid defender of the Law. But after his conversion, he testified with self-deprecating zeal to the impotence of the Law compared with the power of Christ's love and the presence of the Spirit working within the human person. Paul's understanding of the Law, however, was viewed by Jews as a parody of its true nature. For them, the Law was itself God's gift and called forth moral responsibility in man. It upheld human autonomy and good works as necessary elements in the economy of salvation. Paul, too, recognized a role for those elements, but asserted that his own life exemplified the ultimate futility of a Law-governed religiosity. More than human effort, even if divinely legislated, was required for something as fundamental and suprahuman as the redemption of the human soul. Good works and moral responsibility were necessary but not sufficient. Only the supreme gift of Christ's incarnation and self-sacrifice made possible that life in harmony with God which the human soul so deeply desired. Faith in Christ's grace, rather than scrupulous conformity to ethical precepts, was man's surest path to salvation—and the evidence of that faith was the Christian's works of love and service that Christ's grace made possible. For Paul, the Law was no longer the binding authority, because the true end of the Law was Christ.

Similarly underscoring the break from the Judaic Law, John's Gospel proclaimed, "For the law was given through Moses; but grace and truth came through Jesus Christ." The tension between God's will and man's, between external regulation and inner inclination, could be dissolved in the love of God, which would unite human and divine in one unitary spirit. To awaken to this state of divine love was to experience the Kingdom of Heaven. Because of Christ's redemption, man could now attain true righteousness in the eyes of God, not by constraint but in happy spontaneity.

Yet this contrast in the New Testament between moral restriction and divinely graced freedom was not unambiguous. The Gospels' concern with interpersonal ethics was a dominant element in the Christian outlook, but its character seemed open to both interpretations. On the one hand, the tone of Jesus's teachings was often extremely uncompromising and judgmental, phrased in the hard dialectic of the Semitic manner, and intensified in the light of the imminent end times.

In Matthew's Gospel, the Law is made even more strict for Jesus's followers—requiring purity of intention as well as act, love of the enemy as well as friend, unceasing forgiveness, utter detachment from worldly things—and the demand for unconditional moral integrity is pressed to the full under the urgency of the messianic transition. On the other hand, Jesus's emphasis was repeatedly on compassion over self-righteousness, and on the inner spirit over the external letter of the law. His demands for heightened, even absolute, moral purity—judging spontaneous thoughts as well as deliberate acts—seemed to presuppose more than human will to achieve such inner goodness, thus opening the way for faith in God's grace. Often his intention appeared to be that of lending comfort to the poor, the desperate, the outcast and the sinful, while direly warning the proud and self-satisfied, those secure in their spiritual and mundane status. A humble openness to divine grace counted for more than legalistically righteous behavior. The Law was constantly to be measured against God's higher commandment of love. According to the New Testament, the extent to which a legalistic morality had overcome Jewish religious practice was evidence that the Law had become entrenched and frozen in the course of time, an end in itself that was now obscuring rather than mediating the individual's true relation to God and to others.

But even the new Christian revelation of God's graciousness was open to antithetical interpretations and consequences, especially under later historical conditions. The Pauline and Augustinian stress on divine grace over human works and self-dependent righteousness lent itself not just to the unitary notion of human fulfillment in embrace of the immanent divine will, but also to an emphatic reduction of man's positive volitional freedom relative to the omnipotence of God. In the struggle for salvation, man's own efforts were comparatively inconsequential; only God's saving power could be effective. The sole source of good was God, and only his mercy could save mankind from the natural fallen human inclination toward blind perversity. Because of Adam's sin, all human beings were corrupt and guilty, and only Christ's death had atoned for that collective guilt. The resurrection Christ brought to mankind was present in the Church, and the justification that every human being required lest he be condemned was dependent on the Church's sacraments, access to which in turn demanded conformity to specific ethical and ecclesiastical standards.

Since the Church and its sacred institutes were the divinely established vehicles of God's grace, the Church was suprahumanly significant, its hierarchy absolutely authoritative, its laws definitive. Because human beings were intrinsically prone to sin and lived in a world of constant temptation, they required stern Church-defined sanctions against uninhibited actions and thoughts, lest their eternal souls fall to the same debased fate as their temporal bodies. Especially in the West, under the historical exigencies of the Church's responsibility for the newly converted (and, from the Church's perspective, morally primitive) barbarian peoples, a pervasive verticality in the institutional Church was established, with all spiritual authority flowing downward from the supreme papal sovereign. Thus the characteristic tone of the medieval Christian Church—with its absolutist moral precepts, its complex legal-judicial structure, its accounting system of good works and merits, its meticulous distinctions between different categories of sin, its mandatory beliefs and sacraments, its power of excommunication, and its forceful stress on the inhibition of the flesh against the continual threat of damnation—often seemed more reminiscent of the older Judaic concept of God's law, indeed an exaggeration of that concept, than of the new unitary image of God's grace. Yet such elaborate safeguards appeared necessary in the present world of moral waywardness and secular danger, to preserve a genuine Christian morality and to guide the Church's charges into the eternal life.

Athens and Jerusalem

Another dichotomy within the Christian belief system involved the question of its purity and integrity and how these should be preserved. For the Judaic inclination toward religious exclusivism and doctrinal purity also passed itself on to Christianity, maintaining a constant tension with the Hellenic element, which sought and found evidence of a divine philosophy in the works of diverse pagan thinkers, especially Plato. While Paul at times stressed the need for complete differentiation of Christianity from the deceptive ideas of pagan philosophy, which for that reason should be carefully avoided, on other occasions he suggested a more liberal approach, quoting from pagan poets and tacitly infusing elements of Stoic ethics into his Christian teachings (Paul's native city of

Tarsus in Asia Minor was in his time a cosmopolitan university city, especially renowned for its Stoic philosophers). Later Christian theologians in the classical era were often imbued with Greek philosophy before converting to Christianity, and subsequently continued to find value in the Hellenic tradition. A syncretistic mysticism informed many early Christian thinkers as they eagerly recognized identical patterns of meaning in other philosophies and religions, often applying allegorical analysis to compare biblical and pagan literatures. The Truth was one, wherever it was found, for the Logos was all-comprehensive and boundlessly creative.

As early as the second century, Justin Martyr first advanced a theology that saw both Christianity and Platonic philosophy as aspiring toward the same transcendent God, with the Logos signifying at once the divine mind, human reason, and the redemptive Christ who fulfills both the Judaic and Hellenic historical traditions. Later, the Christian Platonist school in Alexandria used as its basis the *paideia,* the classical Greek education system from Plato's time centered on the liberal arts and philosophy, but now with theology as the highest and culminating science of the new curriculum. In this framework, learning per se was a form of Christian discipline, even of adoration. Such learning did not limit itself to the Judaeo-Christian tradition, but moved beyond it to encompass a larger whole, to illuminate all knowledge with the light of the Logos.

A characteristic compromise position, at once employing the admired Greek culture for Christian apologetic purposes and yet keeping distance from it, was presented by Clement of Alexandria in his use of Homer's *Odyssey:* Sailing by the island of the Sirens on his way home to Ithaca, Odysseus tied himself to the mast of his ship so he could hear their seductive singing ("have full knowledge") without succumbing to their temptation and destroying himself on their rocky shores. So too could the mature Christian make his way through the sensual and intellectual enticements of the secular world and pagan culture, having full knowledge of them while tying himself to the cross—the mast of the Church— for spiritual security.

Just as often, however, Christianity more fully resembled its Judaic parent in rejecting virtually all contact with non-Christian philosophical ideas and systems, considering them not only profane but valueless. In this view, the true core of the Christian mystery was so unique and luminous that it could only be blurred, distorted, or falsified by the infusion of other cultural streams. For the Hellenic side of Christianity, the Logos (as God's wisdom, the universal Reason) was seen as operative in non-Christian wisdom preceding the revelation, and in the larger framework of world history outside the Judaeo-Christian tradition. But in the more exclusivist understanding, the Logos (here understood more particularly as God's Word) tended to be recognized solely within the confines of Scripture, Church doctrine, and biblical history. Compared with the secular sophistication of pagan philosophy, the Christian gospel must seem mere foolishness, and any dialogue between the two would be futile. Thus Tertullian in the late second century emphatically questioned the relevance of the Hellenic tradition in his dictum "What has Athens to do with Jerusalem?"

Theological variants and religious innovations—Gnosticism, Montanism, Donatism, Pelagianism, Arianism—were especially abhorrent to Church authorities, because they controverted matters close to the heart of Christianity, and were therefore viewed as heretical, perilous, and requiring effective condemnation. Christianity's demand for uniformity of doctrine and structure, with its attendant intolerance, found part of its basis in the urgent primitive Christian imperative—seen especially in Paul—that the body of Christ (the Church community) be pure and undivided in readiness for the Parousia. Augustine presented, again, an influential stance containing elements of both sides—knowledgeable and respectful concerning classical culture and particularly Platonic philosophy, yet acutely conscious of Christianity's unique doctrinal superiority and, especially as he grew older, forcefully active in repressing heresies. Christian thinking in the centuries following Augustine generally reflected a similar position. Despite constant influences, both conscious and unconscious, from other philosophical and religious systems, the Church officially adopted a restrictive dogmatic stance with little tolerance for other systems on their own terms.

Thus Augustine's sense of the need for restraining or negating (in both himself and others) the pluralistic and heretical, the biological, the worldly, and the human, in favor of God, the spiritual, the one true Church and its one true sacred doctrine, was crystallized in the final moments of the ancient world, and, through his enduring influence on major Church figures like Pope Gregory the Great, given institutional embodiment in the medieval Western Church. Because of the remarkable power of his thought, his writings, and his personality, and because Augustine in some sense articulated the nascent self-consciousness of an era, the development of the Christian sensibility in the West took place largely through his mediation. By the end of the classical period, the exultant and inclusive religious spirit visible in primitive Christianity had taken on a different character: more inward, otherworldly, and philosophically elaborate, yet also more institutional, juridical, and dogmatic.

The Holy Spirit and Its Vicissitudes

The fundamental tensions inhering in Christianity from its outset come to clear focus in the extraordinary doctrine of the Holy Spirit, the third person of the Christian Trinity with God the Father and Christ the Son. The New Testament stated that before Jesus died, he had promised his disciples that God would send the Holy Spirit to remain with them to continue and complete his redemptive task. The subsequent "descent of the Holy Spirit" into a group of the disciples who had gathered together on Pentecost in an upper room in Jerusalem was reportedly experienced as a numinous visitation of great intensity, accompanied by a sound "like the rush of a mighty wind filling the house," with "tongues as of fire" appearing above each disciple. The event was interpreted by those present as an overwhelming and indisputable revelation of Christ's continuing presence among them despite his death and ascension. Immediately afterward, according to the report in Acts of the Apostles, the inspired disciples began preaching ecstatically to the multitudes: Through the Spirit the Word was spoken to the world; now the fruit of Christ's passion could be disseminated to all humanity. As Pentecost for the Jews had marked the revelation of the Law on Mount Sinai, so now for the Christians it marked a new revelation, the pouring forth of the Spirit. A new age had commenced with the Spirit's coming upon all the people of God. This Pentecostal experience—apparently renewed in subsequent communal gatherings, and in other circumstances involving charismatic phenomena such as unexpected healings and prophetic ecstasies—later served as the basis for the Church's doctrine of the Holy Spirit.

This doctrine conceived of the Holy Spirit as the spirit of truth and wisdom (the Paraclete, or Counselor), as well as the divine principle of life manifest in both material creation and spiritual rebirth. In the first, or revelatory, aspect, the Holy Spirit was recognized as the divine source of inspiration that had spoken through the Hebrew prophets. Now, however, the Spirit was democratized, made accessible to all Christians and not just the few. In the second, or procreative, aspect, the Holy Spirit was recognized as the progenitor of Christ within Mary his mother, and as being present at the beginning of Jesus's ministry when he was baptized by John the Baptist. Jesus had died that the Spirit might come to all: only thus could take place humanity's death and rebirth into the fullness of God. Through the continuing influx of the Spirit, a progressive incarnation of God into humanity was being effected, renewing and propelling the divine birth of Christ in the continuing Christian community. Although a human being's mortal reasonings were valueless by themselves, with the inspiration of the Spirit one could attain divine knowledge. Although on one's own resources a human being could not find sufficient love within oneself for others, through the Spirit one could know an infinite love embracing all humanity. The Holy Spirit was the Spirit of Christ, the agent of man's restoration to divinity, God's spiritual force acting through and with the Logos. The presence of the Holy Spirit made possible a sharing in the divine life, and a state of communion within the Church that was in essence a participation in God. Finally, because the Holy Spirit's presence brought divine authority and numinosity to the Church's believing community, the Spirit was seen as the basis for the Church itself, expressing itself in all aspects of the life of the Church—its sacraments, prayer, and doctrine, its developing tradition, its official hierarchy, and its spiritual authority.

The spontaneous experience of the Holy Spirit, however, soon came into conflict with the conservative imperatives of the institutional Church. The New Testament described the Spirit as like a wind that blows "where it wills." But as such, the Spirit possessed inherently spontaneous and revolutionary qualities that placed it, by definition, beyond any control. Individuals claiming the presence of the Spirit tended to produce unpredictably variable revelations and charismatic phenomena. Too often such manifestations—unrestrained and inappropriate activities in Church services, wandering preachers with diverse and unorthodox messages—seemed unconducive to the positive pursuit of the Church's mission. For such phenomena, the Church did not consider the authority of the Holy Spirit to be genuinely present. If not more circumspectly defined, the principle of the Holy Spirit in its more extreme manifestations seemed to lend itself to a blasphemous, or at best premature, human deification that would threaten the traditional separation between Creator and creature, and would contravene the supreme uniqueness of Christ's redemptive act.

In view of these tendencies toward the disruptive and heretical, and mindful of the need to preserve an orderly structure of belief and ritual, the Church came to adopt a generally negative response to self-proclaimed outbursts of the Holy Spirit. The charismatic and irrational expressions of the Spirit—spontaneous spiritual ecstasies, miraculous healings, speaking in tongues, prophecies, new assertions of divine revelation—were increasingly discouraged in favor of more ordered, rational manifestations, such as sermons, organized religious services and rituals, institutional authority, and doctrinal orthodoxy. A fixed canon of specific apostolic writings was carefully selected and permanently established, with no new revelations recognized as God's infallible Word. The authority of the Holy Spirit, invested by Christ in the original apostles, now passed on in a sacredly established order to the bishops of the Church, with the ultimate authority in the West claimed by the Roman pontiff, the successor to Peter. The notion of the Holy Spirit as a divine principle of revolutionary spiritual power, immanent in the human community and moving it toward deification, diminished in Christian belief in favor of a notion of the Holy Spirit as solely invested in the authority and activities of the institutional Church. The stability and continuity of the Church were thereby maintained, though at the expense of more individualistic forms of religious experience and revolutionary spiritual impulses.

The relation of the Holy Spirit to the Father and Son was not precisely defined in the New Testament. The first Christians were plainly more concerned with God's presence among them than with meticulous theological formulations. Later Church councils defined the Holy Spirit as the third person of the triune God, with Augustine describing the Spirit as the mutual spirit of love uniting the Father and Son. For a time in early Christian worship, the Holy Spirit was imaged in feminine terms (symbolized, as it would be later as well, by a dove), and was sometimes referred to as the divine Mother. In the long run, the Holy Spirit was conceived rather in more general and impersonal terms as a mysterious and numinous power, whose intensity seemed to have radically diminished as time grew more distant from the generation of the first apostles, and whose continuing presence, activity, and authority were lodged chiefly in the institutional Church.

Rome and Catholicism

The Judaic influence on Christianity in the West—the sense of a divinely mandated historical mission, the stress on obedience to the will of God, the moral rigor, the doctrinal conformity and exclusiveness—was further amplified and modulated by the influence of Rome. The Church's conception of humanity's relationship to God as a judicial one strictly defined by moral law was partly derived from Roman law, which the Catholic Church, based in Rome, inherited and integrated. The effectiveness of the Roman state's religious cult was based upon meticulous observance of a multitude of regulations. More fundamentally, Roman legal theory and practice were founded on the idea of justification; transposed to the religious sphere, sin was a criminal violation of a legal relationship established by God between himself and man. The doctrine of justification—of sin, guilt, repentance, grace, and restitution—was set forth by Paul in his Letter to the Romans,[12] and was taken up again by Augustine as the foundation of man's relationship to God. Similarly, the Judaic imperative of subordinating the highly developed but refractory human will to that of divine authority found supporting cultural patterns in the political subordination demanded by the immense authoritarian structure of the Roman Empire. God himself was generally conceived in terms reflective of the contemporary political environment—as commander and king, lord and master, inscrutably and unquestionably just, a stern ruler of all who was ultimately generous to his favorites.

The Christian Church, mindful of its spiritual mission and the great responsibility it bore for the religious guardianship of mankind, required an unusually durable form to ensure its survival and influence in the late classical world. The established cultural patterns and structures of both the Roman state and the Judaic religion—psychological, organizational, doctrinal—were particularly suited to the development of a strong and self-conscious institutional entity capable of guiding the faithful and enduring through time. As the Christian religion evolved in the West, its Judaic foundation readily assimilated the kindred juridical and authoritarian qualities of the Roman imperial culture, and much of the Roman Church's distinctive character was molded in those terms: a powerful central hierarchy, a complex judicial structure governing ethics and spirituality, the binding spiritual authority of priests and bishops, the demand for obedience from Church members and its effective enforcement, formalized rituals and institutionalized sacraments, a strenuous defense against any divergence from authorized dogma, a centrifugal and militant expansiveness aimed at converting and civilizing the barbarians, and so forth. The bishop's authority was declared to be God-ordained and unquestionable. He was the living representative of God's authority on earth, a ruler and judge whose decisions regarding sin, heresy, excommunication, and other vital religious matters were considered binding in heaven. Christian truth itself under Rome's influence became a matter for legislative battles, power politics, imperial edicts, military enforcement, and eventually assertions of divinely infallible authority by the new Roman sovereign, the pope. The fluid and communal forms of the primitive Church gave way to the definitively hierarchical institution of the Roman Catholic Church. Yet within such a firm and comprehensive structure, Christian doctrine was preserved, the Christian faith disseminated, and a Christian society maintained throughout medieval Europe.

In the period after Constantine's conversion in the early fourth century, the relationship of Rome to Christianity had undergone a complete reversal: Rome the persecutor had become Rome the defender, progressively uniting itself with the Church. The Church's boundaries now coincided with those of the Roman state, and its role was now allied with the state in maintaining public order and ruling the activities and beliefs of its citizenry. By the time of Pope Gregory the Great—the exemplar and architect of the medieval papacy, who reigned at the turn of the sixth century—Western society had changed so drastically that what had been Augustine's dialectical statement against the spirit of the late pagan era had now become the governing norm of the culture.[13] The public theater, circuses, and festal holidays of paganism had been replaced by Christian sacramental celebrations and processions, holy days and feast days. A new sense of public responsibility entered Christianity as it moved onto the world stage with an unprecedented consciousness of its mission to spiritually master the world. The centralized and hierarchical institution of the Church, the religious counterpart to the Roman Empire, increasingly absorbed and controlled the focus of the Christian spiritual quest. As the Roman Empire became Christian, Christianity became Roman.

The decision by Constantine to move the capital of the Roman Empire eastward from Rome to Byzantium (renamed Constantinople) also had immense consequences for the West, for after the empire's division into an eastern and western sector, and after the western empire's collapse in the wake of the barbarian migrations, a political and cultural vacuum occurred in much of Europe. The Church became the only institution capable of sustaining some semblance of social order and civilized culture in the West, and the bishop of Rome, as the traditional spiritual head of the imperial metropolis, gradually absorbed many of the distinctions and roles previously possessed by the Roman emperor. The Church took over a variety of governmental functions and became the sole patron of knowledge and the arts, its clergy became the West's sole literate class, and the pope became the supreme sacred authority, who could anoint or excommunicate emperors and kings. The new states of Europe that were founded on the ruins of the Western empire, which were successively converted to Christianity, inevitably perceived papal Rome as the sovereign spiritual center of Christendom. In the course of the first millennium, the Western Church not only concentrated its power in the Roman bishop, it also gradually but decisively asserted its independence from the Eastern churches centered in Byzantium and allied there with the still-reigning Eastern emperor. The geographical distances, the differences in language, culture, and political circumstances, the differing effects of the barbarian and Moslem incursions, various major doctrinal conflicts, and finally the West's own autonomous tendencies—all widened the separation between the Latin church of Rome and the Greek church of Byzantium.[14]

In these circumstances, Christianity in the West experienced a unique historical opportunity. Freed from both the church and the state of the East, unimpeded by the previous civil and secular structures of the old empire in the West, and empowered by the religiosity of its peoples and their rulers, the Western church assumed an extraordinarily universal authority in medieval Europe. The Roman Church became not just the Empire's religious counterpart, but its historical successor. The ideal self-image of the ensuing medieval Church was that of a spiritual *Pax Romana* reigning over the world under the guidance of a wise and beneficent priestly hierarchy. Augustine himself had envisioned the fall of the old Rome, the temporal empire, in the light of a new Rome, the spiritual empire of the Christian Church, which began with the apostles and would continue throughout history as a reflection in this world of God's divine Kingdom. In doing so, Augustine mediated that momentous transition taken by Christianity as it reconceived the nature of the promised Kingdom of Heaven in terms of the existing Church.[15] As the Middle Ages progressed and the Church gradually consolidated its authority in Rome, the Roman Catholic Church definitively emerged as the one, true, universally authoritative institution ordained by God to bring salvation to mankind.

The Virgin Mary and the Mother Church

The large-scale conversion of the pagan masses in the late Roman Empire brought about one other remarkable development in the Christian religion. Although the New Testament gave relatively little information about Mary, the mother of Jesus, and little explicit support for any substantial role she might have in the Church's future, in the course of the later classical period and the Middle Ages an extraordinary cult of Mary as the numinous Mother of God spontaneously arose and asserted itself as a dominant element in the popular Christian vision. Both Old and New Testaments were almost uniformly patriarchal in their monotheism, but when the pagan multitudes converted to Christianity in the post-Constantinian empire, they brought with them a deeply ingrained tradition of the Great Mother Goddess (as well as several mythological examples of divine virgins and virgin births of divine heroes), the infusion of which into Christian piety significantly expanded the Church's veneration of Mary. Yet Mary fundamentally differed from the pagan goddesses in being the unique human mother of the Son of God, the pivotal historical figure in the unrepeatable act of Christ's incarnation, rather than a nature goddess governing timeless cycles of death and rebirth. From the pagan mythological ground sprung an intensified devotion to Mary, whose role and character, however, were developed within a specifically Christian understanding.

Given the scriptural background alone, the elevation of Mary to such an exalted role in Christian piety was an unexpected development. References to Mary in the Gospels are not extensive, nor are they entirely congruent. When in Luke's Gospel she receives the angelic announcement that she is to conceive the Son of God, she is portrayed as graciously obedient to God's will, conscious of the special role she is to play in the divine plan, uniquely fitted for that role because of her profound purity in body and soul. Yet passages in the Gospel according to Mark, probably based on an older tradition, portray a more typically human character, suggesting that she may have been unaware of Jesus's divine role during much of his lifetime. In Mark as well are references to Jesus's having several close relatives, possibly brothers and sisters, who, like his mother, seem to have opposed Jesus in the earlier stages of his self-perceived mission. Even the Gospel according to John contains signs of definite tension between Mary and her son. The scriptural evidence for Mary's being a virgin when she conceived and gave birth is also ambiguous. Two Gospels, Mark and John, do not mention the subject at all, nor do Paul's letters. The two Gospels that do, Matthew and Luke, are implicitly inconsistent, since both accounts also present genealogical tables demonstrating Jesus to be from the direct line of David (and, in Luke's case, of Adam), ending in Mary's husband, Joseph, not in Mary.

But with her recognition by the faithful as the virginal Mother of God, and with the theologians' portrayal of her as vessel for the incarnation of the divine Logos, Mary was soon venerated in the early Church as the mediator between humanity and Christ and even as "Coredemptrix" with Christ. Within Mary had taken place the first merging of the divine and the human. As Christ was seen as the second Adam, so Mary was the second Eve, through her obedient virginal conception bringing redemption to humanity and nature, rectifying the virginal Eve's primal disobedience. Mary stood as supreme exemplar for all those virtues so characteristic of the Christian ethos—purity and chasteness, tenderness and modesty, simplicity, meekness, immaculate blessedness, inner beauty, moral innocence, unselfish devotion, surrender to the divine will.

The infusion via Mary of the feminine nurturing element from the pagan Great Mother Goddess, as well as the latter's fundamental relation to nature, served to soften the more austerely transcendent and masculine Judaic God. Mary's elevation to the virtual status of divine Mother also provided a necessary (for the converted pagans) complement to the otherwise inexplicably solitary and absolute God the Father. The recognition and worship of the Virgin Mother made the Christian pantheon more congenial to the classical world's sensibility and served as an effective link between Christianity and the pagan nature religions of rebirth. But where earlier matriarchal goddesses presided over nature, the Virgin Mary's role was in the context of human history. It was of the greatest importance to early theologians that the human Mary's maternal relation to Christ guaranteed the latter's authentic humanity, against some Gnostic claims that Christ was exclusively a superhuman divine being.

At times, the massive popular veneration of Mary seemed from the Church's viewpoint to exceed the bounds of theological justifiability. That problem was resolved, however, both by the Church and in the popular imagination, through the identification of the Virgin Mary with the Church. As Mary was the first believer in Christ upon her acceptance of the divine annunciation of his birth, and the first human to receive Christ within her, she represented the prototype of the entire Church community. In relation to Mary's receptive and virginal aspect, the Church was viewed as the "bride of Christ," to be united in sacred marriage with Christ when humanity would receive the full divine influx at the end of time. But even more significant was the identification of Mary's maternal qualities with the Church: The "Holy Mother Church," under the immanent guardianship of Mary, became not only the embodiment of Christian humanity but also the nourishing matrix within which all Christians could be encompassed, protected, and guided.[16]

Christians thus conceived of themselves as children of the Mother Church as well as children of God the Father. The nurturing maternal image of the Virgin Mary and the Mother Church thereby complemented and ameliorated not only the stern patriarchal image of the biblical Yahweh but also the Church's own tendencies toward strict legalism and patriarchal authoritarianism.[17] Even the architecture of church buildings, with their luminous interiors and sacral uterine structures, culminating in the great medieval cathedrals, re-created this tangible sense of the virginal Mother's numinous womb. And the Catholic Church as a whole took on the universal cultural role of an all-encompassing spiritual, intellectual, moral, and social womb, gestating the nascent Christian community, the mystical body of Christ, prior to its rebirth in the heavenly Kingdom. It would seem to have been particularly in this form—the veneration of Mary and the transference of her maternal numinosity onto the Church—that the unitive element of Christianity was most successfully sustained in the collective Christian psyche.

A Summing Up

Thus the primitive Christian revelation took on various cultural and intellectual inflections—Judaic, Greek and Hellenistic, Gnostic and Neoplatonist, Roman and Near Eastern—which Christianity brought into an often contradictory but singularly durable synthesis. Pluralistic in its origins but monolithic in its developed form, that synthesis would effectively govern the European mind until the Renaissance.

Let us attempt to draw a few summary distinctions between this outlook and that of the Greco-Roman era, focusing particularly here on the character of the Christian vision in the West from the later classical period through the early Middle Ages. Within this frame of reference, and allowing for the inevitable imprecision of such generalities, one may say that the overall effect of Christianity on the Greco-Roman mind was as follows:

(1) to establish a monotheistic hierarchy in the cosmos through the recognition of one supreme God, the triune Creator and Lord of history, thereby absorbing and negating the polytheism of pagan religion while depreciating, though not eliminating, the metaphysics of archetypal Forms;

(2) to reinforce Platonism's spirit-matter dualism by infusing it with the doctrine of Original Sin, the Fall of man and nature, and collective human guilt; by largely severing from nature any immanent divinity, whether polytheistic or pantheistic, though leaving the world an aura of supernatural significance, either theistic or satanic; and by radically polarizing good and evil;

(3) to dramatize the relation of the transcendent to the human in terms of God's rulership of history, the narrative of the Chosen People, the historical appearance of Christ on earth, and his eventual reappearance to save mankind in a future apocalyptic age—thus introducing a new sense of historical dynamism, a divine redemptive logic in history that was linear rather than cyclical; yet gradually relocating this redemptive force in the ongoing institutional Church, thereby implicitly restoring a more static understanding of history;[18]

(4)   to absorb and transform the pagan Mother Goddess mythology into a historicized Christian theology with the Virgin Mary as the human Mother of God, and into a continuing historical and social reality in the form of the Mother Church;

(5)   to diminish the value of observing, analyzing, or understanding the natural world, and thus to deemphasize or negate the rational and empirical faculties in favor of the emotional, moral, and spiritual, with all human faculties encompassed by the demands of Christian faith and subordinated to the will of God; and

(6)   to renounce the human capacity for independent intellectual or spiritual penetration of the world's meaning in deference to the absolute authority of the Church and Holy Scripture for the final definition of truth.

>+X+<

It has been said that a Manichaean cloud overshadowed the medieval imagination. Both popular Christian piety and much medieval theology evidenced a decisive depreciation of the physical world and the present life, with "the world, the flesh, and the devil" frequently grouped together as a satanic triumvirate. Mortification of the flesh was a characteristic spiritual imperative. The natural world was the vale of sorrow and death, a stronghold of evil from which the believer would be mercifully released at the end of this life. One entered the world reluctantly, as would a knight who entered a realm of shadow and sin hoping only to resist, overcome, and pass beyond it. For many early medieval theologians, direct study of the natural world and the development of an autonomous human reason were seen as pernicious threats to the integrity of religious faith. It is true that according to official Christian doctrine the goodness of God's material creation was not ultimately denied, but in itself the world was not considered a worthy focus of human endeavor. If it was not altogether evil, it was, in spiritual terms, largely irrelevant.

The fate of the human soul was divinely preordained, known by God before time began, a belief paralleled and psychologically supported by the apparent powerlessness of early medieval men and women in the face of nature, history, and traditional authority. The drama of human life may have been the central focus of God's will, but the human role was a weak and inferior one. Compared with, say, Homer's Odysseus, the medieval individual could be seen as relatively impotent in the face of evil and the world, a lost soul without the constant guidance and protection of the Church. ("Wandering" in this view was less likely to be a heroic adventure than a heretical slipping into ungodly ways.) Compared with, for example, Socrates, the medieval Christian could be seen as laboring under considerable intellectual confinement. ("Doubt" in this view was less a primary intellectual virtue than a serious spiritual failing.) The assertion of human individuality—so conspicuous, say, in Periclean Athens—now seemed largely negated in favor of a pious acceptance of God's will and, in more practical terms, submission to the Church's moral, intellectual, and spiritual authority. It thus might appear to be the great paradox of Christianity's history that a message whose original substance—the proclamation of the divine rebirth of the cosmos, the turning point of the aeons through the human incarnation of the Logos —had unprecedentedly elevated the significance of human life, human history, and human freedom eventually served to enforce a somewhat antithetical conception.

Yet the Christian world view, even in its medieval form, was not as simple or one-sided as these distinctions might suggest. Both impulses— optimistic and pessimistic, dualistic and unitive—constantly intermingled in inextricable synthesis. Indeed, it was held by the Church that one side of the polarity necessitated the other—that, for example, the great celestial destiny of the Christian faithful and the supreme beauty of the Christian truth demanded such formidable measures of institutional control and doctrinal rigor. In the eyes of many conscientious Christians, the fact that the continuity of sacred revelation and ritual had been successfully maintained century after century far outweighed the passing evils of contemporary Church politics or the temporary distortions of popular belief and theological doctrine. From such a perspective, the Church's saving grace lay finally in the cosmic significance of its earthly mission. The manifest faults of the mundane Church were merely inevitable side effects of the imperfect human attempt to carry out a divine plan the scope of which was inconceivably great. On similar grounds, Christian dogma and ritual were perceived as standing above and beyond the independent judgment of individual Christians—as if all Christians were to absorb themselves in symbolic representations of cosmic truths, the sublimity and magnitude of which were not now directly accessible to the believer, but which eventually might be grown into and comprehended in the course of humanity's spiritual progress. And whatever medieval Christians' apparent existential diminution, they knew themselves to be the potential recipients of Christ's redeeming grace through the Church, which elevated them beyond all other peoples in history and vitiated any negative comparisons with the pagan cultures.

But such religious defenses aside, in comparing one era with another, we have been implicitly contrasting the average person in early medieval Western Christendom with a relatively small group of brilliant Greeks who flourished during a relatively brief period of unique cultural creativity at the start of the classical era. The medieval West was not without its geniuses, even if in the earlier centuries they were few and only occasionally influential. To claim that this dearth was due more to Christianity than to other historical factors would be rash, especially considering not only the decline of classical culture well before the ascendance of Christianity, but also the extraordinary achievements of later Christian culture. And we should not forget that Socrates was put to death by the Athenian democracy for "impiety"; nor was he the only philosopher or scientist of antiquity to be indicted for unorthodox opinions. Conversely, the medieval Arthurian knights of the Holy Grail were not unworthy successors to their Homeric forebears. Adventurousness and dogmatism certainly exist in every age, even if the balance between them shifts, and in the long run one no doubt spurs the other. In any case, a more general psychological comparison between the medieval and classical ages would be more just and perhaps show less disparity.

It certainly could be argued that some cumulative moral and social benefits accrued to the pagan and barbarian peoples who converted to Christianity, and who were instructed week after week, year after year, to place new value on the sanctity of individual life, on concern for the welfare of others, on patience, humility, forgiveness, and compassion. While in classical times the introspective life was characteristic of a few philosophers, the Christian focus on personal responsibility, awareness of sin, and withdrawal from the secular world all encouraged an attentiveness to the inner life among a much wider population. And in contrast to the previous centuries of often distressing philosophical uncertainty and religious alienation, the Christian world view offered a stable, unchanging womb of spiritual and emotional nourishment in which every human soul was significant in the greater scheme of things. An unquestioned sense of cosmic order prevailed, and it would be difficult to overestimate the tremendous charismatic potency contained in the supreme figure of Jesus Christ, binding together the entire Christian universe. Whatever limitations medieval Christians may have felt would seem to have been compensated by an intense consciousness of their sacred status and potential for spiritual redemption. Although human life might be a trial now, the divine plan of history was bringing about a progressive movement of the faithful toward final reunion with God. Indeed, the ultimate power of faith, hope, and love was such that, in principle, nothing was impossible in the Christian universe. In a long era that was often dark and chaotic, the Christian world view held out the reality of an ideal spiritual realm in which all believers, the children of God, might find sustenance.

Viewing now in retrospect the Roman Catholic Church at the height of its glory in the high Middle Ages—with virtually all of Europe Catholic, with the entire calendar of human history now numerically centered on the birth of Christ, with the Roman pontiff regnant over the spiritual and often the temporal as well, with the masses of the faithful permeated with Christian piety, with the magnificent Gothic cathedrals, the monasteries and abbeys, the scribes and scholars, the thousands of priests, monks, and nuns, the widespread care for the sick and poor, the sacramental rituals, the great feast days with their processions and festivals, the glorious religious art and Gregorian chant, the morality and miracle plays, the universality of the Latin language in liturgy and scholarship, the omnipresence of the Church and Christian religiosity in every sphere of human activity—all this can hardly fail to elicit a certain admiration for the magnitude of the Church's success in establishing a universal Christian cultural matrix and fulfilling its earthly mission.[19] And whatever Christianity's actual metaphysical validity, the living continuity of Western civilized culture itself owed its existence to the vitality and pervasiveness of the Christian Church throughout medieval Europe.

But perhaps above all, we must be wary of projecting modern secular standards of judgment back onto the world view of an earlier era. The historical record suggests that for medieval Christians, the basic tenets of their faith were not abstract beliefs compelled by ecclesiastical authority but rather the very substance of their experience. The workings of God or the devil or the Virgin Mary, the states of sin and salvation, the expectation of the Kingdom of Heaven—these were living principles that effectively underlay and motivated the Christian's world. We must assume that the medieval experience of a specifically Christian reality was as tangible and self-evident as, say, the archaic Greek experience of a mythological reality with its gods and goddesses, or the modern experience of an impersonal and material objective reality fully distinct from a private subjective psyche. It is for this reason we must attempt to view the medieval world view from within if we are to approach an understanding of our cultural psyche's development. In a sense, we are talking here of a world as much as of a world view. And, as with the Greeks, we are talking of a world view that the West elaborated and transformed, criticized and negated, but never altogether left.

Indeed, it was the profound contraries within the Christian vision itself—the numerous inner tensions and paradoxes rooted both in Christianity's multiple sources and in the dialectical character of the Christian synthesis—that would constantly subvert the Christian mind's tendency toward monolithic dogmatism, thereby ensuring not only its great historical dynamism, but also, eventually, its radical self-transformation.

IV

The
Transformation
of the Medieval Era

We now engage one of our central tasks: to follow the complex evolution of the Western mind from the medieval Christian world view to the modern secular world view, a long and dramatic transformation in which classical thought would play a pivotal role.

The glories of classical civilization and the Roman Empire were a distant memory for the early medieval West. The barbarian migrations had not only destroyed the West's system of civil authority, but had largely eliminated any higher cultural life and, especially after the Islamic expansion, cut off its access to the original Greek texts. Despite an awareness of their specially graced spiritual status, intellectually conscious Christians of the early Middle Ages knew themselves to be living in the dim aftermath of a golden age of culture and learning. But in the Church's monasteries, a few kept alive the classical spark. In that politically and socially unsettled era, it was the Christian cloister that provided a protected enclosure within which higher pursuits could be safely sustained and developed.

Cultural progress for the medieval mind above all signified, and required, the recovery of the ancient texts and their meaning. The ancient Christian fathers had established an effective tradition according to which the classical pagan achievements were not entirely rejected, but could be reinterpreted and comprehended within the framework of Christian truth, and it was on this basis that the early medieval monks continued some semblance of scholarship. In monasteries, the copying of old manuscripts by many hands became a typical form of manual labor. Boethius, a Christian aristocratic statesman and philosopher in the dying hours of ancient Rome, attempted to preserve the classical intellectual heritage for posterity, and partially succeeded. After his death in the early sixth century, his Latin works and digests—of Platonic and Aristotelian philosophy as well as Christian theology—were passed into the monastic tradition and studied by generations of medieval scholars.[1] Similarly, Charlemagne, after having united much of Europe by military conquest to form a Western Christendom in the late eighth century, encouraged a cultural renascence of scholarship that rested as much on classical ideals as Christian.

But throughout the first half of the Middle Ages, scholars were rare, resources for culture scarce, and original classical texts largely unavailable. Under these conditions, intellectual progress for the newly amalgamated Western peoples was a slow and painstaking process. Just learning the vocabulary and grammar of the conquered empire's language, mastering its already highly developed modes of thinking, and establishing a sound didactic methodology were considerable tasks requiring centuries of scholastic effort.

Nor were these the only impediments, for the absolute primacy of Christian faith over secular concerns discouraged any extensive involvement with classical thought and culture on their own terms. The intellectual energies of the leading monks were absorbed in meditation upon Holy Scripture, whereby the mind could grasp the spiritual meaning of the Word, moving the soul toward mystical union with the divine. This monastic quest and discipline, rooted in the theology of the ancient Church fathers, created little centrifugal desire for other intellectual pursuits that could only have intruded upon the cloister of interior contemplation. The demands of the next world occupied the attention of devout Christians, and so deterred any compelling interest in nature, science, history, literature, or philosophy for their own sake. Because the truths of Scripture were all-comprehensive, the development of human reason was sanctioned and encouraged solely for the purpose of better understanding the mysteries and tenets of Christian doctrine.

But at the midpoint of the medieval period, around the year 1000, with Europe finally attaining a measure of political security after centuries of invasion and disorganization, cultural activity in the West began to quicken on many fronts: population increased, agriculture improved, trade within and beyond the continent grew, contacts with the neighboring Islamic and Byzantine cultures became more frequent, cities and towns emerged along with a literate upper class, guilds of workmen formed, and a general rise in the desire for learning led to the founding of universities. The fixed world of the old feudal order was giving way to something new.

The new social formations—guilds, communes, fraternities—were based on horizontal and fraternal lines rather than the earlier vertical and paternalistic authority of lords and vassals, and their rites of agreement were based on democratic consensus rather than the Church-sanctioned oaths of feudal vassalage. Political rights and institutions were redefined, taking on a more secular cast. Legal procedures moved toward rational proof rather than trial by ordeal. The world of nature took on increased reality for the medieval mind, visible as much in the new eroticism and realism of Jean de Meun's *Roman de la Rose* as in theologians' widespread use of the word *universitas* to signify the concrete universe as a single homogeneous ensemble, a divine harmony of natural diversity. Ancient literature and thought, from Plato's *Timaeus* to Ovid's *Ars Amatoria,* found appreciative audiences. Troubadors and court poets celebrated a new ideal of soul-transfiguring romantic love between free individuals, in implicit rebellion against the widespread feudal convention of marriage as a social-political arrangement ratified by the Church. A more profound sense of history and historical dynamism was awakened, expressed not only in the new chroniclers' accounts of contemporary political events, but also in the theologians' new awareness of Christianity's evolutionary progress over time. On many planes at once, the medieval horizons were rapidly expanding.

Of particular importance in this cultural revolution was the emergence of several major technical innovations in agriculture and the mechanical arts, above all the harnessing of new power sources (windmill, waterwheel, horse collar, stirrup, heavy plow). With such inventions, the natural environment began to be exploited with unprecedented skill and energy. Technical advances highlighted the value of human intelligence for mastering the forces of nature and acquiring useful knowledge.

The world seemed to be humanized by such use of the intellect, and Europeans showed themselves to be extraordinarily resourceful in this realm. The resulting increased productivity spurred the growth of a rudimentary agrarian society with a subsistence economy into the dynamic and progressive culture of the European high Middle Ages. The young and barbarian Christian West was emerging, through its own enterprise, as a vigorous center of civilization.

The Scholastic Awakening

As Western culture as a whole transformed itself, the Catholic Church's attitude toward secular learning and pagan wisdom also underwent a fundamental change. Christianity's earlier need to distinguish and strengthen itself by a more or less rigid exclusion of pagan culture lost some of its urgency. With most of the European continent now Christian, the Church's spiritual and intellectual authority was supreme. Other sources of learning and culture no longer posed such a threat, particularly if the Church could integrate them into its own all-encompassing structure. Moreover, with Europe's increased prosperity, the Church clergy found more time to pursue intellectual interests, which were in turn further stimulated by increased contacts with the older Eastern centers of learning—the Byzantine and Islamic empires—where the ancient manuscripts and Hellenic heritage had been preserved during Europe's darker ages. Under these new circumstances, the Church began to sponsor a tradition of scholarship and education of extraordinary breadth, rigor, and profundity.

Characteristic of this change in intellectual climate was the development of a school in early twelfth-century Paris at the Augustinian Abbey of Saint-Victor. Although working wholly within the tradition of monastic mysticism and Christian Platonism, Hugh of Saint-Victor proposed the radical educational thesis that secular learning, focused on the reality of the natural world, constituted a necessary foundation for advanced religious contemplation and even mystical ecstasy. "Learn everything," Hugh declared; "later you will see that nothing is superfluous." The purpose of the seven liberal arts—the *trivium* (grammar, rhetoric, and dialectic) and the *quadrivium* (arithmetic, music, geometry, and astronomy)—was "to restore God's image in us." From this new commitment to learning arose the composition of the great medieval *summae*, encyclopedic treatises aimed at comprehending the whole of reality, of which Hugh wrote the first.[2] This same educational conception became the basis for the development of universities throughout Europe, among which the University of Paris (founded c. 1170) would be preeminent. The Greek *paideia* was again springing forth in a new incarnation.

The West's increasing interest in the natural world and in the human mind's capacity to understand that world thus found congenial in-

stitutional and cultural support for its new enterprise. In this unprecedented context of Church-sponsored learning, and under the impact of
the larger forces invigorating the cultural emergence of the West, the
stage was set for a radical shift in the philosophical underpinnings of
the Christian outlook: Within the womb of the medieval Church, the
world-denying Christian philosophy forged by Augustine and based on
Plato began giving way to a fundamentally different approach to existence, as the Scholastics in effect recapitulated the movement from Plato
to Aristotle in their own intellectual evolution.

That shift was sparked in the twelfth and thirteenth centuries with the
West's rediscovery of a large corpus of Aristotle's writings, preserved by
the Moslems and Byzantines and now translated into Latin. With these
texts, which included the *Metaphysics,* the *Physics,* and *De Anima* (*On the
Soul*), came not only learned Arabic commentaries, but also other works
of Greek science, notably those of Ptolemy. Medieval Europe's sudden
encounter with a sophisticated scientific cosmology, encyclopedic in
breadth and intricately coherent, was dazzling to a culture that had been
largely ignorant of these writings and ideas for centuries. Yet Aristotle
had such extraordinary impact precisely because that culture was so well
prepared to recognize the quality of his achievement. His masterly
summation of scientific knowledge, his codification of the rules for
logical discourse, and his confidence in the power of the human intelligence were all exactly concordant with the new tendencies of rationalism and naturalism growing in the medieval West—and were attractive to many Church intellectuals, men whose reasoning powers had
been developed to uncommon acuity by their long scholastic education
in the logical disputation of doctrinal subtleties. The arrival of the
Aristotelian texts in Europe thus found a distinctly receptive audience,
and Aristotle was soon referred to as "the Philosopher." This shift in the
wind of medieval thought would have momentous consequences.

Under the Church's auspices, the universities were evolving into
remarkable centers of learning where students gathered from all over
Europe to study and hear public lectures and disputations by the masters.
As learning developed, the scholars' attitude toward Christian belief
became less unthinking and more self-reflective. The use of reason to
examine and defend articles of faith, already exploited in the eleventh
century by Anselm, archbishop of Canterbury, and the discipline of logic
in particular, championed by the fiery twelfth-century dialectician Abelard, now rapidly ascended in both educational popularity and theologi-

cal importance. With Abelard's *Sic et Non* (*Yes and No*), a compilation of apparently contradictory statements by various Church authorities, medieval thinkers became increasingly preoccupied with the possible plurality of truth, with debate between competing arguments, and with the growing power of human reason for discerning correct doctrine. It is not that Christian truths were called into question; rather, they were now subject to analysis. As Anselm stated, "It seems to me a case of negligence if, after becoming firm in our faith, we do not strive to understand what we believe."

Moreover, after long struggle with local religious and political authorities, the universities won the right from king and pope to form their own communities. With the University of Paris's receipt of a written charter from the Holy See in 1215, a new dimension entered European civilization, with the universities now existing as relatively autonomous centers of culture devoted to the pursuit of knowledge. Although Christian theology and dogma presided over this pursuit, these were in turn increasingly permeated by the rationalist spirit. It was into this fertile context that the new translations of Aristotle and his Arabic commentators were introduced.

Initially some ecclesiastical authorities resisted the sudden intrusion of the pagan philosophers, especially their writings on natural philosophy and metaphysics, lest Christian truth be violated. But their early bans on teaching Aristotle quickened scholars' curiosity and provoked deeper study of the censored texts. Aristotle could not in any case be easily dismissed, for his already known works on logic, passed on by Boethius, had been considered authoritative since the beginning of the Middle Ages, forming one of the bases of Christian culture. Despite the misgivings of conservative theologians, the culture's intellectual interests were increasingly Aristotelian in character if not yet in content, and in time the Church's strictures became lax. But the new attitudes were to transform drastically the nature and direction of European thought.

The principal occupation of medieval philosophy had long been the joining of faith with reason, so that the revealed truths of Christian dogma could be explicated and defended with the aid of rational analysis. Philosophy was the handmaid of theology, as reason was faith's interpreter. Reason was thus subordinate to faith. But with the introduction of Aristotle and the new focus on the visible world, the early Scholastics' understanding of "reason" as formally correct logical thinking began to take on a new meaning: Reason now signified not only logic but also empirical observation and experiment—i.e., cognition of the natural world. With the increasingly extended scope of the philosopher's intellectual territory, the tension between reason and faith was now radically heightened. A constantly growing multiplicity of facts about concrete things had to be integrated with the demands of Christian doctrine.

The resulting dialectic between this new reason and faith, between human knowledge of the natural world and the inherited doctrines of divine revelation, emerged fully in the thirteenth century's culminating Scholastic philosophers Albertus Magnus and his pupil Thomas Aquinas. Both men were devoutly loyal to biblical theology, yet also concerned with the mysteries of the physical world, and sympathetic to Aristotle's affirmation of nature, the body, and the human intellect. These scholars of Scholasticism's golden age could not have known the ultimate consequences of their intellectual quest to comprehend all that exists. For by confronting so directly this tension between divergent tendencies—Greek and Christian, reason and faith, nature and spirit—the Scholastics prepared the way in the late medieval universities for the massive convulsion in the Western world view caused by the Scientific Revolution.

Albertus was the first medieval thinker to make the firm distinction between knowledge derived from theology and knowledge derived from science. The theologian is the expert in matters of faith, but in mundane matters the scientist knows more. Albertus asserted the independent value of secular learning and the need for sense perceptions and empirical observations on which to ground one's knowledge of the natural world. In this view, Aristotle's philosophy was regarded as the greatest achievement of the natural human reason working without benefit of Christian inspiration.

After Albertus had grasped the intellectual power of Aristotelianism and established it as a necessary part of the university curriculum, Aquinas was left the philosophical task of coherently integrating the Greek challenge. Devout Dominican, son of Italian nobility, descendant of the Norman and Lombard conquerors, student at Naples, Paris, and Cologne, advisor to Rome—Aquinas knew the breadth and dynamism of European cultural life and did his pivotal teaching at the University of Paris, at the epicenter of the West's intellectual ferment. In Aquinas, the forces at work in the immediately previous centuries came to full articulation. In his relatively brief life he would forge a world view that dramatically epitomized the high Middle Ages' turning of Western thought on its axis, to a new direction of which the modern mind would be the heir and trustee.

The Quest of Thomas Aquinas

The passion for synthesis that Albertus and Aquinas experienced was perhaps inevitable for such men at that moment in history, standing between the past and the future: drawn magnetically toward the opening of the natural world and a new range of intellectual competence, yet imbued with an unshakable, indeed renewed faith in Christian revelation. Moreover, it was the peculiarity of that era, and of those men in particular, that these two loyalties—to the gospel on the one hand, and to the natural world and human reason on the other—were felt not as antithetical but as mutually supportive. Albertus and Aquinas were both members of the Dominican order and thus participants in a sustained and widespread influx of evangelical fervor spearheaded a generation earlier by Dominic and Francis of Assisi. The quickly flourishing Dominican and Franciscan mendicant orders had brought not only new vitality but new values to medieval Christianity.

Francis's mystical joy in the sacred fellowship of nature, Dominic's cultivation of scholarship in the service of the gospel, their dissolution of rigid boundaries between clerical and lay, their more democratic forms of internal government granting greater individual autonomy, their call to leave the monastic cloister to preach and teach actively in the world—all these encouraged a new openness to nature and society, to human reason and freedom. Above all, this fresh infusion of apostolic faith supported a direct dialogue between Christian revelation and the secular world, while recognizing anew an intimate relation between nature and grace. In the eyes of the evangelicals, the Word of God was not a remote truth to be cloistered far from humanity's daily life, but was directly relevant to the immediate particularities of human experience. By its very nature, the gospel required entrance into the world.[3]

Heirs to this religious rapprochement with the secular, Albertus and Aquinas could more freely develop those aspects of the Christian theological tradition, found even in Augustine, that affirmed the Creator's providential intelligence and the resulting order and beauty within the created world. It was a short step to their conclusion that the more the world was explored and understood, the greater knowledge of and reverence for God would result. Since there could be only one valid truth derived from the one God, nothing reason would uncover could ultimately contradict theological doctrine. Nothing that was true and valuable, even if achieved by man's natural intellect, could ultimately be foreign to God's revelation, for both reason and faith derived from the same source. But Aquinas went still further, asserting that nature itself could provide a deeper appreciation of divine wisdom, and that a rational exploration of the physical world could disclose its inherent religious value—not just as a dim reflection of the supernatural but on its own terms, a rationally intelligible natural order discovered in its profane reality.

Traditional theologians opposed the new scientific perspective because its purported discovery of regular determining laws of nature seemed to diminish God's free creativity, while also threatening man's personal responsibility and need for faith in Providence. To assert the value of nature seemed to usurp the supremacy of God. Basing their arguments on the teachings of Augustine concerning nature's fall and the need for God's redemptive grace, they viewed the new science's positive and deterministic conception of nature as a heretical threat to the essence of Christian doctrine.

But Aquinas held that the recognition of nature's order enhanced human understanding of God's creativity and in no way lessened divine omnipotence, which he saw as expressing itself in a continuous creation according to ordered patterns over which God remained sovereign. Within this structure, God willed each creature to move according to its own nature, with man himself given the greatest degree of autonomy by virtue of his rational intelligence. Man's freedom was not threatened either by natural laws or by his relationship to God, but rather was built into the fabric of the divinely created order. And the fact of nature's orderliness allowed man to develop a rational science that would lead his mind to God.

For Aquinas, the natural world was not just an opaque material stage upon which man briefly resided as a foreigner to work out his spiritual destiny. Nor was nature governed by principles alien to spiritual concerns. Rather, nature and spirit were intimately bound up with each other, and the history of one touched the history of the other. Man himself was the pivotal center of the two realms, "like a horizon of the corporeal and of the spiritual." To give value to nature did not, in Aquinas's eyes, usurp God's supremacy. Rather, nature was valuable, as was man, precisely because God gave it existence. To be a creature of the

Creator did not signify a separation from God, but rather a relationship to God. Moreover, divine grace did not vitiate nature, but perfected it.

Aquinas was also convinced that human reason and freedom were valuable on their own account, and that their actualization would further serve the glory of the Creator. Man's autonomy of will and intellect was not limited by the fact of God's omnipotence, nor would their full emergence be an inappropriate presumption of powers by a creature against the Creator. Rather, these special qualities were themselves founded in God's own nature, for man was made in God's image. Man could, by his unique relationship with the Creator, enjoy autonomous intellectual and volitional powers modeled on those of God himself.

Influenced by Aristotle's teleological concept of nature's relation to the highest Form and the Neoplatonic understanding of the all-pervasive One, Aquinas declared a new basis for the dignity and potential of man: Within human nature, as divinely posited, lay the potential for actively moving toward perfect communion with the infinite ground of man's being, God, who was the source of all development toward perfection in nature. Even human language incarnated the divine wisdom, and was therefore a worthy instrument capable of approaching and elaborating the mysteries of creation. Hence human reason could function within faith and yet according to its own principles. Philosophy could stand on its own virtues apart from, and yet complementary to, theology. Human intelligence and freedom received their reality and value from God himself, for God's infinite generosity allowed his creatures to participate in his own being each according to its distinctive essence, and man could do so to the full extent of his ever-developing humanness.

At the heart of Aquinas's vision was his belief that to subtract these extraordinary capacities from man would be to presume to lessen the infinite capacity of God himself and his creative omnipotence. To strive for human freedom and for the realization of specifically human values was to promote the divine will. God had created the world as a realm with immanent ends, and to reach his ultimate ends, man was intended to pass through immanent ends: to be as God intended, man had fully to realize his humanity. Man was an autonomous part of God's universe, and his very autonomy allowed him to make his return freely to the source of all. Indeed, only if man were genuinely free could he be capable of freely loving God, of freely realizing his exalted spiritual destiny.

>⋅✖⋅<

Aquinas's appreciation of human nature extended to the human body, an appreciation that affected his distinctive epistemological orientation. In contrast to Plato's antiphysical stance, reflected in much of the tenor of traditional Augustinian theology, Aquinas incorporated Aristotelian concepts to assert a new attitude. In man, spirit and nature were distinguishable, but they were also aspects of a homogeneous whole: The soul was the form of man, the body was the matter. Man's body was thus intrinsically necessary to his existence.[4] In epistemological terms, it was to man's benefit that his soul was united with a body, for it was only man's physical observations that could activate his potential understanding of things. Aquinas repeatedly quoted from Paul's Letter to the Romans, "the invisible things of God are clearly seen . . . by the things that are made." The divine invisibles, among which Aquinas included the "eternal types" of Augustine and Plato, could be approached only through the empirical, the observation of the visible and particular. By experiencing the particular through the senses, the human mind could then move toward the universal, which made intelligible the particular. Therefore both sense experience and intellect were necessary for cognition, each informing the other. In contrast to Plato's implication, sense and intellect for Aquinas were not opponents in the quest for knowledge, but partners. Like Aristotle, Aquinas believed that the human intellect could not have direct access to transcendent Ideas, but that it required sensory experience to awaken its potential knowledge of universals.

Just as Aquinas's epistemology more deeply stressed the value and even necessity of this-world experience for human knowledge, so did his ontology assert the essential worth and substantiality of this world's existence.[5] Sensible things did not exist merely as relatively unreal images, as shadowy replications of the Platonic Ideas; rather, they had a substantial reality of their own, as Aristotle had maintained. The forms were genuinely embedded in matter, united with matter to produce a composite whole. But here Aquinas went beyond the Aristotelians' tendency to view nature as existing apart from God, arguing that a deeper philosophical understanding of the meaning of existence would fully connect the created world with God. To accomplish this, Aquinas reintroduced the Platonic notion of "participation" in this new context: Created things have true substantial reality because they participate in Existence, which is from God, the infinite self-subsistent ground of all being. For God's essence was precisely his existence, his infinite act of being which underlay the finite existence of all created things, each with its own particular essence.

The essence of each thing, its specific kind of being, is the measure of its participation in the real existence communicated to it by God. What a thing is and the fact that it is at all are two distinct aspects of any created being. In God alone is there absolute simplicity, for what God is and the fact of his being are one and the same: God is "be-ing" itself—unlimited, absolute, beyond definition. Thus every creature is a compound of essence and existence, while God alone is not a compound, for his essence is existence per se. Creatures *have* existence; God *is* existence. Existence for creatures is not self-given, and therein lay Aquinas's fundamental philosophical tenet: the absolute contingency of the finite world on an infinite giver of being.

Thus for Aquinas, God was not only the supreme Form drawing nature forth, but was also the very ground of nature's existence. For both Aristotle and Aquinas, form was an active principle—not just a structure, but a dynamism toward realization; and the entire creation was dynamically moved relative to the highest Form, God. But whereas Aristotle's God was apart from and indifferent to the creation of which he was the unmoved mover, for Aquinas God's true essence was existence. God communicated his essence to his creation, each instance of which became real to the extent of its reception of the act of existence communicated by God. Only in this way was the Aristotelian Prime Mover genuinely connected to the creation he motivated. And conversely, only thus was the Platonic transcendent genuinely connected to the empirical world of multiplicity and flux.

Building on philosophical developments in the Arab and Christian Neoplatonist traditions (which were, besides Augustine and Boethius, the main sources for his knowledge of Plato), and particularly on the thought of the ancient Eastern Christian mystic who used the name Dionysius the Areopagite, Aquinas aspired to deepen Aristotle by using Platonic principles. Yet he also saw Platonism's need for Aristotelian principles. Indeed, for Aquinas, the Platonic theory of participation made full metaphysical sense only when it was deepened to reach the principle of existence itself, beyond the various types of being that existence might lend itself to. And this deepening required an Aristotelian context of a nature that possessed real being—a reality achieved through nature's constant process of becoming, its dynamic movement from potentiality to actuality. Thus Aquinas showed the complementarity of the two Greek philosophers, of Plato's exalted spiritual absolute and Aristotle's dynamically real nature, an integration achieved by using Plato's participation relative not to the Ideas but to Existence. In doing so, he further corrected Aristotle by showing that concrete individuals were not just isolated substances, but were united both to each other and to God by their common participation in existence. Yet he also corrected Plato by arguing that divine Providence did not pertain just to the Ideas, but extended directly to individuals, each of which was created in the image of God and participated, each in its limited fashion, in God's unlimited act of existence.

Aquinas thus gave to God alone what Plato gave to Ideas in general, but by doing so gave increased reality to the empirical creation. Since "to be" is to participate in existence, and since existence is itself the gift of God's own being, then every created thing possesses a true reality founded in God's infinite reality. The Ideas are in a sense the exemplars of God's creation, as formal designs in God's mind; but on the deepest level God is the true and ultimate exemplar of creation, and all the Ideas are inflections of that supreme essence. All created beings participate firstly and most significantly in God's nature, each in its own specific finite manner manifesting a part of God's infinite variety and perfection. In Aquinas's understanding, God was not so much a thing, an entity that was the first of a series of other entities, but was rather the infinite act of existence (*esse*) from which everything derived its own being. In effect, Aquinas synthesized Plato's transcendent reality with Aristotle's concrete reality by means of the Christian understanding of God as the loving infinite Creator, giving freely of his own being to his creation. Similarly, he synthesized the Aristotelian stress on nature's and man's teleological dynamism, striving forward to more perfect realization, with the Platonic emphasis on nature's participation in a superior transcendent reality, by conceiving the divine as standing in absolute ineffable perfection and yet also as bestowing its essence—i.e., existence—to created things. These are then moved dynamically toward realization precisely because they participate in being, which is by its nature a dynamic tendency toward the Absolute. As in Neoplatonism, all creation begins and ends with, goes forth from and returns to, the supreme One. But for Aquinas, God created and gave being to the world not by necessary emanation but by a free act of personal love. And the creature participated not merely in the One as a distant semi-real emanation, but in "be-ing" (*esse*) as a fully real individual entity created by God.

So Aquinas followed Aristotle in his regard for nature, for its reality and dynamism, for individual beings, and for the epistemological necessity of sense experience. Yet in his emphatic awareness of a superior transcendent reality, his belief in the immortality of the individual soul, and his strongly spiritual sensibility which focused on a loving God as the infinite source and goal of being, he continued the Augustinian tradition of medieval theology and thereby more nearly resembled Plato and Plotinus. But the distinction Aquinas made against Plato and Augustine in relation to the Ideas and human knowledge was an epistemologically significant one, for it sanctioned the Christian intellect's explicit recognition of the essential value of sensory experience and empiricism, which Plato and Augustine had devalued in favor of direct illumination from the transcendent Ideas. Aquinas did not deny the existence of the Ideas. Rather, ontologically he denied their self-subsistence apart from material reality (in keeping with Aristotle) and their separate creative status apart from God (in keeping with Christian monotheism and Augustine's placement of the Ideas within the creative mind of God). And epistemologically he denied the human intellect's capacity to know the Ideas directly, asserting the intellect's need for sensory experience to activate an imperfect but meaningful understanding of things in terms of those eternal archetypes. If man would know even imperfectly what God knows perfectly, he would have to open his eyes to the physical world.

For Aquinas, like Aristotle, we know concrete things first, then we can know universals. For Plato and Augustine, the reverse was true. Augustine's theory of knowledge rested on the epistemological certainty that man could know truth by being illuminated directly from within by the knowledge of God's transcendent Ideas. These Ideas constitute the Logos, Christ, Augustine's inward teacher, who contains all Ideas and who in an interior manner illuminates the human intellect. Although Aquinas would retain aspects of Augustine's view, he could not embrace Plato's epistemological dependence on the Ideas alone. Man is matter as well as spirit, and human cognition must reflect both principles: knowledge is derived from the sensory experience of concrete particulars, from which universals can be abstracted, and this knowledge has validity because in recognizing the universal in singular things the human mind is intellectually participating, however indirectly, in the original pattern by which God created that thing. Here Aquinas again integrated Plato with Aristotle by identifying the soul's capacity for such participation with Aristotle's active intellect, or *nous*—though he strenuously opposed those interpreters of Aristotle who would make the *nous* a single separate entity common to all mankind, which would tend to deny individual intelligence and moral responsibility, as well as the immortality of the individual soul.

Aquinas agreed that a kind of reality can be ascribed to the Ideas, as eternal types in the divine intellect akin to the forms that exist in an architect's mind prior to his constructing a building, but he denied that human beings can directly know them in this life. Only a more perfect (i.e., angelic) intelligence can enjoy intimate contact with God's eternal notions and grasp them directly. Earthly man, however, understands things in the light of those eternal types in the same way that he sees things in the light of the Sun. The mind without sensory experience is a blank slate, in a state of potentiality with regard to things intelligible. But sensory experience without the active intellect would be unintelligible, and thus effectively blind. In his present condition, man must focus his active intellect, which contains within it the likeness of the divine light, onto his sensory experience of the physical world if he is going to attempt to grasp truth, and from that point he may proceed by means of discursive reasoning in the Aristotelian manner. In Aquinas's philosophy, the Ideas recede into the background, and emphasis is instead placed on sensory experience as that which provides the necessary particular sense images that the active intellect illuminates so as to abstract intelligible species or concepts.

Aquinas thus offered a solution to one of the central and most enduring problems of Scholastic philosophy, the problem of universals. The early medieval doctrine of universals was characteristically that of "Realism"—i.e., the universal existed as a real entity. Since the time of Boethius, opinion was divided as to whether the universal was real in the Platonic sense, as a transcendent ideal independent of the concrete particular, or in the Aristotelian sense, as an immanent form fully associated with its individual material embodiment. Under Augustine's influence, the Platonic interpretation was usually favored. Yet in either case the reality of universals was so generally affirmed that Anselm, for example, argued from the existence of the Idea to the existence of the particular, the derivative of the Idea. But Roscellinus, a contemporary of Anselm and teacher of Abelard, criticized the belief in real universals, asserting that the latter were merely words or names (*nomina*)—thus giving voice to the philosophical doctrine of nominalism. Aquinas, using distinctions formulated by Albertus Magnus, strove to resolve the dispute by suggesting that the Ideas had three kinds of existence: as exemplars in the mind of God independent of things (*ante rem*), as intelligible forms in things (*in re*), and as concepts in the human mind formed by abstracting from things (*post rem*).

These meticulous epistemological distinctions and others like them were important for Aquinas because for him the nature and processes of human knowledge bore directly on matters of weighty theological concern. In Aquinas's view, man could strive to know things as they are because both the things and man's knowledge of them were determined by and, like man himself, expressive of the same absolute being—God. Like Plato and Aristotle, Aquinas believed in the possibility of human knowledge because he was convinced of an ultimate identity between being and knowledge. Man could know an object by comprehending its formal, or universal, aspect. Man possessed this capacity for comprehension not because his mind was merely impressed by superior separated entities, the Ideas, but because his own mind possessed a superior, "nobler" element by which it could abstract valid universals from sense impressions. This capacity was the light of the active intellect—*lumen intellectus agentis*. The light of human reason derived its power from the divine Truth which contained the eternal types of all things. In endowing man with this light, God had given him the potential for knowledge of the world, just as God had endowed all beings, as possible objects of knowledge, with intelligibility. Thus the human mind could make true judgments.

Yet Aquinas held that, because of the relationship of being and knowledge, something of deeper significance was involved in the process of human cognition. To know a thing was in a sense to have that thing in the knower. The soul received the form of an object into itself. The soul could know a thing by receiving its universal aspect, that which represented every instance of it—the thing's form apart from its individuating material embodiment. As Aristotle had said, the soul was in a sense all things, because it had been created in such a way as to have the whole order of the universe inscribed within it. But the highest condition of this knowledge Aquinas recognized as the vision of God—not so much the state of philosophical contemplation recognized by Aristotle as the final end of man, but rather the supreme beatific vision of Christian mysticism. By expanding his own knowledge, man was becoming more like God, and to be like God was man's true desired end. Because pure being and pure knowledge were both expressive of God (with knowledge constituting the "being to itself" of being, the self-illumination of being), and because a finite being participates, in a partial way, in those absolutes, every act of knowing was not only an expansion of one's own being but an expanding participation in God's nature. And by knowing existence in created things, the mind could gain a positive—though ever imperfect—knowledge of God, by virtue of the analogy between finite being and Infinite Being. Thus for Aquinas, the human effort to know was endowed with profound religious significance: The way of truth was the way of the Holy Spirit.

>·✕·<

The extraordinary impact Aquinas had on Western thought lay especially in his conviction that the judicious exercise of man's empirical and rational intelligence, which had been developed and empowered by the Greeks, could now marvelously serve the Christian cause. For it was the human intellect's penetrating cognition of the multitude of created objects in this world—their order, their dynamism, their directedness, their finiteness, their absolute dependence on something more—that revealed, at the culmination of the universe's hierarchy, the existence of an infinite highest being, an unmoved mover and first cause: the God of Christianity. For God was the sustaining cause of all that exists, the ultimate unconditioned condition for the being of all things. The final result of the metaphysical quest, of which the Greeks were the prime exemplars, was discovered to be identical to that of the spiritual quest, of which Christianity was the definitive expression. Faith transcended reason, but was not opposed by it; indeed, they enriched each other. Rather than view the workings of secular reason as a threatening antithesis to the truths of religious faith, Aquinas was convinced that ultimately the two could not be in conflict and that their plurality would therefore serve a deeper unity. Aquinas thereby fulfilled the challenge of dialectic posed by the earlier Scholastic Abelard, and in so doing opened himself to the influx of the Hellenic intellect.

It is true that rational philosophy could not on its own offer compelling proof for all the spiritual truths revealed in Scripture and Church doctrine. But it could enhance the spiritual understanding of theological matters, just as theology could enhance the philosophical understanding of worldly matters. Because God's wisdom permeated all aspects of creation, knowledge of natural reality could only magnify the profundity of Christian faith, although in ways that might not be knowable in advance. Certainly the philosophy of the natural mind alone could not penetrate fully into the deepest meanings of the creation. For this, Christian revelation was necessary. Human intelligence was imperfect, darkened by the Fall. To approach the highest spiritual realities, human thought required the illumination of the revealed Word; and only love could truly reach the infinite. But the philosophical enterprise was nevertheless a vital element in the human search for spiritual understanding. And if Aristotle for Aquinas (like Plato for Augustine) lacked an adequate conception of the Creator, Aquinas saw how to build on Aristotle while correcting and deepening him wherever necessary— whether by infusing Neoplatonic conceptions, by employing the special insights of Christian revelation, or by drawing on his own philosophical acuity. Thus Aquinas gave to Aristotelian thought a new religious significance—or, as it has been said, Aquinas converted Aristotle to Christianity and baptized him. Yet it is equally true that in the long run Aquinas converted medieval Christianity to Aristotle and to the values Aristotle represented.

Aristotle's introduction into the medieval West as mediated by Aquinas opened Christian thought to the intrinsic worth and autonomous dynamism of this world, of man and nature, while not forsaking the Platonic transcendent of Augustinian theology. In Aquinas's view, an understanding of Aristotle paradoxically allowed theology to become more fully "Christian," more resonant with the mystery of the Incarnation as the redemptive reunion of nature and spirit, time and eternity, man and God. Rational philosophy and the scientific study of nature could enrich theology and faith itself while being fulfilled by them. The ideal was "a theologically based worldliness and a theology open to the world." For Aquinas the mystery of being was inexhaustible, but that mystery opened up to man, radiantly if never completely, through the devout development of his God-given intelligence: so God drew man onward from within to seek perfection, to know a fuller participation in the Absolute, to move beyond himself and return to his source.[6]

Aquinas thus embraced the new learning, mastered all the available texts, and committed himself to the Herculean intellectual task of

comprehensively uniting the Greek and Christian world views in one
great *summa*, wherein the scientific and philosophical achievements of
the ancients would be brought within the overarching vision of Christian
theology. More than a sum of its parts, Aquinas's philosophy was a live
compound that brought the diverse elements of its synthesis to new
expression—as if he had recognized an implicit unity in the two streams
and then set about drawing it out by sheer force of intellect.

Further Developments
in the High Middle Ages

The Rising Tide of Secular Thought

Aquinas's optimistic confidence in the conjunction of reason and revelation was not shared by everyone. Other philosophers, influenced by Aristotle's greatest Arabic commentator, Averroës, taught Aristotle's works without seeing the need for or the possibility of consistently coordinating his scientific and logical conclusions with the truths of Christian faith. These "secularistic" philosophers, centered in the arts faculty at Paris and led by Siger of Brabant, noted the apparent discrepancies between certain Aristotelian tenets and those of Christian revelation—particularly such Aristotelian concepts as the single intellect common to all mankind (which implied the mortality of the individual human soul), the eternity of the material world (which contradicted the creation narrative of Genesis), and the existence of many intermediaries between God and man (which overruled the direct workings of divine Providence). Siger and his colleagues asserted that if philosophical reason and religious faith were in contradiction, then the realm of reason and science must in some sense be outside the sphere of theology. A "double-truth" universe was the consequence. Aquinas's desire for fundamental resolution between the two realms thus found itself opposed not only to the position of the traditional Augustinians, who rejected the intrusion of Aristotelian science altogether, but also to the Averroists' heterodox philosophy, which Aquinas viewed as inimical to an integrated Christian world view and as undercutting the potential of a genuine Christian interpretation of Aristotle. But with better translations of Aristotle's writings and with their gradual separation from the Neoplatonist interpretations with which they had long been conflated, the Aristotelian outlook was increasingly recognized as a naturalistic cosmology not readily combined with a straightforward Christian outlook.

Faced with this disturbing outbreak of intellectual independence in the universities, ecclesiastical authorities condemned the new thought.

Sensing the secularizing threat of the pagan Aristotelian-Arabic science, of an autonomous human reason and its embrace of profane nature, the Church was pressed to take a stand against the antitheological thinking beginning to spread. The truths of Christian faith were supernatural, and needed to be safeguarded against the insinuations of a naturalistic rationalism. Aquinas had not succeeded in resolving the heated differences between the opposing camps, and after his early death in 1274 the rift grew more profound. Indeed, three years later when the Church made its list of condemned propositions, some of those taught by Aquinas were included. Thus the division between the warring adherents of reason and faith was further deepened, for by its initial censure of not only the secularists but also Aquinas, the Church cut off communication between the scientific thinkers and the traditional theologians, leaving the two camps increasingly aloof and distrustful toward each other.

The Church's prohibition did not stop the new thinking. In the eyes of many philosophers, the die was already cast. Having tasted the power of the Aristotelian intellect, they rejected a return to the previous status quo. They recognized that their intellectual duty was to follow the critical judgments of human reason wherever these led, even if that contradicted the traditional verities of faith. Not that the truths of faith could ultimately be doubted; but such truths could not necessarily be justified by pure reason, which had its own logic and its own conclusions, and which found its application in a realm perhaps irrelevant to faith. The potential divorce between theology and philosophy was already visible. And once opened, the Pandora's box of scientific inquiry would not shut.

In these final centuries of the Middle Ages, however, the Church's authority was still secure and could accommodate itself to doctrinal shifts without endangering its cultural hegemony. Despite repeated censure by the Church, the new ideas were too attractive to be altogether suppressed, even among devout Church intellectuals. Half a century after Aquinas's death, his life and work were reevaluated by the Church hierarchy and he was canonized, a scholar-saint. All Thomist teachings were removed from the list of condemned propositions. Recognizing Aquinas's prodigious achievement in interpreting Aristotle in Christian terms, the Church began incorporating this modulated Aristotelianism into ecclesiastical doctrine, with Aquinas as its most authoritative expositor. Aquinas and his Scholastic followers and colleagues thus legitimated Aristotle by working out in painstaking detail the unification of his science, philosophy, and cosmology with Christian doctrine. Without that synthesis, it is questionable whether the force of Greek rationalism and naturalism could have been so fully assimilated into a culture as pervasively Christian as the medieval West. But with the Church's gradual acceptance of that work, the Aristotelian corpus was elevated virtually to the status of Christian dogma.

Astronomy and Dante

With the discovery of Aristotle came as well Ptolemy's works on astronomy explicating the classical conception of the heavens, with the planets revolving around the Earth in concentric crystalline spheres, and with the further mathematical refinements of epicycles, eccentrics, and equants. Although disparities between observation and theory continued to arise and demand new solutions, the Ptolemaic system still reigned as the most sophisticated astronomy known, capable of modifying itself in details while maintaining its basic structure. Above all, it provided a convincing scientific account for the natural perception of the Earth as fixed with the heavens moving around it. Taken together, the works of Aristotle and Ptolemy offered a comprehensive cosmological paradigm representing the best science of the classical era, one that had dominated Arabic science and that now swept the universities in the West.

From the twelfth and thirteenth centuries even the classical astrology codified by Ptolemy was being taught in the universities (often linked to medical studies), and was integrated by Albertus and Aquinas into a Christian context. Astrology in fact had never entirely disappeared during the medieval era, periodically enjoying royal and papal patronage and scholarly repute, and constituting the cosmic framework for an ongoing and growingly vital esoteric tradition. But with paganism no longer an immediate threat to Christianity, theologians of the high Middle Ages more freely and explicitly accepted the relevance of astrology in the scheme of things, especially given its classical pedigree and Aristotelian-Ptolemaic systematization. The traditional Christian objection to astrology—its implicit negation of free will and grace—was met by Aquinas in his *Summa Theologica*. There he affirmed that the planets influenced man, specifically his corporeal nature, but that through the use of his God-given reason and free will man could control his passions and achieve freedom from astrological determinism. Because most individuals did not exercise this faculty and were therefore subject to planetary forces, astrologers were able to make accurate general predictions. In principle, however, the soul was free to choose, just as, according to astrologers, the wise man ruled his stars. Aquinas thus maintained the Christian belief in free will and divine grace while acknowledging the Greek conception of the celestial powers.

Astrology, conjoined with astronomy, rose again to high status as a comprehensive science, capable of disclosing the universal laws of nature. The planetary spheres—Moon, Mercury, Venus, Sun, Mars, Jupiter, Saturn—formed successive heavens surrounding the Earth and affecting human existence. For underlying the restored classical cosmology was Aristotle's fundamental axiom, "The end of every movement must be one of the divine bodies moving in the sky." As the translations from the Arabic continued during the succeeding generations, the esoteric and astrological conceptions forged in the Hellenistic era, enunciated in the Alexandrian schools and Hermetic tradition and carried forward by the Arabs, gradually achieved widespread influence among the medieval intelligentsia.

But it was when the Aristotelian-Ptolemaic cosmology bestowed to Christianity by the Scholastics was embraced by Dante that the ancient world view fully reentered the Christian psyche and was there elaborated and permeated with Christian meaning. Closely following Aquinas in time and spirit, and similarly inspired by the scientific wisdom of Aristotle, Dante realized in his epic poem *La Divina Commedia* what was in effect the moral, religious, and cosmological paradigm of the medieval era. The *Commedia* represented, on several counts, an unprecedented achievement in Christian culture. As a sustained act of the poetic imagination, Dante's epic transcended earlier medieval conventions—in its literary sophistication, in its eloquent use of the vernacular, in its psychological insight and theological innovations, in its expression of a deepening individualism, in its upholding of poetry and learning as instruments of religious understanding, in its implicit identification of the feminine with the mystical knowledge of God, in its bold Platonic amplification of human eros in a Christian context. But especially consequential for the history of the Western world view were certain ramifications of the epic's cosmological architecture. For by integrating the scientific constructs of Aristotle and Ptolemy with a vividly imagined portrayal of the Christian universe, Dante created a vast classical-Christian mythology encompassing the whole of creation that would exert a considerable—and complex—influence on the later Christian imagination.

In Dante's vision, as in the medieval vision generally, the heavens were both numinous and humanly meaningful. The human microcosm directly reflected the macrocosm, and the planetary spheres embodied the various forces influencing human destiny. Dante filled out this general conception by poetically uniting the specific elements of Christian theology with the equally specific elements of classical astronomy. In the *Commedia*, the ascending elemental and planetary spheres that envelop the central Earth culminate in the highest sphere, containing the throne of God, while the circles of Hell, mirroring the celestial spheres in reverse, descend toward the corrupt core of the Earth. The Aristotelian geocentric universe thus became a massive symbolic structure for the moral drama of Christianity, in which man was situated between Heaven and Hell, drawn between his ethereal and earthly abodes, and balanced at the moral pivot between his spiritual and corporeal natures. All of the Ptolemaic planetary spheres now took on Christian references, with specific ranks of angels and archangels responsible for each sphere's motions, even for their various epicyclic refinements. The *Commedia* portrayed the entire Christian hierarchy of being—ranging from Satan and Hell in the dark depths of the material Earth, out through the Mount of Purgatory, and on up through the successive angelic hosts to the supreme God in Paradise at the highest celestial sphere, with man's earthly existence at the cosmological midpoint, all carefully mapped onto the Ptolemaic-Aristotelian system. The resulting Christian universe was a divine macrocosmic womb in which humankind was positioned securely in the center, enclosed on all sides by God's omniscient and omnipotent being. Thus Dante, like Aquinas, achieved an extraordinarily comprehensive ordering of the cosmos, a medieval Christian transfiguration of the cosmic order set forth by the Greeks.

But the very power and vividness of this Greek-Christian integration was to encourage an unexpectedly critical turn of events in the cultural psyche. The medieval mind perceived the physical world as symbolic to its core, and that perception had gained new specificity with the embrace of Aristotle and Greek science by Christian intellectuals. Dante's use of the Ptolemaic-Aristotelian cosmology as a structural foundation for the Christian world view readily established itself in the collective Christian imagination, with every aspect of the Greek scientific scheme now imbued with religious significance. In the minds of Dante and his contemporaries, astronomy and theology were inextricably conjoined, and the cultural ramifications of this cosmological synthesis were profound: for if any essential physical change were to be introduced into that system by future astronomers—such as, for example, a moving Earth— the effect of a purely scientific innovation would threaten the integrity of the entire Christian cosmology. The intellectual comprehensiveness and desire for cultural universality so characteristic of the Christian mind in the high Middle Ages, bringing even the details of classical science into its fold, were leading it into directions that would later prove intensely problematic.

The Secularization of the Church and the Rise of Lay Mysticism

In the high Middle Ages, the Christian world view was still beyond question. The status of the institutional Church, however, had become considerably more controversial. Having consolidated its authority in Europe after the tenth century, the Roman papacy had gradually assumed a role of immense political influence in the affairs of Christian nations. By the thirteenth century, the Church's powers were extraordinary, with the papacy actively intervening in matters of state throughout Europe, and with enormous revenues being reaped from the faithful to support the growing magnificence of the papal court and its huge bureaucracy. By the early fourteenth century the results of such worldly success were both clear and unsettling. Christianity had become powerful but compromised.

The Church hierarchy was visibly prone to financial and political motivation. The pope's temporal sovereignty over the Papal States in Italy involved it in political and military maneuverings that repeatedly complicated the Church's spiritual self-understanding. Moreover, the Church's extravagant financial needs were placing constantly augmented demands on the masses of devout Christians. Perhaps worst of all, the secularism and evident corruption of the papacy were causing it to lose, in the eyes of the faithful, its spiritual integrity. (Dante himself had made the distinction between spiritual merit and the ecclesiastical hierarchy, and felt compelled to consign more than one high Church official to the Inferno for betraying the Church's apostolic mission.) The very success of the Church's striving for cultural hegemony, at first spiritually motivated, was now undermining its religious foundations.

In the meantime, the secular monarchies of the European nation-states had gradually gained power and cohesion, creating a situation in which the papal claim to universal authority was inevitably leading toward serious conflict. At the height of its wealth and worldly expansiveness, the Church suddenly found itself caught up in a century of extreme institutional disruption—first with the transfer of the papacy to Avignon under French control (the "Babylonian captivity") and subsequently with the unprecedented situation of having two, and then three, popes simultaneously claiming primacy (the "Great Schism"). With the sacred papal authority so obviously at the mercy of wayward political forces, worldly pomp, and personal ambition, the Church's actual spiritual role was becoming increasingly obscured and the unity of Western Christendom dangerously threatened.

During these same years of the Church's accelerating secularization, in the late thirteenth and fourteenth centuries, an extraordinary wave of mystical fervor swept through much of Europe, especially the Rhineland, involving thousands of men and women—laypersons as well as priests, monks, and nuns. Intensely devotional, Christ-centered, and aimed at achieving a direct inner union with the divine, this religious outpouring took place largely without regard to the established structures of the Church. The Christian mystical impulse that found in Aquinas and Dante a theological expression of considerable intellectual complexity took a more purely affective and devotional character in the central European lay population. Intellectuality of great subtlety played a role here too in the person of Meister Eckhart, the movement's leading teacher, whose metaphysical vision derived philosophical support from Aquinas and Neoplatonism, and whose original formulations of the mystical experience sometimes appeared to threaten the limits of orthodoxy: "The eye with which God sees me is the eye with which I see him; my eye and his are one." Yet the impact of his widely heard sermons, and of the teachings of his disciples Johann Tauler and Heinrich Suso, was not primarily intellectual or rational but moral and religious. Above all, their concern was with direct religious illumination and a sanctified life of Christian love and service.

But with such an emphasis on internal communion with God, rather than on the need for the Church's institutionalized sacraments and collective forms of worship, the Church itself was seen as less mandatory for the spiritual enterprise. With advanced religious experience now perceived as directly available to lay people as much as to clergy, the priest and bishop were no longer regarded as necessary mediators of spiritual activity. Similarly, the relative unimportance of words and reason in the context of the soul's relationship to God made the highly rationalist development of theology and the contentious subtleties of Church doctrine seem superfluous. From the opposite side of the issue from Scholasticism, but with identical effect, reason and faith were growing ever further apart.

Of greater immediate import was the growing divergence between the ideal of Christian spirituality and the reality of the institutional Church. In the view of the new mystical preachers and lay brotherhoods, personal piety took precedence over ecclesiastical office, just as internal experience superseded external observance. The true Church, the body of Christ, was now increasingly identified with the humble souls of the faithful and the graciously illuminated, rather than with the officially sanctioned Church hierarchy. A new stress on the Bible and faith in God's Word as the basis of that true Church began to displace the institutional Church's stress on dogma and papal sovereignty. A life of renunciation and simplicity was upheld as the authentic path to God, in contrast to the life of wealth and power enjoyed by the privileged officeholders of the ecclesiastical establishment.

All of these widely experienced dichotomies suggested a potential break from the traditional structure of the medieval Church. Yet that break did not occur. Those involved were devout Christians who generally recognized no need for active rebellion against the Church. Where reform and renewal were sought, as these were by several major religious movements in the later Middle Ages, it was still generally within the existing Church framework. But a seed was sown. The life of Christ and the apostles was acknowledged as the paradigm of spiritual existence, but that life appeared to be neither represented nor mediated by the contemporary structures of the Catholic Church. And the new spiritual autonomy embraced by the Rhineland mystics, as well as by others in England and the Low Countries, tended to place the Church in a secondary role in the realm of authentic spirituality. Already at the turn of the thirteenth century, Joachim of Fiore had set forth his influential mystical vision of history as divided into three eras of increasing spirituality—the Age of the Father (the Old Testament), the Age of the Son (the New Testament and Church), and a coming Age of the Spirit, when the whole world would be suffused with the divine and the institutional Church would no longer be necessary.

With the new emphasis given to the individual's direct and private relation to God, the elaborate institutional forms and regulations of the Church were devalued at the same moment that the secularization of the Church made its spiritual mission appear increasingly open to question. As the medieval era reached its final stages, the earnest cries for reform, always present in Church history, found strong voice in a growing diversity of figures—Dante, Marsilius of Padua, Dietrich of Niem, John Wycliffe, Jan Hus—and became, from the hierarchy's perspective, ever more heretical in character.

Critical Scholasticism and Ockham's Razor

While one cultural stream, represented by the new lay mysticism, moved toward religious autonomy, the Scholastic stream continued its remarkable development of the Western intellect under Aristotle's tutelage. And if the Church's spiritual role was now ambiguous, its intellectual role was no less so. On the one hand, the Church was supporting the whole academic enterprise in the universities, where Christian doctrine was explicated with unprecedentedly rigorous logical method and increasingly greater scope. On the other hand, it attempted to keep that enterprise under control, either by condemnation and suppression, or by giving doctrinal status to certain innovations such as those of Aquinas—as if to say, "This far and no further." But within this ambivalent atmosphere, the Scholastic inquiry went on, with increasingly weighty implications.

The Church had largely accepted Aristotle. But the culture's new interest in Aristotle did not stop with the study of his writings, for that interest signified a broader, and ever-broadening, interest in the natural world and a growing confidence in the power of human reason. Aristotelianism in the late Middle Ages was more symptom than cause of the developing scientific spirit in Europe. Already Scholastics in England such as Robert Grosseteste and his pupil Roger Bacon were performing concrete scientific experiments (moved in part by esoteric traditions such as alchemy and astrology), applying the mathematical principles held supreme by the Platonic tradition to the observation of the physical world recommended by Aristotle. This new focus on direct experience and reasoning was beginning to undermine the Church's exclusive investment in the authoritativeness of the ancient texts—now Aristotelian as well as biblical and patristic. Aristotle was being questioned on his own terms, in specifics if not in overall authority. Some of his principles were compared with experience and found lacking, logical fallacies in his proofs were pinpointed, and the corpus of his works was subjected to minute examination.

The Scholastics' exhaustive critical discussions of Aristotle and their often shrewd suggestions of alternative hypotheses were forging a new intellectual spirit, increasingly perceptive, skeptical, and open to fundamental change. In particular, their probings were creating an intellectual climate that not only encouraged a more empirical, mechanistic, and quantitative view of nature, but would in time more easily accommodate the radical shift of view necessary for the conception of a moving Earth. By the fourteenth century, a leading Scholastic such as the Parisian scholar and bishop Nicole d'Oresme could defend the theoretical possibility of a rotating Earth (even while personally rejecting it), out of sheer logical vigor proposing ingenious arguments against Aristotle concerning optical relativity and falling bodies—arguments that would later be used by Copernicus and Galileo to support the heliocentric theory. To solve difficulties presented by Aristotle's theory of projectile motion, Oresme's teacher, Jean Buridan, developed an impetus theory, applying it to both celestial and terrestrial phenomena, which would lead directly to Galileo's mechanics and Newton's first law of motion.[7]

Aristotle continued to provide the terminology, the logical method, and the increasingly empiricist spirit of the developing Scholastic philosophy. But ironically, it was Aristotle's very authority that, by inviting such intense examination, was contributing to his eventual overthrow. And it was the meticulous and energetic attempt to synthesize Aristotelian science with the indubitable tenets of Christian revelation that was bringing forth all the critical intelligence that would ultimately turn against both the ancient and the ecclesiastical authorities. In retrospect, Aquinas's *summa* had been one of the final steps of the medieval mind toward full intellectual independence.

>-✕-<

This new autonomy was portentously asserted in the fourteenth century in the paradoxical figure of William of Ockham, a man at once strangely modern and yet altogether medieval. A British philosopher and priest born soon after Aquinas's death, Ockham looked at matters with the same passion for rational precision as Aquinas, but arrived at sharply different conclusions. In the service of upholding Christian revelation, he employed both a highly developed logical method and an augmented empiricism. Yet in the wake of the Church's condemnation of the Parisian secularists, Ockham strove above all to limit the presumed competence of the natural human reason to grasp universal truths. Although his intentions were entirely to the contrary, Ockham proved to be the pivotal thinker in the late medieval movement toward the modern outlook. And although the modern mind itself would largely dismiss the intellectual conflicts that concerned him as the insignificant quibblings of a decadent and overwrought Scholasticism, it would be precisely those recondite conceptual battles that had to be fought before modern thought could establish its radical revision of human knowledge and the natural world.

The central principle of Ockham's thought, and the most consequential, was his denial of the reality of universals outside of the human mind and human language. Driving Aristotle's stress on the ontological primacy of concrete particulars over Platonic Forms to its logical extreme, Ockham argued that nothing existed except individual beings, that only concrete experience could serve as a basis for knowledge, and that universals existed not as entities external to the mind but only as mental concepts. In the last analysis, what was real was the particular thing outside the mind, not the mind's concept of that thing. Since all knowledge had to be based on the real, and since all real existence was that of individual beings, then knowledge must be of particulars. Human concepts possessed no metaphysical foundation beyond concrete particulars, and there existed no necessary correspondence between words and things. Ockham thereby gave new force and vitality to the philosophical position of nominalism (in its conceptualist version), which held that universals were only names or mental concepts and not real entities. Roscellinus had argued a similar position in the eleventh century, but it was from the time of Ockham that nominalism would play a central role in the evolution of the Western mind.

In the generation before Ockham, another prominent Scholastic known as the "subtle doctor," Duns Scotus, had already modified classical Form theories in the direction of the concrete individual by asserting that each particular had its own individual "thisness" (*haeccitas*), which possessed a positive reality of its own apart from the particular's participation in the universal—or, more precisely, apart from its sharing in a common nature. This added formal quality of individuation Scotus saw as necessary to allow the individual an intelligibility on its own terms, apart from its universal form (otherwise the individual in itself would be unintelligible, perhaps even to the divine mind). He also saw this principle of individuation as a necessary recognition of the individual human free will and especially of God's freedom to choose how he created each individual, rather than God's or man's being bound by the determinism of eternally fixed universals and necessary emanations from the First Cause. These modifications away from fixed universals and determinism in turn encouraged attention to observation and experiment—i.e., to study the unpredictable creation of a free God—and heightened the distinction between rational philosophy and religious truth.

But whereas Scotus, like most of his predecessors back to Augustine, had assumed a direct and real correspondence between human concept and metaphysical existent, Ockham denied that correspondence altogether. Only concrete individual beings were real, and common natures (Scotus), intelligible species (Aquinas and Aristotle), or transcendent Forms (Plato) were conceptual fictions derived from that primary reality. A universal for Ockham was a term signifying some conceptualized aspect of a real, concrete individual being, and did not constitute a metaphysical entity in itself. A separate, independent order of reality populated by universals or Forms was expressly denied. Ockham thus moved to eliminate the last vestige of Platonic Forms in Scholastic thought: Only the particular existed, and any inference about real universals, whether transcendent or immanent, was spurious. So often and with such force did Ockham use the philosophical principle that "entities are not to be multiplied beyond necessity" (*non sunt multiplicanda entia praeter necessitatem*) that the principle came to be known as "Ockham's razor."[8]

Hence, according to Ockham, universals exist only in the human mind, not in reality. They are concepts abstracted by the mind on the basis of its empirical observations of more or less similar individuals. They are not God's pre-existing Ideas governing his creation of individuals, for God was absolutely free to create anything in any way he pleased. Only his creatures exist, not Ideas of creatures. For Ockham, the issue was no longer the metaphysical question as to how ephemeral individuals came from real transcendent Forms, but the epistemological question as to how abstract universal concepts came from real individuals. "Man" as a species signified not a distinct real entity in itself, but a shared similarity in many individual human beings as recognized by the mind. It was a mental abstraction, not a real entity. The problem of universals was therefore a matter of epistemology, grammar, and logic—not of metaphysics or ontology.

Ockham, again following leads established by Scotus, also denied the possibility of moving from a rational apprehension of the facts of this world to any necessary conclusions about God or other religious matters.

The world was utterly contingent on God's omnipotent and indefinable will. Hence man's only certainty derived from direct sensory observation or from self-evident logical propositions, not from rational speculations about invisible realities and universal essences. Because God was free to create or determine things according to his will, any human claim to certain knowledge of the cosmos as a rationally ordered expression of transcendent essences was altogether relativized. God could have created things in any way he arbitrarily wished, without the use of intermediaries such as the celestial intelligences of Aristotelianism and Thomism. There were two realities given to man: the reality of God, given by revelation, and the reality of the empirical world, given by direct experience. Beyond those, or between them, man could not legitimately claim cognitive access, and without revelation he could not know of God. Man could not empirically experience God in the same way he could the material object in front of him. Since all human knowledge was founded on the sensory intuition of concrete particulars, something beyond the senses, such as the existence of God, could only be revealed by faith, it could not be known by reason. The concept of an absolute divine being was only a subjective human construction, and could not therefore serve as a secure foundation for theological reasoning.

In Ockham's understanding, the determinism and necessary causes of Greek philosophy and science, which Aquinas sought to integrate with Christian faith, placed arbitrary limits on God's infinitely free creation, and this Ockham vigorously opposed. Such a philosophy failed to recognize the real limits of human rationality. For Ockham, all knowledge of nature arose solely from what comes through the senses. Reason was a powerful tool, but its power lay only in relation to the empirical encounter with the concrete facts of "positive" reality. The human mind possessed no divine light, as Aquinas taught, by which the active intellect could move beyond the senses to a valid universal judgment grounded in absolute being. Neither the mind nor the world could be said to be ordered in such a coherently interconnected fashion that the mind knows the world by means of real universals that govern both knower and known. Because only particulars demonstrably exist, and not any transcendent relation or coherence between them, speculative reason and metaphysics lacked any real foundation.

Without interior illumination or some other means of epistemological certainty such as Aquinas's light of the active intellect, a newly skeptical attitude toward human knowledge was both inevitable and mandatory.

Since only direct evidence of individual existents provided a basis for knowledge, and since those existents were contingent on a divine omnipotence that knew no determined bounds to its creative activity—anything was possible for God—then human knowledge was limited to the contingent and empirical, and was, finally, not necessary and universal knowledge at all. God's will was not limited by the structures of human rationality, for his absolute volitional freedom and omnipotence could allow him to make what was evil good, and vice versa, if he so wished. There was no mandatory relation between God's freely created universe and the human desire for a world of rational intelligibility. At best, only arguments of probability were legitimate. The human mind could make strict logical demonstrations on the basis of immediate experience, but that experience, being contingent on God's free will, necessarily relativized the absolute certainty of the logic. And because Ockham's ontology was exclusively of concrete individuals, the empirical world had to be viewed from an exclusively physical standpoint. The metaphysical organizing principles of Aristotle or Plato could not be derived from immediate experience.

Ockham therefore attacked the earlier Scholastics' speculative theological rationalism as inappropriate to logic and science (employing unverifiable and superfluous entities like the Forms to explain individual beings), and dangerous to religion (presuming to know God's reasons or to put limits of order and intermediate causes onto his direct free creation, while elevating pagan metaphysics vis-à-vis Christian faith). He thereby severed the unity so painstakingly constructed by Aquinas. For Ockham, there was one truth described by Christian revelation, which was both beyond doubt and beyond rational comprehension, and there was another truth comprising the observable particular facts described by empirical science and rational philosophy. The two truths were not necessarily continuous.

In a sense, Ockham both opposed and fulfilled the secularistic movement of the previous century. He forcefully proclaimed a new form of the double-truth universe, with a religious truth and a scientific truth, effectively cutting the link between theology and philosophy. But the earlier secularists had argued for such a division because they were unwilling to restrict Greek and Arabic philosophy to a subordinate position when it conflicted with Christian belief. Ockham, by contrast, wished to preserve the preeminence of Christian doctrine—especially God's absolute freedom and omnipotence as Creator—by firmly defining the limits of the natural reason. In doing so, however, Ockham negated Aquinas's confidence that God's creation would be warmly open to human efforts at universal understanding. For both Aquinas and Ockham, the human mind had to accommodate its intellectual aspirations to the fact that God's reality and man's rational knowledge were infinitely distant from each other. But where Aquinas left room for a rational knowledge that approached the divine mystery and enhanced theological understanding, Ockham saw the necessity of defining a more absolute limit. A positivist reason could be carefully and modestly employed in approaching the empirical world, but only revelation could illuminate the greater realities of God's will, his creation, and his gratuitously bestowed salvation. There was no humanly intelligible continuity between the empirical and the divine.

Ockham's logical rigor was matched by his moral rigor. Against the worldly magnificence of the Avignon papacy, he endorsed a life of total poverty for true Christian spiritual perfection, following the example of Jesus, the apostles, and Francis of Assisi. For Ockham was himself a fervent Franciscan, whose religious conviction moved him even to risk excommunication by the pope if the latter's policies seemed to conflict with Christian truth. In a series of fateful encounters with the papacy, Ockham not only upheld radical poverty against the secular wealth of the ecclesiastical hierarchy, he also defended the right of the English king to tax Church property (as Jesus, in "rendering unto Caesar," had submitted to temporal authority), condemned the Church's infringement on individual Christian freedom, denied the legitimacy of papal infallibility, and outlined the various circumstances in which a pope could be rightfully deposed. In the personal drama between Ockham and the Church were foreshadowings of an epochal drama to come.

But it was on the philosophical level that Ockham's impact was to be most immediately potent, for in his emphatic assertion of nominalism, the growing medieval tension between reason and faith began to snap. Paradoxically, the very intensity of Ockham's allegiance to God's omnipotent freedom, combined with his acute sense of logical precision, led him to formulate a philosophical position remarkable for its modernity. In Ockham's view, one could not assume that man's mind and God's were fundamentally connected. Empiricism and reason could give a limited knowledge of the world in its particulars, but no certain knowledge of God, for which only God's Word could be a source. Revelation offered certainty, but could be affirmed only through faith and grace, not through natural reason. Reason should rightly focus on nature rather than God, because only nature provided the senses with concrete data upon which reason could ground its knowledge.

Ockham left no bridge between human reason and divine revelation, between what man knows and what he believes. Yet his uncompromising emphasis on the individual concrete things of this world, his trust in the power of human reason and logic to ascertain necessary entities and to differentiate evidence and degrees of probability, and his skeptical attitude toward traditional and institutionally sanctioned ways of thinking all directly encouraged the scientific enterprise. Indeed, from such a dualistic starting point, science could be free to develop along its own lines with less fear of potential doctrinal contradiction—at least until the entire cosmology was called into question. It was not accidental that both Buridan and Oresme, two of the most original scientific thinkers of the late Middle Ages, worked in the Parisian nominalist school in which Ockham had been a central influence. Although Ockham's interests lay principally in philosophy rather than natural science, his elimination of the fixed correspondence between human concept and metaphysical reality, and his assertion that all genuine existence was individual existence, helped open the physical world to fresh analysis. Now direct contact with concrete particulars could overcome the metaphysical mediation by abstract universals. Significantly, as the alliance of nominalism and empiricism represented in Ockham's ideas spread through the universities in the fourteenth century (despite papal censure), Ockham's way of philosophy was known as the *via moderna*, in contrast to Aquinas's and Scotus's *via antiqua*. The traditional Scholastic enterprise, committed to joining faith with reason, was coming to an end.

Thus with the fourteenth century, the long-assumed metaphysical unity of concept and being began to break down. The assumption that the human mind knows things by intellectually grasping their inherent forms—whether through interior illumination by transcendent Ideas, as in Plato and Augustine, or through the active intellect's abstraction of immanent universals from sense-perceived particulars, as in Aristotle and Aquinas—was now challenged. In the absence of that basic epistemological presupposition, the ambitiously comprehensive systems constructed by the thirteenth-century Scholastics were no longer possible. With the displacement of abstract speculation by empirical evidence as the basis of knowledge, the earlier metaphysical systems seemed increasingly implausible. The underlying medieval world view—Christian and Aristotelian—continued intact, but new, more critical interpretations now arose, thereby undoing the earlier synthesis and engendering a new intellectual pluralism. In many matters, probability replaced certainty, as empiricism, grammar, and logic began to supersede metaphysics.

Ockham's vision prefigured the path subsequently taken by the Western mind. For just as he believed the Church must be politically separated from the secular world for the integrity and rightful freedom of both, so he believed God's reality must be theologically distinguished from empirical reality. Only thus would Christian truth preserve its transcendent sacrosanctness, and only thus would the world's nature be properly comprehended on its own terms, in its full particularity and contingency. Herein lay the embryonic foundations—epistemological and metaphysical as well as religious and political—for coming changes in the Western world view to be wrought by the Reformation, the Scientific Revolution, and the Enlightenment.

>+✕+<

And so it was that just as the medieval vision had attained its consummation in the work of Aquinas and Dante, the altogether different spirit of a new epoch began to arise, propelled by the very forces that had achieved the earlier synthesis. The great medieval masterworks had culminated an intellectual development that was starting to break into new territories, even if that meant stepping out of the Church's established structure of education and belief. But Ockham's precocious modernism was still ahead of its time. Paradoxically, the culture of this new era would receive its major initiating impulse not from the line of medieval Scholasticism, natural science, and Aristotle, but from the other pole of classical Humanism, belles lettres, and a revived Plato. For just as Aquinas had his contrasting philosophical successor in Ockham, so did Dante have his contrasting literary successor in Petrarch, born in the same decade Dante began writing *La Divina Commedia,* at the start of the fourteenth century.

The Rebirth of Classical Humanism

Petrarch

It was a pivotal moment in Western cultural history when Petrarch looked back on the thousand years since the decline of ancient Rome and experienced that entire period as a decline of human greatness itself, a diminishment of literary and moral excellence, a "dark" age. In contrast to this impoverishment, Petrarch beheld the immense cultural wealth of Greco-Roman civilization, a seeming golden age of creative genius and human expansiveness. For centuries, medieval schoolmen had been gradually rediscovering and integrating the ancient works, but now Petrarch radically shifted the focus and tone of that integration. Instead of Scholasticism's concern with logic, science, and Aristotle, and with the constant imperative of Christianizing the pagan conceptions, Petrarch and his followers saw value in all the literary classics of antiquity—poetry, essays, letters, histories and biographies, philosophy in the form of elegant Platonic dialogues rather than dry Aristotelian treatises—and embraced these on their own terms, not as needing Christian modification, but as noble and inspirational just as they stood in the radiance of classical civilization. Ancient culture was a source not just for scientific knowledge and rules for logical discourse, but for the deepening and enrichment of the human spirit. The classical texts provided a new foundation for the appreciation of man; classical scholarship constituted the "humanities." Petrarch set about the task of finding and absorbing the great works of ancient culture—Virgil and Cicero, Horace and Livy, Homer and Plato—not just to inculcate a sterile imitation of the past masters, but to instill in himself the same moral and imaginative fire that they had so superbly expressed. Europe had forgotten its noble classical heritage, and Petrarch called for its recollection. A new sacred history was being established, a Greco-Roman testament to be placed alongside the Judaeo-Christian.

Thus Petrarch began the reeducation of Europe. Direct intercourse with the great masters of Latin and Greek literature was to be the key to the radical expansion of the contemporary European mind. Not just Christian theology but classical *litterae humaniores* could now be recognized as a source of spiritual insight and moral development. While Church learning had become increasingly intellectualized and abstract, Petrarch felt the need for a learning that would better reflect the conflicts and vagaries of man's emotional and imaginative depths. Rather than doctrinal formulae for describing man and clerical austerities for educating him, Petrarch turned to undogmatic introspection and observation for his insights into the human condition, and a full life of literature and action, as well as monastic solitude, for his education. *Studia humanitatis* were differentiated from, and elevated to the level of, *studia divinitatis*. Now, under the revived classical model, poetry and rhetoric, style, eloquence, and persuasiveness again became worthy ends in themselves, the necessary accompaniments of moral power. For Petrarch, grace and clarity of literary expression reflected grace and clarity of the soul. In the slow, meticulous labor of working with words and ideas, in the sensitive exploration of each nuance of emotion and perception, the literary discipline became a spiritual discipline, a striving for artistic perfection that demanded a parallel perfecting of the soul.

While Dante's sensibility had in a sense culminated and summed up the medieval era, Petrarch's looked forward to and impelled a future age, bringing a rebirth of culture, creativity, and human greatness. While Dante's poetic work was done in the reverent spirit of the anonymous artisans and craftsmen who built the medieval cathedrals, inspired by God and created for his greater glory, Petrarch's work was motivated by a new spirit, inspired by the ancients and created for the enrichment and greater glory of man himself, the noble center of God's creation. While Dante and the Scholastics were focused on theological precision and scientific knowledge of the natural world, Petrarch was instead engaged by the depths and complexities of his own consciousness. Rather than spiritual and scientific system building, his focus was psychological, humanist, and aesthetic.

Not that Petrarch was unspiritual or even unorthodox; in the end, his Christianity was as devout and firmly rooted as his classicism. Augustine was as important as Virgil for Petrarch, and like all the other notable synthesizers of the two traditions, he believed Christianity to be the divine fulfillment of the classical promise. Petrarch's highest ideal was *docta pietas*, learned piety. Piety was Christian, directed to God, yet learning enhanced that piety, and learning derived from knowledge of the ancient classics. The two streams—Christianity and classical culture—formed a deep harmony, and man achieved a larger spiritual vision when he drank from both. In Petrarch's view, when Cicero spoke of "one single God as the governor and maker of all things," he did so "not in a merely philosophical but in an almost Catholic manner of phrasing it, so that sometimes you would think you were hearing not a pagan philosopher but an apostle."

What was new in the late Middle Ages was not any lack of spirituality in Petrarch, but rather the overall character of his approach to human life. The demands of his religious temperament were in continuous creative battle with his desire for romantic and sensuous love, for secular activity in diplomatic and courtly circles, for literary greatness and personal glory. It was this new self-reflective awareness of human life's richness and multidimensionality, and his recognition of a kindred spirit in the great writers of antiquity, that made Petrarch the first man of the Renaissance.

The Return of Plato

Inspired by Petrarch's call, large numbers of scholars took up the search for the lost manuscripts of antiquity. Whatever they discovered was then carefully collated, edited, and translated to provide as accurate and substantial a basis as possible for their humanistic mission. This activity coincided with more frequent contacts with the Byzantine world, which had preserved much of the Greek heritage intact, and whose scholars started leaving Constantinople for the West under the threat of the Turkish invasion. Western scholars began to study and master the Greek language, and there soon arrived in Italy the Greek *Dialogues* of Plato, the *Enneads* of Plotinus, and other major works of the Platonic tradition and classical Greek culture.

The West's sudden access to these writings precipitated a Platonic revival not unlike the earlier rediscovery of Aristotle. Platonism, of course, had permeated Christian thought in the West from the earliest years of the Middle Ages, passed on first by Augustine and Boethius, and later through the ninth-century philosopher John Scotus Erigena and his translation of and commentaries on the works of Dionysius the Areopagite. Platonism was revivified in the schools at Chartres and Saint-Victor in the twelfth-century renascence, and was plainly visible in the mystical philosophy of Meister Eckhart. Even the high Scholastic tradition of Albertus and Aquinas, although necessarily focused on the challenge of integrating Aristotle, was nevertheless still deeply Platonic in disposition. But this had always been an indirect Plato, highly Christianized, modified through Augustine and the other Church fathers: a Plato known from afar, largely untranslated, passed on by digests and references in another language and mind-set and seldom in his own words. Petrarch himself, eager for a Platonic revival on the basis of allusions in Cicero and Augustine, did not in the fourteenth century have the necessary translators. The recovery of the original Greek works was a fresh revelation for fifteenth-century Western Europe, and Humanists such as Marsilio Ficino and Pico della Mirandola devoted themselves wholeheartedly to the transmission of this stream to their contemporaries.

The Platonic tradition provided the Humanists with a philosophical basis highly compatible with their own intellectual habits and aspirations. Rather than the syllogistic hairsplitting and cerebral abstractness of the later Scholastics in the universities, Platonism offered a richly textured tapestry of imaginative depth and spiritual exaltation. The notion that beauty was an essential component in the search for the ultimate reality, that imagination and vision were more significant in that quest than logic and dogma, that man could attain a direct knowledge of things divine—such ideas held much attraction for the new sensibility growing in Europe. Moreover, Plato's dialogues were themselves refined literary masterpieces, not the stodgy treatises of the Aristotelian-Scholastic tradition, and thus appealed to the Humanists' passion for rhetorical eloquence and aesthetic persuasiveness.

Both Aristotle and Aquinas had been rigidified by the late Scholastics, losing much of their allure for the new Humanists. Late Scholasticism thrived in an academic atmosphere marked by qualities that often exaggerated to the point of caricature Aquinas's almost superhuman intellectual precision and analytical rigor. The open-ended intellectual curiosity displayed by Aristotle and Aquinas in their own times had produced bodies of thought that were eventually transformed by their respectful successors into closed, complete, and inflexible systems. The very success and breadth of Aquinas's work left little for his followers to do but replow the same ground. A too reverential awe of the master's words inevitably lessened the possibility of creative scholarship. Even where conflict and criticism existed, as between Thomists, Scotists, and Ockhamists, the Scholastic dialogue seemed to outsiders to have degenerated into ceaseless argument over sterile subtleties. The *via moderna* initiated by Ockham was especially prone to such minute controversy, where the search for terminological accuracy and the concern with formal logic displaced the *via antiqua*'s interest in metaphysical comprehensiveness. And after the brilliance of Ockham, Buridan, Oresme, and their contemporaries in the fourteenth century, the *via moderna* itself had lost much of its original impetus. By the fifteenth century, Scholasticism's intellectual nerve was failing. The influx of the Platonic tradition thus signified a fresh and expansive wind revitalizing European thought. With the universities trapped in a backwater of intellectual orthodoxy, a Platonic Academy was founded in Florence in the second half of the fifteenth century, under the patronage of Cosimo de Medici and the leadership of Ficino, and this became the flourishing center of the Platonic revival.

In Platonism and Neoplatonism the Humanists discovered a non-Christian spiritual tradition possessing a religious and ethical profundity seemingly comparable to that of Christianity itself. The Neoplatonic corpus implied the existence of a universal religion, of which Christianity was perhaps the ultimate but not the only manifestation. Erasmus, pressing further the spirit of Petrarch's view of Cicero, wrote of his difficulty in refraining from praying to Socrates as to a saint. The Humanists' suddenly expanded reading lists gave evidence of a tradition of learning, of intellectual, spiritual, and imaginative insight, that found expression not only in the classical Greeks but throughout civilized history—in the Hermetic corpus, in Zoroastrian oracles, in the Hebrew Kaballah, in Babylonian and Egyptian texts—a cross-cultural revelation that bespoke a Logos that manifested itself continually and universally.

With the influx of this tradition came a new vision of man, nature, and the divine. Neoplatonism, based on Plotinus's conception of the world as an emanation from the transcendent One, portrayed nature as permeated by divinity, a noble expression of the World Soul. Stars and planets, light, plants, even stones possessed a numinous dimension. Neoplatonist Humanists declared the light of the Sun to be the light of God, as Christ was the light of the world, with all of creation thereby bathed in divinity and with the Sun itself, the source of light and life, possessing divine attributes. The ancient Pythagorean vision of a universe ordered according to transcendent mathematical forms received an intense renewal of interest, and promised to reveal nature as permeated by a mystical intelligence whose language was number and geometry. The garden of the world was again enchanted, with magical powers and transcendent meanings implicit in every part of nature.

The Humanists' Neoplatonic conception of man was equally exalted. Possessing a divine spark, man was capable of discovering within himself the image of the infinite deity. He was a noble microcosm of the divine macrocosm. Ficino asserted in his *Platonic Theology* that man not only was "the vicar of God" in the great extent of his earthly powers, but was of "almost the same genius as the Author of the heavens" in the range of his intelligence. The devoutly Christian Ficino even went on to praise man's soul for being capable "by means of the intellect and will, as by those twin Platonic wings . . . of becoming in a sense all things, and even a god."

With man now attaining, in the light of the revivified classical past, a new consciousness of his noble role in the universe, a new sense of history arose as well. The Humanists embraced the ancient Greco-Roman conception of history as cyclical, rather than only linear as in the traditional Judaeo-Christian vision; they saw their own period as a rebirth out of the barbarian darkness of the Middle Ages, a return to ancient glory, the dawn of another golden age. In the vision of the Neoplatonic Humanists, this world was not so fallen as it had been for Moses or Augustine, and neither was man.

Perhaps the young and brilliant Pico della Mirandola best summed up this new spirit of religious syncretism, broad scholarship, and optimistic reclamation of man's potential divinity. In 1486, at the age of twenty-three, Pico announced his intention to defend nine hundred theses derived from various Greek, Latin, Hebrew, and Arabic writers, invited scholars from all over Europe to Rome for a public disputation, and composed for the event his celebrated *Oration on the Dignity of Man*. In it Pico described the Creation using both Genesis and the *Timaeus* as initial sources, but then went further: When God had completed the creation of the world as a sacred temple of his divine wisdom, he at last considered the creation of man, whose role would be to reflect on, admire, and love the immense grandeur of God's work. But God found he had no archetypes remaining with which to make man, and he therefore said to his last creation:

Neither an established place, nor a form belonging to you alone, nor any special function have We given to you, O Adam, and for this reason, that you may have and possess, according to your desire and judgment, whatever place, whatever form, and whatever functions you shall desire. The nature of other creatures, which has been determined, is confined within the bounds prescribed by Us. You, who are confined by no limits, shall determine for yourself your own nature, in accordance with your own free will, in whose hand I have placed you. I have set you at the center of the world, so that from there you may more easily survey whatever is in the world. We have made you neither heavenly nor earthly, neither mortal nor immortal, so that, more freely and more honorably the molder and maker of yourself, you may fashion yourself in whatever form you shall prefer. You shall be able to descend among the lower forms of being, which are brute beasts; you shall be able to be reborn out of the judgment of your own soul into the higher beings, which are divine.[9]

To man had been given freedom, mutability, and the power of self-transformation: thus Pico affirmed that, in the ancient mysteries, man had been symbolized as the great mythic figure of Prometheus. God had bestowed to man the ability to determine freely his position in the universe, even to the point of ascending to full union with the supreme God. The classical Greeks' sense of man's own glory, of man's intellectual powers and capacity for spiritual elevation seemingly uncontaminated by a biblical Original Sin, was now emerging anew in the breast of Western man.

The new mode of attaining knowledge of the universe was different as well. Imagination now rose to the highest position on the epistemological spectrum, unrivaled in its capacity to render metaphysical truth. Through the disciplined use of imagination man could bring to his consciousness those transcendent living Forms that ordered the universe. Thus could the mind recover its own deepest organization and reunite itself with the cosmos. In contrast to the Scholastics, with their increasing empiricism and concretism, the Neoplatonic Humanists saw archetypal meaning in each concrete fact, used myths as vehicles for communicating metaphysical and psychological insights, and were ever observant for the hidden significance of things.

Following Neoplatonism's integration of astrology and inclusion of the pagan gods in the hierarchy of reality, Renaissance Humanists began employing the pantheon of planetary deities as modes of imaginative discourse. Prominent Scholastics such as the fourteenth-century nominalist Oresme had opposed astrologers' predictive claims, but with the Humanists' influence astrology again flourished—in the Florentine Academy, in royal courts and aristocratic circles, in the Vatican. The Judaeo-Christian God still reigned supreme, but the Greco-Roman gods and goddesses were now given new life and value in the scheme of things. Horoscopes abounded, and references to the planetary powers and zodiacal symbols became ubiquitous. It is true that mythology, astrology, and esotericism had never been absent from even orthodox medieval culture: allegories and artistic images, the planetary names for the days of the week, the classification of the elements and humors, and many other aspects of the liberal arts and sciences all reflected their continuing presence. But now they were rediscovered in a new light that served to revivify their classical status. The gods regained a sacred dignity, their forms portrayed in paintings and sculptures with a beauty and sensuousness resembling that of the ancient images. Classical mythology began to be regarded as the noble religious truth of those who lived before Christ, as a theology in itself, so that its study became another form of *docta pietas*. The pagan Venus, goddess of beauty, was restored as the symbol of spiritual beauty, an archetype in the divine Mind that mediated the soul's awakening to divine love—and as such could be identified as an alternative manifestation of the Virgin Mary. Platonic images and doctrines were reconceived in Christian terms, the Greek deities and daimones seen as Christian angels, Socrates's teacher in the *Symposium*, Diotima, recognized as inspired by the Holy Spirit. A flexible syncretism was emerging, encompassing diverse traditions and perspectives, with Platonism espoused as a new gospel.

Thus while Scholasticism had energetically forwarded the rational mind in the Aristotelian tradition, and while the evangelical orders and Rhineland mystics had nurtured the spiritual heart in the primitive Christian tradition, Humanism now evoked the imaginative intelligence of the Platonic tradition, all of these developments directed in their different ways toward reestablishing man's relation to the divine. Humanism gave man new dignity, nature new meaning, and Christianity new dimensions—and yet less absoluteness. Indeed, man, nature, and the classical heritage were all divinized in the Humanist perception, which provoked a radical expansion of human vision and activity far beyond the medieval horizon, threatening the old order in ways the Humanists did not fully anticipate.

For with the rediscovery of such a sophisticated and viable yet non-Christian spiritual tradition, the absolute uniqueness of the Christian revelation was relativized and the Church's spiritual authority implicitly undermined. Moreover, the Humanists' celebration of interiority and the riches of the individual human imagination overstepped the dogmatic bounds of the Church's traditional forms of spirituality, which abjured an unrestrained private imagination as dangerous in favor of institutionally defined ritual, prayer, and meditation on the mysteries of Christian doctrine. Similarly, Neoplatonism's assertion of the immanent divinity of all nature confronted the orthodox Judaeo-Christian tendency to uphold God's absolute transcendence, his utterly unique divinity which was revealed only in special places like Mount Sinai or Golgotha in a distant biblical past. And especially disturbing were the polytheistic implications of Neoplatonic Humanist writings, in which references to Venus, Saturn, or Prometheus seemed to signify something more than allegorical conveniences.

Equally uncongenial to conservative theologians was the Neoplatonic belief in the uncreated divine spark in man, whereby divine genius could overtake the human personality and exalt man to the summits of spiritual illumination and creative power. While this conception, as well as the ancient polytheistic mythologies, provided a foundation and stimulus for the emerging Renaissance artistic genius (Michelangelo, for example, was Ficino's student in Florence), it also undercut the Church's traditional limitation of divinity to God alone and to the sacramental institutions of the Church. The elevation of man to a God-like status, as described by Ficino and Pico, seemed to contravene the more strictly defined orthodox Christian dichotomy between Creator and creature, and the doctrine of the Fall. Pico's statement in the *Oratio* to the effect that man could freely determine his being at any level of the cosmos, including union with God, without any mention of a mediating savior, could easily be interpreted as a heretical breach of the established sacred hierarchy.

It is not surprising, then, that a papal commission condemned several of Pico's propositions, or that the pope forbade the international public assembly Pico had planned. Yet the Church hierarchy in Rome largely tolerated and even embraced the classical revival, especially as men like the Florentine Medici made their way into papal power and began using Church resources to underwrite the enormous artistic masterworks of the Renaissance (establishing indulgences, for example, to help pay for them). The Renaissance popes were sufficiently enamored of the new cultural movement, with its classical and secular enrichments of life, that the Church's spiritual guardianship of the larger body of Christian souls often seemed altogether neglected. It was the Reformation that would recognize all the infringements on orthodox Christian dogma that the Humanist movement was encouraging—nature as immanent divinity, pagan sensuousness and polytheism, human deification, universal religion—and would therefore call a halt to the Renaissance's Hellenization of Christianity. Yet the Protestants would simultaneously build on those same Humanists' criticisms of the Church and demands for spiritual and institutional reform. The new religious sensibility of the Humanists revitalized the spiritual life of Western culture just as it was decaying under the secularization of the Church and the extreme rationalism of the late medieval universities. Yet by emphasizing Hellenic and trans-Christian religious values, it was also to provoke a purist Judaeo-Christian reaction against this pagan intrusion into the traditional sacrosanct religion based solely on biblical revelation.

The scientific ramifications of the Platonic revival were no less significant than the religious. The Humanists' anti-Aristotelianism strengthened the culture's movement toward intellectual independence from the increasingly dogmatic authority of the Aristotelian tradition dominating the universities. More particularly, the influx of the Pythagorean theory of mathematics, in which quantitative measurement of the world could reveal a numinous order emanating from the supreme intelligence, would directly inspire Copernicus and his successors through Galileo and Newton in their efforts to penetrate nature's mysteries. Neoplatonist mathematics, added to the rationalism and nascent empiricism of the late Scholastics, provided one of the final components necessary for the emergence of the Scientific Revolution. It was Copernicus's and Kepler's tenacious Neoplatonic faith that the visible universe conformed to and was illuminated by simple, precise, and elegant mathematical forms that impelled them to overthrow the complex and increasingly unworkable geocentric system of Ptolemaic astronomy.

The development of the Copernican hypothesis was also influenced by the Neoplatonists' sacralization of the Sun, as celebrated by Ficino in particular. The intellectual force that Copernicus and especially Kepler brought to bear on transforming the Earth-centered universe received an important impetus from their Neoplatonic apprehension of the Sun as reflecting the central Godhead, with the other planets and the Earth revolving around it (or as Kepler put it, moving in adoration around it). Plato's *Republic* had declared that the Sun played the same role in the visible realm as did the supreme Idea of the Good in the transcendent realm. Given the boundless gifts of light, life, and warmth that emanated from the Sun, the most brilliant and creative entity in the heavens, no other body seemed equally appropriate for the role of center of the universe. Moreover, in contrast to the finite Aristotelian universe, the infinite nature of the Neoplatonic supreme Godhead, and its infinite fecundity in creation, suggested a corresponding expansion of the universe that further mediated the break from the traditional architectural structure of the medieval cosmos. Accordingly, Nicholas of Cusa, the erudite Church cardinal and Neoplatonic philosopher-mathematician of the mid-fifteenth century, proposed a moving Earth as part of a centerless (or omnicentered) infinite Neoplatonic universe.

And so the Humanists' Platonic revival extended momentously into the creation of the modern era, not only through its inspiration of the Renaissance proper—with the latter's artistic achievements, philosophical syncretism, and cult of human genius—but also through its direct and indirect consequences for the Reformation and Scientific Revolution. With the recovery of the direct sources of the Platonic line, the medieval trajectory was in a sense complete. Something like the ancient Greek balance and tension between Aristotle and Plato, between reason and imagination, immanence and transcendence, nature and spirit, external world and interior psyche, was again emerging in Western culture—a polarity further complicated and intensified by Christianity itself with its own internal dialectic. From this unstable but fertile balance would issue forth the next age.

At the Threshold

In the course of the long medieval era, a potent maturation had occurred within the Christian matrix on every front—philosophical, psychological, religious, scientific, political, artistic. By the later high Middle Ages, this development was beginning to challenge the limits of that matrix. Extraordinary social and economic growth had provided an ample basis for such cultural dynamism, which was further provoked by the consolidation of political authority by the secular monarchies in competition with that of the Church. Out of the feudal order had grown towns, guilds, leagues, states, international commerce, a new merchant class, a mobile peasantry, new contractual and legal structures, parliaments, corporate liberties, and early forms of constitutional and representative government. Important technological advances were made and disseminated. Scholarship and learning progressed, both in and out of the universities. Human experience in the West was reaching new levels of sophistication, complexity, and expansiveness.

The character of this evolution was visible on a philosophical level in Aquinas's affirmation of the human being's essential dynamic autonomy, of the natural world's ontological significance, and of the value of empirical knowledge, all as intrinsic elements in the unfolding of the divine mystery. More generally, it was evidenced in the Scholastics' long and polemical development of naturalism and rationalism, and in their encyclopedic *summae* integrating Greek philosophy and science into the Christian framework. It was visible in the unparalleled architectural achievement of the Gothic cathedrals and in Dante's great Christian epic. It was conspicuous in the early experimental science advanced by Bacon and Grosseteste, in Ockham's assertion of nominalism and the bifurcation of reason and faith, and in Buridan's and Oresme's critical advances in Aristotelian science. It could be seen in the rise of lay mysticism and private religiosity, in the new realism and romanticism in society and the arts, in the secularization of the sacred found in the celebration of redemptive *amor* by the troubadors and poets. It could be measured by the emergence of sensibilities as complex, subtle, and aesthetically refined as that of Petrarch, and especially in his articulation of a highly individualized temperament at once religious and secular in orientation. It was evident in the Humanists' revival of classical letters, their recovery of the Platonic tradition, and their establishment in Europe of an autonomous secular education for the first time since the fall of the Roman Empire. And perhaps most tellingly, that evolution was visible in the new Promethean image of man proclaimed by Pico and Ficino. A new and growing independence of spirit was everywhere apparent, expressed in often divergent but always expanding directions. Slowly, painfully, but wondrously and with ineluctable force, the Western mind was opening to a new universe.

The medieval gestation of European culture had approached a critical threshold, beyond which it would no longer be containable by the old structures. Indeed, the thousand-year maturation of the West was about to assert itself in a series of enormous cultural convulsions that would give birth to the modern world.

V

The
Modern World View

The modern world view was the outcome of an extraordinary convergence of events, ideas, and figures which, for all their conflicting variety, engendered a profoundly compelling vision of the universe and of the human being's place in it—a vision radically novel in character and paradoxical in its consequences. Those same factors also reflected, and wrought, a fundamental change in the Western character. To understand the historical emergence of the modern mind, we shall now examine the complexly intermingled cultural epochs known as the Renaissance, the Reformation, and the Scientific Revolution.

The Renaissance

The phenomenon of the Renaissance lay as much in the sheer diversity of its expressions as in their unprecedented quality. Within the span of a single generation, Leonardo, Michelangelo, and Raphael produced their masterworks, Columbus discovered the New World, Luther rebelled against the Catholic Church and began the Reformation, and Copernicus hypothesized a heliocentric universe and commenced the Scientific Revolution. Compared with his medieval predecessors, Renaissance man appeared to have suddenly vaulted into virtually superhuman status. Man was now capable of penetrating and reflecting nature's secrets, in art as well as science, with unparalleled mathematical sophistication, empirical precision, and numinous aesthetic power. He had immensely expanded the known world, discovered new continents, and rounded the globe. He could defy traditional authorities and assert a truth based on his own judgment. He could appreciate the riches of classical culture and yet also feel himself breaking beyond the ancient boundaries to reveal entirely new realms. Polyphonic music, tragedy and comedy, poetry, painting, architecture, and sculpture all achieved new levels of complexity and beauty. Individual genius and independence were widely in evidence. No domain of knowledge, creativity, or exploration seemed beyond man's reach.

With the Renaissance, human life in this world seemed to hold an immediate inherent value, an excitement and existential significance, that balanced or even displaced the medieval focus on an afterworldly spiritual destiny. Man no longer appeared so inconsequential relative to God, the Church, or nature. On many fronts, in diverse realms of human activity, Pico's proclamation of man's dignity seemed fulfilled. From its beginnings with Petrarch, Boccaccio, Bruni, and Alberti, through Erasmus, More, Machiavelli, and Montaigne, to its final expressions in Shakespeare, Cervantes, Bacon, and Galileo, the Renaissance did not cease producing new paragons of human achievement. Such a prodigious development of human consciousness and culture had not been seen since the ancient Greek miracle at the very birth of Western civilization. Western man was indeed reborn.

Yet it would be a deep misjudgment to perceive the emergence of the Renaissance as all light and splendor, for it arrived in the wake of a series of unmitigated disasters and thrived in the midst of continuous upheaval. Beginning in the mid-fourteenth century, the black plague swept through Europe and destroyed a third of the continent's population, fatally undermining the balance of economic and cultural elements that had sustained the high medieval civilization. Many believed that the wrath of God had come upon the world. The Hundred Years' War between England and France was an interminably ruinous conflict, while Italy was ravaged by repeated invasions and internecine struggles. Pirates, bandits, and mercenaries were ubiquitous. Religious strife grew to international proportions. Severe economic depression was nearly universal for decades. The universities were sclerotic. New diseases entered Europe through its ports and took their toll. Black magic and devil worship flourished, as did group flagellation, the dance of death in cemeteries, the black mass, the Inquisition, tortures and burnings at the stake. Ecclesiastical conspiracies were routine, and included such events as a papally backed assassination in front of the Florentine cathedral altar at High Mass on Easter Sunday. Murder, rape, and pillage were often daily realities, famine and pestilence annual perils. The Turkish hordes threatened to overwhelm Europe at any moment. Apocalyptic expectations abounded. And the Church itself, the West's fundamental cultural institution, seemed to many the very center of decadent corruption, its structure and purpose devoid of spiritual integrity. It was against this backdrop of massive cultural decay, violence, and death that the "rebirth" of the Renaissance took place.

As with the medieval cultural revolution several centuries earlier, technical inventions played a pivotal role in the making of the new era. Four in particular (all with Oriental precursors) had been brought into widespread use in the West by this time, with immense cultural ramifications: the magnetic compass, which permitted the navigational feats that opened the globe to European exploration; gunpowder, which contributed to the demise of the old feudal order and the ascent of nationalism; the mechanical clock, which brought about a decisive change in the human relationship to time, nature, and work, separating and freeing the structure of human activities from the dominance of nature's rhythms; and the printing press, which produced a tremendous increase in learning, made available both ancient classics and modern works to an

ever-broadening public, and eroded the monopoly on learning long held
by the clergy.

All of these inventions were powerfully modernizing and ultimately
secularizing in their effects. The artillery-supported rise of separate but
internally cohesive nation-states signified not only the overthrow of the
medieval feudal structures but also the empowerment of secular forces
against the Catholic Church. With parallel effect in the realm of
thought, the printing press allowed the rapid dissemination of new and
often revolutionary ideas throughout Europe. Without it, the Reformation would have been limited to a relatively minor theological dispute in
a remote German province, and the Scientific Revolution, with its
dependence on international communication among many scientists,
would have been altogether impossible. Moreover, the spread of the
printed word and growing literacy contributed to a new cultural ethos
marked by increasingly individual and private, noncommunal forms of
communication and experience, thereby encouraging the growth of individualism. Silent reading and solitary reflection helped free the individual from traditional ways of thinking, and from collective control of
thinking, with individual readers now having private access to a multiplicity of other perspectives and forms of experience.

Similarly progressive in its consequences was the development of the
mechanical clock, which with its precisely articulated system of wheels
and gears became the paradigm of modern machines, accelerating the
advance of mechanical invention and machine building of all kinds.
Equally important, the new mechanical triumph provided a basic conceptual model and metaphor for the new era's emerging science—indeed,
for the entire modern mind—profoundly shaping the modern view of
the cosmos and nature, of the human being, of the ideal society, even
of God. Likewise, the global explorations made possible by the magnetic compass greatly impelled intellectual innovation, reflecting and
encouraging the new scientific investigation of the natural world and
further affirming the West's sense of being at the heroic frontier of
civilized history. By unexpectedly revealing the errors and ignorance of
the ancient geographers, the discoveries of the explorers gave the modern intellect a new sense of its own competence and even superiority over
the previously unsurpassed masters of antiquity—undermining, by implication, all traditional authorities. Among these discredited geographers was Ptolemy, whose status in astronomy was therefore affected as
well. The navigational expeditions in turn required more accurate astro-

nomical knowledge and more proficient astronomers, out of whose number would emerge Copernicus. Discoveries of new continents brought new possibilities for economic and political expansion, and hence the radical transformation of European social structures. With those discoveries came also the encounter with new cultures, religions, and ways of life, introducing into the European awareness a new spirit of skeptical relativism concerning the absoluteness of its own traditional assumptions. The West's horizons—geographical, mental, social, economic, political—were changing and expanding in unprecedented ways.

Concurrent with these advances was an important psychological development in which the European character, beginning in the peculiar political and cultural atmosphere of Renaissance Italy, underwent a unique and portentous transformation. The Italian city-states of the fourteenth and fifteenth centuries—Florence, Milan, Venice, Urbino, and others—were in many ways the most advanced urban centers in Europe. Energetic commercial enterprise, a prosperous Mediterranean trade, and continual contact with the older civilizations of the East presented them with an unusually concentrated inflow of economic and cultural wealth. In addition, the weakening of the Roman papacy in its struggles with the incohesive Holy Roman Empire and with the rising nation-states of the north had produced a political condition in Italy of marked fluidity. The Italian city-states' small size, their independence from externally sanctioned authority, and their commercial and cultural vitality all provided a political stage upon which a new spirit of bold, creative, and often ruthless individualism could flourish. Whereas in earlier times, the life of the state was defined by inherited structures of power and law imposed by tradition or higher authority, now individual ability and deliberate political action and thought carried the most weight. The state itself was seen as something to be comprehended and manipulated by human will and intelligence, a political understanding making the Italian city-states forerunners of the modern state.

This new value placed on individualism and personal genius reinforced a similar characteristic of the Italian Humanists, whose sense of personal worth also rested on individual capacity, and whose ideal was similarly that of the emancipated man of many-sided genius. The medieval Christian ideal in which personal identity was largely absorbed in the collective Christian body of souls faded in favor of the more pagan heroic mode—the individual man as adventurer, genius, and rebel. Realization of the protean self was best achieved not through saintly withdrawal from the world but through a life of strenuous action in the service of the city-state, in scholarly and artistic activity, in commercial enterprise and social intercourse. Old dichotomies were now comprehended in a larger unity: activity in the world as well as contemplation of eternal truths; devotion to state, family, and self as well as to God and Church; physical pleasure as well as spiritual happiness; prosperity as well as virtue. Forsaking the ideal of monastic poverty, Renaissance man embraced the enrichments of life afforded by personal wealth, and Humanist scholars and artists flourished in the new cultural climate subsidized by the Italian commercial and aristocratic elites.

The combined influences of political dynamism, economic wealth, broad scholarship, sensuous art, and a special intimacy with ancient and eastern Mediterranean cultures all encouraged a new and expansively secular spirit in the Italian ruling class, extending into the inner sanctum of the Vatican. In the eyes of the pious a certain paganism and amorality was becoming pervasive in Italian life. Such was visible not only in the calculated barbarities and intrigues of the political arena, but also in the unabashed worldliness of Renaissance man's interests in nature, knowledge, beauty, and luxury for their own sakes. It was thus from its origins in the dynamic culture of Renaissance Italy that there developed a distinctive new Western personality. Marked by individualism, secularity, strength of will, multiplicity of interest and impulse, creative innovation, and a willingness to defy traditional limitations on human activity, this spirit soon began to spread across Europe, providing the lineaments of the modern character.

Yet for all the secularism of the age, in a quite tangible sense the Roman Catholic Church itself attained a pinnacle of glory in the Renaissance. Saint Peter's Basilica, the Sistine Chapel, the Stanza della Segnatura in the Vatican all stand as astonishing monuments to the Church's final moments as undisputed sovereign of Western culture. Here the full grandeur of the Catholic Church's self-conception was articulated, encompassing Genesis and the biblical drama (the Sistine ceiling), classical Greek philosophy and science (the *School of Athens*), poetry and the creative arts (the *Parnassus*), all culminating in the theology and supreme pantheon of Roman Catholic Christianity (*La Disputa del Sacramento, The Triumph of the Church*). The procession of the centuries, the history of the Western soul, was here given immortal embodiment. Under the guidance of the inspired albeit thoroughly unpriestlike Pope Julius II, protean artists like Raphael, Bramante, and

Michelangelo painted, sculpted, designed, and constructed works of art of unsurpassed beauty and power to celebrate the majestic Catholic vision. Thus the Mother Church, mediatrix between God and man, matrix of Western culture, now assembled and integrated all her diverse elements: Judaism and Hellenism, Scholasticism and Humanism, Platonism and Aristotelianism, pagan myth and biblical revelation. With Renaissance artistic imagery as its language, a new pictorial *Summa* was written, integrating the dialectical components of Western culture in a transcendent synthesis. It was as if the Church, subconsciously aware of the wrenching fate about to befall it, called forth from itself its most exalted cultural self-understanding and found artists of seemingly divine stature to incarnate that image.

Yet this efflorescence of the Catholic Church in the midst of an era that was so decidedly embracing the secular and the present world was the kind of paradox that was altogether characteristic of the Renaissance. For the unique position in cultural history held by the Renaissance as a whole derives not least from its simultaneous balance and synthesis of many opposites: Christian and pagan, modern and classical, secular and sacred, art and science, science and religion, poetry and politics. The Renaissance was both an age to itself and a transition. At once medieval and modern, it was still highly religious (Ficino, Michelangelo, Erasmus, More, Savonarola, Luther, Loyola, Teresa of Avila, John of the Cross), yet undeniably worldly (Machiavelli, Cellini, Castiglione, Montaigne, Bacon, the Medici and Borgias, most of the Renaissance popes). At the same time that the scientific sensibility arose and flourished, religious passions surged as well, and often in inextricable combination.

The Renaissance integration of contraries had been foreshadowed in the Petrarchian ideal of *docta pietas,* and was now fulfilled in religious scholars like Erasmus and his friend Thomas More. With the Christian Humanists of the Renaissance, irony and restraint, worldly activity and classical erudition served the Christian cause in ways the medieval era had not witnessed. A literate and ecumenical evangelism here seemed to replace the dogmatic pieties of a more primitive age. A critical religious intellectuality sought to supersede naive religious superstition. The philosopher Plato and the apostle Paul were brought together and synthesized to produce a new *philosophia Christi.*

But perhaps it was the art of the Renaissance that best expressed the era's contraries and unity. In the early Quattrocento, only one in twenty paintings could be found with a nonreligious subject. A century later, there were five times as many. Even inside the Vatican, paintings of nudes and pagan deities now faced those of the Madonna and Christ Child. The human body was celebrated in its beauty, formal harmony, and proportion, yet often in the service of religious subjects or as a revelation of God's creative wisdom. Renaissance art was devoted to the exact imitation of nature, and was technically capable of an unprecedented naturalistic realism, yet was also singularly effective in rendering a sublime numinosity, depicting spiritual and mythic beings and even contemporary human figures with a certain ineffable grace and formal perfection. Conversely, that capacity for rendering the numinous would have been impossible without the technical innovations—geometrical mathematization of space, linear perspective, aerial perspective, anatomical knowledge, *chiaroscuro, sfumato*—that developed from the striving for perceptual realism and empirical accuracy. In turn, these achievements in painting and drawing propelled later scientific advances in anatomy and medicine, and foreshadowed the Scientific Revolution's global mathematization of the physical world. It was not peripheral to the emergence of the modern outlook that Renaissance art depicted a world of rationally related solids in a unified space seen from a single objective viewpoint.

The Renaissance thrived on a determined "decompartmentalization," maintaining no strict divisions between different realms of human knowledge or experience. Leonardo was the prime exemplar—as committed to the search for knowledge as for beauty, artist of many mediums who was continuously and voraciously involved in scientific research of wide range. Leonardo's development and exploitation of the empirical eye for grasping the external world with fuller awareness and new precision were as much in the service of scientific insight as of artistic representation, with both goals jointly pursued in his "science of painting." His art revealed an uncanny spiritual expressiveness that accompanied, and was nurtured by, extreme technical accuracy of depiction. It was uniquely characteristic of the Renaissance that it produced the man who not only painted the *Last Supper* and *The Virgin of the Rocks*, but also articulated in his notebooks the three fundamental principles—empiricism, mathematics, and mechanics—that would dominate modern scientific thinking.

So too did Copernicus and Kepler, with Neoplatonic and Pythagorean motivations, seek solutions to problems in astronomy that would satisfy aesthetic imperatives, a strategy which led them to the heliocentric universe. No less significant was the strong religious motivation, usually combined with Platonic themes, impelling most of the major figures in the Scientific Revolution through Newton. For implicit in all these activities was the half-inarticulate notion of a distant mythical golden age when all things had been known—the Garden of Eden, ancient classical times, a past era of great sages. Mankind's fall from this primal state of enlightenment and grace had brought about a drastic loss of knowledge. Recovery of knowledge was therefore endowed with religious significance. And so once again, just as in classical Athens the religion, art, and myth of the ancient Greeks met and interacted with the new and equally Greek spirit of rationalism and science, this paradoxical conjunction and balance was attained in the Renaissance.

Although the Renaissance was in many senses a direct outgrowth of the rich and burgeoning culture of the high Middle Ages, by all accounts, between the mid-fifteenth and early seventeenth centuries, an unmistakable quantum leap was made in the cultural evolution of the West. The various contributing factors can be recognized in retrospect and listed—the rediscovery of antiquity, the commercial vitality, the city-state personality, the technical inventions, and so forth. But when all these "causes" of the Renaissance have been enumerated, one still senses that the essential thrust of the Renaissance was something larger than any of these factors, than all of them combined. Instead, the historical record suggests there was concurrently on many fronts an emphatic emergence of a new consciousness—expansive, rebellious, energetic and creative, individualistic, ambitious and often unscrupulous, curious, self-confident, committed to this life and this world, open-eyed and skeptical, inspired and inspirited—and that this emergence had its own raison d'être, was propelled by some greater and more subsuming force than any combination of political, social, technological, religious, philosophical, or artistic factors. It was not accidental to the character of the Renaissance (nor, perhaps, unrelated to its new sense of artistic perspective) that, while medieval scholars saw history divided into two periods, before and after Christ, with their own time only vaguely separated from the Roman era of Christ's birth, Renaissance historians achieved a decisively new perspective on the past: history was perceived and defined for the first time as a tripartite structure—ancient, medieval, modern—thus sharply differentiating the classical and medieval eras, with the Renaissance itself at the vanguard of the new age.

The events and figures converged on the Renaissance stage with amazing rapidity, even simultaneity. Columbus and Leonardo were both born in the same half decade (1450–55) that brought the development of the Gutenberg press, the fall of Constantinople with the resulting influx of Greek scholars to Italy, and the end of the Hundred Years' War through which France and England each forged its national consciousness. The same two decades (1468–88) that saw the Florentine Academy's Neoplatonic revival at its height during the reign of Lorenzo the Magnificent also saw the births of Copernicus, Luther, Castiglione, Raphael, Dürer, Michelangelo, Giorgione, Machiavelli, Cesare Borgia, Zwingli, Pizarro, Magellan, and More. In the same period, Aragon and Castille were joined by the marriage of Ferdinand and Isabella to form the nation of Spain, the Tudors succeeded to the throne in England, Leonardo began his artistic career with his painting of the angel in Verrocchio's *Baptism of Christ*, then his own *Adoration of the Magi*, Botticelli painted *Primavera* and *The Birth of Venus*, Ficino wrote the *Theologia Platonica* and published the first complete translation of Plato in the West, Erasmus received his early Humanist education in Holland, and Pico della Mirandola composed the manifesto of Renaissance Humanism, the *Oration on the Dignity of Man*. More than "causes" were operative here. A spontaneous and irreducible revolution of consciousness was taking place, affecting virtually every aspect of Western culture. Amidst high drama and painful convulsions, modern man was born in the Renaissance, "trailing clouds of glory."

The Reformation

It was when the spirit of Renaissance individualism reached the realm of theology and religious conviction within the Church, in the person of the German Augustinian monk Martin Luther, that there erupted in Europe the momentous Protestant Reformation. The Renaissance had accommodated both classical culture and Christianity in one expansive if unsystematic vision. But the continued moral deterioration of the papacy in the south now encountered a new surge of rigorous religiosity in the north. The relaxed cultural syncretism displayed by the Renaissance Church's embrace of Greco-Roman pagan culture (including the immense expense of patronage this embrace demanded) helped precipitate the collapse of the Church's absolute religious authority. Armed with the thunderous moral power of an Old Testament prophet, Luther defiantly confronted the Roman Catholic papacy's patent neglect of the original Christian faith revealed in the Bible. Sparked by Luther's rebellion, an insuperable cultural reaction swept through the sixteenth century, decisively reasserting the Christian religion while simultaneously shattering the unity of Western Christendom.

The proximate cause of the Reformation was the papacy's attempt to finance the architectural and artistic glories of the High Renaissance by the theologically dubious means of selling spiritual indulgences. Tetzel, the traveling friar whose sale of indulgences in Germany provoked Luther in 1517 to post his Ninety-five Theses, had been so authorized by the Medici Pope Leo X to raise money for building Saint Peter's Basilica. An indulgence was the remission of punishment for a sin after guilt had been sacramentally forgiven—a Church practice influenced by the pre-Christian Germanic custom of commuting the physical penalty for a crime to a money payment. To grant such an indulgence, the Church drew from the treasury of merits accumulated by the good works of the saints, and in return the recipient made a contribution to the Church. A voluntary and popular arrangement, the practice allowed the Church to raise money for financing crusades and building cathedrals and hospitals. At first applied only to penalties imposed by the Church in this life, by Luther's time indulgences were being granted to remit penalties imposed by God in the afterlife, including immediate release from purgatory.

With indulgences effecting even the remission of sins, the sacrament of penance itself was seemingly compromised.

But beyond the matter of indulgences lay more fundamental sources of the Protestant revolution—the long-developing political secularism of the Church hierarchy, undermining its spiritual integrity while embroiling it in diplomatic and military struggles; the prevalence of both deep piety and poverty among the Church faithful, in contrast to an often irreligious but socially and economically privileged clergy; the rise of monarchical power, nationalism, and local Germanic insurgency against the universal ambitions of the Roman papacy and the Habsburgs' Holy Roman Empire. Yet the more immediate cause, the Church's expensive patronage of high culture, does illuminate a deeper factor behind the Reformation—namely, the anti-Hellenic spirit with which Luther sought to purify Christianity and return it to its pristine biblical foundation. For the Reformation was not least a purist "Judaic" reaction against the Hellenic (and Roman) impulse of Renaissance culture, of Scholastic philosophy, and of much postapostolic Christianity in general. Yet perhaps the most fundamental element in the genesis of the Reformation was the emerging spirit of rebellious, self-determining individualism, and particularly the growing impulse for intellectual and spiritual independence, which had now developed to that crucial point where a potently critical stand could be sustained against the West's highest cultural authority, the Roman Catholic Church.

Luther desperately sought for a gracious God's redemption in the face of so much evidence to the contrary, evidence both of God's damning judgment and of Luther's own sinfulness. He failed to find that grace in himself or in his own works, nor did he find it in the Church—not in its sacraments, not in its ecclesiastical hierarchy, and assuredly not in its papal indulgences. It was, finally, the faith in God's redeeming power as revealed through Christ in the Bible, and that alone, which rendered Luther's experience of salvation, and upon that exclusive rock he built his new church of a reformed Christianity. Erasmus, by contrast, the devoutly critical Humanist, wished to save the Church's unity and mission by reforming it from within. But the Church hierarchy, absorbed in other matters, remained intransigently insensitive to such needs, while Luther, with equal intransigence, declared the necessity of complete schism and independence from an institution he now viewed as the seat of the Antichrist.

Pope Leo X considered Luther's revolt merely another "monk's quarrel," and long delayed any response adequate to the problem. When, almost three years after the Ninety-five Theses were posted, Luther finally received the papal bull to submit, he publicly burned it. At the ensuing meeting of the imperial Diet, the Habsburg Holy Roman Emperor Charles V declared himself certain that a single friar could not be right in denying the validity of all Christianity during the previous thousand years. Wishing to preserve the unity of the Christian religion, yet faced with Luther's obstinate refusal to recant, he placed an imperial ban on Luther as a heretic. But empowered by the rebellious German princes and knights, Luther's personal theological insurgency rapidly expanded to an international upheaval. In retrospect, the post-Constantinian welding of the Christian religion to the ancient Roman state had proved to be a two-edged sword, contributing both to the Church's cultural ascendance and to its eventual decline. The overarching cultural union maintained in Europe for a thousand years by the Catholic Church was now irrevocably split asunder.

But it was Luther's personal religious dilemma that was the sine qua non of the Reformation. In his acute sense of alienation and terror before the Omnipotent, Luther saw it was the whole man who was corrupt and needed God's forgiveness, not just particular sins that one by one could be erased by proper Church-defined actions. The particular sins were but symptoms of a more fundamental sickness in man's soul that required healing. One could not purchase redemption, step by step, through good works or through the legalisms of penance or other sacraments, not to mention the infamous indulgences. Only Christ could save the whole man, and only man's faith in Christ could justify man before God. Only thus could the terrible righteousness of an angry God, who justly damns sinners to eternal perdition, be transformed into the merciful righteousness of a forgiving God, who freely rewards the faithful with eternal bliss. As Luther exultantly discovered in Paul's Letter to the Romans, man did not earn salvation; rather, God gave it freely to those who have faith. The source of that saving faith was Holy Scripture, where God's mercy revealed itself in Christ's crucifixion for mankind. There alone could the Christian believer find the means to his salvation. The Catholic Church—with its cynical marketplace practice of claiming to be dispensing God's grace, distributing the merits of the saints, forgiving men's sins, and releasing them from debts owed in the afterlife, in return for money garnered for its own often irreligious purposes, meanwhile claiming papal infallibility—could only be an impostor. The Church could no longer be reverenced as the sacred medium of Christian truth.

All the accretions brought into Christianity by the Roman Church that were not found in the New Testament were now solemnly questioned, criticized, and often expelled altogether by the Protestants: the centuries' accumulation of sacraments, rituals, and art, the complex organizational structures, the priestly hierarchy and its spiritual authority, the natural and rational theology of the Scholastics, the belief in purgatory, papal infallibility, clerical celibacy, the eucharistic transubstantiation, the saints' treasury of merits, the popular worship of the Virgin Mary, and finally the Mother Church herself. All these had become antithetical to the individual Christian's primary need for faith in Christ's redemptive grace: Justification occurred by faith alone. The Christian believer had to be liberated from the obscuring clutches of the old system, for only by being directly responsible to God could he be free to experience God's grace. The only source of theological authority now lay in the literal meaning of Scripture. The complicated doctrinal developments and moral pronouncements of the institutional Church were irrelevant. After centuries of possessing relatively indisputable spiritual authority, the Roman Catholic Church, with all its accoutrements, was suddenly no longer considered mandatory for humanity's religious well-being.

In defense of the Church and its continued unity, Catholic theologians argued that the Church's sacramental institutions were both valuable and necessary, and that its doctrinal tradition, which interpreted and elaborated the original revelation, held genuine spiritual authority. Moral and practical reforms in the present Church certainly needed to be made, but its inherent sanctity and validity were still sound. Without Church tradition, they held, God's Word would be less potent in the world and less understood by the Christian faithful. Through the inspiration of the Holy Spirit invested in the institutes of the Church, the latter could draw out and affirm elements of Christian truth not fully explicit in the biblical text. For indeed, the Church in its earliest apostolic stages had preceded the New Testament, produced it, and later canonized it as God's inspired Word.

But the reformers countered that the Church had replaced faith in the person of Christ with faith in the doctrine of the Church. It had thereby vitiated the potency of the original Christian revelation and placed the

Church opaquely in the middle of man's relation to God. Only direct contact with the Bible could bring the human soul direct contact with Christ.

In the Protestant vision, true Christianity was founded on "faith alone," "grace alone," and "Scripture alone." While the Catholic Church agreed that those indeed were the fundaments of the Christian religion, it maintained that the institutional Church, with its sacraments, priestly hierarchy, and doctrinal tradition, was intrinsically and dynamically related to that foundation—faith in God's grace as revealed in Scripture—and served the propagation of that faith. Erasmus also argued against Luther that man's free will and virtuous actions were not to be entirely discounted as elements in the process of salvation. Catholicism held that divine grace and human merit were both instrumental in redemption and did not have to be viewed in opposition, with exclusively one or the other operative. Most important, the Church argued, institutional tradition and the Scripture-based faith were not in opposition. On the contrary, Catholicism provided the living vessel for the Word's emergence in the world.

But for the reformers, the Church's actual practice too much belied its ideal, its hierarchy was too manifestly corrupt, its doctrinal tradition too remote from the original revelation. To reform such a degenerate structure from within would be both practically futile and theologically erroneous. Luther argued persuasively for God's exclusive role in salvation, man's spiritual helplessness, the moral bankruptcy of the institutional Church, and the exclusive authority of Scripture. The Protestant spirit prevailed in half of Europe, and the old order was broken. Western Christianity was no longer exclusively Catholic, nor monolithic, nor a source of cultural unity.

>+✳+<

The peculiar paradox of the Reformation was its essentially ambiguous character, for it was at once a conservative religious reaction and a radically libertarian revolution. The Protestantism forged by Luther, Zwingli, and Calvin proclaimed an emphatic revival of a Bible-based Judaic Christianity—unequivocally monotheistic, affirming the God of Abraham and Moses as supreme, omnipotent, transcendent, and "Other," with man as fallen, helpless, predestined for damnation or salvation, and, in the case of the latter, fully dependent on God's grace for his redemption. Whereas Aquinas had posited every creature's participation in God's infinite and free essence, and asserted the positive, God-given autonomy of human nature, the reformers perceived the absolute sovereignty of God over his creation in a more dichotomous light, with man's innate sinfulness making the independent human will inherently ineffective and perverse. While Protestantism was optimistic concerning God, the gratuitously merciful preserver of the elect, it was uncompromisingly pessimistic concerning man, that "teeming horde of infamies" (Calvin). Human freedom was so bound to evil that it consisted merely in the ability to choose among different degrees of sin. For the reformers, autonomy suggested apostasy. Man's true freedom and joy lay solely in obedience to God's will, and the capacity for such obedience arose solely from God's merciful gift of faith. Nothing man did on his own could bring him closer to salvation. Nor could his illumination be achieved through the rational ascents of a Scholastic theology contaminated by Greek philosophy. Only God could provide genuine illumination, and only Scripture revealed the authentic truth. Against the Renaissance's dalliance with a more flexible Hellenized Christianity, with pagan Neoplatonism and its universal religion and human deification, Luther, and more systematically Calvin, reinstituted the more strictly defined, morally rigorous, and ontologically dualistic Augustinian Judaeo-Christian view.

Moreover, this reassertion of "pure" traditional Christianity was given further impetus throughout European culture by the Catholic Counter-Reformation when, beginning in the mid-sixteenth century with the Council of Trent, the Catholic Church finally awakened to the crisis and vigorously reformed itself from within. The Roman papacy again became religiously motivated, often austerely so, and the Church restated the basics of Christian belief (while maintaining the Church's essential structure and sacramental authority) in just as militantly dogmatic terms as the Protestants it opposed. Thus on both sides of the European divide, in the Catholic south and the Protestant north, orthodox Christianity was energetically reestablished in a conservative religious backlash against the Renaissance's pagan Hellenism, naturalism, and secularism.

Yet for all the Reformation's conservative character, its rebellion against the Church was an unprecedentedly revolutionary act in Western culture—not only as a successful social and political insurgency against the Roman papacy and ecclesiastical hierarchy, with the reformers supported by the secular rulers of Germany and other northern countries, but first and foremost as an assertion of the individual conscience against the established Church framework of belief, ritual, and organizational structure. For the fundamental question of the Reformation concerned the locus of religious authority. In the Protestant vision, neither the pope nor the Church councils possessed the spiritual competence to define Christian belief. Luther taught instead the "priesthood of all believers": religious authority rested finally and solely in each individual Christian, reading and interpreting the Bible according to his own private conscience in the context of his personal relationship to God. The presence of the Holy Spirit, in all its liberating, directly inspirational, noninstitutional freedom, was to be affirmed in every Christian against the quenching constrictions of the Roman Church. The individual believer's interior response to Christ's grace, not the elaborate ecclesiastical machinery of the Vatican, constituted the true Christian experience.

For it was the very unflinchingness of Luther's individual confrontation with God that had revealed both God's omnipotence and his mercy. The two contraries characteristic of Protestantism, independent human self and all-powerful Deity, were inextricably interconnected. Hence the Reformation marked the standing forth of the individual in two senses— alone outside the Church, and alone directly before God. Luther's impassioned words before the imperial Diet declared a new manifesto of personal religious freedom:

> Unless I am convinced by Scripture and plain reason—I do not accept the authority of popes and councils, for they have contradicted each other—my conscience is captive to the Word of God. I cannot and I will not recant anything, for to go against conscience is neither right nor safe. God help me. Amen.

The Reformation was a new and decisive assertion of rebellious individualism—of personal conscience, of "Christian liberty," of critical private judgment against the monolithic authority of the institutional Church—and as such further propelled the Renaissance's movement out of the medieval Church and medieval character. Although the conservative Judaic quality of the Reformation was a reaction against the Renaissance in the latter's Hellenic and pagan aspects, on another level, the Reformation's revolutionary declaration of personal autonomy served as a continuation of the Renaissance impulse—and was thus an intrinsic, if partially antithetical, element of the overall Renaissance phenom-

enon. An era that saw both Renaissance and Reformation was revolutionary indeed, and it was perhaps on account of this Promethean
Zeitgeist that the force of Luther's rebellion rapidly amplified far past what
he had anticipated or even desired. For in the end, the Reformation was
but one particularly salient expression of a much larger cultural
transformation taking place in the Western mind and spirit.

>·×·<

Here we encounter the other extraordinary paradox of the Reformation. For while its essential character was so intensely and unambiguously
religious, its ultimate effects on Western culture were profoundly
secularizing, and in multiple, mutually reinforcing ways. By overthrowing the theological authority of the Catholic Church, the internationally
recognized supreme court of religious dogma, the Reformation opened
the way in the West for religious pluralism, then religious skepticism,
and finally a complete breakdown in the until then relatively homogeneous Christian world view. Although various Protestant authorities
would attempt to reinstitute their particular form of Christian belief as
the supreme and exclusively correct dogmatic truth, the first premise of
Luther's reform—the priesthood of all believers and the authority of the
individual conscience in the interpretation of Scripture—necessarily
undercut the enduring success of any efforts to enforce new orthodoxies.
Once the Mother Church had been left behind, no new claims to
infallible insight could long be regarded as legitimate. The immediate
consequence of the liberation from the old matrix was a manifest liberation of fervent Christian religiosity, permeating the lives of the new
Protestant congregations with fresh spiritual meaning and charismatic
power. Yet as time passed, the average Protestant, no longer enclosed by
the Catholic womb of grand ceremony, historical tradition, and sacramental authority, was left somewhat less protected against the vagaries
of private doubt and secular thinking. From Luther on, each believer's
belief was increasingly self-supported; and the Western intellect's critical
faculties were becoming ever more acute.

Moreover, Luther had been educated in the nominalist tradition,
leaving him distrustful of the earlier Scholastics' attempt to bridge reason
and faith with rational theology. There was for Luther no "natural
revelation," given by the natural human reason in its cognition and
analysis of the natural world. Like Ockham, Luther saw the natural
human reason as so far from comprehending God's will and gratuitous

salvation that the rationalist attempts to do so by Scholastic theology appeared absurdly presumptuous. No genuine coherence between the secular mind and Christian truth was possible, for Christ's sacrifice on the cross was foolishness to the wisdom of the world. Scripture alone could provide man with the certain and saving knowledge of God's ways. These assertions held significant and unanticipated consequences for the modern mind and its apprehension of the natural world.

The Reformation's restoring of a predominantly biblical theology against a Scholastic theology helped to purge the modern mind of Hellenic notions in which nature was permeated with divine rationality and final causes. Protestantism thus provided a revolution of theological context that solidified the movement begun by Ockham away from the outlook of classical Scholasticism, thereby supporting the development of a new science of nature. The increased distinction made by the reformers between Creator and creature—between God's inscrutable will and man's finite intelligence, and between God's transcendence and the world's contingency—allowed the modern mind to approach the world with a new sense of nature's purely mundane character, with its own ordering principles that might not directly correspond to man's logical assumptions about God's divine government. The reformers' limiting of the human mind to a this-worldly knowledge was precisely the prerequisite for the opening up of that knowledge. God had graciously and freely created the world, fully distinct from his own infinite divinity. Hence that world could now be apprehended and analyzed not according to its assumed sacramental participation in static divine patternings, in the manner of Neoplatonic and Scholastic thought, but rather according to its own distinct dynamic material processes, devoid of direct reference to God and his transcendent reality.

By disenchanting the world of immanent divinity, completing the process initiated by Christianity's destruction of pagan animism, the Reformation better allowed for its radical revision by modern science. The way was then clear for an increasingly naturalistic view of the cosmos, moving first to the remote rationalist Creator of Deism, and finally to secular agnosticism's elimination of any supernatural reality. Even the Reformation's renewal of the biblical subjection of nature to man's dominion as found in Genesis contributed to this process, encouraging man's sense of being the knowing subject against the object of nature, and of being divinely authorized to exercise his sovereignty over the natural—hence nonspiritual—world. As God's magnitude and distinctness relative to his creation was affirmed, so too was man's magnitude and distinctness relative to the rest of nature. Subduing nature for man's benefit could be seen as a religious duty, eventually taking on a secular momentum of its own as man's sense of self-worth and autonomy, and his powers of dominion, continued to increase in the course of the modern era.

A further and similarly ambiguous effect of the Reformation on the modern mind involved a new attitude to truth. In the Catholic view, the deepest truths were first divinely revealed as recorded in the Bible, and these then became the basis for a continuing growth of truth through Church tradition—each generation of Church theologians inspired by the Holy Spirit, creatively acting upon that tradition and forging a more profound Christian doctrine. Much as Aquinas's active intellect took sense impressions and from them formed intelligible concepts, so did the Church's active intellect take the basic tradition and from it render more penetrating formulations of spiritual truth. But from the Protestant perspective, the truth lay finally and objectively in the revealed Word of God, and fidelity to that unalterable truth alone could render theological certainty. In this view, the Roman Catholic tradition was a long and ever-worsening exercise in subjective distortion of that primal truth. Catholic "objectivity" was nothing other than the establishment of doctrines conforming to the subjective demands of the Catholic mind, not to the external sacrosanct truth of the Word. And the Catholic mind had become especially distorted by its theological integration of Greek philosophy, a system of thought intrinsically alien to biblical truth.

Protestantism's reclamation of the unalterable Word of God in the Bible thus fostered in the emerging modern mind a new stress on the need to discover unbiased objective truth, apart from the prejudices and distortions of tradition. It thereby supported the growth of a critical scientific mentality. To confront entrenched doctrines courageously, to subject all beliefs to fresh criticism and direct testing, to come face-to-face with objective reality unmediated by traditional preconceptions or vested authorities—such a passion for disinterested truth informed the Protestant mind and thence the modern mind generally. But in time, the Word itself would become subject to that new critical spirit, and secularism would triumph.

Indeed, the very foundation for the reformers' appeal to objective truth would provoke its dialectical collapse. Luther's stress on the literal meaning of Scripture as the exclusive reliable basis for knowledge of

God's creation was to present the modern mind with an impossible tension as it confronted the distinctly unbiblical revelations soon to be established by secular science. Two apparently contradictory—or at least incongruent—truths had to be maintained simultaneously, one religious and one scientific. The fundamentalist's Bible was to hasten the long-developing schism between faith and reason experienced by the Western mind as it attempted to accommodate science. The Christian faith was far too deeply ingrained to be readily sloughed off altogether, but neither could the scientific discoveries be denied. Eventually the latter would far outweigh the former in both intellectual and practical significance. In the process of that shift, the West's "faith" would itself be radically realigned and transferred to the victor. In the long term, Luther's zealous reinstatement of a Scripture-based religiosity was to help precipitate its secular antithesis.

The Reformation had another effect on the modern mind contrary to Christian orthodoxy. For Luther's appeal to the primacy of the individual's religious response would lead gradually but inevitably to the modern mind's sense of the interiority of religious reality, the final individualism of truth, and the pervasive role in determining truth played by the personal subject. As time passed, the Protestant doctrine of justification through the individual's faith in Christ seemed to place more emphasis on the individual's faith than on Christ—on the personal relevance of ideas, as it were, rather than on their external validity. The self increasingly became the measure of things, self-defining and self-legislating. Truth increasingly became truth-as-experienced-by-the-self. Thus the road opened by Luther would move through Pietism to Kantian critical philosophy and Romantic philosophical idealism to, finally, the philosophical pragmatism and existentialism of the late modern era.

The Reformation was secularizing too in its realignment of personal loyalties. Previously, the Roman Catholic Church had maintained the general, if sometimes controversial, allegiance of virtually all Europeans. But the Reformation had succeeded not least because it coincided with the potent rise of secular nationalism and German rebelliousness against the papacy and the Holy Roman Empire, especially against the latter's attempts to assert a European-wide authority. With the Reformation, the universal ambition and dream of the Catholic imperium was finally defeated. The resulting empowerment of the various separate nations and states of Europe now displaced the old ideal unity of Western Christendom, and the new order was marked by intensely aggressive competition. There was now no higher power, international and spiritual, to which all individual states were responsive. Moreover, the individual national languages, already spurred forward by the Renaissance literatures, were further strengthened against Latin, the previously universal language of the educated, by the compelling new vernacular translations of the Bible, above all Luther's translation into German and the King James committee's into English. The individual secular state now became the defining unit of cultural, as well as political, authority. The medieval Catholic matrix unifying Europe had disintegrated.

No less significant were the Reformation's complex effects on political-religious dynamics, both within the individual and within the state. With secular rulers now defining the religion of their territories, the Reformation unintentionally moved power from church to state, just as it did from priest to layman. And because many of the principal monarchs chose to remain Catholic, their continuing attempts to centralize and absolutize political power caused Protestantism to be allied with resisting bodies—aristocrats, clergy, universities, provinces, cities—that sought to maintain or increase their separate liberties. Hence the cause of Protestantism became associated with the cause of political freedom. The Reformation's new sense of personal religious self-responsibility and the priesthood of all believers also abetted the growth of political liberalism and individual rights. At the same time, the religious fragmentation of Europe necessarily promoted a new intellectual and religious diversity. From all these factors ensued a succession of increasingly secularizing political and social consequences: first the establishment of individual state-identified churches, then the division of church and state, religious toleration, and finally the predominance of the secular society. Out of the exceedingly illiberal dogmatic religiosity of the Reformation eventually emerged the pluralistic tolerant liberalism of the modern era.

The Reformation had still other unexpected and paradoxically secularizing effects. Despite the reformers' Augustinian demotion of man's inherent spiritual power, they had also given human life in this world new significance in the Christian scheme of things. When Luther eliminated the traditional hierarchical division between clerical and lay, and, in blatant defiance of Catholic law, decided to marry a former nun and father a family, he endowed the activities and relationships of ordinary life with a religious meaning not previously emphasized by the Catholic Church. Holy matrimony replaced chastity as the Christian ideal. Domestic life, the raising of children, mundane work, and the tasks of daily existence were now upheld more explicitly as important areas within which the spirit could grow and deepen. Now occupational work of every variety was a sacred calling, not just monasticism as in the Middle Ages. With Calvin, a Christian's worldly vocation was to be pursued with spiritual and moral fervor in order to realize the Kingdom of God on earth. The world was to be regarded not as the inevitable expression of God's will, to be passively accepted in pious submission, but rather as the arena in which man's urgent religious duty was to fulfill God's will through questioning and changing every aspect of life, every social and cultural institution, in order to help bring about the Christian commonwealth.

Yet in time this religious uplifting of the secular was to take on an autonomous, nonreligious character. Marriage, for example, freed from Church control as a Catholic sacrament and now regulated by civil law, in time became an essentially secular contract, more easily entered into or dissolved, more easily subject to losing its sacramental character. On a larger social scale, the Protestant call to take this world more seriously, to revise society and to embrace change, served to overcome the traditional religious antipathy both to this world and to change, and thereby gave the embryonic modern psyche the religious sanction and internal restructuring it required to propel the progress of modernity and liberalism in many spheres, from politics to science. Eventually, however, this powerful impulse to make over the world became autonomous, not only becoming independent of its originally religious motivation, but finally turning against the religious bulwark itself as yet another, and especially profound, form of oppression to be overcome.

Important social consequences of the Reformation also became evident in its complex relationship to the economic development of the northern European nations. The Protestant affirmation of moral discipline and the holy dignity of one's work in the world seems to have combined with a peculiarity in the Calvinist belief in predestination, whereby the striving (and anxious) Christian, deprived of the Catholic's recourse to sacramental justification, could find signs of his being among the elect if he could successfully and unceasingly apply himself to disciplined work and his worldly calling. Material productivity was often the fruit of such effort, which, compounded by the Puritan demand for ascetic renunciation of selfish pleasure and frivolous spending, readily lent itself to the accumulation of capital.

Whereas traditionally the pursuit of commercial success was perceived as directly threatening to the religious life, now the two were recognized as mutually beneficial. Religious doctrine itself was at times selectively transformed or intensified in accord with the prevailing social and economic temper. Within a few generations, the Protestant work ethic, along with the continued emergence of an assertive and mobile individualism, had played a major role in encouraging the growth of an economically flourishing middle class tied to the rise of capitalism. The latter, already developing in the Renaissance Italian city-states, was further propelled by numerous other factors—the accumulation of wealth from the New World, the opening up of new markets, expanding populations, new financial strategies, new developments in industrial organizations and technologies. In time, much of the originally spiritual orientation of the Protestant discipline had become focused on more secular concerns, and on the material rewards realized by its productivity. Thus religious zeal yielded to economic vigor, which pressed forward on its own.

The Counter-Reformation, for its part, similarly brought on unforeseen developments in a direction opposite from that intended. The Catholic Church's crusade to reform itself and oppose the spread of Protestantism took many forms, from the revival of the Inquisition to the practical reforms and mystical writings of John of the Cross and Teresa of Avila. But the Counter-Reformation was spearheaded above all by the Jesuits, a Roman Catholic order that established itself as militantly loyal to the pope and attracted a considerable number of strong-willed and intellectually sophisticated men. Among their various activities in the secular world designed to accomplish their Catholic mission, which ranged from heroic missionary work overseas to assiduous censorship and Byzantine political intrigue in the courts of Europe, the Jesuits took on the responsibility of educating the young, especially those of the ruling class, to forge a new Catholic elite. Jesuits soon became the most celebrated teachers on the Continent. Their educational strategy, however, involved not only the teaching of the Catholic faith and theology, but also the full humanistic program from the Renaissance and classical era—Latin and Greek letters, rhetoric, logic and metaphysics, ethics, science and mathematics, music, even the gentlemanly arts of acting and fencing—all in the service of developing a scholarly "soldier of Christ": a morally disciplined, liberally educated, critically intelligent Christian man capable of outwitting the Protestant heretics and furthering the great Western tradition of Catholic learning.

Hundreds of educational institutions were founded by the Jesuits throughout Europe, and were soon replicated by Protestant leaders similarly mindful of the need to educate the faithful. The classical humanistic tradition based on the Greek *paideia* was thereby broadly sustained during the following two centuries, offering the growing educated class of Europeans a new source of cultural unity just as the old source, Christianity, was fragmenting. But as a consequence of such a liberal program, with its exposure of students to many eloquently articulate viewpoints, pagan as well as Christian, and with its disciplined inculcation of a critical rationality, there could not but emerge in educated Europeans a decidedly nonorthodox tendency toward intellectual pluralism, skepticism, and even revolution. It was no accident that Galileo and Descartes, Voltaire and Diderot all received Jesuit educations.

And here was the final and most drastic secularizing effect of the Reformation. For with the revolt of Luther, Christianity's medieval matrix split into two, then into many, then seemingly commenced destroying itself as the new divisions battled each other throughout Europe with unbridled fury. The resulting chaos in the intellectual and cultural life of Europe was profound. Wars of religion reflected violent disputes between ever-multiplying religious sects over whose conception of absolute truth would prevail. The need for a clarifying and unifying vision capable of transcending the irresolvable religious conflicts was urgent and broadly felt. It was amidst this state of acute metaphysical turmoil that the Scientific Revolution began, developed, and finally triumphed in the Western mind.

The Scientific Revolution

Copernicus

The Scientific Revolution was both the final expression of the Renaissance and its definitive contribution to the modern world view. Born in Poland and educated in Italy, Copernicus lived during the height of the Renaissance. Though it was destined to become an unquestioned principle of existence for the modern psyche, the central tenet of his vision was inconceivable to most Europeans in his own lifetime. More than any other single factor, it was the Copernican insight that provoked and symbolized the drastic, fundamental break from the ancient and medieval universe to that of the modern era.

Copernicus sought a new solution to the age-old problem of the planets: how to explain the apparently erratic planetary movements by means of a simple, clear, elegant mathematical formula. To recapitulate, the solutions proposed by Ptolemy and all his successors, solutions based on the geocentric Aristotelian cosmos, had required the employment of increasingly numerous mathematical devices—deferents, major and minor epicycles, equants, eccentrics—in the attempt to make sense of the observed positions while maintaining the ancient rule of uniform circular motion. When a planet's movement did not appear to move in a perfect circle, another, smaller circle was added, around which the planet hypothetically moved while it continued moving around the larger circle. Further discrepancies were solved by compounding the circles, displacing their centers, positing yet another center from which motion remained uniform, and so on. Each new astronomer, faced with newly revealed irregularities that contradicted the basic scheme, attempted to resolve them by adding more refinements—another minor epicycle here, another eccentric there.

By the Renaissance, the Ptolemaic strategy had produced, in Copernicus's words, a "monster"—an inelegant and overburdened conception which, despite all the complicated ad hoc corrective devices, still failed to account for or predict observed planetary positions with reliable accuracy. The original conceptual economy of the Ptolemaic model no longer existed. Moreover, different Greek, Arabic, and European astronomers used different methods and principles, different combinations of epicycles, eccentrics, and equants, so that there now existed a confusing multiplicity of systems based on Ptolemy. The science of astronomy, lacking any theoretical homogeneity, was riddled with uncertainty. Further, the accumulation of many centuries of observations since Ptolemy's time had revealed more and worse divergences from the Ptolemaic predictions, so that it seemed to Copernicus increasingly unlikely that any new modification of that system would be tenable. The continued maintenance of the ancient assumptions was making it impossible for astronomers to compute accurately the actual movements of heavenly bodies. Copernicus concluded that classical astronomy must contain, or even be based upon, some essential error.

Renaissance Europe urgently needed a better calendar, and the Church, for which the calendar was indispensable in administrative and liturgical matters, undertook its reform. Such reform depended on astronomical precision. Copernicus, asked to advise the papacy on the problem, responded that the existing confused state of astronomical science precluded any immediate effective reform. Copernicus's technical proficiency as an astronomer and mathematician enabled him to recognize the inadequacies of the existing cosmology. Yet this alone would not have forced him to devise a new system. Another, equally competent astronomer might well have perceived the problem of the planets as intrinsically insoluble, too complex and refractory for any mathematical system to comprehend. It would seem to be above all Copernicus's participation in the intellectual atmosphere of Renaissance Neoplatonism—and specifically his embrace of the Pythagorean conviction that nature was ultimately comprehensible in simple and harmonious mathematical terms of a transcendent, eternal quality—that pressed and guided him toward innovation. The divine Creator, whose works were everywhere good and orderly, could not have been slipshod with the heavens themselves.

Provoked by such considerations, Copernicus painstakingly reviewed all the ancient scientific literature he could acquire, much of which had recently become available in the Humanist revival and the transfer of Greek manuscripts from Constantinople to the West. He found that several Greek philosophers, notably of Pythagorean and Platonist background, had proposed a moving Earth, although none had developed the hypothesis to its full astronomical and mathematical conclusions. Hence Aristotle's geocentric conception had not been the only judgment of the revered Greek authorities. Armed with this sense of kinship with an ancient tradition, inspired by the Neoplatonists' exalted conception of the Sun, and further supported by the university Scholastics' critical appraisals of Aristotelian physics, Copernicus hypothesized a Sun-centered universe with a planetary Earth and mathematically worked out the implications.

Despite the innovation's apparent absurdity, its application resulted in a system Copernicus believed to be qualitatively better than Ptolemy's. The heliocentric model readily explained the apparent daily movement of the heavens and annual motion of the Sun as due to the Earth's daily rotation on its axis and its annual revolution around the central Sun. The appearance of the moving Sun and stars could now be recognized as deceptively created by the Earth's own movements. The great celestial motions were then nothing but a projection of the Earth's motion in the opposite direction. To the traditional objection that a moving Earth would be disruptive to itself and objects on it, Copernicus countered that the geocentric theory necessitated an even swifter movement by the immensely greater heavens, which would constitute a patently worse disruption.

Many particular problems that had long haunted the Ptolemaic tradition seemed more elegantly solved by a heliocentric system. The apparent backward and forward movements of the planets relative to the fixed stars, and their varying degrees of brightness, to explain which astronomers had employed innumerable mathematical contrivances, could now be understood more simply as the result of viewing those planets from a moving Earth—which would produce the retrograde appearances without the hypothetical use of major epicycles. A moving Earth would automatically make regular planetary orbits around the Sun appear to the terrestrial observer as irregular movements around the Earth. Nor were equants any longer necessary, a Ptolemaic device that Copernicus found especially objectionable on aesthetic grounds because it violated the rule of uniform circular motion. Copernicus's new ordering of the planets outward from the Sun—Mercury, Venus, Earth and Moon, Mars, Jupiter, and Saturn—replaced the traditional Earth-centered order, and provided a simple and coherent solution to the previously ill-resolved problem of why Mercury and Venus always appeared close to the Sun. The explanation for these problems and others like them strongly suggested to Copernicus the superiority of the heliocentric theory over the Ptolemaic system. The appearances were saved (albeit still approximately), and with greater conceptual elegance. Despite the obvious commonsense evidence to the contrary, not to mention almost two millennia of scientific tradition, Copernicus was convinced the Earth truly moved.

Having set down a first version of his thesis in a short manuscript, the *Commentariolus*, Copernicus circulated it among his friends as early as 1514. Two decades later, a lecture on the principles of his new system was given in Rome before the pope, who approved. Subsequently, a formal request to publish was made. Yet throughout most of his life, Copernicus held back from full publication of his extraordinary idea. (Later, in his preface to the *De Revolutionibus*, dedicated to the pope, Copernicus confessed his reluctance to reveal publicly his insight into nature's mysteries lest it be scorned by the uninitiated—invoking the Pythagorean practice of strict secrecy in such matters.) But his friends and particularly his closest student, Rheticus, prevailed upon him, and finally Rheticus was allowed to take the completed manuscript from Poland to Germany to be printed. On the last day of his life, in the year 1543, a copy of the published work was brought to Copernicus.

But on that day, and even during the following several decades, there was little indication in Europe that an unprecedented revolution in the Western world view had been initiated. For most who heard of it, the new conception was so contradictory to everyday experience, so patently false, as not to require serious discussion. But as a few proficient astronomers began to find Copernicus's argument persuasive, the opposition began to mount; and it was the religious implications of the new cosmology that quickly provoked the most intense attacks.

The Religious Reaction

In the beginning, that opposition did not come from the Catholic Church. Copernicus was a canon in good standing at a Catholic cathedral and an esteemed consultant to the Church in Rome. His friends urging publication included a bishop and a cardinal. After his death, Catholic universities did not avoid using the *De Revolutionibus* in astronomy classes. Moreover, the new Gregorian calendar instituted by the Church was based on calculations according to Copernicus's system. Nor was this apparent flexibility altogether unusual, for throughout most of the high Middle Ages and Renaissance, Roman Catholicism had allowed considerable latitude in intellectual speculation. Indeed, such latitude was a major source of Protestant criticism of the Church. By tolerating and even encouraging the exploration of Greek philosophy, science, and secular thinking, including the Hellenistic metaphorical interpretation of Scripture, the Church had, in Protestant eyes, allowed pristine Christianity and the literal truth of the Bible to be contaminated.

It was antagonism from the Protestant reformers that arose first and most forcefully, and understandably so: the Copernican hypothesis contradicted several passages in Holy Scripture concerning the fixity of the Earth, and Scripture was Protestantism's one absolute authority. To have biblical revelation questioned by human science was just the kind of Hellenizing intellectual arrogance and interpretive sophistry the reformers most abhorred in Catholic culture. Protestants were therefore quick to recognize the threat of Copernican astronomy and condemn the impiety. Even before the publication of the *De Revolutionibus*, Luther called Copernicus an "upstart astrologer" who foolishly wished to reverse the entire science of astronomy while flagrantly contradicting the Holy Bible. Luther was soon joined by other reformers like Melanchthon and Calvin, some of whom recommended that stringent measures be taken to suppress the pernicious heresy. Quoting a passage from the Psalms, "the world also is established, that it cannot be moved," Calvin asked: "Who will dare to place the authority of Copernicus above that of the Holy Spirit?" When Rheticus took Copernicus's manuscript to Nürnberg to be published, he was forced by reformers' opposition to go elsewhere. Even in Leipzig, where he left the book with the Protestant Osiander to publish, the latter inserted an anonymous preface without Copernicus's knowledge, asserting that the heliocentric theory was merely a convenient computational method and should not be taken seriously as a realistic account of the heavens.

The ploy may have saved the publication, but Copernicus had indeed been serious, as a close reading of the text revealed. And by Galileo's time in the early seventeenth century, the Catholic Church—now with a renewed sense of the need for doctrinal orthodoxy—felt compelled to take a definite stand against the Copernican hypothesis. While in an earlier century, Aquinas or the ancient Church fathers might have readily considered a metaphorical interpretation of the scriptural passages in question, thereby eliminating the apparent contradiction with science, the emphatic literalism of Luther and his followers had activated a similar attitude in the Catholic Church. Both sides of the dispute now wished to secure an uncompromised solidity with respect to the biblical revelation.

Moreover, guilt by association had recently hurt the reputation of Copernicanism in the case of the mystical Neoplatonist philosopher and astronomer Giordano Bruno. Bruno had widely promulgated an advanced version of the heliocentric theory as part of his esoteric philosophy, but had later been tried and executed by the Inquisition for heretical theological views. His stated beliefs that the Bible should be followed for its moral teachings rather than its astronomy, and that all religions and philosophies should coexist in tolerance and mutual understanding, had received little enthusiasm from the Inquisition. In the heated atmosphere of the Counter-Reformation, such liberal views were unwelcome at best, and in the case of Bruno, whose character was as refractory as his ideas were unorthodox, they were scandalous. Certainly the fact that the same man who held heretical views on the Trinity and other vital theological matters had also taught the Copernican theory did not augur well for the latter. After Bruno was burned at the stake in 1600 (though not for his heliocentric teachings), Copernicanism seemed a more dangerous theory—both to religious authorities and to philosopher-astronomers, each for their different reasons.

Yet not only did the new theory conflict with parts of the Bible, it was now apparent that Copernicanism posed a fundamental threat to the entire Christian framework of cosmology, theology, and morality. Ever since the Scholastics and Dante had embraced Greek science and endowed it with religious meaning, the Christian world view had become inextricably embedded in an Aristotelian-Ptolemaic geocentric universe. The essential dichotomy between the celestial and terrestrial realms, the great cosmological structure of Heaven, Hell, and Purgatory, the circling planetary spheres with angelic hosts, God's empyrean throne above all, the moral drama of human life pivotally centered between spiritual heavens and corporeal Earth—all would be cast into question or destroyed altogether by the new theory. Even discounting the elaborate medieval superstructure, the most basic principles of the Christian religion were now being impugned by the astronomical innovation. If the Earth truly moved, then no longer could it be the fixed center of God's Creation and his plan of salvation. Nor could man be the central focus of the cosmos. The absolute uniqueness and significance of Christ's intervention into human history seemed to require a corresponding uniqueness and significance for the Earth. The meaning of the Redemption itself, the central event not just of human history but of universal history, seemed at stake. To be a Copernican seemed tantamount to atheism. In the eyes of the papal advisors, Galileo's *Dialogue Concerning the Two Chief World Systems,* already being applauded throughout Europe, threatened to have worse effects on Christian minds "than Luther and Calvin put together."

With religion and science in such apparent contradiction—and an upstart science at that, a mere novel theory—there was little question for Church authorities as to which system would prevail. Awakened to the dire theological implications of Copernican astronomy, and further traumatized into dogmatic rigidity by decades of Reformation conflict and heresy, the Catholic Church mustered its considerable powers of suppression and condemned in no uncertain terms the heliocentric hypothesis: the *De Revolutionibus* and *Dialogue* placed on the Index of forbidden books; Galileo interrogated by the Inquisition, forced to recant and placed under house arrest; major Catholic Copernicans dismissed from their posts and banished; all teachings and writings upholding the motion of the Earth prohibited. With the Copernican theory, Catholicism's long-held tension between reason and faith had finally snapped.

Kepler

But by the time of Galileo's recantation, the scientific triumph of Copernicanism was already in sight, and the attempts to suppress it by the institutional religions, both Catholic and Protestant, would soon turn against them. Nevertheless, in the early years of the heliocentric theory that triumph did not seem assured. The notion of a moving Earth was generally ridiculed, if noticed at all, by Copernicus's contemporaries and throughout the rest of the sixteenth century. Moreover, the *De Revolutionibus* was obscure enough (perhaps intentionally) and so demanding of technical mathematical proficiency that only a few astronomers could understand it, and even fewer could accept its central hypothesis. But neither could they overlook its technical sophistication, and its author was soon referred to as "a second Ptolemy." During the following decades, increasing numbers of astronomers and astrologers found Copernicus's diagrams and computations useful, even indispensable. New astronomical tables based on more recent observations were published employing his methods, and as these tables were measurably superior to the old ones, the reputation of Copernican astronomy was further enhanced. Yet major theoretical problems still remained.

For Copernicus was a revolutionary who had maintained many traditional assumptions that worked against the immediate success of his hypothesis. In particular, he had continued to believe in the Ptolemaic dictum that the planets must move with uniform circular motion, which forced his system finally to have as much mathematical complexity as Ptolemy's. For his theory to match the observations, Copernicus still required minor epicycles and eccentrics. He still retained the concentric crystalline spheres moving the planets and stars, as well as other essential physical and mathematical components of the old Ptolemaic system. And he had not adequately answered obvious physical objections to a moving Earth, such as why terrestrial objects would not simply fall off the Earth as it swept through space.

Despite the radical quality of the Copernican hypothesis, a planetary Earth was the only major innovation in the *De Revolutionibus*, a work that was otherwise solidly within the ancient and medieval astronomical tradition. Copernicus had caused the first break from the old cosmology, and thereby created all the problems that had to be solved by Kepler, Galileo, Descartes, and Newton before they could offer a comprehensive scientific theory capable of integrating a planetary Earth. As Copernicus had left it—a moving Earth in a cosmos otherwise ruled by Aristotelian and Ptolemaic assumptions—there were too many internal contradictions. And because of its adherence to uniform circular motion, Copernicus's system was finally no simpler or even more accurate than Ptolemy's. Yet despite the remaining problems, the new theory possessed a certain harmonious symmetry and coherence that appealed to a few subsequent astronomers—most significantly, Kepler and Galileo. It was above all not utilitarian scientific accuracy but aesthetic superiority that would attract those crucial supporters to the Copernican cause. Without the intellectual bias created by a Neoplatonically defined aesthetic judgment, the Scientific Revolution might well not have occurred, certainly not in the form it took historically.

For Kepler, with his passionate belief in the transcendent power of numbers and geometrical forms, his vision of the Sun as the central image of the Godhead, and his devotion to the celestial "harmony of the spheres," was yet more impelled by Neoplatonic motivations than Copernicus. Writing to Galileo, Kepler invoked "Plato and Pythagoras, our true preceptors." He believed that Copernicus had intuited something greater than the heliocentric theory was presently capable of expressing, and that, if freed from the Ptolemaic assumptions still resident in the *De Revolutionibus,* the Copernican hypothesis would open up scientific understanding to a new, spectacularly ordered and harmonious cosmos that would directly reflect God's glory. Kepler was also the inheritor of a vast body of unprecedentedly accurate astronomical observations collected by Tycho de Brahe, his predecessor as imperial mathematician and astrologer to the Holy Roman Emperor.[1] Armed both with these data and with his unwavering faith in the Copernican theory, he set out to discover the simple mathematical laws that would solve the problem of the planets.

For almost ten years, Kepler laboriously attempted to fit against Brahe's observations every possible hypothetical system of circles he could devise, focusing particularly on the planet Mars. After many failures, he was forced to conclude that some geometrical figure other than the circle must be the true form of planetary orbits. Having mastered the ancient theory of conic sections developed by Euclid and Apollonius, Kepler at last discovered that the observations precisely matched orbits shaped as ellipses, with the Sun as one of the two foci, and with each planet moving at speeds varying proportionately according to its distance from the Sun—fastest near the Sun, slowest away from the Sun, with equal areas swept out in equal times. The Platonic dictum for uniformity of motion had always been interpreted in terms of measurement along the arc of the circular orbit—equal distance on the arc in equal intervals of time. This interpretation had ultimately failed, despite the ingenuity of astronomers for two thousand years. Kepler, however, discovered a new and subtler form of uniformity which did fit the data: If a line were drawn from the Sun to the planet on its elliptical orbit, that line would sweep out equal areas of the ellipse in equal intervals of time. Subsequently, he conceived and corroborated a third law, which demonstrated that the different planetary orbits were exactly related to each other by mathematical proportions—the ratio of the squares of the orbital periods being equal to the ratio of the cubes of their average distance from the Sun.

Thus Kepler at last solved the ancient problem of the planets and fulfilled Plato's extraordinary prediction of single, uniform, mathematically ordered orbits—and in so doing vindicated the Copernican hypothesis. With elliptical orbits replacing the Ptolemaic circles, and with the law of equal areas replacing that of equal arcs, he was able to dispense with all the complex corrective devices, epicycles, eccentrics, equants, and so forth. Even more significantly, his one simple geometrical figure and his one simple mathematical speed equation produced results that precisely matched observations of the most rigorous quality—something none of the previous Ptolemaic solutions, despite all their ad hoc devices, had ever accomplished. Kepler had taken centuries of diverse and largely inexplicable observations of the heavens and condensed them into a few concise, overarching principles which gave convincing evidence that the universe was arranged in accordance with elegant mathematical harmonies. Empirical data and abstract mathematical reasoning at last meshed perfectly. And of particular importance for Kepler, the most advanced scientific conclusions affirmed both Copernicus's theory and the mathematical mysticism of the ancient Pythagorean and Platonic philosophers.

Moreover, for the first time a mathematical solution to the problem of the planets led directly to a physical account of the heavens in terms of a physically plausible motion. For Kepler's ellipses were continuous straightforward motions of a single shape. By contrast, the complicated Ptolemaic system of indefinitely compounded circles possessed no empirical correlate in everyday experience. Because of this, mathematical solutions in the Ptolemaic tradition had often been considered as merely instumentalist constructions with no ultimate claim to describing a physical reality. Copernicus had nevertheless argued for the physical reality of his mathematical constructions. In the first book of the *De Revolutionibus*, he alluded to the ancient conception of astronomy as "the consummation of mathematics." Yet in the end, even Copernicus offered an implausibly complicated system of minor epicycles and eccentrics to account for the appearances.

With Kepler, however, Copernicus's intuition and imperfect mathematical argument were brought to fruition. For the first time in planetary astronomy, the appearances were "genuinely" saved, not just instrumentally. Indeed, Kepler both saved the phenomena in the traditional sense and "saved" mathematical astronomy itself by demonstrating mathematics' genuine physical relevance to the heavens—its capacity to disclose the actual nature of the physical motions. Mathematics was now established not just as an instrument for astronomical prediction, but as an intrinsic element of astronomical reality. Kepler thus considered that the Pythagorean claim for mathematics as the key to cosmic understanding had been triumphantly validated, thereby revealing the previously hidden grandeur of God's creation.

Galileo

With Kepler's breakthrough, the Copernican revolution would in time have almost certainly succeeded in the scientific world through sheer mathematical and predictive superiority. But coincidentally, in 1609, the same year that Kepler published in Prague his laws of planetary motion, Galileo in Padua turned his recently constructed telescope to the heavens, and through his startling observations made available to astronomy the first qualitatively new evidence it had known since the ancients. And each of his observations—the craters and mountains on the surface of the Moon, the moving spots on the Sun, the four moons revolving around Jupiter, the phases of Venus, the "unbelievably" numerous individual stars of the Milky Way—was interpreted by Galileo as powerful evidence in favor of the Copernican heliocentric theory.

If the Moon's surface was uneven, like the Earth's, and if the Sun had spots that came and went, then these bodies were not the perfect, incorruptible, and immutable celestial objects of Aristotelian-Ptolemaic cosmology. Similarly, if Jupiter was a moving body and yet could also have four moons revolving around it while its entire system revolved in a greater orbit, then the Earth could also do the same with its own moon—thus refuting the traditional argument that the Earth could not move around the Sun, or else the Moon would have long ago spun off its orbit. And again, if phases of Venus were visible, then Venus must be revolving around the Sun. And if the Milky Way, which to the naked eye was just a nebulous glow, now proved to be composed of a multitude of new stars, then the Copernican suggestion of a much larger universe (to explain the lack of visible annual stellar parallax despite the Earth's movement around the Sun) seemed considerably more plausible. And if the planets now appeared through the telescope to have substantial bodies with extended surfaces and were not just points of light, and yet many more stars were visible without any apparent extension, then this also argued in favor of an incomparably larger universe than that assumed by the traditional cosmology. After several months of such discoveries and conclusions, Galileo quickly wrote his *Sidereus Nuncius* (*The Messenger of the Stars*), making public his first observations. The book created a sensation in European intellectual circles.

With Galileo's telescope, the heliocentric theory could no longer be considered merely a computational convenience. It now had visible physical substantiation. Moreover, the telescope revealed the heavens in their gross materiality—not transcendent points of celestial light, but concrete substances appropriate for empirical investigation, just like natural phenomena on the Earth. The time-honored academic practice of arguing and observing exclusively from within the boundaries of Aristotelian thought began giving way to a fresh examination of empirical phenomena with a critical eye. Many individuals not previously involved in scientific studies now took up the telescope and saw for themselves the nature of the new Copernican universe. Astronomy, by virtue of the telescope and Galileo's compelling writings, became of vital interest to more than specialists. Successive generations of late Renaissance and post-Renaissance Europeans, increasingly willing to doubt the absolute authority of traditional doctrines both ancient and ecclesiastical, were finding the Copernican theory not only plausible but liberating. A new celestial world was opening up to the Western mind, just as a new terrestrial world was being opened by the global explorers. Although the cultural consequences of Kepler's and Galileo's discoveries were gradual and cumulative, the medieval universe had effectively been dealt its death blow. The Copernican revolution's epochal triumph in Western thought had begun.

It is possible the Church could have reacted to this triumph otherwise than it did. Seldom in its history had the Christian religion attempted to suppress so rigidly a scientific theory strictly on the basis of apparent scriptural contradictions. As Galileo himself pointed out, the Church had long been accustomed to sanctioning allegorical interpretations of the Bible whenever the latter appeared to conflict with scientific evidence. He quoted the early Church fathers to that effect, and added that it would be "a terrible detriment for the souls if people found themselves convinced by proof of something that it was made then a sin to believe." Moreover, many ecclesiastical authorities recognized Galileo's genius, including several Jesuit astronomers in the Vatican. Indeed, the pope himself was a friend of Galileo and accepted with enthusiasm the dedication of his book, *Assayer,* which had outlined the new scientific method.

Even Cardinal Bellarmine, the Church's chief theologian, who finally made the decision to declare Copernicanism "false and erroneous," had earlier written:

> If there were a real proof that the Sun is in the center of the universe, that the Earth is in the third heaven, and that the Sun does not go round the Earth but the Earth round the Sun, then we should have to proceed with great circumspection in explaining passages of Scripture which appear to teach the contrary, and rather admit that we did not understand them than declare an opinion to be false which is proved to be true.[2]

But a unique and potent combination of circumstances conspired otherwise. The Church's pervasive awareness of the Protestant threat compounded the challenge of any novel and potentially heretical position. With the memory of the Bruno heresy still fresh, Catholic authorities earnestly desired to avoid a new scandal that might further disrupt Reformation-torn Christianity. Making the issue all the more threatening were the new power of the printing press and the lucid persuasiveness of Galileo's vernacular Italian, undermining the Church's attempts to control the beliefs of the faithful. Also complicating the Church's reaction were the intricate political conflicts in Italy involving the pope. A pivotal role was played by the Aristotelian professors in the universities, whose intense opposition to the vociferously anti-Aristotelian and all-too-popular Galileo served to arouse fundamentalist preachers, who in turn aroused the Inquisition. Galileo's own polemical and even vitriolic personality, which alienated his opponents to the point of vengeance, was a contributing factor, as was his insufficient sensitivity to the profound significance of the greater cosmological revolution taking place. Bellarmine's conviction that mathematical hypotheses were only intellectual constructs with no ultimate relation to physical reality; Galileo's espousal of atomism, when the Catholic doctrine of the eucharistic transubstantiation seemed to require an Aristotelian physics; the pope's sense of personal betrayal, exacerbated by his political insecurity; the power struggles between different religious orders within the Church; the Inquisition's voracious appetite for punitive repression—all these factors coalesced with fateful accord to motivate the Church's official decision to prohibit Copernicanism.

That decision caused irreparable harm to the Church's intellectual and spiritual integrity. Catholicism's formal commitment to a stationary

Earth drastically undercut its status and influence among the European intelligentsia. The Church would retain much power and loyalty in the succeeding centuries, but it could no longer justifiably claim to represent the human aspiration toward full knowledge of the universe. After the Inquisition's ban, Galileo's writings were smuggled to the north, where the vanguard of the Western intellectual quest would thereafter reside.[3] Whatever the relative importance of individual factors such as the entrenched Aristotelian academic opposition or the pope's personal motives, the ultimate cultural meaning of the Galilean conflict was that of Church versus science, and, by implication, religion versus science. And in Galileo's forced recantation lay the Church's own defeat and science's victory.

Institutional Christianity as a whole suffered from the Copernican victory, which contravened both religious foundations—Protestantism's literal Bible and Catholicism's sacramental authority. For the present, most European intellectuals, including the scientific revolutionaries, would remain devoutly Christian. But the schism between science and religion—maintained even within the individual mind—had fully announced itself. With Luther, the West's intellectual independence had asserted itself within the realm of religion. With Galileo, it took a step outside of religion altogether, established new principles, and opened new territory.

The Forging of Newtonian Cosmology

Although Kepler's mathematical and Galileo's observational support assured the success of the heliocentric theory in astronomy, the theory still lacked a more encompassing conceptual scheme, a coherent cosmology within which it could fit. Ptolemy had been satisfactorily replaced, but not Aristotle. That the Earth and the other planets moved in elliptical orbits around the Sun seemed clear, but if there were no circling aetheric spheres, then how did the planets, including the Earth, move at all? And what now kept them from flying out of their orbits? If the Earth was moving, thereby destroying the basis of Aristotelian physics, then why did terrestrial objects always fall toward its surface? If the stars were so numerous and distant, then how large was the universe? What was its structure, and where was its center, if any? What happened to the long-recognized celestial-terrestrial division if the Earth was planetary like other heavenly bodies, and if the heavenly bodies now appeared to have Earth-like qualities? And where was God in this cosmos? Until these weighty questions were answered, the Copernican revolution had shattered the old cosmology, but it had not yet forged a new one.

Both Kepler and Galileo had provided vital insights and tools with which to approach these problems. Both had believed and then demonstrated that the universe was organized mathematically, and that scientific progress was achieved by rigorously comparing mathematical hypotheses with empirical observations. And Copernicus's work had already made the most fertile suggestion for the new cosmology; by making the Earth a planet to explain the Sun's apparent motion, he implied that the heavens and the Earth should not and could not be considered absolutely distinct. But Kepler went further, and directly applied notions of terrestrial force to celestial phenomena.

The Ptolemaic (and Copernican) circular orbits had always been considered "natural motions" in the Aristotelian sense: by their elemental nature, the aetheric spheres moved in perfect circles, just as the heavy elements of earth and water moved downward and the light elements of air and fire moved upward. Kepler's ellipses, however, were not circular and constant, but involved the planets in changes of speed and direction at each point in their orbits. Elliptical motion in a heliocentric universe required a new explanation beyond that of natural motion.

Kepler suggested as an alternative the concept of a constantly imposed force. Influenced as always by the Neoplatonic exaltation of the Sun, he believed the Sun to be an active source of movement in the universe. He therefore postulated an *anima motrix,* a moving force akin to astrological "influences," which emanated from the Sun and moved the planets— most powerfully close to the Sun, less so when distant. But Kepler still had to explain why the orbits curved in ellipses. Having absorbed William Gilbert's recently published work on magnetism, with its thesis that the Earth itself was a giant magnet, Kepler extended this principle to all celestial bodies and hypothesized that the Sun's *anima motrix* combined with its own magnetism and that of the planets to create the elliptical orbits. Kepler thereby made the first proposal that the planets in their orbits were moved by mechanical forces, rather than by the automatic geometrical motion of the Aristotelian-Ptolemaic spheres. Despite its relatively primitive form, Kepler's concept of the solar system as a self-governing machine based on notions of terrestrial dynamics correctly anticipated the emerging cosmology.

In the meantime, Galileo had pursued this mechanical-mathematical mode of analysis on the terrestrial plane with systematic rigor and extraordinary success. Like his fellow Renaissance scientists Kepler and Copernicus, Galileo had imbibed from the Neoplatonic Humanists the belief that the physical world could be understood in geometrical and arithmetic terms. With Pythagorean conviction he declared that "the Book of Nature is written in mathematical characters." But with his more down-to-earth sensibility, Galileo developed mathematics less as a mystical key to the heavens than as a straightforward tool for the understanding of matter in motion and for the defeat of his Aristotelian academic opponents. Although Kepler's understanding of celestial motion was more advanced than that of Galileo (who, like Copernicus, still believed in self-sustaining circular motion), it was Galileo's insights into terrestrial dynamics that, when applied by his successors to the heavens, would begin to solve the physical problems created by Copernicus's innovation.

Aristotle's physics, based on perceptible qualities and verbal logic, still ruled most contemporary scientific thinking and dominated the universities. But Galileo's revered model was Archimedes the mathematical physicist (whose writings had been recently rediscovered by the Humanists), rather than Aristotle the descriptive biologist. To combat the Aristotelians, Galileo developed both a new procedure for analyzing phenomena and a new basis for testing theories. He argued that to make accurate judgments concerning nature, scientists should consider only precisely measurable "objective" qualities (size, shape, number, weight, motion), while merely perceptible qualities (color, sound, taste, touch, smell) should be ignored as subjective and ephemeral. Only by means of an exclusively quantitative analysis could science attain certain knowledge of the world. In addition, while Aristotle's empiricism had been predominantly a descriptive and, especially as exaggerated by later Aristotelians, logico-verbal approach, Galileo now established the quantitative experiment as the final test of hypotheses. Finally, to further penetrate nature's mathematical regularities and true character, Galileo employed, developed, or invented a host of technical instruments—lens, telescope, microscope, geometric compass, magnet, air thermometer, hydrostatic balance. The use of such instruments gave a new dimension to empiricism unknown to the Greeks, a dimension that undercut both the theories and the practice of the Aristotelian professors. In Galileo's vision, free exploration of an impersonal mathematical universe was to replace the hidebound academic tradition's interminable deductive justification of Aristotle's organismic universe.

Employing the new categories and new methodology, Galileo set out to demolish the spurious dogma of academic physics. Aristotle had believed that a heavier body would fall at a faster rate than a lighter one, because of its elemental propensity to seek the center of the Earth as its natural position—the heavier the body, the greater the propensity. Through his repeated application of mathematical analysis to physical experiments, Galileo first refuted this tenet and later formulated the law of uniform accelerated motion in falling bodies—a motion that was independent of the weight or composition of the bodies. Building on the impetus theory of Aristotle's Scholastic critics Buridan and Oresme, Galileo analyzed projectile motion and developed the crucial idea of inertia. Contrary to Aristotle, who held that all bodies sought their natural place and that nothing continued to move otherwise without a constantly applied external push, Galileo stated that just as a body at rest would tend to remain so unless otherwise pushed, so too would a moving body tend to remain in constant motion unless otherwise stopped or deflected. Force was required to explain only change in motion, not constant motion. In this way, he met one of the Aristotelians' chief physical arguments against a planetary Earth—that objects on a moving Earth would be forcibly knocked about, and that a projectile thrown directly upward from a moving Earth would necessarily land at some distance away from its point of departure. Since neither of these phenomena was observed, they concluded that the Earth must be stationary. Through his concept of inertia, however, Galileo demonstrated that a moving Earth would automatically endow all its objects and projectiles with the Earth's own motion, and therefore the collective inertial motion would be imperceptible to anyone on the Earth.

In the course of his life's work, Galileo had effectively supported the Copernican theory, initiated the full mathematization of nature, grasped the idea of force as a mechanical agent, laid the foundations of modern mechanics and experimental physics, and developed the working principles of modern scientific method. But the question of how to explain physically the celestial movements, including the motion of the Earth itself, still remained unresolved. Because Galileo had missed the significance of the planetary laws discovered by his contemporary Kepler, he had continued to maintain the traditional understanding of celestial motion as circular orbits, only now centered around the Sun. His concept of inertia—which he understood as applicable on the Earth only to motion on horizontal surfaces (where gravity was not a factor) and which was thus circular motion around the Earths's surface—was applied to the heavens accordingly: The planets continued to move in their orbits about the Sun because their natural inertial tendency was circular. Galileo's circular inertia, however, could not explain Kepler's ellipses. And it was all the more implausible if the Earth, which as the unique center of the universe in Aristotelian cosmology had defined the surrounding space and given an absolute motive and reference point for circling spheres, was now understood to be a planet. The Copernican universe had created and was still plagued by a fundamental enigma.

But now occurred another influx of ancient Greek philosophy: the atomism of Leucippus and Democritus, which would both point toward a solution to the problem of celestial motion and help shape the future course of Western scientific development. The philosophy of atomism, as passed on by Democritus's successors Epicurus and Lucretius, had resurfaced during the Renaissance as part of the Humanists' recovery of ancient literature, particularly through the manuscript of Lucretius's poem *De Rerum Natura* (*On the Nature of Things*), outlining the Epicurean system. Originally developed as an attempt to meet the logical objections against change and motion put forward by Parmenides, Greek atomism had posited a universe made up of invisibly small, indivisible particles moving freely in an infinite neutral void, and creating by their collisions and combinations all phenomena. In this void there was no absolute up or down or universal center, every position in space being neutral and equal to every other. Since the entire universe was composed of the same material particles on the same principles, the Earth itself was merely another chance aggregation of particles and was neither at rest nor at the universe's center. There was therefore no fundamental celestial-terrestrial division. And since both the size of the void and the number of particles were infinite, the universe was potentially populated by many moving earths and suns, each created by the atoms' random movements.

The evolving Copernican universe bore a number of striking resemblances to this conception. Making the Earth a planet had removed the foundation from the Aristotelian idea of an absolute (nonneutral) space centered on the stationary Earth. A planetary Earth also required a much larger universe to satisfy the absence of observable stellar parallax. With the Earth no longer the universal center, the universe did not have to be finite (a universal center requires a finite universe, since an infinite space can have no center). The outermost sphere of stars was now unnecessary as an explanation for the movement of the heavens, and so the stars could be dispersed infinitely, as the Neoplatonists had also suggested. And Galileo's telescopic discoveries had both revealed a multitude of new stars at apparently great distances, and further undermined the celestial-terrestrial dichotomy. The implications of a Copernican universe—a nonunique moving Earth; a neutral, centerless, multipopulated, and perhaps infinite space; and the elimination of the celestial-terrestrial distinction—all coincided with those of the atomistic cosmos. With the comprehensive structure of Aristotelian cosmology collapsing, and with no other viable alternative to replace it, the atomists' universe represented an already well-developed and uniquely appropriate framework into which the new Copernican system could be placed. The esoteric philosopher-scientist Bruno was the first to perceive the congruence between the two systems. Through his work, the Neoplatonic image of an infinite universe enunciated by Nicholas of Cusa was reinforced by the atomistic conception to create an immensely expanded Copernican cosmos.

But atomism was to provide other and no less consequential contributions to the developing cosmology. For not only was the structure of the atomistic cosmos congruent with the Copernican theory, but, in addition, the atomistic conception of matter itself was singularly appropriate to the working principles of the new natural scientists. Democritus's atoms were characterized exclusively by quantitative factors—size, shape, motion, and number—and not by any perceptible qualities, such as taste, smell, touch, or sound. All apparent qualitative changes in phenomena were created by differing quantities of atoms combined in different arrangements, and therefore the atomistic universe was in principle open to mathematical analysis. The material particles possessed neither purpose nor intelligence, but moved solely according to mechanical principles. Thus the cosmological and physical structures of ancient atomism invited the very modes of analysis—mechanistic and mathematical—already being chosen and rapidly developed by seventeenth-century natural scientists. Atomism influenced Galileo in his approach to nature as matter in motion, was admired by Francis Bacon and employed by Thomas Hobbes in his philosophy of mechanistic materialism, and was popularized in European scientific circles by their younger contemporary Pierre Gassendi. But it was finally René Descartes who undertook the task of systematically adapting atomism to provide a physical explanation for the Copernican universe.

The basic principles of ancient atomism offered many parallels to Descartes's image of nature as an intricate impersonal machine strictly ordered by mathematical law. Like Democritus, Descartes assumed that the physical world was composed of an infinite number of particles, or "corpuscles," which mechanically collided and aggregated. As a Christian, however, he assumed that these corpuscles did not move in utterly random fashion, but obeyed certain laws imposed on them by a providential God at their creation. To discover those laws was Descartes's challenge, and his first step was to ask how a single corpuscle would freely move in an infinite universe possessing neither absolute directions nor Aristotelian elemental tendencies to motion. By employing the Scholastics' impetus theory in the new context of an atomistic space, he concluded that a corpuscle at rest would tend to remain at rest unless otherwise pushed, while a corpuscle in motion would tend to continue moving in a straight line at the same speed unless otherwise deflected. Thus Descartes enunciated the first unequivocal statement of the law of inertia—one that included the critical element of inertial linearity (compared with Galileo's more rudimentary and empirically conceived Earth-oriented inertia with its implication of circularity). Descartes additionally reasoned that since all motion in a corpuscular universe must in principle be mechanistic, any deviations from these inertial tendencies must occur as a result of corpuscular collisions with other corpuscles. The basic principles governing these collisions he set out to establish by intuitive deduction.

With its freely moving particles in an infinite neutral space, atomism had suggested a new way of looking at motion. Descartes's notion of corpuscular collision allowed his successors to develop further Galileo's insights into the nature of force and momentum. But of immediate significance for the Copernican theory, Descartes applied his theories of linear inertia and corpuscular collision to the problem of planetary motion, and thereby began to clear away the last residue of Aristotelian physics from the heavens. For the automatic circular motions of the celestial bodies still espoused by Copernicus and Galileo were not possible in an atomistic world in which particles could only move in a straight line or remain at rest. By applying his inertial and corpuscular theories to the heavens, Descartes isolated the crucial missing factor in the explanation of planetary motion: Unless there was some other inhibiting force, the inertial motion of the planets, including that of the Earth, would necessarily tend to propel them in a tangential straight line away from the curving orbit around the Sun. Since, however, their orbits were maintained in continuous closed curves without such centrifugal breaks, it was evident that some factor was forcing the planets toward the Sun—or as Descartes and his successors more revealingly formulated it, something was continually forcing the planets to "fall" toward the Sun. To discover what force caused that fall was the fundamental celestial dilemma facing the new cosmology. The fact that the planets moved at all was now explicable by inertia. But the form that motion took—the planets' constant maintenance of elliptical orbits about the Sun—still demanded explanation.

Many of Descartes's intuitively deduced hypotheses concerning his corpuscular universe—including most of his laws of corpuscular collision and his filling the universe with vortices of moving corpuscles (by which he tried to explain the planets' being pushed back into their orbits)— were not retained by his successors. But his basic conception of the physical universe as an atomistic system ruled by a few mechanistic laws became the guiding model for seventeenth-century scientists grappling with the Copernican innovation. And because the riddle of planetary motion still remained the outstanding problem for post-Copernican science in its efforts to establish a self-consistent cosmology, Descartes's isolation of the "fall" factor was indispensable. With Descartes's concept of inertia applied to Kepler's ellipses, and with the general principle of mechanistic explanation implicit in both their rudimentary theories of planetary motion (Kepler's *anima motrix* and magnetism, Descartes's corpuscular vortices), the problem had gained a definition within which subsequent scientists—Borelli, Hooke, Huygens—could fruitfully work. Galileo's terrestrial dynamics had further defined the problem by effectively contravening Aristotelian physics, and by giving precise mathematical measurements of heavy bodies falling to the Earth. Thus two fundamental questions remained, one celestial and one terrestrial: Given inertia, why did the Earth and other planets continually fall toward the Sun? And given a moving noncentral Earth, why did terrestrial objects fall to the Earth at all?

The possibility that both questions could have the same answer had been constantly growing with the work of Kepler, Galileo, and Descartes. The notion of an attractive force acting between all material bodies had also been developing. Among the Greeks, Empedocles had posited such a force. Among the Scholastics, Oresme had reasoned that if Aristotle were mistaken about the Earth's unique central position, an alternative explanation for bodies' falling to the Earth could be that matter naturally tended to attract other matter. Both Copernicus and Kepler had invoked such a possibility to defend their moving Earth. By the third quarter of the seventeenth century, Robert Hooke had clearly glimpsed the synthesis: that a single attractive force governed both planetary motions and falling bodies. Moreover, he mechanically demonstrated his idea with a pendulum swung in an elongated circular path, its linear motion being continuously deflected by a central attraction. Such a demonstration tellingly illustrated the relevance of terrestrial mechanics for the explanation of celestial phenomena. Hooke's pendulum signaled the extent to which the scientific imagination had radically transformed the heavens from being a transcendent realm with its own special laws to being in principle no different from the mundane realm of the Earth.

It finally fell to Isaac Newton, born on Christmas Day the year of Galileo's death, to complete the Copernican revolution by quantitatively establishing gravity as a universal force—a force that could simultaneously cause both the fall of stones to the Earth and the closed orbits of the planets around the Sun. Indeed, it was Newton's astounding achievement to synthesize Descartes's mechanistic philosophy, Kepler's laws of planetary motion, and Galileo's laws of terrestial motion in one comprehensive theory. In an unprecedented series of mathematical discoveries and intuitions, Newton established that to maintain their stable orbits at the relative speeds and distances specified by Kepler's third law, the planets must be pulled toward the Sun with an attractive force that decreased inversely as the square of the distance from the Sun, and that bodies falling toward the Earth—not only a nearby stone but also the distant Moon—conformed to the same law. Moreover, he mathematically derived from this inverse-square law both the elliptical shapes of the planetary orbits and their speed variation (equal areas in equal times) as defined by Kepler's first and second laws. Thus all the major cosmological problems confronting the Copernicans were at last solved—what moved the planets, how they remained in their orbits, why heavy objects fall toward the Earth, the basic structure of the universe, the issue of the

celestial-terrestrial dichotomy. The Copernican hypothesis had provoked the need for, and now found, a new, comprehensive, and self-
consistent cosmology.

With an exemplary combination of empirical and deductive rigor,
Newton had formulated a very few overarching laws that appeared to
govern the entire cosmos. Through his three laws of motion (of inertia,
force, and equal reaction) and the theory of universal gravitation, he not
only established a physical basis for all of Kepler's laws, but was also able
to derive the movements of the tides, the precession of the equinoxes,
the orbits of comets, the trajectory motion of cannonballs and other
projectiles—indeed, all the known phenomena of celestial and terrestrial
mechanics were now unified under one set of physical laws. Every
particle of matter in the universe attracted every other particle with a
force proportional to the product of their masses and inversely proportional to the square of the distance between them. Newton had
struggled to discover the grand design of the universe, and had patently
succeeded. Descartes's vision of nature as a perfectly ordered machine
governed by mathematical laws and comprehensible by human science
was fulfilled.

Although Newton's working concept of gravity as a force acting at
a distance—a concept transposed from his studies of the sympathies
and antipathies of Hermetic philosophy and alchemy—seemed esoteric
and insufficiently mechanical to continental mechanistic philosophers,
and puzzled even Newton, the mathematical derivations were too spectacularly comprehensive not to be compelling. Through the concept of a
quantitatively defined attractive force, he had integrated the two major
themes of seventeenth-century science—the mechanistic philosophy and
the Pythagorean tradition. It was not long before both his method and
his conclusions were recognized as the paradigm of scientific practice. In
1686–87, the Royal Society of London published Newton's *Principia
Mathematica Philosophiae Naturalis*. During the following decades, his
achievement was celebrated as the triumph of the modern mind over
ancient and medieval ignorance. Newton had revealed the true nature of
reality: Voltaire called him the greatest man who ever lived.

The Newtonian-Cartesian cosmology was now established as the
foundation for a new world view. By the beginning of the eighteenth
century, the educated person in the West knew that God had created the
universe as a complex mechanical system, composed of material particles
moving in an infinite neutral space according to a few basic principles,

such as inertia and gravity, that could be analyzed mathematically. In this universe, the Earth moved about the Sun, which was one star among a multitude, just as the Earth was one planet among many, and neither Sun nor Earth was at the center of the universe. A single set of physical laws governed both the celestial and the terrestrial realms, which were thus no longer fundamentally distinct. For just as the heavens were composed of material substances, so were their motions impelled by natural mechanical forces.

It also seemed reasonable to assume that after the creation of this intricate and orderly universe, God removed himself from further active involvement or intervention in nature, and allowed it to run on its own according to these perfect, immutable laws. The new image of the Creator was thus that of a divine architect, a master mathematician and clock maker, while the universe was viewed as a uniformly regulated and fundamentally impersonal phenomenon. Man's role in that universe could best be judged on the evidence that, by virtue of his own intelligence, he had penetrated the universe's essential order and could now use that knowledge for his own benefit and empowerment. One could scarcely doubt that man was the crown of creation. The Scientific Revolution—and the birth of the modern era—was now complete.

The Philosophical Revolution

The career of philosophy during these pivotal centuries was intimately tied to the Scientific Revolution, which it accompanied and stimulated, for which it provided a foundation, and by which it was critically molded. Indeed, philosophy now acquired an entirely new identity and structure as it entered into its third great epoch in the history of the Western mind. During much of the classical era, philosophy, though influenced by both religion and science, had held a largely autonomous position as definer and judge of the literate culture's world view. With the advent of the medieval period, the Christian religion assumed that preeminent status, while philosophy took on a subordinate role in the joining of faith to reason. But with the coming of the modern era, philosophy began to establish itself as a more fully independent force in the intellectual life of the culture. More precisely, philosophy now commenced its momentous transfer of allegiance from religion to science.

Bacon

In the same decades of the early seventeenth century during which Galileo in Italy was forging the new scientific practice, Francis Bacon in England proclaimed the birth of a new era in which natural science would bring man a material redemption to accompany his spiritual progress toward the Christian millennium. For Bacon, the discovery of the New World by the global explorers demanded a corresponding discovery of a new mental world in which old patterns of thinking, traditional prejudices, subjective distortions, verbal confusions, and general intellectual blindness would be overcome by a new method of acquiring knowledge. This method was to be fundamentally empirical: through the careful observation of nature and the skillful devising of many and varied experiments, pursued in the context of organized cooperative research, the human mind could gradually elicit those laws and generalizations that would give man the understanding of nature necessary for its control. Such a science would bring man immeasurable benefits and reestablish that mastery over nature he had lost with the fall of Adam.

While Socrates had equated knowledge with virtue, Bacon equated knowledge with power. Its practical usefulness was the very measure of its validity. With Bacon, science took on a new role—utilitarian, utopian, the material and human counterpart to God's plan of spiritual salvation. Man was created by God to interpret and hold dominion over nature. The pursuit of natural science was therefore his religious obligation. Man's primal fall required that such a pursuit be painstaking and fallible, but if he would discipline his mind and purify his vision of nature from age-old prejudices, man would achieve his divine right. Through science, the man of the modern era could assert his true superiority over the ancients. History was not cyclical, as was supposed by the ancients, but progressive, for man now stood at the dawn of a new, scientific civilization.

Skeptical of received doctrines and impatient with the syllogisms of the Aristotelian Scholastics, which he saw as nothing more than long-respected obstacles to useful knowledge, Bacon insisted that progress in science required a radical reformulation of its foundations. The true basis of knowledge was the natural world and the information it provided through the human senses. To fill the world with assumed final causes, as did Aristotle, or with intelligible divine essences, as did Plato, was to obscure from man a genuine understanding of nature on its own terms, solidly based on direct experimental contact and inductive reasoning from particulars. No longer should the pursuer of knowledge start from abstract definitions and verbal distinctions and then reason deductively, forcing the phenomena into prearranged order. Instead, he must begin with the unbiased analysis of concrete data and only then reason inductively, and cautiously, to reach general, empirically supported conclusions.

Bacon criticized Aristotle and the Scholastics for depending so heavily on deduction for their knowledge, since the premises from which deduction proceeded might simply be a spurious concoction of the philosopher's mind with no foundation in nature. From Bacon's point of view, all pure reason could accomplish in such circumstances would be to spin out of itself a web of abstractions possessing no objective validity. By contrast, the true philosopher directly approached the real world and studied it, without falsely anticipating and prejudicing the outcome. He cleansed the mind of its subjective distortions. The Aristotelian search for formal and final causes, the a priori belief that nature possessed teleological purposes and archetypal essences, were just such distortions, deceptively attractive to the emotionally tainted intellect. They should be discarded as useless, barren of empirical fruit. The traditional philosophers' Forms were merely fictions, and their words were prone to obscure rather than reveal. Preconceptions and verbiage must be renounced in favor of direct attention to things and their observed orderings. No "necessary" or "ultimate" truths should be so blithely assumed. To discover nature's true order, the mind must be purified of all its internal obstacles, purged of its habitual tendencies to produce rational or imaginary wish fulfillments in advance of empirical investigation. The mind must humble itself, rein itself in. Otherwise science would be impossible.

To assume, as did the ancient and medieval philosophers, that the world was divinely permeated and ordered in a manner directly accessible to the human mind, leading the mind directly to God's hidden purposes, was to bar the mind from insight into nature's actual forms. Only by recognizing the distinction between God and his creation, and between God's mind and man's, could man achieve real progress in science. Thus Bacon expressed the spirit of the Reformation and of Ockham. A "natural theology," as in classical Scholasticism, must be relinquished as a contradiction in terms, a falsifying miscegenation of matters of faith with matters of nature. Each realm had its own laws and its own appropriate method. Theology pertained to the realm of faith, but the realm of nature must be approached by a natural science unhampered by irrelevant assumptions derived from the religious imagination. Kept rightly separate, both theology and science could better flourish, and man could better serve his Creator through understanding the earthly kingdom's true natural causes—thereby gaining power over it as God intended.

Because all the previous systems of philosophy from the Greeks onward lacked a rigorously critical sense-based empiricism, because they relied on rational and imaginative constructions unsupported by careful experiment, they were like grandly entertaining theatrical productions, of no genuine relevance to the real world they so elegantly distorted. Emotional needs and traditional styles of thinking constantly impelled man to misperceive nature, to anthropomorphize it, to make it out to be what he wishes rather than what it is. The true philosopher does not attempt to narrow down the world to fit his understanding, but strives to expand his understanding to fit the world. Hence for Bacon, the business of philosophy was first and foremost the fresh examination of particulars. Through the astute use of experiments, the evidence of the senses could be progressively corrected and enhanced to reveal the truths hidden in nature. Thus could take place at last a marriage between the human mind and the natural universe, the fruit of which Bacon foresaw to be a long line of great inventions to relieve the miseries of mankind. In the future of science lay the restoration of learning and of human greatness itself.

With Bacon was evident the modern turning of the tide in philosophy. The nominalism and empiricism of the later Scholastics, and their growing criticism of Aristotle and speculative theology, now found bold and influential expression. It is true that for all his shrewdness, Bacon drastically underestimated the power of mathematics for the development of the new natural science, he failed to grasp the necessity of theoretical conjecture prior to empirical observation, and he altogether missed the significance of the new heliocentric theory. Yet his forceful advocacy of experience as the only legitimate source of true knowledge effectively redirected the European mind toward the empirical world, toward the methodical examination of physical phenomena, and toward the rejection of traditional assumptions—whether theological or metaphysical—when pursuing the advancement of learning. Bacon was neither a systematic philosopher nor a rigorous practicing scientist. He was, rather, a potent intermediary whose rhetorical power and visionary ideal persuaded future generations to fulfill his revolutionary program: the scientific conquest of nature for man's welfare and God's glory.

Descartes

If it was Bacon in England who helped inspire the distinctive character, direction, and vigor of the new science, it was Descartes on the Continent who established its philosophical foundation, and in so doing articulated the epochal defining statement of the modern self.

In an age faced with a crumbling world view, with unexpected and disorienting discoveries of every sort, and with the collapse of fundamental institutions and cultural traditions, a skeptical relativism concerning the possibility of certain knowledge was spreading among the European intelligentsia. External authorities could no longer be naively trusted, no matter how venerable, yet there existed no new absolute criterion of truth to replace the old. This growing epistemological uncertainty, already exacerbated by the plethora of competing ancient philosophies bestowed by the Humanists to the Renaissance, received additional stimulus through yet another influx from the Greeks—the recovery of Sextus Empiricus's classical defense of Skepticism. The French essayist Montaigne was especially sensitive to the new mood, and he in turn gave modern voice to the ancient epistemological doubts. If human belief was determined by cultural custom, if the senses could be deceptive, if the structure of nature did not necessarily match the processes of the mind, if reason's relativity and fallibility precluded knowledge of God or absolute moral standards, then nothing was certain.

A skeptical crisis in French philosophy had emerged, a crisis that the young Descartes, steeped in the critical rationalism of his Jesuit schooling, experienced acutely. Pressed by the residual confusions of his education, by the contradictions between different philosophical perspectives, and by the lessening relevance of religious revelation for understanding the empirical world, Descartes set out to discover an irrefutable basis for certain knowledge.

To begin by doubting everything was the necessary first step, for he wished to sweep away all the past presumptions now confusing human knowledge and to isolate only those truths he himself could clearly and directly experience as indubitable. Unlike Bacon, however, Descartes was a considerable mathematician, and it was the rigorous methodology characteristic of geometry and arithmetic that alone seemed to promise him the certainty he so fervently sought in philosophical matters. Mathematics began with the statement of simple self-evident first principles, foundational axioms from which further and more complex truths could be deduced according to strict rational method. By applying such precise and painstaking reasoning to all questions of philosophy, and by accepting as true only those ideas that presented themselves to his reason as clear, distinct, and free from internal contradiction, Descartes established his means for the attainment of absolute certainty. Disciplined critical rationality would overcome the untrustworthy information about the world given by the senses or the imagination. Using such a method, Descartes would be the new Aristotle, and found a new science that would usher man into a new era of practical knowledge, wisdom, and well-being.

Skepticism and mathematics thus combined to produce the Cartesian revolution in philosophy. The third term in that revolution, that which was both the impulse behind and the outcome of systematic doubt and self-evident reasoning, was to be the bedrock of all human knowledge: the certainty of individual self-awareness. For in the process of methodically doubting everything, even the apparent reality of the physical world and his own body (which could all be only a dream), Descartes concluded that there was one datum that could not be doubted—the fact of his own doubting. At least the "I" who is conscious of doubting, the thinking subject, exists. At least this much is certain: *Cogito, ergo sum*—I think, therefore I am. All else can be questioned, but not the irreducible fact of the thinker's self-awareness. And in recognizing this one certain truth, the mind can perceive that which characterizes certainty itself: Certain knowledge is that which can be clearly and distinctly conceived.

The *cogito* was thus the first principle and paradigm of all other knowledge, providing both a basis for subsequent deductions and a model for all other self-evident rational intuitions. From the indubitable existence of the doubting subject, which was ipso facto an awareness of imperfection and limitation, Descartes deduced the necessary existence of a perfect infinite being, God. Something cannot proceed from nothing, nor can an effect possess a reality not derived from its cause. The thought of God was of such magnitude and perfection that it self-evidently must have derived from a reality beyond the finite and contingent thinker; hence the certainty of an objective omnipotent God. Only through presupposition of such a God could the reliability of the natural light of human reason, or the objective reality of the phenomenal world, be assured. For if God is God, which is to say a perfect being, then he would not deceive man and the reason that gives man self-evident truths.

Of equal consequence, the *cogito* also revealed an essential hierarchy and division in the world. Rational man knows his own awareness to be certain, and entirely distinct from the external world of material substance, which is epistemologically less certain and perceptible only as object. Thus *res cogitans*—thinking substance, subjective experience, spirit, consciousness, that which man perceives as within—was understood as fundamentally different and separate from *res extensa*—extended substance, the objective world, matter, the physical body, plants and animals, stones and stars, the entire physical universe, everything that man perceives as outside his mind. Only in man did the two realities come together as mind and body. And both the cognitive capacity of human reason and the objective reality and order of the natural world found their common source in God.

Hence on the one side of Descartes's dualism, soul is understood as mind, and human awareness as distinctively that of the thinker. The senses are prone to flux and error, the imagination prey to fantastic distortion, the emotions irrelevant for certain rational comprehension. On the other side of the dualism, and in contrast to the mind, all objects of the external world lack subjective awareness, purpose, or spirit. The physical universe is entirely devoid of human qualities. Rather, as purely material objects, all physical phenomena can in essence be comprehended as machines—much like the lifelike automata and ingenious machines, clocks, mills, and fountains being constructed and enjoyed by seventeenth-century Europeans. God created the universe and defined its mechanical laws, but after that the system moved on its own, the supreme machine constructed by the supreme intelligence.

The universe, therefore, was not a live organism, as Aristotle and the Scholastics supposed, endowed with forms and motivated by teleological purpose. If such preconceptions were set aside and man's analytic reason alone employed to intuit the simplest, most self-evident description of nature, then it was apparent that the universe was composed of nonvital atomistic matter. Such a substance was best understood in mechanistic terms, reductively analyzed into its simplest parts, and exactly comprehended in terms of those parts' arrangements and movements: "The laws of Mechanics are identical with those of Nature." For man to claim to see immanent forms and purposes in nature was to assert a metaphysical impiety, claiming direct access to God's mind. Yet because the physical world was entirely objective, and solidly and unambiguously material, it was inherently measurable. Therefore man's most powerful tool for understanding the universe was mathematics, available to the natural light of human reason.

To support his metaphysics and epistemology, Descartes used Galileo's distinction between primary, measurable properties of objects and secondary, more subjective properties. In seeking to understand the universe, the scientist should not focus on those qualities merely apparent to sense perception, which are liable to subjective misjudgment and human distortion, but should instead attend only to those objective qualities that can be perceived clearly and distinctly and analyzed in quantitative terms—extension, shape, number, duration, specific gravity, relative position. Upon this basis, using experiment and hypothesis, science could proceed. For Descartes, mechanics was a species of a "universal mathematics" by which the physical universe could be fully analyzed and effectively manipulated to serve the health and comfort of mankind. With quantitative mechanics ruling the world, an absolute faith in human reason was justified. Here, then, was the basis for a practical philosophy—not the speculative philosophy of the schools, but one granting man direct understanding of the forces of nature so they could be turned to his own purposes.

Thus human reason establishes first its own existence, out of experiential necessity, then God's existence, out of logical necessity, and thence the God-guaranteed reality of the objective world and its rational order. Descartes enthroned human reason as the supreme authority in matters of knowledge, capable of distinguishing certain metaphysical truth and of achieving certain scientific understanding of the material world. Infallibility, once ascribed only to Holy Scripture or the supreme pontiff, was now transferred to human reason itself. In effect, Descartes unintentionally began a theological Copernican revolution, for his mode of reasoning suggested that God's existence was established by human reason and not vice versa. Although the self-evident certainty of God's existence was guaranteed by God's benevolent veracity in creating a reliable human reason, that conclusion could be affirmed only on the basis of the clear-and-distinct-idea criterion, in which authority was fundamentally rooted in a judgment by the individual human intellect. In the ultimate religious question, not divine revelation but the natural light of human reason had the final say. Until Descartes, revealed truth had maintained an objective authority outside of human judgment, but now its validity began to be subject to affirmation by human reason. The metaphysical independence that Luther had demanded within the parameters of the Christian religion, Descartes now intimated more universally. For whereas Luther's foundational certainty was his faith in God's saving grace as revealed in the Bible, Descartes's foundational certainty was his faith in the procedural clarities of mathematical reasoning applied to the indubitability of the thinking self.

Moreover, by his assertion of the essential dichotomy between thinking substance and extended substance, Descartes helped emancipate the material world from its long association with religious belief, freeing science to develop its analysis of that world in terms uncontaminated by spiritual or human qualities and unconstrained by theological dogma. Both the human mind and the natural world now stood autonomously as never before, separated from God and from each other.

Here, then, was the prototypical declaration of the modern self, established as a fully separate, self-defining entity, for whom its own rational self-awareness was absolutely primary—doubting everything except itself, setting itself in opposition not only to traditional authorities but to the world, as subject against object, as a thinking, observing, measuring, manipulating being, fully distinct from an objective God and an external nature. The fruit of the dualism between rational subject and material world was science, including science's capacity for rendering certain knowledge of that world and for making man "master and possessor of nature." In Descartes's vision, science, progress, reason, epistemological certainty, and human identity were all inextricably connected with each other and with the conception of an objective, mechanistic universe; and upon this synthesis was founded the paradigmatic character of the modern mind.

Thus Bacon and Descartes—prophets of a scientific civilization, rebels against an ignorant past, and zealous students of nature—proclaimed the twin epistemological bases of the modern mind. In their respective manifestos of empiricism and rationalism, the long-growing significance of the natural world and the human reason, initiated by the Greeks and recovered by the Scholastics, achieved definitive modern expression. Upon this dual foundation, philosophy proceeded and science triumphed: It was not accidental to Newton's accomplishment that he had systematically employed a practical synthesis of Bacon's inductive empiricism and Descartes's deductive mathematical rationalism, thereby bringing to fruition the scientific method first forged by Galileo.

After Newton, science reigned as the authoritative definer of the universe, and philosophy defined itself in relation to science—predominantly supportive, occasionally critical and provocative, sometimes independent and concerned with different areas, but ultimately not in a position to gainsay the cosmological discoveries and conclusions of empirical science, which now increasingly ruled the Western world view. Newton's achievement in effect established both the modern understanding of the physical universe—as mechanistic, mathematically ordered, concretely material, devoid of human or spiritual properties, and not especially Christian in structure—and the modern understanding of man, whose rational intelligence had comprehended the world's natural order, and who was thus a noble being not by virtue of being the central focus of a divine plan as revealed in Scripture, but because by his own reason he had grasped nature's underlying logic and thereby achieved dominion over its forces.

The new philosophy did not just mirror the new sense of human empowerment. Its significance as a philosophy, and the cause of its great impact on the Western mind, lay especially in its scientific and then technological corroboration. As never before, a way of thinking produced spectacularly tangible results. Within such a potent framework, progress appeared inevitable. Mankind's happy destiny at last seemed assured, and patently as a result of its own rational powers and concrete achievements. It was now evident that the quest for human fulfillment would be propelled by increasingly sophisticated analysis and manipulation of the natural world, and by systematic efforts to extend man's intellectual and existential independence in every realm—physical, social, political, religious, scientific, metaphysical. Proper education of the human mind in a well-designed environment would bring forth rational individuals, capable of understanding the world and themselves, able to act in the most intelligent fashion for the good of the whole. With the mind cleared of traditional prejudices and superstitions, man could grasp the self-evident truth and thus establish for himself a rational world within which all could flourish. The dream of human freedom and fulfillment in this world could now be realized. Mankind had at last reached an enlightened age.

Foundations of the Modern World View

And so between the fifteenth and seventeenth centuries, the West saw the emergence of a newly self-conscious and autonomous human being—curious about the world, confident in his own judgments, skeptical of orthodoxies, rebellious against authority, responsible for his own beliefs and actions, enamored of the classical past but even more committed to a greater future, proud of his humanity, conscious of his distinctness from nature, aware of his artistic powers as individual creator, assured of his intellectual capacity to comprehend and control nature, and altogether less dependent on an omnipotent God. This emergence of the modern mind, rooted in the rebellion against the medieval Church and the ancient authorities, and yet dependent upon and developing from both these matrices, took the three distinct and dialectically related forms of the Renaissance, the Reformation, and the Scientific Revolution. These collectively ended the cultural hegemony of the Catholic Church in Europe and established the more individualistic, skeptical, and secular spirit of the modern age. Out of that profound cultural transformation, science emerged as the West's new faith.

For when the titanic battle of the religions failed to resolve itself, with no monolithic structure of belief any longer holding sway over civilization, science suddenly stood forth as mankind's liberation—empirical, rational, appealing to common sense and to a concrete reality that every person could touch and weigh for himself. Verifiable facts and theories tested and discussed among equals replaced dogmatic revelation hierarchically imposed by an institutional Church. The search for truth was now conducted on a basis of international cooperation, in a spirit of disciplined curiosity, with a willingness, even eagerness, to transcend previous limits of knowledge. Offering a new possibility of epistemological certainty and objective agreement, new powers of experimental prediction, technical invention, and control of nature, science presented itself as the saving grace of the modern mind. Science ennobled that mind, showing it to be capable of directly comprehending the rational order of nature first declared by the Greeks, but on a level far transcending the achievements of the ancients and the medieval Scholastics. No traditional authority now dogmatically defined the cultural outlook, nor was such authority needed, for every individual possessed within himself the means for attaining certain knowledge—his own reason and his observation of the empirical world.

Thus science seemed to bring the Western mind to independent maturity, out of the encompassing structure of the medieval Church, beyond the classical glories of the Greeks and Romans. From the Renaissance onward, modern culture evolved and left behind the ancient and medieval world views as primitive, superstitious, childish, unscientific, and oppressive. By the end of the Scientific Revolution, the Western mind had acquired a new way of discovering knowledge and a new cosmology. Because of man's own intellectual and physical efforts, the world itself had expanded—immensely, unprecedentedly. And the most astonishing global shift of all had now dawned on the cultural psyche: the Earth moves. The straightforward evidence of the naive senses, the theological and scientific certitude of the naive centuries, that the Sun rises and sets and that the Earth beneath one's feet is utterly stationary at the center of the universe, was now overcome through critical reasoning, mathematical calculation, and technologically enhanced observation. Indeed, not only the Earth but man himself now moved, as never before, out of the finite, static, hierarchical Aristotelian-Christian universe and into new, unknown territories. The nature of reality had fundamentally shifted for Western man, who now perceived and inhabited a cosmos of entirely new proportions, structure, and existential meaning.

The way was now open to envision and establish a new form of society, based on self-evident principles of individual liberty and rationality. For the strategies and principles that science had shown to be so useful for discovering truth in nature were clearly relevant to the social realm as well. Just as the antiquated Ptolemaic structure of the heavens, with its complicated, cumbersome, and finally unsustainable system of epicyclic fabrications, had been replaced by the rational simplicity of the Newtonian universe, so too could the antiquated structures of society—absolute monarchical power, aristocratic privilege, clerical censorship, oppressive and arbitrary laws, inefficient economies—be replaced by new forms of government based not on supposed divine sanction and inherited traditional assumptions, but on rationally ascertainable individual rights and mutually beneficial social contracts. The application of systematic critical thought to society could not but suggest the need for reform of that society, and as modern reason brought to nature a scientific revolution, so would it bring to society a political revolution. Thus did John Locke, and the French *philosophes* of the Enlightenment after him, take the lessons of Newton and extend them to the human realm.

At this point the foundation and direction of the modern mind had been largely established. It is time, then, to summarize some of the major tenets of the modern world view, as we did earlier with the classical Greek and medieval Christian outlooks. Yet to do this, we must define our focus more precisely and extend our analysis forward. For the modern world view was, like its predecessors, not a stable entity but a continually evolving way of experiencing existence, and, what is especially relevant to us here, the views of Newton, Galileo, Descartes, Bacon, and the rest were essentially a Renaissance synthesis of modern and medieval: i.e., a compromise between a medieval Christian Creator God and a modern mechanistic cosmos, between the human mind as a spiritual principle and the world as objective materiality, and so forth. During the two centuries following the Cartesian-Newtonian formulation, the modern mind continued to disengage itself from its medieval matrix. The writers and scholars of the Enlightenment—Locke, Leibniz, Spinoza, Bayle, Voltaire, Montesquieu, Diderot, d'Alembert, Holbach, La Mettrie, Pope, Berkeley, Hume, Gibbon, Adam Smith, Wolff, Kant—philosophically elaborated, broadly disseminated, and culturally established the new world view. By its end, the autonomous human reason had fully displaced traditional sources of knowledge about the universe, and in turn had defined its own limits as those constituted by the boundaries and methods of empirical science. The industrial and democratic revolutions, and the rise of the West to global hegemony, brought forth the concrete technological, economic, social, and political concomitants of that world view, which was thus further affirmed and elevated in its cultural sovereignty. And in modern science's culminating triumph over traditional religion, Darwin's theory of evolution brought the origin of nature's species and man himself within the compass of natural science and the modern outlook. At this juncture, science's capacity to comprehend the world had apparently achieved insuperable dimensions, and the modern world view could assert its mature character.

The following synopsis of the modern outlook thus reflects not only its earlier Cartesian-Newtonian formulation, but also its later form as the modern mind more fully realized itself in the course of the eighteenth and nineteenth centuries. For as the Cartesian-Newtonian framework was drawn out to its logical conclusion, the implications of the new sensibility and the new conceptions that had been initiated in the Renaissance and Scientific Revolution were gradually made explicit. We may describe as the specifically "modern" world view that which was most sharply distinguished from its antecedents, mindful that in reality the latter (e.g., the Judaeo-Christian perspective) continued to play a major role in the culture's understanding, if often in a latent manner, and that a particular individual's outlook in the modern era could occupy any position in a wide spectrum ranging from a minimally affected childlike religious faith to an uncompromisingly tough-minded secular skepticism.

(1) In contrast to the medieval Christian cosmos, which was not only created but continuously and directly governed by a personal and actively omnipotent God, the modern universe was an impersonal phenomenon, governed by regular natural laws, and understandable in exclusively physical and mathematical terms. God was now distantly removed from the physical universe, as creator and architect, and was now less a God of love, miracle, redemption, or historical intervention than a supreme intelligence and first cause, who established the material universe and its immutable laws and then withdrew from further direct activity. While the medieval cosmos was continuously contingent upon God, the modern cosmos stood more on its own, with its own greater ontological reality, and with a diminution of any divine reality either transcendent or immanent. Eventually that residual divine reality, unsupported by scientific investigation of the visible world, disappeared altogether. The order found in the natural world, initially ascribed to and guaranteed by the will of God, was eventually understood to be the result of innate mechanical regularities generated by nature without higher purpose. And while in the medieval Christian view, the human mind could not comprehend the universe's order, which was ultimately supernatural, without the aid of divine revelation, in the modern view, the human mind was capable by its own rational faculties of comprehending the order of the universe, and that order was entirely natural.

(2) The Christian dualistic stress on the supremacy of the spiritual and transcendent over the material and concrete was now largely inverted, with the physical world becoming the predominant focus for

human activity. An enthusiastic embrace of this world and this life as the stage for a full human drama now replaced the traditional religious dismissal of mundane existence as an unfortunate and temporary trial in preparation for eternal life. Human aspiration was now increasingly centered on secular fulfillment. The Christian dualism between spirit and matter, God and world, was gradually transformed into the modern dualism of mind and matter, man and cosmos: a subjective and personal human consciousness versus an objective and impersonal material world.

(3) Science replaced religion as preeminent intellectual authority, as definer, judge, and guardian of the cultural world view. Human reason and empirical observation replaced theological doctrine and scriptural revelation as the principal means for comprehending the universe. The domains of religion and metaphysics became gradually compartmentalized, regarded as personal, subjective, speculative, and fundamentally distinct from public objective knowledge of the empirical world. Faith and reason were now definitively severed. Conceptions involving a transcendent reality were increasingly regarded as beyond the competence of human knowledge; as useful palliatives for man's emotional nature; as aesthetically satisfying imaginative creations; as potentially valuable heuristic assumptions; as necessary bulwarks for morality or social cohesion; as political-economic propaganda; as psychologically motivated projections; as life-impoverishing illusions; as superstitious, irrelevant, or meaningless. In lieu of religious or metaphysical overviews, the two bases of modern epistemology, rationalism and empiricism, eventually produced their apparent metaphysical entailments: While modern rationalism suggested and eventually affirmed and based itself upon the conception of man as the highest or ultimate intelligence, modern empiricism did the same for the conception of the material world as the essential or only reality—i.e., secular humanism and scientific materialism, respectively.

(4) In comparison with the classical Greek outlook, the modern universe possessed an intrinsic order, yet not one emanating from a cosmic intelligence in which the human mind could directly participate, but rather an order empirically derived from nature's material patterning by means of the human mind's own resources. Nor was this an order simultaneously and inherently shared by both nature and the human mind, as the Greeks had understood. The modern world order was not a transcendent and pervasive unitary order informing both inner mind and outer world, in which recognition of the one necessarily signified knowl-

edge of the other. Rather, the two realms, subjective mind and objective world, were now fundamentally distinct and operated on different principles. Whatever order was perceived was now simply the objective recognition of nature's innate regularities (or, after Kant, a phenomenal order constituted by the mind's own categories). The human mind was conceived of as separate from and superior to the rest of nature.[4] Nature's order was exclusively unconscious and mechanical. The universe itself was not endowed with conscious intelligence or purpose; only man possessed such qualities. The rationally empowered capacity to manipulate impersonal forces and material objects in nature became the paradigm of the human relationship to the world.

(5) In contrast to the Greeks' implicit emphasis on an integrated multiplicity of cognitive modes, the order of the modern cosmos was now comprehensible in principle by man's rational and empirical faculties alone, while other aspects of human nature—emotional, aesthetic, ethical, volitional, relational, imaginative, epiphanic—were generally regarded as irrelevant or distortional for an objective understanding of the world. Knowledge of the universe was now primarily a matter for sober impersonal scientific investigation, and when successful resulted not so much in an experience of spiritual liberation (as in Pythagoreanism and Platonism) but in intellectual mastery and material improvement.

(6) While the cosmology of the classical era was geocentric, finite, and hierarchical, with the surrounding heavens the locus of transcendent archetypal forces that defined and influenced human existence according to the celestial movements, and while the medieval cosmology maintained this same general structure, reinterpreted according to Christian symbolism, the modern cosmology posited a planetary Earth in a neutral infinite space, with a complete elimination of the traditional celestial-terrestrial dichotomy. The heavenly bodies were now moved by the same natural and mechanical forces and composed of the same material substances as those found on the Earth. With the fall of the geocentric cosmos and the rise of the mechanistic paradigm, astronomy was finally severed from astrology. In contrast to both the ancient and the medieval world views, the celestial bodies of the modern universe possessed no numinous or symbolic significance; they did not exist for man, to light his way or give meaning to his life. They were straightforwardly material entities whose character and motions were entirely the product of mechanistic principles having no special relation either to human exis-

tence per se or to any divine reality. All specifically human or personal qualities formerly attributed to the outer physical world were now recognized as naive anthropomorphic projections and deleted from the objective scientific perception. All divine attributes were similarly recognized as the effect of primitive superstition and wishful thinking, and were removed from serious scientific discourse. The universe was impersonal, not personal; nature's laws were natural, not supernatural. The physical world possessed no intrinsic deeper meaning. It was opaquely material, not the visible expression of spiritual realities.

(7) With the integration of the theory of evolution and its multitude of consequences in other fields, the nature and origin of man and the dynamics of nature's transformations were now understood to be exclusively attributable to natural causes and empirically observable processes. What Newton had accomplished for the physical cosmos, Darwin, building on intervening advances in geology and biology (and later aided by Mendel's work in genetics), accomplished for organic nature.[5] While the Newtonian theory had established the new structure and extent of the universe's spatial dimension, the Darwinian theory established the new structure and extent of nature's temporal dimension—both its great duration and its being the stage for qualitative transformations in nature. While with Newton planetary motion was understood to be sustained by inertia and defined by gravity, with Darwin biological evolution was seen as sustained by random variation and defined by natural selection. As the Earth had been removed from the center of creation to become another planet, so now was man removed from the center of creation to become another animal.

Darwinian evolution presented a continuation, a seemingly final vindication, of the intellectual impulse established in the Scientific Revolution, yet it also entailed a significant break from that revolution's classical paradigm. For evolutionary theory provoked a fundamental shift away from the regular, orderly, predictable harmony of the Cartesian-Newtonian world in recognition of nature's ceaseless and indeterminate change, struggle, and development. In doing so, Darwinism both furthered the Scientific Revolution's secularizing consequences and vitiated that revolution's compromise with the traditional Judaeo-Christian perspective. For the scientific discovery of the mutability of species controverted the biblical account of a static creation in which man had been deliberately placed at its sacred culmination and center. It was now less certain that man came from God than that he came from lower forms of primates. The human mind was not a divine endowment but a biological tool. The structure and movement of nature was the result not of God's benevolent design and purpose, but of an amoral, random, and brutal struggle for survival in which success went not to the virtuous but to the fit. Nature itself, not God or a transcendent Intellect, was now the origin of nature's permutations. Natural selection and chance, not Aristotle's teleological forms or the Bible's purposeful Creation, governed the processes of life. The early modern concept of an impersonal deistic Creator who had initiated and then left to itself a fully formed and eternally ordered world—the last cosmological compromise between Judaeo-Christian revelation and modern science—now receded in the face of an evolutionary theory that provided a dynamic naturalistic explanation for the origin of species and all other natural phenomena. Humans, animals, plants, organisms, rocks and mountains, planets and stars, galaxies, the entire universe could now be understood as the evolutionary outcome of entirely natural processes.

In these circumstances, the belief that the universe was purposefully designed and regulated by divine intelligence, a belief foundational to both the classical Greek and the Christian world views, appeared increasingly questionable. The Christian doctrine of Christ's divine intervention in human history—the Incarnation of the Son of God, the Second Adam, the Virgin Birth, the Resurrection, the Second Coming—seemed implausible in the context of an otherwise straightforward survival-oriented Darwinian evolution in a vast mechanistic Newtonian cosmos. Equally implausible was the existence of a timeless metaphysical realm of transcendent Platonic Ideas. Virtually everything in the empirical world appeared explicable without resort to a divine reality. The modern universe was now an entirely secular phenomenon. Moreover, it was a secular phenomenon that was still changing and creating itself—not a divinely constructed finality with eternal and static structure, but an unfolding process with no absolute goal, and with no absolute foundation other than matter and its permutations. With nature the sole source of evolutionary direction, and with man the only rational conscious being in nature, the human future lay emphatically in man's hands.

(8) Finally, in contrast with the medieval Christian world view, modern man's independence—intellectual, psychological, spiritual—was radically affirmed, with increasing depreciation of any religious belief or institutional structure that would inhibit man's natural right and potential for existential autonomy and individual self-expression. While the

purpose of knowledge for the medieval Christian was to better obey God's will, its purpose for modern man was to better align nature to man's will. The Christian doctrine of spiritual redemption as based on the historical manifestation of Christ and his future apocalyptic Second Coming was first reconceived as coinciding with the progressive advance of human civilization under divine providence, conquering evil through man's God-given reason, and then was gradually extinguished altogether in light of the belief that man's natural reason and scientific achievements would progressively realize a secular utopian era marked by peace, rational wisdom, material prosperity, and human dominion over nature. The Christian sense of Original Sin, the Fall, and collective human guilt now receded in favor of an optimistic affirmation of human self-development and the eventual triumph of rationality and science over human ignorance, suffering, and social evils.

While the classical Greek world view had emphasized the goal of human intellectual and spiritual activity as the essential unification (or reunification) of man with the cosmos and its divine intelligence, and while the Christian goal was to reunite man and the world with God, the modern goal was to create the greatest possible freedom for man—from nature; from oppressive political, social, or economic structures; from restrictive metaphysical or religious beliefs; from the Church; from the Judaeo-Christian God; from the static and finite Aristotelian-Christian cosmos; from medieval Scholasticism; from the ancient Greek authorities; from all primitive conceptions of the world. Leaving behind tradition generally for the power of the autonomous human intellect, modern man set out on his own, determined to discover the working principles of his new universe, to explore and further expand its new dimensions, and to realize his secular fulfillment.

➤◆◅

The above description is necessarily only a useful simplification, for other important intellectual tendencies existed alongside of, and often ran counter to, the dominant character of the modern mind that was forged during the Enlightenment. It will be the task of later chapters to draw a fuller, more complex, and more paradoxical portrait of the modern sensibility. But first we must examine more precisely the extraordinary dialectic that took place as the dominant modern world view just described formed itself out of its major predecessors, the classical and the Christian.

Ancients and Moderns

Classical Greek thought had provided Renaissance Europe with most of the theoretical equipment it required to produce the Scientific Revolution: the Greeks' initial intuition of a rational order in the cosmos, Pythagorean mathematics, the Platonically defined problem of the planets, Euclidean geometry, Ptolemaic astronomy, alternative ancient cosmological theories with a moving Earth, the Neoplatonic exaltation of the Sun, the atomists' mechanistic materialism, Hermetic esotericism, and the underlying foundation of Aristotelian and Presocratic empiricism, naturalism, and rationalism. Yet the character and direction of the modern mind were such that the latter increasingly disavowed the ancients as scientific or philosophical authorities and depreciated their world view as primitive and unworthy of serious consideration. The intellectual dynamics provoking this discontinuity were complex and often contradictory.

One of the most productive motives impelling sixteenth- and seventeenth-century European scientists to engage in detailed observation and measurement of natural phenomena derived from the heated controversies between orthodox Scholastic Aristotelian physics and the heterodox revival of Pythagorean-Platonic mathematical mysticism. It is no small irony that Aristotle, the greatest naturalist and empirical scientist of antiquity, whose work had served as the sustaining impulse of Western science for two millennia, was jettisoned by the new science under the impetus of a romantic Renaissance Platonism—from Plato, the speculative idealist who most systematically wished to leave the world of the senses. But with Aristotle's transformation by the contemporary universities into a stultified dogmatist, the Platonism of the Humanists had succeeded in opening the scientific imagination to a fresh sense of intellectual adventure. At a deeper level, however, Aristotle's empiricist this-worldly direction was extended and fulfilled by the Scientific Revolution *ad extremum*; and although Aristotle himself was overthrown in that revolution, it could be said that this was no more than the Oedipal rebellion by the modern science of which he was the ancient father.

Yet just as decisively was Plato overthrown. Indeed, if Aristotle was deposed in effigy while maintained in spirit, Plato was vindicated in theory but altogether negated in spirit. The Scientific Revolution from Copernicus to Newton had depended upon and been inspired by a series of strategies and assumptions derived directly from Plato, his Pythagorean predecessors, and his Neoplatonic successors: the search for perfect timeless mathematical forms that underlay the phenomenal world, the a priori belief that planetary movements conformed to continuous and regular geometrical figures, the instruction to avoid being misled by the apparent chaos of the empirical heavens, a confidence in the beauty and simple elegance of the true solution to the problem of the planets, the exaltation of the Sun as image of the creative Godhead, the proposals of nongeocentric cosmologies, the belief that the universe was permeated with divine reason and that God's glory was especially revealed in the heavens. Euclid, whose geometry formed a basis both for Descartes's rationalist philosophy and the entire Copernican-Newtonian paradigm, had been a Platonist whose work was fully constructed on Platonic principles. Modern scientific method itself, as developed by Kepler and Galileo, was founded on the Pythagorean faith that the language of the physical world was one of number, which provided a rationale for the conviction that the empirical observation of nature and the testing of hypotheses should be systematically focused through quantitative measurement. Moreover, all modern science implicitly based itself upon Plato's fundamental hierarchy of reality, in which a diverse and ever-changing material nature was viewed as being ultimately obedient to certain unifying laws and principles that transcend the phenomena they govern. Above all, modern science was the inheritor of the basic Platonic belief in the rational intelligibility of the world order, and in the essential nobility of the human quest to discover that order. But those Platonic assumptions and strategies eventually led to the creation of a paradigm whose thoroughgoing naturalism left little room for the mystical tenor of Platonic metaphysics. The numinosity of the mathematical patterns celebrated by the Pythagorean-Platonic tradition now disappeared, regarded in retrospect as an empirically unverifiable and superfluous appendage to the straightforward scientific understanding of the natural world.

It is true that the Pythagorean-Platonic claim for the explanatory power of mathematics was being constantly vindicated by natural science, and that this apparent anomaly—why should mathematics work so consistently and elegantly in the realm of brute material phenomena?—caused some puzzlement among thoughtful philosophers of science. But for most practicing scientists after Newton, such mathematical consistencies in nature were considered to represent a certain mechanical tendency toward regular patterning, with no deeper meaning per se. They were seldom seen as revelatory Forms by which the mind of man was comprehending the mind of God. Mathematical patterning was simply "in the nature of things," or in the nature of the human mind, and was not interpreted in a Platonic light as giving evidence of an eternal changeless world of pure spirit. The laws of nature, although perhaps timeless, now stood on their own on a material foundation, dissociated from any divine cause.

Thus with the somewhat perplexing exception of mathematics, the Platonic stream of philosophy generally ceased to be viewed as a viable form of thought in the modern context, and science's quantitative character was left with an entirely secular meaning. In the face of the indisputable success of mechanistic natural science and the ascendance of positivistic empiricism and nominalism in philosophy, the idealist claims of Platonic metaphysics—the eternal Ideas, the transcendent reality wherein resided true being and meaning, the divine nature of the heavens, the spiritual government of the world, the religious meaning of science—were now dismissed as elaborately sophisticated products of the primitive imagination. Paradoxically, the Platonic philosophy had served as the sine qua non for a world view that seemed directly to controvert the Platonic assumptions. Thus "the irony of fate built the mechanical philosophy of the eighteenth century and the materialistic philosophy of the nineteenth out of the mystical mathematical theory of the seventeenth."[6]

A further irony lay in the modern defeat of the classical giants— Aristotle and Plato—at the hands of the ancient minority traditions. In the course of the later classical and medieval periods, the mechanistic and materialistic atomism of Leucippus and Democritus; the heterodox (nongeocentric or nongeostatic) cosmologies of Philolaus, Heraclides, and Aristarchus; the radical Skepticism of Pyrrho and Sextus Empiricus—all these had been overshadowed, almost trampled underfoot and extinguished, by the culturally more powerful philosophical triumvirate of Socrates, Plato, and Aristotle and by the dominant Aristotelian-Ptolemaic cosmology.[7] But the minority views' retrieval by the Humanists during the Renaissance eventually served to reverse that hierarchy in the world of science, with many of their tenets enjoying an unexpected validation in the theoretical conclusions and philosophical tenor of the

Scientific Revolution and its aftermath. A similar restoration would come to the Sophists, whose secular humanism and relativistic skepticism found renewed favor in the philosophical climate of the Enlightenment and subsequent modern thought.

But the isolated and seemingly fortuitous insights of a few speculative theorists were not sufficient to offset modern science's critical evaluation of the ancient mind. Nor was the utility of various premises from the Platonic and Aristotelian traditions enough to counterbalance what were seen as their misguided and insufficiently empirical foundations. The retrospective awe felt by medieval and Renaissance thinkers toward the genius and achievements of the classical golden age luminaries no longer seemed appropriate when on every side modern man was proving his practical and intellectual superiority. Thus, having extracted whatever was useful for its present needs, the modern mind reconceived classical culture in terms respectful of its literary and humanistic accomplishments, while generally dismissing the ancients' cosmology, epistemology, and metaphysics as naive and scientifically erroneous.

A more sweeping dismissal was given to the esoteric elements of the ancient tradition—astrology, alchemy, Hermeticism—that had also been instrumental in the genesis of the Scientific Revolution. The ancient birth of astronomy, and of science itself, had been inextricably tied to the primitive astrological understanding of the heavens as a superior realm of divine significance, with the planetary movements carefully observed because of their symbolic import for human affairs. In the ensuing centuries, astrology's ties to astronomy had been essential for the latter's technical progress, for it was the astrological presuppositions that gave astronomy its social and psychological relevance, as well as its political and military utility in matters of state. Astrological predictions required the most accurate possible astronomical data, so that astrology supplied the astronomical profession with its most compelling motive for attempting to solve the problem of the planets. It was no accident that prior to the Scientific Revolution the science of astronomy enjoyed its most rapid development precisely during those periods—the Hellenistic era, the high Middle Ages, and the Renaissance—when astrology was most widely accepted.

Nor did the major protagonists of the Scientific Revolution move to sever that ancient bond. Copernicus made no distinction in the *De Revolutionibus* between astronomy and astrology, referring to them conjointly as "the head of all the liberal arts." Kepler confessed that his astronomical research was inspired by his search for the celestial "music of the spheres." Although outspokenly critical of the lack of rigor in contemporary astrology, Kepler was his era's foremost astrological theoretician, and both he and Brahe served as royal astrologers to the Holy Roman Emperor. Even Galileo, like most Renaissance astronomers, routinely calculated astrological birth charts, including one for his patron the Duke of Tuscany in 1609, the year of his telescopic discoveries. Newton reported that it was his own early interest in astrology that stimulated his epochal researches in mathematics, and he later studied alchemy at considerable length. It is sometimes difficult now to determine the actual extent of these pioneers' commitment to astrology or alchemy, but the modern historian of science looks in vain for a clear demarcation in their vision between the scientific and the esoteric.

For a peculiar collaboration between science and esoteric tradition was in fact the norm of the Renaissance, and played an indispensable role in the birth of modern science: Besides the Neoplatonic and Pythagorean mathematical mysticism and Sun exaltation that ran through all the major Copernican astronomers, one finds Roger Bacon, the pioneer of experimental science whose work was saturated with alchemical and astrological principles; Giordano Bruno, the polymath esotericist who championed an infinite Copernican cosmos; Paracelsus, the alchemist who laid early foundations of modern chemistry and medicine; William Gilbert, whose theory of the Earth's magnetism rested on his proof that the world-soul was embodied in that magnet; William Harvey, who believed his discovery of the circulation of the blood revealed the human body to be a microcosmic reflection of the Earth's circulatory systems and the cosmos's planetary motions; Descartes's affiliation with mystical Rosicrucianism; Newton's affiliation with the Cambridge Platonists, and his belief that he worked within an ancient tradition of secret wisdom dating back to Pythagoras and beyond; and, indeed, the law of universal gravitation itself, modeled on the sympathies of Hermetic philosophy. The modernity of the Scientific Revolution was in many ways ambiguous.

But the new universe that emerged from the Scientific Revolution was not so ambiguous, and appeared to leave little room for the reality of astrological or other explicitly esoteric principles. While the original revolutionaries themselves called no attention to the problems the new paradigm posed for astrology, those contradictions soon became apparent for others. For a planetary Earth seemed to undermine the very foundation of astrological thinking, since the latter assumed the Earth was the absolute central focus of planetary influences. It was difficult to see how without the privileged position of being the fixed universal center, the Earth could continue to deserve such distinctive cosmic attention. The entire traditional cosmography delineated from Aristotle through Dante was shattered as the moving Earth now trespassed into celestial realms previously defined as the exclusive domain of specific planetary powers. After Galileo and Newton, the celestial-terrestrial division could no longer be maintained, and without that primordial dichotomy, the metaphysical and psychological premises that had helped support the astrological belief system began to collapse. The planets were now known to be prosaically material objects moved by inertia and gravity, not archetypal symbols moved by a cosmic intelligence. There had been relatively few thinkers in the Renaissance who were not convinced of astrology's essential validity, but a generation after Newton there were few who considered it worth examining. Increasingly marginalized, astrology went underground, surviving only among small groups of es-otericists and the uncritical masses.[8] After being the classical "queen of sciences" and the guide of emperors and kings for the better part of two millennia, astrology was no longer credible.

With the exception of the Romantics, the modern mind also gradually outgrew the Renaissance's fascination with ancient myth as an autono-mous dimension of existence. That the gods were nothing more than colorful figments of pagan fantasy needed little argument from the Enlightenment on. Just as the Platonic Forms died out in philosophy, their place taken by objective empirical qualities, subjective concepts, cognitive categories, or linguistic "family resemblances," so did the ancient gods assume the role of literary characters, artistic images, useful metaphors without any claim to ontological reality.

For modern science had cleansed the universe of all those human and spiritual properties previously projected upon it. The world was now neutral, opaque, and material, and therefore no dialogue with nature was possible—whether through magic, mysticism, or divinely certified au-thority. Only the impersonal employment of man's critical and empir-ically based rational intellect could attain an objective understanding of nature. Although in fact an astonishing variety of epistemological sources had converged to make possible the Scientific Revolution—the immense imaginative (and antiempirical) leap to the conception of a planetary Earth,[9] Pythagorean and Neoplatonic aesthetic and mystical beliefs, Descartes's revelatory dream and vision of a new universal science and his own mission to forge it, Newton's Hermetically inspired concept of gravitational attraction, all the serendipitous recoveries of the ancient manuscripts (Lucretius, Archimedes, Sextus Empiricus, the Neoplatonists), the fundamentally metaphorical character of the various scientific theories and explanations—these were all later viewed as significant only in the context of scientific discovery. In the context of scientific justification, of ascertaining the truth value of any hypothesis, only empirical evidence and rational analysis could be considered legitimate epistemological bases, and in the wake of the Scientific Revolution these modes dominated the scientific enterprise. The too flexible, syncretistic, and mystical epistemologies of the classical period, and their elaborate metaphysical consequences, were now repudiated.

Classical culture would long remain an exalted realm haunting the West's imaginative and aesthetic creations. It would continue to provide modern thinkers with inspiring political and moral ideas and models. Greek philosophy, the Greek and Latin languages and literatures, the events and personalities of ancient history would all still evoke in the modern mind avid interest and scholarly respect, often bordering on reverence. But the humanistic nostalgia for classicism could not disguise the latter's growing irrelevance for the modern mind. For when the issue at hand was a stringent philosophical and scientific analysis of reality, the classical world view, whatever its historical importance, and whatever its virtues in aesthetic or imaginative terms, could not favorably compare with the intellectual rigor and efficacy modern man could justly claim for his own understanding.

Yet for all that, the ancient Greek mind still pervaded the modern. In the virtually religious zeal of the scientist's quest for knowledge, in his often unconscious assumptions concerning the rational intelligibility of the world and man's capacity to reveal it, in his critical independence of judgment and his ambitious drive to expand human knowledge beyond ever more distant horizons, Greece lived on.

The Triumph of Secularism

Science and Religion: The Early Concord

The fate of Christianity in the wake of the Scientific Revolution was not dissimilar to the fate of classical thought, nor did it lack its own share of paradox. If the Greeks had supplied most of the theoretical provisions requisite for the Scientific Revolution, the Catholic Church, for all its dogmatic strictures, had provided the necessary matrix within which the Western mind was able to develop and from which the scientific understanding could emerge. The nature of the Church's contribution was both practical and doctrinal. From the beginning of the Middle Ages, the Church had provided in its monasteries the only refuge in the West within which the achievements of classical culture could be preserved and their spirit continued. And from the turn of the first millennium, the Church had officially supported and encouraged the vast Scholastic enterprise of scholarship and education without which modern intellectuality might never have arisen.

This momentous act of ecclesiastical sponsorship was justified by a unique constellation of theological positions. The precise and profound comprehension of Christian doctrine required, in the medieval Church's evolving view, a corresponding capacity for logical clarity and intellectual acuity. Beyond that rationale emerged another, for with the increasing recognition of the physical world in the high Middle Ages there arose a corresponding recognition of the positive role a scientific understanding could play in the appreciation of God's wondrous creation. For all its wariness of mundane life and "the world," the Judaeo-Christian religion nevertheless placed great emphasis on the ontological reality of that world and its ultimate relationship to a good and just God. Christianity took this life seriously. Therein lay a significant religious impetus for the scientific quest, which depended not only on a sense of the human being's active responsibility in this world, but also on a belief in this world's reality, its order, and, at the start of modern science, its coherent relationship to an omnipotent and infinitely wise Creator.

Nor was the contribution of the Scholastics merely an imperfect Christianized recovery and sustaining of the Greek ideas. For it was the

Scholastics' exhaustive examination and criticism of those ideas, and their creation of new alternative theories and concepts—rudimentary formulations of inertia and momentum, the uniform acceleration of freely falling bodies, hypothetical arguments for a moving Earth—that allowed modern science from Copernicus and Galileo onward to begin forging its new paradigm. And perhaps most consequential was not the specific nature of the Scholastics' theoretical innovations, nor their revitalization of Hellenic thought, but rather the more intangible existential attitude medieval thinkers passed on to their modern descendants: the theologically founded but decidedly robust confidence that man's God-given reason possessed the capacity, and the religious duty, to comprehend the natural world. Man's intellectual relation to the creative Logos, his privileged possession of the divine light of the active intellect—Aquinas's *lumen intellectus agentis*—was from the Christian perspective precisely what mediated the human understanding of the cosmos. Descartes's natural light of the human reason was the direct half-secularized inheritor of that medieval conception. It was Aquinas himself who had written in his *Summa Theologica* that "authority is the weakest source of proof," a dictum central for the protagonists of the modern mind's independence. Modern rationalism, naturalism, and empiricism all had Scholastic roots.

But the Scholasticism encountered by the sixteenth- and seventeenth-century natural philosophers was a senescent structure of pedagogical dogmatism that no longer spoke to the new spirit of the age. Little or nothing fresh was emerging from within its confines. Its obsession with Aristotle, its oversubtle verbal distinctions and logical quibbles, and its failure to submit theory systematically to the test of experiment all marked late Scholasticism as an outmoded, ingrown institution whose intellectual authority had to be overthrown lest the brave infant science be fatally smothered. After Bacon, Galileo, Descartes, and Newton, that authority had been effectively impugned, and Scholasticism's reputation never recovered. From then on, science and philosophy could move forward without theological justification, without recourse to a divine light in the human intellect, without the colossal supporting superstructure of Scholastic metaphysics and epistemology.

Yet despite the unambiguously secular character of the modern science that eventually crystallized out of the Scientific Revolution, the original scientific revolutionaries themselves continued to act, think, and speak of their work in terms conspicuously redolent of religious illumination.

They perceived their intellectual breakthroughs as foundational contributions to a sacred mission. Their scientific discoveries were triumphant spiritual awakenings to the divine architecture of the world, revelations of the true cosmic order. Newton's joyful exclamation, "O God, I think thy thoughts after thee!" was only the culmination of a long series of such epiphanies marking the milestones of modern science's birth. In the *De Revolutionibus*, Copernicus celebrated astronomy as a "science more divine than human," closest to God in the nobility of its character, and upheld the heliocentric theory as revealing the true structural grandeur and precision of God's cosmos. Kepler's writings were ablaze with his sense of being divinely illuminated as the inner mysteries of the cosmos unfolded before his eyes.[10] He declared astronomers to be "priests of the most high God with respect to the book of nature," and saw his own role as "the honor of guarding, with my discovery, the door of God's temple, in which Copernicus serves before the high altar." In *Sidereus Nuncius*, Galileo spoke of his telescopic discoveries as made possible by God's grace enlightening his mind. Even the worldly Bacon envisioned humanity's progress through science in explicitly religious, pietistic terms, with the material improvement of mankind corresponding to its spiritual approach to the Christian millennium. Descartes interpreted his vision of the new universal science, and a subsequent dream in which that science was symbolically presented to him, as a divine mandate for his life's work: God had shown him the way to certain knowledge, and assured him of his scientific quest's ultimate success. And with Newton's achievement, the divine birth was considered complete. A new Genesis had been written. As Alexander Pope declared for the Enlightenment:

> Nature and nature's laws lay hid in night;
> God said, "Let Newton be," and all was light.

For the great passion to discover the laws of nature that was felt by the scientific revolutionaries derived not least from a sense that they were recovering a divine knowledge that had been lost in the primal Fall. At last the human mind had comprehended God's working principles. The eternal laws governing Creation, the divine handiwork itself, now stood unveiled by science. Through science man had served God's greater glory, demonstrating the mathematical beauty and complex precision, the stupendous order reigning over the heavens and the Earth. The luminous perfection of the discoverers' new universe compelled their awe before the transcendent intelligence which they attributed to the Creator of such a cosmos.

Nor was the religiosity of the major scientific pioneers a generalized religious sentiment with little specific relation to Christianity. Newton was as zealously absorbed in Christian theology and studies of biblical prophecy as he was in physics. Galileo was committed to saving his Church from a costly error and, despite his confrontation with the Inquisition, remained steadfast in his Catholic piety. Descartes lived and died a devout Catholic. And their Christian presuppositions were intellectually pervasive, embedded in the very fabric of their scientific and philosophical theories. Both Descartes and Newton constructed their cosmological systems on the assumption of God's existence. For Descartes, the objective world existed as a stable reality because it stood in the mind of God, and human reason was epistemologically reliable because of God's intrinsically veracious character. Similarly, for Newton, matter could not be explained on its own terms but necessitated a prime mover, a creator, a supreme architect and governor. God had established the physical world and its laws, and therein lay the world's continuing existence and order. Indeed, because of certain unresolved problems in his calculations, Newton concluded that God's intervention was periodically necessary to maintain the system's regularity.

Compromise and Conflict

But the early modern accord between science and Christianity was already displaying tensions and contradictions, for apart from the creationist ontology still underpinning the new paradigm, the scientific universe—with its mechanical forces, its material heavens, and its planetary Earth—was not notably congruent with traditional Christian conceptions of the cosmos. Any central focus of the new universe was maintained only by religious belief, not by scientific evidence. The Earth and mankind might be the metaphysical pivot of God's creation, but that status could not be supported by a purely scientific understanding, which saw both the Earth and the Sun as merely two bodies among countless others moving through a boundless neutral void. "I am terrified," said the intensely religious mathematician Pascal, "by the eternal silence of these infinite spaces." Intellectually sensitive Christians attempted to reinterpret and modify their religious understanding to accommodate a universe drastically different from that of the ancient and medieval cosmology within which the Christian religion had evolved, but the metaphysical hiatus continued to widen. In the Enlightenment's Newtonian cosmos, heaven and hell had lost their physical locations, natural phenomena had lost their symbolic import, and miracles and arbitrary divine interventions into human affairs now appeared increasingly implausible, contradicting the supreme orderliness of a clockwork universe. Yet the deeply rooted principles of Christian belief could scarcely be negated altogether.

Thus arose the psychological necessity of a double-truth universe. Reason and faith came to be seen as pertaining to different realms, with Christian philosophers and scientists, and the larger educated Christian public, perceiving no genuine integration between the scientific reality and the religious reality. Joined together in the high Middle Ages by the Scholastics culminating in Aquinas, then severed in the late medieval period by Ockham and nominalism, faith had moved in one direction with the Reformation, Luther, literal Scripture, fundamentalist Protestantism and Counter-Reformational Catholicism, while reason had moved in another direction with Bacon, Descartes, Locke, Hume, empirical science, rational philosophy, and the Enlightenment. Attempts to bridge the two generally failed to preserve the character of one or the other, as in Kant's delimiting of religious experience to the moral impulse.

With both science and religion simultaneously vital yet discrepant, the culture's world view was by necessity bifurcated, reflecting a metaphysical schism that existed as much within the individual as within the larger society. Religion was increasingly compartmentalized, seen as relevant less to the outer world than to the inner self, less to the contemporary spirit than to revered tradition, less to this life than to the afterlife, less to everyday than to Sunday. Christian doctrine was still believed by most, and indeed, as if in reaction to the abstract mechanical universe of the Enlightenment's physicists and philosophers, a host of fervently emotional religious movements—Pietism in Germany, Jansenism in France, the Quakers and Methodists in England, the Great Awakening in America—emerged and found broad popular support in the seventeenth and eighteenth centuries. Devout religiosity in the traditional Christian mold continued to be widespread; these were the very years in which Western religious music reached its apogee in Bach and Handel, both born within months of Newton's *Principia*. But amidst this pluralism, wherein the scientific and religious temperaments pursued their separate paths, the overriding cultural direction was clear: scientific rationalism was ineluctably on the ascent, demonstrating its sovereignty over ever-larger areas of human experience.

Within two centuries after Newton, the secularity of the modern outlook had fully established itself. Mechanistic materialism had dramatically proved its explanatory power and utilitarian efficacy. Experiences and events that appeared to defy accepted scientific principles—alleged miracles and faith healings, self-proclaimed religious revelations and spiritual ecstasies, prophecies, symbolic interpretations of natural phenomena, encounters with God or the devil—were now increasingly regarded as the effects of madness, charlatanry, or both. Questions concerning the existence of God or a transcendent reality ceased to play a decisive role in the scientific imagination, which was becoming the principal factor in defining the educated public's shared belief system. Already for Pascal in the seventeenth century, faced with his own religious doubts and philosophical skepticism, the leap of faith necessary to sustain Christian belief had become a wager. Now, for many at the leading edge of Western thought, it seemed a losing bet.

What, then, caused this shift from the explicit religiosity of the scientific revolutionaries of the sixteenth and seventeenth centuries to the equally emphatic secularism of the Western intellect in the nineteenth and twentieth? Certainly the metaphysical incongruity of the two outlooks, the cognitive dissonance resulting from the attempt to hold together such innately divergent systems and sensibilities, eventually had to force the issue in one direction or the other. The character and implications of the Christian revelation simply did not cohere well with those of the scientific revelation. Essential to the Christian faith was the belief in Christ's physical resurrection after death, an event that, with its apostolic witness and interpretation, had served as the very foundation of Christianity. But with the near-universal acceptance of the scientific explanation of all phenomena in terms of regular natural laws, that foundational miracle, as well as all the other supernatural phenomena recounted in the Bible, could no longer command unquestioning belief. Raisings from the dead, miraculous healings and exorcisms, a divine-human savior, a virgin birth, manna from heaven, wine from water,

water from rocks, partings of seas—all appeared increasingly improbable
to the modern mind, bearing as they did too many similarities to other
mythical or legendary concoctions of the archaic imagination.

Damaging criticism of the absolute truth of Christian revelation also
emerged from the new academic discipline of biblical scholarship, which
demonstrated Scripture's variable and manifestly human sources. Both
the Renaissance Humanists and the Reformation theologians had pressed
for a return to the original Greek and Hebrew sources of the Bible, which
led to a more critical reading of the original texts and reevaluations of
their historical authenticity and integrity. In the course of several generations of such scholarship, Scripture began to lose its sacral aura of
divine inspiration. The Bible could now be recognized less as the unquestionably authoritative and pristine Word of God than as a heterogeneous collection of writings in various traditional literary genres,
composed, collected, and editorially modified by many human hands
over the centuries. Soon biblical textual criticism was followed by critical
historical studies of Christian dogma and the church, and by historical
investigations into the life of Jesus. The intellectual skills developed for
analyzing secular history and literature were now being applied to the
sacred foundations of Christianity, with unsettling consequences for the
faithful.

By the time such studies were joined by the Darwinian theory's
discrediting of the creation narrative found in Genesis, the validity of
scriptural revelation had become entirely problematic. Man could hardly
have been made in the image of God if he was also the biological
descendant of subhuman primates. The thrust of evolution was not one
of spiritual transfiguration but of biological survival. While up through
Newton the weight of science had tended to support an argument for the
existence of God based on evidence of design in the universe, after
Darwin the weight of science was thrown against that argument. The
evidence of natural history seemed more plausibly comprehended in
terms of evolutionary principles of natural selection and random muta-
tion than in terms of a transcendent Designer.

Certainly some scientists of a Christian persuasion noted the affinity
between the theory of evolution and the Judaeo-Christian notion of
God's progressive and providential plan of history. These drew parallels
with the New Testament's conception of an immanent evolutionary
process of divine incarnation in man and nature, and even attempted to
remedy some of Darwinism's theoretical shortcomings with religious

explanatory principles. Yet for a culture generally accustomed to un-derstanding its Bible at face value, the more glaring inconsistency between the static original creation of species in Genesis and the Dar-winian evidence for their transmutation over aeons of time commanded the greater attention, ultimately encouraging massive agnostic defections from the religious fold. For at bottom, the Christian belief in a God who acted through revelation and grace appeared wildly incompatible with everything common sense and science suggested about the way the world actually worked. With Luther, the monolithic structure of the medieval Christian Church had cracked. With Copernicus and Galileo, the medieval Christian cosmology itself had cracked. With Darwin, the Christian world view showed signs of collapsing altogether.

In an era so unprecedentedly illuminated by science and reason, the "good news" of Christianity became less and less convincing a metaphysi-cal structure, less secure a foundation upon which to build one's life, and less psychologically necessary. The sheer improbability of the whole nexus of events was becoming painfully obvious—that an infinite eternal God would have suddenly become a particular human being in a specific historical time and place only to be ignominiously executed. That a single brief life taking place two millennia earlier in an obscure primitive nation, on a planet now known to be a relatively insignificant piece of matter revolving about one star among billions in an inconceivably vast and impersonal universe—that such an undistinguished event should have any overwhelming cosmic or eternal meaning could no longer be a compelling belief for reasonable men. It was starkly implausible that the universe as a whole would have any pressing interest in this minute part of its immensity—if it had any "interests" at all. Under the spotlight of the modern demand for public, empirical, scientific corroboration of all statements of belief, the essence of Christianity withered.

What was probable, in the judgment of the critical modern intellect, was that the Judaeo-Christian God was a peculiarly durable combination of wish-fulfillment fantasy and anthropomorphic projection—made in man's own image to assuage all the pain and right all the wrongs man found unbearable in his existence. If, by contrast, the unsentimental human reason could adhere closely to the concrete evidence, there was no necessity to posit the existence of such a God, and much that argued against it. The scientific data suggested overwhelmingly that the natural world and its history were expressions of an impersonal process. To say exactly what caused this complex phenomenon, bearing signs of both order and chaos, dramatic and yet evidently purposeless, out of control in the sense of lacking divine government—to go so far as to posit and define what was behind this empirical reality had to be regarded as intellectually unsound, a mere dreaming about the world. The ancient concern with cosmic designs and divine purposes, with ultimate metaphysical issues, with the *why*'s of phenomena, now ceased to engage the attention of scientists. It was patently more fruitful to focus on the *how*'s, the material mechanisms, the laws of nature, the concrete data that could be measured and tested.[11]

Not that science perversely insisted on the hard facts and on a "narrower" vision out of simple myopia. Rather, it was only the *how*'s, the empirical correlations and tangible causes, that could be experimentally confirmed. Teleological designs and spiritual causes could not be subjected to such testing, could not be systematically isolated, and therefore could not be known to exist at all. It was better to deal only with categories that could be empirically evidenced than to allow into the scientific discussion transcendent principles—however noble in the abstract—that in the final analysis could no more be corroborated than could a fairy tale. God was scarcely a testable entity. And in any case, the character and modus operandi of the Judaeo-Christian deity ill fitted the real world discovered by science.

With its apocalyptic prophecies and sacred rituals, its deified human hero and world savior motifs, its miracle stories, moralisms, and veneration of saints and relics, Christianity seemed best understood as a singularly successful folk myth—inspiring hope in believers, giving meaning and order to their lives, but without ontological foundation. In such a light, Christians could be seen as well-meaning but credulous. With the victory of Darwinism (and notably in the wake of the celebrated Oxford debate in 1860 between Bishop Wilberforce and T. H. Huxley), science had unequivocally achieved its independence from theology. After Darwin, there seemed little further possibility of contact of any kind between science and theology, as science focused ever more successfully on the objective world, while theology, virtually incapacitated outside ever-smaller religious intellectual circles, focused exclusively on inward spiritual concerns. Faced by the final severance of the scientifically intelligible universe from the old spiritual verities, modern theology adopted an increasingly subjective stance. The early Christian belief that the Fall and Redemption pertained not just to man but to the entire cosmos, a doctrine already fading after the Reformation, now disappeared altogether: the process of salvation, if it had any meaning at all, pertained solely to the personal relation between God and man. The inner rewards of Christian faith were now stressed, with a radical discontinuity between the experience of Christ and that of the everyday world. God was wholly other than man and this world, and therein lay the religious experience. The "leap of faith," not the self-evidence of the created world or the objective authority of Scripture, constituted the principal basis for religious conviction.

Under such limitations, modern Christianity assumed a new and far less encompassing intellectual role. In its long-held capacity as both explanatory paradigm for the visible world and universal belief system for Western culture, the Christian revelation had lost its potency. It is true that Christian ethics were not so readily depreciated by the new secular sensibility. For many non-Christians, even outspoken agnostics and atheists, the moral ideals taught by Jesus remained as admirable as those of any other ethical system. But the Christian revelation as a whole—the infallible Word of God in the Bible, the divine plan of salvation, the miracles and so forth—could not be taken seriously. That Jesus was simply a man, albeit a compelling one, seemed increasingly self-evident. Compassion for humanity was still upheld as a social and individual ideal, but its basis was now secular and humanistic rather than religious. A humanitarian liberalism thereby sustained certain elements of the Christian ethos without the latter's transcendent foundation. Just as the modern mind admired the loftiness of spirit and moral tone of Platonic philosophy while simultaneously negating its metaphysics and epistemology, so too Christianity continued to be tacitly respected, and indeed closely followed, for its ethical precepts, while increasingly doubted for its larger metaphysical and religious claims.

It is also true that in the eyes of not a few scientists and philosophers, science itself contained a religious meaning, or was open to a religious interpretation, or could serve as an opening to a religious appreciation of the universe. The beauty of nature's forms, the splendor of its variety, the extraordinarily intricate functioning of the human body, the evolutionary development of the human eye or the human mind, the mathematical patterning of the cosmos, the unimaginable magnitude of the heavenly spaces—to some these seemed to require the existence of a divine intelligence and power of miraculous sophistication. But many others argued that such phenomena were the straightforward and relatively random results of the natural laws of physics, chemistry, and

biology. The human psyche, longing for the security of a cosmic providence, and susceptible to personifying and projecting its own capacity for
value and purpose, might wish to see more in nature's design, but the
scientific understanding was deliberately beyond such wishful anthropomorphizing: the entire scenario of cosmic evolution seemed explicable as a direct consequence of chance and necessity, the random
interplay of natural laws. In this light, any apparent religious implications had to be judged as poetic but scientifically unjustifiable
extrapolations from the available evidence. God was "an unnecessary
hypothesis."[12]

Philosophy, Politics, Psychology

Parallel developments in philosophy during these centuries reinforced
the same secular progression. During the Scientific Revolution and the
early Enlightenment, religion continued to hold its own among
philosophers, but was already being transformed by the character of the
scientific mind. In preference to traditional biblical Christianity,
Enlightenment Deists like Voltaire argued in favor of a "rational religion"
or a "natural religion." Such would be appropriate not only to the
rational apprehension of nature's order and the requirement of a universal first cause, but also to the West's encounter with other cultures'
religions and ethical systems—an encounter suggesting to many the
existence of a universal religious sensibility grounded in common human
experience. In such a context, the absolute claims of Christianity could
not enjoy special privilege. Newton's cosmic architecture demanded a
cosmic architect, but the attributes of such a God could be properly
derived only from the empirical examination of his creation, not from
the extravagant pronouncements of revelation. Earlier religious conceptions—primitive, biblical, medieval—could now be recognized as
infantile steps to the more mature modern understanding of an impersonal rational deity presiding over an orderly creation.

The rationalist God, however, soon began to lose philosophical support. With Descartes, God's existence had been affirmed not through
faith but through reason; yet on that basis God's certain existence could
not be indefinitely sustained, as Hume and Kant, the culminating
philosophers of the Enlightenment, noted in their different ways. Much
as Ockham had warned four centuries earlier, rational philosophy could

not presume to pronounce on matters that so far transcended the empirically based intellect. At the start of the Enlightenment, in the late seventeenth century, Locke had systematically pursued Bacon's empiricist directive by rooting all knowledge of the world in sensory experience and subsequent reflection on the basis of that experience. Locke's own inclinations were Deist, and he retained Descartes's certainty that God's existence was logically demonstrable from self-evident intuitions. But the empiricism he championed necessarily limited the human reason's capacity for knowledge to that which could be tested by concrete experience. As successive philosophers drew more rigorous conclusions from the empiricist basis, it became clear that philosophy could no longer justifiably make assertions about God, the soul's immortality and freedom, or other propositions that transcended concrete experience.

In the eighteenth century, Hume and Kant systematically refuted the traditional philosophical arguments for God's existence, pointing out the unwarrantability of using causal reasoning to move from the sensible to the supersensible. Only the realm of possible experience, of concrete particulars registered in sensation, offered any ground for valid philosophical conclusions. For Hume, an entirely secular thinker and more unequivocal in his skepticism, the matter was simple: To argue from the problematic evidence of this world to the certain existence of the good and omnipotent God of Christianity was a philosophical absurdity. But even Kant, though highly religious himself and intent on preserving the moral imperatives of the Christian conscience, nevertheless recognized that Descartes's laudable philosophical skepticism had ceased too abruptly with his dogmatic assertions about God's certain existence derived from the *cogito*. For Kant, God was an unknowable transcendent— thinkable, not knowable, only by attending to man's inner sense of moral duty. Neither human reason nor the empirical world could give any direct or unequivocal indication of a divine reality. Man could have faith in God, he could believe in his soul's freedom and immortality, but he could not claim that these inner persuasions were rationally certain. For the rigorous modern philosopher, metaphysical certainties about God or the like were spurious, lacking as they did a sound basis for verification. The inevitable and proper outcome of both empiricism and critical philosophy was to eliminate any theological substrate from modern philosophy.

At the same time, the bolder thinkers of the French Enlightenment increasingly tended toward not only skepticism but also atheistic materialism as the most intellectually justifiable consequence of the scientific discoveries. Diderot, chief editor of the *Encyclopédie*, the Enlightenment's great project of cultural education, illustrated in his own life the gradual transformation of a reflective man from religious belief to Deism, then to skepticism, and finally to a materialism ambiguously joined with a deistic ethics. More uncompromising was the physician La Mettrie, who portrayed man as a purely material entity, an organic machine whose illusion of possessing an independent soul or mind was produced simply by the interplay of its physical components. Hedonism was the ethical consequence of such a philosophy, which La Mettrie did not fail to advocate. The physicist Baron d'Holbach similarly affirmed the determinisms of matter as the only intelligible reality, and declared the absurdity of religious belief in the face of experience: given the ubiquity of evil in the world, any God must be deficient either in power or in justice and compassion. On the other hand, the random occurrence of good and evil accorded readily with a universe of mindless matter lacking any providential overseer. Atheism was necessary to destroy the chimeras of religious fantasy that endangered the human race. Man needed to be brought back to nature, experience, and reason.

It would be the nineteenth century that would bring the Enlightenment's secular progression to its logical conclusion as Comte, Mill, Feuerbach, Marx, Haeckel, Spencer, Huxley, and, in a somewhat different spirit, Nietzsche all sounded the death knell of traditional religion. The Judaeo-Christian God was man's own creation, and the need for that creation had necessarily dwindled with man's modern maturation. Human history could be understood as progressing from a mythical and theological stage, through a metaphysical and abstract stage, to its final triumph in science, based on the positive and concrete. This world of man and matter was clearly the one demonstrable reality. Metaphysical speculations concerning "higher" spiritual entities constituted nothing more than idle intellectual fantasy, and were a disservice to humanity and its present fate. The duty of the modern age was the humanization of God, who was merely a projection of man's own inner nature. One could perhaps speak of "an Unknowable" behind the world's phenomena, but that was the extent of what could be said with any legitimacy. What was more immediately apparent, and more positively contributive to the modern world view, was that the world's phenomena were being superbly comprehended, to humanity's inestimable benefit, by science, and that the terms of that comprehension were fundamentally naturalistic. The question remained as to who, or what, initiated the whole phenomenon of the universe, but intellectual honesty precluded any certain conclusions or even progress in such an inquiry. Its answer lay epistemologically beyond man's ken and, in the face of more immediate and attainable intellectual objectives, increasingly beyond his interest. With Descartes and Kant, the philosophical relation between Christian belief and human rationality had grown ever more attenuated. By the late nineteenth century, with few exceptions, that relation was effectively absent.

There were also many nonepistemological factors—political, social, economic, psychological—pressing toward this same end, the secularization of the modern mind and its disengagement from traditional religious belief. Even before the Industrial Revolution had demonstrated science's superior utilitarian value, other cultural developments had recommended the scientific view over the religious. The Scientific Revolution had been born amidst the immense turmoil and destruction of the wars of religion that followed the Reformation, wars that in the name of divergent Christian absolutisms had caused over a century of crisis in Europe. In such circumstances much doubt was cast upon the integrity of the Christian understanding, as well as upon its ability to foster a world of relative peace and security, let alone of universal compassion. Despite the increased fervor of religiosity—whether Lutheran, Zwinglian, Calvinist, Anabaptist, Anglican, Puritan, or Catholic—experienced by the European populace in the wake of the Reformation, it was clear to many that the culture's failure to agree on a universally valid religious truth had created the need for another type of belief system, less controversially subjective and more rationally persuasive. Thus the neutral and empirically verifiable world view of secular science soon found an ardent reception among the educated class, offering a commonly acceptable conceptual framework that peacefully cut across all political and religious boundaries. Just as the last major convulsions of post-Reformational bloodshed had been expended, the Scientific Revolution was approaching completion. The final decade of the Thirty Years' War, 1638–48, saw the publication of both Galileo's *Dialogue Concerning Two New Sciences* and Descartes's *Principles of Philosophy,* as well as the birth of Newton.

Circumstances of a more specifically political nature were also to play a part in the modern shift away from religion. For centuries, there had existed a fateful association between the hierarchical Christian world view and the established social-political structures of feudal Europe, centering on the traditional authority figures of God, pope, and king. By the eighteenth century, that association had become mutually disadvantageous. The growingly apparent implausibilities of the one and injustices of the other combined to produce the image of a system whose senile oppressiveness demanded revolt for the larger good of humanity. The French philosophes—Voltaire, Diderot, Condorcet—and their successors among the French revolutionaries recognized the Church itself in its wealth and power as a bastion of reactionary forces, allied inextricably to the conservative institutions of the ancien régime. To the philosophes, the power of the organized clergy posed a formidable obstacle to the progress of civilization. In addition to the issue of economic and social exploitation, the atmosphere of censorship, intolerance, and intellectual rigidity that the philosophes found so abhorrent in contemporary intellectual life was directly attributable to the dogmatic pretensions and vested interests of the ecclesiastical establishment.

Voltaire had seen and admired firsthand the consequences of England's religious toleration, which in turn, with the superior intellectual clarifications of Bacon, Locke, and Newton, he enthusiastically presented to the Continent for emulation. Armed with science, reason, and empirical facts, the Enlightenment saw itself as engaged in a noble struggle against the constricting medieval darkness of Church dogma and popular superstition, tied to a backward and tyrannical political structure of corrupt privilege.[13] The cultural authority of dogmatic religion was recognized as inherently inimical to personal liberty and unhampered intellectual speculation and discovery. By implication, the religious sensibility itself—except in rationalized, deistic form—could well be seen as antagonistic to human freedom.

Yet one philosophe, the Swiss-born Jean-Jacques Rousseau, asserted a very different view. Like his fellows in the vanguard of the Enlightenment, Rousseau argued with the weapons of critical reason and reformist zeal. Yet the progress of civilization they celebrated seemed to him the source of much of the world's evil. Man suffered from civilization's corrupt sophistications, which alienated him from his natural condition of simplicity, sincerity, equality, kindness, and true understanding. Moreover, Rousseau believed religion was intrinsic to the human condition. He contended that the philosophes' exaltation of reason had neglected man's actual nature—his feelings, his depths of impulse and intuition and spiritual hunger that transcended all abstract formulae. Rousseau certainly disbelieved in the organized churches and clergy, and thought absurd the orthodox Christian belief that its form of worship was the exclusively and eternally genuine one—the only religion acceptable to the Creator of a world most of whose inhabitants had never heard of Christianity. Even Christianity notoriously disagreed on what was the exclusively correct form of worship. Rather than through the mediation of theological dogmas, priestly hierarchies, and hostile sectarianism, Rousseau believed humanity could best learn to worship the Creator by turning to nature, for there lay a sublimity that all could understand and feel. The rationally demonstrable God of the Deists was unsatisfactory, for love of God and awareness of morality were primarily feelings, not reasonings. The deity recognized by Rousseau was not an impersonal first cause, but a God of love and beauty whom the human soul could know from within. Reverent awe before the cosmos, the joy of meditative solitude, the direct intuitions of the moral conscience, the natural spontaneity of human compassion, a "theism" of the heart—these constituted the true nature of religion.

Rousseau thus set forth an immensely influential position beyond those of the orthodox Church and the skeptical philosophes, combining the religiosity of the former with the rational reformism of the latter, yet critical of both: if the one was constricting in its narrow dogmatism, the other was scarcely less so in its arid abstractions. And here lay the seed for contradictory developments, for at the same time that Rousseau reaffirmed man's religious nature, he encouraged the modern sensibility in its gradual departure from Christian orthodoxy. He gave a rational reformist's support to the lingering religious impulse of the modern mind, yet he gave that impulse new dimensions that served the Enlightenment's undermining of the Christian tradition. Rousseau's embrace of a religion whose essence was universal rather than exclusive, whose ground was in nature and man's subjective emotions and mystical intuitions rather than in biblical revelation, initiated a spiritual current in Western culture that would lead first to Romanticism and eventually to the existentialism of a later age.

Thus whether it was the anticlerical Deism of Voltaire, the rationalist skepticism of Diderot, the agnostic empiricism of Hume, the materialistic atheism of Holbach, or the nature mysticism and emotional religiosity of Rousseau, the advance of the eighteenth century brought traditional Christianity into ever-lower regard in the eyes of progressive Europeans.

By the nineteenth century, both organized religion and the religious impulse itself had been subjected by Karl Marx to a forceful and acute social-political critique—and prophetically redirected to embrace the revolutionary cause. In Marx's analysis, all ideas and cultural forms reflected material motivations, specifically the dynamics of class struggle, and religion was no exception. Despite their high-minded doctrines, the organized churches seldom seemed to concern themselves with the plight of workers or the poor. This seeming contradiction, Marx held, was in fact essential to the churches' character, for the true role of religion was to keep the lower classes in order. A social opiate, religion effectively served the interests of the ruling class against the masses by encouraging the latter to forgo their responsibility for changing the present world of injustice and exploitation, in exchange for the false security of divine providence and the false promise of immortal life. Organized religion formed an essential element in the bourgeoisie's control of society, for religious beliefs lulled the proletariat into self-defeating inaction. To speak of God and build one's life on such fantasies was to betray man. By contrast, a genuine philosophy of action must start with the living man and his tangible needs. To transform the world, to realize the ideals of human justice and community, man must rid himself of the religious delusion.

The more moderate voices of nineteenth-century liberalism characteristic of the advanced Western societies also argued for the reduction of organized religion's influence on political and intellectual life, and put forth the ideal of a pluralism accommodating the broadest possible freedom of belief consonant with social order. Liberal thinkers of a religious persuasion recognized not only the political necessity of freedom of worship, or freedom not to worship at all, in a liberal democracy, but also the religious necessity of such freedom. To be constrained to be religious, let alone bound to a particular religion, could scarcely encourage a genuinely religious approach to life.

But in such a liberal and pluralistic environment, a more secular sensibility became the increasingly usual outcome, for many the natural one. Religious tolerance gradually metamorphosed into religious indifference. It was no longer mandatory in Western society to be Christian, and in coincidence with this growing freedom, fewer members of the culture found the Christian belief system intrinsically compelling or satisfying. Both liberal utilitarian and radical socialist philosophies seemed to offer the contemporary age more cogent programs for human activity than the traditional religions. Nor was the tenor of materialism unique to Marxism, for while capitalism had earlier been encouraged by certain elements of the Protestant sensibility, the capitalist societies' increasing preoccupation with material progress could not but depreciate the urgency of the Christian salvational message and the spiritual enterprise generally.[14] While religious observance continued to be widely upheld as a pillar of social integrity and civilized values, that observance was often indistinguishable from the conventions of Victorian morality.

Moreover, the Christian churches were themselves unwitting contributors to their own decline. The Roman Catholic Church, in its Counter-Reformational response to the Protestant heresy, had reinforced its conservative structure by crystallizing its past—doctrinally as well as institutionally—thereby leaving it comparatively unresponsive to any changes necessitated by the evolution of the modern era. Catholicism maintained a certain impregnable strength among its still vast membership, but at the cost of its appeal to the growing modern sensibility. Conversely, the Protestant churches in their Reformational response to Catholicism had established a more antiauthoritarian and noncentralized structure by overthrowing the past in its monolithic Catholic form, setting forth literal Scripture alone as a new foundation. But in so doing, Protestantism tended to fray out in ever-diversifying sectarianism, while leaving its later membership, under the impact of scientific discoveries antithetical to literal interpretations of the Bible, more susceptible to the secularizing influences of the modern age. In either case, Christianity lost much of its relevance to the contemporary mind. By the twentieth century, with uncounted thousands quietly leaving their inherited religion, the latter had been radically diminished in cultural importance.

Christianity now experienced itself as not only a divided church but a shrinking one, dwindling away before the ever-widening and ever-deepening onslaught of secularism. The Christian religion now faced a historical situation not unlike that encountered at its inception, when it was one faith among many in a large, sophisticated, urbanized environment—a world ambivalent about religion in general, and distanced from the claims and concerns of the Christian revelation in particular. The once perfervid enmities existing between Protestantism and Catholicism, the mutual distancing between all the various sects of Christianity, now diminished as these recognized their close affinity in the face of a growingly secular world. Kinship even with Judaism, so long the outcast in a Christian world, began to be more warmly acknowledged. In the modern world, all religions seemed to have more in common, a fading precious truth, than in dispute. Many commentators on the modern sensibility believed that religion was in its terminal stages, that it was just a matter of time before the irrationalities of religion would have relinquished their hold on the human mind.

Nevertheless, the Judaeo-Christian tradition sustained itself. Millions of families continued to nurture their children in the tenets and images of their inherited faith. Theologians continued to develop more historically nuanced understandings of Scripture and Church tradition, more flexible and imaginative applications of religious principles to life in the contemporary world. The Catholic Church began to open itself to modernity, to pluralism, ecumenism, and new freedom in matters of belief and worship. Christian churches in general moved to embrace wider congregations by making their structures and doctrines more relevant to the challenges—intellectual, psychological, sociological, political—of modern existence. Efforts were made to reconstruct an idea of God more immanent and evolutionary in character than the traditional one, more congruent with current cosmology and intellectual trends. Prominent philosophers, scientists, writers, and artists continued to claim personal meaning and spiritual comfort in the Judaeo-Christian framework. Yet the general movement of the culture's intellectual elite, of the modern sensibility as a whole—of the religiously reared child as it reached a skeptical and secular modern maturity—was largely otherwise.

For beyond the institutional and scriptural anachronisms discouraging a universal continuation of Christian faith lay a more general psychological discrepancy between the traditional Judaeo-Christian self-image and that of modern man. As early as the eighteenth and nineteenth centuries, the heavy taint of Original Sin ceased to be experienced as a dominant element in the lives of those born into the bright world of modern progress, nor could such a doctrine be readily combined with the scientific conception of man. The traditional image of the Semitic-Augustinian-Protestant God, who creates man too weak to withstand evil temptation, and who predestines the majority of his human creatures to eternal damnation with little consideration of their good works or honest attempts at virtue, ceased to be either palatable or plausible to many sensitive members of modern culture. The internal liberation from religious guilt and fear was as attractive an element in the secular world view as was earlier the external liberation from oppressive Church-dominated political and social structures. It was also increasingly recognized that the human spirit was expressed in secular life or not at all—any division of spiritual and secular was an artificiality, and an impoverishment for both. To locate the human spirit in another reality, transcendent or otherworldly, was to subvert that spirit altogether.

It was Friedrich Nietzsche's epochal pronouncement of "the death of God" that culminated this long evolution in the Western psyche and foreshadowed the existential mood of the twentieth century. With ruthless perceptiveness, he held up a dark mirror to the soul of Christianity—its inculcation of attitudes and values opposed to man's present existence, to the body, to the Earth, to courage and heroism, to joy and freedom, to life itself. "They would have to sing better songs to me that I might believe in their Redeemer: his disciples would have to look more redeemed!" And with this critique many agreed. For Nietzsche, the death of God signified not just the recognition of a religious illusion, but the demise of an entire civilization's world view that for too long had held man back from a daring, liberating embrace of life's totality.

With Freud, the modern psychological evaluation of religion achieved a new level of systematic and penetrating theoretical analysis. The discovery of the unconscious and of the human psyche's tendency to project traumatic memory constellations onto later experience opened up a crucial new dimension to the critical understanding of religious beliefs. In the light of psychoanalysis, the Judaeo-Christian God could be seen as a reified psychological projection based on the child's naive view of its libidinally restrictive and seemingly omnipotent parent. Reconceived in this way, many aspects of religious behavior and belief appeared to be comprehensible as symptoms of a deeply rooted cultural obsessive-compulsive neurosis. The projection of a morally authoritative patriarchal deity could be seen as having been a social necessity in earlier stages of human development, satisfying the cultural psyche's need for a powerful "external" force to undergird society's ethical requirements. But having internalized those requirements, the psychologically mature individual could recognize the projection for what it was, and dispense with it.

An important role in the devaluation of traditional religion was also played by the issue of sexual experience. With the rise in the twentieth century of a broad-mindedly secular and psychologically informed perspective, the long-held Christian ideal of asexual or antisexual asceticism seemed symptomatic more of cultural and personal psychoneurosis than of eternal spiritual law. Medieval practices such as mortification of the flesh were recognized as pathological aberrations rather than saintly exercises. The sexual attitudes of the Victorian era were seen as parochial inhibitions. Both Protestantism's puritanical tradition and the Catholic Church's continuing restrictiveness in sexual matters, particularly its prohibition of contraception, alienated thousands from the fold. The demands and delights of human eros made the traditional religious attitudes seem unhealthily constraining. As Freud's insights were integrated into the ever-growing modern movement of personal liberation and self-realization, a powerful Dionysian impulse arose in the West. Even for more staid sensibilities, it made little sense for human beings systematically to deny and repress that part of their being, their physical organism, that was not only their evolutionary inheritance but their existential foundation. Modern man had committed himself to this world, with all the entailments of such a choice.

Finally, even the long schooling of the Western mind in the Christian value system eventually worked to undermine Christianity's status in the modern era. From the Enlightenment onward, the continuing development of the Western mind's social conscience, its growing recognition of unconscious prejudices and injustices, and its increasing historical knowledge shed new light on the actual practice of the Christian religion over the centuries. The Christian injunction to love and serve all humanity and high valuation of the individual human soul now stood in sharp counterpoint to Christianity's long history of bigotry and violent intolerance—its forcible conversion of other peoples, its ruthless suppression of other cultural perspectives, its persecutions of heretics, its crusades against Moslems, its oppression of Jews, its depreciation of women's spirituality and exclusion of women from positions of religious authority, its association with slavery and colonialist exploitation, its pervasive spirit of prejudice and religious arrogance maintained against all those outside the fold. Measured by its own standards, Christianity fell woefully short of ethical greatness, and many alternative systems, from ancient Stoicism to modern liberalism and socialism, seemed to provide equally inspiring programs for human activity without the baggage of implausible supernatural belief.

The Modern Character

Thus was the movement from the Christian to the secular world view an overdetermined progression. Indeed, it would seem that the overall driving force of secularism did not lie in any specific factor or combination of factors—the scientific discrepancies with biblical revelation, the metaphysical consequences of empiricism, the social-political critiques of organized religion, the growing psychological acuity, the changing sexual mores, and so forth—for any of these could have been negotiable, as they were for those many who remained devout Christians. Secularism, rather, reflected a more general shift of character in the Western psyche, a shift visible in the various specific factors but transcending and subsuming them in its own global logic. The new psychological constitution of the modern character had been developing since the high Middle Ages, had conspicuously emerged in the Renaissance, was sharply clarified and empowered by the Scientific Revolution, then extended and solidified in the course of the Enlightenment. By the nineteenth century, in the wake of the democratic and industrial revolutions, it had achieved mature form. The direction and quality of that character reflected a gradual but finally radical shift of psychological allegiance from God to man, from dependence to independence, from otherworldliness to this world, from the transcendent to the empirical, from myth and belief to reason and fact, from universals to particulars, from a supernaturally determined static cosmos to a naturally determined evolving cosmos, and from a fallen humanity to an advancing one.

The tenor of Christianity no longer suited the prevailing mood of man's self-sustained progress in and mastery of his world. Modern man's capacity to understand the natural order and to bend that order to his own benefit could not but diminish his former sense of contingency upon God. Using his own natural intelligence, and without the aid of Holy Scripture's divine revelation, man had penetrated nature's mysteries, transformed his universe, and immeasurably enhanced his existence. Combined with the seemingly non-Christian character of the scientifically revealed natural order, this new sense of human dignity and power inevitably moved man toward his secular self. The tangible immediacy of this world and man's ability to find his meaning in it, to respond to its demands, and to experience progress within it all relieved him of that incessant striving for and anxiety concerning an afterworldly salvation. Man was responsible for his own earthly destiny. His own wits and will could change his world. Science gave man a new faith—not only in scientific knowledge, but in himself. It was particularly this emerging psychological climate that made the progressive sequence of philosophical and scientific advances—whether by Locke, Hume, and Kant, or by Darwin, Marx, and Freud—so potently effective in undercutting religion's role in the modern world view. The traditional Christian attitudes were no longer psychologically appropriate to the modern character.

Especially consequential for the secularization of the modern character was the nature of its allegiance to reason. The modern mind required of itself, and exulted in, a systematically critical independence of judgment—an existential posture not easily compatible with the pious surrender required for belief in divine revelation or obedience to the precepts of a priestly hierarchy. The modern emergence of autonomous personal judgment, prototypically incarnated in Luther, Galileo, and Descartes, made increasingly impossible any continuation of the medieval era's virtually universal intellectual deference to external authorities, such as the Church and Aristotle, that had been culturally empowered by tradition. And as modern man continued to mature, his striving for intellectual independence grew more absolute.

Thus the advance of the modern era brought a massive shift in the psychological vector of perceived authority. Whereas in earlier periods of the West's history, wisdom and authority were characteristically located in the past—biblical prophets, ancient bards, classical philosophers, the apostles and early fathers of the Church—the modern awareness increasingly located that power in the present, in its own unprecedented achievements, in its own self-consciousness as the evolutionary vanguard of human experience. Earlier eras looked backward, while the modern looked to itself and its future. Modern culture's complexity, productivity, and sophistication plainly put it in a class beyond all predecessors. And whereas the past authority had been typically associated with a transcendent principle—God, mythic deities, a cosmic intelligence—the modern awareness was itself becoming that authority, subsuming that power, making the transcendent immanent in itself. Medieval theism and ancient cosmism had given way to modern humanism.

Hidden Continuities

The West had "lost its faith"—and found a new one, in science and in man. But paradoxically, much of the Christian world view found continued life, albeit in often unrecognized forms, in the West's new secular outlook. Just as the evolving Christian understanding did not fully divorce itself from its Hellenic predecessor but, on the contrary, employed and integrated many of the latter's essential elements, so too did the modern secular world view—often less consciously—retain essential elements from Christianity. The Christian ethical values and the Scholastic-developed faith in human reason and in the intelligibility of the empirical universe were conspicuous among these, but even as fundamentalist a Judaeo-Christian doctrine as the command in Genesis that man exercise dominion over nature found modern affirmation, often explicit as in Bacon and Descartes, in the advances of science and technology. [15] So too did the Judaeo-Christian high regard for the individual soul, endowed with "sacred" inalienable rights and intrinsic dignity, continue in the secular humanist ideals of modern liberalism—as did other themes such as the moral self-responsibility of the individual, the tension between the ethical and the political, the imperative to care for the helpless and less fortunate, and the ultimate unity of mankind. The West's belief in itself as the most historically significant and favored culture echoed the Judaeo-Christian theme of the Chosen People. The global expansion of Western culture as the best and most appropriate for all mankind represented a secular continuation of the Roman Catholic Church's self-concept as the one universal Church for all humanity. Modern civilization now replaced Christianity as the cultural norm and ideal with which all other societies were to be compared, and to which they were to be converted. Just as Christianity had, in the process of overcoming and succeeding the Roman Empire, become Roman itself in the centralized, hierarchical, and politically motivated Roman Catholic Church, so too did the modern secular West, in the process of overcoming and succeeding Christianity and the Catholic Church, incorporate and unconsciously continue many of the latter's characteristic approaches to the world.

But perhaps the most pervasive and specifically Judaeo-Christian component tacitly retained in the modern world view was the belief in man's linear historical progress toward ultimate fulfillment. Modern man's self-understanding was emphatically teleological, with humanity seen as moving in a historical development out of a darker past characterized by ignorance, primitiveness, poverty, suffering, and oppression, and toward a brighter ideal future characterized by intelligence, sophistication, prosperity, happiness, and freedom. The faith in that movement was based largely on an underlying trust in the salvational effect of expanding human knowledge: Humanity's future fulfillment would be achieved in a world reconstructed by science. The original Judaeo-Christian eschatological expectation had here been transformed into a secular faith.

The religious faith in God's eventual salvation of mankind—whether Israel's arrival in the Promised Land, the Church's arrival at the millennium, the Holy Spirit's progressive perfecting of humanity, or the Second Coming of Christ—now became an evolutionary confidence, or revolutionary belief, in an eventual this-worldly utopia whose realization would be expedited by the expert application of human reason to nature and society.

Even in the course of Christianity's own development of the end time expectation, the waiting and hoping for divine action to initiate the world's transfiguration had gradually shifted during the early modern period to a sense that man's own activity and initiative were required to prepare for a Christian social utopia appropriate to the Second Coming. In the Renaissance, Erasmus had suggested a new understanding of Christian eschatology whereby humanity might move toward perfection in this world, with history realizing its goal of the Kingdom of God in a peaceful earthly society—not through apocalypse, divine intervention, and otherworldly escape, but through a divine immanence working within man's historical evolution. In a similar spirit during the Scientific Revolution, Bacon had heralded the coming scientific civilization as a movement toward material redemption coincident with the Christian millennium. As secularization advanced during the modern era, the Christian element in and rationale for the coming utopia dwindled and disappeared, though the expectation and striving remained. In time, the focus on a social utopia merged into futurology, which replaced earlier eras' visions and anticipations of the Kingdom of Heaven. "Planning" replaced "hoping" as human reason and technology demonstrated their miraculous efficacy.

Confidence in human progress, akin to the biblical faith in humanity's spiritual evolution and future consummation, was so central to the modern world view that it notably increased with the decline of Christianity. Expectations of mankind's coming fulfillment found vivid expression even as the modern mind reached its most determinedly secular stages in Condorcet, Comte, and Marx. Indeed, the ultimate statement of belief in evolutionary human deification was found in Christianity's most fervent antagonist, Nietzsche, whose Superman would be born out of the death of God and the overcoming of the old limited man.

But regardless of what attitude was maintained toward Christianity, the conviction that man was steadily and inevitably approaching entrance into a better world, that man himself was being progressively improved and perfected through his own efforts, constituted one of the most characteristic, deep-seated, and consequential principles of the modern sensibility. Christianity no longer seemed to be the driving force of the human enterprise. For the robust civilization of the West at the high noon of modernity, it was science and reason, not religion and belief, which propelled that progress. Man's will, not God's, was the acknowledged source of the world's betterment and humanity's advancing liberation.

VI

The Transformation of the Modern Era

We now approach the last stages of our narrative. What remains for us is to scan the trajectory taken by the modern mind as it developed from the foundations and premises of the modern world view just examined. For perhaps the most momentous paradox concerning the character of the modern era was the curious manner in which its progress during the centuries following the Scientific Revolution and the Enlightenment brought Western man unprecedented freedom, power, expansion, breadth of knowledge, depth of insight, and concrete success, and yet simultaneously served—first subtly and later critically—to undermine the human being's existential situation on virtually every front: metaphysical and cosmological, epistemological, psychological, and finally even biological. A relentless balance, an inextricable intertwining of positive and negative, seemed to mark the evolution of the modern age, and our task here is to attempt to understand the nature of that intricate dialectic.

The Changing Image of the Human
from Copernicus through Freud

The peculiar phenomenon of contradictory consequences ensuing from the same intellectual advance was visible from the start of the modern era with Copernicus's dethroning of the Earth as the center of creation. In the same instant that man liberated himself from the geocentric illusion of virtually all previous generations of mankind, he also effected for himself an unprecedentedly fundamental cosmic displacement. The universe no longer centered on man; his cosmic position was neither fixed nor absolute. And each succeeding step in the Scientific Revolution and its aftermath added new dimensions to the Copernican effect, further propelling that liberation while intensifying that displacement.

With Galileo, Descartes, and Newton, the new science was forged, a new cosmology defined, a new world opened to man within which his powerful intelligence could act with new freedom and effectiveness. Yet simultaneously, that new world was disenchanted of all those personal and spiritual qualities that for millennia had given human beings their sense of cosmic meaning. The new universe was a machine, a self-contained mechanism of force and matter, devoid of goals or purpose, bereft of intelligence or consciousness, its character fundamentally alien to that of man. The premodern world had been permeated with spiritual, mythic, theistic, and other humanly meaningful categories, but all these were regarded by the modern perception as anthropomorphic projections. Mind and matter, psyche and world, were separate realities. The scientific liberation from theological dogma and animistic superstition was thus accompanied by a new sense of human alienation from a world that no longer responded to human values, nor offered a redeeming context within which could be understood the larger issues of human existence. Similarly, with science's quantitative analysis of the world, the methodological liberation from subjective distortions was accompanied by the ontological diminution of all those qualities—emotional, aesthetic, ethical, sensory, imaginative, intentional—that seemed most constitutive of human experience. These losses and gains were noted, but the paradox seemed inescapable if man was to be faithful to his own intellectual rigor. Science may have revealed a cold, impersonal world, but it was the true one nonetheless. Despite any nostalgia for the venerable but now disproved cosmic womb, one could not go backward.

With Darwin, these consequences were further affirmed and amplified. Any remaining theological assumptions concerning the world's divine government and man's special spiritual status were severely controverted by the new theory and evidence: Man was a highly successful animal. He was not God's noble creation with a divine destiny, but nature's experiment with an uncertain destiny. Consciousness, once believed to rule the universe and permeate it, was now understood to have arisen accidentally in the course of matter's evolution, to have been in existence a relatively brief time, and to be characteristic of a limited and relatively insignificant part of the cosmos—Homo sapiens—for which there was no guarantee its ultimate evolutionary fate would be any different from that of thousands of other now extinct species.

With the world no longer a divine creation, a certain spiritual nobility seemed to have departed from it, an impoverishment that also necessarily touched man, its erstwhile crown. While Christian theology had maintained that natural history existed for the sake of human history, and that humanity was essentially at home in a universe designed for its spiritual unfoldment, the new understanding of evolution refuted both claims as anthropocentric delusions. All was in flux. Man was not an absolute, and his cherished values had no foundation outside of himself. Man's character, his mind and will, came from below, not above. The structures not only of religion but of society, of culture, of reason itself now seemed to be relatively arbitrary expressions of the struggle for biological success. Thus too was Darwin liberating and diminishing. Man could now recognize that he rode forth at the crest of evolution's advance, nature's most complex and dazzling achievement; but he was also just an animal of no "higher" purpose. The universe provided no assurance of indefinite success for the species, and certain assurance of individual demise at physical death. Indeed, on the longer-term macroscopic scale, the growing modern sense of life's contingency was further enforced by nineteenth-century physics' formulation of the second law of thermodynamics, which portrayed the universe as moving spontaneously and irreversibly from order to disorder toward a final condition of maximum entropy, or "heat death." The chief facts of human history until the present were fortuitously supportive biophysical circumstances and brute survival, with no apparent larger meaning or context, and with no cosmic security supplied by any providential design from above.

Freud dramatically forwarded these developments as he brought the Darwinian perspective to bear more fully on the human psyche, presenting persuasive evidence for the existence of unconscious forces determining man's behavior and conscious awareness. In so doing, he seemingly both freed the modern mind from its naive unconsciousness (or rather from being altogether unconscious of its unconsciousness), giving it a new profundity of self-understanding, yet also confronted that mind with a dark, deflating vision of its true character. For on the one hand, psychoanalysis served as a virtual epiphany for the early twentieth-century mind as it brought to light the archaeological depths of the psyche, disclosed the intelligibility of dreams, fantasy, and psychopathological symptoms, illuminated the sexual etiology of neurosis, demonstrated the importance of infantile experience in conditioning adult life, discovered the Oedipus complex, unveiled the psychological relevance of mythology and symbolism, recognized the psychic structural components of the ego, superego, and id, revealed the mechanisms of resistance, repression, and projection, and brought forth a host of other insights laying open the mind's character and internal dynamics. Freud thereby represented a brilliant culmination of the Enlightenment project, bringing even the human unconscious under the light of rational investigation.

Yet on the other hand, Freud radically undermined the entire Enlightenment project by his revelation that below or beyond the rational mind existed an overwhelmingly potent repository of nonrational forces which did not readily submit either to rational analysis or to conscious manipulation, and in comparison with which man's conscious ego was a frail and fragile epiphenomenon. Freud thereby furthered the cumulative modern process of casting man out of that privileged cosmic status his modern rational self-image had retained from the Christian world view. Man could no longer doubt that it was not only his body but his psyche as well for which powerful biological instincts—amoral, aggressive, erotic, "polymorphous perverse"—were the most significant motivating factors, and that in the face of these the proud human virtues of rationality, moral conscience, and religious feelings were conceivably no more than reaction-formations and delusions of the civilized self-concept. Given the existence of such unconscious determinants, man's sense of personal freedom could well be spurious. The psychologically aware individual now knew himself to be, like all members of modern civilization, condemned to internal division, repression, neurosis, and alienation.

With Freud, the Darwinian struggle with nature took on new dimensions, as man was now constrained to live in eternal struggle with his own nature. Not only was God exposed as a primitive infantile projection, but the conscious human ego itself with its prize virtue the human reason—man's last bastion separating him from nature—was now dethroned, it too recognized as nothing more exalted than a recent and precarious development out of the primordial id. The true wellspring of human motivations was a seething caldron of irrational, bestial impulses—and contemporary historical events began to provide distressing evidence for just such a thesis. Not just man's divinity but his humanity was coming into question. As the scientific mind emancipated modern man from his illusions, he seemed increasingly swallowed up by nature, deprived of his ancient dignities, unmasked as a creature of base instinct.

Marx's contribution had already suggested a similar deflation, for as Freud revealed the personal unconscious, Marx exposed the social unconscious. The philosophical, religious, and moral values of each age could be plausibly comprehended as determined by economic and political variables, whereby control over the means of production was maintained by the most powerful class. The entire superstructure of human belief could be seen as reflecting the more basic struggle for material power. The elite of Western civilization, for all its sense of cultural achievement, might recognize itself in Marx's dark portrait as a self-deceiving bourgeois imperialist oppressor. Class struggle, not civilized progress, was the program of the foreseeable future—and again, contemporary historical developments appeared to bear out that analysis. Between Marx and Freud, with Darwin behind them, the modern intelligentsia increasingly perceived man's cultural values, psychological motivations, and conscious awareness as historically relative phenomena derived from unconscious political, economic, and instinctual impulses of an entirely naturalistic quality. The principles and directives of the Scientific Revolution—the search for material, impersonal, secular explanations for all phenomena—had found new and illuminating applications in the psychological and social dimensions of human experience. Yet in that process, modern man's optimistic self-estimate from the Enlightenment was subject to repeated contradiction and diminution by his own advancing intellectual horizons.

These horizons were also radically expanded under the force of scientific discoveries that, like the views of Darwin, Marx, and Freud, applied a historical and evolutionary model of change to an increasing array of phenomena. That model had first emerged in the Renaissance and Enlightenment when European man's recently unbound intellectual curiosity was combined with a new and emphatic sense of his dynamic progress. From these grew a heightened interest in the classical and ancient past from which he had developed, and enhanced standards of scholarship and historical investigation. From Valla and Machiavelli to Voltaire and Gibbon, from Vico and Herder to Hegel and Ranke, attention to history increased, as did awareness of historical change and recognition of developmental principles by which historical change could be comprehended. The global explorers had similarly expanded Europeans' geographical knowledge, and with it their exposure to other cultures and other histories. With the continuous growth of information in these areas, it gradually became evident that human history extended back in time far longer than had been assumed, that there existed many other significant cultures past and present, that these possessed views of the world widely divergent from the European, and that there was nothing absolute, immemorial, or secure about modern Western man's present status or values. For a culture long accustomed to a relatively static, abbreviated, and Eurocentric conception of human history—indeed, of universal history (as in Archbishop Ussher's famous dating of the year of Creation in Genesis as 4004 B.C.)—the new perspectives were disorienting in both scope and character. Yet subsequent work by archaeologists pressed the horizon back still further, uncovering ever more ancient civilizations whose entire rise and fall had occurred before Greece and Rome were born. Unending development and variety, decay and transformation, were the law of history, and history's trajectory was disconcertingly long.

When the developmental and historical perspective was applied to nature, as with Hutton and Lyell in geology, and Lamarck and Darwin in biology, the time spans within which organic life and the Earth were known to have existed were exponentially expanded to thousands of millions of years, in comparison with which all of human history had taken place within a startlingly brief period. Yet this was only the beginning, for then astronomers, empowered by increasingly advanced technical tools, applied similar principles toward understanding the cosmos itself, resulting in its unprecedented temporal and spatial expansion.

By the twentieth century, the resulting cosmology had posited the solar system as a vanishingly small part of a gigantic galaxy containing a hundred billion other stars, each comparable to the Sun, with the observable universe containing a hundred billion other galaxies, each comparable to the Milky Way. These individual galaxies were, in turn, members of much larger galactic clusters, themselves seemingly parts of even vaster galactic superclusters, with celestial space conveniently measurable only in terms of distances traveled in years at the speed of light, and with the distances between galactic clusters calculated in hundreds of millions of light-years. All these stars and galaxies were presumed to be involved in enormously long processes of formation and decay, with the universe itself born in a scarcely conceivable, let alone explicable, primordial explosion some ten or twenty billion years past.

Such macrocosmic dimensions forced upon man's awareness a disturbingly humble sense of his own relative minuteness in both time and space, dwarfing the entire human enterprise, not to mention individual human lives, to shockingly minuscule proportions. Superseded by such immensities, the earlier expansions of man's world effected by Columbus, Galileo, and even Darwin seemed comparatively intimate. Thus did the combined efforts of explorers, geographers, historians, anthropologists, archaeologists, paleontologists, geologists, biologists, physicists, and astronomers serve to expand man's knowledge and diminish his cosmic stature. The distant origins of mankind among the primates and primitives, and yet, relative to the age of the Earth, their comparative proximity; the great size of the Earth and the solar system, and yet, relative to the galaxy, their extreme minuteness; the stupendous expanse of the heavens in which the Earth's nearest neighboring galaxies were so unimaginably remote that their light now visible on Earth had left its source over a hundred thousand years earlier, when Homo sapiens was still in the Old Stone Age—faced with such vistas, thoughtful persons had good cause to ponder the apparent insignificance of human existence in the greater scheme of things.

Yet it was not just the radical temporal and spatial diminution of human life effected by science's advance that threatened modern man's self-image, but also science's qualitative devaluation of his essential character. For as reductionism was successfully employed to analyze nature, and then human nature as well, man himself was reduced. With science's increasing sophistication, it seemed likely, perhaps even necessary, that the laws of physics were in some sense at the bottom of everything. The phenomena of chemistry could be reduced to principles of physics, those of biology to chemistry and physics, and, for many scientists, those of human behavior and awareness to biology and biochemistry. Hence consciousness itself became a mere epiphenomenon of matter, a secretion of the brain, a function of electrochemical circuitry serving biological imperatives. The Cartesian program of mechanistic analysis thereby began to overcome even the division between *res cogitans* and *res extensa*, thinking subject and material world, as La Mettrie, Pavlov, Watson, Skinner, and others argued that as the universe as a whole could be best comprehended as a machine, so too could man. Human behavior and mental functioning were perhaps only reflex activities based on mechanistic principles of stimulus and response, compounded by genetic factors that were themselves increasingly susceptible to scientific manipulations. Ruled by statistical determinisms, man was an appropriate subject for the domain of probability theory. Man's future, his very essence, appeared to be as contingent and unmysterious as an engineering problem. Although it was, strictly speaking, only a regulatory assumption, the widespread hypothesis that all the complexities of human experience, and of the world in general, would ultimately be explicable in terms of natural scientific principles increasingly, if often unconsciously, took on the character of a well-substantiated scientific principle itself, with profound metaphysical entailments.

The more modern man strove to control nature by understanding its principles, to free himself from nature's power, to separate himself from nature's necessity and rise above it, the more completely his science metaphysically submerged man into nature, and thus into its mechanistic and impersonal character as well. For if man lived in an impersonal universe, and if his existence was entirely grounded in and subsumed by that universe, then man too was essentially impersonal, his private experience of personhood a psychological fiction. In such a light, man was becoming little more than a genetic strategy for the continuance of his species, and as the twentieth century progressed that strategy's success was becoming yearly more uncertain. Thus it was the irony of modern intellectual progress that man's genius discovered successive principles of determinism—Cartesian, Newtonian, Darwinian, Marxist, Freudian, behaviorist, genetic, neurophysiological, sociobiological—that steadily attenuated belief in his own rational and volitional freedom, while eliminating his sense of being anything more than a peripheral and transient accident of material evolution.

The Self-Critique of the Modern Mind

These paradoxical developments were paralleled by the simultaneous progress of modern philosophy as it analyzed the nature and extent of human knowledge with ever-increasing rigor, subtlety, and insight. For at the same time that modern man was vastly extending his effective knowledge of the world, his critical epistemology inexorably revealed the disquieting limits beyond which his knowledge could not claim to penetrate.

From Locke to Hume

With Newton's synthesis, the Enlightenment began with an unprecedented confidence in human reason, and the new science's success in explicating the natural world affected the efforts of philosophy in two ways: first, by locating the basis of human knowledge in the human mind and its encounter with the physical world; and second, by directing philosophy's attention to an analysis of the mind that was capable of such cognitive success.

It was above all John Locke, Newton's contemporary and Bacon's heir, who set the tone for the Enlightenment by affirming the foundational principle of empiricism: There is nothing in the intellect that was not previously in the senses (*Nihil est in intellectu quod non antea fuerit in sensu*). Stimulated to philosophy by reading Descartes, yet also influenced by the contemporary empirical science of Newton, Boyle, and the Royal Society, and affected as well by Gassendi's atomistic empiricism, Locke could not accept the Cartesian rationalist belief in innate ideas. In Locke's analysis, all knowledge of the world must rest finally on man's sensory experience. Through the combining and compounding of simple sensory impressions or "ideas" (defined as mental contents) into more complex concepts, through reflection after sensation, the mind can arrive at sound conclusions. Sense impressions and inner reflection on these impressions: "These two are the fountains of knowledge, from whence all the ideas we have, or can naturally have, do spring." The mind is at first a blank tablet, upon which experience writes. It is intrinsically a passive receptor of its experience, and receives atomistic sensory impressions that represent the external material objects causing them. From those impressions, the mind can build its conceptual understanding by means of its own introspective and compounding operations. The mind possesses innate powers, but not innate ideas. Cognition begins with sensation.

The British empiricist demand that sensory experience be the ultimate source of knowledge of the world set itself in opposition to the Continental rationalist orientation, epitomized in Descartes and variously elaborated by Spinoza and Leibniz, which held that the mind alone, through its recognition of clear, distinct, and self-evident truths, could achieve certain knowledge. For the empiricists, such empirically ungrounded rationalism was, as Bacon had said, akin to a spider's producing cobwebs out of its own substance. The characteristic imperative of the Enlightenment (soon to be carried by Voltaire from England to the Continent and the French Encyclopedists) held that reason required sensory experience to know anything about the world other than its own concoctions. The best criterion of truth was henceforth its genetic basis—in sense experience—not just its apparent intrinsic rational validity, which could be spurious. In subsequent empiricist thought, rationalism was increasingly delimited in its legitimate claims: The mind without sensory evidence cannot possess knowledge of the world, but can only speculate, define terms, or perform mathematical and logical operations. Similarly, the rationalist belief that science could attain certain knowledge of general truths about the world was increasingly displaced by a less absolutist position, suggesting that science cannot make known the real structure of things but can only, on the basis of hypotheses concerning appearances, discover probable truths.

This nascent skepticism in the empiricist position was already visible in Locke's own difficulties with his theory of knowledge. For Locke recognized there was no guarantee that all human ideas of things genuinely resembled the external objects they were supposed to represent. Nor was he able to reduce all complex ideas, such as the idea of substance, to simple ideas or sensations. There were three factors in the process of human knowledge: the mind, the physical object, and the perception or idea in the mind that represents that object. Man knows directly only the idea in the mind, not the object. He knows the object only mediately, through the idea. Outside man's perception is simply a world of substances in motion; the various impressions of the external world that man experiences in cognition cannot be absolutely confirmed as belonging to the world in itself.

Locke, however, attempted a partial solution to such problems by making the distinction (following Galileo and Descartes) between primary and secondary qualities—between those qualities that inhere in all extended material objects as objectively measurable, like weight and shape and motion, and those that inhere only in the subjective human experience of those objects, like taste and odor and color. While primary qualities produce ideas in the mind that genuinely resemble the external object, secondary qualities produce ideas that are simply consequences of the subject's perceptual apparatus. By focusing on the measurable primary qualities, science can gain reliable knowledge of the material world.

But Locke was followed by Bishop Berkeley, who pointed out that if the empiricist analysis of human knowledge is carried through rigorously, then it must be admitted that *all* qualities that the human mind registers, whether primary or secondary, are ultimately experienced as ideas in the mind, and there can be no conclusive inference whether or not some of those qualities "genuinely" represent or resemble an outside object. Indeed, there can be no conclusive inference concerning even the existence of a world of material objects outside the mind producing those ideas. For there is no justifiable means by which one can distinguish between objects and sensory impressions, and thus no idea in the mind can be said to be "like" a material thing so that the latter is "represented" to the mind. Since one can never get outside of the mind to compare the idea with the actual object, the whole notion of representation is groundless. The same arguments Locke used against the representational accuracy of secondary qualities were equally applicable to primary qualities, for in the end both types of qualities must be regarded as experiences of the mind.

Locke's doctrine of representation was therefore untenable. In Berkeley's analysis, all human experience is phenomenal, limited to appearances in the mind. Man's perception of nature is his mental experience of nature, and consequently all sense data must finally be adjudged as "objects for the mind" and not representations of material substances. In effect, while Locke had reduced all mental contents to an ultimate basis in sensation, Berkeley now further reduced all sense data to mental contents.

The Lockean distinction between qualities that belong to the mind and qualities that belong to matter could not be sustained, and with this breakdown Berkeley, a bishop of the church, sought to overcome the contemporary tendency toward "atheistic Materialism" which he felt had unjustifiably arisen with modern science. The empiricist rightly affirms that all knowledge rests on experience. But in the end, Berkeley pointed out, all experience is nothing more than experience—all mental representations of supposed material substances are finally ideas in the mind— and therefore the existence of a material world external to the mind is an unwarranted assumption. All that can be known with certainty to exist is the mind and its ideas, including those ideas that seem to represent a material world. From a rigorously philosophical point of view, "to be" does not mean "to be a material substance"; rather, "to be" means "to be perceived by a mind" (*esse est percipi*).

Yet Berkeley held that the individual mind does not subjectively determine its experience of the world, as if the latter were a fantasy susceptible to any person's whim of the moment. The reason that objectivity exists, that different individuals continually perceive a similar world, and that a reliable order inheres in that world, is that the world and its order depend on a mind that transcends individual minds and is universal—namely, God's mind. That universal mind produces sensory ideas in individual minds according to certain regularities, the constant experience of which gradually reveals to man the "laws of nature." It is this situation that allows the possibility of science. Science is not hampered by the recognition of sense data's immaterial basis, for it can continue its analysis of objects just as well with the critical knowledge that they are objects for the mind—not external material substances but recurrent groups of sense qualities. The philosopher does not have to worry about the problems created by Locke's representation of an external material reality that evaded certain corroboration, because the material world does not exist as such. The ideas in the mind are the final truth. Thus Berkeley strove to preserve the empiricist orientation and solve Locke's representation problems, while also preserving a spiritual foundation for human experience and natural science.

But Berkeley in turn was followed by David Hume, who drove the empiricist epistemological critique to its final extreme, making use of Berkeley's insight while turning it in a direction more characteristic of the modern mind—more reflective of that secular skepticism growingly visible from Montaigne through Bayle and the Enlightenment. As an empiricist who grounded all human knowledge in sense experience, Hume agreed with Locke's general orientation, and he agreed too with Berkeley's criticism of Locke's theory of representation; but he disagreed with Berkeley's idealist solution. Human experience was indeed of the phenomenal only, of sense impressions, but there was no way to ascertain what was beyond the sense impressions, spiritual or otherwise. Like Berkeley, Hume could not accept Locke's views on representative perception, but neither could he accept Berkeley's identification of external objects with internal ideas, rooted ultimately in the mind of God.

To begin his analysis, Hume made a distinction between sensory impressions and ideas: Sensory impressions are the basis of any knowledge, and they come with a force and liveliness that make them unique. Ideas are faint copies of those impressions. One can experience through the senses an *impression* of the color blue, and on the basis of this impression one can have an *idea* of that color whereby the latter can be recalled. The question therefore arises, What *causes* the sensory impression? If every valid idea has a basis in a corresponding impression, then to what impression can the mind point for its idea of causality? None, Hume answered. If the mind analyzes its experience without preconception, it must recognize that in fact all its supposed knowledge is based on a continuous chaotic volley of discrete sensations, and that on these sensations the mind imposes an order of its own. The mind draws from its experience an explanation that in fact derives from the mind itself, not from the experience. The mind cannot really know what causes the sensations, for it never experiences "cause" as a sensation. It experiences only simple impressions, atomized phenomena, and causality per se is not one of those simple impressions. Rather, through an association of ideas—which is only a habit of the human imagination—the mind assumes a causal relation that in fact has no basis in a sensory impression. All that man has to base his knowledge on is impressions in the mind, and he cannot assume to know what exists beyond those impressions.

Hence the presumed basis for all human knowledge, the causal relation, is never ratified by direct human experience. Instead, the mind experiences certain impressions that suggest they are caused by an objective substance existing continuously and independently of the mind; but the mind never experiences that substance, only the suggestive impressions. Similarly, the mind may perceive that one event, A, is repeatedly followed by another event, B, and on that basis the mind may project that A causes B. But in fact all that is known is that A and B have been regularly perceived in close association. The causal nexus itself has never been perceived, nor can it be said to exist outside of the human mind and its internal habits. Cause must be recognized as merely the accident of a repeated conjunction of events in the mind. It is the reification of a psychological expectation, apparently affirmed by experience but never genuinely substantiated.

Even the ideas of space and time are ultimately not independent realities, as Newton assumed, but are simply the result of experiencing the coexistence or succession of particular objects. From repeated experiences of this kind, the notions of time and space are abstracted by the mind, but actually time and space are only ways of experiencing objects. All general concepts originate in this way, with the mind moving from an experience of particular impressions to an idea of relationship between those impressions, an idea that the mind then separates and reifies. But the general concept, the idea, is only the result of the mind's habit of association. At bottom, the mind experiences only particulars, and any relation between those particulars is woven by the mind into the fabric of its experience. The intelligibility of the world reflects habits of the mind, not the nature of reality.

Part of Hume's intention was to refute the metaphysical claims of philosophical rationalism and its deductive logic. In Hume's view, two kinds of propositions are possible, one based purely on sensation and the other purely on the intellect. A proposition based on sensation concerns obvious matters of concrete fact (e.g., "it is a sunny day"), which are always contingent (they could have been different, though in fact they were not). By contrast, a proposition based purely on intellect concerns relations between concepts (e.g., "all squares have four equal sides"), and these are always necessary—that is, their denial leads to self-contradiction. But the truths of pure reason, such as those of mathematics, are necessary only because they exist in a self-contained system with no mandatory reference to the external world. They are true only by logical definition, by making explicit what is implicit in their own terms, and these can claim no necessary relation to the nature of things. Hence the only truths of which pure reason is capable are tautological. Reason alone cannot assert a truth about the ultimate nature of things.

Moreover, not only does pure reason have no direct insight into metaphysical matters, neither can reason pronounce on the ultimate nature of things by inference from experience. One cannot know the supersensible by analyzing the sensible, because the only principle upon which one can base such a judgment—causality—is finally grounded only in the observation of particular concrete events in temporal succession. Without the elements of temporality and concreteness, causality is rendered meaningless. Hence all metaphysical arguments, which seek to make certain statements about all possible reality beyond temporal concrete experience, are vitiated at their basis. Thus for Hume, metaphysics was just an exalted form of mythology, of no relevance to the real world.

But another and, for the modern mind, more disturbing consequence of Hume's critical analysis was its apparent undermining of empirical science itself, for the latter's logical foundation, induction, was now recognized as unjustifiable. The mind's logical progress from many particulars to a universal certainty could never be absolutely legitimated: no matter how many times one observes a given event-sequence, one can never be certain that that event-sequence is a causal one and will always repeat itself in subsequent observations. Just because event B has always been observed to follow event A in the past cannot guarantee it will always do so in the future. Any acceptance of that "law," any belief that the sequence represents a true causal relationship, is only an ingrained psychological persuasion, not a logical certainty. The apparent causal necessity in phenomena is the necessity only of subjective conviction, of the human imagination controlled by its regular association of ideas. It has no objective basis. One can perceive the regularity of events, but not their necessity. The latter is no more than a subjective feeling induced by the experience of apparent regularity. In such a context, science is possible, but it is a science of the phenomenal only, of appearances registered in the mind, and its certainty is a subjective one, determined not by nature but by human psychology.

Paradoxically, Hume had begun with the intention of applying rigorous Newtonian "experimental" principles of investigation to man, to bring the successful empirical methods of natural science to a science of man. But he ended by casting into question the objective certainty of empirical science altogether. If all human knowledge is based on empiricism, yet induction cannot be logically justified, then man can have no certain knowledge.

With Hume, the long-developing empiricist stress on sense perceptions, from Aristotle and Aquinas to Ockham, Bacon, and Locke, was brought to its ultimate extreme, in which only the volley and chaos of those perceptions exist, and any order imposed on those perceptions was arbitrary, human, and without objective foundation. In terms of Plato's fundamental distinction between "knowledge" (of reality) and "opinion" (about appearances), for Hume all human knowledge had to be regarded as opinion. Where Plato had held sensory impressions to be faint copies of Ideas, Hume held ideas to be faint copies of sensory impressions. In the long evolution of the Western mind from the ancient idealist to the modern empiricist, the basis of reality had been entirely reversed: Sensory experience, not ideal apprehension, was the standard of truth—and that truth was utterly problematic. Perceptions alone were real for the mind, and one could never know what stood beyond them.

Locke had retained a certain faith in the capacity of the human mind to grasp, however imperfectly, the general outlines of an external world by means of its combining operations. But for Hume, not only was the human mind less than perfect, it could never claim access to the world's order, which could not be said to exist apart from the mind. That order was not inherent in nature, but was the result of the mind's own associating tendencies. If nothing was in the mind that did not ultimately derive from the senses, and if all valid complex ideas were based on simple ideas derived from sensory impressions, then the idea of cause itself, and thus certain knowledge of the world, had to be critically reconsidered, for cause was never so perceived. It could never be derived from a simple direct impression. Even the experience of a continuously existing substance was only a belief produced by many impressions' recurring in a regular way, producing the fiction of an enduring entity.

Pursuing this psychological analysis of human experience still further, Hume concluded that the mind itself was only a bundle of disconnected perceptions, with no valid claims to substantial unity, continuous existence, or internal coherence, let alone to objective knowledge. All order and coherence, including that giving rise to the idea of the human self, were understood to be mind-constructed fictions. Human beings required such fictions to live, but the philosopher could not substantiate them. With Berkeley, there had been no necessary material basis for experience, though the mind had retained a certain independent spiritual power derived from God's mind, and the world experienced by the mind derived its order from the same source. But with the more secular skepticism of Hume, nothing could be said to be objectively necessary— not God, not order, not causality, nor substantial existents, nor personal identity, nor real knowledge. All was contingent. Man knows only phenomena, chaotic impressions; the order he perceives therein is imagined, for reasons of psychological habit and instinctual need, and then projected. Thus did Hume articulate philosophy's paradigmatic skeptical argument, one that in turn was to stimulate Immanuel Kant to develop the central philosophical position of the modern era.

Kant

The intellectual challenge that faced Immanuel Kant in the second half of the eighteenth century was a seemingly impossible one: on the one hand, to reconcile the claims of science to certain and genuine knowledge of the world with the claim of philosophy that experience could never give rise to such knowledge; on the other hand, to reconcile the claim of religion that man was morally free with the claim of science that nature was entirely determined by necessary laws. With these several claims in such intricate and pointed conflict, an intellectual crisis of profound complexity had emerged. Kant's proposed resolution of that crisis was equally complex, brilliant, and weighty in its consequences.

Kant was too intimate with Newtonian science and its triumphs to doubt that man had access to certain knowledge. Yet he felt as well the force of Hume's relentless analysis of the human mind. He too had come to distrust the absolute pronouncements on the nature of the world for which a purely rational speculative metaphysics had been pretending competence, and concerning which it had fallen into endless and seemingly irresolvable conflict. According to Kant, the reading of Hume's work had awakened him from his "dogmatic slumber," the residue of his long training in the dominant German rationalist school of Wolff, Leibniz's academic systematizer. He now recognized that man could know only the phenomenal, and that any metaphysical conclusions concerning the nature of the universe that went beyond his experience were unfounded. Such propositions of the pure reason, Kant demonstrated, could as readily be opposed as supported by logical argument. Whenever the mind attempted to ascertain the existence of things beyond sensory experience—such as God, the immortality of the soul, or the infinity of the universe—it inevitably found itself entangled in contradiction or illusion. The history of metaphysics was thus a record of contention and confusion, entirely devoid of cumulative progress. The mind required empirical evidence before it could be capable of knowledge, but God, immortality, and other such metaphysical matters could never become phenomena; they were not empirical. Metaphysics, therefore, was beyond the powers of human reason.

But Hume's dissolution of causality also appeared to undercut the claims of natural science to necessary general truths about the world, since Newtonian science was based on the assumed reality of the now uncertified causal principle. If all human knowledge necessarily came from observation of particular instances, these could never be legitimately generalized into certain laws, since only discrete events were perceived, never their causal connection. Nevertheless, Kant was convinced beyond doubt that Newton, with the aid of experiments, had gotten hold of real knowledge of absolute certainty and generality. Who was correct, Hume or Newton? If Newton had attained certain knowledge, and yet Hume had demonstrated the impossibility of such knowledge, how could Newton have succeeded? How was certain knowledge possible in a phenomenal universe? This was the burden of Kant's *Critique of Pure Reason,* and his solution was to satisfy the claims of both Hume and Newton, of skepticism and science—and in so doing to resolve modern epistemology's fundamental dichotomy between empiricism and rationalism.

The clarity and strict necessity of mathematical truths had long provided the rationalists—above all Descartes, Spinoza, and Leibniz—with the assurance that, in the world of modern doubt, the human mind had at least one solid basis for attaining certain knowledge. Kant himself had long been convinced that natural science was scientific to the precise extent that it approximated to the ideal of mathematics. Indeed, on the basis of such a conviction, Kant himself had made an important contribution to Newtonian cosmology, demonstrating that through strictly necessary measurable physical forces, the Sun and planets had consolidated and assumed the motions defined by Copernicus and Kepler. To be sure, in attempting to extend the mathematical mode of reasoning to metaphysics, Kant became convinced of pure reason's incompetence in such matters. But within the bounds of sensory experience, as in natural science, mathematical truth was patently successful.

Yet because natural science was concerned with the external world given through the senses, it thereby opened itself to Hume's criticism that all its knowledge would then be contingent, its apparent necessity only psychological. By Hume's reasoning, with which Kant had to agree, the certain laws of Euclidean geometry could not have been derived from empirical observation. Yet Newtonian science was explicitly based upon Euclidean geometry. If the laws of mathematics and logic were said to come from within the human mind, how could they be said to pertain with certainty to the world? Rationalists like Descartes had more or less simply assumed a mind-world correspondence, but Hume had subjected that assumption to a damaging critique. Nevertheless, a mind-world correspondence was clearly presupposed, and seemingly vindicated, in the Newtonian achievement, of which Kant was certain.

Kant's extraordinary solution was to propose that the mind-world correspondence was indeed vindicated in natural science, yet not in the naive sense previously assumed, but in the critical sense that the "world" science explicated was a world already ordered by the mind's own cognitive apparatus. For in Kant's view, the nature of the human mind is such that it does not passively receive sense data. Rather, it actively digests and structures them, and man therefore knows objective reality precisely to the extent that that reality conforms to the fundamental structures of the mind. The world addressed by science corresponds to principles in the mind because the only world available to the mind is already organized in accordance with the mind's own processes. All human cognition of the world is channeled through the human mind's categories. The necessity and certainty of scientific knowledge derive from the mind, and are embedded in the mind's perception and understanding of the world. They do not derive from nature independent of the mind, which in fact can never be known in itself. What man knows is a world permeated by his knowledge, and causality and the necessary laws of science are built into the framework of his cognition. Observations alone do not give man certain laws; rather, those laws reflect the laws of man's mental organization. In the act of human cognition, the mind does not conform to things; rather, things conform to the mind.

How did Kant arrive at this epoch-making conclusion? He began by noting that if all content that could be derived from experience was withdrawn from mathematical judgments, the ideas of space and time still remained. From this he inferred that any event experienced by the senses is located automatically in a framework of spatial and temporal relations. Space and time are "a priori forms of human sensibility": they condition whatever is apprehended through the senses. Mathematics could accurately describe the empirical world because mathematical principles necessarily involve a context of space and time, and space and time lay at the basis of all sensory experience: they condition and structure any empirical observation. Space and time are thus not drawn from experience but are presupposed in experience. They are never observed as such, but they constitute that context within which all events are observed. They cannot be known to exist in nature independently of the mind, but the world cannot be known by the mind without them.

Space and time therefore cannot be said to be characteristic of the world in itself, for they are contributed in the act of human observation.

They are grounded epistemologically in the nature of the mind, not ontologically in the nature of things. Because mathematical propositions are based on direct intuitions of spatial relations, they are "a priori"— constructed by the mind and not derived from experience—and yet they are also valid for experience, which will by necessity conform to the a priori form of space. It is true that pure reason inevitably becomes entangled in contradiction if it attempts to apply these ideas to the world as a whole—to ascertain what is true beyond all possible experience—as in trying to decide whether the universe is infinite or finite either in time or space. But as regards the phenomenal world that man does experience, time and space are not just applicable concepts, they are intrinsic components of all human experience of that world, frames of reference mandatory for human cognition.

Moreover, further analysis reveals that the character and structure of the mind are such that the events it perceives in space and time are subject to other a priori principles—namely, the categories of the understanding, such as the law of causation. These categories in turn lend their necessity to scientific knowledge. Whether all events are causally related in the world outside the mind cannot be ascertained, but because the world that man experiences is necessarily determined by his mind's predispositions, it can be said with certainty that events in the phenomenal world are causally related, and science can so proceed. The mind does not derive cause and effect from observations, but already experiences its observations in a context in which cause and effect are presupposed realities: causality in human cognition is not derived from experience but is brought to experience.

As with cause and effect, so too with other categories of the understanding such as substance, quantity, and relation. Without such fundamental frames of reference, such a priori interpretive principles, the human mind would be incapable of comprehending its world. Human experience would be an impossible chaos, an utterly formless and miscellaneous manifold, except that the human sensibility and understanding by their very nature transfigure that manifold into a unified perception, place it in a framework of time and space, and subject it to the ordering principles of causality, substance, and the other categories. Experience is a construction of the mind imposed on sensation.

The a priori forms and categories serve as absolute conditions of experience. They are not read out of experience, but read into it. They are a priori, yet empirically applicable—and applicable only empirically, not metaphysically. For the only world that man knows is the empirical world of phenomena, of "appearances," and that world exists only to the extent that man participates in its construction. We can know things only relative to ourselves. Knowledge is restricted to the sensible effects of things on us, and these appearances or phenomena are, as it were, predigested. Contrary to the usual assumption, the mind never experiences what is "out there" apart from the mind in some clear, undistorted mirroring of objective "reality." Rather, "reality" for man is necessarily one of his own making, and the world in itself must remain something one can only think about, never know.

The order man perceives in his world is thus an order grounded not in that world but in his mind: the mind, as it were, forces the world to obey its own organization. All sensory experience has been channeled through the filter of human a priori structures. Man can attain certain knowledge of the world, not because he has the power to penetrate to and grasp the world in itself, but because the world he perceives and understands is a world already saturated with the principles of his own mental organization. This organization is what is absolute, not that of the world in itself, which ultimately remains beyond human cognition. But because man's mental organization *is* absolute, Kant assumed, man can know with genuine certainty—know, that is, the only world he can experience, the phenomenal world.

Thus man does not receive all his knowledge from experience, but his knowledge in a sense already introduces itself into his experience in the process of cognition. Although Kant criticized Leibniz and the rationalists for believing that reason alone without sense experience can calculate the universe (for, Kant argued, knowledge requires acquaintance with particulars), he also criticized Locke and the empiricists for believing that sense impressions alone, without a priori concepts of the understanding, could ever lead to knowledge (for particulars are meaningless without general concepts by which they are interpreted). Locke was correct to deny innate ideas in the sense of mental representations of physical reality, but wrong to deny innate formal knowledge. As thought without sensation is empty, so is sensation without thought blind. Only in conjunction can understanding and sensibility supply objectively valid knowledge of things.

For Kant, Hume's division of propositions into those based on pure intellect (which are necessary but tautological) and those based on pure sensation (which are factual but not necessary) required a third and more important category, one involving the intimately combined operation of both faculties. Without such a combination, certain knowledge would be impossible. One cannot know something about the world simply by thinking; nor can one do so simply by sensing, or even by sensing and then thinking about the sensations. The two modes must be interpenetrating and simultaneous.

Hume's analysis had demonstrated that the human mind could never attain certain knowledge of the world, for the apparent order of all past experience could not guarantee the order of any future experience. Cause was not directly perceivable in the world, and the mind could not penetrate beyond the veil of phenomenal experience of discrete particulars. It was therefore clear to Kant that if we received all our knowledge of things from sensation alone, there would be no certainty. But Kant then moved beyond Hume because he recognized the extent to which the history of science had progressed only on the basis of conceptual predispositions that were not derived from experience, but were already woven into the fabric of the scientific observation. He knew that Newton's and Galileo's theories could not have been derived simply from observations, for purely accidental observations that have not been prearranged according to human design and hypothesis could never lead to a general law. Man can elicit from nature universal laws not by waiting on nature like a pupil for answers, but only, like an appointed judge, by putting shrewd questions to nature that will be deliberately and precisely revealing. Science's answers derive from the same source as its questions. On the one hand, the scientist requires experiments to ascertain that his hypotheses are valid and thus true laws of nature; only by tests can he be sure there are no exceptions and that his concepts are genuine concepts of the understanding and not only imaginary. On the other hand, the scientist also requires a priori hypotheses even to approach the world, to observe and test it fruitfully. And the situation of science in turn reflects the nature of all human experience. The mind can know with certainty only that which it has in some sense already put into its experience.

Man's knowledge, then, does not conform to objects, but objects conform to man's knowledge. Certain knowledge is possible in a phenomenal universe because the human mind bestows to that universe its own absolute order. Thus Kant proclaimed what has been called his "Copernican revolution": as Copernicus had explained the perceived movement of the heavens by the actual movement of the observer, so

Kant explained the perceived order of the world by the actual order of the observer.[1]

By confronting the seemingly irresolvable dialectic between Humean skepticism and Newtonian science, Kant demonstrated that human observations of the world were never neutral, never free of priorly imposed conceptual judgments. The Baconian ideal of an empiricism totally free of "anticipations" was an impossibility. It could not work in science, nor was it even experientially possible, for no empirical observation and no human experience was pure, neutral, without unconscious assumptions or a priori orderings. In terms of scientific knowledge, the world could not be said to exist complete in itself with intelligible forms that man could empirically reveal if only he would clear his mind of preconceptions and improve his senses by experiment. Rather, the world that man perceived and judged was formed in the very act of his perception and judgment. Mind was not passive but creative, actively structuring. Physical particulars could not simply be identified and then correlated by means of conceptual categories. Rather, the particulars required prior categorization of some kind to be identified at all. To make knowledge possible, the mind necessarily imposed its own cognitive nature on the data of experience, and thus man's knowledge was not a description of external reality as such, but was to a crucial extent the product of the subject's cognitive apparatus. The laws of natural processes were the product of the observer's internal organization in interaction with external events that could never be known in themselves. Hence neither pure empiricism (without a priori structures) nor pure rationalism (without sensory evidence) constituted a viable epistemological strategy.

The task of the philosopher was therefore radically redefined. His goal could no longer be that of determining a metaphysical world conception in the traditional sense, but should instead be that of analyzing the nature and limits of human reason. For although reason could not decide a priori on matters transcending experience, it could determine what cognitive factors are intrinsic to all human experience and inform all experience with its order. Thus philosophy's true task was to investigate the formal structure of the mind, for only there would it find the true origin and foundation for certain knowledge of the world.

>⚬<

The epistemological consequences of Kant's Copernican revolution were not without disturbing features. Kant had rejoined the knower to the known, but not the knower to any objective reality, to the object in itself. Knower and known were united, as it were, in a solipsistic prison. Man knows, as indeed Aquinas and Aristotle had said, because he judges things through the medium of a priori principles; but man cannot know whether these internal principles possess any ultimate relevance to the real world, or to any absolute truth or being outside the human mind. There was now no divine warrant for the mind's cognitive categories, such as Aquinas's *lumen intellectus agentis*, the light of the active intellect. Man could not determine whether his knowledge had some fundamental relation to a universal reality or whether it was merely a human reality. Only the subjective necessity of such knowledge was certain. For the modern mind, the inevitable outcome of a critical rationalism and a critical empiricism was a Kantian subjectivism limited to the phenomenal world: Man had no necessary insight into the transcendent, nor into the world as such. Man could know things only as they appeared to him, not as they were in themselves. In retrospect, the long-term consequences of both the Copernican and the Kantian revolutions were fundamentally ambiguous, at once liberating and diminishing. Both revolutions awakened man to a new, more adventurous reality, yet both also radically displaced man—one from the center of the cosmos, the other from genuine cognition of that cosmos. Cosmological alienation was thereby compounded by epistemological alienation.

It could be said that in one sense Kant reversed the Copernican revolution, since he placed man again at the center of his universe by virtue of the human mind's central role in establishing the world order. But man's claim to be the center of his cognitive universe was only the obverse of his recognition that he could no longer assume any direct contact between the human mind and the universe's intrinsic order. Kant "humanized" science, but in so doing, he removed science from any certain foundation independent of the human mind such as Cartesian and Baconian science—the original programs of modern science—had earlier enjoyed, or presumed. Despite the attempt to ground knowledge in a new absolute—the human mind—and despite, from one point of view, the ennobling status of the mind's being the new epistemological center, it was also evident that human knowledge was subjectively constructed and therefore—relative to the intellectual certainties of other eras, and relative to the world in itself—fundamentally dislocated.

Man was again at the center of his universe, but this was now only *his* universe, not *the* universe.

Yet Kant saw this as a necessary recognition of the limits of human reason, a recognition that would paradoxically open up a larger truth to man. For Kant's revolution had two sides to it, one focused on science, the other on religion: he wished to rescue both certain knowledge and moral freedom, both his belief in Newton and his belief in God. On the one hand, by demonstrating the necessity of the mind's a priori forms and categories, Kant sought to confirm the validity of science. On the other hand, by demonstrating that man can know only phenomena, not things in themselves, he sought to make room for the truths of religious belief and moral doctrine.

In Kant's view, the attempt by philosophers and theologians to rationalize religion, to give the tenets of faith a foundation by pure reason, had succeeded only in producing a scandal of conflict, casuistry, and skepticism. Kant's restriction of reason's authority to the phenomenal world thereby freed religion of reason's clumsy intrusion. Moreover, by such a restriction, science would no longer conflict with religion. Since the causal determinism of science's mechanistic world picture would deny the soul's freedom of will, yet such freedom must be presupposed in any genuine moral activity, Kant argued that his limitation of science's competence to the phenomenal, his recognition of man's ignorance concerning things in themselves, opened up the possibility of faith. Science could claim certain knowledge of appearances, but it could no longer arrogantly claim knowledge over all of reality, and precisely this allowed Kant to reconcile scientific determinism with religious belief and morality. For science could not legitimately rule out the possibility that the truths of religion were valid as well.

Kant thus held that although one could not know that God exists, one must nevertheless *believe* he exists in order to act morally. Belief in God is therefore justified, morally and practically, even if it is not certifiable. It is a matter of faith rather than knowledge. Ideas of God, the soul's immortality, and the freedom of the will could not be known to be true in the same way that the laws of nature established by Newton were so known. Yet one could not justify doing one's duty if there were no God, or if free will did not exist, or if one's soul perished at death. These ideas must therefore be believed as true. They are necessary to postulate for a moral existence. With the advances of scientific and philosophical knowledge, the modern mind could no longer base religion on a cosmological or metaphysical foundation, but instead it could base religion in the structure of the human situation itself—and it was through this decisive insight that Kant, following the spirit of Rousseau and of Luther before him, defined the direction of modern religious thought. Man was freed from the external and objective to form his religious response to life. Inner personal experience, not objective demonstration or dogmatic belief, was the true ground of religious meaning.

In Kant's terms, man could view himself under two different, even contradictory aspects—scientifically, as a "phenomenon," subject to the laws of nature; and morally, as a thing-in-itself, a "noumenon," which could be thought of (not known) as free, immortal, and subject to God. Here the Humean and Newtonian influences in Kant's philosophical development were countered by the universal humanitarian moral ideals of Rousseau, who had stressed the priority of feeling over reason in religious experience, and whose works had made a considerable impression on Kant, reinforcing the deeper roots of Kant's sense of moral duty coming from his strict Pietist childhood. The inner experience of duty, the impulse to selfless moral virtue, permitted Kant to transcend the otherwise daunting limitations of the modern mind's world picture, which had reduced the knowable world to one of appearance and mechanistic necessity. Kant was thereby able to rescue religion from scientific determinism, just as he had rescued science from radical skepticism.

But he rescued these only at the price of their disjunction, and of the restriction of human knowledge to phenomena and subjective certainties. It is clear that at heart, Kant believed that the laws moving the planets and stars ultimately stood in some fundamental harmonious relation to the moral imperatives he experienced within himself: "Two things fill the heart with ever new and always increasing awe and admiration: the starry heavens above me and the moral law within me." But Kant also knew he could not prove that relation, and in his delimitation of human knowledge to appearances, the Cartesian schism between the human mind and the material cosmos continued in a new and deepened form.

In the subsequent course of Western thought, it was to be Kant's fate that, as regards both religion and science, the power of his epistemological critique tended to outweigh his positive affirmations. On the one hand, the room he made for religious belief began to resemble a vacuum, since religious faith had now lost any external support from either the empirical world or pure reason, and increasingly seemed to lack internal plausibility and appropriateness for secular modern man's psychological character. On the other hand, the certainty of scientific knowledge, already unsupported by any external mind-independent necessity after Hume and Kant, became unsupported as well by any internal cognitive necessity with the dramatic controversion by twentieth-century physics of the Newtonian and Euclidean categories which Kant had assumed were absolute.

Kant's penetrating critique had effectively pulled the rug out from under the human mind's pretensions to certain knowledge of things in themselves, eliminating in principle any human cognition of the ground of the world. Subsequent developments in the Western mind—the deepening relativisms introduced not only by Einstein, Bohr, and Heisenberg, but also by Darwin, Marx, and Freud; by Nietzsche, Dilthey, Weber, Heidegger, and Wittgenstein; by Saussure, Lévi-Strauss, and Foucault; by Gödel, Popper, Quine, Kuhn, and a host of others— radically magnified that effect, altogether eliminating the grounds for subjective certainty still felt by Kant. All human experience was indeed structured by largely unconscious principles, but those principles were not absolute and timeless. Rather, they varied fundamentally in different eras, different cultures, different classes, different languages, different persons, different existential contexts. In the wake of Kant's Copernican revolution, science, religion, and philosophy all had to find their own bases for affirmation, for none could claim a priori access to the universe's intrinsic nature.

The Decline of Metaphysics

The course of modern philosophy unfolded under the impact of Kant's epochal distinctions. At first, Kant's successors in Germany pursued his thinking in an unexpectedly idealist direction. In the Romantic climate of European culture in the late eighteenth and early nineteenth centuries, Fichte, Schelling, and Hegel suggested that the cognitive categories of the human mind were in some sense the ontological categories of the universe—i.e., that human knowledge did not point to a divine reality but was itself that reality—and on that basis constructed a metaphysical system with a universal Mind revealing itself through man. For these idealists, the "transcendental ego" (Kant's notion of the human self that imposed categories and heuristic unifying principles on experience to render knowledge) could be radically extended and recognized as an aspect of an absolute Spirit constituting all reality. Kant had held that mind supplied the form taken by experience, but that the content of experience is given empirically by an external world. For his idealist successors, however, it seemed more philosophically plausible that both content and form were determined by the all-encompassing Mind, so that nature was in some sense more an image or symbol of the self than an altogether independent existent.

But among most scientifically inclined modern thinkers, the speculations of idealist metaphysics could not command widespread philosophical acceptance, especially after the nineteenth century, for they were not empirically testable, nor for many did they appear to represent adequately the tenor of scientific knowledge or the modern experience of an objective and ontologically distinct material universe. Materialism, the opposite metaphysical option from idealism, seemed to better reflect the quality of contemporary scientific evidence. Yet it too assumed an ultimate untestable substance—matter, rather than spirit—and seemingly failed to account for the subjective phenomenology of human consciousness and man's sense of being a personal volitional entity different in character from the unconscious impersonal external world. But because materialism, or at least naturalism—the position holding that all phenomena could ultimately be explained by natural causes—appeared most congruent with the scientific account of the world, it constituted a more compelling conceptual framework than did idealism. Still, there was much in such a conception that was not entirely acceptable to the modern sensibility, whether because of doubts concerning the completeness and certainty of scientific knowledge, because of ambiguities within the scientific evidence itself, or because of various conflicting religious or psychological factors.

The other available metaphysical option was therefore some form of dualism reflecting the Cartesian and Kantian positions, one that more adequately represented the common modern experience of disjunction between the objective physical universe and subjective human awareness. But with the increasing reluctance of the modern mind to postulate any transcendent dimension, the nature of the Cartesian-Kantian position was such as to prevent, or at best make highly problematic, any coherent metaphysical conception. Given both the discontinuity of the modern experience (the dualism between man and world, mind and matter), and the epistemological quandary entailed by that discontinuity (how can man presume to know that which is fundamentally separate and different from his own awareness?), metaphysics necessarily lost its traditional preeminence in the philosophical enterprise. One could investigate the world as a scientist, or human experience as an introspective analyst; or one could avoid the dichotomy by admitting the human world's irresolvable ambiguity and contingency, arguing instead for its existential or pragmatic transformation through an act of will. But a universal order rationally intelligible to the contemplative observer was now generally precluded.

Thus modern philosophy, progressing according to principles established with Descartes and Locke, eventually undercut its own traditional raison d'être. While from one perspective the problematic entity for the modern human being was the external physical world in its dehumanized objectification, from another perspective the human mind itself and its inscrutable cognitive mechanisms had become that which could not command full trust and endorsement. For man could no longer assume his mind's interpretation of the world to be a mirrorlike reflection of things as they actually were. The mind itself might be the alienating principle. Moreover, the insights of Freud and the depth psychologists radically increased the sense that man's thinking about the world was governed by nonrational factors that he could neither control nor be fully conscious of. From Hume and Kant through Darwin, Marx, Freud and beyond, an unsettling conclusion was becoming inescapable: Human thought was determined, structured, and very probably distorted by a multitude of overlapping factors—innate but nonabsolute mental categories, habit, history, culture, social class, biology, language, imagination, emotion, the personal unconscious, the collective unconscious. In the end, the human mind could not be relied upon as an accurate judge of reality. The original Cartesian certainty, that which served as foundation for the modern confidence in human reason, was no longer defensible.

Henceforth, philosophy concerned itself largely with the clarification of epistemological problems, with the analysis of language, with the philosophy of science, or with phenomenological and existentialist analyses of human experience. Despite the incongruence of aims and predispositions among the various schools of twentieth-century philosophy, there was general agreement on one crucial point: the impossibility of apprehending an objective cosmic order with the human intelligence. That point of agreement was approached from the various positions as developed by philosophers as diverse as Bertrand Russell, Martin Heidegger, and Ludwig Wittgenstein: Because empirical science alone could render verifiable, or at least provisionally corroborated, knowledge, and such knowledge concerned the contingent natural world of sense experience only, unverifiable and untestable metaphysical propositions concerning the world as a whole were without genuine meaning (logical positivism). Because human experience—finite, conditioned, problematic, individual—was all man could know, human subjectivity and the very nature of human being necessarily permeated, negated, or made inauthentic any attempts at an impartially objective world conception (existentialism and phenomenology). Because the meaning of any term could be found only in its specific use and context, and because human experience was fundamentally structured by language, and yet no direct relation between language and an independent deeper structure in the world could be presumed, philosophy should concern itself only with a therapeutic clarification of language in its many concrete uses without any commitment to a particular abstract conception of reality (linguistic analysis).

On the basis of these several converging insights, the belief that the human mind could attain or should attempt an objective metaphysical overview as traditionally understood was virtually relinquished. With few exceptions, the philosophical enterprise was redirected into the analysis of linguistic problems, scientific and logical propositions, or the raw data of human experience, all without metaphysical entailments in the classical sense. If "metaphysics" still had any viable function, aside from being a handmaid to scientific cosmology, it could only involve the analysis of those various factors that structured human cognition—i.e., to continue Kant's work with an approach at once more relativistic and more sensitive to the multiplicity of factors that can influence and permeate human experience: historical, social, cultural, linguistic, existential, psychological. But cosmic syntheses could no longer be taken seriously.

As philosophy became more technical, more concerned with methodology, and more academic, and as philosophers increasingly wrote not for the public but for each other, the discipline of philosophy lost much of its former relevance and importance for the intelligent layperson, and thus much of its former cultural power. Semantics was now more germane to philosophical clarity than were universal speculations, but for most nonprofessionals, semantics held limited interest. In any case, philosophy's traditional mandate and status had been obviated by its own development: There was no all-encompassing or transcendent or intrinsic "deeper" order in the universe to which the human mind could legitimately lay claim.

The Crisis of Modern Science

With both philosophy and religion in such problematic condition, it was science alone that seemed to rescue the modern mind from pervasive uncertainty. Science achieved a golden age in the nineteenth and early twentieth centuries, with extraordinary advances in all its major branches, with widespread institutional and academic organization of research, and with practical applications rapidly proliferating on the basis of a systematic linkage of science with technology. The optimism of the age was directly tied to confidence in science and in its powers to improve indefinitely the state of human knowledge, health, and general welfare.

Religion and metaphysics continued their long, slow decline, but science's ongoing—indeed, accelerating—progress could not be doubted. Its claims to valid knowledge of the world, even subject to the critique of post-Kantian philosophy, continued to seem not only plausible but scarcely questionable. In the face of science's supreme cognitive effectiveness and the rigorously impersonal precision of its explanatory structures, religion and philosophy were compelled to define their positions in relation to science, just as, in the medieval era, science and philosophy were compelled to do so in relation to the culturally more powerful conceptions of religion. For the modern mind, it was science that presented the most realistic and reliable world picture—even if that picture was limited to "technical" knowledge of natural phenomena, and despite its existentially disjunctive implications. But two developments in the course of the twentieth century radically changed science's cognitive and cultural status, one theoretical and internal to science, the other pragmatic and external.

In the first instance, the classical Cartesian-Newtonian cosmology gradually and then dramatically broke down under the cumulative impact of several astonishing developments in physics. Beginning in the later nineteenth century with Maxwell's work with electromagnetic fields, the Michelson-Morley experiment, and Becquerel's discovery of radioactivity, then in the early twentieth century with Planck's isolation of quantum phenomena and Einstein's special and general theories of relativity, and culminating in the 1920s with the formulation of quantum mechanics by Bohr, Heisenberg, and their colleagues, the long-established certainties of classical modern science were radically undermined. By the end of the third decade of the twentieth century, virtually every major postulate of the earlier scientific conception had been controverted: the atoms as solid, indestructible, and separate building blocks of nature, space and time as independent absolutes, the strict mechanistic causality of all phenomena, the possibility of objective observation of nature. Such a fundamental transformation in the scientific world picture was staggering, and for no one was this more true than the physicists themselves. Confronted with the contradictions observed in subatomic phenomena, Einstein wrote: "All my attempts to adapt the theoretical foundation of physics to this knowledge failed completely. It was as if the ground had been pulled out from under one, with no firm foundation to be seen anywhere upon which one could have built." Heisenberg similarly realized that "the foundations of physics have started moving . . .[and] this motion has caused the feeling that the ground would be cut from science."

The challenge to previous scientific assumptions was deep and multiple: The solid Newtonian atoms were now discovered to be largely empty. Hard matter no longer constituted the fundamental substance of nature. Matter and energy were interchangeable. Three-dimensional space and unidimensional time had become relative aspects of a four-dimensional space-time continuum. Time flowed at different rates for observers moving at different speeds. Time slowed down near heavy objects, and under certain circumstances could stop altogether. The laws of Euclidean geometry no longer provided the universally necessary structure of nature. The planets moved in their orbits not because they were pulled toward the Sun by an attractive force acting at a distance, but because the very space in which they moved was curved. Subatomic phenomena displayed a fundamentally ambiguous nature, observable both as particles and as waves. The position and momentum of a particle could not be precisely measured simultaneously. The uncertainty principle radically undermined and replaced strict Newtonian determinism. Scientific observation and explanation could not proceed without affecting the nature of the object observed. The notion of substance dissolved into probabilities and "tendencies to exist." Nonlocal connections between particles contradicted mechanistic causality. Formal relations and dynamic processes replaced hard discrete objects. The physical world of twentieth-century physics resembled, in Sir James Jeans's words, not so much a great machine as a great thought.

The consequences of this extraordinary revolution were again ambiguous. The continuing modern sense of intellectual progress, leaving behind the ignorance and misconceptions of past eras while reaping the fruits of new concrete technological results, was again bolstered. Even Newton had been corrected and improved upon by the ever-evolving, increasingly sophisticated modern mind. Moreover, to the many who had regarded the scientific universe of mechanistic and materialistic determinism as antithetical to human values, the quantum-relativistic revolution represented an unexpected and welcome broaching of new intellectual possibilities. Matter's former hard substantiality had given way to a reality perhaps more conducive to a spiritual interpretation. Freedom of the human will seemed to be given a new foothold if subatomic particles were indeterminate. The principle of complementarity governing waves and particles suggested its broader application in a complementarity between mutually exclusive ways of knowledge, like religion and science. Human consciousness, or at least human observation and interpretation, seemed to be given a more central role in the larger scheme of things with the new understanding of the subject's influence on the observed object. The deep interconnectedness of phenomena encouraged a new holistic thinking about the world, with many social, moral, and religious implications. Increasing numbers of scientists began to question modern science's pervasive, if often unconscious, assumption that the intellectual effort to reduce all reality to the smallest measurable components of the physical world would eventually reveal that which was most fundamental in the universe. The reductionist program, dominant since Descartes, now appeared to many to be myopically selective, and likely to miss that which was most significant in the nature of things.

Yet such inferences were neither universal nor even widespread among practicing physicists. Modern physics was perhaps open to a spiritual interpretation, but did not necessarily compel it. Nor was the larger population intimately conversant with the arcane conceptual changes wrought by the new physics. Moreover, for several decades the revolution in physics did not result in comparable theoretical transformations in the other natural and social sciences, although their theoretical programs had been based largely on the mechanistic principles of classical physics. Nevertheless, many felt that the old materialistic world view had been irrevocably challenged, and that the new scientific models of reality offered possible opportunities for a fundamental rapprochement with man's humanistic aspirations.

Yet these ambiguous possibilities were countered by other, more disturbing factors. To begin with, there was now no coherent conception of the world, comparable to Newton's *Principia,* that could theoretically integrate the complex variety of new data. Physicists failed to come to any consensus as to how the existing evidence should be interpreted with respect to defining the ultimate nature of reality. Conceptual contradictions, disjunctions, and paradoxes were ubiquitous, and stubbornly evaded resolution.[2] A certain irreducible irrationality, already recognized in the human psyche, now emerged in the structure of the physical world itself. To incoherence was added unintelligibility, for the conceptions derived from the new physics not only were difficult for the layperson to comprehend, they presented seemingly insuperable obstacles to the human intuition generally: a curved space, finite yet unbounded; a four-dimensional space-time continuum; mutually exclusive properties possessed by the same subatomic entity; objects that were not really things at all but processes or patterns of relationship; phenomena that took no decisive shape until observed; particles that seemed to affect each other at a distance with no known causal link; the existence of fundamental fluctuations of energy in a total vacuum.

Moreover, for all the apparent opening of the scientific understanding to a less materialistic and less mechanistic conception, there was no real change in the essential modern dilemma: The universe was still an impersonal vastness in which man with his peculiar capacity for consciousness was still an ephemeral, inexplicable, randomly produced minutia. Nor was there any compelling answer to the looming question as to what ontological context preceded or underlay the "big-bang" birth of the universe. Nor did leading physicists believe that the equations of quantum theory described the actual world. Scientific knowledge was confined to abstractions, mathematical symbols, "shadows." Such knowledge was not of the world itself, which now more than ever seemed beyond the compass of human cognition.

Thus in certain respects the intellectual contradictions and obscurities of the new physics only heightened the sense of human relativity and alienation growing since the Copernican revolution. Modern man was being forced to question his inherited classical Greek faith that the world was ordered in a manner clearly accessible to the human intelligence. In the physicist P. W. Bridgman's words, "the structure of nature may eventually be such that our processes of thought do not correspond to it sufficiently to permit us to think about it at all. . . . The world fades out and eludes us. . . . We are confronted with something truly ineffable. We have reached the limit of the vision of the great pioneers of science, the vision, namely, that we live in a sympathetic world in that it is comprehensible by our minds."[3] Philosophy's conclusion was becoming science's as well: Reality may not be structured in any way the human mind can objectively discern. Thus incoherence, unintelligibility, and an insecure relativism compounded the earlier modern predicament of human alienation in an impersonal cosmos.

When relativity theory and quantum mechanics undid the absolute certainty of the Newtonian paradigm, science demonstrated, in a way that Kant as a convinced Newtonian could never have anticipated, the validity of Kant's skepticism concerning the human mind's capacity for certain knowledge of the world in itself. Because he was certain of the truth of Newtonian science, Kant had argued that the categories of human cognition congruent with that science were themselves absolute, and these alone provided a basis for the Newtonian achievement, as well as for man's epistemological competence in general. But with twentieth-century physics, the bottom fell out of Kant's last certainty. The fundamental Kantian a prioris—space, time, substance, causality—were no longer applicable to all phenomena. The scientific knowledge that had seemed after Newton to be universal and absolute had to be recognized after Einstein, Bohr, and Heisenberg as limited and provisional. So too did quantum mechanics reveal in unexpected fashion the radical validity of Kant's thesis that the nature described by physics was not nature in itself but man's relation to nature—i.e., nature as exposed to man's form of questioning.

What had been implicit in Kant's critique, but obscured by the apparent certainty of Newtonian physics, now became explicit: Because induction can never render certain general laws, and because scientific knowledge is a product of human interpretive structures that are themselves relative, variable, and creatively employed, and finally because the act of observation in some sense produces the objective reality science attempts to explicate, the truths of science are neither absolute nor unequivocally objective. In the combined wake of eighteenth-century philosophy and twentieth-century science, the modern mind was left free of absolutes, but also disconcertingly free of any solid ground.

This problematic conclusion was reinforced by a newly critical approach to the philosophy and history of science, influenced above all by the work of Karl Popper and Thomas Kuhn. Drawing on the insights of Hume and Kant, Popper noted that science can never produce knowledge that is certain, nor even probable. Man observes the universe as a stranger, making imaginative guesses about its structure and workings. He cannot approach the world without such bold conjectures in the background, for every observed fact presupposes an interpretive focus. In science, these conjectures must be continually and systematically tested; yet however many tests are successfully passed, any theory can never be viewed as more than an imperfectly corroborated conjecture. At any time, a new test could falsify it. No scientific truth is immune to such a possibility. Even the basic facts are relative, always potentially subject to a radical reinterpretation in a new framework. Man can never claim to know the real essences of things. Before the virtual infinitude of the world's phenomena, human ignorance itself is infinite. The wisest strategy is to learn from one's inevitable mistakes.

But while Popper maintained the rationality of science by upholding its fundamental commitment to rigorous testing of theories, its fearless neutrality in the quest for truth, Kuhn's analysis of the history of science tended to undercut even that security. Kuhn agreed that all scientific knowledge required interpretive structures based on fundamental paradigms or conceptual models that allowed researchers to isolate data, elaborate theories, and solve problems. But citing many examples in the history of science, he pointed out that the actual practice of scientists seldom conformed to Popper's ideal of systematic self-criticism by means of attempted falsification of existing theories. Instead, science typically proceeded by seeking confirmations of the prevailing paradigm— gathering facts in the light of that theory, performing experiments on its basis, extending its range of applicability, further articulating its structure, attempting to clarify residual problems. Far from subjecting the paradigm itself to constant testing, normal science avoided contradicting it by routinely reinterpreting conflicting data in ways that would support the paradigm, or by neglecting such awkward data altogether. To an extent never consciously recognized by scientists, the nature of scientific practice makes its governing paradigm self-validating. The paradigm acts as a lens through which every observation is filtered, and is maintained as an authoritative bulwark by common convention. Through teachers and texts, scientific pedagogy sustains the inherited paradigm and ratifies its credibility, tending to produce a firmness of conviction and theoretical rigidity not unlike an education in systematic theology.

Kuhn further argued that when the gradual accumulation of conflicting data finally produces a paradigm crisis and a new imaginative synthesis eventually wins scientific favor, the process by which that revolution takes place is far from rational. It depends as much on the established customs of the scientific community, on aesthetic, psychological, and sociological factors, on the presence of contemporary root metaphors and popular analogies, on unpredictable imaginative leaps and "gestalt switches," even on the aging and dying of conservative scientists, as on disinterested tests and arguments. For in fact the rival paradigms are seldom genuinely comparable; they are selectively based on differing modes of interpretation and hence different sets of data. Each paradigm creates its own gestalt, so comprehensive that scientists working within different paradigms seem to be living in different worlds. Nor is there any common measure, such as problem-solving ability or theoretical coherence or resistance to falsification, that all scientists agree upon as a standard for comparison. What is an important problem for one group of scientists is not for another. Thus the history of science is not one of linear rational progress moving toward ever more accurate and complete knowledge of an objective truth, but is one of radical shifts of vision in which a multitude of nonrational and nonempirical factors play crucial roles. Whereas Popper had attempted to temper Hume's skepticism by demonstrating the rationality of choosing the most rigorously tested conjecture, Kuhn's analysis served to restore that skepticism.[4]

With these philosophical and historical critiques and with the revolution in physics, a more tentative view of science became widespread in intellectual circles. Science was still patently effective and powerful in its knowledge, but scientific knowledge was now regarded as, in several senses, a relative matter. The knowledge science rendered was relative to the observer, to his physical context, to his science's prevailing paradigm and his own theoretical assumptions. It was relative to his culture's prevailing belief system, to his social context and psychological predispositions, to his very act of observation. And science's first principles might be overturned at any point in the face of new evidence. Moreover, by the later twentieth century, the conventional paradigm structures of other sciences, including the Darwinian theory of evolution, were coming under increasing pressure from conflicting data and alternative theories. Above all, the bedrock certainty of the Cartesian-Newtonian world view, for centuries the acknowledged epitome and model of human knowledge and still pervasively influential in the cultural psyche, had been shattered. And the post-Newtonian world order was neither intuitively accessible nor internally coherent—indeed, scarcely an order at all.

>-x-<

Yet for all this, science's cognitive status would still have retained its unquestioned preeminence for the modern mind. Scientific truth might be increasingly esoteric and only provisional, but it was a testable truth, continually being improved and more accurately formulated, and its practical effects in the form of technological progress—in industry, agriculture, medicine, energy production, communication and transportation—provided tangible public evidence for science's claims to render viable knowledge of the world. But it was, paradoxically, this same tangible evidence that was to prove crucial in an antithetical development; for it was when the practical consequences of scientific knowledge could no longer be judged exclusively positive that the modern mind was forced to reevaluate its previously wholehearted trust in science.

As early as the nineteenth century, Emerson had warned that man's technical achievements might not be unequivocally in his own best interests: "Things are in the saddle and ride mankind." By the turn of the century, just as technology was producing new wonders like the automobile and the widespread application of electricity, a few observers began to sense that such developments might signal an ominous reversal of human values. By the mid-twentieth century, modern science's brave new world had started to become subject to wide and vigorous criticism: Technology was taking over and dehumanizing man, placing him in a context of artificial substances and gadgets rather than live nature, in an unaesthetically standardized environment where means had subsumed ends, where industrial labor requirements entailed the mechanization of human beings, where all problems were perceived as soluble by technical research at the expense of genuine existential responses. The self-propelling and self-augmenting imperatives of technical functioning were dislodging man and uprooting him from his fundamental relation to the Earth. Human individuality seemed increasingly tenuous, disappearing under the impact of mass production, the mass media, and the spread of a bleak and problem-ridden urbanization. Traditional structures and values were crumbling. With an unending stream of technological innovations, modern life was subject to an unprecedentedly disorienting rapidity of change. Gigantism and turmoil, excessive noise, speed, and complexity dominated the human environment. The world in which man lived was becoming as impersonal as the cosmos of his science. With the pervasive anonymity, hollowness, and materialism of modern life, man's capacity to retain his humanity in an environment determined by technology seemed increasingly in doubt. For many, the question of human freedom, of mankind's ability to maintain mastery over its own creation, had become acute.

But compounding these humanistic critiques were more disturbingly concrete signs of science's untoward consequences. The critical contamination of the planet's water, air, and soil, the manifold harmful effects on animal and plant life, the extinction of innumerable species, the deforestation of the globe, the erosion of topsoil, the depletion of groundwater, the vast accumulation of toxic wastes, the apparent exacerbation of the greenhouse effect, the breakdown of the ozone layer in the atmosphere, the radical disruption of the entire planetary ecosystem—all these emerged as direly serious problems with increasing force and complexity. From even a short-term human perspective, the accelerating depletion of irreplaceable natural resources had become an alarming phenomenon. Dependence on foreign supplies of vital resources brought a new precariousness into global political and economic life. New banes and stresses to the social fabric continued to appear, directly or indirectly tied to the advance of a scientific civilization—urban overdevelopment and overcrowding, cultural and social rootlessness, numbingly mechanical labor, increasingly disastrous industrial accidents, automobile and air travel fatalities, cancer and heart disease, alcoholism and drug addiction, mind-dulling and culture-impoverishing television, growing levels of crime, violence, and psychopathology. Even science's most cherished successes paradoxically entailed new and pressing problems, as when the medical relief of human illness and lowering of mortality rates, combined with technological strides in food production and transportation, in turn exacerbated the threat of global overpopulation. In other cases, the advance of science presented new Faustian dilemmas, as in those surrounding the unforeseeable future uses of genetic engineering. More generally, the scientifically unfathomed complexity of all relevant variables—whether in global or local environments, in social systems, or in the human body—made the consequences of technological manipulation of those variables unpredictable and often pernicious.

All these developments had reached an early and ominous proleptic climax when natural science and political history conspired to produce the atomic bomb. It seemed supremely, if tragically, ironic that the Einsteinian discovery of the equivalence of mass and energy, by which a particle of matter could be converted into an immense quantity of energy—a discovery by a dedicated pacifist reflecting a certain apex of human intellectual brilliance and creativity—precipitated for the first time in history the prospect of humanity's self-extinction. With the dropping of atomic bombs on the civilians of Hiroshima and Nagasaki, faith in science's intrinsic moral neutrality, not to say its unlimited powers of benign progress, could no longer be upheld. During the protracted and tense global schism of the Cold War that followed, the numbers of unprecedentedly destructive nuclear missiles relentlessly multiplied until the entire planet could be devastated many times over. Civilization itself was now brought into peril by virtue of its own genius. The same science that had dramatically lessened the hazards and burdens of human survival now presented to human survival its gravest menace.

The great succession of science's triumphs and cumulative progress was now shadowed by a new sense of science's limits, its dangers, and its culpability. The modern scientific mind found itself beleaguered on several fronts at once: by the epistemological critiques, by its own theoretical problems arising in a growing number of fields, by the increasingly urgent psychological necessity of integrating the modern outlook's human-world divide, and above all by its adverse consequences and intimate involvement in the planetary crisis. The close association of scientific research with the political, military, and corporate establishments continued to belie science's traditional self-image of detached purity. The very concept of "pure science" was now criticized by many as entirely illusory. The belief that the scientific mind had unique access to the truth of the world, that it could register nature like a perfect mirror reflecting an extrahistorical, universal objective reality, was seen not only as epistemologically naive, but also as serving, either consciously or unconsciously, specific political and economic agenda, often allowing vast resources and intelligence to be commandeered for programs of social and ecological domination. The aggressive exploitation of the natural environment, the proliferation of nuclear weaponry, the threat of global catastrophe—all pointed to an indictment of science, of human reason itself, now seemingly in thrall to man's own self-destructive irrationality.

If all scientific hypotheses were to be rigorously and disinterestedly tested, then it seemed that the "scientific world view" itself, the governing metahypothesis of the modern era, was being decisively falsified by its deleterious and counterproductive consequences in the empirical world. The scientific enterprise, which in its earlier stages had presented a cultural predicament—philosophical, religious, social, psychological— had now provoked a biological emergency. The optimistic belief that the world's dilemmas could be solved simply by scientific advance and social engineering had been confounded. The West was again losing its faith, this time not in religion but in science and in the autonomous human reason.

Science was still valued, in many respects still revered. But it had lost its untainted image as humanity's liberator. It had also lost its long-secure claims to virtually absolute cognitive reliability. With its productions no longer exclusively benign, with its reductionist understanding of the natural environment apparently deficient, with its evident susceptibility to political and economic bias, the previously unqualified trustworthiness of scientific knowledge could no longer be affirmed. On the basis of these several interacting factors, something like Hume's radical epistemological skepticism—mixed with a relativized Kantian sense of a priori cognitive structures—seemed publicly vindicated. After modern philosophy's acute epistemological critique, the principal remaining foundation for reason's validity had been its empirical support by science. The philosophical critique alone had been in effect an abstract exercise, without definite influence on the larger culture or on science, and would have so continued if the scientific enterprise had itself continued being so unequivocally positive in its practical and cognitive progress. But with science's concrete consequences so problematic, reason's last foundation was now unfirm.

Many thoughtful observers, not just professional philosophers, were forced to reevaluate the status of human knowledge. Man might think he knows things, scientifically or otherwise, but there was clearly no guarantee for this: he had no a priori rational access to universal truths; empirical data were always theory-soaked and relative to the observer; and the previously reliable scientific world view was open to fundamental question, for that conceptual framework was evidently both creating and exacerbating problems for humanity on a global scale. Scientific knowledge was stupendously effective, but those effects suggested that much knowledge from a limited perspective could be a very dangerous thing.

Romanticism and Its Fate

The Two Cultures

From the complex matrix of the Renaissance had issued forth two distinct streams of culture, two temperaments or general approaches to human existence characteristic of the Western mind. One emerged in the Scientific Revolution and Enlightenment and stressed rationality, empirical science, and a skeptical secularism. The other was its polar complement, sharing common roots in the Renaissance and classical Greco-Roman culture (and in the Reformation as well), but tending to express just those aspects of human experience suppressed by the Enlightenment's overriding spirit of rationalism. First conspicuously present in Rousseau, then in Goethe, Schiller, Herder, and German Romanticism, this side of the Western sensibility fully emerged in the late eighteenth and early nineteenth centuries, and has not since ceased to be a potent force in Western culture and consciousness—from Blake, Wordsworth, Coleridge, Hölderlin, Schelling, Schleiermacher, the Schlegel brothers, Madame de Staël, Shelley, Keats, Byron, Hugo, Pushkin, Carlyle, Emerson, Thoreau, Whitman, and onward in its diverse forms to their many descendants, countercultural and otherwise, of the present era.

To be sure, the Romantic temperament shared much with its Enlightenment opposite, and their complex interplay could be said to constitute the modern sensibility. Both tended to be "humanist" in their high estimate of man's powers and their concern with man's perspective on the universe. Both looked to this world and nature as the setting of the human drama and the focus for human endeavor. Both were attentive to the phenomena of human consciousness and the nature of its hidden structures. Both found in classical culture a rich source of insight and values. Both were profoundly Promethean—in their rebellion against oppressive traditional structures, in their celebration of individual human genius, in their restless quest for human freedom, fulfillment, and bold exploration of the new.

But in each of these commonalities there were deep differences. In contrast with the spirit of the Enlightenment, the Romantic vision perceived the world as a unitary organism rather than an atomistic machine, exalted the ineffability of inspiration rather than the enlightenment of reason, and affirmed the inexhaustible drama of human life rather than the calm predictability of static abstractions. Whereas the Enlightenment temperament's high valuation of man rested on his unequaled rational intellect and its power to comprehend and exploit the laws of nature, the Romantic valued man rather for his imaginative and spiritual aspirations, his emotional depths, his artistic creativity and powers of individual self-expression and self-creation. The genius celebrated by the Enlightenment temperament was a Newton, a Franklin, or an Einstein, while for the Romantic it was a Goethe, a Beethoven, or a Nietzsche. On both sides, the autonomous world-changing will and mind of modern man were apotheosized, bringing the cult of the hero, the history of great men and their deeds. Indeed, on many fronts at once, the Western ego gained substance and impetus, whether in the titanic self-assertions of the French Revolution and Napoleon, the new self-awareness of Rousseau and Byron, the advancing scientific clarities of Lavoisier and Laplace, the incipient feminist confidence of Mary Wollstonecraft and George Sand, or the many-sided richness of human experience and creativity realized by Goethe. But for the two temperaments, Enlightenment and Romantic, the character and aims of that autonomous self were sharply distinct. Bacon's utopia was not Blake's.

Whereas for the Enlightenment-scientific mind, nature was an object for observation and experiment, theoretical explanation and technological manipulation, for the Romantic, by contrast, nature was a live vessel of spirit, a translucent source of mystery and revelation. The scientist too wished to penetrate nature and reveal its mystery; but the method and goal of that penetration, and the character of that revelation, were different from the Romantic's. Rather than the distanced object of sober analysis, nature for the Romantic was that which the human soul strove to enter and unite with in an overcoming of the existential dichotomy, and the revelation he sought was not of mechanical law but of spiritual essence. While the scientist sought truth that was testable and concretely effective, the Romantic sought truth that was inwardly transfiguring and sublime. Thus Wordsworth saw nature as ensouled with spiritual meaning and beauty, while Schiller considered the impersonal mechanisms of science a poor substitute for the Greek deities who had animated nature for the ancients. Both modern temperaments, scientific and Romantic, looked to present human experience and the natural world for fulfillment, but what the Romantic sought and found in those domains reflected a radically different universe from that of the scientist.

Equally notable was the difference in their attitudes toward the phenomena of human awareness. The Enlightenment-scientific examination of the mind was empirical and epistemological, gradually becoming focused on sense perception, cognitive development, and quantitative behavioral studies. By contrast, beginning with Rousseau's *Confessions*—the modern Romantic sequel and response to the ancient Catholic *Confessions* of Augustine—the Romantics' interest in human consciousness was fueled by a newly intense sense of self-awareness and a focus on the complex nature of the human self, and was comparatively unconstrained by the limits of the scientific perspective. Emotion and imagination, rather than reason and perception, were of prime importance. New concern arose not only with the exalted and noble but with the contraries and darkness in the human soul, with evil, death, the demonic, and the irrational. Generally ignored in the optimistic, clarified light of rational science, these themes now inspired the works of Blake and Novalis, Schopenhauer and Kierkegaard, Hawthorne and Melville, Poe and Baudelaire, Dostoevsky and Nietzsche. With Romanticism, the modern eye was turned ever more inward to discern the shadows of existence. To explore the mysteries of interiority, of moods and motives, love and desire, fear and angst, inner conflicts and contradictions, memories and dreams, to experience extreme and incommunicable states of consciousness, to be inwardly grasped in epiphanic ecstasy, to plumb the depths of the human soul, to bring the unconscious into consciousness, to know the infinite—such were the imperatives of Romantic introspection.

In contrast to the scientist's quest for general laws defining a single objective reality, the Romantic gloried in the unbounded multiplicity of realities pressing in on his subjective awareness, and in the complex uniqueness of each object, event, and experience presented to his soul. Truth discovered in divergent perspectives was valued above the monolithic and univocal ideal of empirical science. For the Romantic, reality was symbolically resonant through and through, and was therefore fundamentally multivalent, a constantly changing complex of many-leveled meanings, even of opposites. For the Enlightenment-scientific mind, by contrast, reality was concrete and literal, univocal. Against this view, the Romantic pointed out that even the reality constructed and perceived by the scientific mind was at bottom symbolic, but its symbols were exclusively of a specific kind—mechanistic, material, impersonal—and were interpreted by scientists as uniquely valid. From the Romantic's perspective, the conventional scientific view of reality was essentially a jealous "monotheism" in new clothes, wanting no other gods before it. The literalism of the modern scientific mind was a form of idolatry—myopically worshiping an opaque object as the only reality, rather than recognizing that object as a mystery, a vessel of deeper realities.

The search for a unifying order and meaning remained central for the Romantics, but in that task the limits of human knowledge were radically expanded beyond those imposed by the Enlightenment, and a larger range of human faculties were considered necessary for genuine cognition. Imagination and feeling now joined sense and reason to render a deeper understanding of the world. In his morphological studies, Goethe sought to experience the archetypal form or essence of each plant and animal by saturating the objective perception with the content of his own imagination. Schelling proclaimed that "to philosophize about nature means to create nature," for nature's true meaning could be produced only from within man's "intellectual imagination." The historians Vico and Herder took seriously modes of cognition such as the mythological that had informed the consciousness of other eras, and believed that the historian's task was to feel himself into the spirit of other ages through an empathic "historical sense," to understand from within by means of the sympathetic imagination. Hegel discerned overarching rational and spiritual meaning in the vast data of history by means of a "logic of passion." Coleridge wrote that "deep thinking is attainable only by a man of deep feeling," and that the artist's "esemplastic power of the imagination" gave to the human mind the ability to grasp things in their entirety, to create and shape coherent wholes out of disparate elements. Wordsworth recognized the numinous vision of the natural child as possessing a deeper insight into reality than did the opaque, disenchanted perspective of the conventional adult. And Blake recognized "Imagination" as the sacred vessel of the infinite, the emancipator of the bound human mind, the means by which eternal realities came to expression and consciousness. Indeed, for many Romantics, imagination was in some sense the whole of existence, the true ground of being, the medium of all realities. It both pervaded consciousness and constituted the world.

Like imagination, the will too was considered a necessary element in the attainment of human knowledge, a force preceding knowledge and freely impelling man and universe forward to new levels of creativity and awareness. Here it was Nietzsche who, in a uniquely powerful synthesis of titanic Romantic spiritual passion and the most radical strain of Enlightenment skepticism, set forth the paradigmatic Romantic position concerning the relation of will to truth and knowledge: The rational intellect could not achieve objective truth; nor could any perspective ever be independent of interpretation of some sort. "Against positivism, which halts at phenomena—'There are only facts'—I would say: No, facts are precisely what there are not, only interpretations." This was true not just for matters of morality, but for physics too, which was but a specific perspective and exegesis to suit specific needs and desires. Every way of viewing the world was the product of hidden impulses. Every philosophy revealed not an impersonal system of thought, but an involuntary confession. Unconscious instinct, psychological motivation, linguistic distortion, cultural prejudice—these affected and defined every human perspective. Against the long Western tradition of asserting the unique validity of one system of concepts and beliefs—whether religious, scientific, or philosophical—that alone mirrors the Truth, Nietzsche set forth a radical perspectivism: There exists a plurality of perspectives through which the world can be interpreted, and there is no authoritative independent criterion according to which one system can be determined to be more valid than others.

But if the world was radically indeterminate, it could be shaped by a heroic act of will to affirm life and bring forth its triumphant fulfillment: The highest truth, Nietzsche prophesied, was being born within man through the self-creating power of the will. All of man's striving for knowledge and power would fulfill itself in a new being who would incarnate the living meaning of the universe. But to achieve this birth, man would have to grow beyond himself so fundamentally that his present limited self would be destroyed: "What is great in man is that he is a bridge and not a goal. . . . Man is something that must be overcome." For man was a way to new dawns and new horizons far beyond the compass of the present age. And the birth of this new being was not a life-impoverishing otherworldly fantasy to be believed by ecclesiastical decree, but was a vivid, tangible reality to be created, here and now, through the heroic self-overcoming of the great individual. Such an individual had to transform life into a work of art, within which he could forge his character, embrace his fate, and recreate himself as heroic protagonist of the world epic. He had to invent himself anew, imagine himself into being. He had to will into existence a fictive drama into which he could enter and live, imposing a redemptive order on the chaos of a meaningless universe without God. Then the God who had long been projected to the beyond could be born within the human soul. Then man could dance godlike in the eternal flux, free of all foundations and all bounds, beyond every metaphysical constraint. Truth was not something one proved or disproved; it was something one *created*. In Nietzsche, as in Romanticism generally, the philosopher became poet: a world conception was judged not in terms of abstract rationality or factual verification, but as an expression of courage, beauty, and imaginative power.

Thus the Romantic sensibility advanced new standards and values for human knowledge. Through the self-creating power of imagination and will, the human being could body forth unborn realities, penetrate invisible but altogether real levels of being, comprehend nature and history and the cosmos's unfolding—indeed, participate in the very process of creation. A new epistemology was claimed both possible and necessary. And so the limits of knowledge established by Locke, Hume, and the positivist side of Kant were boldly defied by the Idealists and Romantics of the post-Enlightenment.

The two temperaments held similarly divergent attitudes toward the two traditional pillars of Western culture, Greco-Roman classicism and the Judaeo-Christian religion. As the Enlightenment-scientific mind developed during the modern era, it increasingly employed the thought of the classical era only to the extent that it provided useful starting points for further investigation and theory construction, beyond which ancient metaphysical and scientific schemes were generally perceived as deficient and of mainly historical interest. By contrast, classical culture for the Romantic was still a living realm of Olympian images and personalities, its artistic creations from Homer and Aeschylus onward still exalted models, its imaginative and spiritual insights still pregnant with newly discoverable meaning. Both viewpoints encouraged the recovery of the classical past, but for different motives—one for the sake of accurate historical knowledge, the other to revivify that past, to enable it to live again in the creative spirit of modern man.

It was along such lines that their respective attitudes toward tradition in general differed. While the rational scientific mind viewed tradition in more skeptical terms, valuable only to the extent of providing continuity and structure for the growth of knowledge, the Romantic, although no less rebellious in character and often considerably more so, found in tradition something more mysterious—a repository of collective wisdom, the accrued insights of a people's soul, a living, changing force with its own autonomy and evolutionary dynamism. Such wisdom was not merely the empirical and technical knowledge of the scientific mind, but spoke of deeper realities, hidden to common sense and mechanical experiment. New appreciation thus arose not only for the classical Greco-Roman past, but for the spiritually resonant Middle Ages, for Gothic architecture and folk literature, for the ancient and the primitive, for the Oriental and exotic, for esoteric traditions of all sorts, for the Volksgeist of the Germanic and other peoples, for the Dionysian wellsprings of culture. A new awareness of the Renaissance now emerged, followed in subsequent years by a new consciousness of the age of Romanticism itself. By contrast, such matters concerned the scientific mind not out of empathic appreciation or inspiration, but by virtue of their historical and anthropological interest. In the Enlightenment-scientific vision, modern civilization and its values stood unequivocally above all its predecessors, while Romanticism maintained a profound ambivalence toward modernity in its many expressions. As time passed, ambivalence turned into antagonism as Romantics radically questioned the West's belief in its own "progress," in its civilization's innate superiority, in rational man's inevitable fulfillment.

The issue of religion posed the same contrasts. Both streams were in part predicated on the Reformation, for individualism and personal freedom of belief were common to both, yet each developed different aspects of the Reformation legacy. The spirit of the Enlightenment rebelled against the strictures of ignorance and superstition imposed by theological dogma and belief in the supernatural, in favor of straightforward empirical and rational knowledge and a liberating embrace of the secular. Religion was either rejected altogether or maintained only in the form of a rationalist deism or natural law ethics. The Romantic's attitude toward religion was more complex. His rebellion too was against the hierarchies and institutions of traditional religion, against enforced belief, moralistic constriction, and hollow ritual. Yet religion itself was a central and enduring element in the Romantic spirit, whether it took the form of transcendental idealism, Neoplatonism, Gnosticism, pantheism, mystery religion, nature worship, Christian mysticism, Hindu-Buddhist mysticism, Swedenborgianism, theosophy, esotericism, religious existentialism, neopaganism, shamanism, Mother Goddess worship, evolutionary human divinization, or some syncretism of these. Here the "sacred" remained a viable category, whereas in science it had long since disappeared. God was rediscovered in Romanticism—not the God of orthodoxy or deism but of mysticism, pantheism, and immanent cosmic process; not the juridical monotheistic patriarch but a divinity more ineffably mysterious, pluralistic, all-embracing, neutral or even feminine in gender; not an absentee creator but a numinous creative force within nature and within the human spirit.

Moreover, art itself—music, literature, drama, painting—now took on a virtually religious status for the Romantic sensibility. In a world made mechanical and soulless by science, the pursuit of beauty for its own sake assumed extraordinary psychological importance. Art provided a unique point of conjunction between the natural and the spiritual, and for many modern intellectuals disillusioned with orthodox religion, art became the chief spiritual outlet and medium. The problem of grace, focused on the enigma of inspiration, now seemed of more vital concern to painters, composers, and writers than to theologians. The artistic enterprise was elevated to an exalted spiritual role, whether as poetic epiphany or aesthetic rapture, as divine afflatus or revelation of eternal realities, as creative quest, imaginative discipline, devotion to the Muses, existential imperative, or liberating transcendence from the world of suffering. The most secular of moderns could yet worship the artistic imagination, hold sacred the humanistic tradition of art and culture. The creative masters of the past became the saints and prophets of that culture, the critics and essayists its high priests. In art, the disenchanted modern psyche could yet find a ground for meaning and value, a hallowed context for its spiritual yearnings, a world open to profundity and mystery.

The artistic and literary culture also presented the modern mind with virtually an alternative, if more complex and variable, world picture to that of science. The cultural power of, for example, the novel in reflecting and shaping human experience—from Rabelais, Cervantes, and Fielding, through Hugo, Stendhal, Flaubert, Melville, Dostoevsky, and Tolstoy, and on to Mann, Hesse, Lawrence, Woolf, Joyce, Proust, and Kafka—constituted a constant and often unassimilable counterpoint to the power of the dominant scientific world conception. Having lost belief in the theological and mythological master plots of earlier eras, the literate culture of the modern West turned its instinctive hunger for cosmic coherence, for existential order, to the narrative plots of imaginative fiction. Through the artist's ability to give new contour and significance to experience, in the mystical crucible of aesthetic transfiguration, a new reality could be made—"a rival creation" in Henry

James's words. Here in the novel, as in theater and poetry and the other arts, was expressed a concern with the phenomena of consciousness as such, as well as with the qualitative details of the outer world, so that artistic realism could (again in James's words) "survey the whole field." Here in the realms of art and literature was pursued with penetrating rigor and nuance that broad phenomenology of human experience that was also entering into formal philosophy itself through William James and Bergson, Husserl and Heidegger. Rather than conducting experimental analysis of an objectified world, this tradition focused its attention on "being" itself, on the lived world of human experience, on its unceasing ambiguity, its spontaneity and autonomy, its uncontainable dimensions, its ever-deepening complexity.

In this sense the Romantic impulse continued and expanded the modern mind's overall movement toward realism. Its goal was to delineate all aspects of existence, not just the conventionally acceptable and consensually validated. As Romanticism extended its compass and shifted its focus in the course of the modern period, it sought to reflect the authentic character of modern life in its lived actuality, not limiting itself to the ideal or the aristocratic, or to traditional subjects from classical, mythological, or biblical sources. It mission was to transmute the mundane and commonplace into art, to perceive the poetic and mystical in the most concrete details of ordinary experience, even in the degraded and ugly. Its quest was to show "the heroism of modern life" (Baudelaire), and its antiheroism as well. By expressing ever more precisely the variegated quality of human experience, the Romantic conveyed as well its confusion, its irresolution, and its subjectivity. Pressing ever deeper into the nature of human perception and creativity, the modern artist began to move beyond the traditional mimetic, representational view of art, and the "spectator" theory of reality underlying it. Such an artist sought to be not merely the reproducer of forms, not even their discoverer, but rather their creator. Reality was not to be copied, but to be invented.

These radically broadening conceptions of reality, however, could not easily be integrated with the more positivist side of the modern mind. Also alienating to the scientific temperament was the Romantic's characteristic openness to transcendent dimensions of experience, and characteristic antagonism to science's alleged rationalist reductionism and pretensions to objective certainty. As time passed, what had been the medieval dichotomy between reason and faith, which was followed by the early modern dichotomy between secular science and the Christian religion, now became a more general schism between scientific rationalism on the one hand and the multifaceted Romantic humanistic culture on the other, with the latter now including a diversity of religious and philosophical perspectives loosely allied with the literary and artistic tradition.

The Divided World View

Because both temperaments were deeply and simultaneously expressive of Western attitudes and yet were largely incompatible, a complex bifurcation of the Western outlook resulted. With the modern psyche so affected by the Romantic sensibility and in some sense identified with it, yet with the truth claims of science so formidable, modern man experienced in effect an intractable division between his mind and his soul. The same individual could appreciate, say, both Blake and Locke, but not in a coherent manner. Yeats's esoteric vision of history could scarcely be conjoined with the history taught in modern universities. Rilke's idealist ontology ("We are the bees of the invisible") could not readily be accommodated by the assumptions of conventional science. As distinctly modern and influential a sensibility as T. S. Eliot's was yet closer to Dante than to Darwin.

Romantic poets, religious mystics, idealist philosophers, and counter-cultural psychedelicists would claim (and often describe in detail) the existence of other realities beyond the material and argue for an ontology of human consciousness sharply differing from that of conventional empiricism. But when it came to defining a basic cosmology, the secular scientific mind continued to determine the modern Weltanschauung's center of gravity. For without consensual validation, the Romantic's revelations could not overcome their apparent incompatibility with the commonly accepted truths of scientific observation, the bottom line of modern belief. The dreamer held no fragrant rose, tangible and public, with which to demonstrate to all the truth of his dream.

Thus while Romanticism in this most general sense continued to inspire the West's "inner" culture—its art and literature, its religious and metaphysical vision, its moral ideals—science dictated the "outer" cosmology: the character of nature, man's place in the universe, and the limits of his real knowledge. Because science ruled the objective world, the Romantic perception was by necessity limited to the subjective. The

Romantics' reflections on life, their music and poetry and religious yearnings, richly absorbing and culturally sophisticated as those might be, in the end had to be consigned to only a part of the modern universe. Spiritual, imaginative, emotional, and aesthetic concerns had their place, but could not claim full ontological relevance in an objective world whose parameters were fundamentally impersonal and opaque. The faith-reason division of the medieval era and the religion-science division of the early modern era had become one of subject-object, inner-outer, man-world, humanities-science. A new form of the double-truth universe was now established.

As a consequence of this dualism, modern man's experience of the natural world and his relation to it underwent a paradoxical inversion as the modern period evolved, with the Romantic and scientific streams virtually mirroring each other in reverse. To begin with, a gradual immersion of man into nature was visible on both fronts. On the Romantic side, as in Rousseau, Goethe, or Wordsworth, there was an impassioned striving for conscious unity with nature, both poetic and instinctual. On the scientific side, man's immersion into nature was realized in science's description of man in increasingly, and then entirely, naturalistic terms. But against the harmonious aspirations of the Romantics, man's unity with nature was here placed in the context of a Darwinian-Freudian struggle with a nature of brute unconsciousness—a struggle for survival, for ego integrity, for civilization. In the scientific view, man's antagonism toward nature—and thus the necessity of nature's external exploitation and internal repression—was the inevitable consequence of man's biological evolution and emergence from the rest of nature.

In the longer run, however, the early Romantic sense of harmony with nature underwent a distinct transformation as the modern era grew old. Here the Romantic temperament was complexly influenced by its own internal developments, by the sundering effects of modern industrial civilization and modern history, and by science's view of nature as impersonal, non-anthropocentric, and random. The overdetermined result was an experience of nature almost opposite from the original Romantic ideal: Modern man now increasingly sensed his alienation from nature's womb, his fall from unitary being, his confinement to an absurd universe of chance and necessity. No longer the early Romantic's spiritually glorious child of nature, late modern man was the incongruously sensitive denizen of an implacable vastness devoid of meaning. Wordsworth's vision had been displaced by Frost's:

> Space ails us moderns: we are sick
>   with space.
> Its contemplation makes us out as
>   small.
> As a brief epidemic of microbes
> That in a good glass may be seen to
>   crawl
> The patina of this least of globes.

By contrast, and for different reasons, the temperament allied with science and technological development had lauded man's separation from nature. Human freedom from nature's constraints, man's ability to control his environment, and his intellectual capacity to observe and understand nature without anthropomorphic projection were all indispensable values for the scientific mind. Yet this same strategy paradoxically led science to a deepened awareness of man's intrinsic unity with nature: his ineluctable dependence upon and ecological involvement with the natural environment, his epistemological interrelatedness with the nature he could never completely objectify, and the concrete dangers of the modern attempt at such separation and objectification. Science thereby began to move toward a position not altogether unlike the original Romantic one in its appreciation of man's unity with nature—though generally without spiritual or transcendent dimensions, and without effectively resolving the theoretical and practical problems of the still fundamental human-world divide.

In the meantime, the Romantic position had succumbed to the alienation necessitated by that schism. Nature was still impersonal and non-anthropocentric, and the modern psyche's acute awareness of that cosmic estrangement was scarcely dented by the incipient and partial scientific rapprochement. It is true that in the twentieth century, both scientist and artist simultaneously experienced the breakdown and dissolution of the old categories of time, space, causality, and substance. But the deeper discontinuities between the scientific universe and human aspiration remained unresolved. The modern experience was still vexed by a profound incoherence, with the dichotomies of the Romantic and scientific temperaments reflecting the Western Weltanschauung's seemingly unbridgeable disjunction between human consciousness and unconscious cosmos. In a sense the two cultures, the two sensibilities, were present in varying proportion in every reflective individual of the modern West. And as the full character and implications of the scientific world view became explicit, that inner division was experienced as that of the sensitive human psyche situated in a world alien to human meaning. Modern man was a divided animal, inexplicably self-aware in an indifferent universe.

Attempted Syntheses: From Goethe and Hegel to Jung

There were those who sought to encompass that schism by bridging the scientific and humanistic imperatives in both method and theory. Goethe led a *naturphilosophie* movement that strove to unite empirical observation and spiritual intuition into a science of nature more revealing than Newton's, a science capable of grasping nature's organic archetypal forms. The scientist could not, in Goethe's view, arrive at nature's deeper truths by detaching himself from nature and employing bloodless abstractions to understand it, registering the external world like a machine. Such a strategy guaranteed that the observed reality would be a partial illusion, a picture whose depths had been eliminated by an unconscious filter. Only by bringing observation and imaginative intuition into intimate interaction could man penetrate nature's appearances and discover its essence. Then the archetypal form in each phenomenon could be elicited; then the universal could be recognized in the particular and reunited with it.

Goethe justified this approach with a philosophical stance sharply divergent from that of his older contemporary Kant. For while, like Kant, he recognized the human mind's constructive role in knowledge, he nevertheless perceived man's true relation to nature as overcoming the Kantian dualism. In Goethe's vision, nature permeates everything, including the human mind and imagination. Hence nature's truth does not exist as something independent and objective, but is revealed in the very act of human cognition. The human spirit does not simply impose its order on nature, as Kant thought. Rather, nature's spirit brings forth its own order through man, who is the organ of nature's self-revelation. For nature is not distinct from spirit but is itself spirit, inseparable not only from man but from God. God does not exist as a remote governor over nature, but "holds her close to her breast," so that nature's processes breathe God's own spirit and power. Thus did Goethe unite poet and scientist in an analysis of nature that reflected his distinctively sensuous religiosity.

In a similar spirit, the metaphysical speculations of the German Idealists after Kant culminated in the extraordinary philosophical achievement of Georg W. F. Hegel. Drawing on classical Greek philosophy, Christian mysticism, and German Romanticism to construct his all-encompassing system, Hegel set forth a conception of reality that sought to relate and unify man and nature, spirit and matter, human and divine, time and eternity. At the foundation of Hegel's thought was his understanding of dialectic, according to which all things unfold in a continuing evolutionary process whereby every state of being inevitably brings forth its opposite. The interaction between these opposites then generates a third stage in which the opposites are integrated—they are at once overcome and fulfilled—in a richer and higher synthesis, which in turn becomes the basis for another dialectical process of opposition and synthesis.[5] Through philosophy's comprehension of this fundamental process, Hegel asserted, every aspect of reality—human thought, history, nature, the divine reality itself—could be made intelligible.

Hegel's overriding impulse was to comprehend all dimensions of existence as dialectically integrated in one unitary whole. In Hegel's view, all human thought and all reality is pervaded by contradiction, which alone makes possible the development of higher states of consciousness and higher states of being. Each phase of being contains within itself a self-contradiction, and it is this that serves as the motor of its movement to a higher and more complete phase. Through a continuing dialectical process of opposition and synthesis, the world is always in the process of completing itself. Whereas for most of the history of Western philosophy from Aristotle onward, the defining essence of opposites was that they were logically contradictory and mutually exclusive, for Hegel all opposites are logically necessary and mutually implicated elements in a larger truth. Truth is thus radically paradoxical.

Yet for Hegel the human mind in its highest development was fully capable of comprehending such truth. In contrast to Kant's more circumscribed view, Hegel possessed a profound faith in human reason, believing it was ultimately grounded in the divine reason itself. While Kant had argued that reason could not penetrate the veil of phenomena to reach the ultimate reality, since man's finite reason inevitably became caught in contradiction whenever it attempted to do so, Hegel saw human reason as fundamentally an expression of a universal Spirit or Mind (*Geist*), through the power of which, as in love, all opposites could be transcended in a higher synthesis.

Hegel further argued that Kant's philosophical revolution did not establish the final limits or necessary foundations of human knowledge, but rather was one of a long sequence of such conceptual revolutions by which man as subject repeatedly recognized that what he had thought was a being-in-itself actually received its content by means of the form given to it by the subject. The history of the human mind constantly replayed this drama of the subject's becoming conscious of itself and the consequent destruction of the previously uncriticized form of consciousness. The structures of human knowledge were not fixed and timeless, as Kant supposed, but were historically determined stages that evolved in a continuing dialectic until consciousness achieved absolute knowledge of itself. What at any moment was seen as fixed and certain was constantly overcome by the evolving mind, thereby opening up new possibilities and greater freedom. Every stage of philosophy from the ancient Presocratics onward, every form of thought in human history, was both an incomplete perspective and yet a necessary step in this great intellectual evolution. Every era's world view was both a valid truth unto itself and also an imperfect stage in the larger process of absolute truth's self-unfolding.

This same dialectical process also characterized Hegel's metaphysical and religious understanding. Hegel conceived of the primal being of the world, the universal Mind or Spirit, as unfolding itself through its creation, achieving its ultimate realization in the human spirit. In Hegel's understanding, the Absolute first posits itself in the immediacy of its own inner consciousness, then negates this initial condition by expressing itself in the particularities of the finite world of space and time, and finally, by "negating the negation," recovers itself in its infinite essence. Mind thereby overcomes its estrangement from the world, a world that Mind itself has constituted. Thus the movement of knowledge evolves from consciousness of the object separate from the subject, to absolute knowledge in which the knower and the known became one.

But it was only through a dialectical process of self-negation that the Absolute could achieve its fulfillment. Whereas for Plato the immanent and secular was ontologically dismissed in favor of the transcendent and spiritual, for Hegel this world was the very condition of the Absolute's self-realization. In Hegel's conception, both nature and history are ever progressing toward the Absolute: The universal Spirit expresses itself in space as nature, in time as history. All of nature's processes and all of history, including man's intellectual, cultural, and religious development, constitute the teleological plot of the Absolute's quest for self-revelation. Just as it was only through the experience of alienation from God that man could experience the joy and triumph of rediscovering his own divinity, so it was only through the process of God's becoming finite, in nature and in man, that God's infinite nature could be expressed. For this reason, Hegel declared that the essence of his philosophical conception was expressed in the Christian revelation of God's incarnation as man, the climax of religious truth.

The world is the history of the divine's unfolding, a constant process of becoming, an immense drama in which the universe reveals itself to itself and achieves its freedom. All struggle and evolution are resolved in the realization of the world's *telos,* its goal and purpose. In this great dialectic, all potentialities are embodied in forms of ever-increasing complexity, and all that was implicit in the original state of being gradually becomes explicit. Man—his thought, his culture, his history—is the pivot of that unfolding, the vessel of God's glory. Hence theology for Hegel was replaced by the comprehension of history: God is not beyond the creation, but is the creative process itself. Man is not the passive spectator of reality, but its active co-creator, his history the matrix of its fulfillment. The universal essence, which constitutes and permeates all things, finally comes to consciousness of itself in man. At the climax of his long evolution, man achieves possession of absolute truth and recognizes his unity with the divine spirit that has realized itself within him.

When all this was set forth in the early nineteenth century, and for several decades afterward, Hegel's great structure of thought was regarded by many as the most satisfying and indeed ultimate philosophical conception in the history of the Western mind, the culmination of philosophy's long development since the Greeks. Every aspect of existence and human culture found a place in this world conception, embraced by its all-encompassing totality. Hegel's influence was considerable, first in Germany and later in English-speaking countries, encouraging a renascence of classical and historical studies from an Idealist perspective and providing a metaphysical bulwark for spiritually disposed intellectuals grappling with the forces of secular materialism. A new attentiveness to history and to the evolution of ideas was thereby engendered, with history seen as motivated ultimately not simply by political or economic or biological—i.e., material—factors, though these all played a role, but rather by consciousness itself, by spirit or mind, by the self-unfoldment of thought and the power of ideas.

Yet Hegel also aroused much criticism. For some, the absolutist clo-
sures of his system appeared to limit the unpredictable possibilities of the
universe and the personal autonomy of the human individual. His stress
on the rational determinism of the Absolute Spirit and the ultimate
overcoming of all oppositions seemed to undercut the problematic contingency and irrationality of life, and to ignore the concrete emotional
and existential actuality of human experience. His abstract metaphysical
certitudes seemed to avoid the grim reality of death, and to disregard the
human experience of God's remoteness and inscrutability. Religious
critics objected that belief in God was not simply the solution to a
philosophical problem but required a free and courageous leap of faith
amidst ignorance and dark uncertainty. His philosophy was interpreted
by others as a metaphysical justification for the status quo, and was
therefore criticized as a betrayal of humanity's drive for political and
material betterment. Later critics noted that his exalted view of Western
culture in the context of world history, and of rational civilization's
imposing itself on the contingencies of nature, could be interpreted as a
justification for modern man's hubristic impulse toward domination and
exploitation. Indeed, fundamental Hegelian concepts such as those concerning the nature of God, spirit, reason, history, and freedom appeared
to be open to completely antithetical interpretations.

Often Hegel's historical judgments seemed peremptory, his political
and religious implications ambiguous, his language and style perplexing.
Moreover, his scientific views, though informed, were unorthodox. In
any case Hegelian Idealism did not easily cohere with the naturalistic
view of the world corroborated by science. After Darwin, evolution no
longer seemed to require an all-encompassing Spirit, nor did the conventional scientific view of the evidence suggest one. Nor, finally, did
subsequent historical events provide grounds for confidence in Western
man's inevitable spiritual consummation through history.

Hegel had spoken with the autocratic confidence of one who had
experienced a vision of reality whose absolute truth transcended the
skepticism and demands for detailed empirical tests that other systems
might require. To his critics, Hegel's philosophy was unfounded, fantastic. The modern mind did indeed incorporate much of Hegel, above all
his grasp of dialectic and his recognition of the pervasiveness of evolution
and the power of history. But as an entirety, the Hegelian synthesis was
not sustained by the modern mind. In fulfillment, as it were, of its own
theory, Hegelianism was eventually submerged by the very reactions it

helped provoke—irrationalism and existentialism (Schopenhauer and Kierkegaard), dialectical materialism (Marx and Engels), pluralistic pragmatism (James and Dewey), logical positivism (Russell and Carnap), and linguistic analysis (Moore and Wittgenstein), all movements increasingly more reflective of the general tenor of modern experience. With Hegel's decline there passed from the modern intellectual arena the last culturally powerful metaphysical system claiming the existence of a universal order accessible to human awareness.

In the twentieth century, metaphysically inclined scientists such as Henri Bergson, Alfred North Whitehead, and Pierre Teilhard de Chardin sought to conjoin the scientific picture of evolution with philosophical and religious conceptions of an underlying spiritual reality along lines similar to Hegel. Their eventual fate, however, was also similar, for although regarded by many as brilliant and comprehensive challenges to the conventional scientific vision, for others such speculations did not possess a sufficiently demonstrable empirical basis. Given the nature of the case, there seemed to be no decisive means for verifying such concepts as Bergson's creative élan vital operating in the evolutionary process, Whitehead's evolving God who was interdependent with nature and its processes of becoming, or Teilhard's "cosmogenesis" in which human and world evolution would be fulfilled in an "Omega point" of unitive Christ-consciousness. Although each of these theories of a spiritually informed evolutionary process gained wide popular response and began to influence later modern thought in often subtle ways, the overt cultural trend, especially in academia, was otherwise.

The decline of speculative metaphysical overviews signaled as well the decline of speculative historical overviews, and epic efforts such as Oswald Spengler's and Arnold Toynbee's, though not without admirers, were eventually depreciated like Hegel's before them. Academic history now disengaged itself from the task of discerning great overarching patterns and comprehensive uniformities in history. The Hegelian program of discovering the "meaning" of history and the "purpose" of cultural evolution was now regarded as impossible and misguided. Instead, professional historians saw their competence more properly limited to carefully defined specialized studies, to methodological problems derived from the social sciences, to statistical analyses of measurable factors such as population levels and income figures. The historian's attention was better directed to the concrete details of people's lives, especially to their economic and social contexts—"history from below"—than to the

Idealist image of universal principles working through great individuals to forge world history. Following the directive of the Enlightenment, academic historians saw the need to remove history entirely from the theological, mythological, and metaphysical contexts within which it had long been embedded. Like nature, history too was a nominalist phenomenon, to be examined empirically, without spiritual preconceptions.

Yet as the modern era moved to its later stages, Romanticism would reengage the modern mind from another field altogether. The decline of Hegel and of metaphysical and historical overviews had originated in an intellectual environment in which physical science was the dominant force in determining the cultural understanding of reality. But as science itself began to be revealed, both epistemologically and pragmatically, as a relative and fallible form of knowledge, and with both philosophy and religion having already lost their previous cultural preeminence, many reflective individuals began to turn inward, to an examination of consciousness itself as a potential source of meaning and identity in a world otherwise devoid of stable values. This new focus on the inner workings of the psyche reflected as well an increasingly sophisticated concern with those unconscious structures within the mind of the subject that were determining the ostensible nature of the object—a continuation of the Kantian project on a more comprehensive level. Thus it was that of all the instances of a Romantically influenced science (if we except modern evolutionary theory's complex debt to Romantic ideas of organic evolution in nature and history, of reality as a process of constant becoming), the most enduring and seminal proved to be the depth psychology of Freud and Jung, both deeply influenced by the stream of German Romanticism that flowed from Goethe through Nietzsche.

In its concern with the elemental passions and powers of the unconscious—with imagination, emotion, memory, myth, and dreams, with introspection, psychopathology, hidden motivations, and ambivalence—psychoanalysis brought Romanticism's preoccupations to a new level of systematic analysis and cultural significance. With Freud, who first turned to medical science after hearing Goethe's *Ode to Nature* as a student, and who throughout his life obsessively collected archaic religious and mythological statuary, the Romantic influence was often hidden or inverted by the Enlightenment-rationalist assumptions that pervaded his scientific vision. But with Jung, the Romantic inheritance became more explicit as Freud's discoveries and concepts were expanded and deepened. In the course of analyzing a vast range of psychological and cultural phenomena, Jung found evidence of a collective unconscious common to all human beings and structured according to powerful archetypal principles. Though it was clear that human experience was locally conditioned by a multitude of concrete biographical, cultural, and historical factors, subsuming all these at a deeper level appeared to be certain universal patterns or modes of experience, archetypal forms that constantly arranged the elements of human experience into typical configurations and gave to collective human psychology a dynamic continuity. These archetypes endured as basic a priori symbolic forms while taking on the costume of the moment in each individual life and each cultural era, permeating each experience, each cognition, and each world view.

The discovery of the collective unconscious and its archetypes radically extended psychology's range of interest and insight. Religious experience, artistic creativity, esoteric systems, and the mythological imagination were now analyzed in nonreductive terms strongly reminiscent of the Neoplatonic Renaissance and Romanticism. A new dimension to Hegel's understanding of historical dialectic emerged with Jung's insight into the collective psyche's tendency to constellate archetypal oppositions in history before moving toward a synthesis on a higher level. A host of factors previously ignored by science and psychology were now recognized as significant to the psychotherapeutic enterprise and given vivid conceptual formulation: the creativity and continuity of the collective unconscious, the psychological reality and potency of spontaneously produced symbolic forms and autonomous mythic figures, the nature and power of the shadow, the psychological centrality of the search for meaning, the importance of teleological and self-regulating elements in the psyche's processes, the phenomenon of synchronicities. Freud and Jung's depth psychology thus offered a fruitful middle ground between science and the humanities—sensitive to the many dimensions of human experience, concerned with art and religion and interior realities, with qualitative conditions and subjectively significant phenomena, yet striving for empirical rigor, for rational cogency, for practical, therapeutically effective knowledge in a context of collective scientific research.

But precisely because depth psychology was originally grounded in the broader scientific Weltanschauung, its larger philosophical impact was initially limited. This limitation existed not so much because depth psychology was vulnerable to criticism for being insufficiently "scientific," compared with, for example, behaviorist psychology or statistical mechanics (clinical impressions, it was sometimes argued, could not constitute objective, contamination-free evidence for psychoanalytic theories). Such criticisms were occasionally voiced by more conservative scientists but did not significantly affect depth psychology's cultural acceptance, since most who familiarized themselves with its insights found these to possess a certain internal self-evidence and persuasive logic, often bearing the character of an illumination. But more constraining for depth psychology's impact was the very nature of its study: given the basic subject-object dichotomy of the modern mind, the insights of depth psychology had to be adjudged relevant only to the psyche, to the subjective aspect of things, not to the world as such. Even if "objectively" true, they were objectively true only in relation to a subjective reality. They did not and could not change the cosmic context within which the human being sought psychological integrity.

This limitation was further enforced by the modern epistemological critique of all human knowledge. Jung, though metaphysically more flexible than Freud, was epistemologically more exacting, and repeatedly affirmed throughout much of his life the fundamental epistemological limits of his own theories (though he also reminded more conventional scientists that their epistemological situation was no different). With his philosophical grounding in the Kantian critical tradition rather than in Freud's more conventional rationalist materialism, Jung was compelled to admit that his psychology could have no necessary metaphysical implications. It is true that Jung's granting the status of empirical phenomena to psychological reality was itself a major step past Kant, for he thereby gave substance to "internal" experience as Kant had to "external" experience: *all* human experience, not just sense impressions, had to be included for a genuinely comprehensive empiricism. Yet in a Kantian spirit, Jung stated that whatever the data provided by psychotherapeutic investigations, these could never provide substantial warrant for propositions concerning the universe or reality as such. The discoveries of psychology could reveal nothing with certainty about the world's actual constitution, no matter how subjectively convincing was the evidence for a mythic dimension, an *anima mundi*, or a supreme deity. Whatever the human mind produced could be regarded only as a product of the human mind and its intrinsic structures, with no necessary objective or universal correlations. The epistemological value of depth psychology lay rather in its capacity to reveal those unconscious structural factors, the archetypes, which appeared to govern all mental functioning and hence all human perspectives on the world.

Thus the nature of Jung's field and concepts seemed to require an exclusively psychological interpretation of his findings. They were indeed empirical, but they were only psychologically empirical. Depth psychology had perhaps rendered a deeper inner world for modern man, but the objective universe as known by natural science was necessarily still opaque, without transcendent dimensions. It is true that many striking parallels existed between Jungian archetypes and Platonic archetypes; but for the ancient mind, Platonic archetypes were cosmic, while for the modern mind, Jungian archetypes were only psychic. Therein lay the fundamental difference between the classical Greek and the modern Romantic: Descartes, Newton, Locke, and Kant had intervened. With the bifurcation of the modern mind between Romantic and depth psychology interiority on the one hand and the naturalistic cosmology of the physical sciences on the other, there seemed to be no possibility for a genuine synthesis of subject and object, psyche and world. Yet the therapeutic and intellectual contributions of the Freudian-Jungian tradition to twentieth-century culture were many, and gained more significance with each passing decade.

Indeed, the modern psyche appeared to require the services of depth psychology with increasing urgency, as a profound sense of spiritual alienation and other symptoms of social and psychological distress became more widespread. With the traditional religious perspectives no longer offering effective solace, depth psychology itself, along with its numerous offspring, took on characteristics of a religion—a new faith for modern man, a path for the healing of the soul bringing regeneration and rebirth, epiphanies of sudden insight and spiritual conversion (and other facets of religion as well, with the memorializing of psychology's founding prophets and their initiatory revelations, the development of dogmas, priestly elites, rituals, schisms, heresies, reformations, and the proliferation of protestant and gnostic sects). Yet it seemed that salvation for the cultural psyche was not being widely effected—as if the tools of depth psychology were being employed in a context riddled with a more encompassing pathology than a subjectivist psychotherapy could hope to cure.

Existentialism and Nihilism

As the twentieth century advanced, modern consciousness found itself caught up in an intensely contradictory process of simultaneous expansion and contraction. Extraordinary intellectual and psychological sophistication was accompanied by a debilitating sense of anomie and malaise. An unprecedented broadening of horizons and exposure to the experience of others coincided with a private alienation of no less extreme proportions. A stupendous quantity of information had become available about all aspects of life—the contemporary world, the historical past, other cultures, other forms of life, the subatomic world, the macrocosm, the human mind and psyche—yet there was also less ordering vision, less coherence and comprehension, less certainty. The great overriding impulse defining Western man since the Renaissance—the quest for independence, self-determination, and individualism—had indeed brought those ideals to reality in many lives; yet it had also eventuated in a world where individual spontaneity and freedom were increasingly smothered, not just in theory by a reductionist scientism, but in practice by the ubiquitous collectivity and conformism of mass societies. The great revolutionary political projects of the modern era, heralding personal and social liberation, had gradually led to conditions in which the modern individual's fate was ever more dominated by bureaucratic commercial and political superstructures. Just as man had become a meaningless speck in the modern universe, so had individual persons become insignificant ciphers in modern states, to be manipulated or coerced by the millions.

The quality of modern life seemed ever equivocal. Spectacular empowerment was countered by a widespread sense of anxious helplessness. Profound moral and aesthetic sensitivity confronted horrific cruelty and waste. The price of technology's accelerating advance grew ever higher. And in the background of every pleasure and every achievement loomed humanity's unprecedented vulnerability. Under the West's direction and impetus, modern man had burst forward and outward, with tremendous centrifugal force, complexity, variety, and speed. And yet it appeared he had driven himself into a terrestrial nightmare and a spiritual wasteland, a fierce constriction, a seemingly irresolvable predicament.

Nowhere was the problematic modern condition more precisely embodied than in the phenomenon of existentialism, a mood and philosophy expressed in the writings of Heidegger, Sartre, and Camus, among others, but ultimately reflecting a pervasive spiritual crisis in modern culture. The anguish and alienation of twentieth-century life were brought to full articulation as the existentialist addressed the most fundamental, naked concerns of human existence—suffering and death, loneliness and dread, guilt, conflict, spiritual emptiness and ontological insecurity, the void of absolute values or universal contexts, the sense of cosmic absurdity, the frailty of human reason, the tragic impasse of the human condition. Man was condemned to be free. He faced the necessity of choice and thus knew the continual burden of error. He lived in constant ignorance of his future, thrown into a finite existence bounded at each end by nothingness. The infinity of human aspiration was defeated before the finitude of human possibility. Man possessed no determining essence: only his existence was given, an existence engulfed by mortality, risk, fear, ennui, contradiction, uncertainty. No transcendent Absolute guaranteed the fulfillment of human life or history. There was no eternal design or providential purpose. Things existed simply because they existed, and not for some "higher" or "deeper" reason. God was dead, and the universe was blind to human concerns, devoid of meaning or purpose. Man was abandoned, on his own. All was contingent. To be authentic one had to admit, and choose freely to encounter, the stark reality of life's meaninglessness. Struggle alone gave meaning.

The Romantic's quest for spiritual ecstasy, union with nature, and fulfillment of self and society, previously buttressed by the progressive optimism of the eighteenth and nineteenth centuries, had met the dark realities of the twentieth, and the existentialist predicament was felt by many throughout the culture. Even theologians—perhaps especially theologians—were sensitive to the existentialist spirit. In a world shattered by two world wars, totalitarianism, the holocaust, and the atomic bomb, belief in a wise and omnipotent God ruling history for the good of all seemed to have lost any defensible basis. Given the unprecedentedly tragic dimensions of contemporary historical events, given the fall of Scripture as an unshakable foundation for belief, given the lack of any compelling philosophical argument for God's existence, and given above all the almost universal crisis of religious faith in a secular age, it was becoming impossible for many theologians to speak of God in any way meaningful to the modern sensibility: thus emerged the seemingly self-contradictory but singularly representative theology of the "death of God."

Contemporary narratives increasingly portrayed individuals caught in a bewilderingly problematic environment, vainly attempting to forge meaning and value in a context devoid of significance. Faced with the relentless impersonality of the modern world—whether mechanized mass society or soulless cosmos—the Romantic's only remaining response appeared to be despair or self-annihilating defiance. Nihilism in a multitude of inflections now penetrated cultural life with growing insistence. The earlier Romantic passion to merge with the infinite began to be turned against itself, inverted, transformed into a compulsion to negate that passion. Romanticism's disenchanted spirit increasingly expressed itself in fragmentation, dislocation, and self-parody, its only possible truths those of irony and dark paradox. Some suggested that the entire culture was psychotic in its disorientation, and that those called mad were in fact closer to genuine sanity. The revolt against conventional reality began to take new and more extreme forms. Earlier modern responses of realism and naturalism gave way to the absurd and surreal, the dissolution of all established foundations and solid categories. The quest for freedom became ever more radical, its price the destruction of any standard or stability. As the physical sciences also dismantled long-held certainties and structures, so art met science in the throes of the twentieth century's epistemological relativism.

Already at the beginning of the century, the West's traditional artistic canon, rooted in the forms and ideals of classical Greece and the Renaissance, had begun to be dissolved and atomized. Whereas the nature of human identity reflected in novels of the eighteenth and nineteenth centuries conveyed a sense of human selfhood solidly outlined against large coherent backgrounds of linear narrative logic and historical sequence, the characteristic twentieth-century novel was notable for a constant questioning of its own premises, an incessant disruption of narrative and historical coherence, a confusing of horizons, a sophisticated and convoluted self-doubt that left characters, author, and reader in a state of irreducible suspension. Reality and identity, as Hume had precociously perceived two centuries earlier, were neither humanly ascertainable nor ontologically absolute. They were fictive habits of psychological and pragmatic convenience, and in the acutely introspective, wary, relativist consciousness of the contemporary Western mind, they could no longer be confidently presumed. For many, they were also false prisons, to be seen through and transcended: for where there was uncertainty, there was also freedom.

Half in reflection, half in prophesy, the dissonance and disjunction, radical freedom and radical uncertainty of the twentieth century found full and precise expression in its arts. Palpable life in all its flux and chaos replaced the formal conventions of earlier eras. The marvelous in art was sought through the aleatory, the spontaneous, the happenstance. Whether in painting or poetry, music or theater, an insistent amorphousness and indeterminacy governed artistic expression. Incoherence and disturbing juxtaposition constituted the new aesthetic logic. The anomalous became normative: the incongruous, the fractured, the stylized, the trivial, the allusively obscure. Concern with the irrational and subjective, compounded by the overriding impulse to break free from conventions and expectations, often rendered an art intelligible to but an esoteric few—or so elliptically inscrutable as to preclude communication altogether. Each artist had become the prophet of his own new order and dispensation, courageously breaking the old law and forging a new testament.

Art's task was to "make the world strange," to shock the dulled sensibility, to forge a new reality by fragmenting the old. In art as in social practices, rebellion against a constricting and spiritually destitute society required the earnest, even systematic flouting of traditional values and assumptions. The sacred, made bland and empty by centuries of pious convention, seemed better expressed through the profane and blasphemous. Elemental passion and sensation could best draw forth the aboriginal wellsprings of the creative spirit. In Picasso as in the century he mirrored, there arose a Dionysian compound of unbound eroticism, aggression, dismemberment, death and birth. Alternatively, artistic revolt took the form of simulating the modern world in its metallic aridity, with the minimalists mimicking the scientific positivist in their striving for an expressionless art—an impersonal objectivism stripped of interpretation, flatly depicting gestures, forms, and tones devoid of subjectivity or meaning. In the view of many artists, not just intelligibility and meaning but beauty itself was to be abjured, for beauty, too, could be a tyrant, a convention to be destroyed.

It was not simply that the old formulae had been exhausted, or that artists sought novelty at any cost. Rather, the nature of contemporary human experience demanded the collapse of old structures and themes, the creation of new ones, or the renouncing of any discernible form or content whatever. Artists had become realists of a new reality—of an ever-growing multiplicity of realities—lacking any precedent. Thus their artistic responsibilities sharply diverged from those of their predecessors: radical change, in art as in society, was the century's overriding theme, its dominant imperative and its inescapable actuality.

Yet a price was paid. "Make it new," Ezra Pound had decreed, but later he reflected, "I cannot make it cohere." Radical change and ceaseless innovation lent themselves to unaesthetic chaos, to incomprehensibility and barren alienation. The late modern experiment threatened to fray out into meaningless solipsism. The results of incessant novelty were creative but seldom enduring. Incoherence was authentic but seldom satisfying. Subjectivism was perhaps fascinating but too often irrelevant. The insistent elevation of the abstract over the representational sometimes seemed to reflect little more than the growing incapacity of the modern artist to relate to nature. In the absence of established aesthetic forms or culturally sustained modes of vision, the arts in the twentieth century became notable for a certain quality of graceless transiency, an undisguised self-consciousness regarding their own ephemeral substance and style.

By contrast, what *was* constant and cumulative in twentieth-century art was an increasingly ascetic striving for an uncompromised essence of art that gradually eliminated every artistic element that could be regarded as peripheral or contingent—representation, narrative, character, melody, tonality, structural continuity, thematic relation, form, content, meaning, purpose—moving inevitably toward an end point in which all that remained was a blank canvas, an empty stage, silence. Reversion to distantly past or foreign forms and standards seemed to offer the only way out, but these, too, proved short-lived gambits, incapable of taking deep root in the restless modern psyche. Like philosophers and theologians, artists were finally left with only the self-reflective and fairly paralyzing preoccupation with their own creative processes and formal procedures—and, not infrequently, their destruction of the results. The earlier modernist faith in the great artist who alone was sovereign in an otherwise meaningless world gave way to the postmodernist loss of faith in the artist's transcendence.

The contemporary writer . . . is forced to start from scratch: Reality doesn't exist, time doesn't exist, personality doesn't exist. God was the omniscient author, but he died; now no one knows the plot, and since our reality lacks the sanction of a creator, there's no guarantee as to the authenticity of the received version. Time is reduced to presence, the content of a series of discontinuous moments. Time is no longer purposive, and so there is no density, only chance. Reality is, simply, our experience, and objectivity is, of course, an illusion. Personality, after passing through a stage of awkward self-consciousness, has become . . . a mere locus for our experience. In view of these annihilations, it should be no surprise that literature, also, does not exist—how could it? There is only reading and writing . . . ways of maintaining a considered boredom in face of the abyss.[6]

The underlying powerlessness of the individual in modern life pressed many artists and intellectuals to withdraw from the world, to forsake the public arena. Fewer felt capable of engaging issues beyond those immediately confronting the self and its private struggle for substance, let alone committing to universal moral visions that no longer appeared tenable. Human activity—artistic, intellectual, moral—was forced to find its ground in a standardless vacuum. Meaning seemed to be no more than an arbitrary construct, truth only a convention, reality undiscoverable. Man, it began to be said, was a futile passion.

Underneath the superficial clamor of an often frenetic and hyperstimulated daily existence, an apocalyptic tone started to pervade many aspects of cultural life, and as the twentieth century advanced there could be heard, with accelerating frequency and intensity, bell-tolling declarations concerning the decline and fall, the deconstruction and collapse, of virtually every one of the West's great intellectual and cultural projects: the end of theology, the end of philosophy, the end of science, the end of literature, the end of art, the end of culture itself. Just as the Enlightenment-scientific side of the modern mind found itself undermined by its own intellectual advance and radically challenged by its technological and political consequences in the world, so too the Romantic side, reacting to similar circumstances but with a different and often more prophetic sensibility, found itself both disillusioned from within and thwarted from without, apparently destined to hold transcendent aspirations in a cosmic and historical context devoid of transcendent meaning.

Thus Western man enacted an extraordinary dialectic in the course of the modern era—moving from a near boundless confidence in his own powers, his spiritual potential, his capacity for certain knowledge, his mastery over nature, and his progressive destiny, to what often appeared to be a sharply opposite condition: a debilitating sense of metaphysical insignificance and personal futility, spiritual loss of faith, uncertainty in knowledge, a mutually destructive relationship with nature, and an intense insecurity concerning the human future. In the four centuries of modern man's existence, Bacon and Descartes had become Kafka and Beckett.

Something indeed was ending. And so it was that the Western mind, in response to these many complexly interwoven developments, had followed a trajectory that by the late twentieth century had largely dissolved the foundations of the modern world view, leaving the contemporary mind increasingly bereft of established certainties, yet also fundamentally open in ways it had never been before. And the intellectual sensibility that now reflects and expresses this unprecedented situation, the overdetermined outcome of the modern mind's extraordinary development of increasing sophistication and self-deconstruction, is the postmodern mind.

The Postmodern Mind

Each great epochal transformation in the history of the Western mind appears to have been initiated by a kind of archetypal sacrifice. As if to consecrate the birth of a fundamental new cultural vision, in each case a symbolically resonant trial and martyrdom of some sort was suffered by its central prophet: thus the trial and execution of Socrates at the birth of the classical Greek mind, the trial and crucifixion of Jesus at the birth of Christianity, and the trial and condemnation of Galileo at the birth of modern science. By all accounts the central prophet of the postmodern mind was Friedrich Nietzsche, with his radical perspectivism, his sovereign critical sensibility, and his powerful, poignantly ambivalent anticipation of the emerging nihilism in Western culture. And we see a curious, perhaps aptly postmodern analogy of this theme of archetypal sacrifice and martyrdom with the extraordinary inner trial and imprisonment—the intense intellectual ordeal, the extreme psychological isolation, and the eventually paralyzing madness—suffered at the birth of the postmodern by Nietzsche, who signed his last letters "The Crucified," and who died at the dawn of the twentieth century.

Like Nietzsche, the postmodern intellectual situation is profoundly complex and ambiguous—perhaps this is its very essence. What is called postmodern varies considerably according to context, but in its most general and widespread form, the postmodern mind may be viewed as an open-ended, indeterminate set of attitudes that has been shaped by a great diversity of intellectual and cultural currents; these range from pragmatism, existentialism, Marxism, and psychoanalysis to feminism, hermeneutics, deconstruction, and postempiricist philosophy of science, to cite only a few of the more prominent. Out of this maelstrom of highly developed and often divergent impulses and tendencies, a few widely shared working principles have emerged. There is an appreciation of the plasticity and constant change of reality and knowledge, a stress on the priority of concrete experience over fixed abstract principles, and a conviction that no single a priori thought system should govern belief or investigation. It is recognized that human knowledge is subjectively determined by a multitude of factors; that objective essences, or things-in-themselves, are neither accessible nor positable; and that the value of all truths and assumptions must be continually subjected to direct testing. The critical search for truth is constrained to be tolerant of ambiguity and pluralism, and its outcome will necessarily be knowledge that is relative and fallible rather than absolute or certain.

Hence the quest for knowledge must be endlessly self-revising. One must try the new, experiment and explore, test against subjective and objective consequences, learn from one's mistakes, take nothing for granted, treat all as provisional, assume no absolutes. Reality is not a solid, self-contained given but a fluid, unfolding process, an "open universe," continually affected and molded by one's actions and beliefs. It is possibility rather than fact. One cannot regard reality as a removed spectator against a fixed object; rather, one is always and necessarily engaged in reality, thereby at once transforming it while being transformed oneself. Although intransigent or provoking in many respects, reality must in some sense be hewed out by means of the human mind and will, which themselves are already enmeshed in that which they seek to understand and affect. The human subject is an embodied agent, acting and judging in a context that can never be wholly objectified, with orientations and motivations that can never be fully grasped or controlled. The knowing subject is never disengaged from the body or from the world, which form the background and condition of every cognitive act.

The inherent human capacity for concept and symbol formation is recognized as a fundamental and necessary element in the human understanding, anticipation, and creation of reality. The mind is not the passive reflector of an external world and its intrinsic order, but is active and creative in the process of perception and cognition. Reality is in some sense constructed by the mind, not simply perceived by it, and many such constructions are possible, none necessarily sovereign. Although human knowledge may be bound to conform to certain innate subjective structures, there is a degree of indeterminacy in these that, combined with the human will and imagination, permit an element of freedom in cognition. Implicit here is a relativized critical empiricism and a relativized critical rationalism—recognizing the indispensability both of concrete investigation and of rigorous argument, criticism, and theoretical formulation, yet also recognizing that neither procedure can claim any absolute foundation: There is no empirical "fact" that is not already theory-laden, and there is no logical argument or formal principle that is a priori certain. All human understanding is interpretation, and no interpretation is final.

The prevalence of the Kuhnian concept of "paradigms" in current discourse is highly characteristic of postmodern thought, reflecting a critical awareness of the mind's fundamentally interpretive nature. This awareness has not only affected the postmodern approach to past cultural world views and the history of changing scientific theories, but has also influenced the postmodern self-understanding itself, encouraging a more sympathetic attitude toward repressed or unorthodox perspectives and a more self-critical view of currently established ones. Continuing advances in anthropology, sociology, history, and linguistics have underscored the relativity of human knowledge, bringing increased recognition of the "Eurocentric" character of Western thought, and of the cognitive bias produced by factors such as class, race, and ethnicity. Especially penetrating in recent years has been the analysis of gender as a crucial factor in determining, and limiting, what counts as truth. Various forms of psychological analysis, cultural as well as individual, have further unmasked the unconscious determinants of human experience and knowledge.

Reflecting and supporting all these developments is a radical perspectivism that lies at the very heart of the postmodern sensibility: a perspectivism rooted in the epistemologies developed by Hume, Kant, Hegel (in his historicism), and Nietzsche, and later articulated in pragmatism, hermeneutics, and poststructuralism. In this understanding, the world cannot be said to possess any features in principle prior to interpretation. The world does not exist as a thing-in-itself, independent of interpretation; rather, it comes into being only in and through interpretations. The subject of knowledge is already embedded in the object of knowledge: the human mind never stands outside the world, judging it from an external vantage point. Every object of knowledge is already part of a preinterpreted context, and beyond that context are only other preinterpreted contexts. All human knowledge is mediated by signs and symbols of uncertain provenance, constituted by historically and culturally variable predispositions, and influenced by often unconscious human interests. Hence the nature of truth and reality, in science no less than in philosophy, religion, or art, is radically ambiguous. The subject can never presume to transcend the manifold predispositions of his or her subjectivity. One can at best attempt a fusion of horizons, a never-complete rapprochement between subject and object. Less optimistically, one must recognize the insuperable solipsism of human awareness against the radical illegibility of the world.

The other side of the postmodern mind's openness and indeterminacy is thus the lack of any firm ground for a world view. Both inner and outer realities have become unfathomably ramified, multidimensional, malleable, and unbounded—bringing a spur to courage and creativity, yet also a potentially debilitating anxiety in the face of unending relativism and existential finitude. The conflicts of subjective and objective testings, an acute awareness of the cultural parochialism and historical relativity of all knowledge, a pervasive sense of radical uncertainty and displacement, and a pluralism bordering on distressing incoherence all contribute to the postmodern condition. To even speak of subject and object as distinguishable entities is to presume more than can be known. With the ascendance of the postmodern mind, the human quest for meaning in the cosmos has devolved upon a hermeneutic enterprise that is disorientingly free-floating: The postmodern human exists in a universe whose significance is at once utterly open and without warrantable foundation.

Of the many factors that have converged to produce this intellectual position, it has been the analysis of language that has brought forth the most radically skeptical epistemological currents in the postmodern mind, and it is these currents that have identified themselves most articulately and self-consciously as "postmodern." Again, many sources contributed to this development—Nietzsche's analysis of the problematic relation of language to reality; C. S. Peirce's semiotics, positing that all human thought takes place in signs; Ferdinand de Saussure's linguistics, positing the arbitrary relationship between word and object, sign and signified; Wittgenstein's analysis of the linguistic structuring of human experience; Heidegger's existentialist-linguistic critique of metaphysics; Edward Sapir and B. L. Whorf's linguistic hypothesis that language shapes the perception of reality as much as reality shapes language; Michel Foucault's genealogical investigations into the social construction of knowledge; and Jacques Derrida's deconstructionism, challenging the attempt to establish a secure meaning in any text. The upshot of these several influences, particularly in the contemporary academic world, has been the dynamic dissemination of a view of human discourse and knowledge that radically relativizes human claims to a sovereign or enduring truth, and that thereby supports an emphatic revision of the character and goals of intellectual analysis.

Basic to this perspective is the thesis that all human thought is ultimately generated and bound by idiosyncratic cultural-linguistic forms of life. Human knowledge is the historically contingent product of linguistic and social practices of particular local communities of interpreters, with no assured "ever-closer" relation to an independent ahistorical reality. Because human experience is linguistically pre-structured, yet the various structures of language possess no demonstrable connection with an independent reality, the human mind can never claim access to any reality other than that determined by its local form of life. Language is a "cage" (Wittgenstein). Moreover, linguistic meaning itself can be shown to be fundamentally unstable, because the contexts that determine meaning are never fixed, and beneath the surface of every apparently coherent text can be found a plurality of incompatible meanings. No interpretation of a text can claim decisive authority because that which is being interpreted inevitably contains hidden contradictions that undermine its coherence. Hence all meaning is ultimately undecidable, and there is no "true" meaning. No underlying primal reality can be said to provide the foundation for human attempts to represent truth. Texts refer only to other texts, in an infinite regress, with no secure basis in something external to language. One can never escape from "the play of signifiers." The multiplicity of incommensurable human truths exposes and defeats the conventional assumption that the mind can progress ever forward to a nearer grasp of reality. Nothing certain can be said about the nature of truth, except perhaps that it is, as Richard Rorty put it, "what our peers will let us get away with saying."[7]

Here in a sense the Cartesian critical intellect has reached its furthest point of development, doubting all, applying a systematic skepticism to every possible meaning. With no divine foundation to certify the Word, language possesses no privileged connection to truth. The fate of human consciousness is ineluctably nomadic, a self-aware wandering through error. The history of human thought is a history of idiosyncratic metaphorical schemes, ambiguous interpretive vocabularies having no ground beyond what is already saturated by their own metaphorical and interpretive categories. Postmodern philosophers can compare and contrast, analyze and discuss the many sets of perspectives human beings have expressed, the diverse symbol systems, the various ways of making things hang together, but they cannot pretend to possess an extrahistorical Archimedean point from which to judge whether a given perspective validly represents the "Truth." Since there are no indubitable foundations for human knowledge, the highest value for any perspective is its capacity to be temporarily useful or edifying, emancipatory or creative—though it is recognized that in the end these valuations are themselves not justifiable by anything beyond personal and cultural taste. For justification is itself only another social practice with no foundation beyond social practice.

The most prominent philosophical outcome of these several converging strands of postmodern thought has been a many-sided critical attack on the central Western philosophical tradition from Platonism onward. The whole project of that tradition to grasp and articulate a foundational Reality has been criticized as a futile exercise in linguistic game playing, a sustained but doomed effort to move beyond elaborate fictions of its own creation. More pointedly, such a project has been condemned as inherently alienating and oppressively hierarchical—an intellectually imperious procedure that has produced an existential and cultural impoverishment, and that has led ultimately to the technocratic domination of nature and the social-political domination of others. The Western mind's overriding compulsion to impose some form of totalizing reason—theological, scientific, economic—on every aspect of life is accused of being not only self-deceptive but destructive.

Spurred by these and other, related factors, postmodern critical thought has encouraged a vigorous rejection of the entire Western intellectual "canon" as long defined and privileged by a more or less exclusively male, white, European elite. Received truths concerning "man," "reason," "civilization," and "progress" are indicted as intellectually and morally bankrupt. Under the cloak of Western values, too many sins have been committed. Disenchanted eyes are now cast onto the West's long history of ruthless expansionism and exploitation—the rapacity of its elites from ancient times to modern, its systematic thriving at the expense of others, its colonialism and imperialism, its slavery and genocide, its anti-Semitism, its oppression of women, people of color, minorities, homosexuals, the working classes, the poor, its destruction of indigenous societies throughout the world, its arrogant insensitivity to other cultural traditions and values, its cruel abuse of other forms of life, its blind ravaging of virtually the entire planet.

In this radically transformed cultural context, the contemporary academic world has increasingly concerned itself with the critical deconstruction of traditional assumptions through several overlapping modes of analysis—sociological and political, historical and psychological, linguistic and literary. Texts of every category are analyzed with an acute sensitivity to the rhetorical strategies and political functions they serve. The underlying intellectual ethos is one of disassembling established structures, deflating pretensions, exploding beliefs, unmasking appearances—a "hermeneutics of suspicion" in the spirit of Marx, Nietzsche, and Freud. Postmodernism in this sense is "an antinomian movement that assumes a vast unmaking in the Western mind . . . deconstruction, decentering, disappearance, dissemination, demystification, discontinuity, *difference*, dispersion, etc. Such terms . . . express an epistemological obsession with fragments or fractures, and a corresponding ideological commitment to minorities in politics, sex, and language. To think well, to feel well, to act well, to read well, according to the *épistème* of unmaking, is to refuse the tyranny of wholes; totalization in any human endeavor is potentially totalitarian."[8] The pretense of any form of omniscience—philosophical, religious, scientific—must be abandoned. Grand theories and universal overviews cannot be sustained without producing empirical falsification and intellectual authoritarianism. To assert general truths is to impose a spurious dogma on the chaos of phenomena. Respect for contingency and discontinuity limits knowledge to the local and specific. Any alleged comprehensive, coherent outlook is at best no more than a temporarily useful fiction masking chaos, at worst an oppressive fiction masking relationships of power, violence, and subordination.

Properly speaking, therefore, there is no "postmodern world view," nor the possibility of one. The postmodern paradigm is by its nature fundamentally subversive of all paradigms, for at its core is the awareness of reality as being at once multiple, local and temporal, and without demonstrable foundation. The situation recognized by John Dewey at the start of the century, that "despair of any integrated outlook and attitude [is] the chief intellectual characteristic of the present age," has been enshrined as the essence of the postmodern vision, as in Jean-François Lyotard's definition of *postmodern* as "incredulity toward metanarratives."

Here, paradoxically, we can recognize something of the old confidence of the modern mind in the superiority of its own perspective. Only whereas the modern mind's conviction of superiority derived from its awareness of possessing in an absolute sense more knowledge than its predecessors, the postmodern mind's sense of superiority derives from its special awareness of how little knowledge can be claimed by any mind, itself included. Yet precisely by virtue of that self-relativizing critical awareness, it is recognized that a quasi-nihilist rejection of any and all forms of "totalization" and "metanarrative"—of any aspiration toward intellectual unity, wholeness, or comprehensive coherence—is itself a position not beyond questioning, and cannot on its own principles ultimately justify itself any more than can the various metaphysical overviews against which the postmodern mind has defined itself. Such a position presupposes a metanarrative of its own, one perhaps more subtle than others, but in the end no less subject to deconstructive criticism. On its own terms, the assertion of the historical relativity and cultural-linguistic bondage of all truth and knowledge must itself be regarded as reflecting but one more local and temporal perspective having no necessarily universal, extrahistorical value. Everything could change tomorrow. Implicitly, the one postmodern absolute is critical consciousness, which, by deconstructing all, seems compelled by its own logic to do so to itself as well. This is the unstable paradox that permeates the postmodern mind.

>⊀<

But if the postmodern mind has sometimes been prone to a dogmatic relativism and a compulsively fragmenting skepticism, and if the cultural ethos that has accompanied it has sometimes deteriorated into cynical detachment and spiritless pastiche, it is evident that the most significant characteristics of the larger postmodern intellectual situation—its pluralism, complexity, and ambiguity—are precisely the characteristics necessary for the potential emergence of a fundamentally new form of intellectual vision, one that might both preserve and transcend the current state of extraordinary differentiation. In the politics of the contemporary Weltanschauung, no perspective—religious, scientific, or philosophical—has the upper hand, yet that situation has encouraged an almost unprecedented intellectual flexibility and cross-fertilization, reflected in the widespread call for, and practice of, open "conversation" between different understandings, different vocabularies, different cultural paradigms.

Looked at as a whole, the extreme fluidity and multiplicity of the contemporary intellectual scene can scarcely be exaggerated. Not only is the postmodern mind itself a maelstrom of unresolved diversity, but virtually every important element of the Western intellectual past is now present and active in one form or another, contributing to the vitality and confusion of the contemporary Zeitgeist. With so many previously established assumptions having been called into question, there remain few, if any, a priori strictures on the possible, and many perspectives from the past have reemerged with new relevance. Hence any generalizations about the postmodern mind have to be qualified by a recognition of the continuing presence or recent resurgence of most of its major predecessors, the topics of all the previous chapters of this book. Various still-vital forms of the modern sensibility, of the scientific mind, of Romanticism and the Enlightenment, of Renaissance syncretism, of Protestantism, Catholicism, and Judaism—all of these, at various stages of development and ecumenical interpenetration, continue today to be influential factors. Even elements of the Western cultural tradition going back to the Hellenistic era and classical Greece—Platonic and Presocratic philosophy, Hermeticism, mythology, the mystery religions—have been reemerging to play new roles in the current intellectual scene. Moreover, these in turn have been joined, and affected, by a multitude of cultural perspectives from outside the West, such as the Buddhist and Hindu mystical traditions; by underground cultural streams from within the West itself, such as Gnosticism and the major esoteric traditions; and by indigenous and archaic perspectives antedating Western civilization altogether, such as Neolithic European and Native American spiritual traditions—all gathering now on the intellectual stage as if for some kind of climactic synthesis.

The cultural and intellectual role of religion has of course been drastically affected by the secularizing and pluralistic developments of the modern age, but while in most respects the influence of institutionalized religion has continued to decline, the religious sensibility itself seems to have been revitalized by the newly ambiguous intellectual circumstances of the postmodern era. Contemporary religion has been revitalized as well by its own plurality, finding new forms of expression and new sources of inspiration and illumination ranging from Eastern mysticism and psychedelic self-exploration to liberation theology and ecofeminist spirituality. Although the ascendance of secular individualism and the decline of traditional religious belief may have precipitated widespread spiritual anomie, it is evident that, for many, these same developments ultimately encouraged new forms of religious orientation and greater spiritual autonomy. In growing numbers, individuals have felt not only compelled but free to work out for themselves their relationship to the ultimate conditions of human existence, drawing on a far wider range of spiritual resources to do so. The postmodern collapse of meaning has thus been countered by an emerging awareness of the individual's self-responsibility and capacity for creative innovation and self-transformation in his or her existential and spiritual response to life. Following suggestions implicit in Nietzsche, the "death of God" has begun to be assimilated and reconceived as a positive religious development, as permitting the emergence of a more authentic experience of the numinous, a larger sense of deity. On the intellectual level, religion no longer tends to be understood reductively as a psychologically or culturally determined belief in nonexistent realities, or explained away as an accident of biology, but is recognized as a fundamental human activity in which every society and individual symbolically interprets and engages the ultimate nature of being.

Science too, while no longer enjoying the same degree of sovereignty it possessed during the modern era, continues to retain allegiance for the unrivaled pragmatic power of its conceptions and the penetrating rigor of its method. Because the earlier knowledge claims of modern science have been relativized by both philosophy of science and the concrete consequences of scientific and technological advance, that allegiance is no longer uncritical, yet in these new circumstances science itself has seemingly been freed up to explore new and less-constricted approaches to understanding the world. It is true that individuals who subscribe to an allegedly unified and self-evident "scientific world view" of the modern type are seen as having failed to engage the larger intellectual challenge of the age—thereby receiving the same judgment in the postmodern era that the ingenuous religious person received from science in the modern era. In virtually all contemporary disciplines, it is recognized that the prodigious complexity, subtlety, and multivalence of reality far transcend the grasp of any one intellectual approach, and that only a committed openness to the interplay of many perspectives can meet the extraordinary challenges of the postmodern era. But contemporary science has itself become increasingly self-aware and self-critical, less prone to a naive scientism, more conscious of its epistemological and existential limitations. Nor is contemporary science singular, having given rise to a number of radically divergent interpretations of the world, many of which differ sharply from what was previously the conventional scientific vision.

Common to these new perspectives has been the imperative to rethink and reformulate the human relation to nature, an imperative driven by the growing recognition that modern science's mechanistic and objectivist conception of nature was not only limited but fundamentally flawed. Major theoretical interventions such as Bateson's "ecology of mind," Bohm's theory of the implicate order, Sheldrake's theory of formative causation, McClintock's theory of genetic transposition, Lovelock's Gaia hypothesis, Prigogine's theory of dissipative structures and order by fluctuation, Lorenz and Feigenbaum's chaos theory, and Bell's theorem of nonlocality have pointed to new possibilities for a less reductionist scientific world conception. Evelyn Fox Keller's methodological recommendation that the scientist be capable of empathic identification with the object he or she seeks to understand reflects a similar reorientation of the scientific mind. Moreover, many of these developments within the scientific community have been strengthened and often stimulated by the reemergence of and widespread interest in various archaic and mystical conceptions of nature, the impressive sophistication of which is increasingly recognized.

A further crucial development encouraging these integrative tendencies in the postmodern intellectual milieu has been the epistemological rethinking of the nature of imagination, carried out on many fronts—philosophy of science, sociology, anthropology, religious studies—and spurred perhaps above all by the work of Jung and the epistemological insights of post-Jungian depth psychology. Imagination is no longer conceived as simplistically opposed to perception and reason; rather, perception and reason are recognized as being always informed by the imagination. With this awareness of the fundamental mediating role of the imagination in human experience has also come an increased appreciation of the power and complexity of the unconscious, as well as new insight into the nature of archetypal pattern and meaning. The postmodern philosopher's recognition of the inherently metaphorical nature of philosophical and scientific statements (Feyerabend, Barbour, Rorty) has been both affirmed and more precisely articulated with the postmodern psychologist's insight into the archetypal categories of the unconscious that condition and structure human experience and cognition (Jung, Hillman). The long-standing philosophical problem of universals, which had been partly illuminated by Wittgenstein's concept of "family resemblances"—his thesis that what appears to be a definite commonality shared by all instances covered by a single general word in fact often comprises a whole range of indefinite, overlapping similarities and relationships—has been given new intelligibility through depth psychology's understanding of archetypes. In this conception, archetypes are recognized as enduring patterns or principles that are inherently ambiguous and multivalent, dynamic, malleable, and subject to diverse cultural and individual inflections, yet that possess a distinct underlying formal coherence and universality.

An especially characteristic and challenging intellectual position that has emerged out of modern and postmodern developments is one which, recognizing both an essential autonomy in the human being and a radical plasticity in the nature of reality, begins with the assertion that reality itself tends to unfold in response to the particular symbolic framework and set of assumptions that are employed by each individual and each society. The fund of data available to the human mind is of such intrinsic complexity and diversity that it provides plausible support for many different conceptions of the ultimate nature of reality. The human being must therefore choose among a multiplicity of potentially viable options, and whatever option is chosen will in turn affect both the nature of reality and the choosing subject. In this view, although there exist many defining structures in the world and in the mind that resist or compel human thought and activity in various ways, on a fundamental level the world tends to ratify, and open up according to, the character of the vision directed toward it. The world that the human being attempts to know and remake is in some sense projectively elicited by the frame of reference with which it is approached.

Such a position emphasizes the immense responsibility inherent in the human situation, and the immense potential. Since evidence can be adduced and interpreted to corroborate a virtually limitless array of world views, the human challenge is to engage that world view or set of perspectives which brings forth the most valuable, life-enhancing consequences. The "human predicament" is here regarded as the human adventure: the challenge of being, *in potentia*, a radically self-defining entity—not in the context of the no-exit box of the secular existentialist, which unconsciously assumed specific a priori metaphysical limits, but in a universe that is genuinely open. Because the human understanding is not unequivocally compelled by the data to adopt one metaphysical position over another, an irreducible element of human choice supervenes. Hence there enter into the epistemological equation, in addition to intellectual rigor and social-cultural context, other, more open-ended factors such as will, imagination, faith, hope, and empathy. The more complexly conscious and ideologically unconstrained the individual or society, the more free is the choice of worlds, and the more profound their participation in creating reality. This affirmation of the human being's self-defining autonomy and epistemological freedom has a historical background going back at least to the Renaissance and Pico's *Oratio*, appearing in different forms in the ideas of Emerson and Nietzsche, William James and Rudolf Steiner, among others, but has been given new support and further dimensions by a wide range of contemporary intellectual developments, from philosophy of science to sociology of religion.

More generally, whether in philosophy, religion, or science, the univocal literalism that tended to characterize the modern mind has been increasingly criticized and rejected, and in its place has arisen a greater appreciation of the multidimensional nature of reality, the many-sidedness of the human spirit, and the multivalent, symbolically mediated nature of human knowledge and experience. With that appreciation has also come a growing sense that the postmodern dissolving of old assumptions and categories could permit the emergence of entirely new prospects for conceptual and existential reintegration, with the possibility of richer interpretive vocabularies, more profound narrative coherencies. Under the combined impact of the remarkable changes and self-revisions that have taken place in virtually every contemporary intellectual discipline, the fundamental modern schism between science and religion has been increasingly undermined. In the wake of such developments, the original project of Romanticism—the reconciliation of subject and object, human and nature, spirit and matter, conscious and unconscious, intellect and soul—has reemerged with new vigor.

Two antithetical impulses can thus be discerned in the contemporary intellectual situation, one pressing for a radical deconstruction and unmasking—of knowledge, beliefs, world views—and the other for a radical integration and reconciliation. In obvious ways the two impulses work against each other, yet more subtly they can also be seen as working together as polarized, but complementary, tendencies. Nowhere is this dynamic tension and interplay between the deconstructive and the integrative more dramatically in evidence than in the rapidly expanding body of work produced by women informed by feminism. Carolyn Merchant, Evelyn Fox Keller, and other historians of science have analyzed the influence exerted on the modern scientific understanding by gender-biased strategies and metaphors supporting a patriarchal conception of nature—as a mindless, passive feminine object, to be penetrated, controlled, dominated, and exploited. Paula Treichler, Francine Wattman Frank, Susan Wolfe, and other linguists have meticulously explored the complex relations between language, sex, and society, illuminating the multiplicity of ways women have been excluded or depreciated through the implicit codings of linguistic conventions. New and powerful insights have emerged from the work of Rosemary Ruether, Mary Daly, Beatrice Bruteau, Joan Chamberlain Engelsman, and Elaine Pagels in religious studies; of Marija Gimbutas in archaeology; of Carol Gilligan in moral and developmental psychology; of Jean Baker Miller and Nancy Chodorow in psychoanalysis; of Stephanie de Voogd and Barbara Eckman in epistemology; of a host of feminist scholars in history, anthropology, sociology, jurisprudence, economics, ecology, ethics, aesthetics, literary theory, cultural criticism.

Considered as a whole, the feminist perspective and impulse has brought forth perhaps the most vigorous, subtle, and radically critical analysis of conventional intellectual and cultural assumptions in all of contemporary scholarship. No academic discipline or area of human experience has been left untouched by the feminist reexamination of how meanings are created and preserved, how evidence is selectively interpreted and theory molded with mutually reinforcing circularity, how particular rhetorical strategies and behavioral styles have sustained male hegemony, how women's voices remained unheard through centuries of social and intellectual male dominance, how deeply problematic consequences have ensued from masculine assumptions about reality, knowledge, nature, society, the divine. Such analyses in turn have helped illuminate parallel patterns and structures of domination that have marked the experience of other oppressed peoples and forms of life. Given the context in which it has arisen, the feminist intellectual impulse has been compelled to assert itself with a forceful critical spirit that has often been oppositional and polarizing in character; yet precisely as a result of that critique, long-established categories that had sustained traditional oppositions and dualities—between male and female, subject and object, human and nature, body and spirit, self and other—have been deconstructed and reconceived, permitting the contemporary mind to consider less-dichotomized alternative perspectives that could not have been envisioned within previous interpretive frameworks. In certain respects the implications, both intellectual and social, of feminist analyses are so fundamental that their significance is only beginning to be realized by the contemporary mind.

>+*+<

And so on many fronts, the postmodern mind's insistence on the pluralism of truth and its overcoming of past structures and foundations have begun to open up a wide range of unforeseen possibilities for approaching the intellectual and spiritual problems that have long exercised and confounded the modern mind. The postmodern era is an era without consensus on the nature of reality, but it is blessed with an unprecedented wealth of perspectives with which to engage the great issues that confront it.

Still, the contemporary intellectual milieu is riddled with tension, irresolution, and perplexity. The practical benefits of its pluralism are repeatedly undercut by stubborn conceptual disjunctions. Despite frequent congruence of purpose, there is little effective cohesion, no apparent means by which a shared cultural vision could emerge, no unifying perspective cogent or comprehensive enough to satisfy the burgeoning diversity of intellectual needs and aspirations. "In the twentieth century nothing is in agreement with anything else" (Gertrude Stein). A chaos of valuable but seemingly incompatible interpretations prevails, with no resolution in sight. Certainly such a context provides less hindrance to the free play of intellectual creativity than would the existence of a monolithic cultural paradigm. Yet fragmentation and incoherence are not without their own inhibiting consequences. The culture suffers both psychologically and pragmatically from the philosophical anomie that pervades it. In the absence of any viable, embracing cultural vision, old assumptions remain blunderingly in force, providing an increasingly unworkable and dangerous blueprint for human thought and activity.

Faced with such a differentiated and problematic intellectual situation, thoughtful individuals engage the task of evolving a flexible set of premises and perspectives that would not reduce or suppress the complexity and multiplicity of human realities, yet could also serve to mediate, integrate, and clarify. The dialectical challenge felt by many is to evolve a cultural vision possessed of a certain intrinsic profundity or universality that, while not imposing any a priori limits on the possible range of legitimate interpretations, would yet somehow bring an authentic and fruitful coherence out of the present fragmentation, and also provide a sustaining fertile ground for the generation of unanticipated new perspectives and possibilities in the future. Given the nature of the present situation, however, such an intellectual task appears surpassingly formidable—not unlike having to string the great Odyssean bow of opposites, and then send an arrow through a seemingly impossible multiplicity of targets.

The intellectual question that looms over our time is whether the current state of profound metaphysical and epistemological irresolution is something that will continue indefinitely, taking perhaps more viable, or more radically disorienting, forms as the years and decades pass; whether it is in fact the entropic prelude to some kind of apocalyptic denouement of history; or whether it represents an epochal transition to another era altogether, bringing a new form of civilization and a new world view with principles and ideals fundamentally different from those that have impelled the modern world through its dramatic trajectory.

At the Millennium

Turning and turning in the widening gyre
The falcon cannot hear the falconer;
Things fall apart; the centre cannot hold;
Mere anarchy is loosed upon the world. . . .

Surely some revelation is at hand.

William Butler Yeats
"The Second Coming"

As the twentieth century draws to its close, a widespread sense of urgency is tangible on many levels, as if the end of an aeon is indeed approaching. It is a time of intense expectation, of striving, of hope and uncertainty. Many sense that the great determining force of our reality is the mysterious process of history itself, which in our century has appeared to be hurtling toward a massive disintegration of all structures and foundations, a triumph of the Heraclitean flux. Near the end of his life, Toynbee wrote:

> Present-day man has recently become aware that history has been accelerating—and this at an accelerating rate. The present generation has been conscious of this increase of acceleration in its own lifetime; and the advance in man's knowledge of his past has revealed, in retrospect, that the acceleration began about 30,000 years ago . . . and that it has taken successive "great leaps forward" with the invention of agriculture, with the dawn of civilization, and with the progressive harnessing—within the last two centuries—of the titanic physical forces of inanimate nature. The approach of the climax foreseen intuitively by the prophets is being felt, and feared, as a coming event. Its imminence is, today, not an article of faith; it is a datum of observation and experience.[9]

A powerful crescendo can be sensed in the dramatic series of pronouncements, uttered by some of the West's great thinkers and visionaries, concerning an imminent shift in the ages. Nietzsche, in whom "nihilism became conscious for the first time" (Camus), who had foreseen the cataclysm that would befall European civilization in the twentieth century, realized within himself the epochal crisis that would finally come when the modern mind became conscious of its destruction of the metaphysical world, "the death of God":

> What were we doing when we unchained this earth from its sun? Whither is it moving now? Whither are we moving? Away from all suns? Are we not plunging continually? Backward, sideward, forward, in all directions? Is there still any up or down? Are we not straying as through an infinite nothing? Do we not feel the breath of empty space? Has it not become colder? Is not night continually closing in on us?[10]

And so also the great sociologist Max Weber, who saw the ineluctable consequences of the modern mind's disenchantment of the world, saw the yawning void of relativism left by modernity's dissolution of traditional world views, and saw that modern reason, in which the Enlightenment had placed all its hopes for human freedom and progress, yet which could not on its own terms justify universal values to guide human life, had in fact created an iron cage of bureaucratic rationality that permeated every aspect of modern existence:

> No one knows who will live in this cage in the future, or whether at the end of this tremendous development entirely new prophets will arise, or there will be a great rebirth of old ideas and ideals, or if neither, mechanized petrification, embellished with a sort of convulsive self-importance. For of the last stage of this cultural development, it might well be truly said: "Specialists without spirit, sensualists without heart; this nullity imagines that it has attained a level of civilization never before achieved."[11]

"Only a god can save us," said Heidegger at the end of his life. And Jung, at the end of his, comparing our age to the beginning of the Christian era two millennia ago, wrote:

> [A] mood of universal destruction and renewal . . . has set its mark on our age. This mood makes itself felt everywhere, politically, socially, and philosophically. We are living in what the Greeks called the *kairos*—the right moment—for a "metamorphosis of the gods," of the fundamental principles and symbols. This peculiarity of our time, which is certainly not of our conscious choosing, is the expression of the unconscious man within us who is changing.

Coming generations will have to take account of this momentous transformation if humanity is not to destroy itself through the might of its own technology and science. . . . So much is at stake and so much depends on the psychological constitution of modern man. . . . Does the individual know that *he* is the makeweight that tips the scales?[12]

Our moment in history is indeed a pregnant one. As a civilization and as a species we have come to a moment of truth, with the future of the human spirit, and the future of the planet, hanging in the balance. If ever boldness, depth, and clarity of vision were called for, from many, it is now. Yet perhaps it is this very necessity that could summon forth from us the courage and imagination we now require. Let us give the last words of this unfinished epic to Nietzsche's Zarathustra:

And how could I endure to be a man, if man were not also poet and reader of riddles and . . . a way to new dawns.

VII

Epilogue

We may be seeing the beginnings of the reintegration of our culture, a new possibility of the unity of consciousness. If so, it will not be on the basis of any new orthodoxy, either religious or scientific. Such a new integration will be based on the rejection of all univocal understandings of reality, of all identifications of one conception of reality with reality itself. It will recognize the multiplicity of the human spirit, and the necessity to translate constantly between different scientific and imaginative vocabularies. It will recognize the human proclivity to fall comfortably into some single literal interpretation of the world and therefore the necessity to be continuously open to rebirth in a new heaven and a new earth. It will recognize that in both scientific and religious culture all we have finally are symbols, but that there is an enormous difference between the dead letter and the living word.

Robert Bellah
Beyond Belief

In these final pages, I would like to present an interdisciplinary framework that may help deepen our understanding of the extraordinary history just recounted. I would also like to share with the reader a few concluding reflections on where we, as a culture, may be headed. Let us begin with a brief overview of the background to our present intellectual situation.

The Post-Copernican Double Bind

In a narrow sense, the Copernican revolution can be understood as simply a specific paradigm shift in modern astronomy and cosmology, initiated by Copernicus, established by Kepler and Galileo, and completed by Newton. Yet the Copernican revolution can also be understood in a much wider and more significant sense. For when Copernicus recognized that the Earth was not the absolute fixed center of the universe, and, equally important, when he recognized that the movement of the heavens could be explained in terms of the movement of the observer, he brought forth what was perhaps the pivotal insight of the modern mind. The Copernican shift of perspective can be seen as a fundamental metaphor for the entire modern world view: the profound deconstruction of the naive understanding, the critical recognition that the apparent condition of the objective world was unconsciously determined by the condition of the subject, the consequent liberation from the ancient and medieval cosmic womb, the radical displacement of the human being to a relative and peripheral position in a vast and impersonal universe, the ensuing disenchantment of the natural world. In this broadest sense—as an event that took place not only in astronomy and the sciences but in philosophy and religion and in the collective human psyche—the Copernican revolution can be seen as constituting *the* epochal shift of the modern age. It was a primordial event, world-destroying and world-constituting.

In philosophy and epistemology, this larger Copernican revolution took place in the dramatic series of intellectual advances that began with Descartes and culminated in Kant. It has been said that Descartes and Kant were both inevitable in the development of the modern mind, and I believe this is correct. For it was Descartes who first fully grasped and articulated the experience of the emerging autonomous modern self as being fundamentally distinct and separate from an objective external world that it seeks to understand and master. Descartes "woke up in a Copernican universe":[1] after Copernicus, humankind was on its own in the universe, its cosmic place irrevocably relativized. Descartes then drew out and expressed in philosophical terms the experiential consequence of that new cosmological context, starting from a position of fundamental doubt vis-à-vis the world, and ending in the *cogito*. In doing this, he set into motion a train of philosophical events—leading from Locke to Berkeley and Hume and culminating in Kant—that eventually produced a great epistemological crisis. Descartes was in this sense the crucial midpoint between Copernicus and Kant, between the Copernican revolution in cosmology and the Copernican revolution in epistemology.

For if the human mind was in some sense fundamentally distinct and different from the external world, and if the only reality that the human mind had direct access to was its own experience, then the world apprehended by the mind was ultimately only the mind's interpretation of the world. Human knowledge of reality had to be forever incommensurate with its goal, for there was no guarantee that the human mind could ever accurately mirror a world with which its connection was so indirect and mediated. Instead, everything that this mind could perceive and judge would be to some undefined extent determined by its own character, its own subjective structures. The mind could experience only phenomena, not things-in-themselves; appearances, not an independent reality. In the modern universe, the human mind was on its own.

Thus Kant, building on his empiricist predecessors, drew out the epistemological consequences of the Cartesian *cogito*. Of course Kant himself set forth cognitive principles, subjective structures, that he thought were absolute—the a priori forms and categories—on the basis of the apparent certainties of Newtonian physics. As time passed, however, what endured from Kant was not the specifics of his solution but rather the profound problem he articulated. For Kant had drawn attention to the crucial fact that all human knowledge is interpretive. The human mind can claim no direct mirrorlike knowledge of the objective world, for the object it experiences has already been structured by the subject's own internal organization. The human being knows not the world-in-itself but rather the world as rendered by the human mind. Thus Descartes's ontological schism was both made more absolute and superseded by Kant's epistemological schism. The gap between subject and object could not be certifiably bridged. From the Cartesian premise came the Kantian result.

In the subsequent evolution of the modern mind, each of these fundamental shifts, which I am associating here symbolically with the figures of Copernicus, Descartes, and Kant, has been sustained, extended, and pressed to its extreme. Thus Copernicus's radical displacement of the human being from the cosmic center was emphatically reinforced and intensified by Darwin's relativization of the human being in the flux of evolution—no longer divinely ordained, no longer absolute and secure, no longer the crown of creation, the favored child of the universe, but rather just one more ephemeral species. Placed in the vastly expanded cosmos of modern astronomy, the human being now spins adrift, once the noble center of the cosmos, now an insignificant inhabitant of a tiny planet revolving around an undistinguished star—the familiar litany—at the edge of one galaxy among billions, in an indifferent and ultimately hostile universe.

In the same way, Descartes's schism between the personal and conscious human subject and the impersonal and unconscious material universe was systematically ratified and augmented by the long procession of subsequent scientific developments, from Newtonian physics all the way to contemporary big-bang cosmology, black holes, quarks, W and Z particles, and grand unified superforce theories. The world revealed by modern science has been a world devoid of spiritual purpose, opaque, ruled by chance and necessity, without intrinsic meaning. The human soul has not felt at home in the modern cosmos: the soul can hold dear its poetry and its music, its private metaphysics and religion, but these find no certain foundation in the empirical universe.

And so too with the third of this trinity of modern alienation, the great schism established by Kant—and here we see the pivot of the shift from the modern to the postmodern. For Kant's recognition of the human mind's subjective ordering of reality, and thus, finally, the relative and unrooted nature of human knowledge, has been extended and deepened by a host of subsequent developments, from anthropology, linguistics, sociology of knowledge, and quantum physics to cognitive psychology, neurophysiology, semiotics, and philosophy of science; from Marx, Nietzsche, Weber, and Freud to Heisenberg, Wittgenstein, Kuhn, and Foucault. The consensus is decisive: The world is in some essential sense a construct. Human knowledge is radically interpretive. There are no perspective-independent facts. Every act of perception and cognition is contingent, mediated, situated, contextual, theory-soaked. Human language cannot establish its ground in an independent reality. Meaning is rendered by the mind and cannot be assumed to inhere in the object, in the world beyond the mind, for that world can never be contacted without having already been saturated by the mind's own nature. That world cannot even be justifiably postulated. Radical uncertainty prevails, for in the end what one knows and experiences is to an indeterminate extent a projection.

Thus the cosmological estrangement of modern consciousness initiated by Copernicus and the ontological estrangement initiated by Descartes were completed by the epistemological estrangement initiated by Kant: a threefold mutually enforced prison of modern alienation.

I would like to point out here the striking resemblance between this state of affairs and the condition that Gregory Bateson famously described as the "double bind": the impossibly problematic situation in which mutually contradictory demands eventually lead a person to become schizophrenic.[2] In Bateson's formulation, there were four basic premises necessary to constitute a double bind situation between a child and a "schizophrenogenic" mother: (1) The child's relationship to the mother is one of vital dependency, thereby making it critical for the child to assess communications from the mother accurately. (2) The child receives contradictory or incompatible information from the mother at different levels, whereby, for example, her explicit verbal communication is fundamentally denied by the "metacommunication," the nonverbal context in which the explicit message is conveyed (thus the mother who says to her child with hostile eyes and a rigid body, "Darling, you know I love you so much"). The two sets of signals cannot be understood as coherent. (3) The child is not given any opportunity to ask questions of the mother that would clarify the communication or resolve the contradiction. And (4) the child cannot leave the field, i.e., the relationship. In such circumstances, Bateson found, the child is forced to distort his or her perception of both outer and inner realities, with serious psychopathological consequences.

Now if we substitute in these four premises *world* for mother, and *human being* for child, we have the modern double bind in a nutshell: (1) The human being's relationship to the world is one of vital dependency, thereby making it critical for the human being to assess the nature of that world accurately. (2) The human mind receives contradictory or incompatible information about its situation with respect to the world, whereby its inner psychological and spiritual sense of things is incoherent with the scientific metacommunication. (3) Epistemologically, the human mind cannot achieve direct communication with the world. (4) Existentially, the human being cannot leave the field.

The differences between Bateson's psychiatric double bind and the modern existential condition are more in degree than in kind: the modern condition is an extraordinarily encompassing and fundamental double bind, made less immediately conspicuous simply because it is so universal. We have the post-Copernican dilemma of being a peripheral and insignificant inhabitant of a vast cosmos, and the post-Cartesian dilemma of being a conscious, purposeful, and personal subject confronting an unconscious, purposeless, and impersonal universe, with these compounded by the post-Kantian dilemma of there being no possible means by which the human subject can know the universe in its essence. We are evolved from, embedded in, and defined by a reality that is radically alien to our own, and moreover cannot ever be directly contacted in cognition.

This double bind of modern consciousness has been recognized in one form or another since at least Pascal: "I am terrified by the eternal silence of these infinite spaces." Our psychological and spiritual predispositions are absurdly at variance with the world revealed by our scientific method. We seem to receive two messages from our existential situation: on the one hand, strive, give oneself to the quest for meaning and spiritual fulfillment; but on the other hand, know that the universe, of whose substance we are derived, is entirely indifferent to that quest, soulless in character, and nullifying in its effects. We are at once aroused and crushed. For inexplicably, absurdly, the cosmos is inhuman, yet we are not. The situation is profoundly unintelligible.

If we follow Bateson's diagnosis and apply it to the larger modern condition, it should not be surprising what kinds of response the modern psyche has made to this situation as it attempts to escape the double bind's inherent contradictions. Either inner or outer realities tend to be distorted: inner feelings are repressed and denied, as in apathy and psychic numbing, or they are inflated in compensation, as in narcissism and egocentrism; or the outer world is slavishly submitted to as the only reality, or it is aggressively objectified and exploited. There is also the strategy of flight, through various forms of escapism: compulsive economic consumption, absorption in the mass media, faddism, cults, ideologies, nationalistic fervor, alcoholism, drug addiction. When avoidance mechanisms cannot be sustained, there is anxiety, paranoia, chronic hostility, a feeling of helpless victimization, a tendency to suspect all meanings, an impulse toward self-negation, a sense of purposelessness and absurdity, a feeling of irresolvable inner contradiction, a fragmenting of consciousness. And at the extreme, there are the full-blown psychopathological reactions of the schizophrenic: self-destructive violence, delusional states, massive amnesia, catatonia, automatism, mania, nihilism. The modern world knows each of these reactions in various combinations and compromise formations, and its social and political life is notoriously so determined.

Nor should it be surprising that twentieth-century philosophy finds itself in the condition we now see. Of course modern philosophy has brought forth some courageous intellectual responses to the post-Copernican situation, but by and large the philosophy that has dominated our century and our universities resembles nothing so much as a severe obsessive-compulsive sitting on his bed repeatedly tying and untying his shoes because he never quite gets it right—while in the meantime Socrates and Hegel and Aquinas are already high up the mountain on their hike, breathing the bracing alpine air, seeing new and unexpected vistas.

But there is one crucial way in which the modern situation is not identical to the psychiatric double bind, and this is the fact that the modern human being has not simply been a helpless child, but has actively engaged the world and pursued a specific strategy and mode of activity—a Promethean project of freeing itself from and controlling nature. The modern mind has demanded a specific type of interpretation of the world: its scientific method has required explanations of phenomena that are concretely predictive, and therefore impersonal, mechanistic, structural. To fulfill their purposes, these explanations of the universe have been systematically "cleansed" of all spiritual and human qualities. Of course we cannot be certain that the world *is* in fact what these explanations suggest. We can be certain only that the world is to an indeterminate extent *susceptible* to this way of interpretation. Kant's insight is a sword that cuts two ways. Although on the one hand it appears to place the world beyond the grasp of the human mind, on the other hand it recognizes that the impersonal and soulless world of modern scientific cognition is not necessarily the whole story. Rather, that world is the only kind of story that for the past three centuries the Western mind has considered intellectually justifiable. In Ernest Gellner's words, "It was Kant's merit to see that this compulsion [for mechanistic impersonal explanation] is in us, not in things." And "it was Weber's to see that it is historically a specific kind of mind, not human mind as such, that is subject to this compulsion."[3]

Hence one crucial part of the modern double bind is not airtight. In the case of Bateson's schizophrenogenic mother and child, the mother more or less holds all the cards, for she unilaterally controls the communication. But the lesson of Kant is that the locus of the communication problem—i.e., the problem of human knowledge of the world—must first be viewed as centering in the human mind, not in the world as such. Therefore it is theoretically possible that the human mind has more cards than it has been playing. The pivot of the modern predicament is epistemological, and it is here that we should look for an opening.

Knowledge and the Unconscious

When Nietzsche in the nineteenth century said there are no facts, only interpretations, he was both summing up the legacy of eighteenth-century critical philosophy and pointing toward the task and promise of twentieth-century depth psychology. That an unconscious part of the psyche exerts decisive influence over human perception, cognition, and behavior was an idea long developing in Western thought, but it was Freud who effectively brought it into the foreground of modern intellectual concern. Freud played a fascinatingly multiple role in the unfolding of the greater Copernican revolution. On the one hand, as he said in the famous passage at the end of the eighteenth of his Introductory Lectures, psychoanalysis represented the third wounding blow to man's naive pride and self-love, the first being Copernicus's heliocentric theory, and the second being Darwin's theory of evolution. For psychoanalysis revealed that not only is the Earth not the center of the universe, and not only is man not the privileged focus of creation, but even the human mind and ego, man's most precious sense of being a conscious rational self, is only a recent and precarious development out of the primordial id, and is by no means master of its own house. With his epochal insight into the unconscious determinants of human experience, Freud stood directly in the Copernican lineage of modern thought that progressively relativized the status of the human being. And again, like Copernicus and like Kant but on an altogether new level, Freud brought the fundamental recognition that the apparent reality of the objective world was being unconsciously determined by the condition of the subject.

But Freud's insight too was a sword that cut both ways, and in a significant sense Freud represented the crucial turning point in the modern trajectory. For the discovery of the unconscious collapsed the old boundaries of interpretation. As Descartes and the post-Cartesian British empiricists had noted, the primary datum in human experience is ultimately human experience itself—not the material world, and not sensory transforms of that world; and with psychoanalysis was begun the systematic exploration of the seat of all human experience and cognition, the human psyche. From Descartes to Locke, Berkeley, and Hume, and then to Kant, the progress of modern epistemology had depended on increasingly acute analyses of the role played by the human mind in the act of cognition. With this background, and with the further steps taken by Schopenhauer, Nietzsche, and others, the analytic task established by Freud was in a sense ineluctable. The modern psychological imperative, to recover the unconscious, precisely coincided with the modern epistemological imperative—to discover the root principles of mental organization.

But while it was Freud who penetrated the veil, it was Jung who grasped the critical philosophical consequences of depth psychology's discoveries. Partly this was because Jung was more epistemologically sophisticated than Freud, having been steeped in Kant and critical philosophy from his youth (even in the 1930s Jung was an informed reader of Karl Popper—which comes as a surprise to many Jungians).[4] Partly this was also because by intellectual temperament Jung was less bound than Freud by nineteenth-century scientism. But above all, Jung had the more profound experience to draw upon, and could see the larger context within which depth psychology was operating. As Joseph Campbell used to say, Freud was fishing while sitting on a whale—he didn't realize what he had before him. But of course who of us does, and we all depend on our successors to overleap our own limitations.

Thus it was Jung who recognized that critical philosophy was, as he put it, "the mother of modern psychology."[5] Kant was correct when he saw that human experience was not atomistic, as Hume had thought, but instead was permeated by a priori structures; yet Kant's formulation of those structures, reflecting his complete belief in Newtonian physics, was inevitably too narrow and simplistic. In a sense, just as Freud's understanding of the mind had been limited by his Darwinian presuppositions, so was Kant's understanding limited by his Newtonian presuppositions. Jung, under the impact of far more powerful and extensive experiences of the human psyche, both his own and others, pushed the Kantian and Freudian perspectives all the way until he reached a kind of holy grail of the inner quest: the discovery of the universal archetypes in all their power and rich complexity as the fundamental determining structures of human experience.

Freud had discovered Oedipus and Id and Superego and Eros and Thanatos; he had recognized the instincts in essentially archetypal terms. But at crucial junctures, his reductionist presuppositions drastically restricted his vision. With Jung, however, the full symbolic multivalence of the archetypes was disclosed, and the personal unconscious of Freud, which comprised mainly repressed contents resulting from biographical traumas and the ego's antipathy to the instincts, opened into a vast archetypally patterned collective unconscious which was not so much the result of repression as it was the primordial foundation of the psyche itself. With its progressively unfolding disclosure of the unconscious, depth psychology radically redefined the epistemological riddle that had first been posed by Kant—Freud doing so narrowly and inadvertently as it were, and then Jung doing so on a more comprehensive and self-aware level.

Yet what was the actual nature of these archetypes, what was this collective unconscious, and how did any of this affect the modern scientific world view? Although the Jungian archetypal perspective greatly enriched and deepened the modern understanding of the psyche, in certain ways it too could be seen as merely reinforcing the Kantian epistemological alienation. As Jung repeatedly emphasized for many years in his loyal Kantian way, the discovery of the archetypes was the result of the empirical investigation of psychological phenomena and therefore had no necessary metaphysical implications. The study of the mind rendered knowledge of the mind, not of the world beyond the mind. Archetypes so conceived were psychological, hence in a certain way subjective. Like Kant's a priori forms and categories, they structured human experience without giving the human mind any direct knowledge of reality beyond itself; they were inherited structures or dispositions that preceded human experience and determined its character, but they could not be said to transcend the human psyche. They were perhaps only the most fundamental of the many distorting lenses that distanced the human mind from genuine knowledge of the world. They were perhaps only the deepest patterns of human projection.

But of course Jung's thought was extremely complex, and in the course of his very long intellectually active life his conception of the archetypes went through a significant evolution. The conventional and still most widely known view of Jungian archetypes, just described, was based on Jung's middle-period writings when his thought was still largely governed by Cartesian-Kantian philosophical assumptions concerning the nature of the psyche and its separation from the external world. In his later work, however, and particularly in relation to his study of synchronicities, Jung began to move toward a conception of archetypes as autonomous patterns of meaning that appear to structure and inhere in both psyche and matter, thereby in effect dissolving the modern subject-object dichotomy. Archetypes in this view were more mysterious than a priori categories—more ambiguous in their ontological status, less easily restricted to a specific dimension, more like the original Platonic and Neoplatonic conception of archetypes. Some aspects of this late-Jungian development have been pressed further, brilliantly and controversially, by James Hillman and the school of archetypal psychology, which has developed a "postmodern" Jungian perspective: recognizing the primacy of the psyche and the imagination, and the irreducible psychic reality and potency of the archetypes, but, unlike the late Jung, largely avoiding metaphysical or theological statements in favor of a full embrace of psyche in all its endless and rich ambiguity.

But the most epistemologically significant development in the recent history of depth psychology, and indeed the most important advance in the field as a whole since Freud and Jung themselves, has been the work of Stanislav Grof, which over the past three decades has not only revolutionized psychodynamic theory but also brought forth major implications for many other fields, including philosophy. Many readers will already be familiar with Grof's work, particularly in Europe and California, but for those who are not I will give here a brief summary.[6] Grof began as a psychoanalytic psychiatrist, and the original background of his ideas was Freudian, not Jungian; yet the unexpected upshot of his work was to ratify Jung's archetypal perspective on a new level, and bring it into coherent synthesis with Freud's biological and biographical perspective, though on a much deeper stratum of the psyche than Freud had recognized.

The basis of Grof's discoveries was his observation of several thousand psychoanalytic sessions, first in Prague and then in Maryland with the National Institute of Mental Health, in which subjects used extremely potent psychoactive substances, particularly LSD, and then later a variety of powerful nondrug therapeutic methods, which served as catalysts of unconscious processes. Grof found that subjects involved in these sessions tended to undergo progressively deeper explorations of the unconscious, in the course of which there consistently emerged a pivotal sequence of experiences of great complexity and intensity. In the initial sessions, subjects typically moved back through earlier and earlier biographical experiences and traumas—the Oedipus complex, toilet training, nursing, early infantile experiences—which were generally intelligible in terms of Freudian psychoanalytic principles and appeared to represent something like laboratory evidence for the basic correctness of Freud's theories. But after reliving and integrating these various memory complexes, subjects regularly tended to move further back into an extremely intense engagement with the process of biological birth.

Although this process was experienced on a biological level in the most explicit and detailed manner, it was informed by, or saturated by, a distinct archetypal sequence of considerable numinous power. Subjects reported that experiences at this level possessed an intensity and universality that far surpassed what they had previously believed was the experiential limit for an individual human being. These experiences occurred in a highly variable order, and overlapped with each other in very complex ways, but abstracting from this complexity Grof found visible a distinct sequence—which moved from an initial condition of undifferentiated unity with the maternal womb, to an experience of sudden fall and separation from that primal organismic unity, to a highly charged life-and-death struggle with the contracting uterus and the birth canal, and culminating in an experience of complete annihilation. This was followed almost immediately by an experience of sudden unexpected global liberation, which was typically perceived not only as physical birth but also as spiritual rebirth, with the two mysteriously intermixed.

I should mention here that I lived for over ten years at Esalen Institute in Big Sur, California, where I was the director of programs, and in the course of those years virtually every conceivable form of therapy and personal transformation, great and small, came through Esalen. In terms of therapeutic effectiveness, Grof's was by far the most powerful; there was no comparison. Yet the price was dear—in a sense the price was absolute: the reliving of one's birth was experienced in a context of profound existential and spiritual crisis, with great physical agony, unbearable constriction and pressure, extreme narrowing of mental horizons, a sense of hopeless alienation and the ultimate meaninglessness of life, a feeling of going irrevocably insane, and finally a shattering experiential encounter with death—with losing everything, physically, psychologically, intellectually, spiritually. Yet after integrating this long experiential sequence, subjects regularly reported experiencing a dramatic expansion of horizons, a radical change of perspective as to the nature of reality, a sense of sudden awakening, a feeling of being fundamentally reconnected to the universe, all accompanied by a profound sense of psychological healing and spiritual liberation. Later in these sessions and in subsequent ones, subjects reported having access to memories of prenatal intrauterine existence, which typically emerged in association with archetypal experiences of paradise, mystical union with nature or with the divine or with the Great Mother Goddess, dissolution of the ego in ecstatic unity with the universe, absorption into the transcendent One, and other forms of mystical unitive experience. Freud called the intimations of this level of experience that he had observed the "oceanic feeling," though for Freud this referred only as far back as infant nursing experiences of unity with the mother at the breast—a less profound version of the primal undifferentiated consciousness of the intrauterine condition.

In terms of psychotherapy, Grof found that the deepest source of psychological symptoms and distress reached back far past childhood traumas and biographical events to the experience of birth itself, intimately interwoven with the encounter with death. When successfully resolved, this experience tended to result in a dramatic disappearance of long-standing psychopathological problems, including conditions and symptoms that had proved entirely recalcitrant to previous therapeutic programs. I should emphasize here that this "perinatal" (surrounding birth) sequence of experiences typically took place on several levels at once, but it virtually always had an intense somatic component. The physical catharsis involved in reliving the birth trauma was extremely powerful, and clearly suggested the reason for the relative ineffectiveness of most psychoanalytic forms of therapy, which have been based largely on verbal interaction and by comparison seem scarcely to scratch the surface. The perinatal experiences that emerged in Grof's work were preverbal, cellular, elemental. They took place only when the ego's usual capacity for control had been overcome, either through the use of a catalytic psychoactive substance or therapeutic technique, or through the spontaneous force of the unconscious material.

Yet these experiences were also profoundly archetypal in character. Indeed, the encounter with this perinatal sequence constantly brought home to subjects a sense that nature itself, including the human body, was the repository and vessel of the archetypal, that nature's processes were archetypal processes—an insight that both Freud and Jung had approached, but from opposite directions. In a sense Grof's work gave a more explicit biological ground to the Jungian archetypes, while giving a more explicit archetypal ground to the Freudian instincts. The encounter with birth and death in this sequence seemed to represent a kind of transduction point between dimensions, a pivot that linked the biological and the archetypal, the Freudian and the Jungian, the biographical and the collective, the personal and the transpersonal, body and spirit. In retrospect, the evolution of psychoanalysis can be seen as having gradually pressed the Freudian biographical-biological perspective back to earlier and earlier periods of individual life, until, reaching the encounter with birth itself, that strategy culminated in a decisive negation of orthodox Freudian reductionism, opening the psychoanalytic conception to a radically more complex and expanded ontology of human experience. The result has been an understanding of the psyche that, like the experience of the perinatal sequence itself, is irreducibly multidimensional.

A host of implications from Grof's work could be discussed here— insights concerning the roots of male sexism in the unconscious fear of female birthing bodies; concerning the roots of the Oedipus complex in the far more primal and fundamental struggle against the seemingly punitive uterine contractions and constricting birth canal to regain union with the nourishing maternal womb; concerning the therapeutic importance of the encounter with death; concerning the roots of specific psychopathological conditions such as depression, phobias, obsessive-compulsive neurosis, sexual disorders, sadomasochism, mania, suicide, addiction, various psychotic conditions, as well as collective psychological disorders such as the impulse toward war and totalitarianism. One could discuss the superbly clarifying synthesis Grof's work achieved in psychodynamic theory, bringing together not only Freud and Jung but Reich, Rank, Adler, Ferenczi, Klein, Fairbairn, Winnicott, Erikson, Maslow, Perls, Laing. My concern here, however, is not psychotherapeutic but philosophical, and while this perinatal area constituted the crucial threshold for therapeutic transformation, it also proved to be the pivotal area for major philosophical and intellectual issues. Hence I will limit this discussion to the specific consequences and implications that Grof's work holds for our present epistemological situation.

In this context, certain crucial generalizations from the clinical evidence are relevant:

First, the archetypal sequence that governed the perinatal phenomena from womb through birth canal to birth was experienced above all as a powerful *dialectic*—moving from an initial state of undifferentiated unity to a problematic state of constriction, conflict, and contradiction, with an accompanying sense of separation, duality, and alienation; and finally moving through a stage of complete annihilation to an unexpected redemptive liberation that both overcame and fulfilled the intervening alienated state—restoring the initial unity but on a new level that preserved the achievement of the whole trajectory.

Second, this archetypal dialectic was often experienced simultaneously on both an individual level and, often more powerfully, a collective level, so that the movement from primordial unity through alienation to liberating resolution was experienced in terms of the evolution of an entire culture, for example, or of humankind as a whole—the birth of Homo sapiens out of nature no less than the birth of the individual child from the mother. Here personal and transpersonal were equally present, inextricably fused, so that ontogeny not only recapitulated phylogeny but in some sense opened out into it.

And third, this archetypal dialectic was experienced or registered in several dimensions—physical, psychological, intellectual, spiritual—often more than one of these at a time, and sometimes all simultaneously in complex combination. As Grof has emphasized, the clinical evidence suggests not that this perinatal sequence should be seen as simply reducible to the birth trauma; rather, it appears that the biological process of birth is itself an expression of a larger underlying archetypal process that can manifest in many dimensions. Thus:

• In *physical* terms, the perinatal sequence was experienced as biological gestation and birth, moving from the symbiotic union with the all-encompassing nourishing womb, through a gradual growth of complexity and individuation within that matrix, to an encounter with the contracting uterus, the birth canal, and finally delivery.

• In *psychological* terms, the experience was one of movement from an initial condition of undifferentiated pre-egoic consciousness to a state of increasing individuation and separation between self and world, increasing existential alienation, and finally an experience of ego death followed by psychological rebirth; this was often complexly associated with the biographical experience of moving from the womb of childhood through the labor of life and the contraction of aging to the encounter with death.

• On the *religious* level, this experiential sequence took a wide variety of forms, but especially frequent was the Judaeo-Christian symbolic movement from the primordial Garden through the Fall, the exile into separation from divinity, into the world of suffering and mortality, followed by the redemptive crucifixion and resurrection, bringing the reunion of the divine and the human. On an individual level, the experience of this perinatal sequence closely resembled—indeed, it appeared to be essentially identical to—the death-rebirth initiation of the ancient mystery religions.

• Finally, on the *philosophical* level, the experience was comprehensible in what might be called Neoplatonic-Hegelian-Nietzschean terms as a dialectical evolution from an archetypally structured primordial Unity, through an emanation into matter with increasing complexity, multiplicity, and individuation, through a state of absolute alienation—the death of God in both Hegel's and Nietzsche's senses—followed by a dramatic *Aufhebung,* a synthesis and reunification with self-subsistent Being that both annihilates and fulfills the individual trajectory.

This multileveled experiential sequence holds relevance for an extraordinary range of important issues, but it is the epistemological implications that are especially significant for our contemporary intellectual situation.[7] For from the perspective suggested by this evidence, the fundamental subject-object dichotomy that has governed and defined modern consciousness—that has *constituted* modern consciousness, that has been generally assumed to be absolute, taken for granted as the basis for any "realistic" perspective and experience of the world—appears to be rooted in a specific archetypal condition associated with the unresolved trauma of human birth, in which an original consciousness of undifferentiated organismic unity with the mother, a *participation mystique* with nature, has been outgrown, disrupted, and lost. Here, on both the individual and the collective levels, can be seen the source of the profound dualism of the modern mind: between man and nature, between mind and matter, between self and other, between experience and reality—that pervading sense of a separate ego irrevocably divided from the encompassing world. Here is the painful separation from the timeless all-encompassing womb of nature, the development of human self-consciousness, the loss of connection with the matrix of being, the expulsion from the Garden, the entrance into time and history and materiality, the disenchantment of the cosmos, the sense of total immersion in an antithetical world of impersonal forces. Here is the experience of the universe as ultimately indifferent, hostile, inscrutable. Here is the compulsive striving to liberate oneself from nature's power, to control and dominate the forces of nature, even to revenge oneself against nature. Here is the primal fear of losing control and dominance, rooted in the all-consuming awareness and fear of death—the inevitable accompaniment of the individual ego's emergence out of the collective matrix. But above all, here is the profound sense of ontological and epistemological separation between self and world.

This fundamental sense of separation is then structured into the legitimated interpretive principles of the modern mind. It was no accident that the man who first systematically formulated the separate modern rational self, Descartes, was also the man who first systematically formulated the mechanistic cosmos for the Copernican revolution. The basic a priori categories and premises of modern science, with its assumption of an independent external world that must be investigated by an autonomous human reason, with its insistence on impersonal mechanistic explanation, with its rejection of spiritual qualities in the cosmos, its repudiation of any intrinsic meaning or purpose in nature, its demand for a univocal, literal interpretation of a world of hard facts—all of these ensure the construction of a disenchanted and alienating world view. As Hillman has emphasized: "The evidence we gather in support of a hypothesis and the rhetoric we use to argue it are already part of the archetypal constellation we are in. . . . The 'objective' idea we find in the pattern of data is also the 'subjective' idea by means of which we see the data."[8]

From this perspective, the Cartesian-Kantian philosophical assumptions that have governed the modern mind, and that have informed and impelled the modern scientific achievement, reflect the dominance of a powerful archetypal gestalt, an experiential template that selectively filters and shapes human awareness in such a manner that reality is perceived to be opaque, literal, objective, and alien. The Cartesian-Kantian paradigm both expresses and ratifies a state of consciousness in which experience of the unitive numinous depths of reality has been systematically extinguished, leaving the world disenchanted and the human ego isolated. Such a world view is, as it were, a kind of metaphysical and epistemological box, a hermetically closed system that reflects the contracted enclosure of the archetypal birth process. It is the elabo-

rate articulation of a specific archetypal domain within which human awareness is encompassed and confined as if it existed inside a solipsistic bubble.

The great irony suggested here of course is that it is just when the
modern mind believes it has most fully purified itself from any anthropomorphic projections, when it actively construes the world as
unconscious, mechanistic, and impersonal, it is just then that the world
is most completely a selective construct of the human mind. The human
mind has abstracted from the whole all conscious intelligence and purpose and meaning, and claimed these exclusively for itself, and then
projected onto the world a machine. As Rupert Sheldrake has pointed
out, this is the ultimate anthropomorphic projection: a man-made machine, something not in fact ever found in nature. From this perspective,
it is the modern mind's own impersonal soullessness that has been
projected from within onto the world—or, to be more precise, that has
been projectively elicited from the world.

But it has been the fate and burden of depth psychology, that astonishingly seminal tradition founded by Freud and Jung, to mediate the
modern mind's access to archetypal forces and realities that reconnect
the individual self with the world, dissolving the dualistic world view.
Indeed, in retrospect it would seem that it *had* to be depth psychology
that would bring forth awareness of these realities to the modern mind: if
the realm of the archetypal could not be recognized in the philosophy
and religion and science of the high culture, then it had to reemerge from
the underworld of the psyche. As L. L. Whyte has noted, the idea of the
unconscious first appeared and played an increasing role in Western intellectual history almost immediately from the time of Descartes, beginning its slow ascent to Freud. And when, at the start of the twentieth
century, Freud introduced his work to the world in *The Interpretation of
Dreams*, he began with that great epigraph from Virgil which said it all:
"If I cannot bend the Gods above, then I will move the Infernal regions."
The compensation was inevitable—if not above, then from below.

Thus the modern condition begins as a Promethean movement toward
human freedom, toward autonomy from the encompassing matrix of
nature, toward individuation from the collective, yet gradually and
ineluctably the Cartesian-Kantian condition evolves into a Kafka–
Beckett-like state of existential isolation and absurdity—an intolerable
double bind leading to a kind of deconstructive frenzy. And again, the
existential double bind closely mirrors the infant's situation within the
birthing mother: having been symbiotically united with the nourishing

womb, growing and developing within that matrix, the beloved center of an all-comprehending supportive world, yet now alienated from that world, constricted by that womb, forsaken, crushed, strangled, and expelled in a state of extreme confusion and anxiety—an inexplicably incoherent situation of profound traumatic intensity.

Yet full experience of this double bind, of this dialectic between the primordial unity on the one hand and the birth labor and subject-object dichotomy on the other, unexpectedly brings forth a third condition: a redemptive reunification of the individuated self with the universal matrix. Thus the child is born and embraced by the mother, the liberated hero ascends from the underworld to return home after his far-flung odyssey. The individual and the universal are reconciled. The suffering, alienation, and death are now comprehended as necessary for birth, for the creation of the self: *O Felix Culpa.* A situation that was fundamentally unintelligible is now recognized as a necessary element in a larger context of profound intelligibility. The dialectic is fulfilled, the alienation redeemed. The rupture from Being is healed. The world is rediscovered in its primordial enchantment. The autonomous individual self has been forged and is now reunited with the ground of its being.

The Evolution of World Views

All of this suggests that another, more sophisticated and comprehensive epistemological perspective is called for. Although the Cartesian-Kantian epistemological position has been the dominant paradigm of the modern mind, it has not been the only one, for at almost precisely the same time that the Enlightenment reached its philosophical climax in Kant, a radically different epistemological perspective began to emerge—first visible in Goethe with his study of natural forms, developed in new directions by Schiller, Schelling, Hegel, Coleridge, and Emerson, and articulated within the past century by Rudolf Steiner. Each of these thinkers gave his own distinct emphasis to the developing perspective, but common to all was a fundamental conviction that the relation of the human mind to the world was ultimately not dualistic but participatory.

In essence this alternative conception did not oppose the Kantian epistemology but rather went beyond it, subsuming it in a larger and subtler understanding of human knowledge. The new conception fully acknowledged the validity of Kant's critical insight, that all human knowledge of the world is in some sense determined by subjective principles; but instead of considering these principles as belonging ultimately to the separate human subject, and therefore not grounded in the world independent of human cognition, this participatory conception held that these subjective principles are in fact an expression of the world's own being, and that the human mind is ultimately the organ of the world's own process of self-revelation. In this view, the essential reality of nature is not separate, self-contained, and complete in itself, so that the human mind can examine it "objectively" and register it from without. Rather, nature's unfolding truth emerges only with the active participation of the human mind. Nature's reality is not merely phenomenal, nor is it independent and objective; rather, it is something that comes into being through the very act of human cognition. Nature becomes intelligible to itself through the human mind.

In this perspective, nature pervades everything, and the human mind in all its fullness is itself an expression of nature's essential being. And it is only when the human mind actively brings forth from within itself the full powers of a disciplined imagination and saturates its empirical observation with archetypal insight that the deeper reality of the world emerges. A developed inner life is therefore indispensable for cognition. In its most profound and authentic expression, the intellectual imagination does not merely project its ideas into nature from its isolated brain corner. Rather, from within its own depths the imagination directly contacts the creative process within nature, realizes that process within itself, and brings nature's reality to conscious expression. Hence the imaginal intuition is not a subjective distortion but is the human fulfillment of that reality's essential wholeness, which had been rent asunder by the dualistic perception. The human imagination is itself part of the world's intrinsic truth; without it the world is in some sense incomplete. Both major forms of epistemological dualism—the conventional precritical and the post-Kantian critical conceptions of human knowledge—are here countered and synthesized. On the one hand, the human mind does not just produce concepts that "correspond" to an external reality. Yet on the other hand, neither does it simply "impose" its own order on the world. Rather, the world's truth realizes itself within and through the human mind.

This participatory epistemology, developed in different ways by Goethe, Hegel, Steiner, and others, can be understood not as a regression to naive *participation mystique,* but as the dialectical synthesis of the long evolution from the primordial undifferentiated consciousness through the dualistic alienation. It incorporates the postmodern understanding of knowledge and yet goes beyond it. The interpretive and constructive character of human cognition is fully acknowledged, but the intimate, interpenetrating and all-permeating relationship of nature to the human being and human mind allows the Kantian consequence of epistemological alienation to be entirely overcome. The human spirit does not merely prescribe nature's phenomenal order; rather, the spirit of nature brings forth its *own* order through the human mind when that mind is employing its full complement of faculties—intellectual, volitional, emotional, sensory, imaginative, aesthetic, epiphanic. In such knowledge, the human mind "lives into" the creative activity of nature. Then the world speaks its meaning through human consciousness. Then human language itself can be recognized as rooted in a deeper reality, as reflecting the universe's unfolding meaning. Through the human intellect, in all its personal individuality, contingency, and struggle, the world's evolving thought-content achieves conscious articulation. Yes, knowledge of the world is structured by the mind's subjective contribution; but that contribution is teleologically called forth by the universe for its own self-revelation. Human thought does not and cannot mirror a ready-made objective truth in the world; rather, the world's truth achieves its existence when it comes to birth in the human mind. As the plant at a certain stage brings forth its blossom, so does the universe bring forth new stages of human knowledge. And, as Hegel emphasized, the evolution of human knowledge is the evolution of the world's self-revelation.

Such a perspective suggests of course that the Cartesian-Kantian paradigm, and thus the epistemologically enforced double bind of modern consciousness, is not absolute. But if we take this participatory epistemology, and if we combine it with Grof's discovery of the perinatal sequence and its underlying archetypal dialectic, then a more surprising conclusion is suggested: namely, that the Cartesian-Kantian paradigm, and indeed the entire trajectory into alienation taken by the modern mind, has not been simply an error, an unfortunate human aberration, a mere manifestation of human blindness, but has rather reflected a much deeper archetypal process impelled by forces beyond the merely human. For in this view, the powerful contraction of vision experienced by the modern mind has itself been an authentic expression of nature's unfolding, a process enacted through the growingly autonomous human intellect, and now reaching a highly critical stage of transfiguration. From this perspective, the dualistic epistemology derived from Kant and the

Enlightenment is not simply the opposite of the participatory epistemology derived from Goethe and Romanticism, but is rather an important subset of it, a necessary stage in the evolution of the human mind. And if this is true, several long-standing philosophical paradoxes may now be cleared up.

I shall focus here on one especially significant area. Much of the most exciting work in contemporary epistemology has come from philosophy of science, above all from the work of Popper, Kuhn, and Feyerabend. Yet despite this work, or rather because of this work, which has revealed in so many ways the relative and radically interpretive nature of scientific knowledge, philosophers of science have been left with two notoriously fundamental dilemmas—one left by Popper, the other by Kuhn and Feyerabend.

With Popper the problem of scientific knowledge left by Hume and Kant was brilliantly explicated. For Popper, as for the modern mind, man approaches the world as a stranger—but a stranger who has a thirst for explanation, and an ability to invent myths, stories, theories, and a willingness to test these. Sometimes, by luck and hard work and many mistakes, a myth is found to work. The theory saves the phenomena; it is a lucky guess. And this is the greatness of science, that through an occasionally fortunate combination of rigor and inventiveness, a purely human conception can be found to work in the empirical world, at least temporarily. Yet a gnawing question remains for Popper: How, in the end, are successful conjectures, successful myths, possible? How does the human mind ever acquire genuine knowledge if it's just a matter of projected myths that are tested? Why do these myths ever work? If the human mind has no access to a priori certain truth, and if all observations are always already saturated by uncertified assumptions about the world, how could this mind possibly conceive a genuinely successful theory? Popper answered this question by saying that, in the end, it is "luck"—but this answer has never satisfied. For why should the imagination of a *stranger* ever be able to conceive merely from within itself a myth that works so splendidly in the empirical world that whole civilizations can be built on it (as with Newton)? How can something come from nothing?

I believe there is only one plausible answer to this riddle, and it is an answer suggested by the participatory epistemological framework outlined above: namely, that the bold conjectures and myths that the human mind produces in its quest for knowledge ultimately come from something far deeper than a purely human source. They come from the wellspring of nature itself, from the universal unconscious that is bringing forth through the human mind and human imagination its own gradually unfolding reality. In this view, the theory of a Copernicus, a Newton, or an Einstein is not simply due to the luck of a stranger; rather, it reflects the human mind's radical kinship with the cosmos. It reflects the human mind's pivotal role as vehicle of the universe's unfolding meaning. In this view, neither the postmodern skeptic nor the perennialist philosopher is correct in their shared opinion that the modern scientific paradigm is ultimately without any cosmic foundation. For that paradigm is itself part of a larger evolutionary process.

We can now also suggest a resolution to that fundamental problem left by Kuhn—the problem of explaining why in the history of science one paradigm is chosen over another if paradigms are ultimately incommensurable, if they cannot ever be rigorously compared. As Kuhn has pointed out, each paradigm tends to create its own data and its own way of interpreting those data in a manner that is so comprehensive and self-validating that scientists operating within different paradigms seem to exist in altogether different worlds. Although to a given community of scientific interpreters one paradigm seems to be superior to another, there is no way of justifying that superiority if each paradigm governs and saturates its own data base. Nor does any consensus exist among scientists concerning a common measure or value—such as conceptual precision, or coherence, or breadth, or simplicity, or resistance to falsification, or congruence with theories used in other specialties, or fruitfulness in new research findings—that could be used as a universal standard of comparison. Which value is considered most important varies from one scientific era to another, from one discipline to another, even between individual research groups. What, then, can explain the progress of scientific knowledge if, in the end, each paradigm is selectively based on differing modes of interpretation and different sets of data and different scientific values?

Kuhn has always answered this problem by saying that ultimately the decision lies with the ongoing scientific community, which provides the final basis of justification. Yet, as many scientists have complained, this answer seems to undercut the very foundation of the scientific enterprise, leaving it to the mercy of sociological and personal factors that subjectively distort the scientific judgment. And indeed, as Kuhn himself has demonstrated, scientists generally do *not* in practice fundamentally question the governing paradigm or test it against other alternatives, for many reasons—pedagogical, socioeconomic, cultural, psychological—most of them unconscious. Scientists, like everyone else, are attached to their beliefs. What, then, ultimately explains the progression of science from one paradigm to another? Does the evolution of scientific knowledge have anything to do with "truth," or is it a mere artifact of sociology? And more radically, with Paul Feyerabend's dictum that "anything goes" in the battle of paradigms: If *anything* goes, then why ultimately does *one* thing go rather than another? Why is any scientific paradigm judged superior? If anything goes, why does anything go at all?

The answer I am suggesting here is that a paradigm emerges in the history of science, it is recognized as superior, as true and valid, precisely when that paradigm resonates with the current archetypal state of the evolving collective psyche. A paradigm appears to account for more data, and for more important data, it seems more relevant, more cogent, more attractive, fundamentally because it has become archetypally appropriate to that culture or individual at that moment in its evolution. And the dynamics of this archetypal development appear to be essentially identical to the dynamics of the perinatal process. Kuhn's description of the ongoing dialectic between normal science and major paradigm revolutions strikingly parallels the perinatal dynamics described by Grof: The pursuit of knowledge always takes place within a given paradigm, within a conceptual matrix—a womb that provides an intellectually nourishing structure, that fosters growth and increasing complexity and sophistication—until gradually that structure is experienced as constricting, a limitation, a prison, producing a tension of irresolvable contradictions, and finally a crisis is reached. Then some inspired Promethean genius comes along and is graced with an inner breakthrough to a new vision that gives the scientific mind a new sense of being cognitively connected—reconnected—to the world: an intellectual revolution occurs, and a new paradigm is born. Here we see why such geniuses regularly experience their intellectual breakthrough as a profound illumination, a revelation of the divine creative principle itself, as with Newton's exclamation to God, "I think Thy thoughts after Thee!" For the human mind is following the numinous archetypal path that is unfolding from within it.

And here we can see why the same paradigm, such as the Aristotelian or the Newtonian, is perceived as a liberation at one time and then a constriction, a prison, at another. For the *birth* of every new paradigm is also a *conception* in a new conceptual matrix, which begins the process of gestation, growth, crisis, and revolution all over again. Each paradigm is a stage in an unfolding evolutionary sequence, and when that paradigm has fulfilled its purpose, when it has been developed and exploited to its fullest extent, then it loses its numinosity, it ceases to be libidinally charged, it becomes felt as oppressive, limiting, opaque, something to be overcome—while the new paradigm that is emerging is felt as a liberating birth into a new, luminously intelligible universe. Thus the ancient symbolically resonant geocentric universe of Aristotle, Ptolemy, and Dante gradually loses its numinosity, becomes seen as a problem full of contradictions, and with Copernicus and Kepler that numinosity is fully transferred to the heliocentric cosmos. And because the evolution of paradigm shifts is an *archetypal* process, rather than merely either a rational-empirical or a sociological one, this evolution takes place historically both from within and without, both "subjectively" and "objectively." As the inner gestalt changes in the cultural mind, new empirical evidence just happens to appear, pertinent writings from the past suddenly are unearthed, appropriate epistemological justifications are formulated, supportive sociological changes coincidentally take place, new technologies become available, the telescope is invented and just happens to fall into Galileo's hands. As new psychological predispositions and metaphysical assumptions emerge from within the collective mind, from within many individual minds simultaneously, they are matched and encouraged by the synchronistic arrival of new data, new social contexts, new methodologies, new tools that fulfill the emerging archetypal gestalt.

And as with the evolution of scientific paradigms, so with all forms of human thought. The emergence of a new philosophical paradigm, whether that of Plato or Aquinas, Kant or Heidegger, is never simply the result of improved logical reasoning from the observed data. Rather, each philosophy, each metaphysical perspective and epistemology, reflects the emergence of a global experiential gestalt that informs that philosopher's vision, that governs his or her reasoning and observations, and that ultimately affects the entire cultural and sociological context within which the philosopher's vision is taking form.

For the very possibility of a new world view's appearance rests on the underlying archetypal dynamic of the larger culture. Thus the Copernican revolution that emerged during the Renaissance and Reformation perfectly reflected the archetypal moment of modern humanity's birth out of the ancient-medieval cosmic-ecclesiastical womb. And at the other end, the twentieth century's massive and radical breakdown of so many structures—cultural, philosophical, scientific, religious, moral, artistic, social, economic, political, atomic, ecological—all this suggests the necessary deconstruction prior to a new birth. And why is there evident now such a widespread and constantly growing collective impetus in the Western mind to articulate a holistic and participatory world view, visible in virtually every field? The collective psyche seems to be in the grip of a powerful archetypal dynamic in which the long-alienated modern mind is breaking through, out of the contractions of its birth process, out of what Blake called its "mind-forg'd manacles," to rediscover its intimate relationship with nature and the larger cosmos.

And so we can recognize a multiplicity of these archetypal sequences, with each scientific revolution, each change of world view; yet perhaps we can also recognize one overall archetypal dialectic in the evolution of human consciousness that subsumes all of these smaller sequences, one long metatrajectory, beginning with the primordial *participation mystique* and, in a sense, culminating before our eyes. In this light, we can better understand the great epistemological journey of the Western mind from the birth of philosophy out of the mythological consciousness in ancient Greece, through the classical, medieval, and modern eras, to our own postmodern age: the extraordinary succession of world views, the dramatic sequence of transformations in the human mind's apprehension of reality, the mysterious evolution of language, the shifting relationships between universal and particular, transcendent and immanent, concept and percept, conscious and unconscious, subject and object, self and world—the constant movement toward differentiation, the gradual empowerment of the autonomous human intellect, the slow forging of the subjective self, the accompanying disenchantment of the objective world, the suppression and withdrawal of the archetypal, the constellating of the human unconscious, the eventual global alienation, the radical deconstruction, and finally, perhaps, the emergence of a dialectically integrated, participatory consciousness reconnected to the universal.

But to do justice to this complex epistemological progression and to the other great dialectical trajectories of Western intellectual and spiritual history that have paralleled it—cosmological, psychological, religious, existential—would require another book altogether. Instead, I would like to conclude with a brief, very broad overview of this long historical evolution, a kind of archetypal metanarrative, applying on a large scale the insights and perspectives that have been set forth in the foregoing discussion.

Bringing It All Back Home

Many generalizations could be made about the history of the Western mind, but today perhaps the most immediately obvious is that it has been from start to finish an overwhelmingly masculine phenomenon: Socrates, Plato, Aristotle, Paul, Augustine, Aquinas, Luther, Copernicus, Galileo, Bacon, Descartes, Newton, Locke, Hume, Kant, Darwin, Marx, Nietzsche, Freud. . . . The Western intellectual tradition has been produced and canonized almost entirely by men, and informed mainly by male perspectives. This masculine dominance in Western intellectual history has certainly not occurred because women are any less intelligent than men. But can it be attributed *solely* to social restriction? I think not. I believe something more profound is going on here: something archetypal. The masculinity of the Western mind has been pervasive and fundamental, in both men and women, affecting every aspect of Western thought, determining its most basic conception of the human being and the human role in the world. All the major languages within which the Western tradition has developed, from Greek and Latin on, have tended to personify the human species with words that are masculine in gender: *anthrōpos, homo, l'homme, el hombre, l'uomo, chelovek, der Mensch,* man. As the historical narrative in this book has faithfully reflected, it has always been "man" this and "man" that—"the ascent of man," "the dignity of man," "man's relation to God," "man's place in the cosmos," "man's struggle with nature," "the great achievement of modern man," and so forth. The "man" of the Western tradition has been a questing masculine hero, a Promethean biological and metaphysical rebel who has constantly sought freedom and progress for himself, and who has thus constantly striven to differentiate himself from and control the matrix out of which he emerged. This masculine predisposition in the evolution of the Western mind, though largely unconscious, has been not only characteristic of that evolution, but essential to it.[9]

For the evolution of the Western mind has been driven by a heroic impulse to forge an autonomous rational human self by separating it from the primordial unity with nature. The fundamental religious, scientific, and philosophical perspectives of Western culture have all been affected by this decisive masculinity—beginning four millennia ago with the great patriarchal nomadic conquests in Greece and the Levant over the ancient matriarchal cultures, and visible in the West's patriarchal religion from Judaism, its rationalist philosophy from Greece, its objectivist science from modern Europe. All of these have served the cause of evolving the autonomous human will and intellect: the transcendent self, the independent individual ego, the self-determining human being in its uniqueness, separateness, and freedom. But to do this, the masculine mind has repressed the feminine. Whether one sees this in the ancient Greek subjugation and revision of the pre-Hellenic matrifocal mythologies, in the Judaeo-Christian denial of the Great Mother Goddess, or in the Enlightenment's exalting of the coolly self-aware rational ego radically separate from a disenchanted external nature, the evolution of the Western mind has been founded on the repression of the feminine—on the repression of undifferentiated unitary consciousness, of the *participation mystique* with nature: a progressive denial of the *anima mundi*, of the soul of the world, of the community of being, of the all-pervading, of mystery and ambiguity, of imagination, emotion, instinct, body, nature, woman.

But this separation necessarily calls forth a longing for a reunion with that which has been lost—especially after the masculine heroic quest has been pressed to its utmost one-sided extreme in the consciousness of the late modern mind, which in its absolute isolation has appropriated to itself all conscious intelligence in the universe (man alone is a conscious intelligent being, the cosmos is blind and mechanistic, God is dead). Then man faces the existential crisis of being a solitary and mortal conscious ego thrown into an ultimately meaningless and unknowable universe. And he faces the psychological and biological crisis of living in a world that has come to be shaped in such a way that it precisely matches his world view—i.e., in a man-made environment that is increasingly mechanistic, atomized, soulless, and self-destructive. *The crisis of modern man is an essentially masculine crisis,* and I believe that its resolution is already now occurring in the tremendous emergence of the feminine in our culture: visible not only in the rise of feminism, the growing empowerment of women, and the widespread opening up to feminine values by both men and women, and not only in the rapid burgeoning of women's scholarship and gender-sensitive perspectives in virtually every intellectual discipline, but also in the increasing sense of unity with the planet and all forms of nature on it, in the increasing awareness of the ecological and the growing reaction against political and corporate policies supporting the domination and exploitation of the environment, in the growing embrace of the human community, in the accelerating collapse of long-standing political and ideological barriers separating the world's peoples, in the deepening recognition of the value and necessity of partnership, pluralism, and the interplay of many perspectives. It is visible also in the widespread urge to reconnect with the body, the emotions, the unconscious, the imagination and intuition, in the new concern with the mystery of childbirth and the dignity of the maternal, in the growing recognition of an immanent intelligence in nature, in the broad popularity of the Gaia hypothesis. It can be seen in the increasing appreciation of indigenous and archaic cultural perspectives such as the Native American, African, and ancient European, in the new awareness of feminine perspectives of the divine, in the archaeological recovery of the Goddess tradition and the contemporary reemergence of Goddess worship, in the rise of Sophianic Judaeo-Christian theology and the papal declaration of the *Assumptio Mariae*, in the widely noted spontaneous upsurge of feminine archetypal phenomena in individual dreams and psychotherapy. And it is evident as well in the great wave of interest in the mythological perspective, in esoteric disciplines, in Eastern mysticism, in shamanism, in archetypal and transpersonal psychology, in hermeneutics and other non-objectivist epistemologies, in scientific theories of the holonomic universe, morphogenetic fields, dissipative structures, chaos theory, systems theory, the ecology of mind, the participatory universe—the list could go on and on. As Jung prophesied, an epochal shift is taking place in the contemporary psyche, a reconciliation between the two great polarities, a union of opposites: a *hieros gamos* (sacred marriage) between the long-dominant but now alienated masculine and the long-suppressed but now ascending feminine.

And this dramatic development is not just a compensation, not just a return of the repressed, as I believe this has all along been the underlying goal of Western intellectual and spiritual evolution. *For the deepest passion of the Western mind has been to reunite with the ground of its being.* The driving impulse of the West's masculine consciousness has been its dialectical quest not only to realize itself, to forge its own autonomy, but also, finally, to recover its connection with the whole, to come to terms with the great feminine principle in life: to differentiate itself from but then rediscover and reunite with the feminine, with the mystery of life, of nature, of soul. And that reunion can now occur on a new and profoundly different level from that of the primordial unconscious unity, for the long evolution of human consciousness has prepared it to be capable at last of embracing the ground and matrix of its own being freely and consciously. The *telos*, the inner direction and goal, of the Western mind has been to reconnect with the cosmos in a mature *participation mystique,* to surrender itself freely and consciously in the embrace of a larger unity that preserves human autonomy while also transcending human alienation.

But to achieve this reintegration of the repressed feminine, the masculine must undergo a sacrifice, an ego death. The Western mind must be willing to open itself to a reality the nature of which could shatter its most established beliefs about itself and about the world. *This* is where the real act of heroism is going to be. A threshold must now be crossed, a threshold demanding a courageous act of faith, of imagination, of trust in a larger and more complex reality; a threshold, moreover, demanding an act of unflinching self-discernment. And this is the great challenge of our time, the evolutionary imperative for the masculine to see through and overcome its hubris and one-sidedness, to own its unconscious shadow, to choose to enter into a fundamentally new relationship of mutuality with the feminine in all its forms. The feminine then becomes not that which must be controlled, denied, and exploited, but rather fully acknowledged, respected, and responded to for itself. It is recognized: not the objectified "other," but rather source, goal, and immanent presence.

This is the great challenge, yet I believe it is one the Western mind has been slowly preparing itself to meet for its entire existence. I believe that the West's restless inner development and incessantly innovative masculine ordering of reality has been gradually leading, in an immensely long dialectical movement, toward a reconciliation with the lost feminine unity, toward a profound and many-leveled marriage of the masculine and feminine, a triumphant and healing reunion. And I consider that much of the conflict and confusion of our own era reflects the fact that this evolutionary drama may now be reaching its climactic stages.[10] For our time is struggling to bring forth something fundamentally new in human history: We seem to be witnessing, suffering, the birth labor of a new reality, a new form of human existence, a "child" that would be the fruit of this great archetypal marriage, and that would bear within itself all its antecedents in a new form. I therefore would affirm those indispensable ideals expressed by the supporters of feminist, ecological, archaic, and other countercultural and multicultural perspectives. But I would also wish to affirm those who have valued and sustained the central Western tradition, for I believe that this tradition—the entire trajectory from the Greek epic poets and Hebrew prophets on, the long intellectual and spiritual struggle from Socrates and Plato and Paul and Augustine to Galileo and Descartes and Kant and Freud—

that this stupendous Western project should be seen as a necessary and noble part of a great dialectic, and not simply rejected as an imperialist-chauvinist plot. Not only has this tradition achieved that fundamental differentiation and autonomy of the human which alone could allow the possibility of such a larger synthesis, it has also painstakingly prepared the way for its own self-transcendence. Moreover, this tradition possesses resources, left behind and cut off by its own Promethean advance, that we have scarcely begun to integrate—and that, paradoxically, only the opening to the feminine will enable us to integrate. Each perspective, masculine and feminine, is here both affirmed and transcended, recognized as part of a larger whole; for each polarity requires the other for its fulfillment. And their synthesis leads to something beyond itself: It brings an unexpected opening to a larger reality that cannot be grasped before it arrives, because this new reality is itself a creative act.

But why has the pervasive masculinity of the Western intellectual and spiritual tradition suddenly become so apparent to us today, while it remained so invisible to almost every previous generation? I believe this is occurring only now because, as Hegel suggested, a civilization cannot become conscious of itself, cannot recognize its own significance, until it is so mature that it is approaching its own death.

Today we are experiencing something that looks very much like the death of modern man, indeed that looks very much like the death of Western man. Perhaps the end of "man" himself is at hand. But man is not a goal. Man is something that must be overcome—and fulfilled, in the embrace of the feminine.

Chronology

(Dates for events in antiquity are approximate.)

2000 B.C.	Migrations of Greek-speaking Indo-European peoples into Aegean area begin
1950	Hebrew patriarchs migrate from Mesopotamia to Canaan (traditional biblical dating)
1800	Early Mesopotamian astronomical observations recorded
1700	Minoan civilization on Crete at height during next two centuries, influencing Greek mainland
1600	Gradual Greek fusion of Indo-European and pre-Hellenic Mediterranean religions
1450	Fall of Minoan civilization on Crete after invasions and volcanic disasters
1400	Ascendancy of Mycenaean civilization on Greek mainland
1250	Exodus of Hebrews from Egypt under Moses
1200	Trojan War with Mycenaean Greeks
1100	Dorian invasions, end of Mycenaean dominance
1000	David unites kingdom of Israel with capital at Jerusalem
950	Reign of Solomon, building of Temple
900–700	Early books of Hebrew Bible composed Homer's *Iliad* and *Odyssey* composed
776	First Pan-Hellenic Olympic games held at Olympia
750	Greek colonization of Mediterranean spreads
740	First Isaiah fl. in Israel
700	Hesiod's *Theogony*, *Works and Days*
600	Thales of Miletus fl., birth of philosophy
594	Solon reforms government of Athens, establishes rules for public recital of Homeric poems
590	Jeremiah fl. in Israel
586–538	Babylonian captivity of Jews Ezekiel and Second Isaiah fl., prophesy historical redemption Compilation and redaction of Hebrew Scriptures begins

580	Sappho fl., flowering of Greek lyric poetry
570	Anaximander fl., develops systematic cosmology
545	Anaximenes fl., posits transmutations of underlying substance
525	Pythagoras begins philosophical-religious brotherhood, develops synthesis of science and mysticism
520	Xenophanes fl., concept of human progress, philosophical monotheism, skepticism toward anthropomorphic deities
508	Democratic reforms instituted in Athens by Cleisthenes
500	Heraclitus fl., philosophy of pervasive flux, universal Logos
499	Persian wars begin
490	Athens defeats Persian army at Marathon
480	Greeks defeat Persian fleet at Salamis
478	Establishment of Delian League of Greek states led by Athens Period of Athenian ascendancy begins
472	Aeschylus's *The Persians*, rise of Greek tragedy
470	Pindar fl., apex of Greek lyric poetry Parmenides fl., posits logical opposition between appearances and changeless unitary reality
469	Birth of Socrates
465	Aeschylus's *Prometheus Bound*
460	Anaxagoras fl., concept of universal Mind (Nous)
458–429	Age of Pericles
450	Emergence of Sophists begins
447	Building of Parthenon (completed 432)
446	Herodotus writing *History*
441	Sophocles's *Antigone*
431	Euripides's *Medea*
431–404	Peloponnesian War between Athens and Sparta
430	Democritus fl., atomism
429	Sophocles's *Oedipus Rex*
427	Birth of Plato
423	Aristophanes's *The Clouds*
420	Thucydides writing *History of the Peloponnesian War*
415	Euripides's *Trojan Women*

410	Hippocrates fl., lays foundations of ancient medicine
404	Athens defeated by Sparta
399	Trial and execution of Socrates
399–347	Plato's *Dialogues* written
387	Plato founds Academy in Athens
367	Aristotle begins twenty years of study at Plato's Academy
360	Eudoxus formulates first theory of planetary motion
347	Death of Plato
342	Aristotle tutors Alexander in Macedonia
338	Philip II of Macedon subjugates Greece
336	Death of Philip, accession of Alexander
336–323	Conquests of Alexander the Great
335	Aristotle founds Lyceum in Athens
331	Founding of Alexandria in Egypt
323	Death of Alexander Beginning of Hellenistic era (to c. A.D. 312)
322	Death of Aristotle
320	Pyrrho of Elis fl., founder of Skepticism
306	Epicurus founds Epicurean school in Athens
300	Zeno of Citium founds Stoic school in Athens
300–100	Zenith of Alexandria as center of Hellenistic culture Development of humanistic scholarship, science, astrology
295	Euclid's *Elements* codifying classical geometry
280	Museum (*Mouseion*) built in Alexandria
270	Aristarchus proposes heliocentric theory
260	Skepticism taught at Platonic Academy for next two centuries
250	Hebrew Bible translated into Greek by Alexandrian scholars
240	Archimedes fl., develops classical mechanics and mathematics
220	Apollonius of Perga fl., advances astronomy and geometry
146	Greece conquered by Rome
130	Hipparchus fl., makes first comprehensive chart of heavens, develops classical geocentric cosmology
63	Julius Caesar reforms calendar Cicero prosecutes Catiline conspiracy

60	Lucretius's *De Rerum Natura* propounds Epicurus's atomistic theory of universe
58–48	Caesar conquers Gaul, defeats Pompey
45–44	Cicero's philosophical works
44	Julius Caesar assassinated
31	Octavian (Augustus) defeats Antony and Cleopatra Beginning of Roman Empire
29	Livy begins writing history of Rome
23	Horace's *Odes*
19	Virgil's *Aeneid*
8–4 B.C.	Birth of Jesus of Nazareth
8 A.D.	Ovid's *Metamorphoses*
14	Death of Augustus
15	Manilius's *Astronomica*
23	Strabo's *Geography*
29–30	Death of Jesus
35	Conversion of Paul on way to Damascus
40	Philo of Alexandria fl., integration of Judaism and Platonism
48	Council of Apostles at Jerusalem recognizes Paul's mission to Gentiles
50–60	Letters of Paul written
64–68	Apostles Peter and Paul martyred in Rome under Nero First major persecution of Christians
64–70	Gospel according to Mark
70	Temple in Jerusalem destroyed by Romans
70–80	Gospels according to Matthew and Luke
90–100	Gospel according to John
95	Quintilian's *Institutio Oratoria* codifying humanistic education in Rome
96	First appearance of formula *en Christo paideia*, foreshadowing synthesis of classical humanism with Christianity
100	Nicomachus's *Introduction to Arithmetic*
100–200	Gnosticism flourishes
109	Tacitus's *Historiae*

110	Plutarch fl., writes *Parallel Lives*, comparative biographies of prominent Greeks and Romans
120	Epictetus fl., Stoic moralist
140	Ptolemy's *Almagest* and *Tetrabiblos* codify classical astronomy and astrology
150	Justin Martyr's early synthesis of Christianity and Platonism
161	Marcus Aurelius becomes emperor
170	Galen fl., advances science of medicine
175	Earliest extant authoritative canon of New Testament
180	Irenaeus's *Against Heresies* criticizes Gnosticism Clement assumes leadership of Christian school in Alexandria
190	Sextus Empiricus fl., summarizes classical Skepticism
200	*Corpus Hermeticum* compiled in Alexandria (approx.)
203	Origen succeeds Clement as head of Catechetical school
232	Plotinus begins eleven years' study with Ammonius Saccas in Alexandria
235–285	Barbarian invasions into Roman Empire Beginning of severe inflation, spread of plague, depopulation
248	Origen's *Contra Celsum* defends Christianity against pagan intellectuals
250–260	Persecutions of Christians by emperors Decius and Valerian
265	Plotinus writing and teaching in Rome, emergence of Neoplatonism
301	Plotinus's *Enneads* compiled by Porphyry
303	Final and most severe persecution of Christians begins under Diocletian
312	Conversion of Constantine to Christianity
313	Edict of Milan establishes religious toleration for Christianity in Roman Empire
324	Eusebius's *Ecclesiastical History*, first history of Christian Church
325	Council of Nicaea convened by Constantine establishes orthodox Christian doctrine
330	Constantine moves imperial capital to Constantinople (Byzantium)
354	Birth of Augustine
361–363	Julian the Apostate briefly restores paganism in Roman Empire

370	Huns begin massive invasion of Europe (until 453)
374	Ambrose becomes bishop of Milan
382	Jerome begins translation of Bible into Latin
386	Conversion of Augustine
391	Theodosius prohibits all pagan worship in Roman Empire Destruction of Sarapeum in Alexandria
400	Augustine's *Confessions*
410	Visigoth sack of Rome
413–427	Augustine's *City of God*
415	Death of Hypatia in Alexandria
430	Death of Augustine
439	Carthage captured by the Vandals, West overrun by barbarians
476	End of Roman Empire in West
485	Death of Proclus, last major pagan Greek philosopher
498	Franks under Clovis convert to Catholicism
500	Dionysius the Areopagite fl. (estim.), Christian Neoplatonist
524	Boethius's *Consolation of Philosophy*
529	Closing of Platonic Academy in Athens by Justinian Benedict founds first monastery at Monte Cassino
590–604	Papacy of Gregory the Great
622	Beginning of Islam
731	Bede's *Ecclesiastical History of the English People*, popularizes method of dating events from birth of Christ
732	Muslim forces halted in Europe by Charles Martel at Poitiers
781	Alcuin leads Carolingian renaissance, establishes study of seven liberal arts as basic medieval curriculum
800	Charlemagne crowned emperor of West
866	John Scotus Erigena's *De Divisione Naturae*, synthesis of Christianity and Neoplatonism
1000	Most of Europe under Christian influence
1054	Schism declared between Western and Eastern Churches
1077	Anselm's *Meditation on the Reasonableness of Faith*
1090	Roscellinus teaching nominalism
1095	First Crusade initiated by Urban II

1117	Abelard's *Sic et Non*
1130	Hugh of Saint-Victor writes first medieval *summa*
1150	Rediscovery of Aristotle's works begins in Latin West
1170	Founding of University of Paris Intellectual centers developing at Oxford and Cambridge Court of Eleanor of Aquitaine at Poitiers becomes center of troubador poetry and model of courtly life
1185	André le Chapelain's *Art of Courtly Love*
1190	Joachim of Fiore fl., trinitarian philosophy of history
1194	Building of Chartres Cathedral begins
1209	Francis of Assisi founds Franciscan order
1210	Wolfram von Eschenbach's *Parzival* Gottfried von Strassburg's *Tristan und Isolde*
1215	Signing of Magna Carta
1216	Dominic founds Dominican order
1225	Birth of Thomas Aquinas
1245	Aquinas begins studies under Albertus Magnus in Paris
1247	Roger Bacon begins experimental research at Oxford
1260	Chartres Cathedral consecrated
1266	Siger of Brabant prominent at Paris
1266–73	Aquinas's *Summa Theologica*
1274	Death of Aquinas
1280	Jean de Meun's *Roman de la Rose*
1300–30	Spread of mysticism in Rhineland, Meister Eckhart fl.
1304	Birth of Petrarch
1305	Duns Scotus teaching at Paris
1309	Papacy moved to Avignon ("Babylonian captivity")
1310–14	Dante's *La Divina Commedia*
1319	Ockham teaching at Oxford
1323	Aquinas canonized
1330–50	Spread of Ockham's thought (nominalism) at Oxford and Paris
1335	First public striking clock erected in Milan
1337	Hundred Years' War begins between England and France
1340	Buridan rector at University of Paris

1341	Petrarch crowned poet laureate on the Capitoline in Rome
1347–51	Plague sweeps Europe (Black Death)
1353	Boccaccio's *Decameron*
1377	Oresme's *Book on the Sky and the World* defends theoretical possibility of moving Earth
1378	Great Schism, conflict between rival popes (until 1417)
1380	Wycliffe attacks Church abuses and orthodox doctrine
1400	Chaucer's *Canterbury Tales*
1404	Vergerio's *Concerning Liberal Studies*, first humanist treatise on education
1415	Religious reformer Jan Hus burned at stake
1429	Joan of Arc leads French against English Bruni's *History of Florence* pioneers Renaissance historiography
1434	Accession to power of Cosimo de'Medici in Florence
1435	Alberti's *On Painting* systematizes principles of perspective
1440	Nicholas of Cusa's *On Learned Ignorance* Valla's *On the True Good*
1452	Birth of Leonardo da Vinci
1453	Fall of Constantinople to Ottoman Turks, end of Byzantine Empire
1455	Gutenberg Bible produced, start of printing revolution
1462	Ficino becomes head of Platonic Academy of Florence
1469	Accession of Lorenzo the Magnificent in Florence
1470	Ficino completes first Latin translation of Plato's *Dialogues*
1473	Birth of Copernicus
1482	Ficino's *Theologica Platonica*
1483	Birth of Luther Leonardo's *Virgin of the Rocks*
1485	Botticelli's *Birth of Venus*
1486	Pico's *Oration on the Dignity of Man*
1492	Columbus reaches America
1497	Vasco da Gama reaches India Copernicus studying in Italy, makes first astronomical observation
1498	Leonardo's *Last Supper*

1504   Michelangelo's *David*

1506   Saint Peter's Basilica in Rome begun under Bramante

1508   Erasmus's *Adagia*

1508–11   Raphael's *School of Athens, Parnassus, Triumph of the Church*

1508–12   Michelangelo's Sistine Chapel ceiling

1512–14   Copernicus's *Commentariolus*, first outline of heliocentric theory

1513   Machiavelli's *The Prince*

1513–14   Dürer's *Knight, Death and Devil, St. Jerome in His Study, Melencolia I*

1516   Thomas More's *Utopia*
              Erasmus's Latin translation of New Testament

1517   Luther posts Ninety-five Theses in Wittenburg
              Beginning of Reformation

1519   Luther's *On Christian Liberty*

1521   Luther's excommunication and defiance of the imperial Diet at Worms

1524   Erasmus's defense of freedom of will against Luther

1527   Paracelsus teaching at Basel

1528   Castiglione's *The Courtier*

1530   Melanchthon's Augsburg Confession of Lutheran Churches

1532   Rabelais's *Pantagruel*

1534   Henry VIII issues Act of Supremacy rejecting papal control
              Luther completes translation of Bible into German

1535   Ignatius of Loyola's *Spiritual Exercises*

1536   Calvin's *Institutes of the Christian Religion*

1540   Society of Jesus founded by Loyola
              Rheticus's *Narratio Prima*, first published work describing Copernican theory

1541   Michelangelo's *Last Judgment*

1542   Establishment of Roman Inquisition

1543   Copernicus's *De Revolutionibus Orbium Coelestium*
              Vesalius's *On the Structure of the Human Body*

1545–63   Council of Trent, start of Counter-Reformation

1550   Vasari's *Lives of the Artists*

1554   Palestrina's first book of masses

1564	Birth of Galileo, Shakespeare
1567	Teresa of Avila and John of the Cross promote Carmelite reform
1572	Tycho Brahe observes supernova
1580	Montaigne's *Essays*
1582	Gregorian calendar reform instituted
1584	Bruno's *On the Infinite Universe and Worlds*
1590	Shakespeare's *Henry VI*
1596	Birth of Descartes Kepler's *Mysterium Cosmographicum* Spenser's *Faerie Queene*
1597	Bacon's *Essays*
1600	Shakespeare's *Hamlet* Giordano Bruno executed for heresy by Inquisition Gilbert's *On the Magnet*
1602	Kepler's *On the More Certain Fundamentals of Astrology*
1605	Bacon's *Advancement of Learning* Cervantes's *Don Quixote*
1607	Monteverdi's *Orfeo*
1609	Kepler's *Astronomia Nova*, first two laws of planetary motion
1610	Galileo announces telescopic discoveries in *Sidereus Nuncius*
1611	King James translation of Bible into English Shakespeare's *The Tempest*
1616	Catholic Church declares Copernican theory "false and erroneous"
1618–48	Thirty Years' War
1619	Kepler's *Harmonia Mundi*, third law of planetary motion Descartes's revelatory vision of a new science
1620	Bacon's *Novum Organum*
1623	Galileo's *Assayer* Boehme's *Mysterium Magnum*
1628	Harvey's *On the Movement of the Heart and Blood in Animals*
1632	Galileo's *Dialogue Concerning the Two Chief World Systems*
1633	Galileo condemned by Inquisition
1635	Founding of Académie Française
1636	Founding of Harvard College

1637	Descartes's *Discourse on Method* Corneille's *Le Cid*
1638	Galileo's *Two New Sciences*
1640	Jansen's *Augustinus*, beginning of Jansenism in France
1642–48	English Civil War
1644	Descartes's *Principia Philosophiae* Milton's *Areopagitica*
1647	Lilly's *Christian Astrology*
1648	Peace of Westphalia ending Thirty Years' War
1651	Hobbes's *Leviathan*
1660	Founding of Royal Society Boyle's *New Experiments Physico-Mechanical*
1664	Molière's *Tartuffe*
1665–66	Newton makes early scientific discoveries and develops calculus
1666	Hooke demonstrates mechanical theory of planetary motion Founding of *Académie des Sciences*
1667	Milton's *Paradise Lost*
1670	Pascal's *Pensées*
1675	Spread of Evangelical Pietism in Germany
1677	Spinoza's *Ethica* Racine's *Phaedra* Leeuwenhoek's discovery of microscopic organisms
1678	Bunyan's *Pilgrim's Progress* Simon's *Critical History of the Old Testament* pioneers textual criticism of Bible Huygens proposes wave theory of light
1687	Newton's *Principia Mathematica Philosophiae Naturalis* Quarrel of ancients and moderns begins at Académie Française
1688–89	Glorious Revolution in England
1690	Locke's *Essay Concerning Human Understanding, Two Treatises of Civil Government*
1697	Bayle's *Dictionnaire Historique et Critique*
1704	Newton's *Opticks*
1710	Berkeley's *Principles of Human Knowledge*
1714	Leibniz's *Monadology*
1719	Defoe's *Robinson Crusoe*

1721	Montesquieu's *Persian Letters*
1724	Bach's *Passion According to Saint John*
1725	Vico's *Scienza Nuova*
1726	Swift's *Gulliver's Travels*
1734	Voltaire's *Lettres Philosophiques* Pope's *Essay on Man* Jonathan Edwards fl., beginning of Great Awakening in American colonies
1735	Linnaeus's *Systema Naturae*
1738	Wesley begins Methodist revival in England
1740	Richardson's *Pamela*
1741	Handel's *Messiah*
1747	La Mettrie's *L'Homme-Machine*
1748	Hume's *Enquiry Concerning Human Understanding* Montesquieu's *Spirit of Laws*
1749	Birth of Goethe Fielding's *Tom Jones*
1750	Rousseau's *Discours sur les Sciences et les Arts*
1751	*Encyclopédie* begins publication under Diderot and d'Alembert Franklin's *Experiments and Observations on Electricity*
1755	Johnson's *Dictionary of the English Language*
1756	Voltaire's *Essay on the Manners and Customs of Nations*
1759	Sterne's *Tristram Shandy* Voltaire's *Candide*
1762	Rousseau's *Émile, Social Contract*
1764	Winckelmann's *History of the Art of Antiquity* reawakens European appreciation for classical Greek art and culture
1769–70	Birth of Beethoven, Hegel, Napoleon, Hölderlin, Wordsworth
1770	Holbach's *Système de la Nature*
1771	Swedenborg's *True Christian Religion*
1774	Goethe's *Sorrows of Young Werther*
1775	American Revolution begins
1776	Jefferson et al. draft Declaration of Independence Adam Smith's *Wealth of Nations* Gibbon's *Decline and Fall of the Roman Empire*
1778	Buffon's *Époques de la Nature*

1779   Hume's *Dialogue Concerning Natural Religion*

1780   Lessing's *Education of the Human Race*

1781   Kant's *Critique of Pure Reason*
            Herschel discovers Uranus, first new planet since antiquity

1784   Herder's *Ideas for the Philosophy of the History of Mankind*

1787   Mozart's *Don Giovanni*

1787–88   *The Federalist Papers* by Madison, Hamilton, and Jay

1788   Kant's *Critique of Practical Reason*
            Mozart's *Jupiter* Symphony

1789   French Revolution begins
            Declaration of the Rights of Man and the Citizen
            Blake's *Songs of Innocence*
            Lavoisier's *Elementary Treatise on Chemistry*
            Bentham's *Principles of Morality and Legislation*

1790   Goethe's *Metamorphosis of Plants*
            Kant's *Critique of Judgment*
            Burke's *Reflections on the Revolution in France*

1792   Wollstonecraft's *Vindication of the Rights of Woman*

1793   Blake's *Marriage of Heaven and Hell*

1795   Schiller's *Letters on the Aesthetic Education of Mankind*
            Condorcet's *Sketch for a Historical Picture of the Progress of the
                Human Mind*
            Hutton's *Theory of the Earth*

1796   Laplace's *Exposition du Système du Monde*

1797   Hölderlin's *Hyperion*

1798   Wordsworth and Coleridge's *Lyrical Ballads*
            Schlegel brothers begin Romantic periodical *Athenaeum*
            Malthus's *Essay on the Principle of Population*

1799   Napoleon becomes first consul in France
            Schleiermacher's *On Religion: Speeches to Its Cultured Despisers*

1800   Fichte's *The Vocation of Man*
            Schelling's *System of Transcendental Idealism*

1802   Novalis's *Heinrich von Ofterdingen*

1803   Dalton proposes atomic theory of matter

1803–4   Beethoven's *Eroica* Symphony

1807   Hegel's *Phenomenology of Mind*
            Wordsworth's *Ode: Intimations of Immortality*

1808   Goethe's *Faust I*

1809	Lamarck's *Philosophie Zoologique*
1810	De Staël's *De l'Allemagne (On Germany)*
1813	Austen's *Pride and Prejudice*
1814	Scott's *Waverley*
1815	Waterloo, Congress of Vienna
1817	Keats's *Poems* Coleridge's *Biographia Literaria* Ricardo's *Principles of Political Economy and Taxation* Hegel's *Encyclopaedia of the Philosophical Sciences*
1819	Schopenhauer's *The World as Will and Idea*
1820	Shelley's *Prometheus Unbound*
1822	Stendhal's *De l'Amour* Fourier's *The Analytical Theory of Heat*
1824	Beethoven's *Ninth Symphony* Byron's *Don Juan* Gauss postulates non-Euclidean geometry
1829	Balzac begins *La Comédie Humaine*
1830	Stendhal's *Le Rouge et le Noir* Comte's *Cours de Philosophie Positive* Berlioz's *Symphonie Fantastique*
1831	Pushkin's *Eugene Onegin* Hugo's *Notre-Dame de Paris, Les Feuilles d'Automne* Faraday discovers electromagnetic induction Darwin begins five-year voyage on *Beagle*
1832	Goethe's *Faust II* George Sand's *Indiana*
1833	Lyell's *Principles of Geology* Emerson travels to Europe, meets Coleridge and Carlyle
1834	Carlyle's *Sartor Resartus*
1835	Strauss's *Life of Jesus Critically Examined* Tocqueville's *Democracy in America* Babbage formulates idea of digital computing machine
1836	Emerson's *Nature* initiates Transcendentalism
1837	Emerson's "American Scholar" address Dickens's *Pickwick Papers*
1841	Feuerbach's *The Essence of Christianity*
1843	Kierkegaard's *Either/Or, Fear and Trembling* Mill's *System of Logic* Ruskin's *Modern Painters*

1844	Birth of Nietzsche Emerson's *Essays*
1845	Fuller's *Woman in the Nineteenth Century* Poe's *Tales* Marx and Engels's *Die Heilige Familie*
1848	Marx and Engels's *Communist Manifesto* Revolutions erupt throughout Europe Women's suffrage movement begins in United States
1850	Clausius formulates concept of entropy, second law of thermodynamics Hawthorne's *Scarlet Letter*
1851	Melville's *Moby Dick* Great Exhibition in London
1854	Thoreau's *Walden*
1855	Whitman's *Leaves of Grass*
1857	Flaubert's *Madame Bovary* Baudelaire's *Les Fleurs du Mal*
1858	Darwin and Wallace propose theory of natural selection
1859	Darwin's *Origin of Species* Mill's *On Liberty* Wagner's *Tristan und Isolde*
1860	Burckhardt's *Civilization of the Renaissance in Italy* Oxford debate on evolution between Wilberforce and Huxley
1861	Bachofen's *Mother Right*
1861–65	American Civil War
1862	Hugo's *Les Misérables*
1863	Emancipation Proclamation, Lincoln's Gettysburg Address
1865	Mendel proposes theory of genetic inheritance
1866	Haeckel's *General Morphology of Organisms* Dostoevsky's *Crime and Punishment*
1867	Marx's *Das Kapital*
1869	Tolstoy's *War and Peace* Arnold's *Culture and Anarchy*
1871	Darwin's *The Descent of Man*
1872	Nietzsche's *The Birth of Tragedy* Monet's *Impression: Sunrise* G. Eliot's *Middlemarch*
1873	Maxwell's *Treatise on Electricity and Magnetism*

1875	Blavatsky founds Theosophical Society
1877	Peirce publishes first articles on pragmatism
1878	Wundt founds first laboratory for experimental psychology
1879	Edison invents electric carbon-filament light Frege's *Begriffsclnift* initiates modern logic Ibsen's *A Doll's House*
1880	Dostoevsky's *The Brothers Karamazov*
1881	Ranke's *Universal History*
1883	Dilthey's *Introduction to Human Sciences*
1883–84	Nietzsche's *Thus Spoke Zarathustra*
1884	Twain's *Huckleberry Finn*
1886	Rimbaud's *Illuminations* Nietzsche's *Beyond Good and Evil* Mach's *The Analysis of Sensations*
1887	Michelson-Morley experiment
1889	Van Gogh's *Starry Night*
1890	William James's *Principles of Psychology* Frazer's *The Golden Bough*
1893	Bradley's *Appearance and Reality*
1894	Steiner's *Philosophy of Freedom* Tolstoy's *The Kingdom of God Is Within You* Hertz's *Principles of Mechanics*
1895	Wilde's *The Importance of Being Earnest* Durkheim's *Rules of Sociological Method*
1896	Becquerel's discovery of radioactivity in uranium Jarry's *Ubu Roi* Chekhov's *The Seagull*
1897	James's *The Will to Believe*
1898	Cézanne's *Mont Sainte-Victoire* paintings
1900	Death of Nietzsche Freud's *The Interpretation of Dreams* Planck initiates quantum physics Husserl's *Logical Investigations* initiates phenomenology Rediscovery of Mendelian genetics
1901	Henry James's *The Ambassadors*
1902	William James's *The Varieties of Religious Experience*

1903	Moore's *Refutation of Idealism* and *Principia Ethica*
	Shaw's *Man and Superman*
	Wright brothers make first powered airplane flight
1905	Einstein's papers on special relativity, photoelectric effect, Brownian motion
	Freud's *Three Essays on the Theory of Sexuality*
	Weber's *The Protestant Ethic and the Spirit of Capitalism*
1906	Duhem's *La Théorie Physique*
	Gandhi develops philosophy of nonviolent activism
1907	William James's *Pragmatism*
	Bergson's *L'Évolution Creatrice*
	Picasso's *Les Demoiselles d'Avignon*
	Suzuki's *Outline of Mahayana Buddhism* introduces Buddhism to West
1909	Schoenberg's first atonal work
1910–13	Russell and Whitehead's *Principia Mathematica*
1912	Jung's *Psychology of the Unconscious*, break from Freud
	Wegener proposes theory of continental drift
1913	Steiner founds anthroposophy
	Stravinsky's *Rite of Spring*
	Proust's *À la Recherche du Temps Perdu*
	Lawrence's *Sons and Lovers*
	Unamuno's *The Tragic Sense of Life*
	Royce's *The Problem of Christianity*
	Ford begins mass production of automobiles
1914	Joyce's *Portrait of the Artist as a Young Man*
	Kafka's *The Trial*
1914–18	World War I
1915	Saussure's *Cours de Linguistique Générale*
1916	Einstein's general theory of relativity
1917	Otto's *The Idea of the Holy*
	Russian Revolution
1918	Spengler's *The Decline of the West*
1919	General theory of relativity experimentally confirmed
	Watson's *Psychology from the Standpoint of a Behaviorist*
	Barth's *Epistle to the Romans*
1920	Yeats's "The Second Coming"
	Freud's *Beyond the Pleasure Principle*
	First public radio broadcast
1921	Russell's *The Analysis of Mind*
	Wittgenstein's *Tractatus Logico-Philosophicus*

1922   T.S. Eliot's *The Waste Land*
        Joyce's *Ulysses*
        Weber's *Economy and Society*

1923   Rilke's *Duino Elegies*
        W. Stevens's *Harmonium*
        Freud's *The Ego and the Id*
        Buber's *I and Thou*
        Santayana's *Scepticism and Animal Faith*
        Pavlov's *Conditioned Reflexes*

1924   Piaget's *Judgment and Reasoning in the Child*
        Rank's *The Trauma of Birth*
        Mann's *The Magic Mountain*

1925   Yeats's *A Vision*
        Dewey's *Experience and Nature*
        Whitehead's *Science and the Modern World*

1926   Schrödinger develops wave equation underlying quantum
            mechanics

1927   Heisenberg formulates principle of uncertainty
        Bohr formulates principle of complementarity
        Lemaître proposes big-bang theory
        Heidegger's *Sein und Zeit (Being and Time)*
        Freud's *The Future of an Illusion*
        Reich's *Die Funktion des Orgasmus*
        Hesse's *Der Steppenwolf*

1928   Yeats's *The Tower*
        Carnap's *The Logical Structure of the World*
        Jung's *The Spiritual Problem of Modern Man*

1929   Whitehead's *Process and Reality*
        Vienna Circle manifesto: *Scientific Conception of the World*
        Faulkner's *The Sound and the Fury*
        Woolf's *A Room of One's Own*

1930   Freud's *Civilization and Its Discontents*
        Ortega y Gasset's *The Revolt of the Masses*
        Bultmann's *The Historicity of Man and Faith*

1931   Gödel's Theorem proves undecidability of propositions in
            formalized mathematical systems
        Cassirer's *Philosophy of Symbolic Forms*

1932   Jaspers's *Philosophie*
        Klein's *Psychoanalysis of Children*

1933   Hitler comes to power in Germany

1934   Toynbee's *A Study of History*
        Popper's *Logic of Scientific Discovery*
        Jung's *Archetypes of the Collective Unconscious*
        Mumford's *Technics and Civilization*

1936	Lovejoy's *Great Chain of Being* Ayer's *Language, Truth and Logic* Keynes's *General Theory of Employment, Interest and Money*
1937	Anna Freud's *The Ego and the Mechanisms of Defense* Turing's *On Computable Numbers*
1938	Brecht's *Galileo* Discovery of nuclear fission Sartre's *Nausea*
1939	Death of Freud
1939–45	World War II, Holocaust
1940	Collingwood's *Essay on Metaphysics*
1941	Niebuhr's *The Nature and Destiny of Man* Fromm's *Escape from Freedom* Borges's *Ficciones*
1942	Camus's *The Stranger* and *The Myth of Sisyphus*
1943	Sartre's *Being and Nothingness* Eliot's *Four Quartets*
1945	Merleau-Ponty's *Phénoménologie de la Perception* Schrödinger's *What Is Life?* Atomic bombs dropped on Hiroshima and Nagasaki Founding of United Nations
1946–48	Beginning of Cold War Rise of public television broadcasting First electronic digital computers developed
1947	Pollock's first abstract drip paintings
1948	Wiener's *Cybernetics* Hartshorne's *The Divine Relativity* Graves's *The White Goddess* Merton's *The Seven Storey Mountain*
1949	Orwell's *Nineteen Eighty-Four* Eliade's *The Myth of the Eternal Return* Campbell's *The Hero with a Thousand Faces* De Beauvoir's *Le Deuxième Sex*
1950	Papal declaration of the *Assumptio Mariae*
1951	Tillich's *Systematic Theology* Bonhoeffer's *Letters and Papers from Prison* Quine's *Two Dogmas of Empiricism*
1952	Beckett's *Waiting for Godot* Jung's *Answer to Job, Synchronicity*

1953	Wittgenstein's *Philosophical Investigations*
	Heidegger's *Introduction to Metaphysics*
	Skinner's *Science and Human Behavior*
	Watson and Crick discover structure of DNA

1954	Huxley's *Doors of Perception*
	Rahner's *Theological Investigations*
	Needham's *Science and Civilization in China*

1955	Teilhard de Chardin's *The Phenomenon of Man*
	Marcuse's *Eros and Civilization*
	Ginsburg's *Howl*

| 1956 | Bateson et al. formulate double-bind theory |

1957	Chomsky's *Syntactic Structures*
	Barfield's *Saving the Appearances*
	Watts's *The Way of Zen*
	Sputnik satellite launched

| 1958 | Lévi-Strauss's *Anthropologie Structurale* |
| | Polanyi's *Personal Knowledge* |

| 1959 | Brown's *Life Against Death* |
| | Snow's *Two Cultures and the Scientific Revolution* |

| 1960 | Gadamer's *Truth and Method* |
| | Quine's *Word and Object* |

| 1960–72 | Rise of civil rights movement, student movement, feminism, environmentalism, counterculture |

1961	First space flights
	Watts's *Psychotherapy East and West*
	Foucault's *Histoire de la Folie*
	Fanon's *Les Damnés de la Terre*

1962	Kuhn's *The Structure of Scientific Revolutions*
	Popper's *Conjectures and Refutations*
	Jung's *Memories, Dreams, Reflections*
	Maslow's *Toward a Psychology of Being*
	Carson's *Silent Spring*
	McLuhan's *Gutenberg Galaxy*
	Hess proposes seafloor-spreading hypothesis
	Second Vatican Council begins
	Founding of Esalen Institute, rise of human potential movement
	Psychedelic experiments with Leary and Alpert at Harvard
	Rise of Dylan, Beatles, Rolling Stones
	Students for a Democratic Society adopts Port Huron statement

1963	Civil rights march on Washington, Martin Luther King's "I have a dream" speech
	Friedan's *Feminine Mystique*
	E. N. Lorenz publishes first paper on chaos theory

1964	Free speech movement begins in Berkeley
	Quarks postulated by Gell-Mann and Zweig
	Bellah's *Religious Evolution*
	Barthes's *Essais Critiques*
	Autobiography of Malcolm X

1965   Escalation of U.S. war in Vietnam
          Discovery of background cosmic radiation by Penzias and
              Wilson supports big-bang theory
          Cox's *Religion in the Secular City*
          Heidegger's final interview in *Der Spiegel*

1966   Altizer and Hamilton's *Radical Theology and the Death of God*
          Commoner's *Science and Survival*
          Lacan's *Écrits*
          Bell's theorem of nonlocality

1967   Laing's *Politics of Experience*
          Derrida's *L'Écriture et la Différence*
          White's *Historical Roots of Our Ecologic Crisis*

1968   Habermas's *Knowledge and Human Interests*
          Lakatos's *Criticism and the Methodology of Scientific Research
              Programmes*
          Von Bertalanffy's *General Systems Theory*
          Castaneda's *The Teachings of Don Juan*
          Brand's *The Whole Earth Catalog*
          Ehrlich's *The Population Bomb*

1968–70   Student rebellions, antiwar movement, counterculture
              at height

1969   Landing of astronauts on the Moon
          Lovelock proposes Gaia hypothesis
          Roszak's *The Making of a Counter Culture*
          Millett's *Sexual Politics*
          Abbey's *Desert Solitaire*
          Perls's *Gestalt Therapy Verbatim*
          Kristeva's *Semiotikè*
          Ricouer's *The Conflict of Interpretations*

1970   First Earth Day
          Bellah's *Beyond Belief*

1971   Gutiérrez's *Theology of Liberation*
          Boston Women's Health Book Collective's *Our Bodies, Ourselves*
          Pribram's *Languages of the Brain*

1972   Bateson's *Steps to an Ecology of Mind*
          Meadows's *The Limits to Growth*

1973   Schumacher's *Small Is Beautiful*
Geertz's *Interpretation of Cultures*
Daly's *Beyond God the Father*
Naess's *The Shallow and the Deep Ecology Movements*

1974   Ruether's *Religion and Sexism*
Gimbutas's *The Goddesses and Gods of Old Europe*

1975   Grof's *Realms of the Human Unconscious*
Hillman's *Re-Visioning Psychology*
Capra's *Tao of Physics*
Wilson's *Sociobiology*
Singer's *Animal Liberation*
Feyerabend's *Against Method*

1978   Goodman's *Ways of Worldmaking*
Chodorow's *The Reproduction of Mothering*

1979   Rorty's *Philosophy and the Mirror of Nature*

1980   Emergence of personal computers
Development of biotechnology
Bohm's *Wholeness and the Implicate Order*
Prigogine's *From Being to Becoming*
Merchant's *The Death of Nature*

1981   Sheldrake's *A New Science of Life*

1982   Gilligan's *In a Different Voice*
Aspect experiment confirms Bell's theorem
Schell's *The Fate of the Earth*

1983   Discovery of W and Z subatomic particles

1984   Lyotard's *The Postmodern Condition*

1985   Keller's *Reflections on Gender and Science*
Gorbachev initiates *perestroika* in Soviet Union

1985–90   Rapid rise of public awareness of planetary ecological crisis

1989–90   End of Cold War, collapse of Communism in Eastern Europe

Notes

Introduction

Because the issue of gender is especially significant today, and because it directly affects the language of the present narrative, an introductory comment is in order. In a historical account such as this, the distinction between the author's view and the various views he or she is describing can sometimes be obscured, so that a prior note of clarification can be valuable. Like many others, I do not consider it justifiable for a writer today to use the word "man" or "mankind," or the traditional masculine generic pronouns "he" and "his," when straightforwardly referring to the human species or the generic human individual (as in "the destiny of man" or "man's relationship to his environment" or similar expressions). I recognize that many responsible writers and scholars—mainly men, but some women as well—continue to employ such terms in this way, and I appreciate the problem of changing deeply ingrained habits, but in the long run I do not believe that such usage can be successfully defended for what boils down largely to reasons of style (brevity, elegance, rhetorical vigor, tradition). The motive, worthy in itself, is insufficient to justify the implied exclusion of the female half of the human species.

Such usage, however, is appropriate—and, indeed, necessary for semantic precision and historical accuracy—when the task is specifically that of articulating the mode of thinking, the world view, and the image of the human expressed by most of the principal figures of Western thought from the time of the Greeks until very recently. For most of its existence, the Western intellectual tradition was an unequivocally patrilineal tradition. With a uniform consistency that we today can scarcely appreciate, that tradition was formed and canonized almost exclusively by men writing for other men, with the result that an androcentric perspective was implicitly assumed to be the "natural" one. Perhaps not coincidentally, it has been characteristic of all the major languages within which the Western intellectual tradition developed, both ancient and modern, to denote the human species and the generic human being with words that are masculine in gender and, to varying degrees, in implication (e.g., Greek *anthrōpos*, Latin *homo*, Italian *l'uomo*, French *l'homme*, Spanish *el hombre*, Russian *chelovek*, German *der Mensch*, English *man*). In addition, generalizations about human experience were regularly made using words that in other contexts explicitly denoted members of the male sex alone (e.g., Greek *anēr*, *andres*; English *man*, *men*). Many complexities are involved in analyzing these tendencies: each language has its own grammatical conventions for gender, and its own semantic peculiarities, nuances, and overtones; different words in different contexts suggest different degrees and forms of inclusiveness or bias; and all of these variables can differ from one writer to another and from one era to another. But running through all these complexities is evident a fundamental masculine linguistic bias that has been embedded in and intrinsic to virtually the entire progression of world views discussed in this book. That bias cannot be excised without distorting the essential meaning and structure of those cultural perspectives. The bias does not represent merely an isolated linguistic peculiarity; rather, it is the linguistic manifestation of a deep-seated and systemic, if generally unconscious, masculine predisposition in the character of the Western mind.

When major thinkers and writers of the past used the word "man" or other masculine generics to indicate the human species—as, for example, in *The Descent of Man* (Darwin, 1871), or *De hominis dignitate oratio* ("Oration on the Dignity of Man," Pico della Mirandola, 1486), or *Das Seelenproblem des modernen Menschen* ("The Spiritual Problem of Modern Man," Jung, 1928)—the meaning of the term was pervaded by a fundamental ambiguity. It is usually clear that a writer who employed such an expression in this kind of context intended to personify the entire human species, not only members of the male sex. Yet it is also evident from the larger framework of understanding within which the word appears that such a term was generally intended to denote and connote a decisively masculine contour in what the writer understood to be the essential nature of the human being and the human enterprise. This shifting but persistent ambiguity of diction—*both* gender-inclusive *and* masculine-oriented—must be accurately conveyed if one is to understand the distinctive character of Western cultural and intellectual history. The implicit masculine meaning of such terms was not accidental, even if it was largely unconscious. If the present narrative were to attempt to convey the mainstream traditional Western image of the human enterprise by systematically and unvaryingly using gender-neutral expressions such as "humankind," "humanity," "people," "persons," "women and men," and "the human being" (along with "she or he" and "his or her"), instead of what would actually have been used—man, *anthrōpos, andres, homines, der Mensch*, etc.—the result would be roughly comparable to the work of a medieval historian who, when writing about the ancient Greek view of the divine, conscientiously substituted the word "God" every time the Greeks would have said "the gods," thereby correcting a usage that to medieval ears would have seemed both wrong and offensive.

My aim in this historical narrative has been to recount the evolution of the Western world view as it was articulated within the mainstream Western intellectual tradition, and I have attempted to do so as far as possible *from the unfolding point of view of the tradition itself.* By the careful choice and variation of specific words and expressions within the continuum of the narrative, using the idioms of only one language, modern English, I have tried to capture the spirit of each major perspective that emerged from this tradition. For the sake of historical fidelity, therefore, this narrative employs where appropriate certain English terms and expressions, such as "man," "mankind," "modern man," "man and God," "man's place in the cosmos," "man's emergence from nature," and the like, when these would reflect the spirit and characteristic style of discourse of the individual or era under discussion. To avoid such locutions in this context would bowdlerize the history of the Western mind and misrepresent its fundamental character, making much of that history unintelligible.

The issue of gender ideology, and more deeply the issue of the archetypal dialectic between masculine and feminine, is essential, not peripheral, to understanding the character of a cultural world view, and language provides a vivid reflection of those underlying dynamics. In the retrospective analysis that follows the narrative, I will address this critical subject more fully, and suggest a new conceptual framework for approaching it.

Part I. The Greek World View

1.   John H. Finley, *Four Stages of Greek Thought* (Stanford: Stanford University Press, 1966), 95–96. Closely related to this discussion about gods and Ideas is a valuable point originally made by the German scholar Wilamowitz-Moellendorff, and recounted by W. K. C. Guthrie: ". . . *theos*, the Greek word which we have in mind when we speak of Plato's god, has primarily a predicative force. That is to say, the Greeks did not, as Christians or Jews do, first assert the existence of God and then proceed to enumerate his attributes, saying 'God is good,' 'God is love' and so forth. Rather they were so impressed or awed by the things in life or nature remarkable either for joy or fear that they said 'this is a god' or 'that is a god.' The Christian says 'God is love,' the Greek 'Love is *theos*,' or 'a god.' As another writer has explained it: 'By saying that love, or victory, is god, or, to be more accurate, a god, was meant first and foremost that it is more than human, not subject to death, everlasting. . . . Any power, any force we see at work in the world, which is not born with us and will continue after we are gone could thus be called a god, and most of them were' [Georges M. A. Grube, *Plato's Thought* (Boston: Beacon Press, 1958), 150].

"In this state of mind, and with this sensitiveness to the superhuman character of many things which happen to us, and which give us, it may be, sudden stabs of joy or pain which we do not understand, a Greek poet could write lines like: 'Recognition between friends is *theos*.' It is a state of mind which obviously has no small bearing on the much-discussed question of monotheism or polytheism in Plato, if indeed it does not rob the question of meaning altogether" (W. K. C. Guthrie, *The Greek Philosophers: From Thales to Aristotle* [New York: Harper Torchbook, 1960], 10–11).

2.   By the time of Homer, an essential transformation in the Greek mythological sensibility had taken place, with the more animistic, mystical, and nature-oriented matrifocal mythology—immanent, all-permeating, organic, nonheroic—having been subordinated to the Olympian patriarchal mythology, the character of which was more objectified, transcendent, articulated, heroic and autonomy-supporting. See, for example, Jane Ellen Harrison, *Prolegomena to the Study of Greek Religion* (Cambridge: Cambridge University Press, 1922), and Charlene Spretnak, *Lost Goddesses of Early Greece* (Boston: Beacon Press, 1984). Yet as Joseph Campbell pointed out in *The Masks of God: Occidental Mythology* (New York: Viking, 1964), suggestive signs of the Greeks' dual mythological heritage can be seen even within the Homeric canon itself, in the striking shift from the world of the *Iliad* to that of the *Odyssey*.

The *Iliad* is an historical epic, and sings of the great patriarchal themes: of the wrath of Achilles, of the courage, pride, and excellence of noble warriors, of manly virtue, strength, and warcraft. It is staged in the day-world of public activity, where heroic men strive on the battlefield of life. Yet that life, though glorious, is short, and death tragically final, beyond which is nothing of value. The greatness of the *Iliad* rests especially on its epic rendering of that tragic tension. By contrast, the *Odyssey*, rather than a commemoration of a collective historical event, is an epic of an individual journey with a distinctly imaginal character; it deals throughout with magical and fantastical phenomena, is informed by a different sense of death, and is more concerned with the feminine.

Odysseus, the wisest of the Greek heroes at Troy, undergoes a transformative series of adventures and trials—encountering a succession of magical women and goddesses, entering the underworld, being initiated into dark mysteries, experiencing several sequences of death and rebirth—and is thereby finally enabled to return home in triumph, twice-born, to reunite with Penelope, the beloved feminine. In this reading, the shift from the *Iliad* to the *Odyssey* reflects a continuing dialectic in the Greek cultural psyche between its patriarchal and matriarchal roots, between the Olympian public religion and the ancient mysteries. (See Campbell, *The Masks of God: Occidental Mythology*, 157–176.)

The *Odyssey* still evidences the *Iliad*'s appreciation of the individual and the heroic, rooted in that ancient Indo-European admiration for individual prowess in war that would so profoundly influence the character and history of the West; but the heroism has taken on a decisively new and more complicated form. An important later expression of this same dialectic can be found in Plato's *Symposium*, where it is the wise woman Diotima who plays the pivotal role in Socrates's initiation into the transcendent knowledge of the Beautiful. As with Homer's Odysseus, the element of individual heroism is clearly present in Plato's Socrates, but in a further metamorphosis—more intellectual, spiritual, inward, self-conquering.

3. Both of Thales's successors in Miletus, Anaximander and Anaximenes (both fl. sixth century B.C.), made contributions of importance for later Western thought. Anaximander proposed that the primary substance or essential nature (*archē*) of the cosmos was an infinite and undifferentiated substance he called the *apeiron* (the "boundless"). Within the *apeiron* arose the opposites of hot and cold, whose struggle in turn produced the various phenomena of the world. Anaximander thereby introduced the notion, essential for later philosophy and science, of going beyond perceptible phenomena (such as water) to a more fundamental, nonperceptible substance whose nature was more primitive and indefinite than the familiar substances of the visible world. Anaximander also postulated a theory of evolution in which life originated in the sea, and appears to have been the first person to attempt to draw a map of the entire inhabited Earth.

Anaximander's successor, Anaximenes, in turn posited air as the primary substance, and attempted to demonstrate the manner in which that single substance could change itself into other forms of matter through the processes of rarefaction and condensation. Anaximenes's proposal that a specific element, air, rather than an undifferentiated substance like the *apeiron*, was the origin of things could be viewed as a less sophisticated theory than Anaximander's—a step back toward Thales's water. But by pursuing his analysis of how one primary element underwent change into other types of matter while still retaining its essential nature, Anaximenes introduced the crucial idea that a basic essence could remain itself while undergoing many transformations. Thus the notion of *archē*, which had previously signified the beginning or originating cause of things, now took on the additional significance of "principle"—something that eternally maintains its own nature while transmuting itself into the many transient and changing phenomena of the visible world. Subsequent philosophical and scientific developments concerning first principles, the dependence of phenomena on a continuing underlying primary reality, and the various laws of conservation in physics all owe something to Anaximander's and Anaximenes's rudimentary conceptions. Both men also made pivotal contributions to early Greek astronomy.

4.   Of this important fragment from Xenophanes, W. K. C. Guthrie states: "The emphasis on personal search, and on the need for time, marks this as the first statement in extant Greek literature of the idea of progress in the arts and sciences, a progress dependent on human effort and not—or at least not primarily—on divine revelation" (*A History of Greek Philosophy*, vol. 1, *The Earlier Presocratics and the Pythagoreans* [Cambridge: Cambridge University Press, 1962], 399–400).

5.   The evolution of the Greek view of human history and of the human relation to the divine can be discerned in the shifting nature and status of the mythological Prometheus. Hesiod's earlier depiction of Prometheus as the trickster who stole fire from Olympus for mankind against Zeus's wishes was greatly expanded by Aeschylus in *Prometheus Bound*, whose titanic protagonist gave mankind all the arts of civilization and thereby brought it from a state of primitive savagery to intellectual mastery and dominion over nature. Hesiod's seriocomic figure became for Aeschylus a tragic hero of universal stature; and while Hesiod had viewed human history as an inevitable regress from an aboriginal golden age, Aeschylus's Prometheus celebrated mankind's progress to civilization. Nevertheless, in contrast with later conceptions of the same myth, Aeschylus's version regarded the divine Prometheus, not man, as the source of human progress, thus tacitly acknowledging a divine priority in the scheme of things. While it is difficult to ascertain Aeschylus's precise view of the myth's ontological significance, it would seem that he conceived of Prometheus and man in essentially mythopoeic terms as a symbolic unity.

For fifth-century Greeks after Aeschylus, however, the figure of Prometheus became merely a straightforward allegorical representation of man's own intelligence and restless striving. In a fragment from a comedy called *The Sophists*, Prometheus is simply equated with the human mind; in another work, Prometheus is used as a metaphor for "experience" to explain humanity's progress to civilization. This demythologizing of Prometheus to the status of allegory is also evident in the Sophist Protagoras's account of the myth in Plato's *Protagoras* (see page 14 above). As the Greek mind evolved from archaic poetry to humanist philosophy, with classical tragedy marking a midpoint, the Greek view of history moved from regress to progress, with the source of human achievement moving from the divine to man. See E. R. Dodds, "Progress in Classical Antiquity," in *Dictionary of the History of Ideas,* edited by Philip P. Weiner (New York: Charles Scribner's Sons, 1973) 3: 623–626.

6.   Socrates's combination of intellectual humility with faith in an intelligible order is nicely suggested in R. Hackforth's phrase "an ideal of knowledge unattained" (quoted in Guthrie, *The Greek Philosophers*, 75).

7.   For the Platonic linking of the irrational and physical with the female sex, and of the rational and spiritual with the male sex, and also for the important association of Platonic epistemology with Greek homoeroticism, see Evelyn Fox Keller, "Love and Sex in Plato's Epistemology," in *Reflections on Gender and*

Science (New Haven: Yale University Press, 1985), 21–32. See also the valuable discussion of Plato's homoeroticism by Gregory Vlastos in his essay "The Individual as an Object of Love in Plato," in *Platonic Studies* (Princeton: Princeton University Press, 1973), 3–42. Vlastos points out, however, that Plato's climactic argument in the *Symposium* (206–212) shifts suddenly from a homosexual paradigm to a procreative heterosexual one when Diotima describes the highest fulfillment of Eros as the philosopher's conjugal union with the Idea of Beauty, which brings forth the birth of wisdom. In the same essay, Vlastos offers an illuminating analysis of how Plato's exaltation of the universal Idea of Beauty in the context of personal relations tends to depreciate the concrete individual beloved person as a valuing subject, potentially worthy of love for his or her own sake—just as, in the context of political theory, Plato's exaltation of the ideal republic tends to depreciate individual citizens as ends in themselves, and in so doing deprives them of their civil liberty.

8. "The tradition that detailed astronomical observations supply the principal clues for cosmological thought is, in its essentials, native to Western civilization. It seems to be one of the most significant and characteristic novelties that we inherit from the civilization of ancient Greece" (Thomas S. Kuhn, *The Copernican Revolution: Planetary Astronomy and the Development of Western Thought* [Cambridge: Harvard University Press, 1957], 26).

9. Cited in Sir Thomas L. Heath, *Aristarchus of Samos: The Ancient Copernicus* (Oxford: Clarendon Press, 1913), 140. See also Plato's *Laws*, VII, 821–822.

10. Finley, *Four Stages of Greek Thought*, 2. Owen Barfield, speaking of Coleridge's lectures on the history of philosophy, described the Greek phenomenon in similar terms: "The birth of self-consciousness, the birth of individuality . . . was taking place with the dawn of Greek civilization. . . . The whole thing was like an awakening. When you first awaken in the morning you are very much aware of the world around you in a way that you are not when you get used to it during the course of the day" (Owen Barfield, "Coleridge's Philosophical Lectures," *Towards* 3, 2 [1989]: 29).

Part II. The Transformation of the Classical Era

1. It has been suggested on the basis of passages in the *Laws* and the *Epinomis* that Plato himself may have implicitly supported the hypothesis of a moving Earth as the way to save the appearances mathematically and reveal the single, uniform planetary orbits, and that in the *Timaeus* (40b–d) he may have described a heliocentric system. See R. Catesby Taliaferro, Appendix C to his translation of Ptolemy's *Almagest*, in *Great Books of the Western World*, vol. 16 (Chicago: Encyclopaedia Britannica, 1952), 477–478.

2. The preeminent Hellenistic supreme deity was the Greco-Egyptian Sarapis, a synthesis of Osiris, Zeus, Dionysus, Pluto, Asclepius, Marduk, Helios, and Yahweh. Established as the ruling city-god of Alexandria by Ptolemy I (reigned 323–285 B.C.), and eventually worshiped throughout the Mediterranean world, Sarapis illustrates the Hellenistic tendency of theological syncretism and henotheism (the worship of one deity without denying the existence of others).

3.   Recent scholarship has underscored the abiding vigor of the pagan tradition in the late classical era (see in particular Robin Lane Fox, *Pagans and Christians* [New York: Alfred A. Knopf, 1987]), in contrast with earlier views which tended to suggest the inevitability of the Christian triumph. For vast numbers of pagans, the ancient gods and goddesses continued to hold meaning, and pagan ceremonies and rituals were attended to with energetic piety. Considered as a whole, the Hellenistic period was an era of intense and multiform religiosity of which Christianity was one characteristic expression. The Christian faith spread gradually among the urban populations in the form of small churches led by bishops and fortified by strict ethical and doctrinal norms, yet by the early fourth century it had not penetrated most of the rural areas, and for many pagan intellectuals the Christian arguments still seemed implausible and eccentric. It was the conversion of Constantine (c. 312 A.D.) that marked the great shift in Christianity's fortunes, yet even then its ascendance was significantly challenged in the following generation by the emperor Julian's brief but spirited attempt to restore pagan culture (361–363).

4.   It has also been said that Greco-Roman culture was engrafted onto the Judaeo-Christian religion, or that both were engrafted onto the barbarian Germanic peoples, with what is considered the West's fundamental or primary inheritance changing in each instance. All three perspectives have arguments in their favor, and the truth, like the West itself, can perhaps best be understood as their complex synthesis.

Part III. The Christian World View

1.   "Yahweh" (originally, "YHWH") has been variously translated: e.g., "I Am Who Am"; "He Brings Into Existence Whatever Exists"; and "I Am / Shall Be Who I Am / Shall Be," wherein the complex ambiguity between present and future tense is unresolved. The meaning of the word remains controversial.

2.   Whether the historical Jesus explicitly claimed to be the Messiah as such, or the prophesied "Son of man," remains unclear. Whatever his private self-understanding, it appears unlikely that he publicly claimed to be the Son of God. A similar ambiguity exists as to whether Jesus intended to initiate a new religion or rather a radical eschatological reformation of Judaism. See Raymond E. Brown, " 'Who Do Men Say That I Am?'—A Survey of Modern Scholarship on Gospel Christology," in *Biblical Reflections on Crises Facing the Church* (New York: Paulist Press, 1975), 20–37.

3.   The other side of the Jewish-Christian paradox (that Christianity was comparatively so unsuccessful among the very people from which it sprung) was that Christians in subsequent centuries so pervasively distanced themselves from, deprecated, abused, and persecuted their Jewish contemporaries, while embracing the ancient Judaic scripture and history as the indispensable foundation of their own religion.

4.   The philosophical integration of Hellenism with Judaism was initiated by Philo of Alexandria (b. c. 15–10 B.C.), who identified the Logos in Platonic

terms as the Idea of Ideas, as the summation of all Ideas, and as the source of the world's intelligibility; and in Judaic terms as God's providential ordering of the universe and as mediator between God and man. The Logos was thus both the agent of creation and the agent by which God was experienced and understood by man. Philo taught that the Ideas were God's eternal thoughts, which he created as real beings prior to the creation of the world. Later Christians held Philo in high regard for his views of the Logos, which he called the first-begotten Son of God, the man of God, and the image of God. Philo appears to have been the first person to have attempted to integrate revelation and philosophy, faith and reason—the basic impulse of Scholasticism. Little recognized in Judaic thought, he had a marked influence on Neoplatonism and medieval Christian theology.

5. This generalization about the Greeks' cyclical sense of history should be balanced by the discussion of the Greek experience and conception of progress in the subchapter on the Greek Enlightenment, pages 25–31, and also in note 5, part 1, concerning the figure of Prometheus.

6. Augustine differed from Plotinus in positing an increased distinction between Creator and creation as well as a more personal relation between God and the individual soul; in stressing God's freedom and purposefulness in the creation; in upholding the human need for grace and revelation; and above all in embracing the doctrine of the Incarnation.

7. *Enchiridion,* in Augustine, *Works,* vol. 9, edited by M. Dods (Edinburgh: Clark, 1871–77), 180–181.

8. Ironically, the spirit of Christian dogmatic intolerance was foreshadowed by Plato himself in such dialogues as the *Republic* and the *Laws.* Similarly mindful of the need to protect the young from temptation and misleading thoughts, and similarly certain of possessing knowledge of absolute truth and goodness, Plato outlined a wide range of prohibitions and strictures for his ideal state that were not unlike those later established by Christianity.

9. A few revelant dates and events for the transition from the classical to the medieval era: In the late summer of 386, Augustine experienced his conversion to Christianity in Milan. In 391, the Sarapeum, the Alexandrian temple to the Hellenistic supreme deity Sarapis, was destroyed by the patriarch Theophilus and his followers, marking the triumph of Christianity over paganism in Egypt and throughout the empire. In 415, in the same decade in which the Visigoths overran Rome and Augustine was writing *The City of God,* a Christian mob in Alexandria murdered Hypatia—leader of the Neoplatonic school of philosophy in Alexandria, daughter of the last known member of the Museum, and the personal symbol of pagan learning. With her death, many scholars left Alexandria, marking the beginning of that city's cultural decline. In 485, Proclus, the greatest systematic expositor of late classical Neoplatonism and the last major Greek philosopher of antiquity, died in Athens. In 529, the Christian emperor Justinian closed the Platonic Academy in Athens, the last physical establishment of pagan learning. That year has often been used as a convenient date for the end of the classical period and the beginning of the Middle Ages, for also in

529 Benedict of Nursia, the father of Christian monasticism in the West, founded the first Benedictine monastery at Monte Cassino in Italy (the same monastery where Thomas Aquinas would be brought as a child almost precisely seven hundred years later).

10.   An influential statement of this position was that of the Alexandrian Christian Neoplatonist Origen (c. 185–c. 254), for whom hell could not be absolute because God in his infinite goodness could never finally abandon any of his creatures. The experience of damnation was based on an individual's self-imposed condemnation, a deliberate turning away from God that effectively cut off the individual soul from God's love; hell thus consisted in the complete absence of God. But for Origen this experience of alienation was ultimately a temporary condition in a larger educational process through which every soul would be reunited with God, whose love was all-conquering. In respect of humanity's inherent freedom, God's redemptive process might necessarily be prolonged, but until universal redemption had occurred Christ's mission remained unfulfilled. Similarly, Origen viewed the negative events of human existence not as divine retribution but as instruments of spiritual formation. Popular piety might perceive them as punitive acts of a vengeful God, but such views were based on a distorted understanding of God's activity, which was ultimately informed by unlimited benevolence. As with hell, heaven also was not necessarily absolute, for in their continuing free will the redeemed souls could, at the conclusion of the redemptive process, initiate once again the entire drama. Origen's theology rested throughout on the simultaneous affirmation of God's goodness and the soul's freedom, with the soul's ascent to divinity marked by a hierarchy of stages culminating in mystical union with the Logos: the restoration of the soul from matter to spirit, from image to reality.

Although Origen has been regarded by many as the greatest teacher of the early Church after the apostles, his orthodoxy has been sharply questioned by others on various matters, including his doctrines on universal salvation, the preexistence of the individual soul, the Neoplatonic devaluation of the Son as a hypostatic step down from the One, his spiritualizing of the resurrection of the body, his allegorical transformation of salvational history into a timeless archetypal process, and his speculations on world cycles. See Henry Chadwick, *Early Christian Thought and the Classical Tradition: Studies in Justin, Clement and Origen* (Oxford: Oxford University Press, 1966).

11.   Scholars have often noted the many striking thematic parallels between the biblical Book of Job (c. 600–300 B.C.) and Aeschylus's approximately contemporaneous tragedy *Prometheus Bound.* Comparable historical and literary parallels have been recognized between the earlier Mosaic books of the Bible and the Homeric epics.

12.   In his desire to establish a world church and thus to make the Christian gospel intelligible to those from different cultural backgrounds, Paul modulated his teachings accordingly, speaking "as a Jew to the Jews," "as a Greek to the Greeks." To the church community in Rome, with its strong Jewish influence, he emphasized the doctrine of justification, but in letters to communities with a more Hellenistic background, he described salvation in terms reminiscent of the Greek mystery religions—the new man, sonship with God, the process of divine transformation, and so forth.

13.   The papacy of Gregory the Great (590–604) established many of the most characteristic features of medieval Western Christendom. Born in Rome and deeply influenced by the teachings of Augustine, Gregory centralized and reformed the papal administration, elevated the status of priests, expanded the Church's care for the poor and distressed, and pressed for the pope's recognition as ecumenical leader of Christendom over the claims of the Byzantine patriarch. He also helped establish the papacy's temporal authority by consolidating what would become the Papal States in Italy and, more generally, by his efforts to influence and compel secular authorities through the exercise of ecclesiastical authority. His ideal was to build a universal Christian society pervaded by charity and service to others. It was Gregory who especially recognized the importance of the migrating barbarians for the future of Christianity in the West, and he vigorously pursued missionary activities in Europe (including the historically significant mission to England). Although at times he recommended a sensitive respect for indigenous views and practices, as in England, on other occasions he advocated the use of force in his conversion efforts. A highly popular pope and widely venerated in his own lifetime, Gregory sought to make the Christian faith more comprehensible to the masses of uneducated Europeans by reforming the Mass and by popularizing miracles and the doctrine of purgatory. He encouraged the growth of monasticism, and established rules for the lives of the clergy. Gregorian chant, the liturgical music of the Catholic Church, was named after him, having been codified during his reign.

14.   The separation between the Eastern and Western churches began in the fifth century, and a formal schism was declared in 1054. Whereas the Roman Catholic Church insisted on Roman and papal primacy (on the basis of its interpretation of Christ's words to Peter in the Gospel according to Matthew, 16:18), Eastern Orthodox Christianity remained more of an ecumenical association of churches bound together by the communion of faith, with the laity playing a greater role in religious affairs. On the other hand, instead of the state-church dialectic of the West (created in large part by the barbarian invasions and the consequent political and cultural break with the old Western Roman Empire), the Eastern church remained closely associated with the continuing political system of the Byzantine Empire. The patriarch of Constantinople was often subordinate to the Eastern emperor, who regularly exercised his authority in ecclesiastical matters.

In general, the sense of the need for authoritatively defined and meticulously detailed doctrinal orthodoxy was less pronounced in the East than in the West, and the ecumenical council, rather than the pope, was the highest authority in doctrinal matters. Christian truth was viewed as a living reality experienced within the Church, rather than, as in the West, a fully articulated dogmatic system that attempts to contain that truth according to specific criteria of justification. Whereas the dominant influence in the Latin West was Augustinian, Eastern theology was rooted in the Greek fathers. Its doctrinal tendency was more mystical, placing emphasis not on human beings' individual justification by the Church (as in the West), but on their communal divinization within the Church, as well as on their individual divinization through contemplative asceticism. The juridical relation between God and man characteristic of Western Christianity was absent in the East, where the sovereign themes were the incarnation of God, the deification of humanity, and the divine transfiguration of the cosmos. Generally speaking, Eastern Christianity remained closer to the Johannine unitive mystical impulse in the Christian faith, while the West pursued a more dualistic Augustinian direction.

15. The reconceiving of the Kingdom of Heaven in terms of the Church reflected a fundamental self-transformation of Christian belief which began in the first generations of the Christian religion in response to the delay in Christ's Second Coming. Early Christians had expected an imminent Second Coming, with the arrival of the Kingdom of Heaven to be preceded by a time of rebelliousness and evil, when false prophets and messiahs would arise and lead many astray with signs and wonders; then would occur a global apocalypse, followed by a dramatic opening of the heavens revealing God in his full glory, with Christ descending from the heavens to embrace and liberate the faithful. Already in the New Testament, and particularly in the Gospel according to John, there appeared to be a progressive awareness of the Second Coming's delay—though it was still considered near—and an apparent compensation for that delay expressed through an increasingly exalted interpretation of Jesus's life and death, the coming of the Spirit, and the significance of the young Church community. Jesus's presence in history was seen as having already inaugurated the salvational transformation. In Christ's resurrection was mankind's resurrection, its new life. Through the presence of his Spirit, Christ had risen into the life of the new community of the faithful, his mystical body, the living and growing Church. Thus the delay of the Parousia had been answered for the present: its arrival had been relocated to a more distant future, and Christ's spiritual power had been already claimed and experienced in the continuing life of the Church faithful.

Yet, contrary to expectation, the world continued to endure, and thus the Church, initially conceived as having a brief transitional existence prior to the end time, was encouraged to take on a more substantial role, with a corresponding change in its self-interpretation: rather than the small body of the elect who would be present and saved in the coming apocalypse, the Church now recognized itself as an ongoing, expanding sacramental institution—baptizing, teaching, disciplining, saving. From such a foundation the Church grew, increasingly moving from its earlier, flexible form of communities of the faithful to a complex institution with highly defined structures of hierarchical power and doctrinal tradition, and with an essential distinction drawn between the ecclesiastical elite and the lay congregation over which it presided.

The final outcome of this process emerged in the last centuries of the classical era. With Constantine's conversion, and with the subsequent welding of the Roman state to the Christian religion, a new mood began to appear in the Church: The eschatological expectations of the early Christian community were now submerged by the new sense of a strong earthly Church, whose present triumph overshadowed the demand for and likelihood of an apocalyptic shift. Without persecutions, the Christian community's psychological need for an immediate apocalypse was less intense, and with Christianity now the favored imperial religion, Rome's previous role as the preapocalyptic Antichrist was no longer appropriate.

Concurrently, under the influence of Neoplatonic and Hellenic allegorical thought, Origen and Augustine reformulated the Kingdom of Heaven in terms that were less literal and objective, and instead more spiritual and subjective. For Origen, the genuine religious quest was to experience the Kingdom of Heaven in one's own soul—a metaphysical rather than a historical transformation. Augustine's view was similarly Neoplatonic, but with a more decisively polarized attitude concerning the relationship between this world and the Church. Living during the death throes of classical civilization, Augustine viewed the present world as a realm inherently susceptible to evil, just as did those who had earlier awaited the apocalypse; and he too saw humanity juridically divided between the elect and the damned. Yet the salvational solution he recognized was not that of an apocalyptic renovation of this world, but a sacramental renovation of the soul through the Church. The secular world was not destined for salvation; that condition was a spiritual one only and was already available through the Church.

Thus the Christian anticipation of an imminent end time was substantially weakened and began to disappear as a dominant motivating force in the religion. The institutional Church was thereby solidified and reconceived as the enduring historical representative of the Kingdom of God on earth. Between the Resurrection and the Second Coming was the reign of the Church, and its sacraments were already the means by which Christians began their own "resurrection" and entrance into the heavenly kingdom. Concern with the individual Christian's relation to God and interior spiritual condition replaced the earlier stress on the collective, the universal, and the objectively historical. The collective and historical import of early Christian eschatology was now subsumed by the Church, which enacted its historical imperative by its public responsibility in preserving and propagating the faith, and by providing the community of believers with the grace-giving sacraments. For the established forms of Christianity from Augustine's time on, eschatology was understood symbolically, with its literal historical expectation seen as a primitive mythological misunderstanding of the biblical revelation, without genuine relevance to humanity's present spiritual condition.

The original eschatological impulse, however, never entirely disappeared. On the one hand, it lived on as an undercurrent in which history was still implicitly seen as moving teleologically toward a spiritual climax, but with Christ's return at the end time, though inevitable, postponed to the indefinite future. On the other hand, fresh expectations of an imminent apocalypse and Second Coming periodically emerged in specific individuals and communities, accompanied by a marked intensification of religious fervor, and based on new interpretations of the biblical prophecies or on new recognitions of the evil and chaotic character of the contemporary age. But such expectations were usually fostered on the fringes of the established Church, especially by heretical sects suffering persecutions. The Church discouraged literal interpretations of eschatology and recommended that faith be placed in its sacraments, by which such anxieties could be overcome. To calculate the end time was futile, it taught, since for God a thousand years might equal a day, or vice versa.

Finally, with the rise of modern humanism and the modern mind's increased awareness of history and evolution, Christian conceptions of the millennial transformation took on a more progressive and immanent quality, with humanity's moral, intellectual, and spiritual development culminating in some form of human or cosmic divinization—a conceptual shift visible from the time of

Erasmus and Francis Bacon, and achieving more elaborate formulation in later thinkers such as Hegel and Teilhard de Chardin (and, in a different spirit, in Nietzsche). In connection with some ambiguous symbolism contained in several biblical prophecies, especially in the Book of Revelation, and in response to various historical developments (e.g., the European discovery and settling of America, the papal declaration of the dogma of the Assumption, the nuclear and ecological threats of planetary catastrophe), it has frequently been suggested that the Second Coming would occur at the end of the two-thousand-year Christian aeon, in the late twentieth century. (See, for example, Carl G. Jung's extraordinary discussion in "Answer to Job," in *Collected Works of Carl Gustav Jung*, vol. 11, translated by R. F. C. Hull, edited by H. Read et al. [Princeton: Princeton University Press, 1969].)

16.   As the Mother of the Logos, Mary took on attributes of the Judaic biblical figure of Sophia, or Wisdom—described in Proverbs and Ecclesiasticus as God's eternal creation, a celestial feminine being who personified divine wisdom and mediated humanity's knowledge of God. In Roman Catholic theology, Mary was explicitly identified with Sophia. The relationship of the Old Testament Sophia to the New Testament Logos, both of which represented the divine creative and revelatory wisdom, was thus obliquely reflected in the relationship of Mary to Christ. The figure of the Virgin Mother also absorbed some of the original meaning and function of the Holy Spirit—as principle of divine presence in the Church, as comforter, as mediator of wisdom and spiritual birth, and as instrument of Christ's entrance into the world.

More generally, Catholicism's partial transformation of God into a sheltering and forgiving maternal-like figure prompted Erich Fromm to comment that "Catholicism signified the disguised return to the religion of the Great Mother who had been defeated by Yahweh" (*The Dogma of Christ and Other Essays on Religion, Psychology, and Culture* [New York: Holt, Rinehart & Winston, 1963], 90–91). In the mystical literature of Christian spirituality (e.g., Clement of Alexandria, John of the Cross), explicitly maternal qualities, such as nourishing breasts, were ascribed to God and Christ. For a discussion of both the presence and the suppression of the feminine in Christian theology and worship, see Joan Chamberlain Engelsman, *The Feminine Dimension of the Divine* (Wilmette, Ill.: Chiron, 1987).

17.   Despite the exaltation of the feminine suggested by the Mother Church and Virgin Mary themes, a patriarchal authoritarianism, often theologically justified by reference to the Genesis account of Eve's role in the Fall, continued to express itself through the Church's systematic depreciation of women, of women's spirituality and capacity for religious authority, and (in accord with the sin of Eve and the idealization of the Virgin Mary) of human sexuality.

In both the organization and the self-image of the Church, two polar aspects were expressed which were gender-related. Considered as the ecclesiastical hierarchy, the Church took on the role of Yahweh in the Old Testament, the masculine divine authority of God, with corresponding traits of juridical sovereignty, dogmatic certainty, and paternal guardianship and care. By contrast, considered as the body of the faithful, the Church took on the role of Israel in the Old Testament, the feminine beloved of God (later incarnate in the Virgin Mary), with the corresponding Christian inculcation of such "feminine" virtues as compassion, purity, humility, and obedience. The pope, bishops, and priests represented the divine authority on earth, while the laity represented that which needed to be instructed, justified, and saved. This same polarity was expressed as that of the "head" of the Church and the "body" of the Church. Theologically, the polarity was overcome in the doctrinal understanding of Christ as fulfillment and synthesis of both sides of the Church (just as Christ was seen as fruit of the marriage between Yahweh and Israel).

18. The Church sustained the ancient ordering of events according to archetypal cycles through its liturgical calendar, which provided a ritual living through of the Christian mystery in the context of nature's annual cycle: Christ's Advent in the darkness of winter, his birth at Christmas (coincident with the winter solstice and the birth of the Sun), the preparatory period of purification during Lent in the late winter in anticipation of the Last Supper on Holy Thursday, the Crucifixion on Good Friday, and finally the Resurrection on Easter Sunday amidst the rebirth of spring. Many antecedents for the Christian calendar can be seen in the classical pagan mystery religions.

19. An important qualification should be made here concerning the universality of Christianity in medieval Europe in view of the continuing vestiges of pagan myth and animism in much of the popular culture, as well as the existence of Judaism, Gnosticism, millennialism, witchcraft, Islamic influences, various esoteric traditions, and other minority and underground cultural forces unrelated or resistant to Christian orthodoxy.

Part IV. The Transformation of the Medieval Era

1. Boethius (c. 480–524) was a pivotal figure between the classical and medieval eras—a Roman statesman, one of the last Roman philosophers of antiquity, "the first Christian Scholastic," and the last layman in Christian philosophy for almost a thousand years. Born in Rome of an ancient aristocratic family that had been Christian for a century, he was educated in Athens and became a consul and minister in Roman government. Boethius's unfulfilled goal was to translate and comment upon all the works of Plato and Aristotle, and to forge a "restoration of their ideas into a single harmony." His completed works—especially those on Aristotelian logic, a few short theological treatises, and his Platonist manifesto *The Consolation of Philosophy*—were to have considerable influence on medieval thought. Falsely accused of treason by the barbarian king Theodoric, Boethius was sentenced to prison (where he wrote the *Consolation*) and executed. When Boethius's senatorial colleague Cassiodorus later decided to retire from Roman political life to the monastery he founded, he brought with him his Roman library and placed Boethius's works on the reading list for the education of his monks. Thus the scholarly ideals of the later classical era, and in particular of the educated Roman aristocracy, were transmitted into the Christian monastic tradition. It was Boethius who first formulated the essential Scholastic principle, "As far as possible, join faith to reason." And it was a passage in his commentary on Porphyry's *Isagoge* (a Greek introduction to Aristotelian logic) that initiated the long medieval controversy between nominalism and realism concerning the nature of universals.

2.   Hugh of Saint-Victor (1096–1141) also helped forge the new medieval awareness of human history as a temporal development of inherent significance. He noted, for example, the peculiar tendency of human civilization to move over time from East to West—a fact that suggested to him the approach of the end time, since the limit of the West had apparently already been reached at the Atlantic coast. Hugh also argued against Augustine's interpretation of Genesis as atemporal metaphor, instead affirming a true temporal succession of creative acts, and he upheld the value of salvational history's concrete actuality prior to the imposition of allegorical interpretations of that history. See M. D. Chenu, "Theology and the New Awareness of History" in *Nature, Man and Society in the Twelfth Century: Essays on New Theological Perspectives in the Latin West*, edited and translated by J. Taylor and L. K. Little (Chicago: University of Chicago Press, 1983), 162–201.

3.   The Dominican and Franciscan mendicant orders also represented a force for social revolution in the high Middle Ages. Their commitment to poverty and humility was both a return to the apostolic life of the primitive church and a break from the feudal system and its propertied ecclesiastical hierarchy. In the latter respect, the evangelical friars were similar to the new urban class of merchants and artisans who had also defected from the feudal economy, and it was especially from this class that the orders would draw their numbers. A similar parallel existed in the intellectual revolution that emerged from the Dominican and Franciscan theologians. Just as the evangelical movements found new sources of inspiration in the literal meaning of Scripture against the allegorizing glosses favored by traditional theologians, so this same tendency was reflected in the Scholastics' increasing philosophical respect for the concrete empirical world against the otherworldly idealism of the Augustinian-Platonist tradition. See Chenu, "The Evangelical Awakening," ibid., 239–269.

4.   In a sense, Aquinas outdid Aristotle in his positive valuation of the body. Aquinas's doctrine of the Resurrection held that the perfect human being was a full composite of soul and body, and that with the purification of the soul would come a reunion with and glorification of the body. Whereas for Aristotelians the intimate soul-body relation implied the mortality of the soul, for Aquinas that same intimacy supported the immortality of the redeemed body.

5.   The polarity represented by Aquinas and Augustine (and their respective affinities for Aristotle and Plato) may be understood in part as deriving from their individual intellectual responses to the radically different cultural tempers of their historical periods. If Augustine's Platonic otherworldliness and emphasis on supersensible knowledge can be seen as a reaction to and development out of the pagan sensualism and skeptical secularism of the later classical era, Aquinas's Aristotelian embrace of empiricism and materiality can be seen as a reaction to and development out of the Christian antiworldliness and fideist anti-intellectualism of the earlier medieval era. The contrast of Augustine's pessimism concerning humanity and nature with Aquinas's more optimistic views also has cultural reflections. Living during the last years of the classical era, Augustine was confronted with the decadence and disintegration of Roman civilization amidst the barbarian invasions. Aquinas, however, lived when

European civilization was experiencing a new era of stabilization and rapid development during the high Middle Ages, with the forces of nature increasingly controlled by the human intellect and with the European continent relatively free of external threats. For Augustine, the spirit of the secular world around him must have seemed fraught with decay, suffering, and evil, with the human capacity for positive self-determination minimal; Aquinas's milieu was decidedly more progressive.

6. Aquinas's rationalism was always in tension with a suprarational mysticism showing the influence of Dionysius the Areopagite. Probably a fifth-century Syrian monk who assumed the name of Paul's New Testament convert at Athens, Dionysius set forth a Neoplatonic Christian mysticism that stressed the ultimate unknowability of God: Whatever qualities the human mind attributes to God cannot be considered ultimately valid, for if they are humanly comprehensible, they must be limited to the finiteness of human understanding, and cannot therefore be said to comprehend the infinite nature of God. Even the concepts of "being" and "reality" cannot be attributed to God, since such concepts could only be derived from things that God has created, and the nature of the Creator must be of a fundamentally different character from the nature of his creation. Hence any affirmation of God's nature must be complemented by its negation, and both affirmation and negation are ultimately transcended by God, who surpasses anything the human mind can conceive. These considerations (basic to the *via negativa*, the tradition of negative or apophatic theology which was especially characteristic of Eastern Christianity) perhaps throw light on the statement Aquinas made after a mystical experience he had while celebrating Mass shortly before he died: ". . . such things have been revealed to me that all that I have written seems to me as so much straw."

7. According to Aristotle, any motion other than that caused by the natural tendencies of the different elements must be caused by a constantly applied force. A stone at rest will remain at rest, or will move directly toward the center of the Earth as befits the natural motion of all heavy objects. To explain the difficult case of projectile motion, however, in which a thrown stone continues to move long after it has left the thrower's hand without any visible constantly applied push, Aristotle suggested that the air disturbed by the stone's movement would continue to push the stone after it left the hand. Later Aristotelians criticized this theory for its various weaknesses, but it was Buridan in the fourteenth century who presented a coherent solution: When a projectile is thrown, it is impressed with a motive force, an impetus proportional to its speed and mass, which continues to propel the projectile after it has left its original projector. In addition, Buridan adumbrated the idea that a falling body's weight impresses equal increments of impetus in equal intervals of time.

Buridan also suggested that when God created the heavens, he may have impressed an impetus in the celestial bodies, which continued to move ever afterward (when God rested on the seventh day) by virtue of that impetus, since there was no resistance to their motions. By this means, Buridan could hypothetically dispense with angelic intelligences as the movers of the celestial bodies, since they were neither mentioned in the Bible nor physically necessary to explain the motions. This was perhaps the first major application of a principle of terrestrial physics to celestial phenomena. In turn, Buridan's successor, Oresme, conceived of such a universe as resembling a mechanical clock constructed and left running by God.

Among other contributions, Oresme introduced the use of mathematical tabulations by equivalent graphing, anticipating Descartes's development of analytic geometry. But in reference to the problem of the celestial movements, Oresme argued that the apparent rotation of the entire heavens could just as easily be explained by the rotation of the Earth—a more plausible smaller movement by a single body compared with the immensely greater and swifter movement of all the heavenly bodies through vast spaces in a single day (which Oresme deemed "unbelievable and unthinkable"). In viewing the stars each night or the Sun each day, the observer can be certain only of the fact of movement; whether that movement is produced by the heavens or the Earth cannot be ascertained by the senses, which would register the same phenomenon in either case.

Oresme also argued against Aristotle that material objects may fall to the Earth not because the Earth is the center of the universe, but because material bodies naturally move toward each other. A thrown stone falls back to the Earth wherever in the universe the Earth may be, because the Earth is near the thrown stone and has its own attractive center, while another earth elsewhere would receive nearby loose stones to its own center. Thus matter may be naturally attracted to other matter. Such a theoretical alternative to Aristotle's explanation of falling bodies in terms of a central Earth was prerequisite to the later heliocentric hypothesis. Also, by assuming Buridan's impetus theory, Oresme argued that a vertically falling body would fall straight down to the Earth, even if the Earth was moving, just as a man on a moving ship could move his hand downward in a straight line alongside the mast without noticing any deviation. The ship carries and maintains the hand's straight line relative to itself, just as the Earth would a falling stone. Yet having made these various astute points against Aristotle, and having asserted that only by faith—not by reason or observation or Scripture—could one assert that the Earth is stationary, Oresme then discarded his arguments for the Earth's rotation. In a later and different scientific context, Copernicus and Galileo did not discard them.

The work of Buridan and Oresme in the fourteenth century thus laid the mandatory groundwork for a planetary Earth, the law of inertia, the concept of momentum, the law of uniform accelerated motion for freely falling bodies, analytic geometry, the removal of the terrestrial-celestial distinction, and a mechanistic universe with a clockmaker God. See Thomas S. Kuhn, *The Copernican Revolution: Planetary Astronomy and the Development of Western Thought* (Cambridge: Harvard University Press, 1957), 115–123.

8.   Ockham himself used formulations, somewhat different from that now known as Ockham's razor, such as "Plurality is not to be assumed without necessity" and "What can be done with fewer [assumptions] is done in vain with more."

9.   Translated by Mary Martin McLaughlin in *The Portable Renaissance Reader*, edited by J. B. Ross and M. M. McLaughlin (New York: Penguin, 1977), 478.

Part V. The Modern World View

1. Tycho de Brahe also proposed a system intermediate between those of Copernicus and Ptolemy, in which all the planets except the Earth revolve about the Sun, while the entire Sun-centered system revolves about the Earth. Essentially a modification of the ancient system of Heraclides, the first part preserved many of the superior Copernican insights, while the second part preserved Aristotelian physics, the fixed central Earth, and the literal interpretation of Scripture. Brahe's system furthered the Copernican cause, by explicating some of its advantages and problems, but also because some of the new orbital paths of the Sun and planets intersected each other, bringing into question the physical reality of the separate aetheric spheres within which each planet was supposed to be embedded. In addition, Brahe's observations of comets, now calculated to be beyond the Moon, as well as of a nova that appeared in 1572, began to convince astronomers that the heavens were not immutable, a view subsequently supported by Galileo's telescopic discoveries. Like Brahe's compromise arrangement of the planetary orbits, the observed movements of the comets also made less plausible the existence of the aetheric spheres, which Aristotle had considered to be composed of an invisible but solid crystalline substance. The comets were now recognized as moving through spaces traditionally thought to be filled by the solid crystalline spheres, thereby casting further doubt on their physical reality. Kepler's ellipses would make the circular-moving spheres altogether untenable. See Thomas S. Kuhn, *The Copernican Revolution: Planetary Astronomy and the Development of Western Thought* (Cambridge: Harvard University Press, 1957), 200–209.

2. Translated and quoted by James Brodrick, *The Life and Work of Blessed Robert Francis Cardinal Bellarmine, S.J.*, vol. 2 (London: Longmans, Green, 1950), 359.

3. Galileo's final work and his most important contribution to physics, *Two New Sciences*, was completed in 1634, when he was seventy years old. It was published four years later in Holland, after the manuscript had been smuggled out of Italy (apparently with the assistance of the French ambassador to the Vatican, Galileo's former pupil the Duke of Noailles). In that same year, 1638, John Milton traveled from England to Italy where he visited Galileo, an event later recorded in *Areopagitica* (1644), Milton's classic argument for freedom of the press: "I have sat among their learned men, (for that honor I had,) and been counted happy to have been born in such a place of philosophic freedom, as they supposed England was, while themselves did nothing but bemoan the servile condition into which learning amongst them was brought; that this was it which had damped the glory of Italian wits; that nothing had been there written now these many years but flattery and fustian. There it was that I found and visited the famous Galileo, grown old, a prisoner to the inquisition, for thinking in astronomy otherwise than the Franciscan and Dominican licensers thought" (John Milton, *Areopagitica and Other Prose Writings*, edited by W. Haller [New York: Book League of America, 1929], 41).

4.   Implicit in this division between the human mind and the material world was a nascent skepticism concerning the mind's ability genuinely to penetrate beyond appearances to an intrinsic order in the world—i.e., concerning the capacity of the subject to bridge the gap to the object. Yet this skepticism, broached by Locke, made explicit by Hume, and critically reformulated by Kant, did not generally affect the scientific understanding as it developed through the eighteenth and nineteenth centuries and well into the twentieth.

5.   Mention should be made here of Alfred Russel Wallace's independent formulation of the theory of evolution in 1858, which impelled Darwin to make public his own work after not doing so for twenty years. Among Darwin's and Wallace's important predecessors, Buffon, Lamarck, and Darwin's grandfather Erasmus Darwin stand out, as does Lyell in geology. In addition, Diderot, La Mettrie, Kant, Goethe, and Hegel were all moving toward an evolutionary world conception.

6.   W. Carl Rufus, "Kepler as an Astronomer," in The History of Science Society, *Johannes Kepler: A Tercentenary Commemoration of His Life and Work* (Baltimore: Williams and Wilkins, 1931), 36.

7.   This sentence should be qualified by the fact that the nongeocentric cosmologies were generally offshoots of the Platonic-Pythagorean tradition, and were more emphatically opposed by the Aristotelian-Ptolemaic cosmology than by Platonism. See also note 1, part 2, on Plato's possible heliocentrism.

8.   Recent historical analyses have suggested that the rapid decline of Renaissance esotericism in Restoration England was influenced by the highly charged social and political environment that marked seventeenth-century British history. During the revolutionary upheavals of the English Civil War and Interregnum (1642–60), esoteric philosophies such as astrology and Hermeticism were extremely popular, and their close association with radical political and religious movements was widely perceived as threatening to the established Church and propertied classes. Astrological almanacs outsold the Bible during this period of broken censorship, and influential astrologers such as William Lilly encouraged the forces of rebellion. On a conceptual level, the esoteric philosophies supported a world view highly compatible with the antiauthoritarian political and religious activism of the radical movements, with direct spiritual illumination seen as potentially available to every individual of whatever rank or sex, and with nature seen as alive, permeated at all levels by divinity, and perpetually self-transforming. After the Restoration in 1660, leading philosophers, doctors, and clergymen stressed the importance of a sober natural philosophy, such as the recently published mechanical philosophy of inert material particles governed by permanently fixed laws, to undercut the passion-inflaming "enthusiasm" supported by the esoteric world view and the radical sects.

With the specter of the previous decades' social chaos in the background, Hermetic ideas were increasingly attacked, astrology ceased to be favored by upper-class patronage or taught at the universities, and the science that developed within the Royal Society (founded 1660) upheld the mechanistic view of nature as a despiritualized world of hard matter. Major founding figures in the Royal Society such as Robert Boyle and Christopher Wren continued, at least in private, to consider astrology to be valid (believing, like Bacon, that astrology should be scientifically reformed rather than rejected), but the political climate was increasingly inhospitable; Boyle, for example, did not allow his defense of astrology to be published until after his death. This same context appears to have influenced Newton and his literary executors to suppress the esoteric, Hermetic background of Newton's scientific ideas. See David Kubrin, "Newton's Inside Out: Magic, Class Struggle, and the Rise of Mechanism in the West," in The Analytic Spirit, edited by H. Woolf (Ithaca: Cornell University Press, 1980); Patrick Curry, Prophecy and Power: Astrology in Early Modern England (Princeton: Princeton University Press, 1989); Christopher Hill, The World Turned Upside Down: Radical Ideas During the English Revolution (New York: Viking, 1972); and P. M. Rattansi, "The Intellectual Origins of the Royal Society," in Notes and Records of the Royal Society of London 23 (1968): 129–143.

For two further analyses of the same intellectual revolution in terms of the epistemological conflict between two different perspectives toward gender (the Hermetic ideal of knowledge as an erotic union of masculine and feminine, reflecting a view of the universe as a cosmic marriage, versus the Baconian program of male dominance), see Evelyn Fox Keller, "Spirit and Reason in the Birth of Modern Science," in Reflections on Gender and Science (New Haven: Yale University Press, 1985), 43–65; and Carolyn Merchant, The Death of Nature: Women, Ecology, and the Scientific Revolution (San Francisco: Harper & Row, 1980).

9. Galileo, Dialogue Concerning the Two Chief World Systems, 328: "You wonder that there are so few followers of the Pythagorean opinion [that the Earth moves] while I am astonished that there have been any up to this day who have embraced and followed it. Nor can I ever sufficiently admire the outstanding acumen of those who have taken hold of this opinion and accepted it as true: they have, through sheer force of intellect done such violence to their own senses as to prefer what reason told them over that which sensible experience showed them to be the contrary. For the arguments against [the Earth's rotation] we have examined are very plausible, as we have seen; and the fact that the Ptolemaics and the Aristotelians and all their disciples took them to be conclusive is indeed a strong argument of their effectiveness. But the experiences which overtly contradict the annual movement [of the Earth around the Sun] are indeed so much greater in their apparent force that, I repeat, there is no limit to my astonishment when I reflect that Aristarchus and Copernicus were able to make reason so conquer sense that, in defiance of the latter, the former became mistress of their belief."

10. Kepler, Harmonies of the World, V: "Now, since the dawn eight months ago, since the broad daylight three months ago, and since a few days ago, when the full sun illuminated my wonderful speculations, nothing holds me back. I yield freely to the sacred frenzy; I dare frankly to confess that I have stolen the golden vessels of the Egyptians to build a tabernacle for my God far from the bounds of Egypt. If you pardon me, I shall rejoice; if you reproach me, I shall endure. The die is cast, and I am writing the book—to be read either now or by posterity, it matters not. It can wait a century for a reader, as God himself has waited six thousand years for a witness."

11.   Here was perhaps the most fundamental distinction between classical and modern science: While Aristotle had postulated four causes—material, efficient, formal, and final—modern science considered only the first two empirically justifiable. Thus Bacon praised Democritus for removing God and mind from the natural world, in contrast to Plato and Aristotle who repeatedly introduced final causes into scientific explanations. See also the more recent statement by the biologist Jacques Monod: "The cornerstone of scientific method is . . . the *systematic* denial that 'true' knowledge can be got at by interpreting phenomena in terms of final causes—that is to say, of 'purpose' " (Jacques Monod, *Chance and Necessity: An Essay on the Natural Philosophy of Modern Biology* (translated by A. Wainhouse) [New York: Random House, 1972], 21).

12.   This was the celebrated reply of the French astronomer and mathematician Pierre Simon Laplace to Napoleon, when questioned about the absence of God in his new theory of the solar system, which had perfected the Newtonian synthesis. Because of certain apparent irregularities in the planetary movements, Newton had believed that the solar system required occasional divine adjustments to maintain stability. Laplace's reply reflected his success in demonstrating that every known secular variation (such as the changing speeds of Jupiter and Saturn) was cyclical, and that therefore the solar system was entirely stable on its own account without divine intervention.

13.   The character and composition of the Church clergy in France also played a complex role in these developments. The clergy's upper ranks were typically occupied by the aristocracy's younger sons, who took the positions as sinecures, and whose style of life was generally indistinguishable from that of nonclerical aristocrats. Religious fervor at this level of the Church was infrequent, and was distrusted in others. The interests of the institutional Church seemed to lie less in the pastoral mission of religious salvation than in the enforcement of orthodoxy and the preservation of political advantage. Further complicating the issue was the growing embrace of Enlightenment rationalism by members of the aristocratic clergy itself, thus strengthening the secular forces from within the Church structure. See Jacques Barzun, "Society and Politics," in *The Columbia History of the World,* edited by John A. Garraty and Peter Gay (New York: Harper & Row, 1972), 694–700.

14.   "Those who set out to serve both God and Mammon soon discover that there is no God" (Logan Pearsall Smith).

15.   Such a view was controverted by Christians who interpreted that command as signifying "stewardship" rather than exploitation, the latter seen as reflecting the alienation of the Fall.

Part VI. The Transformation of the Modern Era

1. On the basis of Kant's second preface to the *Critique of Pure Reason,* it has often been said that Kant called his insight a "Copernican revolution" (e.g., by Karl Popper, Bertrand Russell, John Dewey, and the fifteenth edition of the *Encyclopaedia Britannica,* among many others). I. B. Cohen has pointed out (in *Revolution in Science* [Cambridge: Harvard University Press, 1985], 237–243) that Kant does not appear to have made that specific statement. On the other hand, Kant explicitly compared his new philosophical strategy to Copernicus's astronomical theory, and although strictly speaking the term "Copernican revolution" may postdate both Copernicus and Kant, both the term and the comparison are accurate and illuminating.

2. "I can safely say that nobody understands quantum mechanics" (Richard Feynman).

3. Quoted in Huston Smith, *Beyond the Post-Modern Mind,* rev. ed. (Wheaton, Ill.: Quest, 1989), 8.

4. Kuhn's ideas, first set forth in *The Structure of Scientific Revolutions* (1962), were in part the outgrowth of significant advances in the study of the history of science made a generation earlier, notably the work of Alexandre Koyré and A. O. Lovejoy. Also important were major developments within academic philosophy such as those associated with the later Wittgenstein, and with the progress of argument in the school of logical empiricism from Rudolf Carnap through W. V. O. Quine. The widely accepted conclusion of that argument essentially affirmed a relativized Kantian position: i.e., one cannot, in the last analysis, logically compute complex truths out of simple elements based in direct sensation, because all such simple sensory elements are ultimately defined by the ontology of a specific language, and there exist a multiplicity of languages, each with its own particular mode of construing reality, each one selectively eliciting and identifying the objects it describes. The choice of which language to employ is finally dependent on one's purposes, not on objective "facts," which are themselves constituted by the same theoretical and linguistic systems through which those facts are judged. All "raw data" are already theory-laden. See W. V. O. Quine, "Two Dogmas of Empiricism," in *From a Logical Point of View,* 2nd ed. (New York: Harper & Row, 1961), 20–46.

5. The crucial word through which Hegel expressed his concept of dialectical integration was *aufheben,* meaning both "to cancel" and "to lift up." In the moment of synthesis, the antithetical state is both preserved and transcended, negated and fulfilled.

6. Ronald Sukenick, "The Death of the Novel," in *The Death of the Novel and Other Stories* (New York: Dial, 1969), 41. On a less futile note, perhaps the *actor* may be said to epitomize the postmodern artistic ethos, and to personify the postmodern identity generally, for his or her reality remains deliberately and irreducibly ambiguous. Irony pervades action; performance is all. The actor is never univocally committed to an exclusive meaning, to a literal reality. Everything is "as if."

7.   Richard Rorty, *Philosophy and the Mirror of Nature* (Princeton: Princeton University Press, 1979), 176.

8.   Ihab Hassan, quoted in Albrecht Wellmer, "On the Dialectic of Modernism and Postmodernism," *Praxis International* 4 (1985): 338. See also Richard J. Bernstein's discussion of the same passage in his 1988 Presidential Address to the Metaphysical Society of America ("Metaphysics, Critique, Utopia," *Review of Metaphysics* 42 [1988]: 259–260), where he characterizes the postmodern intellectual attitude as sometimes resembling Hegel's description of a self-fulfilling abstract skepticism, "which only ever sees pure nothingness in its result . . .[and] cannot get any further from there, but must wait to see whether something new comes along and what it is, in order to throw it too into the same empty abyss" (G. W. F. Hegel, *The Phenomenology of Spirit*, translated by A. V. Miller [Oxford: Oxford University Press, 1977], 51).

9.   Arnold J. Toynbee, in *Encyclopaedia Britannica*, 15th ed., s.v. "time."

10.   Friedrich Nietzsche, *The Gay Science*, translated by W. Kaufman (New York: Random House, 1974), 181.

11.   Max Weber, *The Protestant Ethic and the Spirit of Capitalism*, translated by Talcott Parsons (New York: Charles Scribner's Sons, 1958), 182.

12.   Carl G. Jung, "The Undiscovered Self," in *Collected Works of Carl Gustav Jung*, vol. 10, translated by R. F. C. Hull, edited by H. Read et al. (Princeton: Princeton University Press, 1970), pars. 585–586.

Part VII. Epilogue

1.   John J. McDermott, "Revisioning Philosophy" conference, Esalen Institute, Big Sur, California, June 1987.

2.   The double bind theory was an application of Bertrand Russell's theory of logical types (from Russell and Alfred North Whitehead's *Principia Mathematica*) to a communications analysis of schizophrenia. See Gregory Bateson et al., "Toward a Theory of Schizophrenia," in Bateson, *Steps to an Ecology of Mind* (New York: Ballantine, 1972), 201–227.

3.   Ernest Gellner, *The Legitimation of Belief* (Cambridge: Cambridge University Press, 1975), 206–207.

4.   Vincent Brome, *Jung: Man and Myth* (New York: Atheneum, 1978), 14.

5.   Jung, "Psychological Commentary on 'The Tibetan Book of the Great Liberation,' " in *Collected Works of Carl Gustav Jung*, vol. 11, translated by R. F. C. Hull, edited by H. Read et al. (Princeton: Princeton University Press, 1969), par. 759.

6. The most comprehensive presentations of Grof's clinical evidence and its theoretical implications can be found in Stanislav Grof, *Realms of the Human Unconscious: Observations from LSD Research* (New York: Viking, 1975) and *LSD Psychotherapy* (Pomona, Calif.: Hunter House, 1980). A more recent popular account is his *Beyond the Brain: Birth, Death, and Transcendence in Psychotherapy* (Albany: State University of New York Press, 1985).

7. The clinical evidence from Grof's research concerning the perinatal experience should not be misunderstood as suggesting the operation of a Freudian, linear-mechanistic kind of causality, in which the individual birth trauma is viewed as mechanically producing specific psychological and intellectual syndromes in the same, more or less "hydraulic" manner that a childhood Oedipal trauma was seen by traditional psychoanalysts as producing specific pathological symptoms. The evidence suggests, rather, what might be called an archetypal form of causation, in which the individual's reliving of the birth process appears to mediate participation in a much larger, transpersonal, archetypal death-rebirth process, with the individual and collective levels of the psyche radically interpenetrating. The perinatal sequence does not seem to be ultimately grounded in or reducible to the individual's original experience of biological birth; instead, biological birth itself appears to reflect a more encompassing archetypal reality which is directly accessed by those undergoing the perinatal process, either spontaneously (as in personal experiences of "the dark night of the soul"), in religious ritual, or in experiential psychotherapy. The birth experience is here viewed not as an ultimate root, a reductionist cause in a closed system, but as an amplifying pivot, an experiential transduction point between personal and transpersonal realities.

Grof's evidence thus suggests a more complex understanding of causation than that offered by the conventional modern scientific conception of linear-mechanistic causality, and, in agreement with recent data and theories emerging from several other fields, points toward a conception that incorporates participatory, morphic, and teleological forms of causation—closer in character to classical Platonic and Aristotelian notions of archetypal, formal, and final causation, as well as to the later Jungian archetypal understanding. The organizing principles of this epistemology are symbolic, nonliteral, and radically multivalent in character, suggesting a nondualistic ontology that is metaphorically patterned "all the way down"—an understanding developed in recent decades by thinkers as diverse as Owen Barfield, Norman O. Brown, James Hillman, and Robert Bellah.

8. James Hillman, *Re-Visioning Psychology* (New York: Harper & Row, 1975), 126.

9. Writers and editors today often comment on the difficulty they have in revising many sentences that were originally written with the traditional generic "man," which they seek to replace with a term that is not gender-biased. Partly the difficulty is created by the fact that no other term simultaneously attempts to denote both the human species (i.e., all human beings) and a single generic human being. That is, the word "man" is uniquely capable of indicating a metaphorically singular and personal entity who is also intrinsically collective in character: "man" denotes a universal individual, an archetypal figure, as "human beings," "humankind," "people," and "men and women" do not. But I believe that the deeper reason for the difficulty in revising such sentences is that the entire meaning of such a sentence as originally conceived was implicitly structured around this specific image of the masculine archetypal human. As a close reading of the many relevant texts—Greco-Roman, Judaeo-Christian, and modern scientific-humanistic—makes clear, both the syntactical structure and the essential meaning of the language that most major Western thinkers have used to represent the human condition and the human enterprise, including its drama, its pathos, and its hubris, are inextricably associated with the unconscious presence of this archetypal figure, "man." At one level, the "man" of the Western intellectual tradition can be seen as simply a socially constructed "false universal," the use of which both reflected and helped shape a male-dominated society. More profoundly, however, "man" has also represented a living archetype in which members of both sexes, willy-nilly, have participated. An entire civilization and world have been constellated by its active, creative, problematic presence. This book has indeed told the story of "Western man," in all his tragic glory, blindness, and, I believe, growth toward self-transcendence.

At some point in the future, unthinking use of masculine generics will very likely disappear. If this book should be read in that new context, the essential role played in the narrative by the particular construction of the human signified by the generic "man" will stand out all the more conspicuously, and the many ramifications of that historical usage—psychological, social, cultural, intellectual, spiritual, ecological, cosmological—will be commensurately more evident. When gender-biased language is no longer the established norm, the entire cultural world view will have moved into a new era. The old kinds of sentences and phrases, the character of the human self-image, the place of humanity in the cosmos and in nature, the very nature of the human drama, all will have been radically transformed. As the language goes, so goes the world view—and vice versa.

10.   Two important complexities in this overarching dialectic may be mentioned here. First, as the narrative and various notes have suggested, the evolution of the Western mind can be seen as having been marked at every stage by a complex interplay of the masculine and feminine, with significant partial reunions with the feminine having occurred in coincidence with the great creative watersheds of Western culture from the birth of Greek civilization onward. Each synthesis and birth has constituted a stage in the much larger overarching dialectic between the masculine and feminine that I believe comprehends the history of the Western mind as a whole.

Yet interwoven with this unfolding masculine-feminine evolution is a second dialectical process, which has played a more explicit role in the historical narrative, and which involves a basic archetypal polarity within the nature of the masculine itself. On the one hand, the masculine principle (again, in both men and women) can be understood in terms of what may be called the Promethean impulse: restless, heroic, rebellious and revolutionary, individualistic and innovative, eternally seeking freedom, autonomy, change, and the new. On the other hand, there is its complement and opposite, what can be called the Saturnian impulse: conservative, stabilizing, controlling, dominating, that which seeks to sustain, order, contain, and repress—i.e., the juridical-structural-hierarchical side of the masculine that has expressed itself in patriarchy.

The two sides of the masculine—Prometheus and Saturn, son and father—are implications of each other. Each requires, calls forth, and grows into its opposite. On a broad scale, the dynamic tension between the two principles can be seen as constituting the dialectic that propels "history" (political, intellectual, spiritual). It is this dialectic that has driven the internal drama throughout *The Passion of the Western Mind*: the unceasing dynamic interplay between order and change, authority and rebellion, control and freedom, tradition and innovation, structure and revolution. I am suggesting, however, that this powerful dialectic ultimately propels and is propelled by—is, as it were, in the service of—yet a larger overarching dialectic involving the feminine, or "life."

Bibliography

Aeschylus. The extant plays in 2 vols. of *The Complete Greek Tragedies*. Edited by D. Grene and R. Lattimore. Chicago: University of Chicago Press, 1953–56.

Aquinas, Thomas. *An Aquinas Reader*. Edited, with an introduction by Mary T. Clark. Garden City, N.Y.: Doubleday, 1972.

————. *Basic Writings of St. Thomas Aquinas*. Edited by A. C. Pegis. 2 vols. New York: Random House, 1945.

————. *Summa Theologica*. Translated by the English Dominican Fathers. 3 vols. New York: Benziger, 1947–48.

Aristotle. *The Complete Works of Aristotle: The Revised Oxford Translation*. Edited by J. Barnes. 2 vols. Princeton: Princeton University Press, 1984.

Armitage, Angus. *Copernicus, The Founder of Modern Astronomy*. New York: Thomas Yoseloff, 1957.

Armstrong, A. H., ed. *The Cambridge History of Later Greek and Early Medieval Philosophy*. Cambridge: Cambridge University Press, 1967.

Augustine. *An Augustine Reader*. Edited, with an introduction by J. J. O'Meara. Garden City, N.Y.: Doubleday, 1973.

————. *Basic Writings of Saint Augustine*. Edited by W. J. Oates. 2 vols. New York: Random House, 1948.

————. *The City of God*. Translated by M. Dods. New York: Modern Library, 1950.

————. *The Confessions*. Translated by J. K. Ryan. Garden City, N.Y.: Doubleday, 1960.

————. *Works*. Edited by M. Dods. Edinburgh: Clark, 1871–77.

Bacon, Francis. *Advancement of Learning; Novum Organum; The New Atlantis*. In *Great Books of the Western World*, Vol. 30. Chicago: Encyclopaedia Britannica, 1952.

Bainton, Roland. *The Reformation of the Sixteenth Century*. Boston: Beacon Press, 1985.

Barbour, Ian. *Myths, Models, and Paradigms: A Comparative Study in Science and Religion*. New York: Harper & Row, 1974.

Barfield, Owen. "Coleridge's Philosophical Lectures." *Towards* 3, 2 (1989): 27–30.

————. *Saving the Appearances: A Study in Idolatry*. 2nd ed. Middletown, Conn.: Wesleyan University Press, 1988.

Barnett, Lincoln. *The Universe and Dr. Einstein*. Rev. ed. New York: William Morrow, 1972.

Barnhart, Bruno. "Monastic Wisdom and the World of Today." *Monastic Studies* 16 (1985): 111–138.

————. "The Sophia Hypothesis." Paper presented at symposium, The Feminine Wisdom Traditions and Creation Spirituality in Christianity; at conference, Gaia Consciousness: The Goddess and the Living Earth, California Institute of Integral Studies, San Francisco, April 1988.

Barzun, Jacques. *Classic, Romantic, and Modern*. Chicago: University of Chicago Press, 1975.

———. *Darwin, Marx, Wagner: Critique of a Heritage*. 2nd ed. Chicago: University of Chicago Press, 1981.

Bate, William Jackson. "The Crisis in English Studies." *Harvard Magazine*, Sept.-Oct. 1982: 46–53.

Bateson, Gregory. *Mind and Nature: A Necessary Unity*. New York: Dutton, 1979.

———. *Steps to an Ecology of Mind*. New York: Ballantine, 1972.

Baudelaire, Charles. *Les Fleurs du Mal*. Translated by F. Duke. Charlottesville: University Press of Virginia, 1961.

Baynes, Kenneth, James Bohman, Thomas McCarthy, eds. *After Philosophy: End or Transformation?* Cambridge: MIT Press, 1987.

Beauvoir, Simone de. *The Second Sex*. Translated and edited by H. M. Parshley. New York: Alfred A. Knopf, 1953.

Beckett, Samuel. *Endgame*. New York: Grove Press, 1958.

———. *Waiting for Godot*. New York: Grove Press, 1954.

Bellah, Robert N. *Beyond Belief: Essays on Religion in a Post-Traditional World*. New York: Harper & Row, 1970.

Benz, Ernst Wilhelm. *The Eastern Orthodox Church: Its Thought and Life*. Translated by R. Winston and C. Winston. Garden City, N.Y.: Doubleday, 1963.

———. *Evolution and Christian Hope: Man's Concept of the Future from the Early Fathers to Teilhard de Chardin*. Translated by H. G. Frank. Garden City, N.Y.: Doubleday, 1968.

Bergson, Henri. *Creative Evolution*. Translated by A. Mitchell. New York: Modern Library, 1944.

Berkeley, George. *The Principles of Human Knowledge*. In *Great Books of the Western World*, Vol. 35. Chicago: Encyclopaedia Britannica, 1952.

Bernstein, Richard J., ed. *Habermas and Modernity*. Cambridge: MIT Press, 1985.

———. "Metaphysics, Critique, Utopia." *Review of Metaphysics* 42 (1988): 255–273.

Bible. *Authorized King James Version*. Wheaton, Ill.: Tyndale House, 1981.

Bible. *The New Oxford Annotated Bible with the Apocrypha*. Expanded ed. Revised Standard Version. Edited by H. G. May and B. M. Metzger. New York: Oxford University Press, 1977.

Blake, William. *The Poetry and Prose of William Blake*. Edited by D. V. Erdman. Commentary by H. Bloom. Garden City, N.Y.: Doubleday, 1970.

Boas, George. *Dominant Themes of Modern Philosophy: A History*. New York: Ronald, 1957.

Boethius. *The Consolation of Philosophy*. Translated by R. Green. Indianapolis: Bobbs-Merrill, 1962.

Bohm, David. *Wholeness and the Implicate Order*. London: Routledge & Kegan Paul, 1980.

Bohr, Niels. *Atomic Physics and the Description of Nature*. Cambridge: Cambridge University Press, 1934.

Bonner, Gerald. "The Spirituality of St. Augustine and Its Influence on Western Mysticism." *Sobornost* 4, 2 (1982): 143–162.

Bornkamm, Gunther. *Jesus of Nazareth.* Translated by I. McLuskey and F. McLuskey with J. M. Robinson. New York: Harper & Row, 1975.

Bouyer, Louis. *The Spirituality of the New Testament and the Fathers.* Translated by M. P. Ryan. New York: Seabury, 1982.

Bridgman, P. W. *The Logic of Modern Physics.* New York: Macmillan, 1946.

Brodrick, James. *The Life and Work of Blessed Robert Francis Cardinal Bellarmine, S.J.* 2 vols. London: Longmans, Green, 1950.

Brome, Vincent. *Jung: Man and Myth.* New York: Atheneum, 1978.

Bronowski, Jacob, and Bruce Mazlish. *The Western Intellectual Tradition: From Leonardo to Hegel.* New York: Harper & Row, 1960.

Brown, Norman O. *Love's Body.* New York: Random House, 1968.

Brown, Raymond E. *Biblical Reflections on Crises Facing the Church.* New York: Paulist Press, 1975.

Burckhardt, Jacob. *The Civilization of the Renaissance in Italy.* Translated by S. G. C. Middlemore. New York: Harper Torchbook, 1958.

Burnaby, J. *Amor Dei: A Study of the Religion of Saint Augustine.* London: Hodder & Stoughton, 1938.

Butterfield, Herbert. *The Origins of Modern Science, 1300–1800.* Rev. ed. New York: Free Press, 1965.

———. *Writings on Christianity and History.* Edited by C. T. McIntyre. Oxford: Oxford University Press, 1979.

Byron, George Gordon. *Lord Byron: Selected Letters and Journals.* Edited by L. A. Marchand. Cambridge: Harvard University Press, 1982.

Campbell, Joseph. *The Hero with a Thousand Faces.* 2nd ed. Princeton: Princeton University Press, 1968.

———. *The Masks of God.* Vol. 3, *Occidental Mythology.* New York: Viking, 1964.

Camus, Albert. *The Myth of Sisyphus and Other Essays.* Translated by J. O'Brien. New York: Random House, 1959.

———. *The Stranger.* Translated by S. Gilbert. New York: Random House, 1954.

Capra, Fritjof. *The Tao of Physics: An Exploration of the Parallels Between Modern Physics and Eastern Mysticism.* Berkeley: Shambhala, 1975.

———. *The Turning Point: Science, Society, and the Rising Culture.* New York: Simon and Schuster, 1982.

Carnap, Rudolf. "The Rejection of Metaphysics." In *20th Century Philosophy: The Analytic Tradition,* edited by M. Weitz. New York: Free Press, 1966.

Caspar, Max. *Kepler.* Translated and edited by C. D. Hellman. London: Abelard-Schuman, 1959.

Cassirer, Ernst. *The Philosophy of Symbolic Forms.* Translated by R. Manheim. 3 vols. New Haven: Yale University Press, 1955–57.

Castiglione, Baldesar. *The Book of the Courtier.* Translated by G. Bull. Baltimore: Penguin, 1976.

Cellini, Benvenuto. *The Autobiography of Benvenuto Cellini*. Translated by J. A. Symonds. New York: Modern Library, 1985.

Chadwick, Henry. *Early Christian Thought and the Classical Tradition: Studies in Justin, Clement and Origen*. Oxford: Oxford University Press, 1966.

Chenu, M. D. *Nature, Man and Society in the Twelfth Century: Essays on New Theological Perspectives in the Latin West*. Edited and translated by J. Taylor and L. K. Little. Chicago: University of Chicago Press, 1983.

———. *Toward Understanding Saint Thomas*. Translated by A. M. Landry and D. Hughes. Chicago: University of Chicago Press, 1964.

Chodorow, Nancy J. *Feminism and Psychoanalytic Theory*. New Haven: Yale University Press, 1989.

———. *The Reproduction of Mothering: Psychoanalysis and the Sociology of Gender*. Berkeley: University of California Press, 1978.

Chroust, Anton-Hermann. *Aristotle: New Light on His Life and on Some of His Lost Works*. 2 vols. Notre Dame: University of Notre Dame Press, 1973.

Cicero, Marcus Tullius. *The Basic Works of Cicero*. Edited by M. Hadas. New York: Modern Library, 1951.

———. *De Natura Deorum; Academica*. With an English translation by H. Rackham. Cambridge: Harvard University Press, 1972.

Clement of Alexandria. *The Exhortation to the Heathen*. In *The Ante-Nicene Fathers*, edited by A. Roberts and J. Donaldson, Vol. 2. Grand Rapids, Mich.: Wm. B. Eerdmans, 1967.

Cohen, I. B. *Revolution in Science*. Cambridge: Harvard University Press, 1985.

Coleridge, Samuel Taylor. *The Portable Coleridge*. Edited by I. A. Richards. New York: Viking, 1950.

Colorado, Pam. "Bridging Native and Western Science." *Convergence* 21, 2/3 (1988): 49–68.

Comte, Auguste. *Introduction to Positive Philosophy*. Edited by F. Ferre. Indianapolis: Bobbs-Merrill, 1970.

Condorcet, Antoine-Nicolas, Marquis de. *Sketch for a Historical Picture of the Progress of the Human Mind*. Translated by J. Barraclough. Westport, Conn.: Hyperion, 1979.

Copernicus, Nicolaus. *On the Revolutions of the Heavenly Spheres*. Translated by C. G. Wallis. In *Great Books of the Western World*, Vol. 16. Chicago: Encyclopaedia Britannica, 1952.

———. *Three Copernican Treatises: The Commentariolus of Copernicus, the Letter against Werner, the Narratio Prima of Rheticus*. Translated, with an introduction by E. Rosen. New York: Columbia University Press, 1939.

Cornford, F. M. *Plato's Cosmology*. London: Routledge, 1966.

Curry, Patrick. *Prophecy and Power: Astrology in Early Modern England*. Princeton: Princeton University Press, 1989.

Cutler, Donald R., ed. *The Religious Situation: 1968*. Boston: Beacon Press, 1968.

Dante. *The Banquet*. Translated by K. Hillard. London: Routledge & Kegan Paul, 1889.

———. *The Divine Comedy*. Translated by C. S. Singleton. 3 vols. Princeton: Princeton University Press, 1973–75.

Danto, Arthur C. *The Philosophical Disenfranchisement of Art.* New York: Columbia University Press, 1986.

Darwin, Charles. *The Descent of Man and Selection in Relation to Sex.* Princeton: Princeton University Press, 1981.

———. *The Origin of Species.* New York: Dutton, Everyman's University Library edition of the 6th ed. (1882), 1971.

de Beer, Sir Gavin. *Charles Darwin: A Scientific Biography.* Garden City, N.Y.: Doubleday, 1965.

Derrida, Jacques. *Margins of Philosophy.* Translated by A. Bass. Chicago: University of Chicago Press, 1982.

———. *Writing and Difference.* Translated by A. Bass. Chicago: University of Chicago Press, 1978.

Descartes, René. *The Philosophical Works of Descartes.* Translated by E. S. Haldane and G. R. T. Ross. 2 vols. New York: Dover, 1955.

Dewey, John. *Experience and Nature.* Rev. ed. La Salle, Ill.: Open Court, 1971.

———. *The Quest for Certainty: A Study of the Relation of Knowledge and Action.* New York: Minton, Balch, 1929.

Dijksterhuis, E. J. *The Mechanization of the World Picture: Pythagoras to Newton.* Translated by C. Dikshoorn. Princeton: Princeton University Press, 1986.

Dodds, E. R. *The Ancient Concept of Progress.* Oxford: Clarendon Press, 1973.

———. *The Greeks and the Irrational.* Berkeley: University of California Press, 1951.

———. *Pagan and Christian in an Age of Anxiety: Some Aspects of Religious Experience from Marcus Aurelius to Constantine.* New York: Norton, 1970.

Dostoevsky, Fyodor. *The Brothers Karamazov.* Translated by C. Garnett. New York: Modern Library, 1933.

———. *Crime and Punishment.* Translated by C. Garnett. New York: Modern Library, 1950.

———. *Notes from Underground.* Edited and translated by M. Katz. New York: Norton, 1989.

Dreyer, J. L. E. *A History of Astronomy from Thales to Kepler.* 2nd ed. New York: Dover, 1953.

Duhem, Pierre. *To Save the Phenomena: An Essay on the Idea of Physical Theory from Plato to Galileo.* Translated by E. Doland and C. Maschler. Chicago: University of Chicago Press, 1969.

Eckhart, Meister. *The Essential Sermons, Commentaries, Treatises, and Defense.* Translated, with an introduction by E. Colledge and B. McGinn. New York: Paulist Press, 1981.

Eckman, Barbara. "Jung, Hegel, and the Subjective Universe." *Spring 1986* (Dallas: Spring Publications, 1986): 88–89.

Edinger, Edward F. *Ego and Archetype: Individuation and the Religious Function of the Psyche.* Baltimore: Penguin, 1973.

Edwards, Jonathan. *Apocalyptic Writings.* In *The Works of Jonathan Edwards,* Vol. 5, edited by S. J. Stein. New Haven: Yale University Press, 1977.

Einstein, Albert. *The Meaning of Relativity.* 5th ed. Princeton: Princeton University Press, 1956.

————. *Relativity: The Special and the General Theory.* Translated by R. W. Lawson. New York: Crown, 1961.

Eliade, Mircea. *Cosmos and History: The Myth of the Eternal Return.* Translated by W. R. Trask. New York: Harper & Row, 1954.

Eliot, T. S. *Complete Poems and Plays.* New York: Harcourt, Brace & World, 1971.

Emerson, Ralph Waldo. *The Collected Works.* 4 vols. Edited by A. R. Ferguson et al. Cambridge: Harvard University Press, 1979–87.

Engelsman, Joan Chamberlain. *The Feminine Dimension of the Divine.* Wilmette, Ill.: Chiron, 1987.

Erasmus. *The Epistles of Erasmus.* Translated by F. M. Nichols. London: Longmans, Green, 1901.

Erikson, Erik. *Childhood and Society.* 2nd ed. New York: Norton, 1950.

Euripides. The extant plays in 5 vols. of *The Complete Greek Tragedies.* Edited by D. Grene and R. Lattimore. Chicago: University of Chicago Press, 1955–59.

Evans, Donald. "Can We Know Spiritual Reality?" *Commonweal,* 13 July 1984.

Fairbairn, W. R. D. *An Object-Relations Theory of the Personality.* New York: Basic Books, 1952.

Fenichel, Otto. *The Psychoanalytic Theory of Neurosis.* New York: Norton, 1945.

Ferenczi, Sandor. *Thalassa: A Theory of Genitality.* Translated by H. A. Bunker. New York: Norton, 1968.

Ferguson, W. K., et al. *Renaissance: Six Essays.* New York: Harper Torchbook, 1962.

Feyerabend, Paul. *Against Method: Outline of an Anarchistic Theory of Knowledge.* Rev. ed. London: Verso, 1988.

————. *Science in a Free Society.* London: Verso, 1978.

Ficino, Marsilio. *The Book of Life.* Translated by C. Boer. Irving, Tex.: Spring Publications, 1980.

————. *The Letters of Marsilio Ficino.* Translated by members of the Language Department of the School of Economic Science, London. 2 vols. Preface by P. O. Kristeller. London: Shepheard-Walwyn, 1975.

————. *Platonic Theology.* Selected passages translated by J. L. Burroughs. *Journal of the History of Ideas,* 5, 2 (1944): 227–239.

Findlay, J. N. *Ascent to the Absolute.* London: Allen and Unwin, 1970.

————. *Hegel: A Re-examination.* New York: Humanities Press, 1958.

Finley, John H. *Four Stages of Greek Thought.* Stanford: Stanford University Press, 1966.

Foucault, Michel. *The Archaeology of Knowledge.* Translated by A. M. Sheridan Smith. London: Tavistock, 1972.

————. *Power/Knowledge: Selected Interviews and Other Writings.* Edited by C. Gordon. New York: Pantheon, 1980.

Fox, Robin Lane. *Pagans and Christians.* New York: Alfred A. Knopf, 1987.

Frank, Francine Wattman, and Paula A. Treichler. *Language, Gender, and Professional Writing.* New York: Modern Language Association, 1989.

Freeman, Kathleen, ed. and trans. *Ancilla to the Pre-Socratic Philosophers: A Complete Translation of the Fragments.* Cambridge: Harvard University Press, 1983.

Freud, Anna. *The Ego and the Mechanisms of Defense.* Rev. ed. New York: International Universities Press, 1966.

Freud, Sigmund. *The Standard Edition of the Complete Works of Sigmund Freud.* Edited by J. Strachey. 21 vols. New York: Hogarth, 1955–61.

Fromm, Erich. *The Dogma of Christ and Other Essays on Religion, Psychology, and Culture.* New York: Holt, Rinehart & Winston, 1963.

Gadamer, Hans-Georg. *Truth and Method.* Translated by G. Barden and J. Cumming. New York: Seabury, 1970.

Galbraith, John Kenneth. *The New Industrial State.* 4th ed. Boston: Houghton Mifflin, 1985.

Galilei, Galileo. *Dialogue Concerning the Two Chief World Systems—Ptolemaic and Copernican.* Translated by S. Drake. Berkeley: University of California Press, 1953.

———. *Discoveries and Opinions of Galileo.* Translated by S. Drake. New York: Doubleday, 1957.

———. *Sidereus Nuncius, or, The Sidereal Messenger.* Translated, with an introduction by A. van Helden. Chicago: University of Chicago Press, 1989.

———. *Two New Sciences.* Translated by S. Drake. Madison: University of Wisconsin Press, 1974.

Garin, Eugenio. *Italian Humanism.* Translated by P. Munz. Oxford: Blackwell, 1965.

Garraty, John A., and Peter Gay, eds. *The Columbia History of the World.* New York: Harper & Row, 1972.

Geertz, Clifford. "From the Native's Point of View: On the Nature of Anthropological Understanding." In *Interpretive Social Science: A Reader,* edited by P. Rabinow and W. M. Sullivan. Berkeley: University of California Press, 1979.

Gellner, Ernest. *The Legitimation of Belief.* Cambridge: Cambridge University Press, 1975.

Geymonat, Ludovico. *Galileo Galilei: A Biography and Inquiry into His Philosophy of Science.* Translated by S. Drake. New York: McGraw-Hill, 1965.

Gibbon, Edward. *The Decline and Fall of the Roman Empire.* 3 vols. New York: Modern Library, 1977.

Gilkey, Langdon. *Religion and the Scientific Future: Reflections on Myth, Science, and Theology.* New York: Harper & Row, 1970.

Gilligan, Carol. *In a Different Voice: Psychological Theory and Women's Development.* Cambridge: Harvard University Press, 1982.

Gilson, Etienne. *The Christian Philosophy of St. Thomas Aquinas.* Translated by L. K. Shook. New York: Random House, 1956.

———. *History of Christian Philosophy in the Middle Ages.* New York: Random House, 1955.

Gimbutas, Marija. *The Goddesses and Gods of Old Europe, 6500–3500 B.C.: Myths and Cult Images.* Rev. ed. Berkeley: University of California Press, 1982.

———. *The Language of the Goddess: Unearthing the Hidden Symbols of Western Civilization.* San Francisco: Harper & Row, 1989.

Gingerich, Owen. "From Copernicus to Kepler: Heliocentrism as Model and as Reality." *Proceedings of the American Philosophical Society* 117 (1973): 513–522.

———. "Johannes Kepler and the New Astronomy." *Quarterly Journal of the Royal Astronomical Society* 13 (1972): 346–373.

Gleick, James. *Chaos: Making a New Science.* New York: Viking, 1988.

Goethe, Johann Wolfgang von. *Faust Parts One and Two.* Translated by G. M. Priest. In *Great Books of the Western World.* Vol. 47. Chicago: Encyclopaedia Britannica, 1952.

Gombrich, E. H. *Art and Illusion: A Study in the Psychology of Pictorial Representation.* 2nd ed., rev. Princeton: Princeton University Press, 1961.

Graves, Robert. *The Greek Myths.* 2 vols. Rev. ed. New York: Penguin, 1960.

Grenet, Paul. *Thomism.* Translated by J. F. Ross. New York: Harper & Row, 1967.

Grof, Stanislav. *Beyond the Brain: Birth, Death, and Transcendence in Psychotherapy.* Albany: State University of New York Press, 1985.

———. *LSD Psychotherapy.* Pomona, Calif.: Hunter House, 1980.

———. *Realms of the Human Unconscious: Observations from LSD Research.* New York: Viking, 1975.

Grube, Georges M. A. *Plato's Thought.* Boston: Beacon Press, 1958.

Gusdorf, Georges. *Speaking.* Translated, with an introduction by P. T. Brockelman. Evanston, Ill.: Northwestern University Press, 1965.

Guthrie, W. K. C. *The Greek Philosophers: From Thales to Aristotle.* New York: Harper Torchbook, 1960.

———. *A History of Greek Philosophy.* 6 vols. Cambridge: Cambridge University Press, 1962–81.

Habermas, Jurgen. *Knowledge and Human Interests.* Translated by J. J. Shapiro. Boston: Beacon Press, 1971.

Hall, Nor. *The Moon and the Virgin: Reflections on the Archetypal Feminine.* New York: Harper & Row, 1980.

Hanson, N. R. *Patterns of Discovery: An Inquiry into the Conceptual Foundations of Science.* Cambridge: Cambridge University Press, 1958.

Harding, Sandra. "Is Gender a Variable in Conceptions of Rationality?" *Dialectica* 36 (1982): 225–242.

Harrison, Jane Ellen. *Prolegomena to the Study of Greek Religion.* 3rd ed. Cambridge: Cambridge University Press, 1922.

Hayman, Ronald. *Nietzsche: A Critical Life.* New York: Oxford University Press, 1980.

Heath, Sir Thomas L. *Aristarchus of Samos: The Ancient Copernicus.* Oxford: Clarendon Press, 1913.

Hegel, G. W. F. *Early Theological Writings.* Translated by T. M. Knox, with an introduction and fragments translated by R. Kroner. Philadelphia: University of Pennsylvania Press, 1971.

———. *The Essential Writings.* Edited by F. G. Weiss. New York: Harper & Row, 1974.

———. *Introduction to the Lectures on the History of Philosophy.* Translated by T. M. Knox and A. V. Miller. Oxford: Oxford University Press, 1987.

———. *The Phenomenology of Spirit.* Translated by A. V. Miller. Oxford: Oxford University Press, 1977.

———. *Philosophy of Mind.* Translated by W. Wallace, with the *Zusätze* in Boumann's text translated by A. V. Miller. Oxford: Clarendon Press, 1971.

———. *Reason in History.* Translated by R. S. Hartman. Indianapolis: Bobbs-Merrill, 1953.

Heidegger, Martin. *Being and Time.* Translated by J. Macquarrie and E. Robinson. New York: Harper & Row, 1962.

———. " 'Only a God Can Save Us': The *Spiegel* Interview (1966)." Translated by W. J. Richardson. In *Heidegger: The Man and the Thinker,* edited by T. Sheehan. Chicago: Precedent, 1981.

Heilbroner, Robert. *The Worldly Philosophers.* New York: Simon and Schuster, 1980.

Heisenberg, Werner. *Physics and Philosophy: The Revolution in Modern Physics.* New York: Harper & Row, 1962.

Herbert, Nick. *Quantum Reality: Beyond the New Physics.* Garden City, N.Y.: Doubleday, 1985.

Herder, Johann Gottfried. *Reflections on the Philosophy of the History of Mankind.* Abridged, with introduction by F. E. Manuel. Chicago: University of Chicago Press, 1968.

Hesiod. *The Works and Days; Theogony; The Shield of Heracles.* Translated by R. Lattimore. Ann Arbor: University of Michigan Press, 1959.

Hesse, Mary. *Revolutions and Reconstructions in the Philosophy of Science.* Bloomington: Indiana University Press, 1980.

Hill, Christopher. *The World Turned Upside Down: Radical Ideas During the English Revolution.* New York: Viking, 1972.

Hillman, James. "Anima Mundi: The Return of the Soul to the World." *Spring 1982* (Dallas: Spring Publications, 1982): 71–93.

———. *Re-Visioning Psychology.* New York: Harper & Row, 1975.

Hollingdale, R. J. *Nietzsche: The Man and His Philosophy.* Baton Rouge: Louisiana State University Press, 1965.

Homer. *The Iliad.* Translated by Robert Fitzgerald. Garden City, N.Y.: Doubleday, 1974.

———. *The Odyssey.* Translated by Robert Fitzgerald. Garden City, N.Y.: Doubleday, 1961.

Hugh of Saint-Victor. *Didascalicon: A Medieval Guide to the Arts.* Translated, with an introduction by J. Taylor. New York: Columbia University Press, 1961.

Hume, David. *An Enquiry Concerning Human Understanding.* In *Great Books of the Western World,* Vol. 35. Chicago: Encyclopaedia Britannica, 1952.

———. *A Treatise of Human Nature.* Edited by L. A. Selby-Bigge. Oxford: Clarendon, 1967.

Huxley, Aldous. *The Doors of Perception.* New York: Harper & Row, 1970.

Irenaeus. *Against Heresies.* In *The Ante-Nicene Fathers,* edited by A. Roberts and J. Donaldson, Vol. 1. Grand Rapids, Mich.: Wm. B. Eerdmans, 1967.

Jackson, Timothy. "The Theory and Practice of Discomfort: Richard Rorty and Pragmatism." *The Thomist* 51, 2 (1987): 270–298.

Jaeger, Werner. *Aristotle: Fundamentals of the History of His Development.* Translated by R. Robinson. New York: Oxford University Press, 1948.

James, Henry. *The Art of Criticism: Henry James on the Theory and Practice of Fiction.* Edited by W. Veeder and S. Griffin. Chicago: University of Chicago Press, 1986.

James, William. *A Pluralistic Universe.* Cambridge: Harvard University Press, 1977.

————. *Pragmatism and the Meaning of Truth.* Cambridge: Harvard University Press, 1978.

————. *The Principles of Psychology.* 2 vols. Cambridge: Harvard University Press, 1981.

————. *Varieties of Religious Experience.* Cambridge: Harvard University Press, 1985.

————. *The Will to Believe.* Cambridge: Harvard University Press, 1979.

Janson, H. W. *History of Art.* 3rd ed. New York: Abrams, 1986.

Jeans, Sir James. *Physics and Philosophy.* New York: Macmillan, 1943.

John of the Cross, Saint. *Dark Night of the Soul.* Translated and edited by E. Allison Peers. Garden City, N.Y.: Image Books, 1959.

Jones, Ernest. *The Life and Work of Sigmund Freud.* 3 vols. New York: Basic Books, 1953–57.

Jung, Carl G. *Collected Works of Carl Gustav Jung.* 20 vols. Translated by R. F. C. Hull; edited by H. Read, M. Fordham, G. Adler, and W. McGuire. Bollingen Series XX. Princeton: Princeton University Press, 1953–79.

————. *Memories, Dreams, Reflections.* Rev. ed. Recorded and edited by A. Jaffe, translated by R. Winston and C. Winston. New York: Pantheon, 1973.

Kafka, Franz. *The Complete Stories.* Edited by N. N. Glatzer. New York: Schocken, 1971.

————. *The Trial.* Translated by W. Muir and E. Muir, revised by E. M. Butler. New York: Modern Library, 1964.

Kant, Immanuel. *Critique of Practical Reason.* Translated by L. W. Beck. New York: Bobbs-Merrill, 1956.

————. *Critique of Pure Reason.* Translated by N. K. Smith. London: Macmillan, 1968.

————. *Religion Within the Limits of Reason Alone.* 2nd ed. Translated by T. M. Greene and H. H. Hudson. La Salle, Ill.: Open Court, 1960.

Keats, John. *Poems.* 5th ed. Edited, with an introduction by E. De Selincourt. London: Methuen, 1961.

Keepin, William. *Some Deeper Implications of Chaos Theory.* Draft. San Francisco: California Institute of Integral Studies, 1990.

Keller, Evelyn Fox. *A Feeling for the Organism: The Life and Work of Barbara McClintock.* San Francisco: Freeman, 1983.

————. *Reflections on Gender and Science.* New Haven: Yale University Press, 1985.

Kempis, Thomas à. *The Imitation of Christ.* Translated by L. Sherley-Price. Harmondsworth, England: Penguin, 1952.

Kepler, Johannes. *The Harmonies of the World* (V), and *Epitome of Copernican Astronomy* (IV and V). Translated by C. G. Wallis. In *Great Books of the Western World,* Vol. 16. Chicago: Encyclopaedia Britannica, 1952.

————. "On the More Certain Fundamentals of Astrology." Foreword and notes by J. B. Brackenridge, translated by M. A. Rossi. *Proceedings of the American Philosophical Society* 123, 2 (1979): 85–116.

Kirk, Geoffrey S. *The Songs of Homer.* Cambridge: Cambridge University Press, 1962.

Kirk, G. S., and J. E. Raven, eds. *The Presocratic Philosophers: A Critical History with a Selection of Texts.* Cambridge: Cambridge University Press, 1957.

Koyré, Alexandre. *The Astronomical Revolution: Copernicus, Kepler, Borelli.* Translated by R. E. W. Maddison. Ithaca: Cornell University Press, 1973.

————. *From the Closed World to the Infinite Universe.* Baltimore: Johns Hopkins University Press, 1968.

Kubrin, David. "Newton's Inside Out: Magic, Class Struggle, and the Rise of Mechanism in the West." In *The Analytic Spirit,* edited by H. Woolf. Ithaca: Cornell University Press, 1980.

Kuhn, Thomas S. *The Copernican Revolution: Planetary Astronomy and the Development of Western Thought.* Cambridge: Harvard University Press, 1957.

————. *The Structure of Scientific Revolutions.* 2nd ed. Chicago: University of Chicago Press, 1970.

Laing, R. D. *The Divided Self.* New York: Penguin, 1965.

————. *The Politics of Experience.* Harmondsworth, England: Penguin, 1967.

Lakatos, Imre, and Alan Musgrave, eds. *Criticism and the Growth of Knowledge.* Cambridge: Cambridge University Press, 1974.

Landes, David S. *A Revolution in Time: Clocks and the Making of the Modern World.* Cambridge: Harvard University Press, 1983.

Lasch, Christopher. *The Culture of Narcissism: American Life in an Age of Diminishing Expectations.* New York: Norton, 1979.

Leff, Gordon. *The Dissolution of the Medieval Outlook: An Essay on Intellectual and Spiritual Change in the Fourteenth Century.* New York: Harper & Row, 1976.

Leonardo da Vinci. *Leonardo da Vinci.* Edited by G. Nicodemi et al. New York: Reynal, in association with William Morrow, 1956.

Letwin, Shirley R. *Pursuit of Certainty.* Cambridge: Cambridge University Press, 1965.

Levi, Albert William. *Philosophy and the Modern World.* Chicago: University of Chicago Press, 1977.

Lévi-Strauss, Claude. *Structural Anthropology.* Translated by C. Jacobson and B. G. Schoepf. New York: Doubleday, 1967.

Locke, John. *An Essay Concerning Human Understanding.* In *Great Books of the Western World,* Vol. 35. Chicago: Encyclopaedia Britannica, 1952.

Lovejoy, Arthur O. *The Great Chain of Being: A Study of the History of an Idea.* Cambridge: Harvard University Press, 1936.

Lovelock, J. E. *Gaia: A New Look at Life on Earth.* Oxford: Oxford University Press, 1979.

Lucretius. *De Rerum Natura.* Edited by C. Bailey. 3 vols. Oxford: Oxford University Press, 1979.

Luther, Martin. *The Bondage of the Will*. Translated by H. Cole, with corrections by H. Atherton. Grand Rapids, Mich.: Wm. B. Eerdmans, 1931.

———. *Martin Luther's Basic Theological Writings*. Edited by T. F. Lull. Minneapolis: Fortress Press, 1989.

Lyotard, Jean-François. *The Postmodern Condition: A Report on Knowledge*. Translated by G. Bennington and B. Massumi. Minneapolis: University of Minnesota Press, 1984.

Machiavelli, Niccolò. *The Prince*. Translated by H. C. Mansfield, Jr. Chicago: University of Chicago Press, 1985.

Magee, Bryan. *Karl Popper*. New York: Viking, 1973.

Marcuse, Herbert. *Eros and Civilization: A Philosophical Inquiry into Freud*. Boston: Beacon, 1974.

Marx, Karl. *Capital*. Translated by S. Moore and E. Aveling. 3 vols. Moscow: Foreign Languages Publishing House, 1954–62.

———. *The Communist Manifesto*. Edited by A. J. Taylor. Baltimore: Penguin, 1968.

———. *Economic and Philosophical Manuscripts*. In *The Marx-Engels Reader*, edited by R. C. Tucker. New York: Norton, 1972.

McDermott, John J. *The Culture of Experience: Essays in the American Grain*. New York: New York University Press, 1976.

McDermott, Robert A. "Toward a Modern Spiritual Cognition." *Revision* 12 (Summer 1989): 29–33.

McInerny, Ralph. *St. Thomas Aquinas*. Notre Dame: Notre Dame University Press, 1982.

McKibben, Bill. *The End of Nature*. New York: Random House, 1989.

McNeill, William H. *The Rise of the West: A History of the Human Community*. Chicago: University of Chicago Press, 1963.

Melville, Herman. *Moby-Dick, or the Whale*. Berkeley: University of California Press, 1981.

Merchant, Carolyn. *The Death of Nature: Women, Ecology, and the Scientific Revolution*. San Francisco: Harper & Row, 1980.

Merton, Thomas. "The Self of Modern Man and the New Christian Consciousness." In *Zen and the Birds of Appetite*, 15–32. New York: New Directions, 1968.

Michelangelo. *The Complete Works of Michelangelo*. Edited by M. Salmi et al. New York: Reynal, in association with William Morrow, 1965.

Miller, David L. *The New Polytheism*. 2nd ed. Dallas: Spring Publications, 1981.

Miller, Jean Baker, ed. *Psychoanalysis and Women*. New York: Penguin, 1973.

Milton, John. *Areopagitica and Other Prose Writings*. Edited by W. Haller. New York: Book League of America, 1929.

Moltman, Jürgen D. *The Theology of Hope: On the Ground and the Implications of a Christian Eschatology*. Translated by J. W. Leitch. New York: Harper & Row, 1976.

Monod, Jacques. *Chance and Necessity An Essay on the Natural Philosophy of Modern Biology*. Translated by A. Wainhouse. New York: Random House, 1972.

Montaigne, Michel de. *The Complete Essays*. Translated by D. M. Frame. Stanford: Stanford University Press, 1958.

Morgan, Elaine. *The Descent of Woman.* London: Souvenir, 1972.

Mumford, Lewis. *The Myth of the Machine.* 2 vols. New York: Harcourt, Brace & World, 1967–70.

Nehamas, Alexander. *Nietzsche: Life as Literature.* Cambridge: Harvard University Press, 1985.

Neugebauer, O. *The Exact Sciences in Antiquity.* 2nd ed. Providence: Brown University Press, 1957.

Newton, Isaac. *Philosophiae Naturalis Principia Mathematica.* 3rd ed. (1726), with variant readings, assembled by A. Koyré, I. B. Cohen, and A. Whitman. 2 vols. Cambridge: Harvard University Press, 1972.

———. *The Opticks.* 4th ed. New York: Dover, 1952.

Nietzsche, Friedrich. *Basic Writings of Nietzsche.* Edited and translated by W. Kaufman. New York: Modern Library, 1968.

———. *The Gay Science.* Translated by W. Kaufman. New York: Random House, 1974.

———. *Thus Spoke Zarathustra.* Translated, with an introduction by R. J. Hollingdale. New York: Penguin, 1969.

Ockham, William of. *Ockham's Theory of Propositions.* Part II of the *Summa Logicae.* Translated by A. J. Freddoso and H. Schuurman, with an introduction by A. J. Freddoso. Notre Dame: University of Notre Dame, 1980.

———. *Ockham's Theory of Terms.* Part I of the *Summa Logicae.* Translated, with an introduction by M. J. Loux. Notre Dame: University of Notre Dame Press, 1975.

O'Meara, John J. *The Young Augustine.* New York: Alba House, 1965.

Origen. *Contra Celsum.* Translated by H. Chadwick. Cambridge: Cambridge University Press, 1980.

Ovid. *Metamorphoses.* Edited by E. J. Kenney. Oxford: Oxford University Press, 1986.

Pagels, Elaine. *The Gnostic Gospels.* New York: Random House, 1979.

Pagels, Heinz R. *The Cosmic Code: Quantum Physics as the Language of Nature.* New York: Simon & Schuster, 1982.

Palmer, R. R., and Joel Colton. *A History of the Modern World.* 5th ed. New York: Alfred A. Knopf, 1978.

Panofsky, Erwin. *Renaissance and Renascences in Western Art.* New York: Harper & Row, 1969.

Pascal, Blaise. *Pensées.* Translated, with an introduction by A. J. Krailsheimer. Harmondsworth, England: Penguin, 1966.

Pauli, Wolfgang. "The Influence of Archetypal Ideas on the Scientific Theories of Kepler." Translated by P. Silz. In C. G. Jung and W. Pauli, *The Interpretation of Nature and the Psyche.* New York: Pantheon, 1955.

Pelikan, Jaroslav. *The Christian Tradition: A History of the Development of Doctrine.* 5 vols. Chicago: University of Chicago Press, 1971–89.

Perls, Fritz. *Gestalt Therapy Verbatim.* New York: Bantam, 1976.

Petrarch, Francesco. *Petrarch, the First Modern Scholar and Man of Letters: A Selection From His Correspondence.* 2nd ed., rev. and enlarged. Translated by J. H. Robinson and H. W. Rolfe. New York: Greenwood, 1969.

Piaget, Jean. *The Child's Conception of the World*. Translated by J. Tomlinson and A. Tomlinson. London: Routledge & Kegan Paul, 1960.

Pico della Mirandola, Giovanni. "The Dignity of Man." In *The Portable Renaissance Reader*, edited by J. B. Ross and M. M. McLaughlin. New York: Penguin, 1977.

Pieper, Josef. *St. Thomas Aquinas*. Translated by D. MacLaren. New York: Sheed & Ward, 1948.

————. *Scholasticism: Personalities and Problems of Medieval Philosophy*. Translated by R. Winston and C. Winston. New York: Pantheon, 1960.

Pindar. *The Odes of Pindar*. Translated by R. Lattimore. Chicago: University of Chicago Press, 1976.

Plato. *The Collected Dialogues*. Edited by E. Hamilton and H. Cairns. Princeton: Princeton University Press, 1961.

————. *Philebus and Epinomis*. Translated by A. E. Taylor, with an introduction by R. Klibansky. London: Thomas Nelson, 1956.

Plotinus. *The Enneads*. Translated by S. MacKenna. 3rd rev. ed., by B. S. Page. Introduction by P. Henry. London: Faber and Faber, 1962.

Plutarch. *Lives*. Translated by J. Dryden. New York: Modern Library, 1967.

Polanyi, Michael. *Personal Knowledge*. New York: Harper & Row, 1964.

Pope, Alexander. *The Poetical Works of Alexander Pope*. Edited by A. W. Ward. London: Macmillan, 1924.

Popper, Karl R. *Conjectures and Refutations: The Growth of Scientific Knowledge*. New York: Harper Torchbook, 1968.

————. *The Logic of Scientific Discovery*. Rev. ed. New York: Harper & Row, 1968.

Prabhu, Joseph. "Blessing the Bathwater." In "On Deconstructing Theology: A Symposium." *Journal of the American Academy of Religion* 54, 3 (1987): 534–543.

Prigogine, Ilya. *From Being to Becoming: Time and Complexity in the Physical Sciences*. San Francisco: Freeman, 1980.

Ptolemy. *The Almagest*. Translated by R. C. Taliaferro. In *Great Books of the Western World*, Vol. 16. Chicago: Encyclopaedia Britannica, 1952.

————. *The Tetrabiblos*. Translated by J. M. Ashmand. North Hollywood, Calif.: Symbols and Signs, 1976.

Quine, W. V. *From a Logical Point of View*. 2nd ed. New York: Harper & Row, 1961.

Rahner, Karl. *Hearers of the Word*. Translated by M. Richards. Montreal: Palm, 1969.

————. *Theological Investigations*. Vol. 13, *Theology, Anthropology, Christology*. Translated by D. Bourke. New York: Seabury, 1975.

Raine, Kathleen. *Blake and Tradition*. Princeton: Princeton University Press, 1968.

Randall, John Herman. *The Making of the Modern Mind*. New York: Columbia University Press, 1976.

Rank, Otto. *The Trauma of Birth*. New York: Harcourt Brace, 1929.

Raphael. *The Complete Work of Raphael*. Edited by M. Salmi et al. New York: Harrison House, 1969.

Rattansi, P. M. "The Intellectual Origins of the Royal Society." *Notes and Records of the Royal Society of London* 23 (1968): 129–143.

Ravetz, Jerome R. *Scientific Knowledge and Its Social Problems.* London: Oxford University Press, 1971.

Redondi, Pietro. *Galileo: Heretic.* Translated by R. Rosenthal. Princeton: Princeton University Press, 1987.

Reich, Wilhelm. *Character Analysis.* New York: Noonday, 1949.

Rilke, Rainer Maria. *Duino Elegies.* Translated by C. F. MacIntyre. Berkeley: University of California Press, 1961.

Ronan, Colin A. *Galileo.* New York: G.P. Putnam's Sons, 1974.

Rorty, Richard. *Philosophy and the Mirror of Nature.* Princeton: Princeton University Press, 1979.

Rosen, Edward. *Copernicus and the Scientific Revolution.* Malabar, Fla.: Krieger Publications, 1984.

Ross, J. B., and M. M. McLaughlin, eds. *The Portable Renaissance Reader.* Rev. ed. New York: Penguin, 1977.

Ross, Sir William David. *Aristotle.* 5th ed. New York: Methuen, 1964.

———. *Plato's Theory of Ideas.* London: Oxford University Press, 1971.

Roszak, Theodore. *The Making of a Counter Culture.* New York: Doubleday, 1969.

Rothberg, Donald. "Philosophical Foundations of Transpersonal Psychology." *Journal of Transpersonal Psychology* 18, 1 (1986): 1–34.

Rouner, Leroy S., ed. *On Nature.* Notre Dame: University of Notre Dame Press, 1984.

Rousseau, Jean-Jacques. *Confessions.* Translated by J. M. Cohen. Baltimore: Penguin, 1953.

———. *Émile, or Treatise of Education.* Translated by B. Foxley. New York: Dutton, 1955.

Ruether, Rosemary Radford, ed. *Religion and Sexism: Images of Woman in the Jewish and Christian Traditions.* New York: Simon & Schuster, 1974.

———. *Sexism and God-Talk: Toward a Feminist Theology.* Boston: Beacon, 1983.

Rufus, W. Carl. "Kepler as an Astronomer." In The History of Science Society, *Johannes Kepler: A Tercentenary Commemoration of His Life and Work.* Baltimore: Williams and Wilkins, 1931.

Rupp, E. Gordon. *Luther's Progress to the Diet of Worms, 1521.* New York: Harper & Row, 1964.

Russell, Bertrand. *The Basic Writings of Bertrand Russell.* Edited by R. E. Egner and L. E. Dennon. New York: Simon and Schuster, 1967.

———. *A History of Western Philosophy.* New York: Simon and Schuster, 1945.

———. *Why I Am Not a Christian and Other Essays on Religion and Related Subjects.* New York: Simon and Schuster, 1967.

Salinger, J. D. *Franny and Zooey.* Boston: Little, Brown, 1961.

Samuels, Andrew. *Jung and the Post-Jungians.* London: Routledge & Kegan Paul, 1985.

Santillana, Giorgio de. *The Crime of Galileo.* Chicago: University of Chicago Press, 1955.

Sarton, George. *Introduction to the History of Science.* 5 vols. Huntington, New York: Krieger, 1975.

Sartre, Jean-Paul. *Being and Nothingness: A Phenomenological Essay on Ontology.* Translated, with an introduction by H. E. Barnes. New York: Citadel Press, 1956.

————. *Existentialism and Humanism.* Translated by P. Mairet. London: Methuen, 1948.

————. *Nausea.* Translated by Lloyd Alexander. New York: New Directions, 1959.

————. *No Exit & The Flies.* Translated by S. Gilbert. New York: Alfred A. Knopf, 1946.

Schilpp, P. A., ed. *Albert Einstein: Philosopher-Scientist.* New York: Tudor, 1951.

————, ed. *The Philosophy of Karl Popper.* 2 vols. La Salle, Ill.: Open Court, 1974.

Scott, Joan Wallach. *Gender and the Politics of History.* New York: Columbia University Press, 1988.

Sextus Empiricus. *Scepticism, Man and God: Selections from the Major Writings.* Translated by S. Etheridge, edited by P. P. Hallie. Middletown, Conn.: Wesleyan University Press, 1964.

Shakespeare, William. *The Complete Works of Shakespeare.* The Cambridge Edition Text, edited by W. A. Wright. Garden City, N.Y.: Doubleday, 1936.

Sheehan, Thomas, ed. *Heidegger: The Man and the Thinker.* Chicago: Precedent, 1981.

Sheldrake, Rupert. *A New Science of Life: The Hypothesis of Formative Causation.* Los Angeles: Tarcher, 1981.

Shelley, Percy Bysshe. *Prometheus Unbound.* Edited by L. J. Zillman. New Haven: Yale University Press, 1968.

Sherrard, Philip. "The Christian Understanding of Man." *Sobornost* 7, 5 (1977): 329–343.

Skinner, B. F. *Beyond Freedom and Dignity.* New York: Bantam, 1972.

Skinner, Quentin, ed. *The Return of Grand Theory in the Human Sciences.* Cambridge: Cambridge University Press, 1985.

Smith, Adam. *An Inquiry into the Nature and Causes of the Wealth of Nations.* Edited, with an introduction by E. Cannan. New York: Modern Library, 1937.

Smith, Huston. *Beyond the Post-Modern Mind.* Rev. ed. Wheaton, Ill.: Quest, 1989.

Snow, C. P. *Two Cultures and the Scientific Revolution.* Cambridge: Cambridge University Press, 1959.

Sophocles. The extant plays in 2 vols. of *The Complete Greek Tragedies.* Edited by D. Grene and R. Lattimore. Chicago: University of Chicago Press, 1954–57.

Spengler, Oswald. *The Decline of the West.* Translated by C. F. Atkinson. 2 vols. New York: Alfred A. Knopf, 1945.

Spretnak, Charlene. *Lost Goddesses of Early Greece.* Boston: Beacon Press, 1984.

Squire, Aelred. "The Doctrine of the Image in the *De Veritate* of St. Thomas." *Dominican Studies* 4 (1951): 164–177.

Stein, Murray, and Robert L. Moore, eds. *Jung's Challenge to Contemporary Religion.* Wilmette, Ill.: Chiron, 1987.

Steiner, Rudolf. *The Essential Steiner.* Edited, with an introduction by Robert A. McDermott. San Francisco: Harper & Row, 1984.

———. *The Riddles of Philosophy.* Spring Valley, N.Y.: Anthroposophic Press, 1973.

———. *A Theory of Knowledge Based on Goethe's World Conception.* Translated by O. Wannamaker. Spring Valley, N.Y.: Anthroposophic Press, 1968.

Stendahl, Kristen. *Meanings: The Bible as Document and Guide.* Philadelphia: Fortress Press, 1984.

Sukenick, Ronald. *The Death of the Novel and Other Stories.* New York: Dial, 1969.

Taylor, A. E. *Socrates: The Man and His Thought.* Garden City, N.Y.: Doubleday, 1954.

Teilhard de Chardin, Pierre. *The Phenomenon of Man.* Translated by B. Wall, with an introduction by Julian Huxley. New York: Harper & Row, 1959.

Tester, S. J. *A History of Western Astrology.* Woodbridge, Suffolk: Boydell, 1987.

Thomas, Keith. *Religion and the Decline of Magic.* New York: Scribner, 1986.

Thorndike, Lynn. *A History of Magic and Experimental Science.* 8 vols. New York: Columbia University Press, 1923–58.

Tolstoy, Leo. *Anna Karenina.* Translated by C. Garnett. New York: Modern Library, 1935.

———. *The Death of Ivan Ilyich.* Translated by L. Solotaroff. New York: Bantam, 1981.

———. *The Kingdom of God Is Within You.* Translated by C. Garnett. Lincoln: University of Nebraska Press, 1984.

———. *War and Peace.* Translated by C. Garnett. New York: Modern Library, 1931.

Tomlin, E. W. F. *The Western Philosophers.* New York: Harper & Row, 1957.

Torrance, Thomas F. *Theological Science.* London: Oxford University Press, 1978.

Toulmin, Stephen. *Human Understanding: The Collective Use and Evolution of Concepts.* Princeton: Princeton University Press, 1972.

Toynbee, Arnold J. *A Study of History.* Abridgement of vols. I–VI, by D. C. Somervell. New York: Oxford University Press, 1947.

Vasari, Giorgio. *Lives of the Most Eminent Painters, Sculptors, and Architects.* Translated by J. Foster. London: George Bell's Sons, 1890.

Virgil. *The Aeneid.* Translated by Robert Fitzgerald. New York: Random House, 1983.

Vlastos, Gregory. *Platonic Studies.* Princeton: Princeton University Press, 1973.

Voltaire. *Philosophical Letters.* Translated by E. Dilworth. Indianapolis: Bobbs-Merrill, 1961.

Voogd, Stephanie de. "C.G. Jung: Psychologist of the Future, 'Philosopher' of the Past." *Spring 1977* (New York and Zurich: Spring Publications, 1977): 175–182.

Vrooman, J. R. *René Descartes: A Biography.* New York: G.P. Putnam's Sons, 1970.

Walsh, William H. *Metaphysics.* New York: Harcourt, Brace & World, 1966.

Watts, Alan. *Beyond Theology.* New York: Pantheon, 1964.

———. *Psychotherapy East and West.* New York: Pantheon, 1961.

Weber, Max. *The Protestant Ethic and the Spirit of Capitalism.* Translated by Talcott Parsons. New York: Charles Scribner's Sons, 1958.

Weinberg, Steven. *The First Three Minutes: A Modern View of the Origin of the Universe.* New York: Basic Books, 1988.

Weinstein, Donald, and Rudolph M. Bell. *Saints and Society: The Two Worlds of Western Christendom, 1000 to 1700.* Chicago: University of Chicago Press, 1986.

Wellmer, Albrecht. "On the Dialectic of Modernism and Postmodernism." *Praxis International* 4 (1985): 337–362.

Westfall, Richard S. *Force in Newton's Physics: The Science of Dynamics in the Seventeenth Century.* New York: American Elsevier, 1971.

White, Lynn. "The Historical Roots of Our Ecologic Crisis." *Science* 155 (1967): 1203–1207.

Whitehead, Alfred North. *Process and Reality.* Corrected ed. Edited by D. R. Griffin and D. W. Sherburne. New York: Free Press, 1978.

———. *Science and the Modern World.* New York: Macmillan, 1925.

Whitehead, Alfred North, and Bertrand Russell. *Principia Mathematica.* 3 vols. Cambridge: Cambridge University Press, 1927.

Whitfield, J. H. *Petrarch and the Renascence.* New York: Haskell House, 1969 (reprint of 1943 edition).

Whorf, Benjamin Lee. *Language, Thought, and Reality: Selected Writings of Benjamin Lee Whorf.* Edited by J. B. Carroll. Cambridge: MIT Press, 1956.

Whyte, Lancelot Law. *The Unconscious Before Freud.* New York: Basic Books, 1960.

Wilkinson, Elizabeth M., and Leonard A. Willoughby. *Goethe, Poet and Thinker.* New York: Barnes & Noble, 1962.

Wind, Edgar. *Pagan Mysteries in the Renaissance.* Rev. and enlarged ed. New York: Norton, 1968.

Wittgenstein, Ludwig. *Philosophical Investigations.* Translated by G. E. M. Anscombe. 3rd ed. New York: Macmillan, 1968.

———. *Tractatus Logico-Philosophicus.* Translated by D. F. Pears and B. F. McGuinness, with an introduction by Bertrand Russell. London: Routledge & Kegan Paul, 1961.

Wollstonecraft, Mary. *Vindication of the Rights of Woman.* Edited by M. Kramick. New York: Viking Penguin, 1978.

Wordsworth, William. *Poetical Works.* Rev. ed. Edited by T. Hutchinson and E. De Selincourt. Oxford: Oxford University Press, 1950.

Wordsworth, William, and Samuel Taylor Coleridge. *Lyrical Ballads, 1798.* 2nd ed. Edited by W. J. Owen. Oxford: Oxford University Press, 1969.

Yates, Frances A. *Giordano Bruno and the Hermetic Tradition.* London: Routledge, 1964.

Yeats, William Butler. *The Collected Poems.* London: Macmillan, 1952.

———. *A Vision.* New York: Macmillan, 1956.

Reference Works

Bullock, Alan, and R. B. Woodings, eds. *20th Century Culture: A Biographical Companion.* New York: Harper & Row, 1983.

Edwards, Paul, ed. *The Encyclopedia of Philosophy.* 8 vols. New York: Macmillan, 1967.

Encyclopaedia Britannica. 15th ed. 30 vols. Chicago: Encyclopaedia Britannica, 1977.

Flew, Antony, ed. *A Dictionary of Philosophy.* 2nd ed. New York: St. Martin's, 1984.

Gillispie, C. C., ed. *Dictionary of Scientific Biography.* 16 vols. New York: Charles Scribner's Sons, 1970.

Harvey, Sir Paul, ed. *The Oxford Companion to Classical Literature.* Oxford: Clarendon Press, 1974.

Kinder, Hermann, and Werner Hilgemann. *The Anchor Atlas of World History.* Translated by E. A. Menze. 2 vols. Garden City, N.Y.: Doubleday, 1974.

Liddell, H. G., and R. Scott. *A Greek-English Lexicon.* 9th ed. Oxford: Clarendon Press, 1968.

Oxford English Dictionary. Compact ed. 2 vols. Oxford: Oxford University Press, 1971.

Rahner, Karl, et al., eds. *Sacramentum Mundi: An Encyclopedia of Theology.* 6 vols. New York: Herder and Herder, 1968.

Trager, James, ed. *The People's Chronology.* New York: Holt, Rinehart and Winston, 1979.

Wiener, Philip P., ed. *Dictionary of the History of Ideas.* 5 vols. New York: Charles Scribner's Sons, 1973.

Acknowledgments

The long project of writing this book has left me deeply indebted to more people than I can hope adequately to acknowledge. I am very grateful to the following men and women who read the manuscript in its entirety, in several cases more than once, and who gave me invaluable critical comment and support: Stanislav Grof, Bruno Barnhart, Robert McDermott, Joseph Campbell, Huston Smith, David L. Miller, Cathie Brettschneider, Deane Juhan, Charles Harvey, Renn Butler, Bruce Newell, William Keepin, and Margaret Garigan. I also wish to thank the many individuals who read and responded to specific sections of the manuscript at various stages of the writing, including James Hillman, Robert Bellah, Fritjof Capra, Frank Barr, William Webb, Gordon Tappan, Aelred Squire, William Birmingham, Roger Walsh, John Mack, and Joseph Prabhu. An especially important reader of the book throughout the many years of its composition has been my wife Heather Malcolm Tarnas, whose meticulous editorial eye, probing questions, and sensitive judgment have deeply influenced the final result.

There are probably few sentences in this work that could not have been footnoted in recognition of some book or essay, lecture, letter, or conversation that has influenced my understanding of an idea or how best to articulate it. The bibliography attempts to list some portion of my many intellectual debts, but brief citations scarcely do justice to the contributions of scholars such as W. K. C. Guthrie, M. D. Chenu, Josef Pieper, Ernst Wilhelm Benz, Herbert Butterfield, William McNeill, Robert Bellah, and Thomas Kuhn, to name only a few of those whose influence on this book was especially marked. In addition, a number of individuals contributed directly to my working out of the book's overall historical conception, and here I particularly wish to acknowledge my appreciation for innumerable stimulating discussions with Stanislav Grof, Bruno Barnhart, James Hillman, Robert McDermott, Deane Juhan, Huston Smith, Joseph Campbell, and Gregory Bateson.

For the publication of the book, I am greatly indebted to my agent Frederick Hill and his associate Bonnie Nadell; to Robert Wyatt and Teri Henry of Ballantine Books; to Peter Guzzardi, Margaret Garigan, James Walsh, and John Michel of Harmony Books; and to Bokara Legendre for initiating the whole process. I am very grateful for the generous financial support provided by Joan Reddish, Arthur Young, Bokara Legendre, Christopher Bird, and Philip Delevett, as well as by members of the Tarnas and Malcolm families, which enabled me to devote sufficient time to the task of writing and research. My work on the book was also aided in important ways by Michael Murphy, Richard Price, Albert Hofmann, Anne Armstrong, Roger Newell, Jay Ogilvy, the Institute for the Study of Consciousness, and the Princeton University Press. A grant from Laurance S. Rockefeller allowed me to participate in the Esalen Project for Revisioning Philosophy, a three-year series of conferences with leading philosophers, theologians, and scientists. The remarkable discussions that took place during these gatherings played a significant role in pressing me to articulate the evolutionary conception of Western intellectual and spiritual history that is set forth in the epilogue of the present book, and that was first presented at the project's concluding conference, "Philosophy and the Human Future," held at Cambridge University in August 1989.

These acknowledgments would be incomplete without mention of my deep appreciation for the formative role played in my life by Esalen Institute, where I lived from 1974 to 1984; by Harvard University, which I attended from 1968 to 1972; and by the Jesuit teachers of my youth. In some sense this book can be seen as the natural outgrowth of having been educated in, and having to integrate the diverse intellectual influences of, just those particular learning communities. I hope this book can also be seen as an act of gratitude to each of them, and to the many dedicated men and women who shared with me their knowledge and insights.

I also want to acknowledge my gratitude to the land and spirit of Big Sur on the Pacific coast, which nurtured, challenged, and inspired me through all the years I worked on the book.

Finally, I wish to thank my parents, my wife, and my children. Without their faith and loving support, this book could not have been written. I am deeply grateful to each of them.

Index